BORDER REGIONS
OF FAITH

*An Anthology of Religion
and Social Change*

Edited by
Kenneth Aman

ORBIS BOOKS

Maryknoll, New York 10545

The Catholic Foreign Mission Society of America (Maryknoll) recruits and trains people for overseas missionary service. Through Orbis Books Maryknoll aims to foster the international dialogue that is essential to mission. The books published, however, reflect the opinions of their authors and are not meant to represent the official position of the society.

© 1987 by Kenneth Aman
Published in the United States of America by Orbis Books, Maryknoll, NY 10545
Manufactured in the United States of America
All rights reserved
Manuscript editor: William Jerman

Library of Congress Cataloging-in-Publication Data

Border regions of faith.

  Bibliography p.
  1. Theology.   2. Church and social problems.
I. Aman, Kenneth.
BT80.B64   1986   230   86-23551
ISBN 0-88344-415-1 (pbk.)

BORDER REGIONS
OF FAITH

Contents

Introduction

There are two questions that quickly move to the foreground when one ponders the relationship between religion and social change. The first is: To what extent does religion contribute to social change?[1] The second, perhaps even more important to the religious person, is: To what extent is religious consciousness itself altered by social change? This book is primarily concerned with the second question, but we also need to look for a moment at the first.

We can view religion and social change as a dynamic relationship, with religion at one pole and society at the other. In this view, there is a whole complex of influences at each pole upon the other. The whole picture becomes even more complicated when we also note that we are not simply speaking of religion and society as simple entities with unchanging meanings. Rather, religious consciousness and social structures are themselves highly dynamic realities, characterized by change as much as by stability. And because they are closely connected, to change one is to set up powerful surges or currents that necessarily affect the other.

One obvious example of religion impacting upon society was the temperance movement and prohibition; religious sentiments concerning alcohol were a major factor in producing legislation in this country, including a constitutional amendment. On the other hand, the recent activism of American Catholic bishops seems a good illustration of the ways society can influence religious reflection and decision-making.

Sociologists of religion, among other scholars, have been interested for some time in the ways religion influences social change. One important question for them is really disjunctive: Does religion *contribute* to social change, or does it act as a *deterrent*? A famous response to this question is Marx's critique of religion (building upon the almost contemporaneous critique by Feuerbach). Here, religion is seen as providing a powerful ideological support to oppressive and alienating social and political conditions and thus as a block to change. I accept this as one very important way in which religion is related to social change. In my view, Marx is right as far as he goes. Religion supports social structures at many levels, ranging from convenient rationalizations ("I shall be rewarded in the next world for the sufferings I am experiencing in this one") to powerful theological systems that draw on the very marrow of contemporary cultural beliefs—and in turn strengthen those beliefs.

I believe that Marx is basically correct, not because he had a very accurate idea of what religion is about (he did not) or because his analysis is in any sense a *complete* description of the interrelationship between religion and society, but because his central insight was overwhelmingly on the mark, just as Freud and Darwin were overwhelmingly on the mark, no matter how many secondary details of their work now seem beside the point or simply wrong. Marx was successful in bringing to our attention the perennial tendency to stabilize a particular social and cultural system by appealing to religion, or by using religion to legitimize the foundation of that system. He of course looked upon this tendency with scorn, because he himself was so convinced of the need to change society, and to change it radically. Others have tended to see the same influence in a far more positive light: as offering solace, comfort, and solidity in a world emptied of them.

Both supporters and detractors of religion are assuming here the same conservative view of religion: society is seen to support religion, and religion society. In recent years, however, students of religion have become increasingly aware of another dialectic working at cross-purposes to this one. Religion can also be a *dealienating* factor in social life, to use Peter Berger's term.[2] It may be precisely religious values and beliefs that give rise to questions about and challenges to social forms. Religious leadership may be able to stand up to other kinds of political and social authority.[3] Religious symbols may act against the prevailing system of secular symbols that support and reinforce that status quo. In the first three centuries of the Christian era, for example, the cross was a powerful influence against emperor worship.

In this counterdialectic, religious men and women may well be the ones to take the initiative in trying to change, even radically, our society and its norms. Thus, the most notable leaders of civil rights struggles are clerics; women become feminists because of their strong Christian or Jewish backgrounds; priests and nuns emerge as the most visible protesters against oppressive regimes in Third World countries.

It seems equally clear that the process has not stopped there. Those who have engaged in these movements for change have returned to religion with new insights and new questions. Religious consciousness in its turn has undergone and continues to undergo significant change. For example, contemporary movements for a nuclear freeze and indeed for disarmament are accompanied by new questions, emphases, and areas of concentration within religious reflection. Some of these are rather obvious: the morality of waging war, the rediscovery of a peace tradition, possible obligations to resist and civilly disobey a particular government. There are, however, a whole host of other, perhaps deeper, religious concepts that may also be affected: the meaning of Christ, the communal character of church, the very concept of God. In short, religious conscious-ness is highly layered, and alterations in that consciousness may well be induced *indirectly* (through related concepts) as well as directly.

It is such changes that are at the basis of this book. It is my thesis that *all* significant social change involves values; that because it is value-laden, *all* significant social change impacts upon religion and religious consciousness. This does not mean that we are always in a position to describe in what way a particular social movement is going to change religious consciousness, particularly when the movement is relatively new. We may well have to wait until the movement has ripened, until religious persons have experienced it and have the intellectual resources to analyze and understand it. Indeed, the theme of "experience," as well as the need to be faithful to it, is perhaps the only one that the social movements featured in this volume have in common.

Of course not all social activists are especially interested in religion. Perhaps only a relatively few are. Those activists who are religiously motivated, however, are likely to take to their religion the conviction that the social ideal for which they are striving has something about it of religious truth. More, to be actively engaged in attempting to achieve a social ideal is to experience a kind of religious revelation. Fundamental shifts in their perception of the world will inevitably have a significant effect on their religious understanding. The very *meaning* of such terms as "grace," "salvation," "the Spirit," and "sin" are apt to undergo basic changes. This volume, then, takes most seriously and seeks to explore such statements as the following: "Racism is sin." "Nuclear armaments are diabolical." "Revelation impels us to make a preferential option for the poor." And "the Spirit leads us to resist."

QUESTIONS AND COUNTERQUESTIONS

Each of the social movements touched on in this book has produced a virtual library of theological and religious works. Just because of this, very few of the specialists in one area have had time or energy to do much work in any of the others.[4] Many of these areas have in fact been so rich and suggestive that they have quickly spawned subspecialties. It is very difficult, for example, for a feminist theologian to keep track of all the work being done under the general rubric "women and religion." Among other disciplines, this field includes psychology, history, biblical studies, and anthropology. The inevitable consequence is a certain isolation and compartmentalization. It is one of the primary purposes of this book simply to put in one place a representative sampling of alterations of religious consciousness that have resulted from research done in a *number* of separate disciplines.

Another outcome of the vitality of this kind of reflection is that frontiers move outward very rapidly. New questions arise, receive tentative answers, and are dropped, developed, or replaced by newer questions. This is partly because of the nature of social change. Inasmuch as social movements go through different phases, the religious agendas coming out of these movements are bound to change also. But another reason for this drive to development lies in the inner logic of religious reflection itself. It inevitably extends its vision further, probes deeper. In addition to being urged on by external factors, it has an internal urgency. Thus the commitment to the poor of early Latin American liberation theologians was logically followed by a growing emphasis on the popular character of the church, which in turn led to a new interest in popular religiosity.

Those active in relating religious belief to a particular social movement share a kind of "tradition." They agree that certain questions must be taken as the starting point, even if they have moved well beyond that starting point. They share an interest in attacking a given problem, which can often be reduced to an "ism": racism, sexism, (neo)colonialism. There is a bond of unity among those working for a particular movement as they face a common opponent, even when they sharply disagree on other matters. Also, there are usually a few significant writings that have shaped the consciousness of most if not all contemporary religious writers in a particular field. For example, most black theologians are indebted to James Cone. Gustavo Gutiérrez's *A Theology of Liberation* is accorded a special place of honor by liberation theologians, even if he has never claimed such a distinction. Both friends and foes of the Radical Right have probably read Jerry Falwell's *Listen, America;* they certainly have seen and heard of Falwell himself. *Border Regions of Faith* attempts to represent the unity present in these various "traditions" by mirroring these diverse sources of unity. To begin with, articles giving a sense of the problems that have generated a particular social movement have been chosen. In addition, some of the landmark writings in a particular area, as well as pertinent responses to those writings, have been gathered into a single collection. Besides offering the uninitiated easy access to these important statements, their replication here may provide readers with the basic framework presupposed by those currently doing creative work in one or another area.

Although most of these religious writers have kept the bulk of their research within a particular field, many of them have been quite interested in other areas of change. To explore the roots of a particular social problem is almost inevitably to see its connections with other problems. Solutions, too, are seen as inextricably bound together. For example, a freeze on weaponry is also seen as an important step toward international social justice. On the other hand, tensions between various movements (as well as within a particular movement) also appear frequently. Questions of priority, causality, co-option, and the like, can easily be troubling or even divisive. Feminists note that male revolutionaries often exhibit quite sexist attitudes, whereas activists concerned primarily with the gap between rich and poor may feel that many feminist concerns are middle-class. Those who theologize from these social movements are quite likely to reflect some of these tensions. By the same token, they are perhaps more likely to look for convergences between movements. The selections in this volume only hint at these areas of agreement and disagreement. The discerning reader will begin to recognize a number of regions where participants in these movements will need to discuss differences and convergences. It is my belief that both common concerns and tensions will serve as a rich source of further religious reflection and theology.

Is it possible to construct a theological synthesis from these social movements? Is it possible to develop a *general* theory of religion in the face of social change, and in particular, a theology of social change? If individual social movements have been so richly suggestive to men and women of faith, should they not, then, if taken together, imply something at least equally profound?

The answer to these questions may well be affirmative, but we should perhaps first note that activists and theoreticians in these movements (often the same persons) are, in many instances, stubbornly particularistic. By this I mean that they insist on the reality of the problem or evil that gave birth to the social movement in the first place. They will not permit any reduction to another "more basic" oppression or contradiction. Abstractions are part of the problem, not of the solution. In so insisting, these writers prevent us from finding easy exits from the dilemmas that concern them.

And what is true of social analysis is also true of theological reflection. The theologian must be willing to trace the complete anatomy of a particular social evil, and not move to a theoretical standpoint that would leave it behind, or distance it.

Still, there are commonalities in the very processes of their religious reflection that we can and should pay attention to. Not forgetting the above caveat, we not only can but must begin to ask questions such as these: How is religion affected by social change? What is the stance of theology vis-à-vis this relationship? What is the meaning of faith in the light of all this? In what sense can it be said to be unchanging or unswerving? Do Christians today accept a necessity for changing religious concepts in a way that would have been virtually unthinkable even a couple decades ago? What kind of theological evaluation can we make of social change itself? Can we typify some social change as humane, liberating, and self-fulfilling, and other change as debasing, alienating, and antihuman? If so, what are the criteria for such a classification, and whence are they drawn? Can some change—for example, political revolution—be described as both liberating and oppressive at the same time? What is the relationship of religious consciousness to *reactionary* change, if we define reactionary change as movement to more alienating and oppressive social structures? Should we distinguish between religion and religious consciousness, and if so, how are we to distinguish? How are we to compare religious consciousness to nonreligious consciousness?[5]

Ultimately, we may need to explore the meaning of religion itself. In some of these movements there is already a tendency to broaden or narrow the concept of religion. For example, Christian feminists may take quite seriously Gnostic forms of early Christianity and even early pagan religions, particularly insofar as these religions incorporate goddess-worship. In contrast, pacifists might be inclined to utterly disavow forms of "religion" that uncritically embrace militarism.

It seems to me that this second-order form of reflection has hardly begun. It also appears to me that some thoughtful religious persons must eventually take up the task. This book therefore concludes with an epilogue, some reflections on what might constitute basic features of a "theology of social change" (itself part of a broader canvas, that of postmodern theology).

SOME LIMITATIONS

Let me conclude by acknowledging some unavoidable limitations of this collection. These limitations can be discerned from both poles described earlier. From the point of view of social change, there are certainly many features of society and many social movements that have affected the consciousness of Christians and are not represented here, at least as a major category. There are minority groups in the United States, for example, who are finding their own voice in a culture that had previously not given them much recognition. Thus, Amerindians, Asian-Americans, and Hispanic-Americans are demanding to be heard. And there are whole areas of life that are quite neglected in these pages; religion and politics, and experimental communities are just two areas that come easily to mind. There are also currents or tendencies in our culture that are not so easily defined, but which may be as real or more real than the ones represented here. Many thinkers, for example, have detected a movement to narcissism in the 1970s and some have noticed a trend to commitment (of a personal kind) in the 1980s.

My excuse of course is that one has to stop somewhere, and that these six areas seem quite representative of ways in which social movements have affected Christianity. I have wanted to be as simple as possible; to stay therefore with a handful of movements easily recognizable as such. These six are that, if for no other reason than the large number of persons willing to write letters to editors, make telephone calls to talk shows, or even take to the streets in support of their convictions. I am not looking for completeness, but for interesting and instructive representatives of an important phenomenon.

As far as the other pole, religion, is concerned, it is clear from the briefest glance at the selections included here that I have focused almost exclusively on Christianity. There are a few references to Judaism, but any anthology doing justice to Judaism would have a substantially different list of selections, including, for example, representatives of Jewish feminism. Islam and other non-Western religions have been completely left out, although a comparative study of the impact of social change on them would make fascinating reading. Here, too, I can only plead that this volume had to be kept within manageable boundaries. Sacrifice in breadth has perhaps allowed for more richness elsewhere. The pieces that are included here do reflect a wide variety of themes and traditions within Christianity. Perhaps more importantly, they convey a sense of the kind of exploration that deserves the designation "religious."

NOTES

1. This question implies its converse: To what extent does religion impede or block social change?
2. Peter Berger, *The Sacred Canopy* (New York, Doubleday, 1967), chap. 4.
3. A remarkable instance of this was the 1983 meetng of Pope John Paul II with General Jaruselski in Poland. The general was widely described as trembling in the presence of the pontiff.

4. There are significant exceptions to this observation. Perhaps the most notable is Rosemary Ruether, who has made valuable contributions to a number of these areas. Several of her books and articles have the clear purpose of relating one social movement to another.

5. Struggling for social change seems to diminish the differences between the religious and the nonreligious. Religious feminists are comfortable with NOW; Christian peace groups work closely with SANE. And vice versa.

PART ONE
RELIGION AND FEMINISM

Perhaps more than any other social movement in recent years, the women's movement has had a very clear, very direct, and very immediate impact on religious perceptions and religious attitudes. (Whether it has had equally profound effects on religious institutions themselves, I leave others to judge.) This does not mean that the women's movement is more important or more crucial than the others; it simply indicates that it is in some ways easier to trace its effects on religious consciousness.

Feminist religious studies have already developed numerous subdivisions, each with its own eminent specialists. These specialists have a dual task; to keep in touch with one another, and to stay abreast of developments in at least one secular discipline or theological or biblical field that is not particularly feminist. The result has been an astonishing output, as diverse and imaginative as it is large in quantity. Nor does this torrent of materials show any sign of abating. Although earlier feminist writers (Daly, Swidler, Ruether, Russel) are still contributing significantly, a whole host of slightly younger writers are adding their voices. The result is not exactly a unified chorus; yet for all their diversity, there is an amazing sense of camaraderie, good will, and just plain good humor among these women. There is also a shared rage, amply evidenced in the selections included here.

Some of the feminist religious writers work principally within a particular religious tradition. Usually this is Jewish or Christian, although there has recently been a noticeable increase in studies of the role of women in Moslem societies. On the other hand, there is a significant group of women who are more interested in forms of religiousness outside the familiar traditions. For many of these women, the very structure of Western religion speaks blatantly of patriarchy and hierarchy, therefore of domination. Even the names of some of these women (Hallie Mountainwing, Starhawk, Z. Budapest) suggest their desire to make a clean break with the past as it is usually presented to us.

It is important to observe, however, that these women are not outside *all* tradition. They appeal to traditions that reach outside and well beyond Western religion; traditions that extend to Yucatan and the ancient Middle East, to religions of fertility and of the Great Goddess. Nonfeminists may be tempted to dismiss these writers as "far-out," but their sisters listen to them and learn from them. As they see it, the experimentation of their "less orthodox" sisters has an essential role in pushing religious consciousness outward.

The very methods of religious study and of theology are undergoing important changes at the hands of feminists. Several years ago I attended a meeting at which a number of presentations were offered in behalf of various liberal and radical theologies. The *manner* of the feminist presentation was quite unique. For all the other groups, a single advocate was chosen, or perhaps several representatives spoke briefly in succession. When it was the turn of feminist theology, Rosemary Ruether, Sheila Collins, Beverly Harrison, and a number of other representatives simply sat in a semicircle and faced the audience. The *female community* was the advocate. In this case, McLuhan's oft-repeated maxim, "the medium is the message," seemed especially apt.

Symbol takes on a special importance for feminist theology and feminist religious thinking. As Kay Turner points out below, mere structural change frequently fails to be very liberating, and this is particularly true when one speaks of liberation from subordinate sexual roles. A loosening from this kind of bondage requires new concepts, new ways of perceiving. An examination of the symbols that guide us and shape our thinking is essential in making a new consciousness possible. And this process is surely more than intellectual. Action, ritual, celebration, and song—to mention just a few forms of expression—will be necessary ingredients.

On the other hand, it is not difficult to point to *substantive* changes in religious consciousness and theology derived from feminism. Here there is room for a few words about the history of religion, biblical studies, systematic theology, liturgy, and leadership within the church.

For Carol Christ and other feminists, 'the very existence of a scriptural canon, of hierarchy and dogma, indicates the tendency of Judaism and Christianity to see reality and particularly religious reality in terms of insiders versus outsiders. This suppression of dissent, or rather of pluralism, within a religious tradition, is at the very core of patriarchalism. In fact, the history of Judaism and Christianity is not a single tradition at all. Rather, it is the history of an underground and an "overground" or unfolding of the dominant tradition, in which the very existence of a countertradition is a scandal and a threat. It is no coincidence that women have been prominent in the countertraditions. Diffuse, naturalistic, and antihierarchical modes of thinking and organizing have either attracted women, or women have tended to foster them, or both. It makes little difference. What we need to note is the upsurge of such moments in history, as well as their systematic suppression.

Carol Christ gives three historical examples. The first was the elimination of any notion of "goddess" in Hebrew religion. Indeed, she suggests that it was in order to further such a clarification and definition that all-out war was necessary to rid Israel of polytheism. The second was the need within Christianity to define orthodox doctrine and to eliminate heresy, in particular Gnosticism. One of the principal threats of Gnosticism was its suggestion of female authority. The third example was the prolonged war carried on against witchcraft at the beginning of the modern era. Again, by far the greater share of the victims were women. From recent historical studies, it appears that witchcraft was not a turn to devil-worship at all, but was a continuation of pagan and folk religion. That women should have considerable power in these cults was the very crux of the problem. Thus the sexual overtones of many of the diatribes against witches and witchcraft.

The conclusion Christ draws from her brief study of these historical examples is that the very exclusivity of Western religion has been directly related to the issue of power. To share power with women has been to raise disturbing questions concerning the nature and source of that power. Even today, scholars must be careful in evaluating this side of history, because they are likely to be affected by the presuppositions that shaped the canonical tradition in the first place.

In her research on the Gnostic gospels, Elaine Pagels provides the kind of study Carol Christ calls for. Pagels shows us that not only is there a different theoretical notion of woman in these texts, but also women are concretely portrayed as effective leaders: prophets, seers, apostles, ritualists. Not surprisingly, large numbers of women were attracted to the sects that made use of these gospels. On the other hand, the fathers of the church generally reacted to them with horror and vituperation. The fact that we *do* refer to them as *fathers* indicates to what an extent later Christianity has been affected by their sentiments. Pagels's historical detective work may well lead us to question our neat picture of what the church was and is. Any such questioning is bound to lead to a new understanding of authority and leadership within the church.

As the biblical scholar Phyllis Trible points out, feminist biblical studies can pursue several alternatives to traditional approaches. One option is to expose, with appropriate outrage, the indignities and humiliations to which women have been subjected in biblical religion. This can lead to outright rejection of such religion, but perhaps this is the price we must pay for the truth. Another (more revisionist?) stance is to look for the positive liberationist elements in biblical texts, and stress them as normative. A third possibility is to read the texts not judgmentally at all, but in a spirit of solidarity and of "being-there" with the named and unnamed women whom we witness as suffering in the pages of the Bible.

An outstanding example of the second approach (without ever being at all apologetic) is the work of Elisabeth Schüssler Fiorenza. In her thoroughly scholarly study of the pre-Pauline and Pauline church, she brings to our attention the significant role women played in the early church. Her research is especially helpful in reinterpreting the letters of St. Paul, so often used to justify the subordination of women. Schüssler Fiorenza reminds us of how often he refers to women as "co-workers," "apostles," and "deacon-nesses." What is significant is the matter-of-fact way Paul assumes their independence and equality. These women, like Paul himself, are empowered by the Spirit. And these texts are passed on to us *despite* the fact that the tradition in which they appear is male-dominated.

In the case of Jesus, we do not have any biblical texts that carry a negative image of women. He does not accept even passively the sexist views of his time and social environment. In an article that does not appear here, Schüssler Fiorenza puts it quite clearly: "It is remarkable that the canonical literature does not transmit a single androcentric statement or sexist story of Jesus, although he lived and preached in patriarchal culture and society." Leonard Swidler, in his brief but effective "Jesus Was a Feminist," brings out forcefully how sensitive Jesus was to women. His acts and words signified a profound commitment to sexual equality, all the more noteworthy in that such behavior was directly opposed to the common practice of rabbis of his day.

Feminist theologians have recognized for some time that if sexual inequality on the one hand and women's experience on the other are to be taken seriously, then a whole recasting of religious concepts will be necessary. Not only will the "maleness" of God, Christ, and the church have to be reassessed, but also the exclusivity and rigidity already mentioned will have to be first uncovered and then addressed. Despite the considerable work done in systematic theology by such scholars as Rosemary Ruether, Letty Russel, Beverly Harrison, and perhaps most notably by Mary Daly, I think it only fair to say that the task has barely been begun.

One area on which they have concentrated has been that of language. Some hearers or readers are startled or amused by such unfamiliar phases as "hallowed be her name" and "faith of our mothers." The small element of shock involved in these reactions, though, might help all of us understand the sense of exclusion that has been the natural consequence of so many all-male religious formulas.

Mary Daly has bigger game in mind than semantics. To depict God as male (even when denying that there is any *real* sexual identification) is to reflect patterns of exclusion at the very heart of religious faith. This tendency is dramatically increased when we see God as incarnated, literally embodied, in the male human Jesus. The power for legitimation of sexual stereotypes carried by these twin symbols is enormous. We need not join in Daly's emphatic renunciation of Christianity to appreciate that she and her sister theologians have presented us with significant problems we ought not to avoid.

The novelist Mary Gordon tackles a problem of particular importance to Catholics. What are we to make of Mary, so clearly central to the Catholic tradition, if we wish to be faithful to the criterion of sexual equality? Feminists generally agree that devotion to Mary has usually gone hand in hand with outrageous forms of discrimination against women. For detailed scholarly assessments, one can read Rosemary Ruether's *Mary, the Feminine Face of the Church* and Marina Warner's *Alone of All Her Sex.* Mary Gordon's attempt to do a contemporary mariology is attractive precisely because it is what many of us must eventually do: make sense of a historical tradition, but also of our own roots, our own personal story.

For many, no matter what their tradition, the issue of women and church leadership has boiled down to the question: Should women be ordained priests? Even the question invites misunderstanding and misinterpretation, for it may not be clear which church we are speaking of: Catholic, Anglican, Orthodox. . . . Then there is the very different question of whether women should become rabbis, with the contrasting sets of problems and attitudes represented by each of the three Jewish traditions most prominent in the United States.

And of course there is already a whole history of experiences, of failures and successes, of women clergy within Protestant churches. This experience raises as many questions as it answers, for few feminists would claim that the churches that have accepted women as leaders have been or are completely free of sexism. In her "Women in the Ministry Face the '80's," Barbara Brown Zikimund reveals how women ministers are plagued by attitudes of paternalism, jealousy (sexual and professional), and insensitivity. In contrast with this, Patricia Park, one of the recently ordained Episcopal priests, gives us a sense of what a woman priest can bring to life within the church.[1] To invest authority in the female is automatically to make the church more democratic, to change therefore the nature of the *entire* assembly.

Nevertheless, for those churches that have not yet permitted the ordination of women, the question "Should women be ordained?" continues to be felt with a mixture of pain, confusion, and anger. Arguments continue to be offered on both sides, although polls show a trend favoring women's ordination. Mary O'Connell does a nice job of lining up some of the more common arguments, and showing us what the debate tends to hinge upon. For example, if the church is radically sacramental, to what extent is representation of Christ crucial to those sacraments? And how literally are we to understand representation? As a more or less photographic likeness? Meanwhile, groups such as the Women's Ordination Conference are moving beyond this narrow question. As they see it, broader issues of discrimination could easily be swept under the rug, even if women are somehow brought into the hierarchical network. Indeed, such an inclusion might effectively co-opt women. Structures that have supported domination would then continue to do so.

Rosemary Ruether suggests that the meaning of sacrament itself may need to be reexamined. If "dispensing" the sacraments is understood merely in terms of power, so that a select few have the ability to admit them or shut them off, then the church will have drifted far from genuine Christianity.[2] Women may not wish to give up the perspective that enables them to recognize malformations such as these, simply to become "insiders."

NOTES

1. Patricia Park, "Women and Liturgy," in Judith Weidman, ed., *Women Ministers* (New York, Harper, 1981).

2. Rosemary Ruether, "Ordination: What is the Problem?" in Ann Marie Gardiner, ed., *Women and the Catholic Priesthood: An Expanded Vision* (New York, Paulist, 1976). 30–34.

Chapter 1

Carol P. Christ

Heretics and Outsiders

The Struggle over Female Power in Western Religion

I approach this topic as one who views herself as an outsider to the canons and traditions of the West. It is no secret that the "great works" of the Western tradition are written from a male-centered perspective in which the experiences specific to women are ignored, suppressed, or treated only in relation to the interests of men.

The *Iliad* is a case in point. Its major dramatic conflict between Achilles and Agamemnon generates Achilles' "metaphysical dilemma" of whether to seek honor and live a short but glorious life, or to refuse honor and live long but unmemorably. Critics rarely note that both the dramatic conflict and the metaphysical dilemma are generated by an argument between two men over one of the most precious spoils of war, the "spear captive" Briseis. Briseis is a raped woman, a victim of the wars of men, yet her tragedy is treated simply as the occasion for the conflicts of men. How can I find myself in such a tradition without losing my identity as a woman?

This sense of myself as outsider has led me to question many conventional pieties about canons and traditions, particularly the largely unexamined premise that the so-called "great works" have become central and authoritative primarily because they express the struggles and aspirations of humanity in a compelling and beautiful way.

Biblical scholar James Sanders, for example, expresses such a view when he says that his book *Torah and Canon* is a "quest *for the essence of the power of life the Bible demonstrably has*. This power is evident not only in the Bible's remarkable survival for over 2,500 years," he writes, "but in its function as the vehicle of survival to the communities whose identities and life-styles issue from their adherence to it."[1] Sanders apparently assumes that canonical works survive because of an intrinsic vision which commends itself to the hearts and minds of communities. Certainly the Bible has had a compelling power for some in the West; I only note that this view is deceptively one-sided. Sanders does not ask to what extent the survival of the Bible might also be due to political struggles, including slander and repression of rival traditions. Nor does he ask for whom Biblical tradition is a power of life, and for whom, perhaps, a power of death.

First published in *Soundings,* 61 (1978), pp. 260–80. Used by permission.

It is precisely this mundane question which I wish to address here. My first point is simple, obvious, and often overlooked: *the existence of a canon or a canonical tradition implies the existence of outsiders and heretics.* Now the consequences of being outside a canonical tradition (in the West at least) are as follows: texts outside the canon are slandered, often suppressed, sometimes destroyed; groups existing outside canonical authority are often declared heretical; adherents of heretical groups are often persecuted, sometimes killed.

My second point is an hypothesis which I will explore through the discussion of three historic struggles between the proponents of the traditions which became canonical and those whom they declared to be outsiders and heretics. This hypothesis is as follows: myths suppressed by the canonical tradition often contained powerful female symbolism; the texts or traditions transmitting this symbolism may often have had a special appeal for women because they offered greater opportunities for the expression of female power; and the persons persecuted by the canonical tradition may have been disproportionately female.

I will explore this hypothesis by examining some intriguing evidence concerning the struggles between the proponents of views which became canonical and persons whom they identified as outsiders and heretics. Instances of such struggles will be drawn from ancient Hebrew religion, early Christianity, and the middle Christian period. The juxtaposition of these three periods presents a disturbing pattern of suppression of female symbolism and power by the traditions which became canonical in the West.

I do not wish to belabor the feminist criticism of Western religion as male-centered in its specific teachings on the place of women in family, church, and society, and in its core symbolism of divinity. Rather, I wish to examine the apologetic argument which states that the male symbolisms and hierarchies of the Jewish and Christian religions were a spontaneous and natural development given their historical contexts. I will argue to the contrary that the Jewish and Christian traditions were not passive with regard to their environments. At crucial points proponents of the canonical traditions engaged in ideological struggles with competing religious traditions in the course of which female symbolism and female power were actively suppressed.

The historical arguments which I make here are more difficult to document than the familiar charges of sexism in Western religion. Because histories of Western religion do not usually ask how Western religion came to be male-centered, there is no body of secondary scholarship to which to appeal. Moreover, the practitioners of defeated religious traditions have been slandered as idol worshippers, whores, and worse in the official texts of the canonical tradition, and few scholars have been willing to challenge this official view. Finally, the texts of competing religious traditions were often destroyed by the canonical groups, for example, in the burning of the library at Alexandria and the book-burnings of the middle Christian period. Because the evidence on which a clear picture of the outsiders and heretics in Western tradition could be constructed is too often nonexistent or not adequately interpreted by scholarship, the argument of this paper will have to be somewhat more hypothetical than I could wish.

The interest of non-canonical groups in female power and female symbols is no longer hypothetical in the contemporary period, however. In the traditions being developed by some of today's most conspicuous outsiders and heretics, the women in the women's spirituality movement and the feminist witches, there is a resurgence of interest in female power and female symbolism. In a final section of this paper I will briefly discuss this new development in contemporary religious consciousness, particularly as it bears on the relation of canon and anti-canon.

THE SUPPRESSION OF THE GODDESS IN ANCIENT HEBREW RELIGION

According to a widely held view, the official religion of ancient Israel was largely a monotheistic worship of one God, Yahweh. The Hebrew people held to their monotheistic tradition against the temptations presented by the polytheistic traditions of neighboring peoples, because monotheism was ethically and religiously superior to polytheism. Only rarely did the people of Israel succumb to polytheistic practices, referred to as "Baalism," "fetishism" (often synonymous with goddess worship), and "cult prostitution." The prophets criticized these "excesses" and "aberrations" of faith and returned the people to monotheism.

Recent scholarship and archaeological discoveries have challenged this interpretive paradigm. Scholars have discovered that the religion of the Hebrew people was more pluralistic than the monotheistic paradigm indicates, and that the religion of the Canaanites was not mere fetishism and idolatry. Nonetheless the paradigm of a dominant Yahwistic monotheism remains a major interpretive scheme through which the history of biblical religion is taught.[2]

In his book, *Palestinian Parties and Politics Which Shaped the Old Testament,*[3] Morton Smith questioned the standard paradigm of biblical religion. He argued that widespread adherence to monotheism in ancient Israel was a fiction created by ultimately victorious "Yahweh-alone" groups which established control of Israelite religion after the Babylonian exile. These "Yahweh alone" groups edited and rewrote the texts which became the biblical canon to make them conform to their view that the worship of Yahweh alone was the true religion of ancient Israel and Judah from the beginning and that worship of gods and goddesses other than Yahweh constituted heretical deviation. According to Smith the dominant groups in ancient Israel and Judah were polytheistic, worshipping several gods and goddesses, including Baal, Anath, Asherah, El, and others, alongside Yahweh. The defining characteristic of ancient Hebrew religion was worship of Yahweh, but not worship of Yahweh only.

Mythologist Raphael Patai's work, *The Hebrew Goddess,*[4] complements Smith's work. Patai also argues that goddess-worship was prevalent in the official religions of ancient Israel and Judah. He cites the books of I and II Kings as one record of struggles between worshippers of Yahweh and worshippers of other gods and goddesses. Though these books were edited to slander the worshippers of gods and goddesses other than Yahweh as followers after "abomination," they acknowledge the widespread occurrence of polytheism and goddess worship in the biblical period, not only among the populace, but in the official state cults. According to Patai's count the goddess Asherah was worshipped in the temple of Solomon in Jerusalem for 236 of its 370 years of existence. In the Northern Kingdom Asherah was consistently worshipped in the capital city of Samaria from the time of Jezebel. Even if these precise figures are rendered problematic by the recognition that they may be the product of partisan editorship, as Smith suggests they are, the general picture of polytheistic worship in both kingdoms must be accepted. This picture is further supported by the discovery of female figures in archaeological digs at sites connected with worship in ancient Israel and Judah.

Based on the evidence brought forth by Smith and Patai, we might reverse the conventional notion of ancient Hebrew religion, and speak instead of a dominant tradition of polytheism and goddess-worship in the official cult, which was broken only occasionally by the victories of Yahweh-alone groups.

It should be stressed that the struggles between the Yahweh-alone groups and the others were not mere ideological battles. They were political struggles in which force was often used. *Exodus* records that the Levites ordained themselves for the service of Yahweh by murdering 3000 worshippers of the golden calf (Exodus 32:25-29).[5] After Elijah's victory over Elisha, 450 prophets of Baal were killed (I Kings 18:40).[6] Jehu killed the worshippers of Baal in the house of Baal in order to solidify his ascension to the throne following the slaying of Jezebel (II Kings 10:18-30).

Clearly the struggles between the Yahweh-alone groups and the other groups were not simple struggles between women worshippers of the goddess and men worshippers of Yahweh. Men and women were involved in both the worship of Yahweh and the worship of gods and goddesses other than Yahweh. And the polytheistic groups were not exclusively devoted to the goddess. Still we may note that one consequence of the suppression of polytheism by the Yahweh-alone groups was the elimination of goddess-worship. And we may ask whether women may have been particularly attracted to the worship of the goddess as an expression of female power. There is some evidence to suggest that this may have been the case.

In the books of *I* and *II Kings* and *I* and *II Chronicles* the worship of the goddess in the cult sites is often blamed on the influence of foreign queens, wives of the kings. Jezebel is the most notorious example. Now it is possible that the queens worshipped the goddess because they were foreign, not because they were women. And it is also possible, though unlikely, that the misogynist biblical editors attributed everything they considered evil to the influence of women, but that women were not in fact central figures in the institution and defense of goddess worship. Nonetheless it is intriguing to speculate that foreign and native women, like the queens of Israel and Judah, were attracted to the worship of the goddess as a symbol for female power. The murder of Jezebel (II Kings 9:30-37) would then have been a political attack on the religion of the goddess.[7] And the prohibitions at the time of the second Temple against Israelite men taking foreign wives would have been part of an attempt finally to suppress goddess worship and polytheism since women who had been reared in goddess-worshipping traditions would not easily give up the symbol of female power.

The book of *Jeremiah* offers further evidence in support of the view that women were especially devoted to the goddess. In *Jeremiah* the following words are put in the mouth of "all the people":

> As for the word that you have spoken to us in the name of Yahweh—we shall not listen to you. But we shall do everything as we said: we shall burn incense to the Queen of Heaven, and shall pour her libations as we used to do, we, our fathers, our kings, and our princes, in the cities of Judah and in the streets of Jerusalem. For then we had plenty of food, and we all were well and saw no evil.

To these words the women added:

> Is it we alone who burn incense to the Queen of Heaven and pour her libations? Is it without our husbands that we make her cakes in her image and that we pour her libations? [44:15-17].

Though the passage indicates that all the people participated in the worship of the Queen of Heaven, it also suggests that women performed many of the acts related to the cult and that women may have been viewed as the instigators or special devotees of goddess-worship.

Women's attraction to goddess worship may not have been only a symbolic preference. In *When God Was a Woman* Merlin Stone brings together a great deal of evidence in support of her view that the status of women was higher in matrilineal goddess-worshipping cultures than it was in patrilineal Israel and Judah. In Egypt the woman was often head of the family, while in Babylon the wife could acquire property, take legal action and make contracts.[8] In Israel and Judah these rights were curtailed.

These lines of evidence point to the conclusion that the Bible was shaped by politically victorious Yahweh-alone groups whose victory had the effect (if not the intent) of slandering and prohibiting goddess worship, declaring the religious inclinations of many women to be outside the tradition, and depriving women of many of the rights which they had had in goddess-worshipping cultures. If this conclusion is correct, then we must ask whose "power of life" the Biblical tradition expressed, and we must entertain the conclusion that it was not women's.

SUPPRESSION OF GNOSTIC "HERETICS"

The victory of Christianity signaled the suppression of goddess-worship in the ancient world. The temples of the goddess-at Aphaca, Eleusis, Rome, Ephesus, Athens, and elsewhere were forcibly closed in the fourth and fifth centuries C.E. This was the end of public goddess-worship in the Christian West. However, it is not the struggle between Christianity and other religions over female symbolism and female power which I wish to consider here. Rather I wish to consider a suppression of female symbolism and power which occurred *within* the Christian tradition in the struggles which led to the formation of the Christian canon.

A study of the religion of the gnostic Christians suggests that the question of female symbolism and power was also a significant factor in their struggle with those who became orthodox Christians. In fact, if we are to believe the recent Vatican declaration denying the priesthood to women, the ordination of women by the gnostics was one of the reasons the orthodox church suppressed them. "A few heretical sects in the first century, especially gnostic ones, entrusted the priestly ministry to women," the Vatican reports, and "this innovation was immediately noted and condemned by the fathers."[9]

A common paradigm used to interpret early Christian history assumes that the early Christian communities which grew up after the death of Jesus were founded by Peter and Paul and the other male disciples, and that there was a fairly smooth transition between these groups and the early orthodox Church. If they are mentioned at all, the gnostics are viewed as libertine heretics who denied the central Christian doctrine of the unity of the spirit and the flesh, and whose factionalizing influence was rightly suppressed by the Church Fathers. So widespread is this view that "gnosticism" has become a pejorative theological shorthand for any antinomian spiritualizing tendency.

As recent discoveries of gnostic gospels have proved, this conventional view is more polemical than factual. Early Christianity seems to have been far more pluralistic than is generally recognized. Both the gnostic Christians and those groups which later declared themselves orthodox and canonical had their own gospels and claimed to be followers of the religion of Jesus Christ. Only after political struggles did some groups emerge victorious and declare the others heretical.

Elaine Pagels's recent study[10] offers convincing evidence that the gnostic Christian groups provided more avenues for the expression of female symbolism and female power than did their orthodox Christian opponents. Gnostic Christian groups, as Pagels describes them, abounded in female imagery of God. The Valentinians, for example, imaged the divine as a Dyad consisting of two elements: on the one hand, the Ineffable, the Source, the Primal Father, and on the other, the Silence, the Mother of All

Things. Other gnostics viewed the Holy Spirit as a divine Mother, and still others characterized the female element in God as the Holy Wisdom, following Hebrew traditions of Wisdom as the companion of God.

Were the gnostics declared heretical primarily because they employed female symbolism? Pagels rejects this conclusion as simplistic. However, among the "scandals" the victorious Christian groups claimed to find in the heretics, she notes the often repeated charge that they allowed women authority in their communities. Gnostic works like the *Gospel of Mary* provide further evidence of a political struggle between female and male disciples of Jesus over the issue of female leadership. In the *Gospel of Mary,* Peter objects to Mary's claim to have received a special revelation from Jesus and he is rebuked by Levi who says, "Peter, you are always irascible. You object to the women as our enemies do. Surely the Lord knew her very well, and indeed loved her more than us. . . ." Mary is then allowed to speak with authority of the revelation Jesus entrusted to her.[11]

From this evidence Pagels concludes that, whether or not it was the primary cause, one of the effects of the condemnation of the gnostics by the canonical tradition was that female symbolism and leadership were suppressed.

This evidence from the early Christian era suggests that the suppression of female symbolism and power was one of the results of the political struggles which led to the establishment of the Christian canon, a pattern similar to that which seems to have occurred in the establishment of the Hebrew canon. Again we must ask whose "power of life" the victorious tradition reflected. Perhaps women found themselves better represented by the traditions which were declared heretical.

WITCH PERSECUTION IN THE MIDDLE CHRISTIAN PERIOD

The story of the suppression of female symbolism and female power by the canonical traditions of the West could be continued through a discussion of other "heretical" movements which surfaced within Christianity.[12] But I will instead focus on a conflict between the tradition and the outsiders in which the suppression of female power was carried out in particularly violent fashion, the witch persecution of the middle Christian period.

As with the goddess-worshippers and the gnostics, the canonical view of the witches has impeded unbiased treatment of their practices and beliefs. It is commonly thought that witches worshipped the devil in bizarre rites in which children were sacrificed and that participants engaged in perverse sexual practices.

This view is the product of Christian polemic such as that found in the *Malleus Maleficarum,* but it has also influenced two standard paradigms used in scholarship concerning witchcraft. On the one side "ultraconservative" scholars accept the charges of the persecutors that witchcraft was an anti-Christian rite inspired by the devil. On the other side "liberal rationalists" view witchcraft as the creation of the witch persecutors and deny the historical reality of witch practice.[13] A third and different view is reflected in the much disputed hypothesis of Margaret Murray that witchcraft was a survival of the pagan religions of Western Europe. Murray's work has been widely challenged by scholars but her general theory has recently been defended by Mircea Eliade, a leading historian of religions.

Unfortunately, less is known about witch practice and belief than about the religions of the goddess-worshippers and the gnostics. After the forced closing of their temples and the suppression of their priesthoods and priestesshoods in the early Christian period, European pagan traditions survived only in folk custom and in secret societies, and were communicated orally. The major written documents concerning witch practice and belief are the trial documents, and writings and decrees of Christian theologians and Church councils, which are biased. Thus the picture of witchcraft presented here will have to be somewhat hypothetical.

Though scholars disagree about what witchcraft was, except for the ultraconservatives, they agree that many of the charges against the witches were fabricated by their persecutors. It is further agreed by all that large numbers of people were killed as witches between the years 1400 and 1700 as a result of persecutions carried out in the name of the Catholic and Protestant faiths. Estimates of the numbers killed range from 100,000 to nine million or more, with some scholars settling on one million as a reasonably *conservative* estimate,[14] staggering numbers considering the smaller population of Europe at the time. Though scholars are also agreed that women figured disproportionately among those persecuted as witches, few have asked why this was so.[15]

Often portrayed as resulting from peasant hysteria, the witch persecutions were in fact instigated by an educated elite who saw themselves as defenders of canonical tradition. In 1484 Pope Innocent issued a bull[16] which made official the Church's intention to persecute witches. Two Dominican theologians, Heinrich Kramer and James Sprenger, were the authors of the *Malleus Maleficarum,*[17] which became the classic text for witch "hammering." Kramer and Sprenger argue that women are more attracted to witchcraft than men, providing arguments from scripture and tradition to support their view. In answer to the question, "Why is it that women are chiefly addicted to evil superstitions?" they assert that women are more credulous and lightminded, more impressionable, and more given to gossip than men. But the most compelling reason is that "a woman is more carnal than a man, as is clear from her many carnal abominations." Or as they sum it up, "All witchcraft comes from carnal lust which in women is insatiable."[18] The crimes of the witches which Kramer and Sprenger find most objectionable are related to women's alleged sexual nature, including copulating with devils, obstructing the act of generation, making the male organ disappear, and offering newborn children to the devil. Other crimes Sprenger and Kramer allege against witches can be interpreted as species of folk magic, folk medicine, and folk psychology, including methods of preventing conception, procuring abortion, harming animals or crops, producing hail, and predicting the future through a variety of means.

The preoccupation of Sprenger and Kramer with crimes relating to female sexuality, female control over the birth process, and male impotence suggest that the witch persecutions were an attempt to suppress a form of female power which was threatening to the male authorities of church and state.

The question is, What sort of female power did witchcraft represent? Was it simply female sexuality which threatened the witch persecutors, or was witchcraft a competing religious system in which female symbolism and female power were recognized to a greater extent than they were in Christianity? A conclusive answer to this question cannot be obtained at present, but a number of lines of evidence suggest that the witch persecutions may fit into the pattern of suppression of female symbolism and female power which was hypothesized for the periods in which the Hebrew and Christian canons were formed.

Two recent feminist interpretations, which fall into the liberal-rationalist camp, offer intriguing interpretations of the nature of the female power which was suppressed. Barbara Ehrenreich and Dierdre English in their study, *Witches, Nurses, and Midwives,*[19] suggest that many of those persecuted as witches were country doctors, midwives, and herbalists, women who delivered babies, cured the sick, and of course had patients who died. Ehrenreich and English argue that women healers were persecuted because their power over life and death challenged the Church's claim that God and his male deputies, the priests, held all power over life and death. This hypothesis is supported by those portions of the *Malleus* which specifically accuse midwives of using witchcraft to control conception and produce abortion.

In "Why Witches Were Women"[20] Mary Nelson proposes a plausible explanation of some of the more scandalous charges against the witches. The common allegation that witches took away men's generative powers, killed infants, and publicly indulged their sexual lust were projections, she believes, of men's fear of a type of female power which had some basis in social reality. According to Nelson, the years of witch persecution were periods of massive social displacement and poverty, bringing about increases in the numbers of prostitutes (women who publicly indulged sexual lust) and making it necessary to limit family size. Moreover, the most common methods of birth control may have been *coitus interruptus* (women who took away men's generative power) and infanticide of female babies (women who killed infants). Poor women's only ways of surviving the poverty produced by social disruption may have led to their persecution.

In 1921 Margaret Murray[21] challenged both the Christian and the rationalist views of witchcraft and proposed the then startling thesis that witchcraft was a pagan religion and that the persecution of witches was part of a religious war. While many of the details of Murray's view of witch religion have been challenged, her basic hypothesis that witchcraft was a pagan survival has been supported by such scholars of religion as Mircea Eliade[22] and Rosemary Ruether.

Briefly, Murray's hypothesis, deduced from coherences she discovered in the testimony given at witch trials, is that witchcraft in Western Europe was an organized religion with a fairly uniform set of symbols, rituals, and social structures. The witches worshipped a deity who could be incarnate as a male figure (Janus or Dianus), a female figure (Diana), or an animal. The deity personified natural energy and was associated with fertility. Witches met in covens of thirteen and their major celebrations were on May Eve and November Eve. Women had access to leadership positions in the covens.

Rosemary Ruether[23] disputes Murray's theory that witchcraft was an organized religion at the time of the persecutions. She believes that Christianity had already succeeded in destroying the official cults and priesthoods or priestesshoods of pagan religions by the middle Christian period. What survived, Ruether believes, was folk religion, that stratum of religion which belongs to village daily life, the rituals of home and farming life which people carry on by themselves. It included group celebrations such as dances and festivals at planting and harvest times, folk magic, and folk superstition. Ruether believes that women were the primary cultivators of folk magic, or the use of charms, spells, and herbal remedies for curing. According to Ruether, those persecuted as witches were female charismatics, inheritors of traditions of folk religion and the powers derived from it.

In my opinion the theories of witches as midwives and healers should not be set over against the theories of witches as inheritors and transmitters of folk religion, for in these traditions, religion, medicine, and magic probably were not clearly distinguished. If the more spectacular charges of the witch persecutors (copulation with the devil, sacrifice of children) are discounted, a remarkably coherent picture of the practices of the witches can be suggested. Witches were wise and powerful women, practitioners of folk religion, magic, and medicine, whose knowledge of charms, spells, and herbal lore brought them to the bedside at times of birth, illness, and death. The wise woman was summoned at the crises of the life cycle *before* the priest; she delivered the baby, while the priest was called upon later to perform baptism. She was the first to be called upon to cure illness or treat the dying, while the priest was called in after all other remedies had failed, to administer the last rites. Moreover, if the wise woman had knowledge of herbs which could aid or prevent conception or cause abortion, she had a power over the life process which clearly was superior to that of the priest, and which according to official theology made her a rival of God himself. If, moreover, she appealed to pagan deities, some of them probably female, in the performance of divinations or blessings and spells used to promote healing and ward off evil, then it is not difficult to see why she was persecuted by an insecure and misogynist Church which could not tolerate rival power, especially the power of women.

Though the evidence concerning witchcraft is inconclusive due to the lack of direct verification from the free testimony or written texts of witches, the lines of evidence cited here suggest that witch persecution followed the pattern of suppression of female symbolism and female power which seems to have occurred in the formative periods of the Hebrew and Christian traditions.

A METHODOLOGICAL NOTE

This examination of three instances of conflict between the proponents of traditions which were or became canonical and the outsiders or heretics suggests that one of the issues at stake in the definition and defense of canonical tradition in the West was the suppression of female symbolism and power.

Given the persistence of this pattern in the history of the Western tradition, we must ask why scholarship has not been more vigorous in exploring it. The answer to this question seems to be that even the so-called objective traditions of scholarship in the university are not entirely free from certain biases of the canonical tradition. Specifically, the scholarly tradition has largely accepted three canonical views: (1) the ethical and religious superiority of monotheism to polytheism; (2) the inferiority of religious traditions in which sexuality and fertility are central concerns, and the equation of female symbolism with sexuality and fertility; and (3) the importance of maintaining order, and the interpretation of challenges to authorities as antinomian and therefore bad.

In addition the androcentrism of the scholarly tradition, which renders questions about women, female power, or female symbolism trivial and uninteresting because it accepts the subordinate status of women as a given, has blinded scholars to the fascinating history of the suppression of female power and symbolism by the traditions they study. But since an examination of androcentric and other biases in the *scholarly* tradition[24] could form the subject of another paper, I will not pursue it here.

REEMERGENCE OF THE GODDESS AS SYMBOL FOR FEMALE POWER

The suppression of female symbolism and female power by the canonical traditions of the West is being reversed as modern women lay claim to their own forms of spirituality and power. If female symbolism was suppressed at least in part because it was viewed as an expression of female power, then it should not be surprising to discover that symbols of female sacrality are reemerging as women begin to reclaim their spiritual power.

The battles for the ordination of women in the major denominations of Protestantism and in the liberal wings of Judaism are only the most apparent manifestation of a widespread spiritual resurgence among women. During the past several years, a non-institutionalized women's spirituality movement has become one of the major currents in the new wave of feminism. Susan Rennie and Kirsten Grimstad describe this current in their introduction to the spirituality section of *The New Women's Survival Source-book:*

> We found that wherever there are feminist communities, women are exploring psychic and nonmaterial phenomena: reinterpreting astrology; creating and cele-brating feminist rituals around birth, death, menstruation; reading the Tarot; studying pre-patriarchal forms of religion; reviving and exploring esoteric goddess-centered belief systems such as wicce; developing and cultivating dream analysis, ESP, astral projection, precognition; learning psychic and homeopathic healing; rescuing the wholistic perspective of the right hemisphere of the brain from the contempt of left-brain linear mindedness. . . .[25]

Out of the key motifs of this spirituality movement is a new naming of ultimate power or powers. Many women are rediscovering that *one of the oldest names for the fundamental energy*—the energy of natural processes, the energy of life and death, the energy of sexual attraction and repulsion, the energy concentrated in meditation and ritual, the energy felt vibrating in a room when people are really speaking to one another, the energy of psychic healing—*is goddess.*

Barbry MyOwn described the experience of the goddess as energy in a womanspirit circle called Ursa Major. "We have not defined 'goddess' except in loose terms, 'woman-energy.' We hope to invoke a materialization of that woman energy, to love it, to play with it, exult in it."[26] "Spiritually we see our bodies as divine manifestations of womanenergy."[27] Barbry MyOwn and Hallie Mountainwing created a menstruation ritual in which they named themselves sisters of the same mother and invoked "the Goddess whose blood, like our blood, flows with the cycles of the universe."[28] A combination of deep seriousness and playfulness is characteristic of a new attitude toward religion in these women's groups. Knowledge that they are invoking and connecting with fundamental power accounts for the deep seriousness of these women; but they dare to create new ritual forms because they do it playfully and only for themselves at a certain time and place—not for all times and places, not for other women whose experiences may be different.

WomanSpirit magazine[29] provides a space for women from around the country to name the sources of their power by sharing fantasies, rituals, poems, stories, drawings, and photographs on the themes of energy, healing, power, process, nature, wise women, the goddess, and many more. Through *WomanSpirit* women are discovering, creating, choosing their own religious identities. Though the goddess was less frequently men-tioned in the early issues, it is not surprising that her presence as a symbol for female power is becoming increasingly felt as the journal's contributors gather and share power with each other.

Although an important center, *WomanSpirit* is not the only expression of the new feminist spirituality movement. In 1976 a conference in Boston called "Through the Looking Glass" brought together hundreds of women from around the country who shared notes on witchcraft, healing, tarot, the goddess, and much more.[30] Similar conferences have followed. A new journal, *Lady-Unique-Inclination-of-the-Night,*[31] dedicated to a Mayan moon goddess and the expression of feminine spirituality, has recently issued forth from New Brunswick, New Jersey. Most important, women are beginning to gather together in their own womanspirit circles and feminist witchcraft covens all around the country.

The new manifestations of the goddess are manifold. A woman named Mountain-spirit expressed her sense of the goddess in the following way:

I believe the goddess is within and without. . . . Energy is within and without. Exterior and interior, all the dualities we function under lose their meaning when you go deep enough. But we are not all conscious of the goddess within us.[32]

Gail Walker sought the goddess through a study of the mythology associated with the moon and wrote:

The time seems ripe to explore the Moon as a spiritual reflection of the Goddess. . . . The moon's rhythm never misses a beat as her curved shape and arc path vary. The new moon increases and decreases in crescents, bits of her own elemental form. . . . The moon is everchanging, reaching all of her points but rhythmically and in due time.[33]

A third woman, Sarah Wisdom, wrote of encountering the goddess in a dream:

> A wise woman
> sat there in the twilight
> "You must watch ahead," she said,
> "You must walk only on the edge of the sea.
> There is danger in the deep
> But in the sandy desert you will lose your way."
>
> So it is my sisters
> We are on empty shores
>
> uncreated spaces,
>
> filled with echoes of the primitive and the timeless
> and the mysteries of the deep.[34]

Wisdom's poem seems to me to express the situation of women who stand outside the canon on the "empty shores," but who sense their unique opportunity to reconnect with sources of wisdom deeper than those expressed in the canon.

Z Budapest, high priestess of the Susan B. Anthony coven in Los Angeles, has begun to develop a feminist witchcraft tradition in which female power and female symbolism have a central place. Budapest believes that Western religion was developed to celebrate and legitimate male power and that women's liberation requires a secure grounding in women's religion. Budapest's Dianic tradition celebrates the female principle of the universe, the birthing power, as the ultimate sacred power and traces its heritage back to the goddess worshippers of the ancient world and the witches of the middle Christian period.[35]

WOMEN AS ANTI-CANON OR CREATORS OF A NEW CANON?

One might ask whether these developments in women's spirituality signal the creation of a new canon in which women will name God and define reality for themselves, claiming the power denied them in the canonical traditions of the West. This is an intriguing notion. However, it is not surprising to find that many women who stand outside the traditional canon object to the formation of a new canon.

Joan Mallonee states the view of many women in the women's spirituality movement when she says:

I became reluctant to set down interpretations of the Goddess image in my dreams because of a sense that not only was I violating my own material but also in so doing the material would evolve into a dogma, a theology. I had a strong desire to speak about the images which were so strong and powerful, so individual and personal, but I had no desire to create the implication that She would be the same for others as She was for me.[36]

Mary Daly also has taken her stand against canonical traditions. In *Beyond God the Father* she speaks of "sisterhood" as "Anti-Church," a symbol which expresses women's position as outsiders in Western canonical tradition. For Daly, the essence of Anti-Church would be negated if women were to create a new authoritative tradition with official texts and liturgies. Daly envisions a "world without models" as the ideal, and speaks of a feminist liturgy as a contradiction in terms, an "attempt to put new wine, women's awareness, into the old skins of forms that kill female self-affirmation and turn female consciousness against itself."[37] Jean Mountaingrove is even more explicit about the destructive potential of fixed feminist liturgies:

> I think it is important that we do not create new ways for women to fail, because we all have had so much failure. That's why I think it is important for rituals to be open and for each woman to feel her own way so that no one has to feel that they did it wrong. . . . We don't want to say that there is one way to be a feminist spiritual person and you are bad if you don't do it that way.[38]

Like Jean Mountaingrove, Daly sees a need for developing new rituals, but asserts that they must remain open. "There is every reason for women to celebrate our history," Daly writes, "but in ever new ways, not encrusted in stagnant, repetitious ritual."[39]

Women who reject the idea of forming a new canon have a negative view of the canonical process as one which rigidly defines reality and declares certain texts, rituals, and experiences as authoritative while slandering and suppressing those which reflect alternate views of reality. They view canons as promoting conformity and authoritarian mind-sets while denying individual experience and initiative. There is no question that canons function in this way, at least at some times and for some people, perhaps much of the time for women. But there is a second and more positive notion of canon. In this view a canon functions, as Sanders noted, as a "power of life" for a community, reflecting shared histories and shared perceptions of reality. Indeed, as Ralph Norman has argued,[40] there is a sense in which the possibility of communication and community requires implicit acceptance of a minimal canon.

If canon is understood as the shared perceptions of reality which make communication possible, then a community which is totally anti-canon is an impossibility. And certainly the women's spirituality movement is not without a canon in this second sense. Conversations about women's spirituality are deeper and more meaningful if those who participate have read Mary Daly, Rosemary Ruether, Z Budapest, and *Woman-Spirit*.

Rather than rejecting the notion of canon, women might better assume the responsibility for the creation of a new canon. It is important for women to celebrate their shared perceptions of ultimate reality and their power of life in rituals. Women need a heritage and a tradition which will enable them to express and act out the vision of female power which they have discovered outside the canons and traditions of patriarchy.

If the creation of a new canon is inevitable, then the question is whether a new canon can be created which will not also repeat the most destructive features of the old canon: the suppression of individual experience, and the slander and destruction of rival traditions and their adherents. While it is probably not possible for a community to support and legitimate in the same degree the experiences of all its members, it may be possible to create a tradition which is less oppressive than the ones we have known in the West. As Susan Wittig has stated,[41] one sign of a vital tradition is the image which the tradition holds of itself and its relation to the outsiders and heretics, or as she names them, the innovators on the periphery of the canon. The canonical traditions of Western religion do not fare well when judged by this criterion. Perhaps this is the reason many people, especially women, consider the traditional canons moribund. The challenge facing those who have deeply experienced exclusion as part of their own history is to create new traditions that do not exclude others.

NOTES

1. Philadelphia, Fortress, 1974, p. x.
2. Bernard W. Anderson's widely used text, *Understanding the Old Testament* (Englewood Cliffs, N.J., Prentice Hall, 2nd ed., 1966) typifies the problem created when the new evidence about Canaanite religion is discussed within the old paradigm of dominant monotheism. Anderson takes account of the latest historical and archaeological evidence. However, the narrative structure of *Understanding the Old Testament* follows the Yahwistic narrative line, from the exodus covenant with Yahweh at Sinai (chap. 1 and 2) to struggle between faith and culture (chap. 4) to prophetic criticism (chap. 7) to renewal of covenant (chap. 12–14), etc. Within the chapter on Canaanite religion, Anderson improves on previous scholarship: "In many respects, this [the religion portrayed in the Ras Shamra texts] was a highly developed, sophisticated religion, far ahead of the belief in local fertility spirits which scholars once thought the religion of the Baals and Ashtarts to have been (p. 104)." Yet Anderson's discussion of Canaanite religion is set within a chapter in which the narrative line stresses "the great dangers and temptations of life in Canaan" (p. 100), a Yahwistic interpretation which Anderson adopts without acknowledging that he is presenting a Yahwistic viewpoint which may have been a minority opinion in Israel at the time of settlement in Canaan. A work on the religion of the Hebrew people not biased by the Yahwistic viewpoint would not speak of Canaanite religion as a "temptation," but rather as a plausible "solution" to the problems engendered by the settlement.
3. Columbia University Press, 1971.
4. New York, KTAV, 1967. See esp. pp. 42–43, 50, 58–61.
5. The "J" or Yahwistic source in *Exodus,* which records the political-religious murders of the worshippers of the golden calf in the presettlement period, may not be historically reliable. Still it reflects a pattern of murder of opponents of Yahwism which the "J" editors wished to legitimate by reading it back into the presettlement period.
6. The precise figures may not be historical but the pattern of suppression of competing religious groups through murder probably is. Also note that *I Kings* 18:19 mentions that Elijah called 450 prophets of Baal and 400 prophets of Asherah, but the test is waged only with the prophets of Baal, for some reason that the text leaves unexplained.
7. See Merlin Stone, *When God Was A Woman* (New York, Dial, 1976) 57–58.
8. Ibid., esp. pp. 30–61, and Roland de Vaux, *Ancient Israel,* vol. 1, *Social Institutions* (New York, McGraw-Hill, 1965) 39–40.
9. "Excerpts from Vatican's Declaration Affirming Prohibition on Women Priests," *New York Times* (Jan. 28, 1977), p. 8.
10. "What Became of God the Mother? Conflicting Images of God in Early Christianity," *Signs,* 2/2 (Winter 1976) 293–303, esp. 295, 299, 300–301.
11. Ibid., pp. 300–301.
12. Gnosticism is not the only heretical movement which provided greater outlets for female power than canonical tradition. Elisabeth Schüssler Fiorenza notes that women had authority and leading positions in Montanism, Gnosticism, Manichaeism, Donatism, Priscillianism, Messalianism, and Pelagianism, and that they were found among the bishops and priests of the Quintillians ("Feminist Theology as a Critical Theology of Liberation," *Theological Studies,* 36/4 [Dec. 1975] 618). See also Robert E. Lerner, *The Heresy of the Free Spirit in the Later Middle Ages*

(University of California Press, 1972, pp. 228–30) and Gottfried Koch, *Frauenfrage und Ketzertum im Mittelalter* (Berlin, 1962), both cited by Anne Driver in "Materials Not Included in the Canon of Religious Studies: A Neolithic Goddess Cult" (unpublished paper), p. 6.

13. Mircea Eliade divides scholarship on witchcraft into the two groups discussed here. See his "Some Observations on European Witchcraft," *History of Religions,* 14/3 (Feb. 1975) 150–51. He notes that the ultraconservative view is also held by some modern occultists and Luciferians.

14. Rosemary Ruether, *New Woman/New Earth: Sexist Ideologies and Human Liberation* (New York, Seabury, 1975) 111.

15. See, e.g., Margaret Murray, *The Witch-Cult in Western Europe,* (Oxford University Press, 1971) 255–70, and Ruether, *New Woman,* 89.

16. See Heinrich Kramer and James Sprenger, *The Malleus Maleficarum,* translated with an introduction and notes by Montague Summers (New York, Dover, 1971) xliii-xlv.

17. Ibid., esp., 41, 44, 47, 54–61, 66, 80–82, 144–50.

18. Ibid., pp. 44, 47.

19. *A History of Women Healers,* Old Westbury, N.Y., Feminist Press, 1931.

20. Published in Jo Freeman, ed., *Women: A Feminist Perspective* (Palo Alto, Mayfield Publ., 1975) 335–50.

21. See n. 15, above.

22. Eliade, "Some Observations." Eliade discusses evidence which shows how pagan religious groups gradually came to incorporate practices alleged of them by their persecutors.

23. *New Woman/New Earth,* 89–114.

24. See Rita Gross, "Methodological Remarks on the Study of Women and Religion: Review, Criticism, and Redefinition," in Judith Plaskow and Joan Arnold Romero, eds., *Women and Religion* (Missoula, Mont., AAR and Scholars Press, 1974) 153–65; also see Valerie Saiving, "Androcentrism in Religious Studies," *Journal of Religion,* 56/2 (April 1976) 177–96.

25. New York: Knopf, 1975, p. 191.

26. "A Ritual Celebration," *WomanSpirit,* 2/5 (Fall Equinox 1975) 27.

27. Ibid., p. 25.

28. Ibid., p. 28.

29. Published quarterly from Box 263, Wolf Creek, Oregon.

30. See the movie "Musereel #1—A Tapestry of Womanspirit," by Denise Bostrom, Carol Clement, Ariel Dougherty, Nancy Peck, Marilyn Ries.

31. Sowing Circle Press, New Brunswick, N.J.

32. *WomanSpirit,* 3/9 (Fall Equinox 1976) 5.

33. "Moon Change," *Lady-Unique,* 1 (Autumn 1976) 5.

34. "Sea Dream," *WomanSpirit,* 3/10 (Winter Solstice 1976) 30. Used by permission of the author.

35. See Z Budapest, *The Feminist Book of Lights and Shadows,* Luna Publications, 1976.

36. *Lady-Unique,* 1 (Autumn 1976) 12.

37. Boston, Beacon, 1973, pp. 145, also see pp. 69ff. and 132ff.

38. "What Is This Goddess Business," *WomanSpirit,* 3/9 (Fall Equinox 1976) 9.

39. Daly, *Beyond God the Father,* 146.

40. *Soundings,* 61 (1978).

41. Ibid.

Chapter 2

Elaine H. Pagels

What Became of God the Mother?

Conflicting Images of God
in Early Christianity

Unlike many of his contemporaries among the deities of the ancient Near East, the God of Israel shares his power with no female divinity, nor is he the divine Husband or Lover of any.[1] He scarcely can be characterized in any but masculine epithets: King, Lord, Master, Judge, and Father.[2] Indeed, the absence of feminine symbolism of God marks Judaism, Christianity, and Islam in striking contrast to the world's other religious traditions, whether in Egypt, Babylonia, Greece, and Rome or Africa, Polynesia, India, and North America.

Jewish, Christian, and Islamic theologians, however, are quick to point out that God is not to be considered in sexual terms at all. Yet the actual language they use daily in worship and prayer conveys a different message and gives the distinct impression that God is thought of in exclusively *masculine* terms. And while it is true that Catholics revere Mary as the mother of Jesus, she cannot be identified as divine in her own right: if she is "mother of God," she is not "God the Mother" on an equal footing with God the Father.

Christianity of course, added the trinitarian terms to the Jewish description of God. And yet of the three divine "Persons," two—the Father and Son—are described in masculine terms, and the third—the Spirit—suggests the sexlessness of the Greek neuter term *pneuma*. This is not merely a subjective impression. Whoever investigates the early development of Christianity—the field called "patristics," that is, study of "the fathers of the church"—may not be surprised by the passage that concludes the recently discovered secret *Gospel of Thomas:*

> Simon Peter said to them [the disciples]: Let Mary be excluded from among us, for she is a woman, and not worthy of Life. Jesus said: Behold I will take Mary, and make her a male, so that she may become a living spirit, resembling you males. For I tell you truly, that every female who makes herself male will enter the Kingdom of Heaven.[3]

First published in *Signs: Journal of Women in Culture and Society,* 2/2 (1976), pp. 293ff. Used by permission.

Strange as it sounds, this only states explicitly what religious rhetoric often assumes: that men form the legitimate body of the community, while women will be allowed to participate only insofar as their own identity is denied and assimilated to that of men.

Further exploration of the texts which include this *Gospel*—written on papyrus, hidden in large clay jars nearly 1,600 years ago—has identified them as Jewish and Christian gnostic works which were attacked and condemned as "heretical" as early as A.D. 100–150. What distinguishes these "heterodox" texts from those that are called "orthodox" is at least partially clear: they abound in feminine symbolism that is applied, in particular, to God. Although one might expect, then, that they would recall the archaic pagan traditions of the Mother Goddess, their language is to the contrary specifically Christian, unmistakably related to a Jewish heritage. Thus we can see that certain gnostic Christians diverged even more radically from the Jewish tradition than the early Christians who described God as the "three Persons" or the Trinity. For instead of a monistic and masculine God, certain of these texts describe God as a dyadic being, who consists of *both* masculine and feminine elements.

One such group of texts, for example, claims to have received a secret tradition from Jesus through James, and significantly, through Mary Magdalene.[4] Members of this group offer prayer to *both* the divine Father and Mother: "From Thee, Father, and through Thee, Mother, the two immortal names, Parents of the divine being, and thou, dweller in heaven, mankind of the mighty name. . . ."[5] Other texts indicate that their authors had pondered the nature of the beings to whom a single, masculine God proposed, "Let us make mankind in our image, after our likeness" (Gen. 1:26). Since the Genesis account goes on to say that mankind was created "male and female" (1:27), some concluded, apparently, that the God in whose image we are created likewise must be both masculine and feminine—both Father and Mother.

DIVINE MOTHER

The characterization of the divine Mother in these sources is not simple since the texts themselves are extraordinarily diverse. Nevertheless, three primary characterizations merge. First, a certain poet and teacher, Valentinus, begins with the premise that God is essentially indescribable. And yet he suggests that the divine can be imagined as a Dyad consisting of two elements: one he calls the Ineffable, the Source, the Primal Father; the other, the Silence, the Mother of all things.[6] Although we might question Valentinus's reasoning that Silence is the appropriate complement of what is Ineffable, his equation of the former with the feminine and the latter with the masculine may be traced to the grammatical gender of the Greek words.

Followers of Valentinus invoke this feminine power, whom they also call "Grace" (in Greek, the feminine term *charis*), in their own private celebration of the Christian eucharist: they call her "divine, eternal Grace, She who is before all things."[7] At other times they pray to her for protection as the Mother, "Thou enthroned with God, eternal, mystical Silence."[8] Marcus, a disciple of Valentinus, contends that "when Moses began his account of creation, he mentioned the Mother of all things at the very beginning when he said, 'In the beginning God created the heavens and the earth.'"[9] for the word "beginning" (in Greek, the feminine *arche*) refers to the divine Mother, the source of the cosmic elements.

When they describe God in this way different gnostic writers have different interpretations. Some maintain that the divine is to be considered masculo-feminine—the "great male-female power." Others insist that the terms are meant only as metaphors—for, in reality, the divine is *neither* masculine nor feminine. A third group suggests that one can describe the Source of all things in *either* masculine or feminine terms, depending on which aspect one intends to stress.[10] Proponents of these diverse views agree, however, that the divine is to be understood as consisting of a harmonious, dynamic relationship of opposites—a concept that may be akin to the eastern view of *yin* and *yang* but remains antithetical to orthodox Judaism and Christianity.

A second characterization of the divine Mother describes her as Holy Spirit. One source, the *Secret Book of John*, for example, relates how John, the brother of James, went out after the crucifixion with "great grief," and had a mystical vision of the Trinity:

> As I was grieving . . . the heavens were opened, and the whole creation shone with an unearthly light, and the universe was shaken. I was afraid . . . and behold . . . a unity in three forms appeared to me, and I marvelled: how can a unity have three forms? [To John's question the vision answers:] It said to me, "John, John, why do you doubt, or why do you fear? . . . I am the One who is with you always: I am the Father; I am the Mother; I am the Son."[11]

John's interpretation of the Trinity—as Father, Mother, and Son—may at first seem shocking but is perhaps the more natural and spontaneous interpretation. Where the Greek terminology for the Trinity, which includes the neuter term for spirit (*pneuma*), virtually requires that the third "Person" of the Trinity be asexual, the author of the *Secret Book* looks to the Hebrew term for spirit, *ruah*—a feminine word. He thus concludes, logically enough, that the feminine "Person" conjoined with Father and Son must be the Mother! Indeed, the text goes on to describe the Spirit as Mother: ". . . the image of the invisible virginal perfect spirit. . . . She became the mother of the all, for she existed before them all, the mother-father *[matropater]*."[12] This same author, therefore, alters Genesis 1:2 ("the spirit of God moved upon the face of the deep") to say "the Mother then was moved. . . ."[13]

The secret *Gospel to the Hebrews* likewise has Jesus speak of "my Mother, the Spirit."[14] And in the *Gospel of Thomas*, Jesus contrasts his earthly parents, Mary and Joseph, with his divine Father—the Father of Truth—and his divine Mother, the Holy Spirit. The author interprets a puzzling saying of Jesus in the New Testament ("whoever does not hate his father and mother is not worthy of me") by adding: "whoever does not love his father and his mother in my way cannot be my disciple; for my [earthly] mother gave me death but my true Mother gave me the Life."[15] Another secret gnostic gospel, the *Gospel of Philip*, declares that whoever becomes a Christian "gains both a father and a mother."[16] The author refers explicitly to the feminine Hebrew term to describe the Spirit as "Mother of many."[17]

If these sources suggest that the Spirit constitutes the maternal element of the Trinity, the *Gospel of Philip* makes an equally radical suggestion concerning the doctrine that later developed as the virgin birth. Here again the Spirit is praised as both Mother and Virgin, the counterpart—and consort—of the Heavenly Father: "If I may utter a mystery, the Father of the all united with the Virgin who came down,"[18] that is, with the Holy Spirit. Yet because this process is to be understood symbolically, and not literally, the Spirit remains a virgin! The author explains that "for this reason, Christ was 'born of a virgin'"—that is, of the Spirit, his divine Mother. But the author ridicules those "literal-minded" Christians who mistakenly refer the virgin birth to Mary, Jesus' earthly mother, as if she conceived apart from Joseph: "Such persons do not know what they are saying; for when did a female ever impregnate a female?"[19] Instead, he argues, virgin birth refers to the mysterious union of the two divine powers, the Father of the All with the Holy Spirit.

Besides the eternal, mystical Silence, and besides the Holy Spirit, certain gnostics suggest a third characterization of the divine Mother as Wisdom. Here again the Greek feminine term for wisdom, *sophia*, like the term for spirit, *ruah*, translates a Hebrew feminine term, *hokhmah*. Early interpreters had pondered the meaning of certain biblical passages, for example, Proverbs: "God made the world in Wisdom." And they wondered if Wisdom could be the feminine power in which God's creation is "conceived." In such passages, at any rate, Wisdom bears two connotations: first, she bestows the Spirit that makes mankind wise; second, she is a creative power. One gnostic source calls her the "first universal creator";[20] another says that God the Father was speaking to her when he proposed to "make mankind in our image."[21] The *Great Announcement*, a mystical writing, explains the Genesis account in the following terms: ". . . One Power that is above and below, self-generating, self-discovering, its own mother; its own father; its own sister; its own son: Father, Mother, unity, Root of all things."[22]

The same author explains the mystical meaning of the Garden of Eden as a symbol of the womb: "Scripture teaches us that this is what is meant when Isaiah says, 'I am he that formed thee in thy mother's womb' [Isaiah 44:2]. The Garden of Eden, then, is Moses' symbolic term for the womb, and the Eden the placenta, and the river which comes out of Eden the navel, which nourishes the fetus. . . ."[23] This teacher claims that the Exodus, consequently, symbolizes the exodus from the womb, "and the crossing of the Red Sea, they say, refers to the blood." Evidence for this view, he adds, comes directly from "the cry of the newborn,"a spontaneous cry of praise for "the glory of the primal being, in which all the powers above are in harmonious embrace."[24]

The introduction of such symbolism in gnostic texts clearly bears implications for the understanding of human nature. The *Great Announcement*, for example, having described the Source as a masculo-feminine being, a "bisexual Power," goes on to say that "what came into being from that Power, that is, humanity, being one, is found to be two: a male-female being that bears the female within it."[25] This refers to the story of Eve's "birth" out of Adam's side (so that Adam, being one, is "discovered to be two," an androgyne who "bears the female within him"). Yet this reference to the creation story of Genesis 2—an account which inverts the biological birth process, and so effectively denies the creative function of the female—proves to be unusual in gnostic sources. More often, such sources refer instead to the first creation account in Genesis 1:26–27. ("And God said, let us make mankind in Our image, after Our image and likeness . . . in the image of God he created him: male and female he created them").

Rabbis in Talmudic times knew a Greek version of the passage, one that suggested to Rabbi Samuel bar Nahman that "when the Holy One . . . first created mankind, he created him with two faces, two sets of genitals, four arms, and legs, back to back: Then he split Adam in two, and made two backs, one on each side."[26] Some Jewish teachers (perhaps influenced by the story in Plato's *Symposium*) had suggested that Genesis 1:26–27 narrates an androgynous creation—an idea that gnostics adopted and developed. Marcus (whose prayer to the Mother is given above) not only concludes from this account that God is dyadic ("Let *us* make mankind"), but also that "mankind, which was formed according to the image and likeness of God [Father and Mother] was masculo-feminine."[27] And his contemporary, Theodotus, explains: "the saying that Adam was created 'male and female' means that the male and female elements together constitute the finest production of the Mother, Wisdom."[28] We can see, then, that the gnostic sources which describe God in both masculine and feminine terms often give a similar description of human nature as a dyadic entity, consisting of two equal male and female components.

OUTRIGHT REJECTION

All the texts cited above—secret "gospels," revelations, mystical teachings—are among those rejected from the select list of twenty-six that comprise the "New Testament" collection. As these and other writings were sorted and judged by various Christian communities, every one of these texts which gnostic groups revered and shared was rejected from the canonical collection as "heterodox" by those who called themselves "orthodox" (literally, straight-thinking) Christians. By the time this process was concluded, probably as late as the year A.D. 200, virtually all the feminine imagery for God (along with any suggestion of an androgynous human creation) had disappeared from "orthodox" Christian tradition.

What is the reason for this wholesale rejection? The gnostics themselves asked this question of their "orthodox" attackers and pondered it among themselves. Some concluded that the God of Israel himself initiated the polemics against gnostic teaching which his followers carried out in his name. They argued that he was a derivative, merely instrumental power, whom the divine Mother had created to administer the universe, but who remained ignorant of the power of Wisdom, his own Mother: "They say that the creator believed that he created everything by himself, but that, in reality, he had made them because his Mother, Wisdom, infused him with energy, and had given him her ideas. But he was unaware that the ideas he used came from her: He was even ignorant of his own Mother."[29] Followers of Valentinus suggested that the Mother herself encouraged the God of Israel to think that he was acting autonomously in creating the world; but, as one teacher adds, "It was because he was foolish and ignorant of his Mother that he said, 'I am God; there is none beside me.' "[30] Others attribute to him the more sinister motive of jealousy, among them the *Secret Book of John:* "He said, 'I am a jealous God, and you shall have no other God before me,' already indicating that another god does exist. For if there were no other god, of whom would he be jealous? Then the Mother began to be distressed. . . ."[31] A third gnostic teacher describes the Lord's shock, terror, and anxiety "when he discovered that he was not the God of the universe." Gradually his shock and fear gave way to wonder, and finally he came to welcome the teaching of Wisdom. The gnostic teacher concluded: "This is the meaning of the saying, 'The fear of the Lord is the beginning of wisdom.' "[32]

All these are, of course, mythical explanations. To look for the actual, historical reasons why these gnostic writings were suppressed is an extremely difficult proposition, for it raises the much larger question of how (i.e., by what means and what criteria) certain ideas, including those expressed in the texts cited above, came to be classified as heretical and others as orthodox by the beginning of the third century. Although the research is still in its early stages, and this question is far from being solved, we may find one clue if we ask whether these secret groups derived any practical, social consequences from their conception of God—and of mankind—that included the feminine element? Here again, the answer is yes and can be found in the orthodox texts themselves. Irenaeus, an orthodox bishop, for example, notes with dismay that women in particular are attracted to heretical groups—especially to Marcus's circle, in which prayers are offered to the Mother in her aspects as Silence, Grace, and Wisdom; women priests serve the eucharist together with men; and women also speak as prophets, uttering to the whole community what "the Spirit" reveals to them.[33] Professing himself to be at a loss to understand the attraction that Marcus's group holds, he offers only one explanation: that Marcus himself is a diabolically successful seducer, a magician who compounds special aphrodisiacs to "deceive, victimize, and defile" these "many foolish women!" Whether his accusation has any factual basis is difficult, probably impossible, to ascertain. Nevertheless, the historian notes that accusations of sexual license are a stock-in-trade of polemical arguments.[34] The bishop refuses to admit the possibility that the group might attract Christians—especially women—for sound and comprehensible reasons.

While expressing his own moral outrage, Tertullian, another "father of the church," reveals his fundamental desire to keep women out of religion: "These heretical women—how audacious they are! They have no modesty: they are bold enough to teach, to engage in argument, to enact exorcisms, to undertake cures, and, it may be, even to baptize!"[35] Tertullian directs yet another attack against "that viper"—a woman teacher who led a congregation in North Africa.[36]

Marcion had, in fact, scandalised his "orthodox" contemporaries by appointing women on an equal basis with men as priests and bishops among his congregations.[37] The teacher Marcillina also traveled to Rome to represent the Carpocratian group, an esoteric circle that claimed to have received secret teaching from Mary, Salome, and Martha.[38] And among the Montanists, a radical prophetic circle, the prophet Philumene was reputed to have hired a male secretary to transcribe her inspired oracles.[39]

Other secret texts, such as the *Gospel of Mary Magdalene* and the *Wisdom of Faith*, suggest that the activity of such women leaders challenged and therefore was challenged by the orthodox communities who regarded Peter as their spokesman. The *Gospel of Mary* relates that Mary tried to encourage the disciples after the crucifixion and to tell them what the Lord had told her privately. Peter, furious at the suggestion, asks, "Did he then talk secretly with a woman, instead of to us? Are we to go and learn from *her* now? Did he love her more than us?" Distressed at his rage, Mary then asks Peter: "What do you think? Do you think I made this up in my heart? Do you think I am lying about the Lord?" Levi breaks in at this point to mediate the dispute: "Peter, you are always irascible. You object to the woman as our enemies do. Surely the Lord knew her very well, and indeed, he loved her more than us. . . ." Then he and the others invite Mary to teach them what she knows.[40]

Another argument between Peter and Mary occurs in *Wisdom of Faith*. Peter complains that Mary is dominating the conversation, even to the point of displacing the rightful priority of Peter himself and his brethren; he urges Jesus to silence her—and is quickly rebuked. Later, however, Mary admits to Jesus that she hardly dares to speak freely with him, because "Peter makes me hesitate: I am afraid of him, because he hates the female race." Jesus replies that whoever received inspiration from the Spirit is divinely ordained to speak, whether man or woman.[41]

As these texts suggest, then, women were considered equal to men, they were revered as prophets, and they acted as teachers, traveling evangelists, healers, priests, and even bishops. In some of these groups they played leading roles and were *excluded* from them in the orthodox churches, at least by A.D. 150–200. Is it possible, then, that the recognition of the feminine element in God and the recognition of mankind as a male and female entity bore within it the explosive social possibility of women acting on an equal basis with men in positions of authority and leadership? If this were true it might lead to the conclusion that these gnostic groups, together with their conception of God and human nature, were suppressed only because of their positive attitude toward women. But such a conclusion would be a mistake—a hasty and simplistic reading of the evidence. In the first place, orthodox Christian doctrine is far from wholly negative in its attitude toward women. Second, many other elements of the gnostic sources diverge in fundamental ways from what came to be accepted as orthodox Christian teaching. To examine this process in detail would require a much more extensive discussion than is possible here. Nevertheless the evidence does indicate that two very different patterns of sexual attitudes emerged in orthodox and gnostic circles.

In simplest form, gnostic theologians correlate their description of God in both masculine and feminine terms with a complementary description of human nature. Most often they refer to the creation account of Genesis 1, which suggests an equal (or even androgynous) creation of mankind. This conception carries the principle of equality between men and women into the practical social and political structures of gnostic communities. The orthodox pattern is strikingly different: it describes God in exclusively masculine terms, and often uses Genesis 2 to describe how Eve was created from Adam and for his fulfillment. Like the gnostic view, the orthodox also translates into sociological practice: by the late second century, orthodox Christians came to accept the domination of men over women as the proper, God-given order—not only for the human race, but also for the Christian churches. This correlation between theology, anthropology, and sociology is not lost on the apostle Paul. In his letter to the disorderly Corinthian community, he reminds them of a divinely ordained chain of authority: as God has authority over Christ, so the man has authority over the woman, argues Paul citing Genesis 2: "The man is the image and glory of God, but the woman is the glory of man. For man is not from woman, but woman from man; and besides, the man was not created for the woman's sake, but the woman for the sake of the man."[42] Here the three elements of the orthodox pattern are welded into one simple argument: the description of God corresponds to a description of human nature which authorizes the social pattern of male domination.

A striking exception to this orthodox pattern occurs in the writings of one revered "father of the church," Clement of Alexandria. Clement identifies himself as orthodox, although he knows members of gnostic groups and their writings well; some scholars suggest that he was himself a gnostic initiate. Yet his own works demonstrate how all three elements of what we have called the "gnostic pattern" could be worked into fully "orthodox" teaching. First, Clement characterizes God not only in masculine but also feminine terms:

> The Word is everything to the child, both father and mother, teacher and nurse. . . . The nutriment is the milk of the Father . . . and the Word alone supplies us children with the milk of love, and only those who suck at this breast are truly happy. . . . For this reason seeking is called sucking; to those infants who seek the Word, the Father's loving breasts supply milk."[43]

Second, in describing human nature, he insists that "men and women share equally in perfection, and are to receive the same instruction and discipline. For the name 'humanity' is common to both men and women; and for us 'in Christ there is neither male nor female.' "[44] Even in considering the active participation of women and men in the Christian community, Clement offers a list—unique in orthodox tradition—of women whose achievements he admires. They range from ancient examples like Judith, the assassin who destroyed Israel's enemy, to Queen Esther, who rescued her people from genocide, as well as others who took radical political stands. He speaks of Arignole the historian, of Themisto the Epicurean philosopher, and of many other women philosophers including two who studied with Plato and one trained by Socrates. Indeed, he cannot contain his praise: "What shall I say? Did not Theano the Pythagoran make such progress in philosophy than when a man, staring at her, said, 'Your arm is beautiful,' she replied, 'Yes, but it is not on public display.' "[45] Clement concludes his list with famous women poets and painters.

If the work of Clement, who taught in Egypt before the lines of orthodoxy and heresy were rigidly drawn (ca. A.D. 160–80) demonstrates how gnostic principles could be incorporated even into orthodox Christian teaching, the majority of communities in the western empire headed by Rome did not follow his example. By the year 200, Roman Christians endorsed as "canonical" the pseudo-Pauline letter to Timothy, which interpreted Paul's views: "Let a woman learn in silence with full submissiveness. I do not allow any woman to teach or to exercise authority over a man; she is to remain silent, *for* [note Gen. 2!] Adam was formed first, then Eve, and furthermore, Adam was not deceived, but the woman was utterly seduced and came into sin. . . ."[46]

How are we to account for this irreversible development? The question deserves investigation which this discussion can only initiate. For example, one would need to examine how (and for what reasons) the zealously patriarchal traditions of Israel were adopted by the Roman (and other) Christian communities. Further research might disclose how social and cultural forces converged to suppress feminine symbolism—and women's participation—from western Christian tradition. Given such research, the history of Christianity never could be told in the same way again.

NOTES

1. Where the God of Israel is characterized as husband and lover in the Old Testament, the spouse of God is described as the community of Israel (e.g., Isa. 50:1; 54:1–8; Jer. 2:2–3, 20–25; 3:1–20) or as the land of Israel (Isa. 62:1–5).

2. One may note several exceptions to this rule: Deut. 32:11; Hos. 11:1; Isa. 66:12ff.; Num. 11:12.

3. *The Gospel according to Thomas*, A. Guillaumont, H. C. Puech, G. Quispel, W. Till, and Yassah 'Abd-al-Masih, eds. (London, Collins, 1959), logion 113–14.

4. Hippolytus, *Refutationis Omnium Haeresium*, L. Dunker, and F. Schneidewin, eds. (Göttingen, 1859), 5.7

5. Ibid., 5.6.

6. Irenaeus, *Adversus Haereses*, W. W. Harvey, ed. (Cambridge, 1857) 1.11.1.

7. Ibid., 1.13.2.

8. Ibid., 1.13.6.

9. Ibid., 1.18.2.

10. Ibid., 1.11.5; 21.1.3. Hippolytus, *Refutationis*, 6.29.

11. *Apocryphon Johannis*, S. Giverson, ed. (Copenhagen, Prostant apud Munksgaard, 1963), 47.20–48.14.

12. Ibid., 52.34–53.6.

13. Ibid., 61.13–14.

14. Origen, *Commentary on John*, 2.12; *Homily on Jeremiah*, 15.4.

15. *Gospel . . . Thomas*, 101. The text of this passage is badly damaged; I follow here the reconstruction of G. MacRae of Harvard Divinity School.

16. *L'Evangile selon Philippe*, J. E. Ménard, ed. (Leiden, Brill, 1967), logion 6.

17. Ibid., logion 36.

18. Ibid., logion 82.

19. Ibid., logion 17.

20. *Extraits de Théodote*, F. Sagnard, ed. (Paris, Sources Chrétiennes, vol. 23, 1948).

21. *Haereses*, 1.30.6.

22. *Refutationis*, 6.17.

23. Ibid., 6.14.

24. *Haereses*, 1.14.7–8.

25. *Refutationis*, 6.18.

26. Genesis Rabba, 8.1; 17.6; cf. Leviticus Rabba, 14. For an excellent discussion of androgyny, see Wayne Meeks, "The Image of the Androgyne: Some Uses of a Symbol in Earliest Christianity," *History of Religions*, 13 (1974) 165–208.

27. *Haereses*, 1.18.2.

28. *Extraits*, 21.1.

29. *Refutationis*, 6.33.

30. *Haereses*, 1.5.4; *Refutationis*, 6.33.

31. *Apocryphon*, 61.8–14.

32. *Refutationis*, 7.26.

33. *Haereses*, 1.13.7.

34. Ibid., 1.13.2–5.

35. Tertullian, *De Praescriptione Haereticorum*, E. Oehler, ed. (Lipsius, 1853–54), p. 41.

36. *De Baptismo*, 1. I am grateful to Cyril Richardson for calling my attention to this passage and the following three.

37. Epiphanes, *De Baptismo*, 42.5.

38. *Haereses*, 1.25.6.

39. *Praescriptione*, 6.30.

40. "The Gospel according to Mary," Codex Berolinensis, *BG*, 8502, 1.7.1–1.19.5, G. MacRae, trans. (unpublished manuscript).

41. *Pistis Sophia*, Carl Schmidt, ed. (Berlin, Academie-Verlag, 1925), 36(57), 71(161).

42. 1 Cor. 11:7–9. For discussion, see R. Scroggs, "Paul and the Eschatological Woman: Revisited," *Journal of the American Academy of Religion,* 42 (1974) 532–37; and E. Pagels, "Paul and Women: A Response to Recent Discussion," ibid., 42 (1974) 538–49.

43. Clemens Alexandrinus, *Paidagogos*, O. Stählin, ed. (Leipzig, 1905), 1.6.

44. Ibid., 1.4.

45. Ibid., 1.19.

46. 2 Tim. 2:11–14.

Chapter 3

Leonard Swidler

Jesus Was a Feminist

Thesis: *Jesus was a feminist.*

Definition of terms: By *Jesus* is meant the historical person who lived in Palestine two thousand years ago, whom Christians traditionally acknowledge as Lord and Savior, and whom they should "imitate" as much as possible. By a *feminist* is meant a person who is in favor of, and who promotes, the equality of women with men, a person who advocates and practices treating women primarily as human persons (as men are so treated) and willingly contravenes social customs in so acting.

To prove the thesis it must be demonstrated that, so far as we can tell, Jesus neither said nor did anything which would indicate that he advocated treating women as intrinsically inferior to men, but that on the contrary he said and did things which indicated that he thought of women as the equals of men, and that in the process he willingly violated pertinent social mores.

The negative portion of the argument can be documented quite simply by reading through the four Gospels. Nowhere does Jesus treat women as "inferior beings." In fact, Jesus clearly felt especially sent to the typical classes of "inferior beings," such as the poor, the lame, the sinner—and women—to call them all to the freedom and equality of the Kingdom of God. But there are two factors which raise this negative result exponentially in its significance: the status of women in Palestine at the time of Jesus, and the nature of the Gospels. Both need to be recalled here in some detail, particularly the former.

THE STATUS OF WOMEN IN PALESTINE

The status of women in Palestine during the time of Jesus was very decidedly that of inferiors. Despite the fact that there were several heroines recorded in the Scriptures, according to most rabbinic customs of Jesus' time—and long after—women were not allowed to study the Scriptures (Torah). One first-century rabbi, Eliezer, put the point sharply: "Rather should the words of the Torah be burned than entrusted to a woman. . . .Whoever teaches his daughter the Torah is like one who teaches her lasciviousness."

In the vitally religious area of prayer, women were so little thought of as not to be given obligations of the same seriousness as men. For example, women, along with children and slaves, were not obliged to recite the *Shema,* the morning prayer, nor

First published in *Catholic World* (January 1971), pp. 177–83. Used by permission.

prayers at meals. In fact, the Talmud states: "Let a curse come upon the man who [must needs have] his wife or children say grace for him." Moreover, in the daily prayers of Jews there was a threefold thanksgiving: "Praised be God that he has not created me a gentile; praised be God that he has not created me a woman; praised be God that he has not created me an ignorant man." (It was obviously a version of this rabbinic prayer that Paul controverted in his letter to the Galatians: "There is neither Jew nor Greek, there is neither slave nor free, there is neither male nor female; for you are all one in Christ Jesus."

Women were also grossly restricted in public prayer. It was (is) not even possible for them to be counted toward the number necessary for a quorum to form a congregation to worship communally—they were again classified with children and slaves, who similarly did not qualify (there is an interesting parallel to the current canon 93 of the *Codex Juris Canonici* which groups married women, minors, and the insane). In the great temple at Jerusalem they were limited to one outer portion, the women's court, which was five steps below the court for the men. In the synagogues the women were also separated from the men, and of course were not allowed to read aloud or take any leading function. (The same is still true in most synagogues today—canon 1262 of the CJC also states that "in church the women should be separated from the men.")

Besides the disabilities women suffered in the areas of prayer and worship there were many others in the private and public forums of society. As one Scripture scholar, Peter Ketter, noted:

> A rabbi regarded it as beneath his dignity, as indeed positively disreputable, to speak to a woman in public. The "Proverbs of the Fathers" contain the injunction: "Speak not much with a woman." Since a man's own wife is meant here, how much more does not this apply to the wife of another? The wise men say: "Who speaks much with a woman draws down misfortune on himself, neglects the words of the law, and finally earns hell." If it were merely the too free intercourse of the sexes which was being warned against, this would signify nothing derogatory to woman. But since the rabbi may not speak even to his own wife, daughter, or sister in the street, then only male arrogance can be the motive. Intercourse with uneducated company is warned against in exactly the same terms. "One is not so much as to greet a woman."

In addition, save in the rarest instances, women were not allowed to bear witness in a court of law. Some Jewish thinkers, as for example, Philo, a contemporary of Jesus, thought women ought not leave their households except to go to the synagogue (and that only at a time when most of the other people would be at home); girls ought even not cross the threshold that separated the male and female apartments of the household.

In general, the attitude toward women was epitomized in the institutions and customs surrounding marriage. For the most part the function of women was thought rather exclusively in terms of childbearing and rearing; women were almost always under the tutelage of a man, either the father or husband, or if a widow, the dead husband's brother. Polygamy—in the sense of having several wives, but *not* in the sense of having several husbands—was legal among Jews at the time of Jesus, although probably not heavily practiced. Moreover, divorce of a wife was very easily obtained by the husband—he merely had to give her a writ of divorce. Women in Palestine, on the other hand, were not allowed to divorce their husbands.

Rabbinic sayings about women also provide an insight into the attitude toward women:

It is well for those whose children are male, but ill for those whose children are female. . . . At the birth of a boy all are joyful, but at the birth of a girl all are sad. . . .When a boy comes into the world, peace comes into the world: when a girl comes, nothing comes. . . . Even the most virtuous of women is a witch. . . . Our teachers have said: four qualities are evident in women: They are greedy at their food, eager to gossip, lazy and jealous.

The condition of women in Palestinian Judaism was bleak.

THE NATURE OF THE GOSPELS

The Gospels, of course, are not the straight factual reports of eyewitnesses of the events in the life of Jesus of Nazareth as one might find in the columns of *The New York Times* or the pages of a critical biography. Rather, they are four different faith statements reflecting at least four primitive Christian communities who believed that Jesus was the Messiah, the Lord, and Savior of the world. They were composed from a variety of sources, written and oral, over a period of time and in response to certain needs felt in the communities and individuals at the time; consequently they are many-layered. Since the Gospel writer-editors were not twentieth-century critical historians, they were not particularly intent on recording *ipsissima verba Christi,* nor were they concerned to winnow out all of their own cultural biases and assumptions. Indeed, it is doubtful they were particularly conscious of them.

This modern critical understanding of the Gospels, of course, does not impugn the historical character of the Gospels; it merely describes the type of historical documents they are so their historical significance can more accurately be evaluated. Its religious value lies in the fact that modern Christians are thereby helped to know much more precisely what Jesus meant by certain statements and actions as they are reported by the first Christian communities in the Gospels. With this new knowledge of the nature of the Gospels it is easier to make the vital distinction between the religious truth that is to be handed on and the time-conditioned categories and customs involved in expressing it. When the fact that no negative attitudes by Jesus toward women are portrayed in the Gospels is set side by side with the recently discerned "communal faith-statement" understanding of the nature of the Gospels, the importance of the former is vastly enhanced. For whatever Jesus said or did comes to us only through the lens of the first Christians. If there was no very special religious significance in a particular concept or custom, we would not expect that current concept or custom to be reflected by Jesus. The fact that the overwhelmingly negative attitude toward women in Palestine did not come through the primitive Christian communal lens by itself underscores the clearly great religious importance Jesus attached to his positive attitude—his feminist attitude—toward women: feminism, that is, personalism extended to women, is a constitutive part of the Gospel, the Good News, of Jesus.

WOMEN AND RESURECTION FROM THE DEAD

One of the first things noticed in the Gospels about Jesus' attitude toward women is that Jesus'first appearance after his resurrection to any of his followers was to a woman (or women), who was then commissioned by him to bear witness of the risen Jesus to the Eleven (John 20:11ff.; Mt. 29:9f.; Mk. 16:9ff.). In typical male Palestinian style, the Eleven refused to believe the woman since, according to Judaic law, women were not allowed to bear legal witness. As one learned in the Law, Jesus obviously was aware of this stricture. His first appearing to and commissioning women to bear witness to the most important event of his career could not have been anything but deliberate: it was clearly a dramatic linking of a very clear rejection of the second-class status of women with the center of his Gospel, his resurrection. The effort of Jesus to centrally connect these two points is so obvious that it is an overwhelming tribute to human intellectual myopia not to have discerned it effectively in two thousand years.

The intimate connection of women with resurrection from the dead is not limited in the Gospels to that of Jesus. There are accounts of three other resurrections in the Gospels—all closely involving a woman. The most obvious connection of the woman with a resurrection account is that of the raising of a woman, Jairus's daughter (Mt. 9:18ff.; Mk. 5:22ff.; Lk. 8:41ff.). A second resurrection Jesus performed was that of the only son of the widow of Nain: "And when the Lord saw her, he had compassion on her and he said to her, 'Do not weep' "(Lk. 7:11ff.). The third resurrection Jesus performed was Lazarus's, at the request of his sisters Martha and Mary (Jn. 11). From the first it was Martha and Mary who sent for Jesus because of Lazarus's illness. But when Jesus finally came, Lazarus was four days dead. Martha met Jesus and pleaded for his resurrection: "Lord, if you had been here, my brother would not have died. And even now I know that whatever you ask from God, God will give you." Later Mary came to Jesus and said much the same. "When Jesus saw her weeping, and the Jews who came with her also weeping, he was deeply moved in spirit and troubled; and he said, 'Where have you laid him?' They said to him, 'Lord, come and see.' Jesus wept." Then followed the raising from the dead. Thus, Jesus raised one woman from the dead, and raised two other persons largely because of women.

There are two further details that should be noted in these three resurrection stories. The first is that only in the case of Jairus's daughter did Jesus touch the corpse—which made him ritually unclean. In the cases of the two men, Jesus did not touch them, but merely said, "Young man, I say to you, arise," and "Lazarus, come out." One must at least wonder why Jesus chose to violate the laws for ritual purity in order to help a woman, but not a man. The second detail is in Jesus' conversation with Martha after she pleaded for the resurrection of Lazarus. Jesus declared himself to be the resurrection ("I am the resurrection and the life"), the only time he did so that is recorded in the Gospels. Jesus here again revealed the central event, the central message, in the Gospel—the resurrection, *his* resurrection, his *being* the resurrection—to a woman.

WOMEN DISCIPLES OF JESUS

There are numerous occasions recorded in the Gospels where Jesus discussed the Scriptures, and religious truths in general, with women. When it is recalled that in Judaism it was considered improper, and even "obscene," to teach women the Scriptures, this action of Jesus was an extraordinary, deliberate decision to break with a custom invidious to women.

Moreover, women became disciples of Jesus not only in the sense of learning from him, but also in the sense of following him in his travels and ministering to him. A number of women, married and unmarried, were regular followers of Jesus. In Luke 8:1ff. several are mentioned by name in the same sentence with the Twelve: "He made his way through towns and villages preaching and proclaiming the Good News of the kingdom of God. With him went the Twelve, as well as certain women . . . who provided for them out of their own resources" (Mk. 15:40f.; the Greek word translated here as "provided for" *diekonoun,* the same basic word as "deacon"; indeed apparently the tasks of the deacons in early Christianity were much the same as these women undertook).

The significance of this phenomenon of women following Jesus about, learning from and ministering to him, can be properly appreciated when it is recalled that not only were women not to read or study the Scriptures, but in the more observant settings they were not even to leave their household, whether as a daughter, a sole wife, or a member of a harem.

WOMEN AS SEX OBJECTS

Within this context of women being disciples and ministers, Jesus quite deliberately broke another custom disadvantageous to women. There were situations where women were treated by others not at all as persons but as sex objects, and it could be expected that Jesus would do the same. The expectations were disappointed. One such occasion occurred when Jesus was invited to dinner at the house of a skeptical Pharisee (Lk. 7:36ff.) and a woman of ill repute entered and washed Jesus' feet with her tears, wiped them with her hair, and anointed them. The Pharisee saw her solely as an evil sexual creature: "The Pharisee . . . said to himself, 'If this man were a prophet, he would know who this woman is who is touching him and what a bad name she has.' " But Jesus deliberately rejected this approach to the woman as a sex object. He rebuked the Pharisee and spoke solely of the woman's human, spiritual actions; he spoke of her love, her unlove, that is, her sins, of her being forgiven, and her faith. Jesus then addressed her (although it was not "proper" to speak to women in public, especially "improper" women) as a human person: "Your sins are forgiven . . . . Your faith has saved you; go in peace."

A similar situation occurred when the scribes and Pharisees used a woman reduced entirely to a sex object to set a legal trap for Jesus (Jn. 8:3ff.). It is difficult to imagine a more callous use of a human person than the "adulterous" woman was put to by the enemies of Jesus. First, she was surprised in the act of sexual intercourse (quite possibly a trap was set up ahead of time by the suspicious husband), and then dragged before the scribes and Pharisees, and then by them before an even larger crowd that Jesus was instructing: "making her stand in full view of everybody." They told Jesus that she had been caught in the very act of committing adultery and that Moses had commanded that such women be stoned to death (Dt. 22:22f.). "What have you to say?" The trap was partly that if Jesus said yes to the stoning he would be violating the Roman law, which restricted capital punishment, and if he said no, he would appear to contravene Mosaic law. It could also partly have been to place Jesus' reputation for kindness toward, and championing the cause of, women in opposition to the law and the condemnation of sin.

Jesus eluded their snares by refusing to become entangled in legalism and abstractions. Rather, he dealt with both the accusers and the accused directly as spiritual, ethical, human persons. He spoke directly to the accusers in the context of their own personal ethical conduct: " 'If there is one of you who has not sinned, let him be the first to throw a stone at her.' . . . When they heard this they went away one by one." To the accused woman he likewise spoke directly with compassion, but without approving her conduct: "Woman, where are they? Has no one condemned you?" She said, "No one, Lord." And Jesus said, "Neither do I condemn you; go, and do not sin again."

One detail of this encounter provides the basis for a short excursus related to the status of women. The Pharisees stated that the woman had been caught in the act of adultery and according to the Law of Moses was therefore to be stoned to death. Since the type of execution mentioned was stoning, the woman must have been a "virgin betrothed," as referred to in Deut. 22:23f. There provision is made for the stoning of *both* the man and the woman, although in the Gospel story only the woman is brought forward. However, the reason given for why the man ought to be stoned was not because he had violated the woman, or God's law, but: "because he had violated the wife of his neighbor." It was the injury of the man by misusing his property—wife—that was the great evil.

JESUS' REJECTION OF THE BLOOD TABOO

All three synoptic Gospels insert into the middle of the account of raising Jairus's daughter from the dead the story of the curing of the woman who had had an issue of blood for twelve years (Mt. 9:20ff.; Mk. 5:22ff.; Lk. 8:43ff.). Especially touching about this story is that the affected woman was so reluctant to project herself into public attention that she "said to herself, 'If I only touch his garment, I shall be made well.'"

Her shyness was not because she came from the poor, lower classes, for Mark pointed out that over the twelve years she had been to many physicians—with no success—on whom she had spent all her money. It was probably because for twelve years, as a woman with a flow of blood, she was constantly ritually unclean (Lv. 15:19ff.), which not only made her incapable of participating in any cultic action and made her in some sense "displeasing to God," but also rendered anyone and anything she touched (or anyone who touched what she had touched!) similarly unclean. (Here is the basis for the Catholic Church not allowing women in the sanctuary during Mass—she might be menstruating and hence unclean.)

The sense of degradation and contagion that her "womanly weakness" worked upon her over the twelve years doubtless was oppressive in the extreme. This would have been especially so when a religious teacher, a rabbi, was involved. But not only does Jesus' power heal her, in one of his many acts of compassion on the downtrodden and afflicted, including women, but Jesus also makes a great to-do about the event, calling extraordinary attention to the publicity-shy woman:

And Jesus, perceiving in himself that power had gone forth from him, immediately turned about in the crowd, and said, "Who touched my garments?" And his disciples said to him, "You see the crowd pressing around you, and yet you say, 'Who touched me?'" And he looked around to see who had done it. But the woman, knowing what had been done to her, came in fear and trembling and fell down before him and told him the whole truth. And he said to her, "Daughter, your faith has made you well; go in peace, and be healed of your disease."

It seems clear that Jesus wanted to call attention to the fact that he did not shrink from the ritual uncleanness incurred by being touched by the "unclean" woman (on several occasions Jesus rejected the notion of ritual uncleanness), and by immediate implication rejected the "uncleanness" of a woman who had a flow of blood, menstruous or continual. Jesus apparently placed a greater importance on the dramatic making of his point, both to the afflicted woman herself and the crowd, than he did on avoiding the temporary psychological discomfort of the embarrassed woman, which in light of Jesus' extraordinary concern to alleviate the pain of the afflicted, meant he placed a great weight on teaching this lesson about the dignity of women.

JESUS AND THE SAMARITAN WOMAN

On another occasion Jesus again deliberately violated the then common code concerning men's relationship to women. It is recorded in the story of the Samaritan woman at the well of Jacob (Jn. 4:5ff.) Jesus was waiting at the well outside the village while his disciples were getting food. A Samaritan woman approached the well to draw water. Normally a Jew would not address a Samaritan, as the woman pointed out: "Jews, in fact, do not associate with Samaritans." But also normally a man would not speak to a woman in public (doubly so in the case of a rabbi). However, Jesus startled the woman by initiating a conversation. The woman was aware that on both counts, her being a Samaritan and being a woman, Jesus' action was out of the ordinary for she replied: "How is it that you, a Jew, ask a drink of me, a woman of Samaria?" As hated as the Samaritans were by the Jews, it is nevertheless clear that Jesus' speaking with a woman was considered a much more flagrant breach of conduct than his speaking with a Samaritan, for John related: "His disciples returned, and were surprised to find him speaking to a woman, though none of them asked, 'What do you want from her?' or, 'Why are you talking to her?' " However, Jesus' bridging of the gap of inequality between men and women continued further, for in the conversation with the woman he revealed himself in a straightforward fashion as the Messiah for the first time: "The woman said to him, 'I know that the Messiah is coming.' . . . Jesus said to her, 'I who speak to you am he.' "

Just as when Jesus revealed himself to Martha as "the resurrection," and to Mary as the "risen one" and bade her to bear witness to the apostles, Jesus here also revealed himself in one of his key roles, as Messiah, to a woman—who immediately bore witness of the fact to her fellow villagers. (It is interesting to note that apparently the testimony of women carried greater weight among the Samaritans than among the Jews, for the villagers came out to see Jesus: "Many Samaritans of that town had believed in him on the strength of the woman's testimony . . . ." It would seem that John the Gospel-writer deliberately highlighted this contrast in the way he wrote about this event, and also that he clearly wished to reinforce thereby Jesus' stress on the equal dignity of women.)

One other point should be noted in connection with this story. As the crowd of Samaritans was walking out to see Jesus, he was speaking to his disciples about the fields being ready for the harvest and how he was sending them to reap what others had sown. He was clearly speaking of conversion and salvation, and most probably was referring directly to the approaching Samaritans. Such exegesis is standard. It is also rather standard to refer to others in general and only Jesus in particular as having been the sowers whose harvest the apostles were about to reap (e.g., in the Jerusalem Bible). But it would seem that the evangelist also meant specifically to include the Samaritan woman among those sowers, for immediately after he recorded Jesus' statement to the disciples about their reaping what others had sown, he added the above-mentioned verse: "Many Samaritans of that town had believed in him on the strength of the woman's testimony . . . ."

MARRIAGE AND THE DIGNITY OF WOMAN

One of the most important stands of Jesus in relation to the dignity of women was his position on marriage. His unpopular attitude toward marriage (Mt. 19:10: "The disciples said to him, 'If such is the case of a man with his wife, it is not expedient to marry.'") presupposed a feminist view of women; they had rights and responsibilities equal to men. It was quite possible in Jewish law for men to have more than one wife (this was probably not frequently the case in Jesus' time, but there are recorded instances, e.g., Herod, Josephus), though the reverse was not possible. Divorce, of course, also was a simple matter, to be initiated only by the man.

In both situations women were basically chattels to be collected or dismissed as the man was able and wished to; the double moral standard was flagrantly apparent. Jesus rejected both by insisting on monogamy and the elimination of divorce; both the man and the woman were to have the same rights and responsibilities in their relationship toward each other (Mk. 10:2ff.; Mt. 19:3ff.).

This stance of Jesus was rather thoroughly assimilated by the Christian church (in fact, often in an over-rigid way concerning divorce—but, how to understand the ethical prescriptions of Jesus is another matter), doubtless in part because it was reinforced by various sociological conditions and other historical accidents, such as the then current strength in the Greek world of the Stoic philosophy. However, the notion of equal rights and responsibilities was not extended very far within Christian marriage. The general role of women was *Kirche, Kinder, Küche*—and only a suppliant's role in the first.

THE INTELLECTUAL LIFE FOR WOMEN

Jesus clearly did not think of woman's role in such restricted terms; she was not to be limited to being *only* a housekeeper. Jesus quite directly rejected the stereotype that the proper place of all women is "in the home," during a visit to the house of Martha and Mary (Lk. 10:38ff.).

Martha took the typical woman's role: "Martha was distracted with much serving." Mary, however, took the supposedly "male" role: she "sat at the Lord's feet and listened to his teaching." Martha apparently thought Mary was out of place in choosing the role of the "intellectual," for she complained to Jesus. But Jesus' response was a refusal to force all women into the stereotype; he treated Mary first of all as a person (whose highest faculty is the intellect, the spirit) who was allowed to set her own priorities, and in this instance had "chosen the better part." And Jesus applauded her: "it is not to be taken from her."

Again, when one recalls the Palestinian restriction on women studying the Scriptures or studying with rabbis, that is, engaging in the intellectual life or acquiring any "religious authority," it is difficult to imagine how Jesus could possibly have been clearer in his insistence that women were called to the intellectual, the spiritual, life just as were men. There is at least one other instance recorded in the Gospels when Jesus uttered much the same message (Lk. 11:27f.). One day as Jesus was preaching a woman from the crowd apparently was very deeply impressed and, perhaps imagining how happy she would be to have such a son, raised her voice to pay Jesus a compliment. She did so by referring to his mother, and did so in a way that was probably not untypical at that time and place. But her image of a woman was sexually reductionist in the extreme (one that largely persists to the present): female genitals and breasts: "Blessed is the womb that bore you, and the breasts that you sucked!"

Although this was obviously meant as a compliment, and although it was even uttered by a woman, Jesus clearly felt it necessary to reject this "baby-machine" image of women and insist again on the personhood, the intellectual and moral faculties, being primary for all: "But he said, 'Blessed rather are those who hear the word of God and keep it!'"

Looking at this text it is difficult to see how the primary point could be anything substantially other than full personhood. Luke and the tradition and Christian communities he depended on must also have been quite clear about the sexual significance of this event. Otherwise, why would he (and they) have kept and included such a small event from all the years of Jesus' public life? It was not retained *merely* because Jesus said "Blessed are those who hear and keep God's word," but because that was stressed by Jesus as being primary in comparison to a woman's sexuality. Luke, however, seems to have had a discernment here and elsewhere concerning what Jesus was about in the question of women's status that has not been shared by subsequent Christians (nor apparently by many of *his* fellow Christians), for, in the explanation of this passage, Christians for two thousand years did not see its plain meaning—doubtless because of unconscious presuppositions about the status of women inculcated by their cultural milieu.

GOD AS WOMAN

In many ways Jesus strove to communicate the notion of the equal dignity of women. In one sense that effort was capped by his parable of the woman who found the lost coin (Lk. 15:8ff.), for here Jesus projected God in the image of a woman! Luke recorded that the despised tax-collectors and sinners were gathering around Jesus, and consequently the Pharisees and scribes complained. Jesus, therefore, related three parables in a row, all of which depicted God's being deeply concerned for that which was lost. The first story was of the shepherd who left the ninety-nine sheep to seek the one lost—the shepherd is God. The third parable is of the prodigal son—the father is God. The second story is of the woman who sought the lost coin—the woman is God! Jesus did not shrink from the notion of God as feminine. In fact, it would appear that Jesus included this womanly image of God quite deliberately at this point, for the scribes and Pharisees were among those who most of all disparaged women—just as they did the "tax-collectors and sinners."

There have been some instances in Christian history when the Holy Spirit has been associated with a feminine character, as, for example, in the Syrian *Didascalia* where, in speaking of various offices in the church, it states: "The Deaconess, however, should be honored by you as the image of the Holy Spirit."

It would make an interesting investigation to see if these images of God presented here by Luke were ever used in a Trinitarian manner—thereby giving the Holy Spirit a feminine image. A negative result to the investigation would be as significant as a positive one, for this passage would seem to be particularly apt for Trinitarian interpretation: the prodigal son's father is God the Father (this interpretation has in fact been quite common in Christian history); since Jesus elsewhere identified himself as the Good Shepherd, the shepherd seeking the lost sheep is Jesus, the Son (this standard interpretation is reflected in, among other things, the often-seen picture of Jesus carrying the lost sheep on his shoulders); the woman who sought the lost coin should "logically" be the Holy Spirit.

If such an interpretation has existed, it surely has not been common. Should such lack of "logic" be attributed to the general cultural disparagement of women or the abhorrence of pagan goddesses—although Christian abhorrence of pagan gods did not result in a Christian rejection of a male image of God?

From this evidence it should be clear that Jesus vigorously promoted the dignity and equality of women in the midst of a very male-dominated society: Jesus was a feminist, and a very radical one. Can his followers attempt to be anything less *in imitatione Christi?*

Chapter 4

Elisabeth Schüssler Fiorenza

Women in the Pre-Pauline and Pauline Churches

In his letter to the Corinthian church, Paul explicitly refers twice to the behavior of women in the worship service of the community. However, both references, 1 Cor. 11:2–16 and 14:33–36, present for the exegete and historian great difficulties of interpretation. It is very doubtful whether we will be able to reconstruct the correct meaning of these passages at all. Not only is the logic of the argument in 1 Cor. 11:2–16 difficult to trace, but it is also debated whether Paul demands the veiling of women or pleads for a special form of hairstyle. Since both passages seem to contradict Gal. 3:28 and Paul's own theology of freedom from the Law, some scholars attribute 1 Cor. 11:2–16[1] and most scholars 14:33b–36[2] to the early catholic theology of the post-Pauline school.

The exegesis of these texts is even more hampered by the apologetic, theological controversy surrounding them. From the outset of the women's movement these Pauline passages were used against women's demand for equality.[3] Antifeminist preachers and theologians maintained and still maintain that the submission of women and their subordinate role in family, society, and church was ordained and revealed through Paul. Whenever women protest against societal degradation and ecclesial discrimination, Paul's arguments are invoked: Woman was created after man, she is not the image of God, she brought sin into the world and therefore she has to be submissive and is not allowed to speak in church or to teach men. And those theologians rejecting patriarchal submission but upholding an "equal but different" or "two-human-nature"[4] theology point out that Paul maintains the creational difference between women and men without denying their equality.

Feminist thinkers on the other hand argue that Paul's statements give evidence that Christianity was at a very early stage sexist and that therefore a revisionist feminist appropriation of Christian theology is doomed to failure. They criticize the Pauline texts for their patriarchal theology which legitimizes our contemporary patriarchal structures in society and church.[5]

Christian apologists respond to this feminist challenge by defending Paul as a "liberationist."[6] Paul's writings, they argue, correctly understood and interpreted, support women's equality and dignity.[7] Not the Pauline message but the patriarchal or feminist misunderstanding of this message preaches the subjugation of women. The gist

First published in *Union Seminary Quarterly Review*, 33/3–4 (Spring and Summer 1978), pp. 153–66. Used by permission.

of the controversy is summed up in a book title: *Chauvinist or Feminist?*[8]

Because of the apologetic interest to defend Paul against his feminist critics this revisionist approach does not sufficiently take into account the methodological issues and hermeneutical decisions involved on both sides of the debate. The hermeneutical discussion[9] and the sociology of knowledge[10] have underlined how important it is for exegetes and theologians to reflect on their presuppositions and on the theoretical models which they employ to assemble historical "data." This is of special consequence for the reconstruction of early Christian history because our sources do not have an immediate historical interest but rather are written for pastoral and theological purposes. Our understanding of the significance of the Pauline injunctions therefore does not only depend on a perceptive historical-critical interpretation of the texts but much more on the theoretical model of early Christian history in the context of which we formulate our questions and organize our exegetical results.

Since not only Biblical exegesis but historiography in general is a selective view of the past, its scope is not only limited by extant sources and materials but also shaped by the interests and perspectives of the present. As contemporary societal-cultural perspectives shift, the historian's perception and selection of what was important in the past and is worthwhile studying today also shifts.[11] Historians are not able to abstract from their presuppositions, ideologies, and the interests of the powerstructures determining the questions and models with which they assemble the accessible information. The reconstruction and understanding of the past is never determined solely by so-called historical facts but always also by the presuppositions and interests of historians whose methodological approaches are decisively influenced by personal experiences and social mythologies.

Feminist scholars have therefore rightly pointed out that historians study historical sources in general and biblical texts in particular from a patriarchal perspective.[12] Our Western conceptual framework and historical paradigm is determined by the understanding that "humanity is male and man defines woman not in herself but as relative to him; she is not regarded as an autonomous being. He is the subject, the absolute. She is the other."[13] This conceptual framework functions as a social mythology that determines women's and men's socialization and self-perceptions.[14] It marginalizes women and justifies the present structures of power that make women to be the weaker, "second" sex.

The problem with revisionist apologetics therefore is not so much that it has Christian or feminist presuppositions and criteria but rather that it fails to question the androcentric or patriarchal model underlying the scholarly reconstructions of early Christian history. Insofar as scholars single out the "role of women" as a special problem, they reflect our own cultural, androcentric perspective according to which male existence is the standard expression of human existence and Christian history. In such an androcentric paradigm only the role of women becomes a special historical problem while the androcentric presuppositions of such an historiography remain unexamined. In order to understand and theologically evaluate the Pauline injunctions for women it is therefore necessary to critically analyze how scholars reconstruct early Christian history and how they define the role of women in the early Christian communities.

THE ANDROCENTRIC RECONSTRUCTION
OF EARLY CHRISTIAN HISTORY

Since the academic writing of early Christian history shares in the androcentric paradigm of Western culture, it reconstructs the history of the early church according to the model of male dominance that marginalizes women. This becomes evident when we analyze the presuppositions underlying the study of women in early Christianity.[15]

First: Such studies generally presuppose that men have initiated the early Christian missionary movement and that only they had leadership in it. The discussions of discipleship, apostleship,[16] church order, worship, or missionary activity tacitly assume that these leadership functions were exercised by males only. In analyzing 1 Cor. 11:2–16 and 14:33–36 exegetes neglect to place these texts into their historical situation and their immediate context. Instead scholars presume that only these texts speak about women, whereas the rest of chapters 11–14 deals with male prophets and enthusiasts. In a similar fashion the information which the "people of Chloe" gave to Paul is characterized as gossip.[17] The "people of Chloe" are not considered as her followers or associates but as her slaves,[18] although we find a similar genitive construction in the immediate context, where Paul speaks of the different parties that claim different apostles as their spiritual leaders (1 Cor. 1:11ff). Another example of such an androcentric interpretation is the understanding that Rom. 16:7 refers to two male apostles, although Junia or Julia was a common female name of the time and patristic exegesis acknowledged that the passage refers to a woman apostle.[19] Because of the unquestioned presupposition that the early church was a "man's church" such androncentric studies understand the women mentioned in the Pauline letters as helpers of the apostles who supported especially Paul in his missionary work. This androcentric model has no room for the alternative possibility that women were missionaries and leaders of churches *before* Paul and on the same level with Paul. It could well be that Paul had no other choice than to work with women whose leadership was already well established in the pre-Pauline and Pauline churches.

Second: In such an androcentric model masculine terminology[20] is understood in a twofold way: as generic and as gender specific. On the one hand most exegetes would agree that standard masculine terms such as elect, saints, brothers or sons do not designate males over against females but apply to all members of the Christian community. Masculine language in these instances is not used in a gender specific but in a generic inclusive way. On the other hand, when discussing leadership titles as e.g. apostles, prophets or teachers, exegetes assume that these titles apply to men only although we have one instance in the Pauline literature where such a masculine title is applied to a woman. In Rom. 16:1f Phoebe is characterized by the masculine form of the title *diakonos*. Therefore, we can assume that NT androcentric language on the whole is inclusive of women until proven otherwise.

Third: Androcentric interpretations still propose that the available information on women in early Christianity reflects the actual situation and roles women had in the nascent church, although NT scholarship generally recognizes that the NT authors do not give us accurate historical information about the life of Jesus or about the earliest communities. Source- and redaction-critical studies have demonstrated that the NT writers did not incorporate all available information into their works, but that they selected the materials according to their own theological purposes. A few examples for such an androcentric traditioning process should suffice. Paul's letters refer to women as co-missionaries in the early Christian movement, whereas Acts only mentions the contributions of wealthy women as patronesses but does not picture women as missionaries. Or: While all four gospels know of Mary Magdalene as the first witness to the resurrection, Paul does not list any woman among the resurrection witnesses.[21] Or: The Fourth Gospel claims that a woman had an important role in the beginnings of the Samaritan mission (Jn. 4:4–42), whereas Acts mentions Philip as the first missionary in Samaria (Acts 8:4–13). Since the NT authors write from an androcentric point of view and select their information accordingly we can conjecture that they transmit only a small fraction of the information on women available to them. Therefore, the sparse NT references to women do not at all adequately reflect women's actual role and contributions to the history of early Christianity. They allow us, however, a glimpse of the possibly rich traditions which we have lost.

Fourth: One could argue that such an androcentric model of interpretation is methodologically appropriate because early Christianity mirrored its patriarchal culture and religion. However, the studies of the socio-cultural attitudes of the Jesus-movement in Palestine point out that this movement was a socially and religiously deviant group.[22] Jesus and his first followers were not well adjusted members of their society but were in opposition to many cultural and religious values of their time. Jesus did not call into his fellowship the righteous, pious, and powerful, but all those who "did not belong": tax collectors, sinners, prostitutes, poor people, and women. This inclusive egalitarian movement of itinerant disciples understood itself in kinship terms and thereby replaced traditional family roles and bonds. Women, like men, are no longer defined by patriarchal marriage and procreative family roles but by their allegiance to the community of disciples.

However, G. Theissen, whose work is influential in the social study of early Christianity, has argued that the early Christian missionary movement outside Palestine did not stand in conflict to its society but was well integrated into it. The radicalism of the Jesus movement in Palestine was assimilated by the urban Hellenistic communities into a family-style love-patriarchalism which perpetuated the social, hierarchal relationships of the patriarchal family in a softened, milder form.[23] The classic expression of this love-patriarchalism is found in the household-codes of the Deutero- and Postpauline literature. (Cor. 3:18f; Eph. 5:21–33; Tit. 2:4f; 1 Pet. 3:1-7).

In my opinion, however, it must be questioned whether these can be used to establish such a love-patriarchalism for the pre-Pauline and Pauline communities. The allusions of the genuine Pauline letters to the leadership of women suggest that the subordination demands of the household-codes were not yet operative in the earliest congregations of the urban Hellenistic centers. Not the patriarchal family but the egalitarian community-structures of collegia or cultic associations, which accorded women and slaves equal standing within the community, appear to have provided the model for the early Christian missionary movement in the Greco-Roman world.[24]

WOMEN IN THE PRE-PAULINE AND PAULINE CHURCHES

Only when we reconstruct the history of the early Christian movement according to an egalitarian, non-androcentric model are we able to adequately integrate the available information on women's leadership that is found in the letters of Paul. Although this information is very fragmentary it nevertheless permits us to trace women's roles in the churches before Paul and associated with Paul.

First: The Pauline letters mention women as Paul's co-workers but they do not give any indication that these women were dependent on Paul or subordinate to him. Only five of Paul's co-workers (Erastus, Mark, Timothy, Titus, and Tychicus) "stand in explicit subordination to Paul, serving him or being subject to his instructions."[25] The genuine Pauline letters apply missionary titles and characterizations as e.g. co-worker (Prisca), brother/sister (Apphia), *diakonos* (Phoebe), and apostle (Junia) also to women. They usually equate co-workers and "those who toil." In 1 Cor. 16:16ff Paul admonishes the Corinthians to be "subject to every co-worker and laborer" and to give recognition to such persons. 1 Thess. 5:12 exhorts the Thessalonians to "respect those who labor among you, and are over you in the Lord, and admonish you." It is therefore significant that Paul uses the same Greek verb "to labor" or "to toil" not only to characterize his own missionary evangelizing and teaching but also with reference to women. In Rom. 16:6, 12 he commends Mary, Tryphaena, Tryphosa, and Persis for having "labored hard" in the Lord.

Paul also affirms that women have worked with him on an equal basis. Phil. 4:2f explicitly states that Euodia and Syntyche have "contended" side by side with him. As in an athletic race these women have competed alongside with Paul, Clemens, and the rest of Paul's co-missionaries in the cause of the gospel. Paul considers the authority of both women in the community at Philippi so great that he fears that their dissensions could do serious damage to the Christian community.[26] These women missionaries commanded the same esteem and respect as Paul's male co-workers in the community at Philippi.

Second: The house-churches were a decisive factor in the missionary movement insofar as they provided space, support, and actual leadership for the community.[27] The house-churches were the place where the early Christians celebrated the Lord's supper and preached the good news. Theologically the community is called the "house of God," the "new temple" in which the Spirit dwells.[28] Since women were among the wealthy and prominent converts (cf. Acts 17:4–12), they played an important role in the founding, sustaining, and promoting of such house-churches. The following texts which speak of women as leaders of house-churches demonstrate this: Paul greets Apphia "our sister" who together with Philemon is written (Philem. 2).[29] Paul also mentions twice the missionary couple Prisca and Aquila and "the church in their house" (1 Cor. 16:19; Rom. 16:5). In a similar fashion the author of the letter to the Colossians refers to Nympha of Laodicea and the "church in her house" (Col. 4:15). According to Acts the church at Philippi began with the conversion of the business-woman Lydia from Thyatira who offered her house to the Christian mission (Acts 16:14). We also know from Acts that a prayer-meeting was held in the house of Mary, the mother of John Mark.

We have therefore no reason to assume that women were excluded from the leadership of such house-churches and from presiding at their worship. The love-patriarchalism of the household code tradition could therefore be a later patriarchal reaction to the leadership of women within the house-churches, but cannot express the original order of the pre-Pauline churches. This hypothesis is supported by 1 Tim. 2 where the injunctions that women should be submissive are given in the context of regulations for prayer-meetings and teaching as well as in the context of patriarchal requirements for church leadership.

Third: One of the most prominent heads of a house-church and outstanding co-worker of Paul is Prisca or Priscilla who together with her husband Aquila worked with Paul. Yet like Barnabas or Apollos she too was independent from the Apostle and did not stand under his authority.[30] Paul is grateful to the couple because they have risked their lives for him. Yet not only he but all the Gentile churches have reasons to give thanks to these outstanding missionaries (Rom. 16:4). Their house-church in Corinth, Ephesus, and Rome (if Rom. 16 is addressed to that community) was a missionary center at each place. 1 Cor. 16:19 has greetings from the couple. Even though Prisca is mentioned here after her husband, it is remarkable that she is referred to by name at all, since normally the husband alone is named in such greetings. However, it is significant that whenever Paul sends greetings to them (Rom. 16:3f) he addresses Prisca first, thus underlining that she is the more important of the two (cf. also 2 Tim. 4:19).

Acts also mentions Prisca before her husband, which corresponds to the information of the Pauline letters (Acts 18:2ff; 18:26).[31] Since Luke concentrates in the second part of Acts on the greatness of Paul, he refers to the couple only in passing. Even these brief remarks, however, indicate the great influence of the couple. We therefore can assume that Luke had much more information about them than he transmits to us. Like Paul, Priscilla and Aquila were by trade tentmakers and supported their missionary activity through their own work. Like Paul they were Jewish Christians and financially independent of the churches they served. Like Paul they travelled to spread the gospel and suffered for their missionary activity. When Claudius banished the Jews from Rome, they were expelled from there and moved to Corinth. In Ephesus they converted Apollos, one of the greatest apostles and missionaries alongside Paul (18:26), and taught him "the way of God more accurately." The text clearly assumes that Prisca was the catechist and teacher of Apollos.[32]

While Prisca and Aquila are not explicitly called apostles, another couple receives this title in Rom. 16:7. Like Aquila and Prisca, Andronicus and Junia (Julia) were a missionary couple who were apostles before Paul. Since apostles had to have had a missionary task and vision of the resurrected Lord,[33] we can conjecture that the couple was among the more than 500 "brethren" to whom the Lord appeared and of whom most were alive when Paul wrote 1 Corinthians (15:6). Andronicus and Junia are at the writing of Rom. 16 fellow prisoners with Paul and they are praised as "outstanding" among the apostles. We can conclude from 1 Cor. 9:5 that the couples Priscilla and Aquila and Andronicus and Junia were not exceptions among the early Christian missionaries since the other apostles on their missionary journeys had "sisters" with them as "wives" (lit. women). If the term "brother" can characterize a particular group of missionary co-workers (Phil 4:21ff),[34] then we can surmise that "sister" refers likewise to the women as missionary co-workers. The double accusative object (sister, woman) is best explained in this way. We therefore can assume that many early Christian missionaries were couples. When Paul stresses celibacy as the best precondition for missionary work (1 Cor. 7:23ff) he is expressing his own opinion but does not concur with the practice of the early missionary church. Moreover we have no indication that the work of such missionary women, who labored in tandem with their husbands, was restricted to women.[35]

Fourth: Phoebe appears to have been one of the most prominent women in the early church. In Rom. 16:1f she is characterized by three titles: Paul calls her "our sister," a *diakonos* of the church at Cenchreae, and a *prostatis* "of many and myself as well." Exegetes take pains to downplay the significance of these titles because they are given to a woman. Whenever Paul uses the title *diakonos* to refer to himself or another male leader, scholars translate it with "minister", "missionary", or "servant", whereas in the case of Phoebe they usually render it with deaconess. After characterizing Phoebe as an "obviously well-to-do and philanthropic lady," Lietzmann goes on to say: "Even at that time there had long been women deacons in the Christian church who, when *their sex made them especially suitable*, came forward and gave signal help in caring for the poor and sick, and at the baptism of women"[36] (emphasis mine). Unconsciously Lietzmann projects here back into the first century the duties of the deaconesses of a later period whose service was restricted to the ministry to women. Yet the text does not indicate any limitations of the office of Phoebe by prescribed gender-roles. She is not a deaconess of the women in the church at Cenchreae but a minister of the whole church.

Paul uses the term *diakonos* in tandem with *synergos* (co-worker) in 1 Cor. 3:5, 9 and 2 Cor. 6:1, 4. According to 1 Cor. 16:15 the co-workers and laborers are those who "have devoted themselves to the *diakonia* of the saints." However, in distinction to the co-workers the *diakonoi* appear to be not only travelling missionaries but leaders of local congregations. The term is used in the NT and in secular sources to refer to preaching and teaching.[37] Thus the *diakonoi* served in the recognized and designated "official" capacity of teachers and preachers. We therefore can presume that Phoebe was an "official" minister and teacher in the church at Cenchreae.

The importance of Phoebe's position as minister in the church at Cenchreae is underlined by the title *prostatis*, which is usually translated "helper" or "patroness," although in the literature of the time the term has the connotation of leading officer, president, governor, or superintendent.[38] Since Paul claims that Phoebe was a *prostatis* "of many and also of himself," scholars here reject such a meaning. However, in 1 Thess. 5:12 the verb characterizes persons with authority in the community, and in 1 Tim. 3:4f and 5:17 it designates the functions of the bishop, deacon, or elder. We therefore can assume that Phoebe had a position of great authority within the community of Cenchreae and that her authority was not limited to this congregation but was widely respected even by Paul himself. Phoebe receives a recommendation similar to that of Timothy in 1 Cor. 16:10f.[39]

In conclusion: Paul's letters indicate that women were among the most prominent missionaries and leaders of the early Christian communities. They were co-workers with Paul but did not stand under his authority. They were teachers, preachers, and prophets. As leaders of house-churches they had great influence and probably presided also at the worship celebrations. If we compare their leadership with the ministry of the later deaconesses it is striking that their authority was *not* restricted to the ministry for women nor to specific feminine functions.

Such a leadership of women in pre-Pauline Christianity was legitimized by the theology expressed in Gal. 3:28. In the Christian community all distinctions of race, religion, class, and gender are abolished. All members are equal and one in Christ. Gal. 3:28 probably is a traditional baptismal formula[40] which was quoted by Paul in this letter in order to support his view that there is no longer any distinction between Jew and Gentile in the Christian community. This pre-Pauline baptismal formula expresses the self-understanding of the newly initiated Christians over against the societal-religious differences accepted in the Greco-Roman culture of the time. It was a rhetorical commonplace that the Hellenistic man was grateful that he was born a human being and not a beast, a Greek and not a Barbarian, a man and not a woman. This pattern seems to have been adopted by Judaism and found its way into the synagogue liturgy. Three times daily the Jew thanked God that he did not create him a Gentile, a slave, or a woman. In distinction to this cultural-religious pattern shared by Hellenists and Jews alike,[41] the Christians affirmed at their baptism that all cultural-religious differences are abolished among them.

It is important to note, however, that this baptismal formula does not yet reflect the same notion of unification and androcentric perspective found in later gnostic writings.[42] Whereas according to various gnostic texts, to become a disciple means for a woman to become "male" and "like man" because the male principle stands for the heavenly, divine realm while the female principle is secondary, Gal. 3:28 does not extoll maleness as the standard and form of the new life[43] but Jesus Christ, in whose body—the church—male and female gender roles are transcended. Since the pairs "Jews and Greek" as well as "free and slave" indicate the abolition of cultural-religious differences within the Christian community (1 Cor. 12:12ff), we safely can assume that the same applies to the third pair "male and female." The legal-societal and cultural-religious distinctions between Jews and Greeks and slaves and free are transcended in the Christian community insofar as, on the one hand, Jews and Greeks and slaves and free remain legally and socially what they are, but on the other hand have equal standing in the church. In a similar fashion the biological-sexual-legal differences between men and women remain but gender roles and their cultural-religious significance[44] are no longer valid for the Christian community.[45] This new egalitarian Christian self-understanding did away with all distinctions and privileges of religion, class, and caste and thereby allowed not only Gentiles and slaves but also women to exercise leadership functions within the community. Since even wealthy women were marginal people in antiquity, they must have been very attracted to such an egalitarian movement, which granted them authority and leadership within the church. Therefore not the love-patriarchalism of the post-Pauline school but the egalitarian ethos of pre-Pauline and Pauline Christianity provides in my opinion the context for Paul's injunctions concerning the behavior of women in the Corinthian community.

WOMEN'S BEHAVIOR IN THE WORSHIP SERVICE OF THE COMMUNITY

Although we have only scanty information on women in early Christianity, we have seen that the community of Corinth had at least three outstanding women leaders in their midst. The followers of Chloe approached Paul with questions to which he responds in the letter and Prisca lived and worked at Corinth. Most renowned is of course Phoebe who was a minister of the church at Cenchreae, the nearby seaport of Corinth.

However, it is also significant that the Corinthian Christians understood their faith in terms of Hellenistic-Jewish Sophia theology.[46] "The Spirit" was believed to be "the 'Wisdom of God'" and the Spirit-Wisdom bestows the gift of wisdom on those who cultivate her gifts, and who live upon her supramundane level."[47] The Corinthians understand the significance of Jesus Christ in terms of Jewish-Hellenistic Sophia-speculation, which also has determined the pre-Pauline christological NT hymns[48] and which was developed in connection with the Isis-religion.[49] They are convinced that they are able to receive divine Wisdom because God has given them a pneumatic-spiritual nature (Gen. 2:7). This Sophia-theology is found not only here but also in the Synoptic tradition and we must be careful not to quickly label it "gnostic"[50] and therefore heretical.

Since in this theology Wisdom was conceived as a semi-hypostatic female figure we can surmise that women were especially attracted to become her devotees. In the worship service of the community where the divine Wisdom-Spirit was present and all received her "spiritual" gifts, women as well as men were pneumatics and therefore had equal leadership within the community. The immediate context of Paul's injunctions concerning women's behavior in the worship service of the community gives evidence that women as well as men do share in the pneumatic gifts of Wisdom-Spirit, and pray and prophesy publicly under the influence of the divine Spirit. Paul explicitly affirms that in doing so the Corinthians have followed his teachings and example (11:2) and he does not disqualify this "spiritual" self-understanding and practice of the Corinthian pneumatics. The contrast between 1 Cor. 11:2 and 11:17 underlines that Paul does not refer here to any particular abuse but introduces regulations and customs which were observed in other Christian communities (11:16; 14:33).

The injunctions concerning women's behavior, however, are not peripheral to Paul's argument but of great concern to him as their place in the structure of the letter indicates. The whole section of chapters 11–14[51] speaks of the pneumatic worship service of the community and is composed in the form of a thematic inclusion insofar as the section begins and ends with the problem of women's correct behavior in the worship assembly. The concluding verses, 14:37–40, indicate how serious the issues are for Paul and how much he expects resistance to his viewpoint. Paul appeals to the prophets and pneumatics to accept his arguments as a revelatory word of the Lord himself (v. 37).[52] He assures the Corinthians that he does not want to hinder prophetic and ecstatic speaking but that he is concerned that everything "should happen decently and in the right order" (v. 40). Thus it seems to be Paul and not the Corinthians who attempts to qualify or to change the pneumatic behavior of the community. His major line of argument is decency and the right order—values which are not specifically Christian.[53] At the same time Paul is in a difficult position since he had originally spoken to them about the new life in the Spirit and the Christian freedom evolving from it.[54] In order to understand Paul's position more fully we have to analyze the injunctions of 1 Cor. 11:2–16 and 14:33–36 more in detail.

1 Cor. 11:2–16: We no longer are able to decide with certainty which behavior Paul criticizes and which custom he means to introduce in this passage. Traditionally, exegetes have conjectured that Paul insists that the pneumatic women leaders should wear the veil according to Jewish custom.[55] Yet v. 15 maintains that women have their hair instead of a head-covering and thus militates against such an interpretation. It is therefore more likely that Paul speaks here about the manner in which women should wear their hair[56] when praying and prophesying (v. 13). It seems that the women prophets and pneumatics have let down their hair during the worship celebration as the worshippers of Isis appear to have done. For instance a woman friend of the poet Tibullus is said to have had to let her hair down twice daily in the worship of Isis to "say lauds."[57] Archeological evidence also shows that the female devotees of Isis usually wore long hair "with a band around the forehead and curls falling on the shoulder"[58] while the male initiates had their head shaven. Hence Paul's sarcastic statement in vv. 5f that the women who loosen their hair might as well have it cut short or shaven. It is as disgraceful to loosen ones hair as it is to shave it.

The Corinthian pneumatics presumably took over such a hair-fashion because they understood their equality in the community and their devotion to Sophia-Spirit in analogy to the Isis cult since Isis was also said to have made the power of women equal to men[59] and her associations admitted, like the Christian communities, women and slaves to equal membership and active participation.[60] Paul, on the other hand, insists on a different hairstyle probably because loose hair had a completely different meaning in a Jewish-Christian context.

According to Jewish sources, loosened hair continued to be a sign of uncleanness even to Paul's day.[61] Num. 4:18 (*LXX*) prescribes that the women accused of adultery be marked publicly by loosening her hair. Similarly in Lev. 13:45 (*LXX*) one of the signs for the uncleanness of a leper is loosed hair. The Jewish woman very artfully braided her hair and pinned it up so that it formed a kind of tiara on her head (Judith 10:3; 16:8), an effect highlighted by adorning it with gold, jewelry, ribbons, or a silvery gauze.[62] In view of this hairstyle the exegetically difficult statement in v. 10 becomes more understandable. Paul argues: Since the angels[63] are present in the pneumatic worship service of a community that speaks the "tongues of angels," women should not worship as cultically unclean persons by letting their hair down, but they should pin it up in the form of a tiara or crown as a sign of their spiritual power.

However, Paul not only insists on a different hairstyle but also on the differences between women and men. He adduces the following scriptural and theological arguments for his position: *Firstly*, Paul sets forth a descending hierarchy: God-Christ-man-woman,[64] in which each preceding member as "head" stands above the other "in the sense that he establishes the other's beings."[65] *Secondly*, Paul declares that man is created to be the image and manifestation of God, while woman is only the glory or reflection of man, because man was created prior to woman and woman was created because of him

(vv. 7–9).[66] Of course, this interpretation of Gen. 2 flies directly in the face of the Corinthian Jewish-Hellenistic interpretation of Gen. 2:7 which insisted on the pneumatic-spiritual nature of all persons. "A rabbinic reason for denying women the image-of-God status was precisely that they did not have the same religious duties as men."[67] Another rabbinic tradition thinks that the image-of-God status consists in circumcision and therefore a woman is ipso facto not the image of God. *Thirdly*, in vv. 11–12 Paul maintains that his insistence on the creational difference and hierarchy between men and women does not deny the interdependence of men and women within the Christian community.[68] However, that Paul does not want to speak here of the equality of men and women is evident by the fact that he refers shortly afterward in 1 Cor. 12:13 to the baptismal formula of Gal. 3:28 but omits the pair "male and female." This is significant because it is exactly at this point that Paul stresses that all are equal members of the body of Christ although they have different pneumatic gifts and functions. *Fourthly*, Paul employs the Stoic argument from nature[69] which was widely used against emancipatory tendencies in the Greco-Roman world to insist on the difference between men and women. *Finally*, Paul has to resort to an authoritarian appeal, probably because he himself senses that his arguments are not very convincing theologically. Therefore he declares that it is party-spirit and contentiousness if the Corinthians do not accept his injunctions, and he insists that he and the other churches do not acknowledge another practice. Nevertheless, Paul's argument does not deny that women are pneumatics, and pray and prophecy in the worship service of the community. He argues, however, that they should retain the traditional hairstyle and respect the differences between women and men.[70]

1 Cor. 14:33–36: It is debated whether 14:33b–35(36) is an authentic Pauline injunction or whether the passage was added by a later editor of the Pauline school. However, since the verses cannot be excluded on textual-critical grounds but are usually declared to be inauthentic on theological grounds, it is exegetically more sound to accept them as an original Pauline statement and to explain them within their present context. As in chapter 11 so in chapters 12–14 Paul seeks to persuade the Corinthians that decency and order should be more highly esteemed than the spiritual status and exercise of the individual. While the Corinthians seem to have valued glossolalia most, Paul favors the gift of prophecy and interprets it in terms of reason, order, and mission (14:4, 5, 19).[71] The Corinthian pneumatics should not be concerned with the exhibition of their spiritual greatness but with the building up of the community (14:4f) and with the impression they make on interested outsiders (14:16, 17, 23ff).

1 Cor. 14:26–36 are best understood to be a church order[72] with rules for glossolalists (vv. 27ff), for prophets (vv. 29–32), and for wives (vv. 33b–36). These three rules are formulated in a structurally similar fashion. A general sentence of regulation (vv. 27, 29, 34) is complemented by a sentence that concretizes it (vv. 28, 30, 35). The second and third rule are expanded with reasons for the regulation (vv. 31–32, 34a, 35b). However, the rule for wives is different insofar as it has an introduction (v. 33a) and ends with a double rhetorical question (v. 36). These stylistic additions seem to underline the importance of the last regulation.

1 Cor. 14:33–36 is often understood to speak about women in general and therefore to contradict 11:2–16 which presupposes that women are pneumatics and as such pray and prophesy within the worship of the community. However, the difficulty is resolved if we recognize that the injunction does not pertain to all women but solely to wives, since chapter 7 documents that not all women in the community were married and could ask their husbands at home. 1 Cor. 7:32–35 confirms the interpretation that the prohibition in 14:33–36 applies just to wives. Although in 1 Cor. 7 Paul acknowledges the equality

and reciprocity of husband and wife,[73] his ascetic preference for the unmarried state is plain.[74] In 7:32-35 he interprets the apocalyptic "as if not" tradition of 7:29-31 in a christological missionary perspective. The married person, Paul argues, is divided and concerned with the issues of marriage and family, while the unmarried person is completely dedicated to the affairs of the Lord. It is apparent that Paul, here, is "taking over bourgeois moral concepts which denote not absolute but conventional values."[75] Paul's argument is surprising, especially since we know of leading missionary couples who spent their life in the service of the Lord.

However, only the singleminded dedication of the unmarried woman and the virgin and not that of the unmarried man is further qualified with the subordinate clause "that she may be holy in body and spirit" (7:34). Paul ascribes here a special holiness to the unmarried woman and virgin apparently because she is not touched by men (7:1).[76] We therefore can surmise that Paul is able to accept the pneumatic participation of such "holy" women in the worship service of the community but argues in 14:34f against such an active participation of wives.

Paul derives his theological argument from the Jewish-Hellenistic propaganda tradition that places the demand for the subordination of wives in the context of the Law.[77] This tradition has also influenced the household-codes of the post-Pauline literature. However, one could argue that the *hypotassein* of v. 34 does not demand submission to husbands but to the regulations of the community. As in 7:35, so here Paul concludes his injunction by pointing to propriety (v. 35b).

The subsequent rhetorical questions in v. 36 indicate the counter-argument which Paul expects. It is often suggested that these questions refer to the whole community because the wives could not have argued that the word of God originated with them or that they were the only ones whom it reached. However, when we consider that leading early Christian missionaries such as Prisca, Junia, and perhaps Apphia were married and that in general the other leading women mentioned in the Pauline letters are not characterized as virgins, widows, or unmarried, such a counter-argument becomes plausible. Since we have seen that wives were called to missionary preaching and were founders of house-churches, Paul's claim that these women should be silent and ask their husbands at home sounds preposterous. Paul realizes that this regulation goes against the accepted practice of the missionary churches in the Hellenistic urban centers. He therefore claims for his regulations the authority of the Lord (v. 37). In the final analysis, however, not theological reasons but the concern for decency and order determines Paul's regulation concerning the behavior of pneumatic women and men in the worship service of the community (v. 40).

In Conclusion: In the preceding analysis I have attempted to argue that the Pauline injunctions for women in 1 Cor. should be understood in the context of women's leadership in early Christianity. 1 Cor. 11:2-16 on the one hand does not deny women's prophecy and prayer in the worship assembly but insists that in the Christian community women and men are interdependent. However, they should not deny in their behavior the creational differences and hierarchal relationships. The community rule of 14:33-36 on the other hand has a specific situation in mind, namely the speaking and questioning of wives in the public worship assembly. Here as in 7:34 and 9:5 Paul appears to limit the active participation of wives in the "affairs of the Lord." His concluding rhetorical questions indicate that he does not expect his regulation will be accepted without protest by the Corinthian community which knows wives as leading Christian apostles and missionaries. Yet Paul is more concerned that order and propriety be preserved so that an outsider cannot accuse the Christians of religious madness.

In both passages, then, Paul places a limit and qualification on the pneumatic participation of women in the worship service of the community. We do not know whether the Corinthian women and men accepted his limitations and qualifications. However, the love-patriarchalism of the Deutero-Pauline household-codes and the injunctions of the Pastoral Epistles[78] are a further development of Paul's argument that will lead in the future to the exclusion of all women from ecclesial office and to a gradual patriarchalization of the church.[79]

In response to R. Scrogg's attempt to rescue Paul from uninformed attacks of his feminist critics, Elaine Pagels has maintained as a hermeneutical principle:

> It is really not my intent to put Paul on trial before a panel of NT scholars or debate whether he is 30 percent, 75 percent, or 100 percent a feminist. After all, these are criteria that have emerged from our own present situation. To attempt simply to judge Paul by such standards seems to me anachronistic and a waste of time.[80]

I have attempted to show, to the contrary, that firstly, the feminist quest for the equality of women was alive in pre-Pauline and Pauline Christianity, and that Paul for the sake of "order" and for the sake of attracting outsiders appears to react to it. Secondly, the hermeneutical discussion has driven home that a value-free historical inquiry unencumbered by present-day concerns is intellectually not possible. Feminist scholarship is not the exception to the rule but openly demonstrates that all scholarship is determined by contemporary issues. Finally, in my opinion, scholars cannot refrain from passing judgment on biblical texts, because the NT is not just a historical work of the first century but functions as holy Scripture for Christian communities today. Insofar as the Bible is not only a document of past history but inspired Scripture for today, exegetical-biblical studies cannot avoid the question of the *meaning* of NT texts for today.

A hermeneutic-theological approach that is concerned with the contemporary meaning and authority of the Pauline injunctions in a postpatriarchal society and church, however, has to insist that solely non-sexist and non-oppressive traditions of the NT and non-androcentric models of historical reconstruction and biblical interpretation do justice to divine revelation, if the word of God is not to become a tool for the patriarchal oppression of women and a theological justification of sexist societal and ecclesial structures. The theological significance of Paul's injunctions for today has to be judged accordingly. After all, Paul himself has insisted: "For freedom Christ has set us free; stand fast therefore, and do not submit again to a yoke of slavery" (Gal. 5:1, RSV).

NOTES

1. W. Munro, "Patriarchy and Charismatic Community in 'Paul,' " in Plaskow and Romero, eds., *Women and Religion* (Missoula, Mont., Scholars Press, 2nd ed., 1974) 189–98; William O. Walker, "1 Cor. 11:2–16 and Paul's View Regarding Women," JBL, 94 (1975) 94–110; and the critical review of this proposal by Jerome Murphy-O'Connor, "The Non-Pauline Character of 1 Cor. 11:2–16?" JBL 95 (1976) 615–21.

2. G. Fitzer, *Das Weib schweige in der Gemeinde* (Munich, Kaiser, 1963), and H. Conzelmann, *1 Corinthians* (Philadelphia, Fortress, 1975) 246, for arguments against the authenticity of the passage.

3. See E. Cady Stanton, *The Original Feminist Attack on the Bible (Woman's Bible)*, (New York, Arno, 1974), esp. the Introduction by B. Welter; see also "Pastoral Letter of the Massachusetts Congregationalist Clergy (1837)," in A.S. Kraditor, ed., *Up From the Pedestal* (Chicago, Quadrangle, 1968) 50ff.

4. See "Vatican Declaration: Women in the Priesthood," *Origins*, 6 (1977) 518-24, and the supporting comment by D. Burrell, "The Vatican Declaration: Another View," *America* (April 2, 1977) 289-92: " . . . for I cannot but suspect that Lawrence would find the Vatican Declaration profoundly accurate in the way it links sexuality with the symbolic dynamics of human salvation." For a feminist analysis of the political implications of this "two-human-nature" concept, see B. W. Harrison, "The New Consciousness of Women: A Socio-Political Resource," *Cross-Currents*, 24 (1975) 445-62; idem, "Sexism in the Contemporary Church: When Evasion Becomes Complicity," in A.L. Hagemann, ed., *Sexist Religion and Women in the Church* (New York, Association Press, 1974) 195-216.

5. See M. Daly, *Beyond God the Father* (Boston, Beacon, 1973) and the review article by C. Christ, "The New Feminist Theology: A Review of the Literature," *Religious Studies Review*, 3 (1977) 203-12.

6. See, e.g., R. Scroggs, "Paul Chauvinist or Liberationist?" *Christian Century*, 89 (1972) 307-9; idem, "Paul and the Eschatological Woman," JAAR, 40 (1972) 283-303 and 42 (1974) 532-49.

7. E.g., A. Feuillet, "La dignité et le rôle de la femme d'après quelques textes Pauliniens: Comparison avec *L'Ancien Testament*," NTS, 21 (1975) 157-91; J. Massyngberde Ford, "Biblical Material Relevant to the Ordination of Women," JES, 19 (1973) 669-94.

8. R. and J. Boldrey, *Chauvinist or Feminist? Paul's View of Women* (Grand Rapids, Baker Book House, 1976); see also P. J. Ford, "Paul the Apostle: Male Chauvinist?" *Biblical Theology Bulletin*, 4 (1975) 302-11.

9. For a general discussion, see K. Frör, *Biblische Hermeneutik* (Munich, Kaiser, 1961); R. Funk, *Language, Hermeneutic and Word of God* (New York, Harper & Row, 1966); E. Schillebeeckx, *The Understanding of Faith* (New York, Seabury, 1974); J. A. Sanders, "Hermeneutics," *Suppl. Vol.,* JDB (Nashville, Abingdon, 1976) 402-7; and my attempt to apply the hermeneutical principles of the Constitution on Divine Revelation of Vatican II to the problem of how to evaluate the teachings of the NT on women: "Understanding God's Revealed Word," *Catholic Charismatic*, 1 (1977) 7-10.

10. For the heuristic value of "models," see I. G. Barbour, *Myth, Models, and Paradigms* (New York, Harper & Row, 1974).

11. See K. Mannheim, *Ideology and Utopia* (London, Routledge, 1954) 243: "Every epoch has its fundamentally new approach and its characterisitc point of view and consequently sees the 'same' objects from a new perspective." For a feminist analysis, see H. Smith, "Feminism and the Methodology of Women's History," in B. A. Carrol, ed., *Liberating Women's History* (University of Illinois Press, 1976) 368-84.

12. I use "patriarchal" in the sense of a societal system of male dominance and female submission and marginality.

13. Simone de Beauvoir, *The Second Sex* (New York, Knopf, 1953) xv-xvi.

14. E. Janeway, *Man's World, Woman's Place* (New York, Dell, 1971) 307, points to the emotional component of social mythology. Therefore not logic but only "an answer *in reality* to those needs which the myth answers in phantasy" will bring about change in such a social mythology (emphasis added).

15. See my forthcoming article "The Study of Women in Early Christianity" to appear in *Proceedings of the College Theology Society's 1977 Annual Meeting.*

16. See my articles "The Twelve" and "The Apostleship of Women in Early Christianity" in Leonard and Arlene Swidler, eds., *Women Priests: A Catholic Commentary on the Vatican Declaration* (New York, Paulist, 1977) 114-23 and 135-40. In my writings I have consistently pointed to the apostleship of Mary Magdalene: E. Schüssler, *Der vergessene Partner* (Düsseldorf, Patmos, 1964) 57ff.; "Mary Magdalene—Apostle to Apostles," *UTS Journal*, April 1975, 22f.; "Die Rolle der Frau in der urchristlichen Bewegung," *Concilium*, 12 (1976) 3-9.

17. See, e.g., W. A. Meeks, *The Writings of St. Paul* (New York, Norton, 1972) 23: 1 Corinthians "is a response to reports which have come to Paul by two means: 1. a letter, brought by an official delegation, Stephanus, Fortunatus, and Achaicus (16:17; cf. 7:1) and 2. *gossip* from 'Chloe's people' (1:11), otherwise unknown" (emphasis added).

18. See the discussion by G. Theissen, "Soziale Schichtung in der korinthischen Gemeinde. Ein Beitrag zur Soziologie des hellenistischen Urchristentums," ZNW 65 (1974) 255. However, Paul writes *ek* with genitive when speaking about slaves of a household (Rom. 16:10f; Phil. 4:22).

19. See Bernadette Brooten, "Junia . . . Outstanding among the Apostles (Romans 16:7)," in L. and A. Swidler, *Women Priests*, 141-44, and J. M. Lagrange, *Saint Paul: Epître aux Romans* (Paris, 1916), 366.

20. For the problem of masculine language, see R. Lakoff, *Language and Woman's Place* (New York, Harper, 1975); Miller/Swift, *Words and Women* (Garden City, N.Y., Anchor, 1976); L.

Russel, "Changing Language and the Church," in *The Liberating Word* (Philadelphia, Westminster, 1976) 82–98, and the extensive bibliographical review by M. R. Key, *Male/Female Language* (Metuchen, N.J., Scarecrow Press, 1975).

21. See 1 Cor. 15:3–10. The conclusion drawn by R.E. Brown is therefore questionable: "The priority given to Peter in Paul and in Luke is a priority among those who became official witnesses to the Resurrection. The secondary place given to the tradition of an appearance to a woman or women probably reflects the fact that women did not serve at first as official preachers of the church. . . ." ("Roles of Women in the Fourth Gospel," in W. Burkhardt, *Woman: New Dimensions* [New York, Paulist, 1977] 116n. 12).

22. See J.G. Gager, *Kingdom and Community: The Social World of Early Christianity* (Englewood Cliffs, N.J., Prentice Hall, 1975) 22–37; R. Scroggs, "The Earliest Christian Communities as Sectarian Movement," in J. Neusner, *Christianity, Judaism, and Other Greco-Roman Cults* (Leiden, Brill, 1975) I, 1–23; G. Theissen, "Itinerant Radicalism: The Tradition of Jesus Sayings from the Perspective of the Sociology of Literature," in *Radical Religion: The Bible and Liberation* (Community for Religious Research and Education, 1976) 84–93; idem, *Sociology of Early Palestinian Christianity* (Philadelphia, Fortress, 1978).

23. See Theissen, "Soziale Schichtung," 268–72; idem, "Itinerant Radicalism," 91f; idem, "Die Starken und die Schwachen in Korinth," *EvTh, 35* (1975) 171ff. Theissen owes the expression "love-patriarchalism" to E. Troeltsch, *The Social Teachings of the Christian Churches* (New York, Harper, 1960) I, 78, who characterizes it as follows: "This is the type of Christian patriarchalism founded upon the religious recognition of and the religious overcoming of an earthly inequality."

24. For the participation of women in cult associations and in philosophical schools, see L. Swidler, "Greco-Roman Feminism and the Reception of the Gospel," in Jaspert & Mohr, eds., *Traditio-Krisis-Renovatio aus theologischer Sicht* (Marburg, Elwert, 1976) 49–52; W.A. Meeks, "The Image of the Androgyne: Some Uses of a Symbol in Earliest Christianity," *History of Religion,* 13 (1974) 169–74.

25. See E. E. Ellis, "Paul and his Co-Workers," NTS, 17 (1970/71) 439; see also the essay of M.A. Getty on *synergos* in L. & A. Swidler, *Women Priests*, 176–82.

26. See W. D. Thomas, "The Place of Women in the Church at Philippi," *Expository Times,* 83 (1972) 117–20; R. W. Graham, "Women in the Pauline Churches: A Review Article," *Lexington Theological Quarterly,* 11 (1976) 29f.

27. See F. F. Filson, "The Significance of the Early House Churches," JBL, 58 (1939) 105–12; E.A. Judge, *The Social Patterns of Christian Groups in the First Century* (London, Tyndale, 1960) 36: "Not only was the conversion of a household the natural or even necessary way of establishing the cult in unfamiliar surroundings, but the household remained the soundest basis for the meeting of Christians."

28. See R. J. M. Kelvey, *The New Temple, The Church in the New Testament* (Oxford University Press, 1969) and my article "Cultic Language in Qumran and in the New Testament," CBQ, 38 (1976) 159–79.

29. See, however, E. Lohse, *Colossians and Philemon* (Philadelphia, Fortress, 1971) 190: "The lady of the house had to deal daily with the slaves. Therefore she had to give her opinion when the question of taking back a runaway slave was raised." The tendency is clear. Apphia is reduced to a wife and mistress, although like the two men she is given a Christian characterization.

30. See E. Käsemann, *An die Römer* (Tübingen, Vandenhoeck & Ruprecht, 1973) 394, asserts that we are justified to count the couple among the most outstanding early Christian missionaries in the dispersion.

31. The writer of Codex D (2nd century) mentions the name of Prisca in second place in Acts 18:26. Not only does he make Aquila the subject of the sentence in 18:2 by writing "Aquila with his wife Priscilla" but he also mentions Aquila three times (18:3,7,22) without referring to Priscilla.

32. Therefore A. V. Harnack, "Probabilia über die Addresse und den Verfasser des Hebraerbriefes," ZNW, 1 (1900) 16–41, suggests that she authored the Epistle to the Hebrews. It is significant that scholars always assume male authorship, although in most cases we do not know who wrote the NT books.

33. See my article, "The Apostleship of Women," 136ff.

34. See E. E. Ellis, "Paul and his Co-Workers," 445–51.

35. See B. Bauer, "Uxores Circumducere 1 Kor 9:53" BZNF, 3 (1959) 94–102. E. Käsemann suggests that the missionary couples follow the synoptic injunction that the apostles should go out "two by two" (Mk. 6:7 par.). See also the interpretation of Clement of Alexandria (Strom. 111.6.53,3f) ". . . and took their wives with them not as women with whom they had marriage relations but as sisters, that they might be their fellow-ministers (*syndiakonous*) in dealing with housewives. It was through them that the Lord's teaching penetrated also the women's quarters

without any scandal being aroused." However, the text does not give any indication of Encratite behavior.

36. *The History of the Early Church,* 1 (London, Lutterworth, 1963) 146.

37. See A. Lemaire, "From Services to Ministries: Diakonia in the First Two Centuries," *Concilium,* 14 (1972) 35–49; K. H. Schelkle, "Ministry and Ministers in the NT Church," *Concilium,* 11 (1969) 5–11; A. Lemaire, "The Ministries in the NT: Recent Research," *Biblical Theology Bulletin,* 3 (1973) 133–66.

38. See B. Reicke, *"prohistemi,"* TDNT, VI, 703: The verb as well as the substantive "have the twofold sense of leadership and care."

39. See H. Gamble, *The Textual History of the Letter to the Romans* (Grand Rapids, 1977) 87.

40. H. D. Betz, "Spirit, Freedom and Law: Paul's Message to the Galatian Churches," *Svensk Exeg. Arsbok,* 39 (1974) 145–60; M. Bouttier, "Complexio Oppositorum: Sur les formules de 1 Cor xii. 13; Gal iii. 26–28; Col iii. 10.11," NTS, 23 (1976) 1–19; W. A. Meeks, "The Androgyne," 181.

41. See A. Oepke, *"gyne"* TDNT, 1, 777 n. 4. The prayer therefore expresses a commonly accepted cultural attitude toward women and should not be used to denounce Judaism since we have Rabbinic passages similar to Gal. 3:28; see J. Leipoldt, *Jesus und die Frauen* (Leipzig, Quelle & Meyer, 1921) 14f. For the critique of anti-Jewish tendencies in feminist theology, see J. Plaskow, "Christian Feminism and Anti-Judaism."

42. This is maintained by W. Schmithals, *Die Gnosis in Korinth* (FRLANT 66; Göttingen, Vandenhoeck & Ruprecht, 1956) 227 n 1; cf. also W. A. Meeks, "The Androgyne," 180ff and R. Scroggs, "Paul and the Eschatological Woman: Revisited," JAAR 42 (1974) 536. However these authors appear to identify gender roles with sexual-biological roles. H. D. Betz, *op. cit.,* correctly stresses that here male and female societal cultural gender roles are abolished in the Christian community.

43. Cf. the Gospel of Thomas, the Gospel of Mary, and Pistis Sophia. See my analysis of gnostic perceptions and attitudes toward women "Word, Spirit, and Power: Women in Early Christian Communities," to appear in Ruether & McLaughlin (eds), *Women of Spirit* (New York: Simon & Schuster, 1979).

44. For the definition and distinction of sex and gender, see A. Oakley, *Sex, Gender, and Society* (New York, Harper, 1972) 158ff.

45. Exegetes often understand the text not as applying to the church but to the equality of souls, to eschatological equality, or to equality in heaven, or they maintain that the differences are only overcome sacramentally or spiritually *coram deo.* For a criticism of such an interpretation, see K. Stendahl, *The Bible and the Role of Women* (Philadelphia, Fortress, 1966) 32ff.

46. See B. L. Mack, *Logos und Sophia. Untersuchungen zur Weisheitstheologie im Hellenistischen Judentum* (Göttingen, Vandenhoeck & Ruprecht, 1973); R. Marcus, "On Biblical Hypostases of Wisdom," HUCA 23 (1950/51) 157–171.

47. B. A. Pearson, *The Pneumatikos-Psychikos Terminology in 1 Corinthians* (Missoula, Mont., Scholars Press, 1973) 37.

48. See my article "Wisdom Mythology and the Christological Hymns of the New Testament," in R. Wilken, ed., *Aspects of Wisdom in Judaism and Early Christianity* (Notre Dame Univ. Press, 1976) 17–41.

49. See my article "Wisdom Mythology," 30ff; J.M. Reese, *Hellenistic Influences on the Book of Wisdom and its Consequences* (Rome, Biblical Institute, 1970) 33–50.

50. See *Terminology,* 82ff; H. Conzelmann, *1 Corinthians,* 58ff idem, "Paul und die Weissheit," NTS, 12 (1965/66) 231–34. Conzelmann, however, maintains that it is Paul and not the Corinthians who profess a Jewish-Hellenistic wisdom theology. See, however, B. A. Pearson, "Hellenistic-Jewish Wisdom Speculation and Paul," in R. Wilken, Aspects of Wisdom, 43–66.

51. See Wendland, *Die Briefe an die Korinther* (Göttingen, Vandenhoeck & Ruprecht, 1965) 80; H. Conzelmann (*1 Corinthians, 182*) points to a certain tension in chaps. 11–14, because 11:2–16 already deals with behavior at divine worship, while a new topic is introduced only in 12:1. E. Kähler (*Die Frau in den Paulinischen Briefen* [Zurich, Gotthelf, 1960] 43f.) suggests that 10:32–11:2 is the introduction and headline to 11:3–16.

52. Conzelmann *1 Corinthians* suggests that "this idea is better suited to interpolation than to Paul, and is suggested by it" (246). For the prophetic self-understanding of Paul, see U. B. Müller, *Prophetie und Predigt im Neuen Testament* (Güterslo, Mohn, 1975) 117–233.

53. For the concept of "good order," see G. Dautzenberg, *Urchristliche Prophetie. Ihre Erforschung, ihre Voraussetzungen im Judentum und ihre Struktur im 1. Korinterbrief* (Tübingen, Mohr, 1974) 278–84.

54. J. C. Hurd, Jr., *The Origin of 1 Corinthians* (New York, Seabury, 1965) 287: "We have suggested that much of the 'wisdom' and 'knowledge' to which they clung had been given them by

Paul himself. . . . Here we meet a younger, more vigorous Paul, fired with enthusiasm in his new faith, less cautious in his theological statements than he later became, little conscious of the weaknesses of human nature." See also J. W. Drane, "Tradition, Law, and Ethics in Pauline Theology" (Nov. 16 [1974] 167–87), who points out the shift in Paul's theology in Gal. and 1 Cor.

55. See G. Delling, *Paulus Stellung zu Frau and Ehe* (Stuttgart, Kohlhammer, 1931) 96–105; S. Lösch, "Christliche Frauen in Korinth," *Theologische Quartalschrift*, 127 (1947) 216–61; M. D. Hooker, "Authority on Her Head: An Examination of 1 Cor 11:10," NTS, 10 (1963/64) 410–16; A. Joubert, "Le voile des femmes," NTS, 18 (1972) 419–430.

56. See Lösch, "Christliche Frauen," 240ff.; J. B. Hurley, "Did Paul Require Veils or the Silence of Women? A Consideration of 1 Cor 11:2–16 and 1 Cor 14:33b–36," *Westminister Theological Journal*, 35 (1972/73) 190–220; W. J. Martin, "1 Cor 11:2–16: An Interpretation," in Gasque and Martin, eds., *Apostolic History and the Gospel* (Grand Rapids, Eerdmans, 1970) 231–34; J. Murphy-O'Connor, *L'Existence chétienne selon saint Paul* (Paris, Cerf, 1974) 103–4 n. 37; A. Isaakson, *Marriage and Ministry in the New Temple* (Lund, Gleerup, 1965) 165–86.

57. Tib. 1, 3, 29–32; For other cults, see Lösch, *Frauen.*

58. S. Kelly Heyob, *The Cult of Isis among Women in the Greco-Roman World* (Leiden, Brill, 1975) 60.

59. Ibid., 52.

60. Ibid., 105f; see also R.E. Witt, *Isis in the Graeco-Roman World* (Cornell University Press, 1971).

61. W. C. Van Unnik, "Les cheveux défaits des femmes baptisées," VigChr, 1 (1947) 77–100.

62. See Strack/Billerbeck, *Kommentar zum Neuen Testament und Midrasch* (Munich, Beck, 1926) III, 428f. for the hairstyle of Jewish women.

63. See J.A. Fitzmyer, "A Feature of Qumran Angelology and the Angels of 1 Cor 11:10," NTS, 4 (1957/58) 48–58.

64. J. B. Schaller ("Gen 1, 2 im antiken Judentum" [unpubl. dissertation] Göttingen, 1961) points out that the series God-Adam-Eve is found in the targum translation of Gn. 1:26f and 2:18. Therefore he argues that Paul enlarged this series by introducing Christ (188f).

65. H. Schlier, "*kephale*," TDNT, 111, 679.

66. J. Jervell (*Imago Dei. Gen 1, 26f im Spätjudentum, in der Gnosis und in den Paulinischen Briefen* [Göttingen, Vandenhoeck & Ruprecht, 1960] 110) claims that "the tendency of rabbinic theology is not only to deny image-of-God status to Eve . . . but also to every woman."

67. Ibid., 301; see also 109. For the religious duties of women, L. Swidler, *Women in Judaism: The Status of Women in Formative Judaism* (Metuchen, N.J., Scarecrow Press, 1976) 82ff. The rabbinic evidence can be used only with great caution for the interpretation of Pauline texts, since the rabbinic passages are hard to date.

68. See Gnr. 22 (14d) in Strack/Billerbeck, *Kommentar*, 111, 440: "man not without woman, woman not without man, neither of them without the Shekinah."

69. See Conzelmann, *1 Corinthians*, 190, esp. n. 96 and 97.

70. W. A. Meeks, "The Androgyne," 200: "Paul seems primarily concerned to reassert the distinction between male and female and the inferiority of the woman to the man." Similar R. Scroggs, who claims that Paul intends to eliminate the inequality between the sexes but not the distinctions.

71. See esp. the works of G. Dautzenberg and U. Müller. W. A. Meeks ("'Since Then You Would Need to Go Out of the World': Group Boundaries in Pauline Christianity," [forthcoming]) characterizes the Pauline church as "an open sect, concerned not to offend 'those outside' but attract them to its message and if possible to its membership." However, it is questionable whether this describes the attitude of the Pauline church or of Paul himself.

72. See Dautzenberg, Prophetie, 253–88.

73. See R. Scroggs, "The Eschatological Woman," 295–97. See also W. Schrage, "Zur Frontstellung der Paulinischen Ehebewertung in 1 Kor 7:1–7," ZNW, 67 (1976) 214–34.

74. K. Niederwimmer, *Askese und Mysterium* (Göttingen, Vandenhoeck & Ruprecht, 1975) 80–123.

75. Conzelmann, *1 Corinthians*, 134; S. Schulz, "Evangelium und Welt. Hauptprobleme einer Ethik des Neuen Testaments," in Betz/Schottroff, *Neues Testament und christliche Existenz* (Tübingen, Mohr, 1973) 483–501.

76. See Niederwimmer, *Askese*, 115.

77. J. E. Crouch, *The Origin and Intention of the Colossian Haustafel* (Göttingen, Vandenhoeck & Ruprecht, 1972) 138ff.

78. See my article "Interpreting Patriarchal Traditions," in L. Russel, ed., *Liberating Word*, 55–59.

79. For the impact of this development on the contemporary church, see my articles "Feminist Theology as a Critical Theology of Liberation," *Theological Studies*, 36 (1975) 605–25; "Feminist Spirituality, Christian Identity, and Catholic Vision," *NICM Journal*, (1976) 20–34.

80. E. Pagels, "Paul and Women: A Response to a Recent Discussion," JAAR, 42 (1974) 547.

Chapter 5

Mary Daly

Glory to God the Verb

As a result of the [publication] of *The Church of the Second Sex* . . . I "lectured" to academic audiences and women's groups across the country about the sexism of the Christian tradition. Often in the late sixties I encountered hostility in women, not toward the patriarch whose misogynism I exposed, but toward me for exposing them.

By about 1970 this phenomenon of misplaced anger had almost disappeared. More and more people had caught up with the [Mary] Daly [who had written that book], and the lines that formerly had elicited hostility brought forth cheers. But the "I" who was then standing before the friendly audiences and tossing out the familiar phrases was already disconnected from the words, already moving through a new time/space. I often heard the old words as though a stranger were speaking them—some personage visiting from the past. My concern was no longer limited to "equality" in the church or anywhere else. I did not really care about unimaginative reform but instead began dreaming new dreams of women's revolution. This was becoming a credible dream, because a community of sisterhood was coming into being, into be-ing. In the hearing/healing presence of my sisters I had grown ready to try writing/speaking New Words.

The breakthrough to New Words found expression in *Beyond God the Father: Toward a Philosophy of Women's Liberation,* which is excerpted here. In the Introduction to that book I explained:

> To exist humanly is to name the self, the world, and God. The evolving spiritual consciousness of women is nothing less than this beginning to speak humanly—a reclaiming of the right to name. The liberation of language is rooted in the liberation of ourselves.
>
> It would be a mistake to imagine that the new speech of women can be equated simply with women speaking men's words. What is happening is that women are really *hearing* our*selves* and each other, and out of this supportive hearing emerge *new words.*

The biblical and popular image of God as a great patriarch in heaven, rewarding and punishing according to his mysterious and seemingly arbitrary will, has dominated the imagination of millions over thousands of years. The symbol of the Father God,

First published in *Ms.,* 3 (December 1974), pp. 58–62. Used by permission spawned in the human imagination and sustained as plausible by patriarchy, has in turn rendered service to this type of society by making its mechanism for the oppression of women appear right and fitting. If God in "his" heaven is a father ruling "his" people, then it is in the "nature" of things and according to divine plan and the order of the universe that society be male-dominated. Within this context a mystification of roles takes place: the husband dominating his wife represents God "himself."

As the Women's Movement begins to have its effect upon the fabric of society, transforming it from patriarchy into something that never existed before, into a diarchal situation that is radically new, it can become the greatest single challenge to the major religions of the world, Western and Eastern—all of which are essentially sexist. Beliefs and values that have held sway for thousands of years will be questioned as never before. This revolution may well be also the greatest single hope for survival of spiritual consciousness on this planet.

THE CHALLENGE: EMERGENCE OF WHOLE HUMAN BEINGS

There are some who persist in claiming that the liberation of women will only mean that new characters will assume the same old roles, and that nothing will change essentially in structures, ideologies, and values. This supposition is often based on the observation that the very few women in "masculine" occupations often behave much as men do. This kind of reasoning is not at all to the point, for it fails to take into account the fact that tokenism does not change stereotypes or social systems but works to preserve them, since it dulls the revolutionary impulse. The minute proportion of women in the United States who occupy such roles (such as congresswomen, judges, business executives, doctors, and so on) have been trained by men in institutions defined and designed by men, and they have been pressured subtly to operate according to male rules. There are no alternate models.

What is to the point is an emergence of woman-consciousness such as has never before taken place. It is unimaginative and out of touch with what is happening in the Women's Movement to assume that the becoming of women will simply mean uncritical acceptance of structures, beliefs, symbols, norms, and patterns of behavior that have been given priority by a society under male domination. Rather, this becoming will act as catalyst for radical change in our culture . . . .What *can* effect basic alteration in the system is a potent influence from *without*. Women who reject patriarchy have this power and indeed *are* this power of transformation that is ultimately threatening to things as they are.

The roles and structures of patriarchy have been developed and sustained in accordance with an artificial polarization of human qualities into the traditional sexual stereotypes. The image of the person in authority and the accepted understanding of "his" role has corresponded to the eternal masculine stereotype, which implies hyperrationality (in reality, frequently reducible to pseudorationality), "objectivity," agressivity, the possession of dominating and manipulative attitudes toward persons and the environment, and the tendency to construct boundaries between the self (and those identified with the self) and "the Other." The caricature of human being which is represented by this stereotype depends for its existence upon the opposite caricature— the eternal feminine. This implies hyperemotionalism, passivity, self-abnegation, and so on.

By becoming whole persons women can generate a counterforce to the stereotype of the leader, challenging the artificial polarization of human characteristics into sex-role identification. There is no reason to assume that women who have the support of each other to criticize not only the feminine stereotype but the masculine stereotype as well will simply adopt the latter as a model for ourselves. On the contrary, what is happening is that women are developing a wider range of qualities and skills. This is beginning to encourage and in fact demand a comparably liberating process in men—a phenomenon which has begun in men's liberation groups and which is taking place every day within the context of personal relationships. The becoming of androgynous human persons implies a radical change in the fabric of human consciousness and in styles of human behavior.

This change is already threatening the credibility of the religious symbols of our culture. Since many of these have been used to justify oppression, such a challenge should be seen as redemptive. Religious symbols fade and die when the cultural situation that gave rise to them and supported them ceases to give them plausibility. Such an event generates anxiety, but it is part of the risk involved in a faith which accepts the relativity of all symbols and recognizes that clinging to these as fixed and ultimate is self-destructive and idolatrous.

BEYOND THE INADEQUATE GOD

The various theologies that in one way or another objectify "God" as *a being,* thereby attempt in a self-contradictory way to envisage transcendent reality as finite. "God" then functions to legitimate the existing social, economic, and political status quo, in which women and other victimized groups are subordinate.

"God" can be used oppressively against women in a number of ways. First, it occurs in an overt manner when theologians proclaim women's subordination to be God's will.

Second, even in the absence of such explicitly oppressive justification, the phenomenon is present when one-sex symbolism for God and for the human relationship is used. The following passage from Gregory Baum's *Man Becoming* illustrates the point:

> To believe that God is Father is to become aware of oneself not as a stranger, not as an outsider or an alienated person, but as a son who belongs or a person appointed to a marvelous destiny, which he shares with the whole community. To believe that God is Father means to be able to say "we" in regard to all men.

A woman whose consciousness has been aroused can say that such language makes her aware of herself as a stranger, as an outsider, as an alienated person, not as a daughter who belongs or who is appointed to a marvelous destiny. She cannot belong to *this* without assenting to her own lobotomy.

Third, even when the basic assumptions of God-language appear to be nonsexist, and when language is somewhat purified of fixation upon maleness, it is damaging and implicity compatible with sexism if it encourages detachment from the reality of the human struggle against oppression in its concrete manifestations.

The new insight of women is bringing us to a point beyond such direct and indirect theological oppressiveness that traditionally has centered around discussions of "God." It is becoming clear that if God-language is even implicity compatible with oppressiveness, failing to make clear the relation between intellection and liberation, then it will either have to be developed in such a way that it becomes explicitly relevant to the problem of sexism or else dismissed. In my thinking, the specific criterion which implies a mandate to reject certain forms of God-talk is expressed in the question: Does this language hinder human becoming by reinforcing sex-role socialization? Expressed positively, the question is: Does it *encourage* human becoming toward psychological and social fulfillment, toward an androgynous mode of living, toward transcendence?

WOMEN'S LIBERATION AND REVELATORY COURAGE

Many questions that are of burning importance to women now simply have not occurred in the past (and to a large extent in the present) to those with "credentials" to do theology. Other questions may have been voiced timidly but quickly squelched as stupid, irrelevant, or naive. Therefore, attempts by women theologians now merely to "update" or to reform theology within acceptable patterns of question-asking are not likely to get very far.

Moreover, within the context of the prevailing social climate it has been possible for scholars to be aware of the most crudely dehumanizing texts concerning women in the writings of religious "authorities" and theologians—from Augustine to Aquinas, to Luther, to Knox, to Barth—and at the same time to treat their unverified opinions on far more imponderable matters with utmost reverence and respect. That is, the blatant misogynism of these men has not been the occasion of a serious credibility gap even for those who have disagreed on this "point." It has simply been ignored or dismissed as trivial. By contast, in the emerging consciousness of women this context is beginning to be perceived in its full significance and as deeply relevant to the world view in which such "authorities" have seen other seemingly unrelated subjects, such as the problem of God. Hence the present awakening of the hitherto powerless sex demands an explosion of creative imagination that can withstand the disapproval of orthodoxy and overreach the boundaries cherished by conventional minds.

The driving revelatory force that is making it possible for women to speak—and to *hear* each other speak—more authentically about God is courage in the face of the risks that attend the liberation process. Since the projections of patriarchal religion have been blocking the dynamics of existential courage by offering the false security of alienation—that is, of self-reduction in sex roles—there is reason to hope for the emergence of a new religious consciousness in the confrontation with sexism that is now in its initial stages. The becoming of women may be not only the doorway to deliverance which secular humanism has passionately fought for, but also a doorway *to* something—that is, a new phase in the human spirit's quest for God.

This becoming who we really are requires existential courage to confront the experience of nothingness. All human beings are threatened by non-being. I am suggesting that at this point in history women are in a unique sense called to be the bearers of existential courage in society.

People attempt to overcome the threat of nonbeing by denying the self. The outcome of this is ironic: that which is dreaded triumphs, for we are caught in the self-contradictory bind of shrinking our being to avoid non-being. The only alternative is self-actualization in spite of the ever-present nothingness. Part of the problem is that people, women in particular, who are seemingly incapable of a high degree of self-actualization have been made such by societal structures that are products of human attempts to create security. Those who are alienated from their own deepest identity do receive a kind of security in return for accepting very limited and undifferentiated identities. The woman who single-mindedly accepts the role of "housewife," for example, may to some extent avoid the experience of nothingness but also avoids a fuller participation in being, which would be her only real security and source of community. Submerged in such a role, she cannot achieve a breakthrough to creativity. Many strong women are worn out in the struggle to break out of these limits before reaching the higher levels of intellectual discovery or of creativity.

The beginning of breakthrough means a realization that there is an existential conflict between the self and structures that have given such crippling security. This requires confronting the shock of non-being with the courage to be. It means facing the nameless anxieties of fate, which become concretized in loss of jobs, friends, social approval, health, and even life itself. Also involved is anxiety of guilt over refusing to do what society demands, a guilt which can hold one in its grip long after it has been recognized as false. Finally, there is the anxiety of meaninglessness, which can be overwhelming at times when the old simple meanings, role definitions, and life expectations have been rooted out and rejected openly and one emerges into a world without models.

This confrontation with the anxiety of non-being is revelatory, making possible the relativization of structures that are seen as human products, and therefore not absolute and ultimate. It drives consciousness beyond fixation upon "things as they are." Courage to be is the key to the revelatory power of the feminist revolution.

With the rise of feminism, women have come to see the necessity of conflict, of letting rage surface, and of calling forth a will to liberation. Yet, partially because there is such an essential contrast between feminism and patriarchal religion's destructive symbols and values, and partially because women's lives are intricately bound up with those men—biologically, emotionally, socially, and professionally—it is clear that Women's Liberation is essentially linked with full human liberation.

Women generally can see very well that the Movement will self-destruct if we settle for vengeance. The more imminent danger, then, is that some women will seek premature reconciliation, not allowing themselves to see the depth and implications of feminism's essential opposition to sexist society. It can be easy to leap on the bandwagon of "human liberation" without paying the price in terms of polarization, tensions, risk, and pain that the ultimate objective of real human liberation demands.

WHY SPEAK ABOUT "GOD"?

It might seem that the women's revolution should just go about its business of generating a new consciousness, without worrying about God. I suggest that the fallacy involved in this would be an overlooking of a basic question that is implied in human existence and that the pitfall in such an oversight is cutting off the radical potential of the Movement itself.

It is reasonable to take the position that sustained effort toward self-transcendence requires keeping alive in one's consciousness the question of ultimate transcendence—that is, of God. It implies recognition of the fact that we have no power *over* the ultimately real, and that whatever authentic power we have is derived from *participation* in ultimate reality. This awareness, always hard to sustain, makes it possible to be free of idolatry even in regard to one's own cause, since it tells us that all presently envisaged goals, lifestyles, symbols, and societal structures may be transitory. This is the meaning that the question of God should have for liberation, sustaining a concern that is really open to the future—in other words, that is really ultimate. Such concern will not become fixated upon limited objectives.

Feminists in the past have in a way been idolatrous about such objectives as the right to vote. Indeed, this right is due to women in justice and it is entirely understandable that feminists' energies were drained by the efforts needed to achieve even such a modicum of justice. But from the experience of such struggles we are in a position now to distrust token victories within a societal structural framework that renders them almost meaningless. The new wave of feminism desperately needs to be not only many-faceted but cosmic and ultimately religious in its visions. This means reaching outward and inward toward the God beyond and beneath the gods who have stolen our identity.

The idea that human beings are "to the image of God" is an intuition whose implications could hardly be worked through under patriarchal conditions. If it is true that human beings have projected "God" in their own image, it is also true that we can evolve beyond the projections of earlier stages of consciousness. It is the creative potential itself in human beings that is the image of God. As the essential victims of the archaic God-projection, women can bring this process of creativity into a new phase. This involves iconoclasm—the breaking of idols. Even—and perhaps especially— through the activity of its most militantly atheistic and areligious members, the Movement is smashing images that obstruct the becoming of the image of God. The basic idol-breaking will be done on the level of internalized images of male superiority, on the plane of exorcising them from consciousness and from the cultural institutions that breed them.

One of the false deities to be dethroned is the God of explanation, or "God as a stopgap for the incompleteness of our knowledge," as Dietrich Bonhoeffer called "him." This serves sometimes as the legitimation of such anomic (purposeless) occurrences as the suffering of a child. Such phenomena are "explained" as being God's will. So also are socially prevailing inequalities of power and privilege, by justifying a process which easily encourages masochistic attitudes. Clearly, this deity does not encourage commitment to the task of analyzing and eradicating the social, economic, and psychological roots of suffering. As marginal beings who are coming into awareness, women are in a situation to see that "God's plan" is often a front for men's plans and a cover for inadequacy, ignorance, and evil. Our vantage point offers opportunities for dislodging this deity from its revered position on the scale of human delusions.

Another idol is the God of otherworldliness. The most obvious face of this deity in the past has been that of the Judge whose chief activity consists in rewarding and punishing after death. As Simone de Beauvoir indicated, women have been the major consumers of this religious product. Since there has been so little self-realization possible by the female sex "in this life," it was natural to focus attention on the next. As mass consumers of this image, women have the power to remove it from the market, mainly by living full lives here and now. I do not mean to advocate a mere reutterance of the "secularization" theology that was so popular in the sixties. If women can sustain the courage essential to liberation, this can give rise to a deeper "otherworldliness"—an awareness that the process of creating a counterworld to the the counterfeit "this world" presented to consciousness by the societal structures that oppress us is participation in eternal life.

A third idol, intimately related to those described above, is the God who is the Judge of "sin," who confirms the rightness of the rules and roles of the reigning system, maintaining false consciences and self-destructive guilt feelings. Women have suffered both mentally and physically from this deity, in whose name we have been informed that birth control and abortion are unequivocally wrong, that we should be subordinate to husbands, that we must be present at rituals and services in which men have all the leadership roles and in which we are degraded not only by enforced passivity but also verbally and symbolically. Although this is most blatant in the archconservative religions, the God who imposes false guilt is hardly absent from liberal Protestantism and Judaism, where "his" presence is more subtle. Women's growth in self-respect will deal the death blow to this as well as to the other demons dressed as gods.

WOMEN'S LIBERATION AS SPIRITUAL REVOLUTION

I have indicated that because the becoming of women involves a radical encounter with nothingness, it bears with it a new surge of ontological (concerning the nature and relations of being) hope. This hope is essentially active. The passive hope that has been so prevalent in the history of religious attitudes corresponds to the objectified God from whom one may anticipate favors. Within that frame of reference, human beings have tried to relate to ultimate reality as an object to be known, cajoled, manipulated. The tables are turned, however, for the objectified "God" has a way of reducing "his" producers to objects who lack capacity for autonomous action. In contrast to this, the God who is power of being acts as a moral power summoning women and men to act out our deepest hope and to become who we can be.

This hope is communal rather than merely individualistic, because it is grounded in the two-edged courage to be. That is, it is hope coming from the experience of individuation *and* participation. It drives beyond the objectified God that is imagined as limited in benevolence, bestowing blessing upon "his" favorites. The power of being is that in which all finite beings participate, but not on a "one-to-one" basis. Since this power is in all, while transcending all, communal hope involves in some manner a profound interrelationship with other finite beings, human and nonhuman. Ontological communal hope, then, is cosmic. Its essential dynamic is directed to the universal community.

Finally, ontological hope is revolutionary. Since the insight in which it is grounded is the double-edged intuition of non-being and of being, it extends beyond the superstitious fixations of technical reason. The latter, when it is cut off from the intuitive knowledge of ontological reason, cannot get beyond superstition. The rising consciousness that women are experiencing of our dehumanized situation has the power to turn attention around from the projections of our culture to the radically threatened human condition. Insofar as women are true to this consciousness, we have to be the most radical revolutionaries, since the superstition revealed to us is omnipresent and plagues even the other major revolutionary movements of our time. Knowing that black or white, Marxist or capitalist, countercultural or bourgeois male chauvinist deity (human or divine) will not differ essentially from "his" opposite, women will be forced in a dramatic way to confront the most haunting of human questions, the question of God. This confrontation may not find its major locus within the theological academy or the institutional churches and it may not always express itself in recognizable theological or philosophical language. However, there is a dynamism in the ontological affirmation of self that reaches out toward the nameless God. In hearing and naming ourselves out of the depths, women are naming toward God, which is what theology always should have been about. Unfortunately, it tended to stop at fixing names *upon* God, which deafened us to our own potential for self-naming.

THE UNFOLDING OF GOD

It has sometimes been argued that anthropomorphic symbols for "God" are important and even necessary because the fundamental powers of the cosmos otherwise are seen as impersonal. One of the insights characteristic of the rising woman-consciousness is that this kind of dichotomizing between cosmic power and the personal need not be. That is, it is not necessary to anthropomorphize or to reify transcendence in order to relate to this personally. In fact, the process is demonic in some of its consequences. The dichotomizing-reifying-projecting syndrome has been characteristic of patriarchal consciousness, making "the Other" the repository of the contents of the lost self. Since women are now beginning to recognize in ourselves the victims of such dichotomizing processes, the insight extends to other manifestations of the pathological splitting-off of reality into falsely conceived opposites.

Why indeed must "God" be a noun? Why not a verb—the most active and dynamic of all? Hasn't the naming of "God" as a noun been an act of murdering that dynamic Verb? And isn't the Verb infinitely more personal than a mere static noun? The anthropomorphic symbols for God may be intended to convey personality, but they fail to convey that God is Be-ing. Women now who are experiencing the shock of non-being and the surge of self-affirmation against this are inclined to perceive transcendence as the Verb in which we participate—live, move, and have our being.

This Verb—the Verb of verbs—is intransitive. It need not be conceived as having an object that limits its dynamism. That which it is over against is non-being. Women in the process of liberation are enabled to perceive this because our liberation consists in refusing to be "the Other" and asserting instead "I am"—without making another "the Other." Unlike Sartre's "us versus a third" (the closest approximation to love possible in his world), the new sisterhood is saying "us versus nonbeing." When Sartre wrote that "man [sic] fundamentally is the desire to be God," he was saying that the most radical passion of human life is to be a God who does not and cannot exist. The ontological hope of which I am speaking is neither this self-deification nor the simplistic reified images often lurking behind such terms as "Creator," "Lord," "Judge," that Sartre rightly rejects. It transcends these because its experiential basis is courageous *participation* in being. It enables us to break out of this prison of subjectivity because it implies commitment together.

NEW SPACE: NEW TIME

The unfolding of God, then, is an event in which women participate as we participate in our own revolution. The process involves the creation of new space, in which women are free to become who we are, in which there are real and significant alternatives to the prefabricated identities provided within the enclosed spaces of patriarchal institutions. As opposed to the foreclosed identity allotted to us within those spaces, there is a diffused identity—an open road to discovery of the self and of each other.

The new space is located always "on the boundary." Its center is on the boundary of patriarchal institutions, such as churches, universities, national and international politics, families. Its center is the lives of women whose experience of becoming changes the very meaning of center for us by putting it on the boundary of all that has been considered central.

The new space, then, has a kind of invisibility to those who have not entered it. It is therefore inviolable. At the same time it communicates power which, paradoxically, is experienced both as power of presence and power of absence. It is not political power in the usual sense but rather a flow of healing energy which is participation in the power of being. For women who are becoming conscious, that participation is made possible initially by casting off the role of "the Other" which is the nothingness imposed by a sexist world. The burst of anger and creativity made possible in the presence of one's sisters is an experience of becoming whole, of overcoming the division within the self that makes nothingness block the dynamism of being. Instead of settling for being a warped half of a person, which is equivalent to a self-destructive nonperson, the emerging woman is casting off role definitions and moving toward androgynous being.

This is not a mere "becoming equal to men in a man's world"—which would mean settling for footing within the patriarchal space. It is, rather, something like God speaking forth, God-self in the new identity of women. While life in the new space may be "dangerous" in that it means living without the securities catered by the patriarchal system for docility to its rules, it offers a deeper security that can absorb the risks that such living demands. This safety is participation in *being,* as opposed to inauthenticity, alienation, non-identity—in a word, nonbeing.

The power of presence that is experienced by those who have begun to live in the new space radiates outward, attracting others. For those who are fixated upon patriarchal space, it apparently is threatening. Indeed this sense of threat is frequently expressed. For those who are thus threatened, the presence of women to each other is experienced as an absence. Such women are no longer empty receptacles to be used as "the Other," and are no longer internalizing the projections that cut off the flow of being. Men who need such projection screens experience the power of absence of such "objects" and are thrown into the situation of perceiving nothingness.

Women's confrontation with the experience of nothingness invites men to confront it also. Many of course respond with hostility. The hostility may be open or, in some cases, partially disguised both from the men who are excercising it and from the women to whom it is directed. When disguised, it often takes seductive forms, such as invitations to "dialogue" under conditions psychologically loaded against the woman, or invitations to quick and easy "reconciliation" without taking seriously the problems raised. Other men react with disguised hostility in the form of being "the feminist's friend," not in the sense of really hearing women but as paternalistic supervisors, analysts, or "spokesmen" for the Movement. Despite many avenues of nonauthentic response to the threat of women's power of absence, some men do accept the invitation to confront the experience of nothingness that offers itself when "the Other" ceases to be "the Other" and stands back to say "I am." In so doing men begin to liberate themselves toward wholeness, toward androgynous being. This new participation in the power of being becomes possible for men when women move into the new space.

Entry into the new space whose center is on the boundary of the institutions of patriarchy also involves entry into new time. To be caught up in these institutions is to be living in time past. By contrast, when women live on the boundary, we are vividly aware of living in time present/future. Participation in the unfolding of God means also this time breakthrough, which is a continuing (but not ritually "repeated") process. The center of the new time is on the boundary of patriarchal time. What it is, in fact, is women's *own* time. It is our *life-time.* It *is* whenever we are living out of our own sense of reality, refusing to be possessed, conquered, and alienated by the linear, measured-out, quantitative time of the patriarchal system. Women, in becoming who we are, are living in a qualitative, organic time that escapes the measurements of the system. For example, women who sit in institutional committee meetings without surrendering to the purposes and goals set forth by the male-dominated structure, are literally working on our own time while perhaps appearing to be working "on company time." The center of our activities is organic, in such a way that events are more significant than clocks. This boundary living is a way of being in and out of "the system." It entails a refusal of false clarity. Essentially it is being alive now, which in its deepest dimension is participation in the unfolding God.

Chapter 6

Mary Gordon

Coming to Terms with Mary

Meditations on Innocence, Grief, and Glory

Queens in the nineteen sixties had almost as many Catholic high schools as bakeries. Toward the spring of the year, the approach of Senior Proms meant big business for the local merchants. There was one store—which girls in my school were urged to patronize—that had a special section devoted to what were called "Mary-like gowns." The Mary-like gown was an invention of nuns and a coalition of sodalists, and its intent, I think, was to make prom dresses as much like habits as possible. We used to go and try the dresses on for a laugh. They were unbelievably ugly. The yardage of material could have dressed even an Irish family for a year. Nobody I or my friends ever talked to would wear them. We always figured that people who bought prom dresses like that were going to the prom with their cousins. For the purpose of them was to conceal the body, to underplay as much as possible the natural allure of young, female flesh.

In my day, Mary was a stick to beat smart girls with. Her example was held up constantly: an example of silence, of subordination, of the pleasure of taking the back seat. With the kind of smile they would give to the behavior of Margaret, the wife in "Father Knows Best," they talked about the one assertion of Mary's recorded in the Gospel: her request at the wedding feast at Cana. It was noted that she didn't ask her son directly for anything; she merely said: "They have no wine." Making him think it was his decision. Not suggesting it was her idea, no, nothing like that. Then disappearing, once again, into the background, into silence.

For women like me, it was necessary to reject that image of Mary in order to hold onto the fragile hope of intellectual achievement, independence of identity, sexual fulfillment. Yet we were offered no alternative to this Marian image; hence, we were denied a potent female image whose application was universal. There were a few saints one could, in desperation, turn to: Theresa of Avila, who was reported to have had a fresh mouth (If this is the way you treat your friends, Lord, what do you do to your enemies? Henny Youngman in Carmel. Who wouldn't like her?) talked back to bishops, reformed her order, had visions whose power and authenticity were unassailable. But any saint, however celebrated, is venerated out of choice, only by some. The appeal of Mary is that devotion to her is universal, ancient. And she is the mother of God.

First published in *Commonweal,* 109 (January 15, 1982), pp. 11–14. Used by permission.

Women who were independent and intelligent rejected the Virgin Mary in favor of her son in the way that some feminists, particularly in the beginning of the movement, felt it necessary to radically reject those things that were associated exclusively with the female: dresses, make-up, domestic work, relations with men, children. But life has changed. The most interesting and sophisticated thought by feminists now sees that in rejecting those things that were traditionally thought of as female, we are going with the male system of values that rates them as inferior. What we are doing now is trying to salvage the valuable things that the past ascribed to females, and to say that, if they are valuable, why reserve them to only 53 percent of the human race? It is this impulse to re-examine and to understand in a deeper way the history of women, female genius, female work, often anonymous, hidden, uncredited, to look for new values that are not simply male values dressed for success, that is leading women back to Mary.

But there is still a problem. Most of what we know about Mary we know from men. Much of the thought about her has been poisoned by misogyny, and a hatred of the body, particularly female sexuality. The Fathers did not like women—and in setting Mary apart from the rest of the female sex what they were saying was that she was only acceptable because she did not share the corruption that was inevitably attached to the female condition. In an ancient and popular symmetry, the image of Mary as the second Eve has been present in Marian thought from earliest times. In talking about Eve, the early writers gave vent to their disgust for sex, and for female sexuality in general. Consider Tertullian:

> Do you not realize, Eve, that it is you? The curse God pronounced on your sex weighs still on the world. Guiltily, you must bear its hardships. You are the devil's gateway, you desecrated the fatal tree, you first betrayed the law of God, you softened up with your cajoling words the man against whom the devil could not prevail by force.

The tradition suggests that Eve is *cursed* to bear children, rather than being *blessed* with motherhood. Augustine refers to the "feces and urine" of childbirth. In the sixth century, Venantius Fortunatus writes, "Happy virgin . . . she does not weigh down sluggish limbs with an imprisoned embryo; she is not depressed and worn out by its awkward weight." In the seventeenth century, St. Jean Eudes writes, touching on the unbaptized fetus as the victim of original sin:

> It is a subject of humiliation of all the mothers of the children of Adam to know that while they are with child, they carry with them an infant . . . who is the enemy of God, the object of his hatred and malediction, and the shrine of the demon.

The identification of women with the flesh, men with the spirit, was a commonplace of ancient thought, and thinkers about women have used this idea to depict woman as inevitably lower—by virtue of her physical existence—than men. St. Jerome informs us:

> As long as a woman is for birth and children she is different from man as body is from soul. But when she wishes to serve Christ more than the world, then she will cease to be a woman, and will be called man.

St. John Chrysostom, speaking of women's physical nature, opines:

The whole of her bodily beauty is nothing less than phlegm, blood, bile, rheum, and the fluid of digested food. . . . If you consider what is stored up behind those lovely eyes, the angle of the nose, the mouth and cheeks you will agree that the well-proportioned body is merely a whitened sepulcher.

Woman does not have to be sexually active to be threatening and disgusting; the threat and the horror are inherent in her physical nature. It is difficult to understand the transition between this disgust-filled thinking about woman and the veneration accorded to the Virgin Mary. What hope is there for the rest of us, who eat, breathe, menstruate, make love, bear children? How do we bridge the gap between ordinary woman, that repository of phlegm, bile, rheum, and the fluid of digested food, and the Tower of Ivory, the House of Gold, the *floures floure,* the one of whom the twelfth-century poet says: "Your breasts are as fragrant as wine; their whiteness whiter than milk and lilies; their scent lovelier than flowers and balsam wood."

We must begin by the radical and frightening understanding that the history of human thought about women has been a history of error. Christianity is not unique in this error; it is possible to say that its ideas about women are slightly more humane than those of many groups in history. For a woman to try to take her place in any tradition, taking seriously that tradition's history, the only option is a forgiving vigilance. One must forgive, or one must give up history; one must be vigilant to ensure that the tendencies so inbred in all human beings—ourselves as well as men—are passed on as little as possible. For they are in all of us, blood and bone; we cannot expect them to disappear in a lifetime. Those of us whose hearts are moved by those who have gone before us, who wish to keep the connection with them alive, must reject the temptation of historical romanticism. We must not forget the history of woman has been a history of degradation, oppression, the idealization whose other side is tyranny. But we must resist as well the temptation to reject the lovely, the exalted, the resonant life built up for centuries by living men and women.

I have wanted to create for myself a devotion to Mary that honors her as woman, as mother, that rejects the wickedness of sexual hatred and sexual fear. I wanted this particularly as I grew older; I longed for it with a special poignance as I experienced motherhood for the first time. It has come to me, then, that one must sift through the nonsense and hostility that has characterized thought and writing about Mary, to find some images, shards, and fragments, glittering in the rubble. One must find isolated words, isolated images; one must travel the road of metaphor, of icon, to come back to that figure who, throughout a corrupt history, has moved the hearts of men and women, has triumphed over the hatred of woman and the fear of her, and abides shining, worthy of our love, compelling it.

I have chosen three qualities in my thoughts about her; innocence, grief, and glory. I offer here, no system, but a set of meditations. I offer no final words, since, for a woman to come to terms with this woman who endures beloved despite a history of hatred, she must move lightly and discard freely; she must take upon herself the ancient labor of women: she must become a gatherer, a hoarder. She must put out for those around her scattered treasure, isolates without a pattern whose accumulated meaning comes from the relations of proximity.

INNOCENCE

Innocence, grief, glory: they are potent words, ideas, and like all human things that take on power are susceptible to perversion and corruption. The beautiful idea of innocence can be perverted, in the face of a generalized hostility to female power, to an ideal of subservience, of a loss of individual identity and autonomy, of an enforced childishness which barters the responsibilities of freedom for the privileges of a protected object. But the ideal of innocence has nothing to do with weakness. On the contrary, real innocence is capable of understanding and confronting evil in its most radical terms: it is undeceived about the Powers of Darkness, and does not confuse them with human frailty; it never forgets compassion.

Innocence: it is a rare and a powerful quality; it is not the failure of the imagination to imagine wrong, but the naturally bestowed inability to choose malice, selfishness. It is the inborn lack of that instinct to touch others for their harm; the absence of the desire to inflict pain. Mary embodies our love for this instinctive purity of life. I imagine her in one of Leonardo's Annunciations covered over with light, sure in her youthful self-knowledge. Humble—"Behold the handmaid of the Lord"—yet never cringing, always aware of the great dignity of her position: "All generations shall call me blessed." Her consent asked for by God, not enforced.

Innocence suggests an inviolable goodness, not striven after, but lavishly and freely given. Hence we value it. It is not the virtue some of us struggle a lifetime trying to attain. It is a kind of luck. Grace, we call it. The love of innocence is the celebration of grace.

I call up more images. A sixteenth-century sculpture I saw in Winchester cathedral. Mary the young girl looks amused. Her mouth, a thin indentured curve, turns up with pleasure. Her downcast eyes show what might be fear, but finally is not, but only an inward looking, an understanding, wary, perhaps, but not overwhelmed. I think of the curve of the body of a thirteenth-century statue of the young mother with her child. At ease in its own native swaying almost with the rhythms of maternal love, ready for life, radically open to experience, to love.

This radical openness is what Karl Rahner sees as the importance of the idea of virginity for Christians regardless of their sexual vocation:

> This attitude of expectation, of readiness and receptivity to grace, this awareness that the ultimate thing is grace and grace alone, is something which, as an attitude of mind, every Christian must have, even if it does not find concrete expression in virginity.

I think of the young woman in Fra Angelico's Annunciation; thunderstruck from the force of the Angel's entrance, serene, and pleased. I remember the face of the young Mary in Pasolini's Gospel According to St. Matthew. A sensual girl, her wide mouth turned up in a smile of comprehending expectation. A girl of the Middle East, of the warm air of a temperate climate, picking fruit, walking on warm nights under stars we can no longer in the modern world imagine.

Yet these images have nothing to do with the false images of innocence used in our culture to sell everything from designer jeans to membership in the Moral Majority. Contrast the image of the girl in Pasolini's movie, of Fra Angelico's virgin, of the thirteenth-century young mother, the sensual curve of her hip ready for motion— contrast these images with the image of a young woman in Jerry Falwell's school. The sureness of the young Mary is a sureness born of grace; it is a sureness that never excludes understanding of human suffering, that does not assert, with every flick of its coiffed head, the exclusive rightness of its position. It is an innocence that is rooted in the love of the physical world. It is an innocence saddened by much, surprised at nothing. It is an innocence that knows it will be pierced by a sword, ground under by great scandal of an unjust world. It is an innocence that lives with the knowledge of its own impending grief.

GRIEF

The grieving mother. *Mater Dolorosa.* The second word I think about is grief. I note that in our culture, fixated as it is on youth, there are far fewer images of the sorrowing mother who would have to be at least middle-aged, than of the young virgin with child. I listen to Pergolesi's *Stabat Mater.* A mature grief, grief rescued from the danger of madness, not Clytemnestra raging, vengeful over her lost child, but a mother silenced by sorrow. Only in the heart, the great music of a resignation that is anything but a flat giving in: a lifting of the heart to God in the face of the absurd. The death of one's child. It is, for many of us, the worst we can imagine, the greatest stumbling block to faith. To witness the ignominious death of one's most innocent child!

In Mary we have the emblem of all human sorrow, innocence victimized by injustice, by the incomprehensible exigencies of the cruel God who is the God of love. I see her overcome with grief, swooning from the violence of the blows of God, her Father and her Son, in Grünewald's rendering of the sorrowing mother. For this woman, there is no comfort. The heart pierced with the sword, now open to the world. The sweet compassion of the innocent girl deepened beyond our comprehension. Spared nothing. We bring to her the scandal of the fallen world; we give our despair, the failure of all human consolation to assuage us.

GLORY

I see Bellini's Pietà. The Virgin is bent over the dead body of her Son. But behind her, the winter landscape blossoms with the first flowers of spring. She is the mother of the Resurrected Christ; that too is in her fate as she lies holding her dead child. We can, in a romantic love of suffering, fixate on the Sorrowing Virgin, perverting even that image in the belief that we are facing the true nature of life. But for a Christian, the final nature of life is triumphant. Christ rises from the dead: his mother takes her place beside him at the throne of God.

Triumph. How easily that too can be perverted to the triumphalism that attaches to the queenship of Mary when the church sees itself politically beleaguered, in danger of losing its power on earth. Marina Warner notes:

> In times of stasis and entrenchment, as under Popes Pius XII and to some extent Paul VI, veneration of the Virgin is encouraged, and in times of strong ecumenism and change, when the church is less self-righteous and assured, devotion to the Virgin, especially under her triumphant aspect, is restrained and declines.

What can we make of this? The image of the woman brought out as a weapon to threaten the rebellious? Yes, of course, if we confuse the queenship of Mary with a human rule whose first goal is to keep everyone in line. But how ridiculous. The triumph of Mary is beyond law, and lawlessness; the notion of disobedience is a paltry irrelevance if one imagines choirs of angels and the mother of God enthroned, not above her children, but in the midst of them, their voices raised in a harmony impossible to them in their life on earth. I see gold and ivory; I imagine the music of Handel, Alexander's Feast. The mother of God is the queen of heaven; she presides over a feast, secure that all her children are, at last, well fed.

In the end, it is beyond reason, beyond argument. In the end, devotion to Mary is the objective correlative of all the primitive desires that lead human beings to the life of faith. She embodies our desire to be fully human yet to transcend death. The hatred of women is the legacy of death; in Mary, mother and queen, we see, enfleshed in a human form that touches our most ancient longings, the promise of salvation, of deliverance, through flesh, from the burdens of flesh.

As Hopkins says:

> If I have understood,
> She holds high motherhood
> Toward all our ghostly good
> And plays in grace her part
> About man's beating heart,
> Laying, like air's fine flood,
> The deathdance in his blood.

I think, finally, it is through poetry, through painting, sculpture, music, through those human works that are magnificently innocent of the terrible strain of sexual hatred by virtue of the labor, craft, and genius of their great creators, that one finds the surest way back to the mother of God.

Chapter 7

Kay Turner

Contemporary Feminist Rituals

Comprend, we sweat out our rituals together. We change them, we're all the time changing them! But they body our sense of good!
            —Marge Piercy, *Woman at the Edge of Time*

The body is the image relator. In ritual, we *embody* and activate images of the archetypal, the eternal feminine, the goddess. Images of power, of transformation, of harmony and of duality. One woman empowering another. The crucial exchange of gifts. I cross the circle to give you something; you cross the circle to give her something. And so on until we have all changed places.

Power held is powerless; power given is power for all. In feminist ritual we maintain a center of which we are all aware. It is our collective heart which beats there. We hold together, our center endures. Even the most painful separation, the dispersal which is feared but necessary, cannot disconnect us from that ritual circle. Once that circle is created and affirmed, chaos is subdued. We survive. We thrive.

Although some theoretical attention has been given to the recent spiritual awakening within the women's movement, very little writing has been directed toward analysis of the use of ritual by women. What do these ritual acts mean to contemporary U.S. feminists? And what is their significance in terms of the women's movement?

Feminists are primarily at work revising the male-biased ideological bases of culture; some are now engaged in the creation of rituals to promote and sanction this serious turning away from the old to the new. As in traditional societies, feminist ritual provides an emotional, descriptive, intensified, and sanctifying version of emergent ideological systems. Feminist ritual offers an imagistic revitalization for women, participation in the concrete, bodily expressive creation of new images of the feminine which will help alleviate the stress of a liminality.

The evaluation of culture by Michelle Zimbalist Rosaldo in her theoretical overview for *Woman, Culture and Society,* serves as useful background material for answering why women have created rituals as an expression of the need for revitalization and as an impetus for political action. First, Rosaldo establishes a model for interpreting the difference in status between men and women, a model based on extensive contemporary cross-cultural analysis of male/female roles and behavior. She states that "an asymmetry in the cultural evaluations of male and female, in the importance assigned to

First published in *Heresies: A Feminist Publication on Art and Politics* (New York, Heresies Collective, 1982), pp. 20–26. Used by permission.

women and men, appears to be universal."[1] This asymmetry is manifested in the fact
that:

> Male, as opposed to female, activities are always recognized as predominantly
> important, and cultural systems give authority and value to the roles and activities
> of men. Everywhere, from those societies we might want to call most egalitarian
> to those in which sexual stratification is most marked, men are the locus of
> cultural value.[2]

Over the past few thousand years women have not been culturally granted a legitimate, overt way of demonstrating their power, their personhood. Only men define,
possess, and confer power or authority, and power is the necessary ingredient for the
creation of culture. Women are therefore consigned to live on the fringes of culture,
locked in domestic zones which are rarely defined as part of the cultural territory.
Rosaldo elaborates this point by using Mary Douglas's notion of "the anomalous":

> Recent studies of symbolic culture have suggested that whatever violates a
> society's sense of order will be seen as threatening, nasty, disorderly, or wrong.
> Douglas has called this sort of thing "anomalous." The idea of "order" depends,
> logically, on "disorder" as its opposite, yet society tries to set such things aside. .
> . . Insofar as men . . . define the public order, women are their opposite. Where
> men are classified in terms of ranked, institutional positions, women are simply
> women and their activities, interests, and differences receive only idiosyncratic
> note.[3]

Women are anomalies in most cultures and have no cultural recourse for demonstrating the reality of female power. Female power is almost without exception displayed
covertly under the rubric of influence or association with the right man. But Rosaldo
makes a unique claim for the possible use women may make of their anomalous or
liminal positions. Even though women's status is lowest in those societies where there is
the greatest distinction between the public and domestic realms and where women are
isolated from each other, "their position is raised when they can challenge those claims
of male authority, either by taking on men's roles or by establishing social ties, by
creating a sense of rank, order, and value in a world in which women prevail."[4] It is also
clear that historically women have taken on very active roles in social systems by
"manipulating, elaborating, or undermining" their domestic roles and by stressing their
differences from men. In other words, by giving special attention to their anomalous
status, women have been able "to take on powers uniquely their own."[5]

Especially pertinent to our discussion, Rosaldo mentions the roles of nun, midwife,
witch, and religious prostitute as making particularly positive use of women's "anomalous" sexuality:

> These examples suggest that the very symbolic and social conceptions [the
> notions of purity and pollution associated with women] that appear to set women
> apart and to circumscribe their activities may be used by women as a basis for
> female solidarity and worth.[6]

Of course it is most significant that these roles include the classic examples of women
who have been allowed to utilize ritual means as a source of gaining and transferring
power. Men have tenaciously held the rights to ritual use since the suppression of the
ancient priestesses of the goddess. In fact the participation in ritual by men has been

their most profound display of cultural authority and their most direct access to it. The performance of ritual in most societies, "primitive" and "civilized," is a simultaneous acknowledgement of men's warrant to create and define culture and, by exclusion, a sign to women to keep in their place, a place which we have already designated as outside culture and without the symbolic or real attributes of power.

Here we see a further distinction between the sacred and the profane based on the asymmetry of male-female relationships. Men have claimed sacred space as their locus for effecting control over and/or maintaining harmony with each other and the fates. As Mircea Eliade has shown, sacred space is "manifested space," it is created as sacred by men and in most societies women have little or no access to it.[7] Women live in the profane world, the world that is, the world that is incapable of being transformed or of transforming those who live in the profane world too (in fact we all live there most of the time), but when they choose to do so (or when the "gods" command them to do so) they may enter another world, a world of the sacred, and through ritual practice they may take part in ordering that world and themselves. The sacred realm is that of being and becoming, a realm saturated with power and critically "off-limits" to the female half of the human species.

That women in the United States and elsewhere have begun to claim sacred space for themselves, to create rituals which emphasize their loyalty to each other and finally name the powers which men have found "anomalous" (i.e., nameless) is indeed an ultimate, radical (proceeding from the root) affirmation of the revolutionary potential of the feminist movement. Asserting the right to ritual means as a source of power, vision, and solidarity is the symbolic corollary of equal pay, choice of abortion, domestic freedom, the establishment of women's business, etc. Successful and enduring change in the status of women will come only through the parallel transformation of symbols and realities. Feminist ritual practice is currently the most important model for symbolic and, therefore, psychic and spiritual change in women.

FEMINIST RITUALS

Here I would like to describe briefly a number of feminist rituals which characterize the kind and variety of expression this form has taken.

In her *Spotted Bundle Enclosures* Jody Pinto digs out old brick wells outside Philadelphia. At the bottom of these wells she leaves personal and found objects wrapped in animal skins. Next to these bundles Pinto makes a primitive fireplace with shards and cooking utensils. She constructs a ladder and leaves it down the side of the well as an invitation for others to come in. Reflecting on the creation of these ritual sites and her activity in them, Pinto writes:

> The other day I spread wings
> split a man in half
> spent a year in the earth
> excavated my own tomb
> rolled over
> cut out my heart
> and ate it.[8]

Donna Henes's *Spider Woman Series* involves web-building in natural and urban environments. Henes defines web-making as the "most basic female instinct" and has made a personal ritual of web-making over the past three years.[9]

Margi Gumpert, a witch by trade and by faith, performs a specific ritual whenever she enters a public bathroom:

> I often notice that the mirror reflects an image which makes me question myself, feel critical or dissatisfied with my appearance. I don't ignore it as trivial, because I recognize that the mirror is infested with a very common political poison, virus hollywoodius or televisioniensis, subtle pressure to measure up to a pattern designed to enslave. Just to free myself of that pressure isn't a magical operation. But hundreds of other women will use that mirror. So after I have cleared my own image of that false cloud, I usually perform some sort of magical activity to neutralize the poison. I pour suggestive energy into the mirror, encouraging anyone who might look in it to see herself in her true beauty. I reinforce the suggestion with all the power of my will and call on the Goddess of Beauty Herself, blessed Aphrodite, to banish that which would deny Her, as She exists in all of us.[10]

A ritual for the Autumn Equinox is performed yearly by a group of women living in the country near Wolf Creek, Oregon:

> Let friends gather, each bringing with her an article which represents a recent accomplishment—some self-chosen task she has completed. Let a circle form and each one place her article in front of her, and next to it a fruit, seed, or cone. Join hands and chant in unison the names of all present—several times till the energy is high. Then pause and chant the months of the year from the Winter Solstice to the Autumn Equinox.
>
> Now let each one in turn hold her article while she tells her friends of her accomplishment and something she has learned from it. When all have spoken all shall pick up the fruit, seed, or cone in front of them and picture inwardly the process of its change from seed to plant to flower to seed.
>
> Again let each woman speak in turn of what her accomplishment has meant to her growth and how she thinks it may be useful to her self and others. At this time if she feels grateful, let her give thanks. If she wants to dance, let her move. When all have expressed their feeling, with closed eyes ask yourself "What is the next stage in the process of my growth?" Ask your inner self for energy and guidance to continue.
>
> Let all join hands, moving closer into a hugging circle and repeat:
> > After the joy of harvest
> > After the work of the day
> > After the time of fulfillment
> > Comes the time of rest.
> > After the seed is planted
> > Nature takes care of the rest.[11]

On the streets of downtown Boston a woman wearing a high feather headdress makes a circle of cornmeal, places three ears of corn in the center of the circle, and begins a rhythmic chant naming the goddesses of the Americas before the conquest (Tonantzin, Chicomecoaltl, Blue Corn Girl, IxChel, etc.). After the chant is finished, she calls on women passing by, invites them into the circle, and blesses them by saying in litany form an ancient Aztec poem from the *Poesia Nahautl:*

Now o friends
Listen to the words of a dream
Each spring brings us new life
The golden corn refreshes us
And the pink corn makes us a necklace.
At least this we know:
The hearts of our friends are true.

While the women alternate in speaking the lines of the poem to each other, they hold an ear of corn between them and tear the sheaves down, exposing the fresh corn. This ritual has been performed from coast to coast with at least 300 women receiving the blessing since it was first done in 1975.[12]

In northern California several women have constructed menstrual huts as ritual retreats where they can go during their monthly periods. Painting the red quarter moon on their foreheads as a symbol of their special condition, they use the time spent in the hut for experiencing and affirming the culmination of cyclic process. It is a time for meditation and separation, but separation without the patriarchal connotations of impurity, defilement, and unworthiness. The menstrual flow is equated with the particular power of the feminine and time spent apart in the hut is for personally determining the course of that power.[13]

The following ritual was recounted in *Sundance,* a journal devoted to the study and sharing of dreams:

In a past issue of *Womanspirit* there is an article by Hallie Mountainwing describing an overnight wilderness event attended by twelve women. The purpose of the venture was to share dreams, become deeper friends, and explore the meaning to each of them of being women. To prepare for dreaming together, the twelve women arranged their sleeping bags into a "wheel" surrounding a central pole. In addition, each woman had two strands of ribbon attached to her sleeping bag, which were then attached to the pole, making a "dream net." The arrangement is quite similar to the May Pole and Sun Dance ceremonies; except, in this case, the people are lying down, asleep, and dreaming. As an approximation to a contemporary experiment in revelation, a twelve-person "dream wheel" inspires continued exploration.[14]

By way of contrast and comparison, I want to present a woman's ritual which has been practiced on the Yucatan Peninsula for centuries. A form of this ritual is still performed today but the following account was recorded in 1930 by Basauri and translated by J. Eric Thompson in his "The Moon Goddess in Central America." The ceremony is called "the song of the roses," KAIK' MIKTE:

A hollow is made in a level place and filled with water. This hollow should be of sufficient size so that a woman may take a bath in it. The woman who hopes to benefit from the ceremony is placed in it completely naked. Once she is in and the liquid reaches to the height of her breasts, they (other women who participate in the ceremony) cover the surface with flowers. Several women, friends of the one to be benefited, the number of which may vary, but never falls below five, take hands and dance around the bather, some singing and others saying a prayer in Maya. The dance lasts an hour, and during that time the dancers take flowers

which they have already prepared, stoop down to moisten them in the water in
which the principal bathes and throw them on the breast of the woman making
the ceremony (*la solicitante*). During the dance it is the custom to make nine turns
in one direction, stop a moment to moisten the flowers, and then repeat the same
number of turns in the opposite direction. When the ceremony is ended, the
dancers retire, the woman remains alone in the water, and, on coming out, she
takes a quantity of it, which she carries with her to employ in the preparation of
her husband's or lover's food.[15]

Although the ritual is ostensibly practiced to make their lovers remain faithful, the
beauty of the ceremony lies in its kinship with all ritual acts, both past and present,
which describe the healing, nurturing effect of tribal sisterhood. The overt goal of the
ritual is not the only reason for performing it; something significant is taking place in
the act of performance too. An individual woman is uplifted and sacralized by her
sisters, her *comadres,* her C-R group, her kind.

The above presentation of women's rituals is by no means exhaustive. In fact the
range of expressive material in current feminist ritual sets is so diverse, multivocal, and
widespread that one of the major tasks of the historical branch of the women's
movement must be to document the growth of ritual events. Someone must also take on
the project of assembling what cross-cultural historical evidence exists of women's
rituals such as the KAIK' MIKTE.

OPENNESS TO CHANGE

In "The Qualitative Leap Beyond Patriarchal Religion," theologian Mary Daly
makes the following statement:

> The women's revolution is not merely about equality within a patriarchal society
> (a contradiction in terms). It is about *power* and redefining power. Within
> patriarchy, power is generally understood as power over people, the environment,
> things. In the rising consciousness of women, power is experienced as *power of
> presence* to ourselves and to each other, as we affirm our own being against and
> beyond the alienated identity bestowed upon us within the patriarchy. This is
> experienced as *power of absence* by those who would objectify women as "the
> other," as magnifying mirrors.[16]

Daly's insistence that redefinition of power is a central goal of the women's movement
is crucial for understanding the use of ritual by feminists, a symbolic model for
discovering how to give and get "power of presence." One woman empowers another
(or herself) through reaffirmation of the body as an instrument of communion (not
alienation).

None of the rituals mentioned above would be considered effective if a transfer of
power had not resulted. Yet it is of critical importance to note that power is rarely
considered an object of possession which the group or individual may get hold of during
ritual activity. What is stressed through ritual is the dynamic quality of power, the
continual exchange of gifts which heightens the affirmative identity of all who participate. Power emanates from within as it is simultaneously received from without.

For women in revolution it is imperative to create an entirely new value system, the
heart of which will be a dramatic reassessment of the use of power. Ritual serves as a
primary way of affirming commitment to that reassessment. The ritual setting provides
a place for knowing the easy, direct exchange and sharing of power. Certainly ritual is an

idealized microcosmic experience, but it may be an endurably important means of invoking a new order of things in the macrocosm. At the very least it has been a useful mode for envisioning what a different world for women might *feel* like.

The word "feeling" deserves special mention in connection with women's rituals. In fact it is a word we must never neglect in talking about any ritual. Evon Vogt once asked a ritual participant, "Why do you go through the ceremonies? Why do you do what you do?" The participant replied, "To feel better, I want to make myself feel better."[17] In the context of ritual, women are creating a space in which to feel better, to feel more, to feel the past as well as the future. Perhaps most important is the way in which ritual upholds and celebrates the validity of feeling as a mode of revelation, communication, and transvaluation. In some of the rituals described above, the flow of feelings, change in feelings or sharing of feelings with others is a highly desirable goal in performing the ritual.

In discussing the reasons underlying the performance of ritual acts in the feminist community, we must underscore the importance of ritual as a formalized consecration of female bonding. The ritual concretization of the idea reflected in the popular feminist slogan "Sisterhood is Powerful" is extremely important in demonstrating the cohesiveness and commitment of the feminist community. A primary function of ritual is to connect the individual with the group—dramatically, indissolubly. In ritual the desire is to achieve shared emotion, not to promote private images or dreams. The specific rites which comprise many feminist rituals reaffirm relationship, belonging, and identity. Ritual acts maintain a symbolic center of which all the participants are aware. This center is a place to which one can return for support and comfort long after the ceremony has ended. A relational or ideological bond cemented formally through ritual procedure is nothing if not enduring.

Being capable of membership in a group and finding ways of expressing that membership and acting it out are necessary for the success of any political revolution. Let us not forget that less than ten years ago Lionel Tiger told us "women do not bond"[18] and in so saying implied women are incapable of creating significant political institutions. It is already evident that women have effected widespread social change (to enumerate the accomplishments to date would fill pages) since the formal resumption of the feminist movement in 1967. Ritual participation will no doubt stimulate further and deeper political change, for there is, indeed, a continuum between ritual and everyday life for feminists. The female bonds established in ritual lend incentive to the female bonds that inspire social change. The use of ritual is significant as a source for the renewal of commitment to evolving and transforming society as a whole.

Many feminists in fact consider the ritual setting and experience to serve as a visionary mode. In feminist rituals which utilize peyote, a good portion of the night-long ceremony is given over to envisioning the future of the self, the group, and the world. In authentic ritual experience, something, an ability to break through the present, is available which can lead to discovery and creativity. Ritual is a potent source of invention because the participants feel the extreme intensity, sometimes the ecstasy, of openness to possibility and revelation. This sense of extreme openness and creativity is rare for women who have been traditionally circumscribed by severe limitation, constrained by custom, with no hope for a changed future.

PRIESTESS AND GODDESS

Another important consideration is the way feminist ritual purposefully imparts information of a special kind, information which has been unavailable to women and

actually suppressed for hundreds of years. I refer specifically to the ritual communication of feminine images, primarily the communication of images of the goddesses. The
suppression of the goddess in our culture has meant the loss of images which identify
personal and collective power in women. Invocations to the goddesses, references to
their attributes, a reclamation of the wealth of literature which remains to describe
them, the putting on of their symbols—none of these ritual actions indicates a desire to
return to a golden matriarchal age as some critics have suggested. It is much more crucial
for feminists, for all women, to uncover and recover their imagistic heritage (as
represented in the powers and tales of the goddesses) and to create new images which
represent women's recent emergence (as many women in the plastic and performing arts
are now doing) than it is to prove the absolute historical existence of a widespread
matriarchy. I have no doubt that some matriarchies did exist. The important consideration, however, is not the fact that women ruled over men but that they "ruled"
themselves and that they had culturally approved or at least culturally active models for
distinguishing their powers from others. In many ancient civilizations the feminine
world was not as "anomalous" as it currently is. Women had access to powerful images
and used them to order and maintain their particular spheres of life.

One of the most important shrines in the pre-Conquest Mayan world was located on
Cozumel Island twenty miles off the coast of the Yucatan. It was dedicated to IxChel,
the preeminent goddess of the moon, water, childbirth, weaving, and love, who was
equal in status to the great father god, Itzamma. Her shrine was visited by women from
all over the Mayan world, some traveling hundreds of miles from Guatemala and El
Salvador. Inside the shrine a giant image of the goddess served as an oracle for these
women pilgrims. The statue was hollowed out in back; a priestess would stand in that
profound cavity and impersonate the goddess, become a speaking image of the goddess
and in fact *imagine* herself the goddess.

To imagine is to make an image or become an image; impersonation of this sort was
an achievement of relation with the goddess and a means of absorbing her powers.
Images are sources of identification; they tell us who we most profoundly, most
archetypally are. The Mayan women who visited the shrine at Cozumel were seeking
affirmation of their own powers (primarily the power to give birth, to be fruitful) and
they received it through the pilgrimage itself (the association with peers), idol worship
(intense identification with an image) through the blessing bestowed by the personified
goddess, the priestess.

SHAMAN AND RITUALIST

Much the same identificaiton is sought and achieved in feminist rituals. Ritual is a
special vehicle of communication for feminists; ritual speaks a visceral language of
restoration of symbols and provides an opportunity to utilize them personally. Sherry
Ortner says:

> Efforts directed solely at changing the social institutions cannot have far-reaching
> effects if cultural language and imagery continue to purvey a relatively devalued
> view of women.[19]

The imagery conveyed woman-to-woman in ritual experience is imagery that upholds
the value of women and symbolizes the varied kinds of their power. If, as Vogt
maintains, "Ritual perpetuates knowledge essential to the survival of the culture,"[20]

women are just now learning how important it is to their survival to store and transmit feminine knowledge through ritual means.

Much of the available data on women's rituals reveal the prominence of one individual as instigator or leader of the ritual. This is not always the case, as many rituals are performed without a leader, including rituals which follow a format and are repeated the same way every time, rituals which rely on group spontaneity, group meditation or chanting, etc. Nevertheless, a number of women in the feminist community have emerged as ritualists, the counterpart to the shaman in traditional societies. Most women involved in introducing ritual performance, however, do not call themselves as such; they are most widely known simply as ritualists (or practitioners or witches if they adhere solely to the witchcraft tradition). The comparison between shamans and feminist ritualists is instructive only in demonstrating that their goals in performance are similar and, to a certain extent, their conception of self is analogous.

If the ultimate goal of ritual experience is to effect transformation (i.e., to change the order of things), in most cases someone must prepare the group to undergo change. A procedure must be decided upon (in traditional societies, custom determines procedure) and followed correctly to lead the participants from one state of feeling to another.

Both the shaman and feminist ritualist make preparations and later facilitate the group's progress in the actual ritual; both are capable of helping transformation to take place if the participants will trust them. I am stressing here the fact that both shaman and feminist ritualist express a powerful sense of capability, that they can serve as links, as surrogates, that they can connect different realms of reality and facilitate change and are concerned with enabling the change of others.

Eliade says of the shaman: "He is, above all, a sick man who has been cured, who has succeeded in curing himself."[21] The feminist ritualist is also one who has been "sick" in the sense that oppression makes one feel sick. She who is now cured of the tyranny of oppression offers that new sense of well-being to others. A traditional shaman may become a "professional transformer" practicing his art as occupation, whereas a feminist ritualist may rise to the occasion of transformation only once in her lifetime (although many ritualists practice somewhat regularly). Still, the necessity of their individual acceptance of their power to change is crucial to the ultimate effect of the ritual.

An obvious similarity between the traditional shaman and the feminist ritualist is that both do their work through performing (singing, dancing, displaying, holding, hugging) and, moreover, the performance is quite often geared to awakening and stimulating the participant's body. For both ritualist and shaman see the body, not the mind, as the locus of transformation. The body is our first and last outward reality; it defines and conditions our life experience and gives us personal identity and continuity. Both shaman and ritualist take the body to be the clearest, purest expression of self. And it is that aspect of self which must feel change before the intellectual or soul self can change. A chant I used in a ritual performance called *See the Voice* expresses the bodily concerns of the transformer:

> My hands
> Open the curtains of your being
> Clothe you in a further nudity
> Uncover the bodies of your body.
> My hands
> Invent another body for your body.[22]

The body is also recognized by both, especially by the ritualist, as the means for making conscious interconnections and unions that were unconscious or suppressed. Ritual, through those who perform it, creates a new body, one body made of many, through which can be understood and realized the extremes of fear and love, the truly political dimensions of humanness.

Finally, the relation between the shaman and his participant community and the parallel relation between the feminist ritualist and her participant community bears notation. Richard Schechner maintains:

> The deep structure of shamanistic performance is a protagonist-antagonist conflict by means of which the secret wishes of the community are exposed and redistributed. . . . The Shaman is the vessel through which all that is powerful chooses to express itself. And these powers are inherent in community itself, are the community.[23]

Thus both shaman and ritualist exist primarily within a community and the powers they exemplify ultimately belong not to them as individuals but to the community which is the actual source of their power. The work of both the shaman and the ritualist is to make available, clarify, and intensify powers that are the essence of community. Transformation is useless in isolation.

RITUALIST AND ARTIST

A different comparison might be drawn between the artist and the ritualist. Here two items seem important: (1) feminist ritual has some of its deepest roots in the art of the 1960s and 70s which gave rise to ritual-like forms such as the happening, and (2) some feminist ritualists have come to ritual performance as a direct result of their previous interest in manipulating symbolic forms in other media (painting, sculpture, film, etc.).

I said earlier that a primary objective of ritual is to achieve shared meanings and a sense of shared goals, not to promote private images or dreams. This is the crucial difference between the ritualist and the artist. The artist takes herself, her content, and ability to express that content as commendable to the world of meaning and aesthetics. She is a source of new meaning, novelty acting as a basis for determining accomplishment. The ritualist is constantly at work to leave the self, to become a channel for transcendent experience. Gathering the group members, nourishing their need for each other and themselves through the manipulation of dramatic forms—these are her aims.

As Donna Henes once told me in a personal communication, "Making art locks me in myself; making rituals sets me free. I don't want to make art anymore." The ritualist occupies a unique space between individual and group, between self-expression and group cohesion. She is the exemplary mediatrix, simultaneously the weaver and the process of weaving. A quote from Octavio Paz, though not written with the ritualist in mind, helps to define the sense she has of herself:

> I am the other when I am myself, my acts are more my own when they are everybody's. Because to be myself I must be other, go out of myself, seek myself among others, those others who are not if I do not exist.[24]

This dynamic of self loss and group gain epitomized as the ritualist's view of her role is crucial to the transfer of power which the ritual mode promises. The ritualist defines her sense of powerfulness by her capacity to share it with others while the artist is concerned with obtaining power (through manipulation of media) and maintaining it for others to observe or partake of vicariously.

In stressing the communal nature of the ritual experience, it may appear that the concept of the self and its nurturance are served by some means other than ritual. As the examples given earlier indicate, some feminist rituals are performed solely for the purpose of self-revelation. From its inception the women's movement has insisted on the importance of realizing the way in which political change comes out of reinterpretation and reinvention of the personal dimension (the personal is political).

All women have suffered the loss of affirmative, positive self-images as a direct result of their second-class status and consequent objectification in the male-dominant society. It is painful to consider the countless lives wasted, the talents atrophied, and the sickness suffered by women who were never allowed, least of all encouraged, to know themselves, and take strength and happiness in that knowledge. Surely one of the most highly regarded uses of ritual in traditional societies is the curing of "soul loss" of one form or another. Twentieth-century, postindustrial, special-privileged American women are engaged in ritual practice for much the same reason, metaphorically speaking.

For women, the ritual setting is often a place for naming individual powers and sharing the affirmation of those powers with the group or simply internalizing them through private ritual procedure. Ritual provides a mode for getting in touch with the self and staying in touch. Also, by definition, the ritual space and activity are sacred in the sense of representing the possibility of self-transformation.

Part of the power and the fear experienced in ritual is the realization that one may change, become ultimately different, as a result of the experience, or that the experience may suddenly make recognizable change that has been slowly rising from the depths of personality and ideology. Victor Turner states that "When a ritual does work . . . it can cause in some cases real transformations of character and of social relationships."[25] I would venture to say that many women have been profoundly affected and, in some cases, redirected through their experience in ritual. A lost self is recovered, nurtured, and allowed to emerge fully named.

Ritual facilitates transition for the participant in specific ways. As Turner clearly states, "Practically all rituals of any length and complexity represent a passage from one position, constellation, or domain of structure to another."[26] This passage occurs in individual women most dramatically, and not without fear, separation anxiety, and trauma. Before women can enter new roles they must leave old roles behind, roles that once provided the comforts of self-definition and reality structure. Ritual participation can ease transition by rendering it in dramatic, metaphorical terms and providing a support group to encourage and enable the necessary catharsis to take place.

The transfer of values from one framework to another leaves a woman just as vulnerable, suspended between two lifestyles. It is a dangerous time for the individual, one which requires the support of the feminist community and the use of ritual to promote ease in the transfer. Women are realizing that this is a responsibility and a desire: to help other women cross boundaries in their lives not as aggressive individuals, proving themselves, but as new members of a community who deserve the help and protection of those who have gone before. We have all been guarded and we must all become guardians. The ritual setting allows women to know the power of guarding and the comfort of being guarded in a space that does not demand immediate resolution of the passage crisis. The crisis period may continue through many phases of recognition, adjustment, and readjustment, the assimilation of which will fall primarily on the individual. But the community has developed ritual means by which that transformation may be asserted and its painful aspects somewhat absorbed by a formal claim made on the individual—a claim that she is new, that she is one of many, that she is welcome.

For feminists, as for other practitioners of ritual, doing the ritual is more important than knowing the ritual. The efficacy of ritual is always in the acting of it, in becoming bodily involved with the elements, not in understanding the text of belief or ideology which may underlie it. The essence of ritual is in physical relationship, one woman to another (or one woman to herself) in the circle they have created for each other.

This article only begins the necessary process of defining and evaluating the emergence of ritual as an important component of the greater liberation movement. To my knowledge, only Lucy Lippard's article in *Chrysalis* specifically deals with the meaning of ritual for feminists. No other theoretical material is available although movement media sources such as *Womanspirit, Lady-Unique-Inclination-of-the-Night,* and *Quest* have been documenting ritual practices among women since 1974. My sense of the importance of ritual for the feminist community comes out of an understanding of its historical importance for humanity. Ritual marks the ultimate ideal of relationship between self and community, the fusion of two distinct realities rather than separation.

NOTES

1. Michelle Zimbalist Rosaldo, "A Theoretical Overview," in Michelle Z. Rosaldo and Louise Lamphere, eds., *Woman, Culture, and Society* (Stanford University Press, 1974) 19.
2. Ibid., 19–20.
3. Ibid., 31.
4. Ibid., 36.
5. Ibid., 38.
6. Ibid., 39.
7. Mircea Eliade, *Shamanism* (Princeton University Press, 1964).
8. Lucy Lippard, "Quite Contrary: Body, Nature, Ritual in Women's Art," *Chrysalis* (Autumn 1977) 38.
9. Ibid., 43.
10. Margi Gumpert, "Witchcraft," *Country Women* (April 1974) 27.
11. Jean Mountaingrove, "Speaking to Ourselves," *Womanspirit* (June 1976) 64.
12. Observed at the conference, "Through the Looking Glass: A Gynergenetic Experience," Boston, Mass., April 23–25, 1976.
13. Ruth Mountaingrove and Emily Culpepper, "Menstruation: Body and Spirit," *Womanspirit* (June 1976) 64.
14. Henry Reed, ed., *Sundance* (Spring 1977) 262.
15. J. Eric Thompson, "The Moon Goddess in Central America" (Carnegie Institute of Washington, publ. 509, contribution 29, 1939); cited in *Lady-Unique-Inclination-of-the-Night* (Cycle 1) 49.
16. Mary Daly, "The Qualitative Leap Beyond Patriarchal Religion," *Quest,* 1/1, p. 21.
17. Evon Vogt, *Tortillas for the Gods* (Harvard University Press, 1976).
18. Lionel Tiger, *Men in Groups* (New York, Random House, 1969).
19. Sherry Ortner, "Is Female to Male as Nature Is to Culture?" in Rosaldo and Lamphere, *Woman,* 87.
20. Vogt, *Tortillas,* 8.
21. Eliade, *Shamanism,* 27.
22. Octavio Pax, "Touch," in *Configurations* (New York, New Directions, 1971) 63.
23. Richard Schechner, *Environmental Theater* (New York, Hawthorne, 1973) 189–90.
24. Paz, "Touch," 63.
25. Victor Turner, *Dramas, Fields, and Metaphors* (Cornell University Press, 1974) 56.
26. Ibid., 238.

Chapter 8

Barbara Brown Zikmund

Women in Ministry Face the '80s

A recent study sponsored by the Ford Foundation reports that female enrollment in the seminaries of nine leading Protestant denominations has jumped dramatically in the past decade. From 1972 to 1980, the number of women in these seminaries grew from 3,358 to 10,830. Many people in theological education readily admit that if it were not for the women, seminaries would be in deep financial trouble. In the mainline Protestant schools women make up 30 to 50 percent of the student bodies. And although most laypeople in the churches have had little experience with women ministers, the situation is changing rapidly.

People are always asking why this change has come about so quickly. Why do women choose ministry? Why would a woman today seek out a career so obviously dominated by men? Yet it makes sense. As women have moved outside the home to seek employment, the church has offered great appeal. Many women have received excellent educations. In the economy of American Protestant values, when one has a talent or a resource, it is wasteful not to use it. Women are seeking meaningful ways to use the benefits of education. Women are newly aware of their talents. Furthermore, the inflationary spiral has forced many women into the marketplace to supplement shrinking family incomes.

Historically, women have been the backbone of American churches; their volunteer efforts have kept many mainline churches going. Consequently, when women begin looking around society for employment outside the home, the church is very appealing. Women know the church. They know that they can carry on its ministries effectively, because they have been serving the church as volunteers for years. And when the church preaches a theology that celebrates the gifts of all people, regardless of race and sex, women feel comfortable openly seeking more direct leadership. Women who have never claimed their sense of calling are coming forward to do what they have thought about for years.

Although women are challenging the sexist patterns of the past, most women who choose to prepare for ministry are not on a crusade. They are responding to a genuine call to service. While they are hurt and angry that the church has limited the exercise of women's talents in the past, they are hopeful that a new era for women's ministries is emerging.

Women in seminaries today and women moving out to serve in local churches in increasing numbers have shared some unique experiences. In talks with such women, three common concerns emerge: credibility, rivalry, and calling.

CREDIBILITY

Women want to be accepted and effective—and women ministers, like women in many predominantly male professions, do not have the automatic acceptance and unthinking support which their male colleagues enjoy. Consequently they must spend considerable energy establishing and maintaining their credibility as ministers. It begins with externals.

Because women are often quickly judged in our society by "appearances," concerns about what to wear and how one's voice carries cannot be ignored. Women clergy work very consciously on the interrelationship between their private lives and their roles as ministers. How to nourish meaningful relationships with the opposite sex? What to ask of their husbands? Whether to have children? How to balance home responsibilities with the job? These are common concerns for all professional women. In the Protestant ministry, however, these questions have special implications for a woman pastor.

Throughout the history of the American church, the minister's wife has contributed to her husband's credibility. She tended his home, supported the women's program, sang in the choir, and generally supplemented his image as a stable family man. In recent years this ideal has faded with clergy divorces and clergy wives who take less part in the church. But it remains a special problem for women clergy. Laity worry about the personal happiness of an unmarried female pastor; but if she is married, they have even more trouble knowing what to do with her husband. Sometimes he is unwittingly forced into a pseudo-pastoral role he does not choose. At other times, if he maintains a career and identity outside the church or is not even a church member, his wife's ministry (and/ or the marriage) may be questioned.

If both members of a couple are ministers, it might appear to be easier, but the woman/wife usually has a difficult time gaining credibility as a pastor in her own right. People turn to male leadership first and view her work as secondary; or they squeeze her into the sex-stereotyped ministry of Christian education. Clergy couples find that the double demands of their ministries on one marriage make it especially difficult to separate their private lives from their professional obligations.

When a woman pastor chooses to have a family, the situation gets even more complicated. In today's economy many mothers work because their families need the money. But as one pregnant minister told me, "People don't go into ministry for money." So when she tells people that she has no intention of leaving her position when the baby comes, they cannot understand. Everyone seems to assume that she ought to choose between motherhood and ministry. Somehow a woman's call to ordained service is thought to be more easily compromised by parenthood.

Yet ironically, when the pastor is a mother, her credibility is often enhanced. One minister recalled an introduction at a regional women's fellowship meeting. After spelling out the educational and ecclesiastical credentials of the speaker, the woman making the introduction said, "But I know that you will really want to hear what Reverend X has to say, because she is the mother of a two-year-old son." And in that audience her credibility was increased. For the same reasons, divorced and widowed women clergy sometimes gain credibility from the fact that they once were married (and had/have children).

Credibility is measured in many little things. Women clergy often notice that people are overly concerned with how they sound and how they look. If they are single, they are more vulnerable to matchmaking and overprotective laity. If they are married, their husbands and families are regularly measured by parsonage standards which do not fit.

It is a double standard, but until our society becomes less preoccupied with women's appearances and relationships, female clergy cannot ignore these concerns.

RIVALRY

Rivalry is another issue for women moving into ordained ministries. Because ministry is a profession which rewards individual excellence and builds upon unique personal gifts and talents, staff relationships are often difficult. Successful ministers are strong leaders who attract followers, and in many cases they are not skilled team workers.

Yet many seminary graduates, male and female, receive their first appointment or call as the assistant or associate pastor in a large church. Although it is good not to begin one's ministry all alone, working in team ministry is invariably difficult—especially for women. The rivalries that emerge are complex. If the senior pastor (who is usually male) is threatened by a competent woman, her energies will be dissipated in frustration and anger. If he is young and attractive, there may be sexual innuendos and jealousies. If he is supportive, his best intentions sometimes come out in paternalistic ways. In all cases it is difficult to obtain the helpful feedback necessary for professional growth.

Often denominational staff people seek out a new woman pastor to serve on commit-tees and to take a visible role in regional or conference meetings. Being a token, or being pushed into leadership before one is ready, is lonely and frightening. The situation gets worse when patronizing executives lean over backward to help. One well-meaning moderator changed all the "brother in Christ" language at an ordination service to "daughter in Christ." Not until someone pointed it out to him did he realize that "sister in Christ" would have been more appropriate.

Rivalry among clergy is commonplace. For everyone starting out in the Christian ministry, it is disillusioning to function within the hierarchical and patriarchal patterns of church power. It is common for assistant and associate pastors to become discour-aged and cynical. For women, however, the rivalries are more intense and layered with sexism. Male seminary classmates see women as favored candidates for those jobs that take heed of affirmative-action goals. Established male pastors worry about how they will measure up when compared with exceptionally able women. Clergy wives become uneasy after a woman joins the ministerial staff. Active laywomen feel devalued because they have not been to seminary. Even other women clergy sometimes begrudge sharing the limelight with another woman. Rivalry is a powerful reality in the lives of many women clergy.

CALLING

The calling to ordained ministry in much of Protestantism today has a double meaning . On the one hand, to have a call means to have a job, a particular invitation from a church to become its pastor. On the other hand, a call to the gospel ministry is a theological and spiritual reality. Women ministers have special concerns about their calling in both senses.

Placement of women seminarians is a major issue in many denominations. Special educational programs and bureaucratic efforts are under way to help the increasing numbers of women ministerial candidates find employment after graduation. Although some free-church denominations have been ordaining women for over 100 years, they have done little to help place women in other than small, out-of-the-way and marginal pastorates. Many women have had meaningful and significant ministries in these unprestigious places, but their salaries and their capacity to move through a normal ministerial career have been severely curtailed. Where each local church is free to call its own pastor, pressures to change common preferences for male pastors must be indirect. It is a slow process, but the sheer numbers of women graduating from seminaries at the present time are helping to change attitudes.

In those connectional denominations that deploy clergy through an appointment system, change has been even more rapid. When a bishop accepts a female candidate for ministry, the aspirant has powerful forces on her side. Although some ecclesiastical systems are saturated with candidates and there is an oversupply of clergy, when positions do open up, and when the appointment officer is a strong advocate for women, women move into significant pastorates.

For many women, their first call or appointment is not the problem. In today's economy there are many small churches seeking fresh seminary graduates to be their pastors, and there continue to be fair numbers of openings for assistant or associate pastors. Although it usually takes longer than placement for a male graduate, most women who want a position eventually get one.

After several years, however, in a typical minister's career, it becomes time to move to a slightly larger church, or to graduate from being an assistant or associate minister to having a parish of one's own. At this point many women find themselves trapped. They have lost touch with the support networks they developed during seminary. They have learned some things about themselves, and they are less willing to settle for the lowest salary. They have developed greater self-confidence so that they are able to state what they want to do in ministry, not simply to respond in gratitude to whatever is available. Furthermore, women clergy seeking their second placements are often limited geographically because of their husband's job, or they may be limited because they have or want to have children. Single women have a bit more flexibility at this stage, but they too have developed ties and relationships they cherish. Those clergy couples who settled for team ministry when they wanted churches of their own (or the other way around) may become impatient.

At the very practical level, ecclesiastical systems of all types do not have structures that are supportive of the career/life cycle of women ministers. Consequently the burn-out and drop-out rate for women clergy runs high.

Those who do survive often have trouble getting another job, and they struggle with the issue of calling in its deeper meaning. Some women ministers learn to adapt to current definitions of "success" in ministry. They are usually strong personalities with a willingness to sacrifice aspects of their personal life to God's service. Others, however, keep reaching for a new balance between their identity as women and as ministers. It is a difficult life, because there are few models.

These women raise basic questions about Christian vocation and professional ministry. They want to succeed by past expectations, but they believe that the calling to ministry is itself changing. When they reflect upon their situation, it is not easy to interpret. As one woman put it, "I keep wondering if I am successful because I am a woman, or because I am competent?" Or if something goes wrong, "Is it sexism or me?" With increasing numbers of ordained women these concerns are common. What is normal? How do we measure "success"? What structures and leadership resoures are best for the church of tomorrow?

Without necessarily seeking to do so, women clergy are presenting some serious questions about the nature of Christian vocation. In their efforts to gain credibility, to deal with rivalry, and to claim their calling, women ministers raise issues which ought to concern all Christians.

Chapter 9

Mary O'Connell

Why Don't Catholics Have Women Priests?

GOSPEL TRUTH?

What are some of the theological issues surrounding the question of whether women can be priests?

The first one is suggested by the . . . example of Jesus.

Opponents of women's ordination find the practice of Jesus consistent and compelling. Jesus did not call any women to be among the twelve Apostles. Jesus did not share the Eucharist, or the admonition to "do this in my memory," with any women on the night before he died. "Even his Mother," notes the Vatican Declaration, "who was so closely associated with the mystery of her Son, . . . was not invested with the apostolic ministry."

To those who respond that Jesus was merely following the conventions of his times, the Vatican "Declaration on the Question of the Admission of Women to the Ministerial Priesthood" (1976) insists that, in other ways, "his attitude towards women was quite different from that of his milieu, and he deliberately and courageously broke with it." He spoke publicly with the Samaritan women; he had women disciples and friends; he went against Mosaic traditions by affirming the equality of women before the law. But conservatives maintain that he did not ordain women. Theologian Father Louis Bouyer insists that the church is bound by his example:

> To introduce a Christian priesthood of women accepts, at least by implication, the idea that the founder of Christianity, Christ himself, could be wrong on a central point of his teaching practice.

Those on the other side warn against taking the details of Jesus' practice too literally, lest we end up limiting the priesthood to bearded married Jewish males, preferably fishermen. It's the symbolic meanings that are important, suggests Bible scholar Father Carroll Stuhlmueller, C.P., of the Catholic Theological Union. Of the twelve Apostles, for example:

Slightly shortened version of an article first published in *U.S. Catholic*, 49 (January 1984), pp. 8–12. Reprinted with permission from *U.S. Catholic*, published by Claretian Publications, 221 W. Madison St., Chicago, Ill. 60606.

The Church was to be the New Israel, and the twelve tribes of Israel were designated by twelve men, the children and grandchildren of Jacob. The twelve apostles of the New Testament represent a continuation of that tradition.

But they never continued as a distinct order in the Catholic Church—there are no twelve men, consisting of the pope and his immediate associates, leading the church today. If we have to abide by the twelve apostles, then I think the number twelve would be just as important as the male sex. On the other hand, John's gospel doesn't stress twelve apostles, it talks of three beloved disciples; and in Luke's gospel Jesus sends forth the 70 (or 72), and there's no proof that they were all male.

Proponents of women's ordination contend that while the example of Jesus in his earthly life must be judged against Jewish history, the Resurrection transcends history. The risen Jesus, Paul writes, overcomes the specifics of "Jew and Greek, slave and free, male and female." "He rises as the universal human being who is not affected by these particularities anymore," says scripture scholar Father Eugene La Verdiere, S.S.S., "and so everybody is able to relate to him." Others add that the first people to relate to him after his Resurrection—the first to be witnesses of that transcendent event—were women.

WOMEN MINISTERS IN THE EARLY CHURCH

What did the followers of Jesus do after the Resurrection? Asking this brings [up] the question . . . of the theological meaning of tradition.

The reformers of the 16th century broke with the church over this very issue. They aimed to smash what they saw as superstitious accretions of many centuries and to return faithfully to the teaching and example of Jesus as revealed in the New Testament. The official church stoutly insisted that its teachings and traditions through the ages were guided by the Holy Spirit, and thus represented an authentic part of Christian truth.

The commentary that accompanied the 1976 Declaration reiterates the latter position when it says that the question of women's ordination cannot be settled by "keeping to the sacred text alone. We cannot omit the study of tradition: it is the Church that scrutinizes the Lord's thought by reading Scripture, and it is the Church that gives witness to the correctness of its interpretation."

Not all traditions have equal status, of course; those that come and go in different times and places have to be defended by their appropriateness in a given context. But those that go back unchanged to the beginnings of Christianity have a stronger claim to universal acceptance.

That's why the example of the early church is so important. And, unfortunately, in this regard, the evidence is scanty and unclear.

Some observers see no evidence at all of women priests. Father Louis Bouyer, for example, writes:

From the very beginning of the Christian Church, women were admitted to take part . . . in the prayers of the faithful, in the offering of the gifts for the Eucharist, in the communion [and in] diaconal ministry . . . but they were never called, nor supposed to be able to be called, to the apostolic functions of exercising pastoral responsibility, together with publicly announcing the Word, and presiding at the eucharistic consecration.

But it is difficult to prove a negative. Christians of the first century had other things on their minds besides keeping records for posterity on the fine points of church organization. Indeed, Christians of later centuries are wrong when they read back into the early church a formal structure—priests, bishops, and the rest—that just wasn't put together yet, suggests Father Carroll Stuhlmueller:

> It was a visibly different church in the first century. People met in homes, the Eucharist was part of a normal meal, the agape. I suspect that for a woman in this setting to be main celebrant—especially a prophetess or an outstanding woman— would be nothing unusual. But this practice could have been lost as the church solidified its structure.

There is evidence that some slightly later Christian groups did have women priests— groups that were eventually condemned as heretical. But the significance of this is disputed. Was the ordination of women considered part of the heresy, so that the condemnation illustrates continuous church opposition to the practice? Or did the women priests suffer guilt by association—just as the Catholic Church for centuries rejected liturgy in the vernacular because Protestants had come up with the idea?

ADAM'S RIB

No discussion of the early church can avoid coming face to face with the apostle Paul. Passages from his letters have been cited for centuries to define women's place in the church, just as his admonition "wives be subject to your husbands" has been used to define their place in marriage.

There is the passage in 1 Corinthians where Paul instructs women to cover their heads: "A man should certainly not cover his head, since he is the image of God and reflects God's glory; but woman is the reflection of man's glory. For man did not come from woman, but woman was created for the sake of man" (11:7-9). A later passage in the same letter directs that "women are to remain quiet at meetings since they have no permission to speak; they must keep in the background"; other translations say "be subordinate" (14:34). Finally, there is the passage from 1 Timothy:

> I am not giving permission for a woman to teach or to tell a man what to do. A woman ought not to speak, because Adam was formed first and Eve afterward; and it was not Adam who was led astray but the woman who was led astray and fell into sin" [2:12-14].

These are strong statements. The Anglican scholar Roger Beckwith concludes from them (and from the Genesis passages referred to) that "the exclusion of the subordinate partner in the human race from the principal offices in the Christian ministry . . . is as inevitable today as it was in the first century."

Perhaps the strongest of the three statements, the one from Timothy, is today thought to have come not from Paul himself but from a later writer, according to scripture scholar Father John L. McKenzie. All the statements give strong evidence of Christianity's roots in Judaism and the rabbinical tradition. But, notes McKenzie, "Paul was not entirely consistent in his dealings with women. Few men are." Elsewhere Paul lists women among his disciples and thanks "fellow workers" who include at least one woman. And he is also the source of the statement that Christ overcomes human divisions, including male and female.

Paul's statements about the subordination of women, interestingly, do not refer back to the teachings of Christ but rather to the Genesis accounts of Creation. The idea that woman was created second and sinned first is the reason given for her subordinate status. As both Rosemary Ruether and Roger Beckwith point out, that idea of subordination has for centuries been the basis for excluding women from the ministry and confining them to secondary status in Christian society.

Ruether explains:

> The tradition from Genesis and the post-Pauline writings in Timothy was elaborated by Aquinas. He added to it, from Aristotelian biology, the idea that woman was a defective or imperfect representative of the human species. The idea was that the male is the embryo, and the female is a kind of incubator, providing it with the matter to grow. When the male principle partially fails, it produces a female, who is defective morally, mentally, and physically, and therefore necessarily under subjugation because she doesn't represent the fullness of human capacity.
>
> Aquinas added to this the christological assumption that Christ represented humanity in its fullness. The priest, as the representative of Christ, must be male because only a male could represent humanity in its fullness. In other words, in this tradition, it's not a historical accident that God came to earth as a male.

The 1976 Vatican Declaration doesn't use this line of argument; it would not go far with a contemporary audience. Besides, such thinking clashes with other Vatican documents affirming the dignity of women as human persons (although, as Sister M. Nadine Foley, O.P., points out, the documents tend to view women only in relation to men—as wives and mothers—or to the male-dominated church—as nuns; the idea that women might have dignity in themselves is conspicuously lacking). In any case, the omission of the "women are inferior and subordinate" line, understandable though it is, leaves a large hole in the document on ordination. As Rosemary Ruether notes, "A declaration that declares its hands tied, unable to change any tradition so long established, actually goes about its business by sweeping away a 2000-year-old tradition and pretending that it never existed!"

JESUS LOOK-ALIKES

In place of theories about the nature of women, the Declaration substitutes theories about the nature of priesthood. For those who oppose women's ordination, this is the key theological argument: that the nature of priesthood is such that women—even if they are equal—could not validly assume that role.

Central to the arguments is the fact that "the priest represents Christ," explains James Hitchcock of St. Louis University. "Christ stands in relation to the church, as it says in Scripture, in the marital relationship of a man to a woman. The priest is the other Christ in that sense. To permit a female priest would destroy that symbolism."

To those skeptical that a piece of biblical symbolism should carry so much weight, the defenders insist that the symbolism is crucial because a sacrament is involved. The signs of the sacraments cannot be changed at will; they depend for their power on faithful adherence to the actions and intentions of Christ.

Father John Sheets elaborates this idea by drawing on the philosophical concept of "intentionality." The word expresses the idea that people exist, not as isolated units, but in relation to people and objects outside themselves. Our eyes and ears, for example, lead us to perceive outside objects; our emotions require outside people for fulfillment. Sexuality is part of intentionality; that is, it is part of the way a person relates to the outside world. Since Christ was a man, maleness is part of his intentionality—not just an incidental feature, but a crucial element of his "body-person."

Sheets goes on to argue that the transmission of the sacraments "demands a congruence of symbolism, that is, the same mode of intentionality, in both the primary symbol, Christ, and the secondary symbol, the minister." Only a male priest could have the same "mode of intentionality" as the male Christ.

Thomas Aquinas made a similar point by declaring that "Sacramental signs represent what they signify by natural resemblance." His reasoning lies behind the Declaration's famous statement that women cannot be priests because they lack "natural resemblance" to Jesus. If the priest were a woman, says the Declaration, "it would be difficult to see in (her) the image of Christ. For Christ himself was and remains a man."

Feminists, of course, are furious at the statements that women cannot bear the image of Christ. They see it as denying what it means to be a Christian. "People see a natural resemblance to Jesus in the love conveyed, the service rendered, the self shared, much more than they look to a physical characteristic like sex," writes Sister Elizabeth Carroll, R.S.M. "Women as well as men will be accepted as bearing a natural resemblance to Christ as they grow like (him), as they 'put on the Lord Jesus Christ.' "

REVOLUTIONARY ROLE

Other theologians go further and challenge the idea that the priest directly represents Christ. The Catholic Theological Society of America argues that the priest represents both Christ *and* the church. According to Sister Sara Butler, M.S.B.T., of the CTSA research team, "the church is the sacrament and locus of Christ's presence, because of its faith. . . . The priest represents the faith of the church and thereby represents Christ." The Eucharist isn't a sacred drama where the priest portrays Christ; Christ is present, as he promised, in his church, and the priest represents Christ by representing the church. Women share in the faith of the church and can rightfully stand to represent it—and thereby represent Christ.

Opponents charge that such thinking is not, as James Hitchcock puts it, "the classical Catholic doctrine of priesthood," which stresses the priest's sacramental powers over his communal ministry:

Catholics believe that through ordination a sacramental power is imparted, and that it's permanent—that even an ex-priest still has that power. The priest doesn't depend on being "called" or supported by the community; that's a Protestant view.

I see the popularity of this term "ministry" as being part of the downgrading of the priesthood. The notion of ministry implies something that a person is called to by the community, that is held as long as it is exercised, that can be given up. It isn't permanent. And it doesn't depend on ordination. I would say that the ordination of women is not independent of a radical revolution in the notion of priesthood.

Many advocates of women's ordination do talk about changes in the priesthood. Some of these changes are happening already, in response to the shortage of priests and the independence of laypeople. Others will certainly occur if women are integrated into a role whose symbols are entirely male (what do you call a priest when you can't call her "Father"?). But Father Carroll Stuhlmueller, for one, argues that ordaining women will help *preserve* the sacramental priesthood, not destroy it:

> If we keep on as we are now, increasing the number of lay ministers, but do not ordain them, we will become increasingly nonsacramental and, to that extent, Protestant. Or, we could follow the route of the church in France, and simply dwindle and die. Or, finally, we can consider new styles of ordination and priestly ministry. I'm not talking about ordaining women and forcing them on a congregation. It's more a matter of acknowledging people's ministries and linking them with the sacramental ministry of the church.

The belief that women priests would have to be "forced" on Catholic congregations is debatable. A 1982 Gallup Poll revealed that 44 percent of American Catholics agree that "it would be a good thing if the Church decided to ordain women." That figure is up from 29 percent in 1974, while the number strongly opposed has fallen from 47 percent to 34 percent. Interestingly, women are more opposed than men; and Southern and rural Catholics are more likely to favor the idea, perhaps because they suffer most from priest shortages and have encountered more women in pastoral roles.

To William McCready of the National Opinion Research Center, the Gallup figures suggest growing popular perception that church refusal to ordain women is "not a creditable position. People can't figure out exactly why it is that women can't be ordained. Is it an organ that they lack, or what?" Asked if it's seen as a theological issue, McCready scoffs: "Most people in the parish wouldn't know a theological issue if it came up and hit 'em in the head. It's whatever the church says it is."

Right now what "the church" says is no. Theologians on both sides are quick to point out that, because the question is theological, that answer can't be changed by majority vote. Father John Sheets writes that popular pressure "might improve social conditions, and rectify what is within human power, (but) not all of the agitation in the world can create or destroy or change a sacramental sign."

But it is clear that a substantial body of theological opinion disputes the official church position on the nature of that sacramental sign. The Pontifical Biblical Commission in Rome (a different body from the one that issued the Declaration) undermined one of the Declaration's main arguments by concluding that the question could not be settled one way or the other on the basis of New Testament evidence. Theologian Father Hans Küng has stated that "there are no dogmatic or biblical reasons against it." The research team of the Catholic Theological Society of America does not find "any serious grounds to justify the exclusion of women." Other theologians go further and argue that a fully Christian theology would support the ordination of women as a sign of their equal participation in creation and redemption.

Rosemary Ruether insists:

> Scripture teaches, and the Christian Church should teach, that women are whole persons. They have equivalent humanity with men, and they possess equally with men the image of God. Further, redemption in Christ overcomes as sinful those structures in the world that would subordinate women. Galatians 3:28 is a baptismal text: It is a conscious repudiation of the formulae in Jewish and Greek thought that it is better to be Jew than Gentile, to be free than slave, to be male than female. Christ opposed those distinctions. To exclude women from the

priesthood is to reject their equivalent humanity and their equivalent status in redemption.

The official Declaration denies that ordination can be seen in this way, as a matter of the rights of women as redeemed human persons. "Ordination," it says, "is of another order"; it is part of "the mystery of Christ and the Church." It concludes that "the Church, in fidelity to the example of the Lord, does not consider herself authorized to admit women to priestly ordination."

Many in the broader church, however, are working on a different idea of what "the example of the Lord" was all about. And they think they've got the Spirit with them.

PART TWO

RELIGION, PEACE, AND WAR

The response of religious belief to social change is always complex. This is particularly true of Christian (and other) reflections today on war and peace. Why? Is it because of the depth of feeling generated by the nuclear cloud hovering over us all? That these feelings are *more* passionate than those of women on sexism, or those of Third World peoples opposed to First World interventions, is not immediately evident. The breadth of the demonstrations for peace and against the use and deployment of nuclear weapons is indeed impressive. As Walter Wink points out below, the international character and size of these demonstrations are almost unprecedented. But there is nothing in the demonstrations themselves that suggests theological depth or profound reflection. Nevertheless, there is today a tide of religious books, articles, formal statements, even films on war and nuclear armaments. What this suggests is that Christians and the Christian churches find peace or at least the avoidance of war not only an unusual opportunity, but also a formidable task, one that involves an internal taking of stock as well as a detailed examination of weaponry.

The complexity of modern warfare and of modern armaments certainly contributes to the difficulty of achieving both these goals. Theologically, though, the effort takes place in a rich context of Christian reflection on the legitimacy and illegitimacy of war, and on the nature of peace. Questions of war and peace, unlike many other issues that appear in this book, are hardly new to Christian communities. Just because of this tradition, or more properly these traditions, of religious reflection, they cannot be so easily resolved today. The traditions themselves have become an element to be factored into the ultimate resolution. Then there is the impact of that tradition on history. If Christians have honed carefully crafted positions (such as the just war position) on war and peace, it is not clear that these positions have had a beneficial influence or any influence at all on the history of the West.

Most of us would admit that our history has been marked by a shocking tendency to use military means to secure political and economic ends. Even more disturbing: this tendency appears to have increased during the twentieth century. Further, Western nations have developed on an enormous scale the manufacture and sale of armaments to other parts of the earth. This traffic in arms has reached such proportions that one might well argue that it is now essential to the economic well-being of the more developed nations. In sum, military and economic realities all appear to testify that ethical and theological reflection has not yet made a practical difference.

And this might be said even if we confine the discussion to conventional war! When we turn to nuclear war, our reflections become at once more complex and more urgent. There seems to be not merely a quantitative but a qualitative difference between conventional and nuclear warfare. As one philosopher recently noted, the criteria of traditional ethical theories appear not just outmoded but literally monstrous when applied to nuclear warfare. For example, utilitarianism might justify a given policy on the grounds that it would produce the greatest benefit to the greatest number of persons.

But what benefit could possibly justify an exchange of nuclear explosives, with the projected loss of human life? The very question borders on the ludicrous.

It is impressive how many moral and theological dimensions the authors of the following chapters have found in the basic topic of war and peace. And it is equally impressive how courageously they have faced each of these dimensions. They have refused to yield to despair. They have consistently found the seeds of hope and life in the midst of darkness and death.

Wink's article makes precisely this point. Paralysis is an understandable reaction in a culture facing the horrendous possible effects of nuclear war. This glimpse of our own mortality can, however, be an occasion for faith. In this view, the awareness of our own destructive potential is also an opportunity, a grace. Wink is simply extending the resurrection motif to its ultimate conclusion. Out of death *can* emerge life. Nothing certain, nothing guaranteed: just a hope. But for this to happen, we must together create a vision of what that life can be.

The United States Catholic Bishops' pastoral letter cannot be omitted from this collection, but neither can more than a fraction of it be included. Even before it was completed, the bishops' letter had enormous political and theological significance. As George Kennan makes clear, the *process* by which it came about was as important as its conclusions. Whether we agree or disagree with those conclusions, we ought to admire the valor of church leaders determined to communicate with the entire spectrum of moral opinion in the United States, including purely secular opinion. Nor have they avoided the tougher ethical issues, such as questions revolving around deterrence. They recognized that threatening someone who is a danger to oneself is quite different from preemptively injuring that same person. But when we are speaking of nuclear retaliations as the principal threat, it is imperative to understand more clearly the nature of deterrence.

One articulate opponent of the bishops' stance has been Michael Novak. In the piece included here, he presents a very stark picture indeed of possible Soviet actions, military and political, if the United States does not adopt a posture of overwhelming strength. Inasmuch as he himself is careful to point out that the 1980s offer the Soviets a unique mismatch vis-à-vis military capabilities, we might wonder about his fundamental warning to the bishops and all Americans, not to give up on deterrence. For if strength is the only basis for both deterrence and fruitful negotiations, why argue so strenuously for deterrence with the present unprecedented weakness of the United States?

What really guides Novak's thinking, though, is the certainty that the Soviets are profoundly dangerous and will stop short of worldwide domination only if deterred through fear. The moral weakness of the bishop's statement, then, is that it would lead to the incalculable evil of a "socialist world." Novak believes that we must be exceedingly careful in measuring the evil of nuclear annihilation against the evil of worldwide Soviet domination. We must keep in mind that the *threat* of the first is less evil than the likelihood of the second. Although Novak does not say this in so many words, he implies that our very willingness to destroy the enemy (and perhaps ourselves in the process) is what prevents the other very real amd imminent evil.

The problem as Novak well knows is: How can we deter without intending to *use* these weapons? And how can we so intend if their actual use is immoral? In his most elaborate reflection on the problem, "Moral Clarity in the Nuclear Age," Novak finally says:

> The fundamental moral intention in nuclear deterrence is never to have to use the
> deterrent force. That this is so is shown by the honorable discharge of military

officers, after their term of duty expires, who have succeeded in their fundamental intention. Besides this fundamental intention, however, deterrence requires a secondary intention. For the physical, material weapon is by itself no deterrent without the engagement of intellect and will on the part of the entire public which called it into being. . . . Thus a secondary intention cannot be separated from deterrence.[1]

But making the intention secondary hardly solves the problem. All one need do to see this is to substitute "engage in systematic torture of as many of the enemy as can be seized" for "use nuclear weapons." We might manufacture such a horrifying threat in order to ward off a particular evil, but if we in addition intend what we threaten, we are clearly already implicated in what is evil. In other words, the moral person needs to examine carefully the content of any threat and certainly of any intention. That we hope never to implement our threat will not change this moral requirement.

The practical equivalent to the bishop's formal statement has been a whole series of incidents in which rank-and-file Christians have directly attacked armaments, invaded military installations, and in general made concrete the opposition between faith and United States military policy. Here is a theology of deed that both parallels and challenges the more traditional theology of meditation and word. Ched Myers in "Storming the Gates of Hell" offers us some much needed reflections on these actions. These activists, says Myers (popular notions to the contrary notwithstanding), are sober and prayerful, clear-eyed and clear-minded. Many of them are middle-aged. From their collective actions is emerging a new concept of the Spirit, which they repeatedly appeal to. On the other hand, they are becoming more aware of the reality of evil, indeed of the diabolical.

Contemporary Christians struggling with this issue may well desire a clearer vision of scriptural teaching on war and peace, as well as of early Christian practice. Only Alan Kreider's brief summary can be offered here, but it is remarkably successful in conveying how pacifist the early Christians were. At the same time, he is careful to measure his conclusions and avoid absolutes where they should be avoided.

William Mahedy's meditation provides a very different service. He peers into the moral and theological vacuum that is the aftermath of Vietnam. The landmark work (fiction or nonfiction) on Vietnam has yet to be written. Mahedy, though, begins where perhaps we too should begin: with the personal experiences of Vietnam veterans. He compassionately probes their sense of defilement and their shattered faith. His insight: that this "faith" was really a pseudo-faith, based on the assumption of American omnipotence and innocence. Its collapse has been painful, but precisely this collapse can make possible a genuine faith based on the cross.

Finally, a few words from Thomas Merton, whose life was so engaged with the cause of peace. Many have noted the Alice-in-Wonderland character of the discussion of nuclear war. For example, there is something bizarre, almost lunatic, in debating whether to build more weapons when there are already enough to destroy the world three times over. Or is it five times? And we can debate that too! The ultimate problem for Merton is our difficulty with truth. We confuse our need to be right with finding the truth. We then convert untruth to "truth." What we need is to rediscover the gift-like nature of truth.

There are at least a few relatively new theological themes that are emerging from these discussions taken as a whole. Thus, even though one of the preoccupations on this issue has been to retain continuity with the past, it is apparent that a new religious consciousness *is* being formed. For example, the very nature of nuclear armaments has given ethical reflections on war a new urgency. This new urgency in turn often produces a striking blend of boldness and calm in those taking an antiwar stance. The issues are too serious for the usual polemics or for any posturing. At the same time, the continuity between faith and action is more apparent for these activists. Reflection alone is downright perverse, in the light of what is at stake.

The danger of nuclear holocaust has also changed in important ways the answers to the age-old question: When, if ever, is war justified? Christian pacifism is now seen as an attractive and defensible position even within churches not usually known as "peace churches." And the traditional peace churches have for their part recovered and intensified the strong emphasis on peace that gave them the name in the first place. Because of both these tendencies, theologians and other scholars have continued to explore the pacifist nature of early Christian belief and practice.

Specific beliefs, too, are being developed and deepened in the light of the increasing menace of war. An example is faith. Faith is seen now as both more difficult and more crucial than ever before. Because the individual cannot escape the nuclear shadow, faith has now a distinctly social cast. If it is the individual who clings to faith, his or her faith is nevertheless against a social and political backdrop that cannot be ignored. For the first time in history, the issue of one's own mortality has merged with the possible self-annihilation of the human race. Faith now includes a response to this possibility.

Finally, the very meaning of theology and theological method is changing, partly as a result of the war/peace debate. The method now emerging is one not so much of consensus as of conversation. The conversation can take place across many dividing lines. Bishops confer with lay persons, including nonbelievers, in forums that once were exclusively ecclesiastical and hierarchical. Lay persons listen to pastors with remarkable interest and responsiveness, but not uncritically. Christians of various denominations, and Jews, listen to one another. Politicians and military professionals read what theologians and bishops have to say, and comment in detail. Prominent laypersons respectfully but quite clearly declare their disagreement with religious leaders. Church leaders in turn seem remarkably secure, almost serene, in the face of these differing responses. In short, the church and its self-understanding have begun to change fundamentally. It has entered a new age—the nuclear age.

NOTE

1. Michael Novak, "Moral Clarity in the Nuclear Age," *National Review,* 25 (April 1, 1983) 384–85.

Chapter 10

Walter Wink

Faith and Nuclear Paralysis

Fear of nuclear annihilation stalks the land. Polls tell us that many young people do not expect to survive the decade. Some are no longer planning to marry or have children. Many try to mask the nuclear terror by a kind of psychic numbing. A few have developed insomnia, apparently induced by the dread of atomic incineration.

The reasons are all too clear. Try to escape them as we may, the facts continue to penetrate our defenses: the MX debate, the European protests, the blasphemy of naming one of the most lethal weapons ever developed, a Trident submarine, Corpus Christi—"The Body of Christ."

Even a fraction of the data is the stuff of which nightmares are spun. Every American city of 25,000 or more is targeted. This means that even most rural dwellers would not be spared in the event of an all-out war (and once either side attacks, no other kind is conceivable). The fireball from each bomb would set firestorms raging over millions of acres, consuming most plant and animal life. The flesh and bones of those at ground zero would be vaporized, while people in shelters would be either incinerated, killed by concussion, or suffocated as a result of oxygen depletion during the firestorms. Some experts believe that the heat released might melt the polar ice caps, flooding much of the planet. Destruction of the earth's ozone layer would result in increased exposure to cosmic and ultraviolet radiation, leading to a rise in the incidence of skin cancer.

Exposure to gamma radiation near the epicenter of the blast would kill many more within two weeks. Those who survived in more remote areas would face a world stripped of all life-support systems. Food, air, and water would be poisonously radioactive. Psychological trauma over the loss of loved ones and the total devastation would drive some mad. Survivors would begin developing leukemia within five years, or solid cancers over the next 15 to 50 years—if they lived so long. More likely, bacteria, viruses, and disease-bearing insects would mutate, adapt, and multiply in extremely virulent forms. Human beings, with no immunity to these new forms, and already weakened by exposure to excessive radiation, would be wiped out in large numbers by the resulting plagues.

We have tolerated such risks now for decades, believing that the system of "Mutually Assured Destruction" (MAD) was our best defense. But what if a computer malfunctions—as has already happened at least four times—falsely signaling a Soviet attack? What if, like Dr. Strangelove, someone in power becomes deranged, or decides to launch a "pre-emptive strike"? Several weeks before President Nixon resigned, concerned administration officials reportedly removed the mechanisms by which he could start a nuclear war. Soviet Premier Leonid Brezhnev has been treated with cortisone, a drug that occasionally induces acute psychosis. And at least 30 of the soldiers who sit in the cramped quarters of Titan missile silos, ready to launch these weapons, have suffered serious psychological disturbances, according to Dr. Helen Caldicott (*Nuclear Madness* [Bantam, 1980]).

"NOTHING CAN SAVE US THAT IS POSSIBLE"

I have long opposed nuclear weapons, ever since I observed an atmospheric test in Nevada in 1957. But this past summer I began to notice a subtle change in myself and others. A loud blast would make me jump, wondering, "Oh my God, did they really do it?" And more and more people have shared with me dreams of conflagrations, explosions, firestorms. We are internalizing the genuine threat at last—but not in a way that leads to action.

Instead, people are paralyzed. The issue is too vast, the government too unresponsive and paranoid, the public too powerless. We believe that nothing can save us that is possible. And so we quietly make ready to die together. We are stricken by a state of advanced nuclear paralysis.

The public assessment is correct: "Nothing can save us that is possible." But we need to finish that line from Auden: "We who must die demand a miracle" (*For the Time Being*). Suddenly an entire epoch has been brought face to face with its mortality. We are confronted with our need for a transcendent source of faith and hope that can mobilize us into what may be our last chance to end the nuclear nightmare.

The *Bulletin of Atomic Scientists* has moved the hands of the Doomsday clock closer to midnight than ever before; jingoism and nationalistic mania have reached a new pitch after the embarrassments of Vietnam and Iran. In this situation, what grounds exist for faith in any achievable alternatives?

That question is the one faith *always* faces, in every age and every situation. It is precisely such situations that evoke faith. It thrives on desperation. It is never so exhilarated as when nothing else is possible.

Jesus said, "If you had faith as a grain of mustard seed, you could say to this sycamine tree, 'Be rooted up, and be planted in the sea,' and it would obey you" (Luke 17:6). All you need is this much (picture his fingers forming a tiny hole the size of a small seed). That's enough. You have faith, or you do not. There are no degrees. You already have enough faith if you have any at all.

Faith is the recognition that God really is a living presence with us, powerful to save. It is like sight. It sees God's reality and knows it to be true. Now the focus is entirely off us and on God.

We do not even have to shoulder the burden of trying to have faith. In fact, we might try the reverse: try having no faith in God at all. If you cannot, if there is even the slightest suspicion that God may be real; if you doubt your capacity completely to doubt, then you know that you have at least a tiny seed of faith. And that, according to Jesus, is enough to uproot trees or transplant mountains—or even to disarm a missile on its pad.

This passage about faith is one of the most frequently repeated of all Jesus' sayings in the Gospels. In these sayings, and in those dealing with prayer, Jesus gives us the secret of his own miracle-working power. Mark's version (11:22–24) is instructive:

Have faith in God. Truly, I say to you, whoever says to this mountain, "Be taken up and cast into the sea," and does not doubt in his heart [this phrase may have been added by Mark; it is missing in all the other versions of the saying, and draws attention to ourselves], but believes that what he says will come to pass [literally, "is happening"], it will be done for him. Therefore I tell you, whatever you ask in prayer, believe that you receive it, and you will.

How odd: why are we to pray for something which we know perfectly well we have not received (why else would we be praying for it?) as if we have already obtained it?

"PRACTICE THE FUTURE"

Perhaps the key lies in visualization. We are to see the thing for which we pray as already transformed, made new according to the divine will. We are to believe it into being, begin acting as if it were the new reality, rehearse its advent, see it coming.

We live every minute of every day by pictures that put us into the future. We are constantly visualizing other alternatives. No one is without faith. We must believe in elevators, airplanes, people. Business people understand this better than anyone else. They know that unless they believe they can make a go of it, can visualize very concrete inventory and budgetary objectives for a year, two years, five years, then there is little chance of success.

And now everyone seems to have learned about visualizing, from basketball coaches to holistic healers. You must "see" the ball going into the basket; you must "see" your cancer healed. But faith is a two-edged sword. It can also be invested in images of destruction, failure, despair. We believe in the coming world depression. We believe that we are unworthy of love. We believe in the power of cancer. We believe in a nuclear holocaust. And by our very belief, we help to bring these things to pass.

That is why it is so important to take care as to what we visualize. For we are always already visualizing a future of some sort, and letting our lives be conformed to its pattern. If we believe that nuclear suicide is inevitable, then we will act, consciously or unconsciously, to speed it up.

The moderator of the United Presbyterian Church, Robert Davidson, was speaking about the initiative for a nuclear freeze at a local church. Afterward a retired army colonel spoke up, saying he opposed disarmament, that it was against the will of God, that the Soviets can't be trusted. Davidson responded, "If you hold that view, we're liable to end by blowing each other up." "That's right," the colonel snapped, "and the sooner the better."

Take care what you believe: it may come about.

The importance of visualization in shaping the future is by no means a recent discovery. Cross-cultural studies of faith healers, shamans, witch doctors, and other "unorthodox" healers have shown that, regardless of the means used or the system of belief, all share one factor in common: they seemed to be most successful when they could see the person they were treating as whole.

Faith, then, is not something "supernatural." It is the very cornerstone of life. Jesus significantly speaks of faith simply as a reality, often without any reference to God. Faith just *is*; its object is what is variable. When it is focused on the Kingdom of God, when its object is to make God's will effective in the world, faith becomes the very means of God's operation.

I recently woke from a dream with this sentence echoing in my ears: "Faith is practicing the future." I had been studying Ezekiel's vision of the dry bones (Ezek. 37) with a group, and had been particularly struck by the role of the prophet in the "resurrection" of the people. Israel in captivity, he saw, was like a valley filled with dry bones. When God asks if these bones can live, Ezekiel can scarcely muster an answer. Yet Yahweh orders *him*—this prophet who was just as dry as his people—to prophesy to the bones, and say to them:

> O dry bones, hear the word of the Lord. Thus says the Lord God to these bones: Behold, I will cause breath to enter you, and you shall live. And I will lay sinews upon you, and will cause flesh to come upon you, and cover you with skin, and put breath in you, and you shall live; and you shall know that I am the Lord [Ezek. 37:4-7, RSV].

The prophet spoke as he was commanded, and there was a rattling noise as bone was rejoined to bone, and flesh once again covered them. But there was no breath in them. Once again the prophet was commanded to speak, to call on the four winds, to breathe upon those slain, that they might live. And they revived, and stood on their feet, "an exceedingly great host."

How similar to us. For our people also cry out, "Our bones are dried up, and our hope is lost." How can the prophet's mere vision change all that? First, he forces them to face the depth of their despair. Some may have adjusted tolerably well in Babylon (since so many chose to remain there after liberation). Others perhaps were anguished. But had any of them seen themselves as *slain?* The prophet first declares them dead, and only then offers hope.

But he does not stop with the vision of resurrection and return to the land. He goes on, in chapters 40-48, to describe, in meticulous detail, the actual layout of the restored temple. To these captives, only 25 years into captivity and still a full generation from release, the prophet reveals the measurements of the outer and inner walls and courts of the temple, the location of side rooms and vestibules, the thickness of walls, and the height and breadth of doorjambs. The steps of every stairway are numbered, as are all the tables for sacrifice and incense. We are given even the measurement of the metal hooks to hold the sacrifices and the placement of ornamental palms and cherubim. This is more than a sketch; these are architect's specifications. They are matched by a vision of the restored city, Jerusalem, and the boundaries of the resettled tribes, plus rules governing priests, weights, and balances, and the proper offerings.

Why all this incredibly minute detail? Because God is trying to get the people to begin visualizing the temple rebuilt. Nothing less could heal their hopelessness and fire them with a vision of the liberation to come. No doubt Ezekiel's city planning schemes and temple specifications inspired sharp disagreement and debate (compare Ezekiel 44:6-8 with Isaiah 56:6-8); no matter, for even in disagreeing, people were forced to visualize a preferred alternative.

If we were to follow Ezekiel's pattern today, it would mean facing the public with our real status: we are as good as dead. Israel was only "dry bones"; we are as though vaporized. Until we face the enormity of this horror, we will continue blindly to trust to the vision of our blind leaders.

But that grim prospect must be matched with an alternative vision as well. It must not be utopian, romantic, mere wishful thinking. It does no good to talk of a world without violence, of absolute peace, of political perfection. Short of the Kingdom itself, that will not happen, and such fantasies only serve to crush hope further by their impracticality. Ezekiel's vision is short-term, practical, and achievable. It is something that God can do, working with the agents of history.

Our own prophets have already articulated key elements of such a vision. For starters, there is Senator Mark Hatfield's campaign simply to freeze all further testing, production, and deployment of nuclear weapons by mutual treaty with the Soviet Union. Beyond that, we can begin visualizing agreements that will lead to the genuine reduction and decommissioning of in-place nuclear weapons as a step toward total nuclear disarmament. But even a fraction of the existing weapons could be fatal to the future of humanity. We must let ourselves be possessed by a vision of a world in which all nuclear arsenals have been effectively outlawed, just as slavery was successfully outlawed over 100 years ago.

It is already too late to rid ourselves of the nuclear menace entirely. We will be living with the wastes of nuclear production and utilities for hundreds of thousands of years to come. Nor can we prevent isolated cases of nuclear blackmail of cities by mobsters, maniacs, or militants. There was a time when that could perhaps have been prevented, and we squandered it. We must not fail this time.

To begin with, we can visualize the churches of North America organizing the mightiest grass-roots campaign in our hemisphere's history. Imagine an effective peace group or coalition in half the congregations in America. (It has already been achieved in half the churches of the New York City Presbytery!) We can see them praying, studying Scripture, educating themselves on the realities of nuclear war and pollution, organizing, demonstrating, refusing to pay war taxes, engaging in nonviolent civil disobedience, supporting each other in the long-term struggle and linking the nuclear issue to other concerns for justice.

This miracle of the churches organized and acting is the easiest of all these miracles to believe, for the European churches have already done it. It was only in November 1980 that the General Synod of the Netherlands Reformed Church voted for the removal of all nuclear weapons from Holland. Now, a year later, largely through the work of the Interchurch Peace Council over a decade, 400,000 people marched against the missiles in Amsterdam. In Bonn, another 200,000 demonstrated, also largely through organization by the churches. The numbers heap up: 200,000 in Rome, 150,000 in London, 200,000 in Brussels, 200,000 in Paris, more than 200,000 in Athens; and in the Eastern bloc, 300,000 in Bucharest. A year ago, who would not have called this impossible?

"Nothing can save us that is possible. We who must die demand a miracle." This is a struggle that we simply must win. We alone can make the difference. The whole world is looking to the churches of the U.S. and Canada to stop the madness, because no one else is able to believe in the "impossible."

We are freed from our paralysis by practicing the future. The prophets' visions established us in the space where faith is possible. And we do not need more faith than we already have. We only need to exercise the bit we do have. Just the urge to do something is enough.

We can even see our paralysis for what it has become: a kind of self-indulgence. There is something soothing and consoling about it, after all, like shock after massive injury. It excuses us from having to act, and numbs the pain of the impending horror. But it is also a great deception. For powerlessness is always the sign of being duped by the principalities and powers. They want us to feel helpless; that is their best means of constraining us.

But we are not helpless. None of us, no matter how desperate the situation, is ever completely helpless, even if we are free only to choose the attitude with which we shall die. We can today choose faith or paralysis. Which we choose may well determine the future of the earth.

Chapter 11

American Catholic Bishops

The Challenge of Peace: God's Promise and Our Response

Pastoral Letter on War and Peace

INTRODUCTION

"The whole human race faces a moment of supreme crisis in its advance toward maturity." Thus the Second Vatican Council opened its treatment of modern warfare.[1] Since the council, the dynamic of the nuclear arms race has intensified. Apprehension about nuclear war is almost tangible and visible today. As Pope John Paul II said in his message to the United Nations concerning disarmament: "Currently the fear and preoccupation of so many groups in various parts of the world reveal that people are more frightened about what would happen if irresponsible parties unleash some nuclear war."[2]

As bishops and pastors ministering in one of the major nuclear nations, we have encountered this terror in the minds and hearts of our people—indeed, we share it. We write this letter because we agree that the world is at a moment of crisis, the effects of which are evident in people's lives. It is not our intent to play on fears, however, but to speak words of hope and encouragement in time of fear. Faith does not insulate us from the challenges of life; rather, it intensifies our desire to help solve them precisely in light of the good news which has come to us in the person of Jesus, the Lord of history. From the resources of our faith we wish to provide hope and strength to all who seek a world free of the nuclear threat. Hope sustains one's capacity to live with danger without being overwhelmed by it; hope is the will to struggle against obstacles even when they appear insuperable. Ultimately our hope rests in the God who gave us life, sustains the world by his power, and has called us to revere the lives of every person and all peoples.

The crisis of which we speak arises from this fact: Nuclear war threatens the existence of our planet; this is a more menacing threat than any the world has known. It is neither tolerable nor necessary that human beings live under this threat. But removing it will require a major effort of intelligence, courage, and faith. As Pope John Paul II said at

Pages 1-4 of *Origins, NC Documentary Service,* 13/1 (May 19, 1983), published by the National Catholic News Service, Washington, D.C. Excerpts from *The Challenge of Peace: God's Promise and Our Response*, copyright © 1983 by the United States Catholic Conference, Washington, D.C., are used with permission.

Hiroshima: "From now on it is only through a conscious choice and through a deliberate policy that humanity can survive."[3]

As Americans, cititzens of the nation which was first to produce atomic weapons, which has been the only one to use them and which today is one of the handful of nations capable of decisively influencing the course of the nuclear age, we have grave human, moral, and political responsibilities to see that a "conscious choice" is made to save humanity. This letter is therefore both an invitation and a challenge to Catholics in the United States to join with others in shaping the conscious choices and deliberate policies required in this "moment of supreme crisis."

PEACE IN THE MODERN WORLD: RELIGIOUS PERSPECTIVES AND PRINCIPLES

The global threat of nuclear war is a central concern of the universal church, as the words and deeds of recent popes and the Second Vatican Council vividly demonstrate. In this pastoral letter we speak as bishops of the universal church, heirs of the religious and moral teaching on modern warfare of the last four decades. We also speak as bishops of the church in the United States, who have both the obligation and the opportunity to share and interpret the moral and religious wisdom of the Catholic tradition by applying it to the problems of war and peace today.

The nuclear threat transcends religious, cultural, and national boundaries. To confront its danger requires all the resources reason and faith can muster. This letter is a contribution to a wider common effort meant to call Catholics and all members of our political community to dialogue and specific decisions about this awesome question.

The Catholic tradition on war and peace is a long and complex one, reaching from the Sermon on the Mount to the statements of Pope John Paul II. Its development cannot be sketched in a straight line, and it seldom gives a simple answer to complex questions. It speaks through many voices and has produced multiple forms of religious witness. As we locate ourselves in this tradition, seeking to draw from it and to develop it, the document which provides profound inspiration and guidance for us is the Pastoral Constitution on the Church in the Modern World of Vatican II, for it is based on doctrinal principles and addresses the relationship of the church to the world with respect to the most urgent issues of our day.[4]

A rule of interpretation crucial for the pastoral constitution is equally important for this pastoral letter, although the authority inherent in these two documents is quite distinct. Both documents use principles of Catholic moral teaching and apply them to specific contemporary issues. The bishops at Vatican II opened the pastoral constitution with the following guideline on how to relate principles to concrete issues:

> In the first part, the church develops her teaching on man, on the world which is the enveloping context of man's existence, and on man's relations to his fellow men. In Part II, the church gives closer consideration to various aspects of modern life and human society; special consideration is given to those questions and problems which, in this general area, seem to have a greater urgency in our day. As a result, in Part II the subject matter which is viewed in the light of doctrinal principles is made up of diverse elements. Some elements have a permanent value; others, only a transitory one. Consequently, the constitution must be interpreted according to the general norms of theological interpretation. Interpreters must bear in mind—especially in Part II—the changeable circumtances which the subject matter, by its very nature, involves.[5]

In this pastoral letter too we address many concrete questions concerning the arms race, contemporary warfare, weapons systems, and negotiating strategies. We do not intend that our treatment of each of these issues carry the same moral authority as our statement of universal moral principles and formal church teaching. Indeed, we stress here at the beginning that not every statement in this letter has the same moral authority. At times we reassert universally binding principles (e.g., non-combatant immunity and proportionality). At still other times we reaffirm statements of recent popes and the teaching of Vatican II. Again, at other times we apply moral principles to specific cases.

When making application of these principles we realize—and we wish readers to realize—that prudential judgments are involved based on specific circumstances which can change or which can be interpreted differently by people of good will (e.g., the treatment of "no first use"). However, the moral judgments that we make in specific cases, while not binding in conscience, are to be given serious attention and consideration by Catholics as they determine whether their moral judgments are consistent with the Gospel.

We shall do our best to indicate, stylistically and substantively, whenever we make such applications. We believe such specific judgments are an important part of this letter, but they should be interpreted in light of another passage from the pastoral constitution:

> Often enough the Christian view of things will itself suggest some specific solution in certain circumstances. Yet it happens rather frequently, and legitimately so, that with equal sincerity some of the faithful will disagree with others on a given matter. Even against the intention of their proponents, however, solutions proposed on one side or another may be easily confused by many people with the gospel message. Hence it is necessary for people to remember that no one is allowed in the aforementioned situations to appropriate the church's authority for his opinion. They should always try to enlighten one another through honest discussion, preserving mutual charity and caring above all for the common good.[6]

This passage acknowledges that on some complex social questions the church expects a certain diversity of views even though all hold the same universal moral principles. The experience of preparing this pastoral letter has shown us the range of strongly held opinion in the Catholic community on questions of war and peace. Obviously, as bishops we believe that such differences should be expressed within the framework of Catholic moral teaching. We urge mutual respect among different groups in the church as they analyze this letter and the issues it addresses. Not only conviction and commitment are needed in the church, but also civility and charity.

The pastoral constitution calls us to bring the light of the Gospel to bear upon "the signs of the times." Three signs of the times have particularly influenced the writing of this letter. The first, to quote Pope John Paul II at the United Nations, is that "the world wants peace, the world needs peace."[7] The second is the judgment of Vatican II about the arms race: "The arms race is one of the greatest curses on the human race and the harm it inflicts upon the poor is more than can be endured."[8] The third is the way in which the unique dangers and dynamics of the nuclear arms race present qualitatively new problems which must be addressed by fresh applications of traditional moral principles. In light of these three characteristics, we wish to examine Catholic teaching on peace and war.

The Catholic social tradition as exemplified in the pastoral constitution and recent papal teachings is a mix of biblical, theological, and philosophical elements which are brought to bear upon the concrete problems of the day. The biblical vision of the world, created and sustained by God, scarred by sin, redeemed by Christ, and destined for the kingdom, is at the heart of our religious heritage. This vision requires elaboration, explanation, and application in each age; the important task of theology is to penetrate ever more adequately the nature of the biblical vision of peace and relate it to a world not yet at peace. Consequently, the teaching about peace examines both how to construct a more peaceful world and how to assess the phenomenon of war.

At the center of the church's teaching on peace and at the center of all Catholic social teaching, are the transcendence of God and the dignity of the human person. The human person is the clearest reflection of God's presence in the world; all of the church's work in pursuit of both justice and peace is designed to protect and promote the dignity of every person. For each person not only reflects God, but is the expression of God's creative work and the meaning of Christ's redemptive ministry. Christians approach the problem of war and peace with fear and reverence. God is the Lord of life, and so each human life is sacred; modern warfare threatens the obliteration of human life on a previously unimaginable scale. The sense of awe and "fear of the Lord" which former generations felt in approaching these issues weighs upon us with new urgency. In the words of the pastoral constitution: "Men of this generation should realize that they will have to render an account of their warlike behavior; the destiny of generations to come depends largely on the decisions they make today."[9]

Catholic teaching on peace and war has had two purposes: to help Catholics form their consciences and to contribute to the public policy debate about the morality of war. These two purposes have led Catholic teaching to address two distinct but overlapping audiences. The first is the Catholic faithful, formed by the premises of the Gospel and the principles of Catholic moral teaching. The second is the wider civil community, a more pluralistic audience, in which our brothers and sisters with whom we share the name Christian, Jews, Moslems, other religious communities, and all people of good will also make up our polity. Since Catholic teaching has traditionally sought to address both audiences, we intend to speak to both in this letter, recognizing that Catholics are also members of the wider political community.

The conviction, rooted in Catholic ecclesiology, that both the community of the faithful and the civil community should be addressed on peace and war has produced two complementary but distinct styles of teaching. The religious community shares a specific perspective of faith and can be called to live out its implications. The wider civil community, although it does not share the same vision of faith, is equally bound by certain key moral principles. For all men and all women find in the depth of their consciences a law written on the human heart by God.[10] From this law reason draws moral norms. These norms do not exhaust the gospel vision, but they speak to critical questions affecting the welfare of the human community, the role of states in international relations, and the limits of acceptable action by individuals and nations on issues of war and peace.

Examples of these two styles can be found in recent Catholic teaching. At times the emphasis is upon the problems and requirements for a just public policy (e.g., Pope John Paul II at the U.N. Special Session, 1982); at other times the emphasis is on the specific role Christians should play (e.g., Pope John Paul II at Coventry, England, 1982). The same difference of emphasis and orientation can be found in Pope John XXIII's "Peace on Earth" and Vatican II's pastoral constitution.

As bishops we believe that the nature of Catholic moral teaching, the principles of Catholic ecclesiology, and the demands of our pastoral ministry require that this letter speak both to Catholics in a specific way and to the wider political community regarding public policy. Neither audience and neither mode of address can be neglected when the issue has the cosmic dimensions of the nuclear arms race.

We propose, therefore, to discuss both the religious vision of peace among peoples and nations, and the problems associated with realizing this vision in a world of sovereign states devoid of any central authority and divided by ideology, geography, and competing claims. We believe the religious vision has an objective basis and is capable of progressive realization. Christ is our peace, for he has "made us both one, and has broken down the dividing wall of hostility... that he might create in himself one new man in place of the two, so making peace, and might reconcile us to God" (Eph. 2:14-16). We also know that this peace will be achieved fully only in the kingdom of God. The realization of the kingdom, therefore, is a continuing work progressively accomplished, precariously maintained, and needing constant effort to preserve the peace achieved and expand its scope in personal and political life.

Building peace within and among nations is the work of many individuals and institutions; it is the fruit of ideas and decisions taken in the political, cultural, economic, social, military, and legal sectors of life. We believe that the church, as a community of faith and social institution, has a proper, necessary, and distinctive part to play in the pursuit of peace.

The distinctive contribution of the church flows from her religious nature and ministry. The church is called to be in a unique way the instrument of the kingdom of God in history. Since peace is one of the signs of that kingdom present in the world, the church fulfills part of her essential mission by making the peace of the kingdom more visible in our time.

Because peace, like the kingdom of God itself, is both a divine gift and a human work, the church should continually pray for the gift and share in the work. We are called to be a church at the service of peace, precisely because peace is one manifestation of God's word and work in our midst. Recognition of the church's responsibility to join with others in the work of peace is a major force behind the call today to develop a theology of peace. Much of the history of Catholic theology on war and peace has focused on limiting the resort to force in human affairs; this task is still necessary and is reflected later in this pastoral letter, but it is not a sufficient response to Vatican II's challenge "to undertake a completely fresh reappraisal of war."[11]

A fresh reappraisal which includes a developed theology of peace will require contributions from several sectors of the church's life: biblical studies, systematic and moral theology, ecclesiology, and the experience and insights of members of the church who have struggled in various ways to make and keep the peace in this often violent age. This pastoral letter is more an invitation to continue the new appraisal of war and peace than a final synthesis of the results of such an appraisal. We have some sense of the characteristics of a theology of peace, but not a systematic statement of relationships.

A theology of peace should ground the task of peacemaking solidly in the biblical vision of the kingdom of God, then place it centrally in the ministry of the church. It should specify the obstacles in the way of peace, as these are understood theologically and in the social and political sciences. It should both identify the specific contributions a community of faith can make to the work of peace, and relate these to the wider work of peace pursued by other groups and institutions in society. Finally, a theology of peace must include a message of hope. The vision of hope must be available to all, but one source of its content should be found in a church at the service of peace.

We offer now a first step toward a message of peace and hope. It consists of a sketch of the biblical conception of peace; a theological understanding of how peace can be pursued in a world marked by sin; a moral assessment of key issues facing us in the pursuit of peace today; and an assessment of the political and personal tasks required of all people of good will in this most crucial period of history. . . .

NOTES

1. Vatican II, "The Pastoral Constitution of the Church in the Modern World," 77. . . . Several collections of papal and conciliar texts exist, although no single collection is comprehensive; see the following: *Peace and Disarmament: Documents of the World Council of Churches and the Roman Catholic Church* (Geneva and Rome, 1982); Joseph Gremillion, *The Gospel of Peace and Justice: Catholic Social Teaching since Pope John* (Maryknoll, N.Y., 1976); D. J. O'Brien and T. A. Shannon, eds., *Renewing the Earth: Catholic Documents on Peace, Justice, and Liberation* (New York, 1977); Austin Flannery, ed., *Vatican Council II: The Conciliar and Post Conciliar Documents* (Collegeville, Minn., 1975); Walter Abbott, ed., *The Documents of Vatican II* (New York, 1966).

2. John Paul II, "Message to the Second Special Session of the United Nations General Assembly Devoted to Disarmament" (June 1982) 7.

3. John Paul II, "Address to Scientists and Scholars," 4 (*Origins,* 10 [1981] 621).

4. The pastoral constitution is made up of two parts; yet it constitutes an organic unity. By way of explanation: The constitution is called "pastoral" because, while resting on doctrinal principles, it seeks to express the relationship of the church to the world and modern humankind. The result is that, on the one hand, a pastoral slant is present in the first part and, on the other hand, a doctrinal slant is present in the second part. ("Pastoral Constitution," n.1).

5. "Pastoral Constitution," n.1.

6. Ibid., 43.

7. John Paul II, "Message . . . Disarmament," 2.

8. "Pastoral Constitution," 81.

9. Ibid., 80.

10. Ibid., 16.

11. Ibid., 80.

Chapter 12

George F. Kennan

The Bishops' Letter

The results of the two world wars of this century, representing setbacks for European civilization, already began to draw a veil of doubt over the validity, in this modern age, of most of the theoretical principles worked out in earlier centuries to relate the use of the armed power of the state to politics and morals. But the development of the nuclear weapon, bringing the power of existing arsenals to a point that made their use in warfare suicidal and threatening to the very intactness of civilization, heightened the significance of these questions many times over, presenting dilemmas to which the wisdom of the past provided no sure answers, and raising the demand for a fundamental rethinking of the role of armed force in the strategy and the moral philosophy of the modern state.

Numbers of individuals have struggled, over the years, with this challenge and have published their findings. Many conferences of scholars and individual officials have been devoted to it. But these efforts involved no collective discipline, and they departed from no unified, accepted platform of moral philosophy.

Nearly two years ago, a committee, set up at the instance of Archbishop John R. Roach, president of the National Conference of Catholic Bishops, undertook the drafting of a pastoral letter designed to develop and to perfect, as the authors of the letter described it, "a theology of peace suited to a civilization poised on the brink of self-destruction." The paper went through two preliminary drafts. These came, repeatedly, before the membership of the Conference. They were reviewed in international ecclesiastical gatherings held under Vatican auspices. They were discussed at length with senior officials of the present, and previous, American Administrations. The third and final draft, reflecting the results of all these consultations, has now been completed and is to be given final consideration at a special meeting of the Conference in Chicago tomorrow and Tuesday [May 2–3, 1983].

This paper, which is now available to the public, may fairly be described as the most profound and searching inquiry yet conducted by any responsible collective body into the relations of nuclear weaponry, and indeed of modern war in general, to moral philosophy, to politics and to the conscience of the national state.

Not all of the paper is directed to a non-Roman Catholic readership; the final and fourth part, dealing with "The Pastoral Challenge and Response," is addressed directly to the members of the faith. But most of the remainder represents an effort "to share the moral wisdom of the Catholic tradition with the larger society . . . and to participate in

First published on the Op Ed page of the *New York Times*, May 1, 1983. Copyright © 1983 by the New York Times Company. Reprinted by permission.

a common effort with all men and women of good will who seek to reverse the arms race and secure the peace of the world."

Whatever else may be said of this paper, no one can say that its authors made it easy for themselves. They confronted, without flinching, the challenges that nuclear weapons present, not just to all previous Catholic teachings on the relationships of war to morals and politics but to Western public philosophy on these questions generally. Both tone and language of the document bear witness to the earnestness that this effort involved.

The entire question of war, as a legitimate recourse of the national state, is reexamined here with relation to the conditions of this present age. Is there still such a thing as "just war" in the traditional sense? Can there, in other words, be circumstances in which the state would be justified in waging war?

Yes, reply the authors, there can be, but the conditions in which war might be legitimately resorted to are narrowly circumscribed, and the manner in which warfare can then properly be waged is subject to a whole series of restrictions. The cause must be just. The authority that takes the responsibility of launching hostilities must be competent. Resort to the force of arms must be a last resort; all other alternatives must have been previously explored and tested. Above all, the principle of "proportionality" must be observed: The damage to be inflicted and the costs incurred by war must, that is, "be proportionate to the good expected by taking up arms." And the action must be discriminate. The security of noncombatants must be respected. War must be directed "against unjust aggressors, not against innocent people caught up in a war not of their making." There must, in particular, be no aiming of any act of war at the destruction of entire cities or of extensive areas along with their populations.

Are there, in the light of these principles, any circumstances in which the inauguration of nuclear warfare would be justifiable? No, say the authors, there are none. Nuclear weapons are too indiscriminate; even if they are not launched with the aim of destroying innocent civilian life, they inevitably subject it to a wholly unacceptable jeopardy.

But how about "deterrence"? "May a nation threaten what it may never do? May it possess what it may never use?" And is nuclear deterrence, then, a justifiable concept? Yes, say the authors, it is—but not as a purpose in itself—only as a step toward progressive disarmament. It can be invoked as a means of preventing others from using nuclear weapons; but concepts that run to "prevailing" in nuclear war must be seen as going unacceptably far beyond that, as does any attempt to achieve nuclear superiority, as distinct from sufficiency.

In support of these principles, the letter recommends a whole series of arms control measures, including in effect a general stop in the arms races, deep bilateral cuts in arsenals, a comprehensive test ban treaty, and removal of the short-range weapons "which multiply dangers disproportionate to their deterrent value." It recognizes, however, that arms control agreements alone are insufficient if not accompanied by vigorous parallel efforts to reduce political tensions.

The authors avoid the mistake of allowing it to be inferred that if only the nuclear danger were overcome, all would be well. They recognize the wholly unacceptable destructiveness of even the so-called conventional weapons in this modern age. They quote Pope John Paul II to the effect that "the scale and the horror of modern warfare—whether nuclear or not—makes it totally unacceptable as a means of settling differences between nations." They reject the suggestion that to remove the possibility of nuclear war would be to enhance the probability of a nonnuclear one. Means must be found of defending peoples, they insist, that "do not depend upon the threat of annihilation."

The authors do not rule out the possibility that there might have to be a strengthening of Western conventional forces to fill whatever gap might be created, at least psychologically, by the removal of the nuclear option; but they prefer to see the emphasis placed on a new and more determined effort to achieve mutual reductions in conventional forces with a view to disarming both the real possibilities and the public fears of a conventional conflict.

That these propositions meet with the hearty approval of this writer will be evident. But my purpose is not to point that out, but rather to emphasize that the beauty of the pastoral letter lies precisely in the limitations it defines—in the moral perimeters it establishes for the use of force in international affairs.

The paper is firm in its insistence that military values, even when they legitimately exist, must never be treated as absolutes and hence carried to self-defeating extremes—that they must rather be seen, invariably, as relative and conditional: relative to the fundamental need of civilization for survival, conditional on the observance of those elementary moral scruples beyond which horror becomes unlimited, and hope impossible. There is surely no lesson that this generation of Americans needs more to learn.

Chapter 13

Ched Myers

Storming the Gates of Hell

Reflections on Christian Witness in Nuclear Security Areas

> Through the church the great widsom of God is to be made known to the principalities and powers in high places . . . [Eph. 3:10].

On a clear, brisk pre-dawn September morning in 1979, two dozen Christians gathered at the eastern edge of the sprawling Rocky Flats nuclear weapons trigger plant near Denver, Colorado. As they sang, six persons cut through a fence, walked with flickering candles a half-mile over rough terrain to a hill overlooking the humming bomb factory below. There they commenced a "liturgy of light." As the sun rose almost an hour later, the six were brusquely gathered into four-wheel-drive overland security vehicles and hauled off to jail. Citing the gospel in defense, they were convicted of trespass and served six months in Colorado jails.

On the Feast of the Epiphany 1980, two "prayer commandos" climbed a fence and entered the Bangor naval submarine base near Seattle, Washington. For 24 hours they hiked through the woods on the sprawling property, unnoticed by patrol vehicles. Early the next morning, the two men clambered over a 12-foot double-security fence into the maximum-security weapons storage depot at the heart of the base, where guards have orders to use "deadly force" against intruders. The two Christian pilgrims were not fired upon, and they proceeded to pray at each of six nuclear weapons bunkers before being arrested and taken away by marines armed with rifles. They have recently been released after serving one year in federal prison.

In September 1980, six men and two women entered General Electric's King of Prussia manufacturing plant near Philadelphia before the morning shift. They found their way into the security assembly line area, where GE's Mark 12-A re-entry vehicles for nuclear warheads were awaiting shipment. With hammers, some of the peacemakers began to "beat swords into plowshares," while others spilled blood, the biblical symbol for life, on nearby blueprints. They were arrested after having begun the "conversion" of several missile nose cones. After six months' imprisonment, the "Plowshares Eight"

---

were tried, but were not allowed to present in their defense expert testimony on international law, the arms race, or conscience. All eight were convicted, receiving three-to-ten year prison sentences.

A few months after the King of Prussia action, another small group of Christians gathered outside the Pantex plant near Amarillo, Texas, where components for nuclear weapons receive their final assembly. It was early morning, foggy and unseasonably cold. Six of them, using makeshift ladders, glided over the outside fence of the maximum-security area. As their feet touched the ground, overhead lights beamed on and blue security lights flashed. The prayer pilgrims made their way to a second fence, which was electrified, and there fell on their knees in prayer and praise. Found and arrested, they are now serving sentences ranging from six months to a year.

On March 11, 1981, four Christians slipped unnoticed into the security manufacturing area of Lockheed Missiles and Space Corporation near San Jose, California. The three men and one woman, after searching for 15 minutes, located a room filled with Trident submarine-launched strategic missile parts. The activists poured their own blood from bottles over the missile midsections, as well as over nearby files and blueprints. They were discovered and arrested 20 minutes later; they have served from two to six months in a county jail.

ACHIEVING VISION IN AN AGE OF RESIGNATION

What are we to make of such behavior? Are these people lunatics? Are their efforts— no matter how well-intentioned—misguided, irresponsible, and cavalier?

It is clear enough that these actions are nonviolent and firmly grounded within the political tradition of civil disobedience. But they also represent a new kind of tenacity that deserves thoughtful reflection. Although only a few of these and similar actions (at Commander-in-Chief-Pacific [CINCPAC] headquaters in Hawaii, Strategic Air Command bases in Montana, or naval shipyards in Connecticut) have received significant media attention, they are making an impact. It is important to try to understand the nature and context of these actions, and to reflect on their political and theological implications for all who are working for peace.

The politics of the peace movement in the U.S. has always been ambiguous. Like any dissenting political effort trying to achieve vision from within an imperial belly, the movement is riddled with internal disagreements and full of contradictions. Yet two things ought to be clear when we consider the possibilities for peacemaking in the coming decade. First, there is no longer any ground for believing that the governmental, industrial, and academic managers of the arms race will, on their own initiative, do anything significant to slow the present rush to nuclear conflagration. Given the present momentum of militarism, historical realism compels us to acknowledge that we do not have time for official arms negotiators to do a turnabout. This fact demands that political approaches of petition need to be buttressed more and more by popular refusal to cooperate with continued governmental procrastination. In short, the politics of exhortation must become a politics of resistance.

There are signs that this may be happening. The practice of military tax refusal, which was an important, concrete tactic of opposition to the Vietnam war, is beginning to spread again, and in the wake of the "middle-class tax revolt," has real political potential. Similarly, statistics have shown that tens of thousands of young men did not comply with recently renewed draft registration orders. There are other stirrings of hope as well. Nevertheless, we are far from the kind of popular outrage necessary to stop an arms race that threatens to grind history to a halt.

It must be admitted that the traditional peace movement has so far failed to embody a moral and political vitality or creativity able to ignite the consciences of American people. The dictum of C. Wright Mills in his famous 1959 polemic, "The Causes of World War Three," still stands:

The paralysis of nuclear stand-off has all but stifled political imagination in the West. The cold shadow of impending apocalypse has created a psychological and social cul-de-sac, wherein indeed "hearts grow cold" and even the elect are deceived.

Sociopolitical resistance and moral imagination must be linked. The lack of such a synthesis, however, has compelled many astute and committed activists secretly to concede to the view that only when nuclear weapons are used will people wake with sufficient force to stop the nuclear juggernaut. The hope, then, is that nuclear first-use will be tactical and limited! The "politics of resignation" soberly concludes that only the Damoclean sword is adequate to cut the Gordian knot.

There is something to be said for this "new realism." Political renewal can never be based on illusion. All signs point to the fact that nuclear conflict could erupt soon. The official mood of government is brinksmanship, while the new strategic wisdom appears to have embraced the viability and inevitability of tactical nuclear war.

At the popular level, socialization for acceptance of nuclear battle is broad and deep. Theologian Harvey Cox tells of a recent poll in which a random sample of people were asked if they believed there would be a nuclear war in their lifetime, and whether they thought they would survive it. Astonishingly, 85 percent of those surveyed answered that they *did* expect a nuclear war, which they would not survive. The end of the world, as peace activist Elizabeth McAllister has suggested, has become virtually platitudinous. We are a people with a deep sense of futurelessness.

Yet it is precisely in the face of this growing paralysis that a new spirit of resistance is arising, struggling for some kind of "moral equivalent" to thermonuclear holocaust, and calling for a resurrection of political imagination. It is being initiated by Christian people who believe that an atmosphere of capitulation in nuclear nations challenges Christian faith and political hope to come together. These people agree with Thomas Merton, who wrote in the darkest days of the Cuban missile crisis (a moment of similar paralysis) that "Christian faith *begins* at the point where all others stand frozen stiff in the face of the Unspeakable."

THE HOLY SPIRIT AS SUBVERSIVE CO-CONSPIRATOR

As people responsible to both Word and world, Christian activists have long been seeking new ways to keep pressing moral questions upon the nation, the church, and themselves. At stake is the integrity of faith, of democracy, and of freedom in a culture resigned to the destruction of life.

Beginning in the mid-60's, a particular vitality was forged by religious antiwar activists who joined the nonviolent politics of Mahatma Gandhi and Martin Luther King, Jr., with "symbolic" actions informed by the biblical-prophetic tradition. From Catonsville to the recent women's Pentagon action, symbolic direct action has persisted in the grass-roots resistance to atomic weaponry and the nuclear economy.

In its better moments, symbolic direct action has been neither a politics of token pressuring nor fixation upon "kamikaze herosim," as its detractors maintain. Its use of a new political language (symbolic and suggestive rather than ideological or propositional) and a new political locale (e.g., weapons factories rather than Senate chambers) has attempted to create a public moral/political crisis through confrontation. Whether particular actions have succeeded in this aim is not always clear, but this "tradition" of activism has been a consistent goal to political creativity and self-examination.

Theologian-activist Jim Douglass has written:

> Resistance must deepen in a way that might begin to correspond to the depth of the nuclear crisis. Nuclear weapons, and their security measures, remain when mass demonstrations are over. The test of nonviolence is to maintain its commitment just as steadily as our friends in the military maintain their commitment.

Along these lines, some Christians are trying to escalate their witness in proportion to the crisis, confronting the bomb with a militant gospel, employing prayer pilgrimages, hammers of hope, symbols of life.

Though these actions have multiplied without coordination, they do share a common orientation. The participants are all experienced activists with years of more conventional organizing behind them. They undergo rigorous physical, mental, and spiritual preparation for their ventures into high-security areas. The actions are small and controlled, carried out by people deeply committed to non-violence as a way of life.

There is clear recognition that these actions are risky; one does not climb double-security fences without understanding the implications: jail, possible personal injury, even maiming or death. All participants have had to grapple personally with these questions as well as discuss them with family and friends. Thus, the actions become, literally as well as symbolically, faith journeys of life and death.

It is also important to understand that each action commences with and culminates in prayer. Moreover, those "inside" are supported by wider networks of praying co-conspirators. As one Pantex pilgrim put it:

> All the unknowns of this prayer venture [inside the weapons plant] met with more unknowns—the mystery of mustard seeds, seeds of prayer thoughout Christian people and communities across the country and beyond.

In prayer lie both the poverty and the strength of these witnesses.

Perhaps most scandalous of all, however, is the resisters' claim to be led by the Holy Spirit. All have felt the deep security of the Spirit's protection during high-risk witness ventures. To some this claim may seem presumptuous, but to those familiar with security measures at nuclear facilities, the "success" of these actions is indeed remarkable, and the active conspiring of the Spirit is perhaps the only explanation.

THE POLITICS OF TRANSGRESSION

The question must be pressed, however, as to whether this "new spirit" of direct action is in fact the right direction to take in seeking "moral equivalency." Is this new escalation in itself a concession to a kind of desperation? Can't these aims be achieved just as effectively in a more representative fashion, outside the danger of high-security areas, or even (as many argue) outside the boundaries of factories and bases altogether?

It will help in considering these questions to reflect on how the use of nonviolent direct action has developed in the peace movement. We are concerned here not with the question of mass demonstration versus small actions, but rather with the question of "political geography." It is quite arguable that a major breakthrough in the consciousness of the peace movement has come as a result of shifting the locus of action from Senate offices to bomb plants, from the White House to military installations.

Those who consider this tactic naïve (managers and workers don't make the decisions!) need to understand that perhaps the single most important factor determining popular acceptance of the nuclear status quo has been the very anonymity of the bomb itself. The existence of the nuclear economy and of bomb factories was largely hidden from public consciousness for years, with only the respectable and sterile mask of official policies visible. When popular opposition to nuclear terror waned in the early '60s after the phasing out of civil defense drills and the retreat underground by the nuclear testing program, the suspicion was confirmed that in a society gripped by the spell of "mutual assured destruction," ignorance was, by definition, bliss.

The key, then, to suppressing dissent in an age of widespread nuclear fatalism has been to keep the crisis out of sight and mind, something masterfully achieved in the Soviet Union. In opposition to such secrecy, protests at the location of management, research, and development, production and deployment of nuclear weapons have stimulated popular sensitivity to the reality of nuclear destruction. A map of "nuclear America" is today considered a standard organizing tool for resisters, and the intricate network that makes up the nuclear weapons complex has, through research, investigation, and dissenting presence, been exposed to public view.

Even though weapons installations have been identified, however, the weapons themselves remain apparently untouchable. High security is, after all, high security. The Department of Defense policy of "neither confirming nor denying" the presence of nuclear weapons at any particular place, and its strict secrecy surrounding nuclear weapons accidents serves to promote this sense of "nonexistence." As researcher-organizer Jim Albertini has argued in a campaign to expose nuclear weapons storage near the Honolulu International Airport, this secrecy is not to hide the fact from the Russians, who through their intelligence know where most of our weapons are; rather, the weapons must be hidden from the American people, the very constituency they purport to protect. Would you want to raise your children next to a nuclear stockpile?

Another "breakthrough" has been needed to strip away the last myth of the sacredness of nuclear weapons, for the sanctity of weapons installations has had in fact a kind of neo-religiosity about. Nuclear weapons and delivery vehicles reside in the "holy of holies," the high-security bunkers and buildings. Members of the "priesthood" need security clearance to approach these military altars; others who venture too close will surely meet their doom. Clearly, this idolatrous "theology of secrecy" must be challenged, on both democratic and Christian grounds.

This, then, is the context out of which escalated resistance grows. In a historical situation giving such power to nuclear weapons and the policies behind them, it is not enough simply to refuse to accept them, though that is the beginning of liberation. We must begin to transgress their "holy ground" in order to challenge the deepest assumptions about nuclear weaponry, to journey to the very point where the sanctity of their violence is most strongly defended and justified. In unmasking the genocidal instruments themselves, the most crucial crisis is opened up: do these weapons, delivery systems, assembly lines, fences, and bunkers have a right to exist? Will we kill, maim, or jail nonviolent people in order to protect *this* property right? If these vehicles of death are scratched or stained with hammers or blood, shall we then be forced to defend the sanctity of *this* private property?

Depending on what we believe concerning the legitimacy of nuclear weapons, as the resisters at the Bangor base near Seattle have pointed out, we will either regard barbed-wire fences that protect the weapons from us as a deterrent or an invitation, as a red light or a green one. Jim Douglass has posed the question with particular clarity:

> No one believes in nuclear weapons as such, but many Americans have given up hope of reversing the world's (and our own) reliance on them. Thus for the sake of security the premise of the "real world" carries with it the escalating threat of nuclear weapons and all the heightened security measures necessary to protect the weapons: . . . intruders should be shot on sight. A belief in nuclear weapons demands it. . . . To those who see a different reality, . . . that we're now living in global Jonestown and that a different world is possible, then bet your life on the truth of climbing . . . fences to spill those nuclear vats across the public con-science, to awaken us as a people from insanity to responsibilty. Let the "real world" beliefs of those who defend [nuclear] weapons and nonviolent resisters who see the terror as already there, meet as conflicting truths at those fences.

BRINGING DARKNESS TO LIGHT

There is a powerful biblical logic to this kind of peacemaking. While most of these resisters will appeal to the Nuremburg principle or to international law as a kind of moral "hermeneutic" in the courts and in informing the public, the real source of discernment and guidance comes from biblical visions. It is remarkable how all those engaging in actions in high-security areas have gathered around one text in particular:

> Don't be deceived with empty rhetoric
>   For judgment is coming because of the children of disobedience;
> Therefore: Do not associate with them:
> For once you were yourselves darkness, but now in the Lord you are light;
> Live then as children of light!
> (Remember that the fruit of light is all that is good, just, and true.)
> Struggle then to discern what the Lord's will is.
> Not only should you not cooperate with the unfruitful works of darkness,
> But more than that you must unmask them!
> Indeed it is shameful even to discuss the things done in secret these days;
> But when anything is brought to the light it becomes manifest,
>   for light brings to light!
> For this reason we read:
>   "Awake, you who sleep, arise from the dead,
>   "Christ will give you light!"
> Watch carefully therefore how you live your lives,
>   not as unwise people but as wise,
> Seizing the moment, because the times are evil;
> Do not be fooled, but discern what the Lord calls us to do . . .
>   [Eph.5:6-17; author's translation]

This Pauline exhortation, which offers a clear statement of the politics of the Kingdom in bad times, has long been a difficult one for the church to interpret, perhaps because it speaks of a vocation foreign to most Christian experience. It has been unintelligible to us because of our moral ambivalence. In light of present resistance to the bomb, however, the text has come alive as a manifesto of engagement with the unleashed powers of militarism in a national security state. Because this scriptural manifesto has been exemplified in the lives of Christian peacemakers, we can now better understand its summons for militance in truth-telling, for nonviolent steadfastness at the heart of a cosmic conflict between the forces of death and the spirit of life (Eph. 3:10, 6:10ff.).

It stands to reason that direct action taken in this spirit and this hope can break open both Christian faith and political imagination. As we are observing in El Salvador's present struggle, for example, a renewal of faith can indeed offer direction and vitality for a politics of "hope against hope." We must not marginalize actions such as the witness of Central American Christians, either through romanticizing or sacramentalizing—or through dismissal.

To those in the peace movement, such acts, and the efforts of those who invade nuclear production sites and missile bases, are meant to extend a call to deeper "response-ability" to the growing madness of U.S. nuclear policies. To those in the churches, they must be seen as an invitation to renewed and costly discipleship, "because the times are evil." The actions are offered to us not for imitations, but in the hope of engendering deeper experimentation with the truth. It ought to be increasingly clear that nothing short of militant resistance, nothing less than bold ventures of faith and conscience, and nothing other than betting our lives on the truth of nonviolence will awaken our people to the historical ultimatum of nuclear weapons.

Chapter 14

Alan Kreider

Rediscovering Our Heritage

The Pacifism of the Early Church

"The early church was pacifist." "No it wasn't!" Both assertions are common ones; but both can't be right. Which is better? And why does it matter?

Many anti-pacifists admit that the early church appeared to be pacifist. In their attempts to explain this, they have made two points. First, they have claimed that the "pacifism" of the early Christians was limited to a few intellectuals—perverse men who were out of touch with the real world. Most Christians in the Roman empire had better sense and expressed their disdain for these theologians by serving in the legions.

Second, the anti-pacifists have asserted that these theologians were not actually anti-military. It was not killing to which they objected. Rather, they were offended by the idolatry that was an unavoidable part of army life in an empire whose emperors were divinized.

In his book *It Is Not Lawful for Me to Fight: Early Christian Attitudes Toward War, Violence, and the State*, Jean-Michel Hornus responds to these claims. He does not assert that all early Christians were pacifists according to modern definitions of the term. He does not deny that some Christians were in the army. He admits that there were changes in the course of several centuries. And he bends over backwards to report individual cases which are hard to fit into his interpretation.

Nevertheless, in Hornus's careful study a pattern of early church thought and practice does emerge which is more in keeping with the pacifist than the anti-pacifist interpretation. One can summarize it in five statements:

• No Christian writer before Constantine's reign justified the participation of believers in warfare. Every writer who commented on this—and lots of them did—condemned it.

•The objection of these writers was based not just on their obvious revulsion to idolatry but also on their concern to be obedient to Jesus. His teachings had instilled in them a profound respect for life and a desire to love their enemies, even the "barbarians." He also had warned them of the impossibility of serving two masters; and this teaching applied in a special way to soldiers, who were in an authority structure which required absolute obedience. Furthermore, believers were undergirded by an eschatological hope. In their worship and in their personal and communal life, they were experiencing a new reality which expressed God's will and would in the end be victorious. Until then they would be sojourners in conflict with an alien world.

• As early as A.D. 180 there were Christians in the army. And during the ensuing 130 years the number of these grew. Their total numbers, however, were never large, as the almost total absence of soldiers among the Christian grave inscriptions indicates. Most believers in the legions appear to have been either officers' sons, who were required to serve, or men who were converted while in the army. Some new converts submitted to martyrdom in their struggle to be released from the forces. Others stayed in. During the *Pax Romana*, the army was as much a civil service and police force as it was a military organization. It was therefore possible to spend a lifetime in the army without killing. And some Christians with a good conscience chose to remain in this non-combatant role.

• The early church's disciplinary measures, in agreement with the teaching of theologians, disapproved of believers serving in the army. The *Apostolic Tradition*, for example, forbade converts to enter the forces. It permitted believers already in the army to remain there, but only under strict conditions: they were not allowed to be officers, and they were forbidden to kill. Anyone who disobeyed these regulations was to be excommunicated.

• In the fourth century, after the "conversion" of the Emperor Constantine in 312 and the forcible "christianization" of the Roman empire, the church's position changed. Theologians gradually abandoned their pacifism and adopted a new position: acceptance of "just war." Christians, who up to then had been non-conformist sojourners, made their peace with the world, settled down, and lost their distinctiveness. By the early years of the following century, one had to be a Christian to be in the army. Pacifism lived on, however, among professional non-conformists—the priests and monks who continued to uphold the position which earlier had been that of all believers.

Why is this important to us, Christians seeking to be peacemakers in the 1980s? It is not that the early church was pure and to be copied without question. Hornus gives ample illustrations of the compromise, self-seeking, and sin that were present among the early believers. And some of the positions which they adopted—for example, the willingness of many of them to wear military uniform in civil-service jobs—are not ones that would appeal to all of us.

But there are six ways in which I am convinced that we, both in our own lives and in our conversations with fellow Christians who are not yet pacifist, can profit from the early church.

• The early church is not normative for our belief or practice: Scripture is. But the attitudes of the early believers can shed important light on the original meaning of the New Testament. After all, the early Christians were close in time to Jesus Christ and the apostolic church. Their understandings of certain biblical passages may well be rooted in a tradition which accurately reflected the intentions of their authors. We therefore need to listen seriously to the early Christians. And when they say that Jesus' "love your enemies" meant *all* enemies (national and personal), and when the post-Constantinian theologians say that he meant only individual enemies, we will have some reason to prefer the former interpretation.

• We are often told that pacifism "doesn't work." We, on the basis of the early church's experience, can point to a lengthy period in which believers were convinced that it was working. For almost three centuries Christians lived lives of radical non-conformity, which included pacifism. Their social strategy was to seek a new society in the church which would be faithful to Christ; it was not to seize control in Rome in order to enforce a moral empire. During the period, the church grew in grace and numbers.

• Pacifism is an important part of the radical non-conformity of the early church; but it is only one part of a much larger package, each part of which was essential. Thus the Christians not only trusted God to protect them (pacifism); they also trusted God to provide for them (simplicity of life and economic sharing). Their trust was undergirded by their sense of God's presence in the Spirit, their common worship, and their sharing of their lives.

• Since the early church was pacifist, it provides us with a common ground for discussing the Christian attitude toward war with friends from many Christian traditions. In the thinking of most Christians, the early church occupies a special place. Orthodox and Catholic Christians root their traditions in it; the Reformers and the Anabaptists in their differing ways sought to restore its lost purity; and modern charismatic Christians long to revive the dynamism of church life "as at the beginning." Thus we do not need to appeal to the historic peace churches for models of Christian pacifism. We can appeal to a common Christian heritage, which all of us share in the early church. Our pacifist appeal thus does not need to be sectarian; it can be genuinely ecumenical.

• Most traditions, of course, are also the product of the Constantinian centuries, during which Christians coerced belief and coupled the cross with the sword. But we are now living in a post-Constantinian world. With rare exceptions Christianity has once again become a voluntary, minority religion. It now makes sense, as it did for the early Christians, for *all* believers to live as sojourners—radically, communally, nonviolently.

• All of us can thus turn to the early church for encouragement. Many of the stories told by Hornus, and many of the passages from early Christian writings which he quotes, are inspiring. Let me close by citing one of these, from the early fourth-century apologist Lactantius:

> For when God forbids us to kill, he not only prohibits us from open violence, which is not even allowed by the public laws, but he warns us against the commission of those things which are esteemed lawful among men. Thus it will not be lawful for a just man to engage in warfare, since his warfare is injustice itself. . . .

Chapter 15

William P. Mahedy

"It Don't Mean Nothin' ": The Vietnam Experience

"When I went to Vietnam, I believed in Jesus Christ and John Wayne. After Vietnam, both went down the tubes. It don't mean nothin'." Though I have heard other veterans say the same thing a thousand times in different ways, this statement made by a vet in a rap group is, for me, the most concise unmasking of American civil religion and its mythology of war. The loss of faith and meaning experienced by countless Vietnam veterans is now widely known, despite the best efforts of the religious and political right to incorporate Vietnam into the classical mythology of war.

If the United States government is to rearm the country for the struggle against "godless communism"—including preparation for a protracted nuclear war—it must first encourage the remythologizing of America. Foreign policy must be consistent with our national myth: we are God's chosen people in all that we undertake. We believe America has a divine mandate to evangelize the world to its own political and economic systems. War is the sacred instrument, the great cultic activity, whereby this mission is achieved. Jesus Christ and John Wayne must again be linked after their brief separation by Vietnam.

President Reagan has declared the Vietnam war a noble cause and the right wing has unleashed its fury against those who question the traditional mythology. The Reagan administration's attempt to dismantle the controversial Vietnam Veterans' Outreach Program shortly after taking office was consistent with this remythologizing: If the administration were to admit that the last war caused serious psychological, moral, and spiritual problems, then it would be more difficult to prepare the public for a similar conflict or for a much larger conflagration. The truth about the pain, danger, and disillusionment of the Vietnam veterans cannot be admitted if one espouses the traditional American civil religion. Having invested our political and cultural systems with religious characteristics, we must necessarily interpret our historical experience in terms of a sacred dimension. We must forever remain the chosen people, the "city on the hill" of our myth of origin. We cannot wage mere wars; we must fight crusades against the infidels.

It is, therefore, not surprising that the American people greeted with utter silence the anger and disillusionment of the Vietnam veterans. When at last some legitimacy was granted to their protest, it was only within the domesticated categories of psychotherapy. By now their rage, moral pain, and loss of faith have been almost completely contained within the psychiatric construct "post-traumatic stress disorder."

Peter Marin believes that this containment is a misrepresentation of the condition and avoids the real issue. He writes of a "massive, unconscious cover-up in which those who fought and those who did not hide from themselves the true nature of the experience . . . ." ("Living in Moral Pain," *Psychology Today* [November 1981], p. 72). What was experienced was the harshness of war: brutality, death, and atrocity without a comprehensive rationale to "seal over" the reality. The Vietnam war provided no transcendent meaning by which the national purpose could be reinterpreted and transposed into a new key. War was, for the first time in American history, experienced by great numbers of its participants as sin. Psychotherapy is uneasy with the notion of sin, as are most Americans of the late 20th century. As a result, much of what the veterans have to say cannot even be articulated, much less understood. The language and the concepts they need no longer exist within the arena of public discourse.

A large segment of the American religious community (which does possess the linguistic and philosophical tools necessary to deal with the moral and religious questions raised by Vietnam) chooses not to see the war as sin. In *The Unfinished War: Vietnam and the American Conscience* (Beacon, 1982), Walter Capps argues that the "rise of Protestant conservatism . . . or the new religious right bears direct connection with individual and corporate wrestling over the ramifications of the Vietnam experience." Viewing the outcome of the war as a defeat of the forces of good at the hands of the powers of evil, the religious right has enshrouded itself within the American myth of origin. The Soviet Union is seen as a supernaturally evil entity which must be defeated by the United States—God's Kingdom—in an apocalyptic drama. But this false mythology, unmasked by the Vietnam experience, is certain to prove once again its utter moral and religious bankruptcy. Reflecting on Vietnam might provide some insights into the religious underpinnings which seem always to lock us into paths leading to disaster.

W. Taylor Stevenson diagnoses the nature of the Vietnam wound as "defilement", i.e., coming into contact with an object which "has been culturally designated as being unclean" ("The Experience of Defilement," *Anglican Theological Review* [January 1982], p. 18). That there is a good bit of truth in this assessment is demonstrated by the curious fact that many Vietnam veterans describe themselves as unclean. They lament the absence (or, in the case of the recent Washington observance, the delay) of the cleansing rituals of return, such as parades or a hero's welcome, that a society usually grants to its warriors. The almost total inability both of veterans and of the American public to discuss Vietnam for so many years is a clear indication of defilement.

Stevenson sees this defilement as resulting from the breaking of two prerational taboos. These two sacred beliefs are part of American civil religion: (1) America is innocent, and (2) America is powerful. Stevenson writes:

America is innocent/powerful. It is an implication of this innocency that America deserves to be peaceful and properous. A further implication here is that America's exercise of power is an innocent exercise of power necessary for our peace and prosperity. We were not "taught" this in any formal sense. It was not necessary to be taught this because this innocency is not a matter of idea or concept or doctrine; rather, it is a part of the texture of growing up in the United States. It is part of our story of how things *are*, how reality is structured, how life flows for us, and so on. Any violation of this asserted innocency is profoundly disturbing to our individual and social sense of structure and power. . . .

What breaks this taboo and brings a sense of defilement? Any situation or event which challenges or defeats the taboo and all that taboo protects. Did we go into Vietnam originally under the taboo "America is innocent"? The evidence is overwhelming that, for the vast majority of Americans, we did (whatever reservations some had concerning Asian land wars).

Those on both sides of the Vietnam conflict were exposed to and participated in consciousness-altering, irreversible, massive evil. Atrocity, hatred, wholesale slaughter, and barbarous acts of all kinds are the stuff of war. In the name of innocent America and its god, the GIs performed their duty in the great cultic act of war. But the myth was shattered. Neither they nor their country and its god were innocent. Perhaps, had the wages of sin been victory, a belief in our innocence could have been restored; but we were defeated.

The other illusion, that of power, was also shattered. The warriors, their nation and its god were shown to be powerless. The taboos had been broken. We had sinned, and the wages of sin was death. Only in this context can the pervasive loss of faith among the veterans be understood and discussed.

If, as John Wheeler writes, "God acting about us and through us redeems the brokenness of Vietnam" ("Theological Reflection Upon the Vietnam War," *Anglican Theological Review* [January 1982], p. 14), then this God can only be the God revealed to us in the Hebrew and Christian Scriptures. The veteran who told me that 500 years of life would not be sufficient to atone for what he did in Vietnam is quite correct, for those he killed would still be dead. Only death will erase the emotional and spiritual scars inflicted upon the widows and orphans of his victims. The veteran who asked me, "Where was God, that son-of-a-bitch, when the rounds were coming in at Khe Sanh?" asked the right question. The mystery of iniquity is too profound for the American tribal god.

Religious conservatives who retreat from evil and identify religion with feeling good about Jesus, with the conversion experience and with the better life, are not really prepared to grapple with the questions raised by war. Neither are the liberals who believe that personhood and human fulfillment are the end products of religion. The former construct religious and emotional defenses to insulate themselves from evil, and the latter often underestimate its power.

The only God who seems to make any sense is the one who refused to let Moses see his face, the God whose ways are not our ways. When confronted with the problem of Job, many vets ask the questions Job asked. The answer given to Job makes more religious sense than anything else: "Where were you when I laid the foundation of the earth?" (Job 38:4). All human words—even religious words—are frivolous in the face of evil and in the presence of the transcendent God. For veterans who have been seeking some vindication from the American people and its tribal god, it becomes clear that the only real vindication comes from the God of absolute holiness and mercy. Five hundred years may be insufficient for atonement in any human sense, but with the God to whom a thousand years are as a day, everything is possible. Having been expelled from the garden for tasting the forbidden fruit, we can find real hope only in the promise of redemption.

For post-Christian vets, those whose faith was destroyed by Vietnam, I believe the most powerful single utterance in Scripture is the utterance of Jesus on the cross: "My

God, my God, why have you abandoned me?" Quite clearly, they too have walked the way of the cross, and the words of the psalmist are their words too. The tragedy is that no one has pointed out this connection.

Nor has anyone dealt with the next and crucial step that must be taken by those who have experienced great evil and perceived its relationship to the cross. With Jesus, one must be able to say, "Father, into your hands I commend my spirit." All that has happened to the veterans in Vietnam and since Vietnam—their broken lives, broken bodies, and shattered dreams—must be placed in the hands of the Father. Experiential knowledge of the monstrous evil in the world and the recognition of humankind's utter inability to achieve any real shalom elicit the cry of agony.

The next step requires the leap of faith, for the experience of evil is really the perception of God's absence from the world precisely in those situations which seem to demand a providential presence. To understand the apparent absence of God as one mode of his presence requires, first of all, the destruction of the American graven image, with its promise of innocence restored and power regained.

In more than ten years of working with Vietnam veterans, I have seen many discover the true nature of their wound. Although therapy, jobs, and benefits may be helpful in healing some of the hurt, the real source of the alienation and rage is gradually disclosed: it is the death of the national god. For many veterans this abyss is too deep. To survive they must rewrite the history of Vietnam in their own minds and hearts. Beating the drums of war again seems the only way to justify their own war.

For others, a life of service to fellow veterans and to society is the way to overcome the evil they have experienced. The enormous dedication and selflessness shown by those in the self-help centers, in the outreach programs, and in the political groups can be explained in terms of deliverance from evil. Some even articulate their ideals in religious terms: the Beatitudes and the prayer of St. Francis.

What is lacking for most veterans, however, is the willingness of Job to be silent, or the committing of one's own life and death and of all things to the Father as Jesus did. I have seen veterans break into tears of amazement and relief when they begin to understand, in the words of the anonymous author of *The Cloud of Unknowing*:

> You . . . will feel nothing and know nothing except a naked intent toward God in the depths of your being. You will feel frustrated for your mind will be unable to grasp him and your heart will not relish the delight of his love. . . . If, in this life, you hope to see and feel God as he is in himself it must be within this darkness and this cloud. . . . God in his goodness will bring you to a deeper experience of himself [quoted in W. H. Capps and W. M. Wright, *The Silent Fire* (Harper, 1978), p. 104].

The Vietnam experience has not yet been publicly connected with the dark night of the soul or with any theology of the cross. Yet I am aware of no other Christian point of reference adequate to it. Everything else "don't mean nothin'."

Unfortunately, veterans seldom find help from the clergy. Most pastors—of any denomination—do not articulate the Christian faith in these terms. A veteran has, I believe, a better chance of finding a competent guide in a contemplative monk or nun. A person who has spent years in prayer and solitude—however lacking he or she may be in the experience of war or of ministry or of the world—will be more able to relate to one who has undergone the shattering of culturally dominant images of God. The desolation of spirit so common in the life of solitude enters also into the lives of those who are touched by monstrous evil. A person who has encountered God in the darkness of unknowing is, I believe, the best guide for one who is groping in that darkness but who is unable to identify the cloud.

If the church wishes to learn to confront the evils which irrevocably alter consciousness (genocide, mass starvation, systemic injustice, nuclear war), then it must understand and be willing to live in the dark night of the soul and in the cloud of unknowing. If the church is to work actively in the world in behalf of justice and peace, it must not only do so in obedience to God but it must also be prepared to encounter God as present and active precisely in those situations where he seems most painfully absent.

The idolatrous character of American civil religion is nowhere more clearly disclosed than in the variety of props it constructs to insulate its adherents from evil. In striking at the idol, however, American Christianity should be aware that its favorite images of God are also inadequate. The divine guarantor of success, personal healing, charismatic enthusiasm, social betterment, and psychological fulfillment also crumbles when confronted with monstrous evil. I think the Vietnam experience should teach us this if nothing else.

The only God who remains is the Totally Other, who commands us to empty ourselves in imitation of him who became obedient to the death on the cross. The neon lights of our idolatries fail in the darkness of evil that surrounds the cross. They "don't mean nothin'." To God alone belongs the power to redeem the broken world. Within the shadow of the cross all religious images are illusions and all religious discourse is cheap talk. The one remaining Christian possibility is to bend the knee and to confess that Jesus Christ is Lord, to the glory of God the Father.

Chapter 16

Michael Novak

The Bishops and Soviet Reality

At one time there was no comparison between the strength of the U.S.S.R. and your own. Then it became equal to yours. Now, as all recognize, it is becoming superior to yours. Perhaps today the ratio is just greater than equal, but soon it will be 2 to 1. Then 3 to 1. Finally it will be 5 to 1. . . . With such nuclear superiority it will be possible to block the use of your weapons, and on some unlucky morning they will declare: "Attention. We're sending our troops into Europe, and if you make a move, we will annihilate you." And this ratio of 3 to 1 or 5 to 1 will have its effect: you will not make a move [Aleksandr Solzhenitsyn].

Unlike Solzhenitsyn, the U.S. bishops do not urge the West to rearm itself to meet the present danger. They throw their weight, instead, on the side of those who counsel disarmament. At a moment of maximum danger, they counselled the ways of good will, negotiations, and trust. What if they were wrong? The bishops have, therefore, exercised their right to political judgment. They have committed themselves to a line of thought and action which some applaud and others find terribly mistaken.

History alone will show whether what the bishops declared in their pastoral letter on nuclear deterrence is an act of moral illumination, as some judge, or rather of moral obscurantism and appeasement, as others judge. Bishops in the past have erred. It cannot be said with certainty that, in this case, they have not. But it is not foolish to recognize that such final judgment will depend disproportionately on the deeds of the Soviets.

One major vision of the period 1980–1989 is that it is a moment of clear and present danger for the United States, a period during which the correlation of forces between the Soviet Union and the United States is temporarily in favor of the Soviet Union to a degree never reached before nor likely to be reached again, once America has rearmed itself.

Throughout their letter, the bishops seem to assume that the threat of nuclear war emanates most from American actions; their arguments are couched for American ears. Yet the Soviet Union has a doctrine which imposes on its loyal believers an obligation to make socialism triumph universally. Secondly, the succession of leadership in the U.S.S.R. is still unsettled; the military, KGB, and the Party compete under fragile rules.

First published in *New Catholic World*, 1983, pp. 258–61. Used by permission.

Thirdly, Russian traditions of imperial prerogative gain strength from the Soviet viewpoint that socialism is the tide of history, the Soviet state its vanguard, the Red Army its sword.

SOVIET MILITARY BUILDUP AND ITS POSSIBLE CONSEQUENCES

During the past ten years three fundamental changes have occurred in the correlation of forces between the U.S.S.R. and the U.S.A., which seem to confirm the Soviet vision. (1) After the Cuban missile crisis, Soviet *strategic* nuclear forces made such dramatic leaps forward that they were announced to be at "rough parity" to American strategic forces by the time of the SALT 1 agreements of 1972; since then, they have leapt forward again to several forms of superiority. (2) Soviet *theater* nuclear weapons have placed European cities under the unchecked threat of almost instant annihilation through the SS–20s. (3) Soviet *conventional* forces have reached virtual qualitative parity with Western conventional forces, while retaining enormous advantages in the quantities of tanks, aircraft, and artillery pieces.

The balance of power has been dramatically shifted by these advances. Many forms of military initiative have now passed into Soviet hands. They act; the West reacts.

If one looks at the planet strategically, observing the key pressure points, Soviet assets have grown steadily. The Soviet navy now maintains fleets in the South China Sea (with bases in Vietnam), in the Indian Ocean, and in the Mediterranean Sea, where Western shipping was earlier unchallenged. Moreover, the Soviets maintain armed nuclear submarines near both coasts of the United States and in the Caribbean (with bases in Cuba). The Soviet capacity to cut Africa off from America in the South Atlantic is also growing steadily. Finally, Soviet air and naval power in the North Atlantic can no longer be halted by U.S. forces in Iceland and Greenland. The Soviets have assets where they never had them before.

It is obvious that the bishops pay scant attention to the changed quantity and quality, location and activities of Soviet armed power. In calling for "an end to the arms race" the bishops do not assess the present balance of power or its recent sharp shifts. They judge that peace will become more likely if the United States cuts back military spending and continues on its relative decline vis-à-vis Soviet power. They mention no "present danger" from Soviet arms growth.

One day, in the not too distant future, the advance of Soviet military power may nonetheless awaken the American public as never before. At that point, even the bishops will discover how weak, relative to Soviet military power, the U.S. power has become. The Soviets now have both the strategic potential, which they never had before, and the structural proclivities, of which over the years they have given ample evidence, to expand their military control over any one of many new targets of opportunity. Already in Central America, there is an active legion of East German, Bulgarian, Czech, Russian, Cuban, Libyan, and PLO combatants.

Nor is it difficult to imagine that, by 1990, Iran and Iraq may join Afghanistan as forward bases for Soviet aircraft, intelligence units, and rapid deployment forces.

With adroit boldness, Soviet leadership might also re-negotiate the borders of Poland and East Germany, expanding East German control over the poorly performing industrial cities of Western Poland. Simultaneously, without formal reunification, West and East Germany would be pressured to sign pacts committing both to "disarmament" and "neutralization." Soviet military power would ensure the Swedenization of the strongest nation in NATO.

Moreover, a rising genius in the Soviet military might well argue that the worldwide "correlation of forces" is more in favor of the U.S.S.R. than it has even been, or is likely to be in the future, and that, before the current weapons systems became obsolete they ought to be used to ensure Soviet security for generations to come.

The strategic calculation would run as follows: No U.S. leader will commit U.S. cities to destruction in order to defend Europe. The Soviets could, therefore, force Western Europe to capitulate in one of two ways. The most daring way would be to destroy one European city—perhaps Hamburg—with a sudden rain of SS–20s. According to the U.S. Catholic bishops, no nuclear retaliation by the West would be morally permissible; in any case, no retaliation would be likely. Citizens in the U.S. would be loath to have the scenes from Hamburg, witnessed on television, repeated in Minneapolis–St. Paul. The Soviets would offer a non-aggression pact, holding Soviet troops out of Western Europe. All they would ask in exchange is European disarmament.

In Europe, many on the left already champion European neutralism. Political pressure in this direction would be strengthened by the overwhelming military power of the Soviets, poised for further destruction.

Once Europe had preemptively surrendered in the largest matter, many smaller surrenders would be demanded. Anti-Soviet publications would be considered violations of neutrality. Broadcasting services to Eastern Europe—the Vatican, the B.B.C., Radio Free Europe—would be banned. Anything violating Soviet sovereignty and privilege would be punished. Leaders from European Communist parties would be favored as the most appropriate representatives to send to Moscow for the conduct of trade and other matters. Waves of assassinations of anti-peace leaders would routinely occur and routinely be "deplored" by Moscow. American companies in Europe would be nationalized if possible, often expelled. Anti-American propaganda would gain intensity. The European media would be restricted to friends of peace, neutrality, and solidarity.

This is one scenario. Another would be more brutal. Intent on demonstrating that the Red Army is invincible, the bold Soviet general staff would unleash its full fury on the Northern German Plain, warning that resort to tactical nuclear weapons by NATO would be met by the swift destruction of one city after another by SS–20s. Following Soviet battle doctrine, the Red Army would strike in massed formations, wave after wave, breaking through thin NATO defenses at will in three selected corridors, aiming to reach the Rhine within three weeks.

Fleeing refugees would clog every highway with millions of personal automobiles, making effective reinforcement by conventional arms hopeless. Modern cities being easier than ancient cities to paralyze, ten thousand intelligence officers now under deep cover in Western Germany would move to assigned assaults upon communications and information systems. Almost as swiftly as General Jaruzelski broke the back of Solidarity in a single night, West Germany would be stricken. The negotiated non-aggression pact would provide that all American forces humbly disembark within thirty days.

"PROGRESSIVE DISARMAMENT"?

The lesson to the world would be stark. If NATO cannot resist the Red Army, can Pakistan, Iran, or Saudi Arabia? Can Israel? Concessions everywhere would flow toward Moscow. The Catholic bishops of the U.S. may have read the "signs of the time" correctly. But history may judge them guilty of immense miscalculations.

For talking of peace is a proven Leninist tactic; when the Soviets prepare for war (as in Afghanistan) they invariably launch a "peace offensive." Talking of peace is cheap; and it easily feeds illusions and complacence. It suggests a readiness to surrender without a fight. It may, as it often has, quicken brutal instincts.

In the face of this unprecedented build-up of Soviet military power the bishops place great faith in negotiations. They recommend a "halt" to the further deployment and testing of nuclear weapons. They urge negotiated deep cuts in the nuclear arsenals of both sides. And they call for an "early and successful conclusion of negotiations of a comprehensive test ban treaty." These recommendations derive from the bishops' general principle: "Nuclear deterrence should be used as a step on the way toward progressive disarmament." "Progressive" sounds odd here. Can the bishops possibly mean "progressive" in the generic sense of "socialist"? They cannot mean *unilateral* disarmament, which they say they are against. So they must mean "negotiated" disarmament. But far from being "progressive," disarmament efforts during the last century or so are extremely disheartening. Consider the judgment cited by Barbara Tuchman:

> The trouble with disarmament was (and still is) that the problem of war is tackled upside down and at the wrong end . . . . Nations don't distrust each other because they are armed; they are armed because they distrust each other. And therefore to want disarmament before a minimum of common agreement on fundamentals is as absurd as to want people to go undressed in winter.

Even Theodore Draper, writing in *The New York Review of Books*, is not very encouraging:

> Once different weapons and even different weapons systems must be evaluated and balanced off against each other, negotiations inevitably degenerate into endlessly futile haggling sessions, brought to a close only by agreement on a crazy quilt of trade-offs and loopholes. Negotiations of this sort become more important for the mere consolation that the deadly antagonists are negotiating than for anything the negotiations may bring forth. . . . Short of abolishing all nuclear weapons forever and everywhere, deterrence is all we have.

Has disarmament been "progressive" since the Napoleonic wars? Since the Civil War, or 1914, or 1945? Has the Soviet Union ever disarmed in any respect whatever? After 1968, Defense Secretary McNamara expected that a virtual U.S. nuclear freeze would enable the Soviets to come up to parity and halt. They did not.

Indeed, two major examples of "progressive disarmament" that historians can point to—apart from the enforced disarming of West Germany and Japan following World War II—have been conducted by the U.S. The first was the demobilization of U.S. forces in Europe within eighteen months of the cessation of hostilities, which F. D. Roosevelt rashly promised the unbelieving Stalin at Yalta. The second was the *relative* nuclear disarmament of the U.S. since 1968, under the McNamara illusion of Soviet imitation. Congress after Congress was elected in the 1970s to "cut the defense budget." Indeed, the U.S. budget for defense went *down* by 19 percent in constant 1983 dollars from 1970 until 1983—from $223 billion to $182 billion. Moreover, since 1968, the number of land-based missile launchers has remained constant at 1054. The number of strategic bombers has fallen by attrition from 1364 in 1964 to 316 in 1983. The nuclear warheads in its arsenal have been reduced in number and size. The total throw-weight of all its nuclear warheads has been reduced by more than half.

Oddly, the bishops do not *praise* the United States for such "progressive disarmament." To do so would call attention to the feverish and herculean efforts of the U.S.S.R. to achieve something far beyond nuclear parity (which was publicly declared to exist in 1972): both nuclear and conventional superiority in every field. Here, the bishops enter the field of moral wistfulness. They write: "We must continually say no to the idea of nuclear war." Such words are not like the words of transubstantiation; saying no does not change reality. Nor will "progressive disarmament" occur because the bishops need it in order to justify, by their lights, moral reliance on deterrence. Deterrence is morally obligatory *whether or not* "progressive disarmament" leaps from the world of myth into the world of fact. It will be even more necessary if it does not.

For the bishops assume that the Soviets *will* disarmament. This is a fundamental misunderstanding. Neither the Marxist ideology about the moral *obligation* to use force in history nor the practice of the Soviets since 1917 gives any empirical support to such an assumption. When the U.S. reduced its nuclear forces, the U.S.S.R. could have caught up and rested; it did not. We must assume that the U.S.S.R. does what it wills to do. The U.S.S.R. wills to negotiate nothing except the permanent inferiority of the United States, and a consequent patter of subservience to the "laws of history." This cannot be negotiated in justice.

The world has long had a moral theory about justice in war. A classical statement of moral guidance for justice in negotiations does not yet exist. For it cannot be asserted that all negotiations are morally just. Some negotiations succeed through intimidation; some through cowardice. The ill and dying Roosevelt at Yalta was rude toward Churchill, fawning toward Stalin, and catastrophically unjust to the peoples of Eastern Europe. These same peoples had already suffered more than their share through earlier unjust negotiations, the Molotov-Ribbentrop Pact. Some believe the Helsinki Accords added to the injustice, in as yet unmeasured ways.

Whatever the moral status of particular cases, it seems obvious that negotiations between great powers cannot escape moral scrutiny. The Catholic bishops have given thought to the morality of warfare, but very little to the calculus of moral evils involved inevitably at every negotiation aimed at peace.

Two more examples bear on the point. The "unconditional surrender" imposed by the allies on Germany after World War II was not clearly an act of moral justice. Neither were the negotiations at Versailles at the end of World War I.

In all negotiations, the weaker party may be obliged to accept injustice. One cannot, therefore, as the bishops do, simply judge deterrence by the outcome of negotiations. One must, rather, judge the outcome of negotiations by the power of deterrence. Factors of power are of elementary importance.

Further, the asymmetry between democratic states and totalitarian states *ipso facto* injures the moral standing of negotiations. Democratic peoples reach consensus through public contests, and therefore typically negotiate first against themselves; totalitarian powers wait and watch. (They also penetrate domestic debates within open societies.)

TOTALITARIAN AND DEMOCRATIC DIFFERENCES

Power in totalitarian states rests in the will of a collective few, insulated from public discussion, operating in secrecy, and bound to no moral law but their own aggrandizement. In democratic states, one government is not always like another; public consensus shifts; moral standards and public laws have enormous public power even in compelling presidential resignations. It is difficult, therefore, to imagine wholly moral and just relations between democratic and totalitarian states. Agreements between them can only be codified statements of existing correlations of force and national interest.

Finally, as between democratic and totalitarian powers, the aim of negotiations, once entered into, is quite different. Totalitarian states have no need to reach an agreement. They can be sublimely indifferent. They can concentrate every energy upon one sole aim: increasing their power by every possible degree. For their legitimacy does not flow from the esteem of others but from their own tightly clenched power.

By contrast, once negotiations are entered into by democratic powers, democratic leaders are quickly blamed according to standards of universal reason and moral principle. To come home with "nothing" is for them, but not for totalitarian leaders, a public failure. Consequently, it is relatively easy for totalitarian masters of the dynamics of negotiations to concentrate attention upon cosmetic concessions, amounting to words meaningful only within free, open, and moral societies and having no substance whatever within regimes based upon lies. Furthermore, Western negotiators typically want agreements that are simple, clear, and easy to "verify." They define weapons systems and other military matters in this light, which is often a false light.

In a word, negotiating with a totalitarian power like the Soviet Union can never be like negotiating with partners who share a similar moral vision, intellectual tradition, or common meanings to undergird bare words on documents. The language of such negotiations is, inevitably, like Alice in Wonderland. Typically, too, serious issues are relegated to unsigned appendices and memoranda of understanding, with a proviso that all parties understand them according to their own laws, institutions, customs, and authorities.

From these plain facts, there is a strong case to be made that *any* negotiation with a totalitarian power is *inherently* unjust and, if just, only so by accident, as it suits the totalitarian power. Parchment barriers do not bind those whose power comes from no parchment. "Justice" can have no meaning to a party not bound to it.

"Progressive disarmament" is, therefore, a touching plea. It is a phrase uttered by those who despair of the real-world competition of military power. Giving up *that* struggle, they plead with the stronger power to do likewise. Whatever else it is, this plea is not Christian morality, only a Nietzschean parody thereof.

While negotiations with the Soviets must, for various reasons, go on, they can only be as effective as the military power which bends Soviet will. What Soviet morality compels Soviet will to desire in the absence of constraining force is shown in sixty-six years of bloody history. Since 1923, Soviet authorities have put 65 million of their own citizens to death for political reasons; they have also subjugated some 31 nations.

Indeed, one has only to alter the subject of "progressive disarmament" from "Soviets" to "Nazis" to see the absurdity of identifying religious hope with confidence in the reasonable mercies of totalitarian leaders.

It will be better for all of us if the bishops are correct and I am wrong. But I am fearful that the reverse is true. Just when the West needed a call to disciplined deterrence, the net geopolitical impact of the bishops' letter was to contribute to illusions. The bishops did resist pacifism; that is to their credit. They did not, despite much activism, destroy deterrence; that, too, is to their credit. But they failed to strengthen the clarity of soul necessary to make deterrence work, and that marks a grave religious as well as political failure.

Chapter 17

Robert F. Drinan

Is Nuclear Deterrence Immoral in Catholic Tradition?

. . . If there is questionable validity and viability in the centuries-old norms on a just war, what norms can be utilized in evaluating the morality of a nuclear clash? It may be that Vatican II applied the just-war test and concluded . . . that nuclear war may never be allowed whether it is employed offensively or defensively or on a first- or second-strike basis. The only question left open by Vatican II is whether a nation can morally continue the possession of nuclear weapons that it may not morally use.

That question was addressed by the U.S. Catholic bishops in 1979 when Cardinal John Krol of Philadelphia, testifying officially for the U.S. Catholic Conference on behalf of SALT II before the U.S. Senate, stated:

> Not only the use of strategic nuclear weapons but also the declared intent to use them involved in our deterrence policy is wrong. This explains the Catholic dissatisfaction with nuclear deterrence and the urgency of the Catholic demand that the nuclear arms race be reversed.

The demand for a reversal is urgent, and:

> As long as there is hope of this occurring, Catholic moral theology is willing, while negotiations proceed, to tolerate the possession of nuclear weapons for deterrence as the lesser of two evils. If that hope were to disappear, the moral attitude of the Catholic Church would almost certainly have to shift to one of uncompromising condemnation of both the use and the possession of such weapons.

The only issue still unresolved, therefore, is the nature of the "hope" for reversal of the arms race that justifies the "toleration" of the possession of atomic weapons that can never be used. Will this "toleration" of the lesser evil—that is, the possession of superlethal weapons—cease to be allowed if the greater evil—the threat of attack—becomes more and more dubious? How does one assess the malice in each of these two evils? What if leaders of the Soviet Union expressly state, as they did in 1982, that they will never use the nuclear weapon on a first-strike basis? Those who agree with the Catholic teaching that the use, the threatened use, and the possession of nuclear weapons is immoral must regularly continue to evaluate the depths of the greater evil, since its existence and its threat is the only justification for the possession of the lesser evil.

Cardinal Krol's statement said that Catholics may tolerate the possession of nuclear weapons "while negotiations proceed." There were no negotiations during the first several months of the Reagan administration. Why, moreover, should anyone be able to rely on negotiations when not a single weapon has been destroyed by negotiation in the whole history of the nuclear era?

The United States manufactures three more nuclear weapons each day—1,300 per year. What should Catholics do if an administration announced the cancellation of all negotiations, stating that the Soviets are not willing to bargain in good faith? Even more complicated, what should Catholics do if the Kremlin broke off talks, claiming that the White House was not sincere?

The U.S. Catholic bishops became more concerned with the issue of nuclear war in 1981 for the same reasons that the Western world did. In 1980 President Carter issued Presidential Directive 59, which expanded the range of targets of nuclear weapons beyond the urban-industrial community that had been the focus of strategic planning for two decades. Presidential Directive 59 seemed to modify the previous policy of "mutually assured destruction" by suggesting that nuclear weapons were to be used to win a war and not just for deterrence. In 1981 Vice-President George Bush stated that a nuclear war is "winnable"; at the same time the Pentagon appeared to be preparing to strengthen the offensive capabilities of nuclear strategy.

The European demonstrations against nuclear war undoubtedly aroused the Catholic bishops to a greater concern over America's nuclear policy. The protests in Europe were supported, even initiated, by a wide variety of ecclesiastical and other organizations. The Catholic communities in Europe, along with their bishops, were deeply involved. The religious press in Europe pointed to the responsibility of the Catholics in America as the largest single religious denomination in the nation that started the nuclear madness. One religious periodical noted that at Vatican II 10 percent of the bishops attending came from the United States but that they gave little leadership on the nuclear issue.

For whatever reasons, the Catholic hierarchy in 1981 entered a pilgrimage that might well lead them to an active condemnation of a central premise of America's defense policy. In 1981 over 40 bishops joined in statements vigorously critical of U.S. nuclear policy. In March 1981, 17 bishops, members of Pax Christi, asked Archbishop Joseph Bernardin, chairman of a committee established by the bishops to examine war-peace issues, if there could be any morally justifiable warfare in view of the savagery of modern weaponry. In August Archbishop John Roach of Minneapolis–Saint Paul and chairman of the National Conference of Catholic Bishops, reiterated the conference's previous criticism of the neutron warhead. Also in August Bishop Leroy Matthiesen of Amarillo, Texas, counseled Catholics in his diocese to disengage themselves from work in places in his diocese where nuclear weapons were finally assembled; he was later joined by the 12 Catholic bishops of Texas. In October Archbishop John Quinn of San Francisco supported the nuclear freeze movement—as did at later times 133 of the nation's 280 active bishops. Archbishop Quinn also opposed cooperation in civilian defense measures, since they tend to presume survivability in nuclear war.

In November Archbishop Roach in his presidential address at the annual bishops' meeting declared that the Church must act since the "secular debate is openly discussing the use of limited weapons and winning nuclear wars."

The series of initiatives for peace taken by the bishops in 1981 prompted Monsignor Vincent A. Yzermans, former information director of the U.S. Catholic Conference, to write in the *New York Times* on November 14, 1981, that the episcopal activity on nuclear war was "the most significant revolution within the Catholic Church since Lord Baltimore's contingent of Catholics disembarked on Maryland shores in 1634." He predicted an "explosion between church and state that will make the abortion issue, the school-aid controversy, and the tax-exempt status of churches look like a child's sparklers on the Fourth of July." Summarizing the proliferation of antinuclear episcopal pronouncements in 1981, Richard McCormick, S.J., noted moral theologian, remarked in *Theological Studies* for March 1982 that "religious leaderhip in the United States, especially Catholic, is on a collision course with the U.S. government. That just may be the best thing to happen to both in a long time."

ARCHBISHOP HUNTHAUSEN: UNILATERAL DISARMAMENT

But perhaps the most extraordinary occurrence in 1981 was the endorsement of unilateral disarmament by Archbishop Raymond Hunthausen of Seattle. In a very moving address on June 12 to the Pacific Northwest Synod of the Lutheran church, he expressed regret at not speaking out earlier against nuclear arms and the "nearby construction of the Trident submarine base . . . the first-strike nuclear doctrine which Trident represents." He startled his community and no doubt outraged some by stating that the "Trident is the Auschwitz of Puget Sound."

He acted, he revealed, because "politics is . . . powerless to overcome the demonic in its midst." He cites the words of Christ in Mark (8:34) that persons desirous of following Christ must "take up the cross." To Archbishop Hunthausen "one obvious meaning of the cross is unilateral disarmament." He concedes the force of the argument against this unilateral course but then poses this telling challenge: "To ask one's country to relinquish its security in arms is to encourage risk—a more reasonable risk than constant nuclear escalation—but a risk nevertheless."

He goes on with these moving words: "I am struck by how much more terrified we Americans often are by talk of disarmament than by the march of nuclear war. We whose nuclear arms terrify millions around the globe are terrified by the thought of being without them."

The archbishop concludes his powerful statement by advocating what he himself has done—refusing to pay 50 percent of one's federal taxes as a protest against "nuclear murder and suicide." He is convinced that "our paralyzed political system needs that catalyst. . . ." Finally he lashes out angrily at the government because "it concentrates its efforts on shipping arms to countries which need food" and because "it accords the military an open checkbook while claiming that the assistance to the poor must be slashed in the name of balancing the budget" and because "it devotes most of its time and energy and money to developing war strategy and not peace strategy."

In balancing the risks involved in unilateral disarmament the archbishop appears to come out against the "toleration" of the possession of nuclear arms as the lesser of two evils. He thinks the possession of these lethal weapons to be an evil greater than "constant nuclear escalation." The adverse reaction in Seattle and elsewhere to Archbishop Hunthausen's approach is an indication of the depths of the fears in the psyche of countless Americans and also their self-interest, since, as the archbishop put it in his statement, "our economic policies towards other countries require nuclear weapons."

BISHOPS' PASTORAL LETTER: FIRST DRAFT

The restiveness among American bishops in 1981 led, as has been noted, to the appointment of a committee chaired by Archbishop Bernardin with members that included Thomas Gumbleton, president of Pax Christi USA, Bishop John O'Connor, vicar-general of the Military Ordinariate, and Bishops George Fulcher of Columbus, Ohio, and Daniel Reilly of Norwich, Connecticut. The Conference of Major Superiors of Men and the Leadership Conference of Women Religious were invited to appoint representatives as consultants to the committee. Father J. Bryan Hehir, director of the USCC Office of International Justice and Peace, acted as staff. The committee held fourteen meetings and received the view of a wide variety of witnesses.

The seventy-five-page report of the Bernardin committee is possibly the most complete review of the moral problems of nuclear war ever issued by a Catholic body. It reiterates Vatican II by outlawing all use of nuclear weapons on civilian targets, prohibiting any threatened use, and prohibiting the first use. It allows the use of nuclear weapons only in retaliation for a nuclear attack and then "only in an extremely limited, discriminating manner against military targets."

The sophisticated and nuanced proposed pastoral seeks to appreciate to the utmost the horrors of nuclear war and confesses that "continued reliance on nuclear weapons is fundamentally abhorrent." The pastoral does not "demand unilateral nuclear disarmament by the United States or its allies," but the use of nuclear weapons against an assault brought by conventional warfare is forbidden, since "non-nuclear attacks by another state must be deterred by other than nuclear means." The pastoral repeats the 1976 message of the bishops that not only is it wrong to attack civilian populations, but it is also wrong to threaten to attack them as part of a strategy of deterrence. Indeed the *only* use permitted is the possibility of employing a nuclear weapon—presumably a tactical one—on a retaliatory basis against a specific military target. This one exception has been the most severely criticized recommendation of the pastoral. Most of the critics feel that such a situation could hardly arise and that if it did a conventional weapon would suffice.

The pastoral concedes that if this one exception were not permitted and that if every conceivable use of nuclear weapons were rejected, "we would face the very difficult question whether it is permissible ever to continue to possess nuclear weapons." The pastoral weighs the arguments for and against possession: "Abandonment of nuclear deterrence might invite an attack on the United States . . . other people deny that nuclear deterrence is in fact needed . . . perhaps . . . elimination of our nuclear weapons might, by eliminating what other countries perceived as a threat, actually contribute to, and help point the way towards, more constructive means of achieving security."

The pastoral concludes that these positions "are not subject to positive proof" and that, therefore, "we cannot lightly demand abandonment of possession of all nuclear weapons at this moment." A "temporary toleration" is permitted. *Toleration,* a technical term in Catholic theology, was used prominently in the pre–Vatican II era when the official Catholic position was that in a nation overwhelmingly Catholic the presence of non-Catholic religious bodies could be "tolerated." Toleration of the possession of nuclear weapons, the pastoral insists, is not "a comforting moral judgment" but "an urgent call to efforts to change the present relationship among nuclear powers."

The pastoral openly admits that its acceptance of "toleration" will be controversial:

Some will find toleration of the deterrent too much of a concession; they will urge a posture of disengagement and vigorous protest. Others will find toleration as far as they can go. We do not think the facts are so clear, or the moral imperative so compelling, that we can advance a judgment that is more stringent than toleration of the deterrent. But our tolerations must be conditional upon sincere, substantial efforts to modify current policy as well as ultimately to eliminate these weapons.

The difficulty, of course, is that the norms for improvement are so unclear that "toleration" might continue indefinitely. If the "sincere, substantial efforts" are not successful, is there a moment in time when the nuclear escalation is so dangerous that the "temporary toleration" of the possession of nuclear arms is no longer justifiable?

The pastoral stresses repeatedly its urgent call for reduction in arms and powerfully outlines the need to give economic assistance to the Third World in order to decrease injustice and thereby to promote international stability. The episcopal letter also contains thoughtful suggestions to bring about peace, including a very firm approval of "non-violent resistance," which "deserves a serious place in any positive theology of peace."

The authors of the pastoral make note of the Catholic critics of the bishops' approach and state, without naming William Buckley or Michael Novak, that "some people who have entered the public debate on nuclear warfare . . . appear not to understand or accept some of the clear teaching of the Church as contained in papal and conciliar documents."

The pastoral expressly repudiates the position of the twelve Catholic bishops of Texas by affirming that "we cannot at this time require Catholics who manufacture nuclear weapons, sincerely believing they are enhancing a deterrent capabilty and reducing the likelihood of war, to leave such employment." But the document is silent about Archbishop Hunthausen's counsel to withhold taxes in order to avoid complicity in the nuclear war machine.

Reaction to the pastoral is hard to evaluate, since the document was never officially released and was subsequently withdrawn. But the reactions that the pastoral itself predicted were forthcoming. The sharpest criticism came from Archbishop Philip Hannan from New Orleans, who felt that the possesion of nuclear weapons should be tolerated. Bishop Gumbleton in an interview in the *National Catholic Reporter* on July 30, 1982, admitted that he, as an acknowledged nuclear pacifist, would have preferred a stronger statement but, he felt, this will not happen "until we get to the point where we rule out the possiblity of a just-war theology."

The August 13, 1982 issue of *Commonweal* magazine features the comments of nine Catholics on the draft pastoral. They seem to agree that the statement hovered between nuclear pacifism and a restatement of the just-war theory for a nuclear age. There was general approval of the utopian yearning of the message but serious reservations about its pragmatic compromises. Sister Joan Chittister, past president of the Leadership Conference of Women Religious, calls the document "morally schizophrenic." The position she desires is clear: "Let them say a clear no to nuclear war and the possession and manufacture of nuclear weapons as well."

In an unusual and unique comment, Sister Joan claims that the bishops' failure to be "morally absolute in their repudiation of the manufacture or use of nuclear weapons" undermines their credibility on the abortion issue. Her words are worth noting.

It is troublesome to note that the bishops show no such hesitations or ambivalence about abortion. In that case from a given principle they draw universal and absolute implications with ease. Catholic hospitals may not permit abortions; Catholic doctors may not perform them; Catholic nurses may not assist at them; Catholic monies may not be used to sponsor abortion clinics. Nevertheless, the arguments for abortion are the same: the promotion of a greater good and the deterrence of evil for the parents or for a handicapped child itself, for instance. What is a woman to think? That when life is in the hands of a woman, then to destroy it is always morally wrong, never to be condoned, always a grave and unusual evil? But when life is in the hands of men, millions of lives at one time, all life at one time, then destruction can be theologized and some people's needs and lives can be made more important than other people's needs and lives? It is a theological imperative that we confront this dichotomy.

James Finn, a noted writer on peace issues, praises the bishops because "after more than three decades of the nuclear era, during which time there has accumulated a vast literature almost totally unmarked by contribution from American bishops," the bishops have taken up the responsiblity that is theirs in a nation that is "the principal shaper of Western strategic policies." But Mr. Finn finds some of the moral arguments used by the bishops to be "murky." He seems to prefer a statement from the Holy See made on June 11, 1982, to be more acceptable. It was sent as a message by Pope John Paul II to the UN disarmament session:

In current conditions, "deterrence" based on balance, certainly not as an end in itself but as a step in the way towards progressive disarmament, may still be judged morally acceptable. Nonetheless in order to ensure peace it is indispensable not to be satisfied with this minimum, which is always susceptible to the real danger of explosion.

Gordon C. Zahn, a veteran peace activist who was a conscientious objector during World War II, sees in the pastoral a "troubled ambivalence and a yearning for a compromise on essentially irreconcilable issues." He fears that the document will fail to inspire and that "even the slightest indication of willingness to condone the possession and production of weapons that are admittedly immoral to use or even to threaten to use can only undermine the credibility of the entire document."

Father Charles Curran, professor of moral theology at Catholic University, perceptively points out the ambiguity in the nature of the evil that the pastoral "tolerates." Is the evil that is tolerated the intention to threaten population centers? If so, is this different from the concept of toleration as used by Catholic moral theologians in the past? If the evil that is tolerated is one's own evil intentions, then there is "a new proposal in Catholic ethical thought." If, on the other hand, the evil that is tolerated is the possession of those weapons, there is a question whether the possession, absent an intention to use them, will really deter. Father Curran avers to the point mentioned by Father McCormick in the article referred to above where he states that distinctions between possession and use "are regarded as quaint by policy makers." Policy makers who possess weapons intend to use them. Consequently, "there is no such thing, at the present time and realistically, as having nuclear weapons with no intention to use them." As a result, Father McCormick concludes, "it is this that makes the case against mere possession of such weapons so powerful."

Only one of the commentators in *Commonweal* feels that the pastoral distorts reality. "The letter misrepresents the mainline of American nuclear strategy," says Philip Odeen, a former assistant secretary of defense and a professional defense planner. Mr. Odeen asserts that "the focus of our strategy and targeting is Soviet military power not Soviet population." As a result, he feels that the pastoral accepts a "caricature of mutual assured destruction," followed in the United States, he suggests, by "a small minority on the right pushing 'war-winning' approaches. . . . "

Most of the comments in *Commonweal* and elsewhere generally credit the pastoral with coming up with the least unsatisfactory treatment possible of an intractable topic. But no one is very certain what the next steps are or where the bishops go from here.

OTHER NATIONAL HIERARCHIES

Clearly, the entire worldwide Church is watching to see what America's bishops will do. This is particularly true for the Catholic bishops within the NATO Alliance, where their flocks are protected by the nuclear umbrella.

The opinions of these bishops are summarized in a fascinating article in the September 1982 issue of *Theological Studies* by Francis X. Winters, S.J., an articulate writer on nuclear issues and professor of moral theology at Georgetown University. The Canadian bishops are the most militant nuclear pacifists in the West. In a statement in February 1982 they "advocated the dismantling of nuclear weapons installations in Canada, the discontinuation of Canadian manufacture of component parts of nuclear weapons," and a reexamination of Canada's role in NATO.

England's hierarchy, however, has not advanced beyond what Vatican II said about nuclear war—although Cardinal Basil Hume of Westminster has given eloquent leadership to the issue, as has Anglican Archbishop Robert Runcie. But they neither counsel unilateral nuclear disarmament nor condemn the possession of the bomb. The bishops of Scotland appear firmer than their English counterparts in condemning all use of the nuclear weapon and protest the fact that the momentous decisions about retaliations are left exclusively to government officials.

A statement in June 1982 made jointly by the French and German hierarchies speaks copiously about any alteration in the policies on nuclear deterrence. Ironically, it was members of the French hierarchy more than any other group that urged nuclear pacifism at Vatican II. These efforts to bring the Church to a radical stand were countered by some American bishops—a group that now, after the Canadians, may be the strongest anti-nuclear critics in the Catholic world.

Neither the Dutch nor Belgian hierarchies have spoken about the morality of nuclear deterrence. The Belgian Bishops Conference issued a statement in 1978 summarizing previous papal and conciliar pronouncements on the topic. Both this group and the bishops of the Netherlands are preparing new statements, but it does not seem likely that either group will advance beyond Vatican II.

Father Winters concludes his excellent survey by reminding us that "the urgency to pass judgment on the doctrine of assured destruction weighs more heavily on the American church than on any other." The reasons for this are clear—the Americans are the only ones that ever used the nuclear weapon and they are the principals in keeping nuclear threats credible.

BISHOPS' PASTORAL LETTER: SECOND DRAFT

In November 1982, the Catholic bishops discussed a second draft of their proposed pastoral on the moral aspects of nuclear warfare. Critical comments on the first draft from both the "hawks" and "doves" did little to alter the basic approach of the pastoral. Dropped, however, was the passage that conceded the possiblity of a morally permissible attack by a nuclear weapon on a first-strike basis against a military installation. The language about deterrence and the possession of the nuclear bomb being the lesser of two evils was also eliminated. The language about "toleration" of the possession of nuclear weapons was altered. But the general thrust of the overall approach was not changed in any significant way. The twenty-five-thousand-word pastoral was, however, perceived by many to be strengthened or, at least, made more specific. Indeed, it was so specific that the White House sent a seven-page letter of protest to each of the bishops. What appeared to annoy the Reagan Administration the most was the failure of the bishops' statement even to mention the President's program for arms reduction— START. The White House letter authored by William Clark, a Catholic who is national security advisor to the President, insisted that the bishops misunderstood the Reagan approach to arms control.

The bishops forthrightly stood their ground against the contentions of the White House. The exchange of views could not be described exactly as a confrontation, but widespread comments throughout the nation showed that the position of the Catholic bishops was perceived to be a challenge to one of the fundamental premises of U.S. foreign policy since the early 1950's—the reliance on nuclear weapons as an essential component of America's military strategy.

Final approval of the bishops' statement, the text of which appeared in the *National Catholic Reporter* for November 5, 1982, is scheduled for May 1983. Some refinements on the statement may be made by that time, but the essential thrust of it will remain basically unchanged. That thrust is not essentially different from the position of America's Protestant churches or of other church-related bodies around the world. (The major statements made by religious groups on nuclear warfare are gathered together in the 1982 volume edited by Robert Heyer entitled *Nuclear Disarmament—Key Statements of Popes, Bishops, Councils and Churches.)*

Comments in large part critical of the draft pastoral of the American bishops will continue to appear. In *Theological Studies* for December 1982, David Hollenback, S.J., a moral theologian, offers arguments on behalf of the case against the morality of possession for the sake of deterrence. More and more the Catholic bishops will feel required to follow the path of either the nuclear pacifist Pax Christi, to which a minority of them belong, or the position that possession for the sake of deterrence can be "tolerated." There will, of course, be the tendency and the temptation to forget about the agonizing questions involved in the nuclear issue. And this course may be possible depending upon events and developments. But if the nuclear freeze movement continues in some altered form, and if the scientists, the physicians, and the lawyers continue to command public attention, the Catholic bishops will not be able to lapse into silence or to simply reissue previous proclamations.

Is it entirely fanciful to hope and pray that in God's providence that Catholic bishops in America may provide the moral and metaphysical framework by which the United States could extricate itself from the moral morass that it has created for itself? Can we dare to hope that the bishops, relying on a well-developed Catholic doctrine on the morality of war, might join an alliance with most religious groups in the nation and bring forth a consensus that would allow America to end the nuclear age, which it alone created?

This is a fanciful hope, of course, in the sense that the elements of that consensus have yet not been identified. That consensus must bring together a new hope and a deeper faith that can overcome the fear that for almost forty years Americans have had of the Soviets and the communists. That fear is profound, pervasive, and perhaps paranoid.

Chapter 18

Thomas Merton

Truth and Violence

. . . this is no longer a time of systematic ethical speculation for such speculation implies time to reason, and the power to bring social and individual action under the concerted control of reasoned principles upon which most men agree.

There is no time to reason out, calmly and objectively, the moral implications of technical developments which are perhaps already superseded by the time one knows enough to reason about them.

Action is not governed by moral reason but by political expediency and the demands of technology—translated into the simple abstract formulas of propaganda. These formulas have nothing to do with reasoned moral action, even though they may appeal to apparent moral values—they simply condition the mass of men to react in a desired way to certain stimuli.

Men do not agree in moral reasoning. They concur in the emotional use of slogans and political formulas. There is no persuasion but that of power, of quantity, of pressure, of fear, of desire. Such is our present condition—and it is critical!

Bonhoeffer wrote, shortly before his death at the hands of the Nazis, that moral theorizing was outdated in such a time of crisis—a time of villains and saints, and of Shakespearian characters:

> The villain and the saint have little to do with systematic ethical studies. They emerge from the primeval depths and by their appearance they tear open the infernal or the divine abyss from which they come and enable us to see for a moment into mysteries of which they had never dreamed.

And the peculiar evil of our time, Bonhoeffer continues, is to be sought not in the sins of the good, but in the apparent virtues of the evil. A time of confirmed liars who tell the truth in the interest of what they themselves are—liars. A hive of murderers who love their children and are kind to their pets. A hive of cheats and gangsters who are loyal in pacts to do evil. Ours is a time of evil which is so evil that it can do good without prejudice to its own iniquity—it is no longer threatened by goodness.

Such is Bonhoeffer's judgment of a world in which evil appears in the form of probity and righteousness. In such a time the moral theorist proves himself a perfect fool by

First published in *Conjectures of a Guilty Bystander* (Garden City, N.Y., Image Books, 1968), pp. 65–66, 78–81. Used by permission.

142

taking the "light" at its face value and ignoring the abyss of evil underneath it. For him, as long as evil takes a form that is theoretically "permitted," it is good. He responds mentally to the abstract moral equation. His heart does not detect the ominous existential stink of moral death. . . .

We live in crisis, and perhaps we find it interesting to do so. Yet we also feel guilty about it, as if we *ought not to be* in crisis. As if we were so wise, so able, so kind, so reasonable, that crisis ought at all times to be unthinkable. It is doubtless this "ought," this "should" that makes our era so interesting that it cannot possibly be a time of wisdom, or even of reason. We think we know what we ought to be doing, and we see ourselves move, with the inexorable deliberation of a machine that has gone wrong, to do the opposite. A most absorbing phenomenon which we cannot stop watching, measuring, discussing, analyzing, and perhaps deploring! But it goes on. And, as Christ said over Jerusalem, we do not know the things that are for our peace. . . .

We are all convinced that we desire the truth above all. Nothing strange about this. It is natural to man, an intelligent being, to desire the truth. (I still dare to speak of man as "an intelligent being"!) But actually, what we desire is not "the truth" so much as "to be in the right." To seek the pure truth for its own sake may be natural to us, but we are not able to act always in this respect according to nature. What we seek is not the pure truth, but the partial truth that justifies our prejudices, our limitations, our selfishness. This is not "the truth." It is only an argument strong enough to prove us "right." And usually our desire to be right is correlative to our conviction that somebody else (perhaps everybody else) is wrong.

Why do we want to prove them wrong? Because we need them to be wrong. For if they are wrong, and we are right, then our untruth becomes truth: our selfishness becomes justice and virtue: our cruelty and lust cannot be fairly condemned. We can rest secure in the fiction we have determined to embrace as "truth." What we desire is not the truth, but rather that our lie should be proved "right," and our iniquity be vindicated as "just." This is what we have done to pervert our natural, instinctive appetite for truth.

No wonder we hate. No wonder we are violent. No wonder we exhaust ourselves in preparing for war! And in doing so, of course, we offer the enemy another reason to believe that *he* is right, that he must arm, that he must get ready to destroy us. Our own lie provides the foundation of truth on which he erects his own lie, and the two lies together react to produce hatred, murder, disaster.

Is there any vestige of truth left in our declaration that we think for ourselves? Or do we even trouble to declare this any more? Perhaps the man who says he "thinks for himself" is simply one who does not think at all. Because he has no fully articulate thoughts, he thinks he has his own incommunicable ideas. Or thinks that, if he once set his mind to it, he could have his own thoughts. But he just has not got around to doing this. I wonder if "democracies" are made up entirely of people who "think for themselves" in the sense of going around with blank minds which they imagine they *could* fill with their own thoughts if need be.

Well, the need has been desperately urgent, not for one year or ten, but for fifty, sixty, seventy, a hundred years. If, when thought is needed, nobody does any thinking, if everyone assumes that someone else is thinking, then it is clear that no one is thinking either for himself or for anybody else. Instead of thought, there is a vast, inhuman void full of words, formulas, slogans, declarations, echoes—ideologies! You can always reach out and help yourself to some of them. You don't have to reach at all. Appropriate echoes already rise up in your mind—they are "yours." You realize of course that these are not yet "thoughts." Yet we "think" these formulas, with which the void in our hearts is provisionally entertained, can for the time being "take the place of thoughts"—while the computers make decisions for us.

Nothing can take the place of thoughts. If we do not think, we cannot act freely. If we do not act freely, we are at the mercy of forces which we never understand, forces which are arbitrary, destructive, blind, fatal to us and to our world. If we do not use our minds to think with, we are heading for extinction, like the dinosaur: for the massive physical strength of the dinosaur became useless, purposeless. It led to his destruction. Our intellectual power can likewise become useless, purposeless. When it does, it will serve only to destroy us. It will devise instruments for our destruction, and will inexorably proceed to use them. . . . It has already devised them.

Thinking men. Better still, *right-thinking* men! Who are they? The right-thinking man has an instinctive flair for the words and formulas that are most acceptable to his group: and in fact he is partly responsible for making them acceptable. He is indeed a man of timely ideas, opportune ideas.

He is the man whose formulas are replacing the outworn formulas of the year before. And no doubt the formulas of the year before were his also: they were the ones with which he supplanted the formulas of two years ago, which perhaps were his too. The right-thinking man has a knack of expressing, and indeed of discovering, the attitudes that everyone else is unconsciously beginning to adopt. He is the first one to become conscious of the new attitude, and he helps others to become aware of it in themselves. They are grateful to him. They respect him. They listen to his utterances. He is their prophet, their medicine man, their shaman. They talk like him, they act like him, they dress like him, they look like him. And all this brings them good luck. They despise and secretly fear others who have different formulas, dress differently, act differently, speak differently.

Fortunately, though, all right-thinking men think the same these days. At least all who belong to the same tribal society. Even those who do not conform are in their own way a justification of the right-thinking man: the beatnik is necessary to make the square unimpeachably respectable.

The right-thinking men are managers, leaders, but not eggheads. Hence they can be believed. They can justify any wrong road, and make it seem the *only* road. They can justify everything, even the destruction of the world.

Gandhi saw that Western democracy was on *trial*. On trial for what? On trial to be judged by its own claims to be the rule of the people by themselves. Not realizing itself to be on trial, assuming its own infallibility and perfection, Western democracy has resented every attempt to question these things. The mere idea that it might come under judgment has seemed absurd, unjust, diabolical. Our democracy is now being judged, not by man but by God. It is not simply being judged by the enemies of the West and of "democracy." When anyone is judged by God, he receives, in the very hour of judgment, a gift from God. The gift that is offered him, in his judgment, is *truth*. He can receive the truth or reject it; but in any case truth is being offered silently, mercifully, in the very crisis by which democracy is put to the test. For instance, the problem of integration.

When one is on trial in this life, he is at the same time receiving mercy: the merciful opportunity to anticipate God's decision by receiving the light of truth, judging himself, changing his life. Democracy has been on trial in Berlin, in Alabama, in Hiroshima. In World War II. In World War I. In the Boer War. In the American Civil War. In the Opium

War. What have we learned about ourselves? What have we seen? What have we admitted? What is the truth about us? Perhaps we still have time, still have a little light to see by. But the judgment is getting very dark. . . . The truth is too enormous, too ominous, to be seen in comfort. Yet it is a great mercy of God that so many of us can recognize this fact, and that we are still allowed to *say* it.

PART THREE

BLACK AND MEXICAN-AMERICAN THEOLOGIES

At least since the time of St. Anselm, theology has been described as "faith seeking understanding." A more apt description of black theology might be "experience seeking understanding."

With all their diversity, black theologians unanimously and repeatedly emphasize how their theology grows directly out of the black experience in America. No doubt much of the experience to which they refer is from recent decades (the black power movement of the 1960s for James Cone, for example). But they also insist that the experience from which they draw is deep and textured, going back to and beyond slavery itself. This emphasis on experience is itself theological. The very criteria of faith are the truths that have been laboriously uncovered in field, factory, home, street. The church, university, and seminary have their roles, but these roles are secondary and derivative.

It is the task of the churchperson and academic to articulate the more fundamental experience of the black community. All the writers included in this section go to great pains to express and clarify that experience. Some commentators, like Vincent Harding (not represented here), range across the entire history of blacks in America in striving to define the nature of that experience.

If there is a single expression that best describes what has emerged theologically from the black experience it is perhaps "a sense of humanity." Or perhaps "a deeper, fuller sense of humanity." Blacks have been forced to probe this notion and in the process their theology has taken on new emphases. In this humanity, we can detect some of the following qualities:

• Profound humiliation: having to absorb that white society has judged one to be something less than human.

• Self-esteem: realizing that no one can take away one's basic dignity when one is prepared to hold onto it and assert it.

• Determination to struggle: understanding that only resistance and courage can overcome the debasement that is the result of deep-seated bigotry.

• Hope: grasping that one *can* overcome, one *will* overcome.

Religious categories (such as "the divine") are not alternatives to this perception of humanity, but emerge within its context. God, Jesus, the cross, the Holy Spirit, the Bible, and the church: all are seen, indeed felt, with a special vividness and intensity. They are both very real and very liberating: very real *because* liberating, liberating *because* they are real. And because black theology *is* experiential, it shares certain advantages of Evangelical and liberal theologies. With the Evangelicals, it insists on the directness and immediacy of revelation. Yet it avoids fundamentalism. With the liberals, it stresses the humane and reformative nature of Christian belief. Unlike liberalism, though, it avoids the tendency to fall into abstractions. We might wish to describe black theology as relevant—except that the very word "relevance" smacks of a white, middle-

147

class society straining to make its religion and theology come alive. In contrast, the best of black theology has a remarkable vitality. It possesses this simply because it is close to the lives of blacks—where they have been, where they are going.

Selections in this section range from Cone's reflections on black power and Christianity, one of the early landmarks in black theology, to the opening of new ground by the young philosopher and theologian Cornel West. As West himself points out,[1] Cone's work is situated at the onset of a particularly creative period of black theology, one in which the very terms "black theology" and "theology of liberation" first gained wide currency in the United States.

Cone's *Black Theology and Black Power* remains a significant statement for both black and white Christians, despite the near demise of the term "black power." The book still percolates with the righteous anger that boiled over in the black power movement of the 1960s.

Albert Cleage's *The Black Messiah*, which was published just before *Black Theology and Black Power*, made it clear that not all blacks are satisified with a political strategy that rests on gradualism and nonviolence. Black consciousness consists in more than self-assertion and the retrieval of all that is valuable in black history and black culture. It must also locate and reject all that represents enslavement, racism, the dehumanization of the black person. To that extent, blacks can be authentic only if they emphatically say no. To that extent, Brother Malcolm was more representative of contemporary blacks than was Brother Martin (Luther King). As Cleage has made clear, Malcolm X's struggle was one against almost impossible odds. At least Jesus walked in a world prepared for a Messiah. Such was not the case for Malcolm. Black theology should include the perspective of disillusionment, even despair. Perhaps one of the truths that Cleage underlines with his provocative title *The Black Messiah* is that if Jesus was not black, he *should* have been; in a society divided between white and black, he *would* have been.

Cone's early work reflects some of the same anger, but he works in a more explicitly theological framework. The norms for this theology, though, are somewhat different from prevailing theologies of the past. What is more real, most truth-full for the contemporary black, is not the Bible itself, but the black experience. At its heart, this experience is one of encounter with oppression and struggle against that oppression. Thus the move to "black power." It is in the light of this experience that black Christians read the Bible and approach the person of Jesus. They are able, therefore, to see him as liberator and his work as liberation. There is no contradiction between the black movements of the 1960s and the gospel.

Cone's later work is both an extension and a development of these themes. In another chapter on Christ, in *The God of the Oppressed*, he reiterates that the Bible and specifically Jesus Christ can be seen as already anticipated in the lives of black Americans. Now, however, Cone gives us an added theological dimension with which we can formalize this correspondence. For the black, there is a past, present, and future aspect to Christ. The past is the gritty humanity of Jesus, always very real in black culture and especially in evidence in the spirituals. The present is the Jesus vibrantly alive in the current struggles of American blacks (and also appealed to in song). The future is bound up with the hope for liberation: not the general, rather philosophical hope discussed at length by European theologians, but the hope that has appeared over and over in black life (again, particularly in the spiritual).

Cornel West sees himself at the beginning of a new stage in black theology. As he describes it, the first three stages were efforts to cope with the dominant white culture (as represented by slavery, segregation, and white theology itself). The fourth stage takes a more global perspective; it views the situation of blacks against the backdrop of

American capitalism and American imperialism. Inevitably, black theologians will take more seriously the work of Marx and of certain Marxists, notably Antonio Gramsci— which is not at all to say that they should remain uncritical of Marx or Marxists. Indeed, it is precisely the total reliance of Marxists upon a particular historical self-projection that Christians *must* remain critical of. Also, insofar as Marxism has remained aloof from popular culture and values, it has proven elitist—and historically impotent. Still, the two perspectives have much to offer one another, and the black theologian ought to be willing to explore their intersection.[2]

Black theologians are particularly sensitive to the story of America, to American history and American cultural geography. The desire to integrate a vision of America with Christian perceptions is not something new with blacks. But blacks place a particular emphasis on the need to create a new America. The black vision necessarily excludes much of the "old America," for that America has not only excluded blacks, but systematically debased them. Still, blacks are fundamentally in harmony with wider American themes of creativity and development, of inclusion and opportunity. As Vincent Harding views it, black spirituals, black revival movements, "back-to-Africa" movements, black Islam, even the Father Divine cult were all manifestations of this need to carve out a "new America," a "Second Coming of America." Blacks do not spend a great deal of energy fighting or attempting to transcend patriotism or "Americanism," even though these attitudes can indeed be destructive. Blacks are striving for a new, more Christian vision of this land that will force their white compatriots to reevaluate their own understanding of America. Whites, too, need a more open homeland, where the creativity of blacks can be utilized. An exclusively white America will not in fact survive in a nonwhite world; white America requires blacks.[3]

This theme of the white need for a black theology appears in the article by Robert Osborne. All liberation theologies bring out a fundamental dimension of Christianity, and indeed of the Bible. God's word *delivers* us from oppression. Often the greatest difficulty is to recognize that we need such a deliverance. This is particularly so when we are also oppressors. Then we must turn to the group in our society that is most obviously oppressed. For American whites, this is clearly the black community. In finding their way *out of* oppression, in rejecting despair, blacks speak to whites. As Osborne puts it, it is not that whites must adopt black theology, but the presence of black theology makes possible a genuine, a whole white theology.

Cheryl Townsend shows us one of the ways in which the black experience can instruct the white. Taking from R.D. Laing the notion of "asylum," she suggests that blacks have found in the church a place where they can truly express, articulate suffering. The "Balm in Gilead" is also a curative ointment in a cruel oppressive world. This does not make the black church a place for escape; it transforms it into an environment where I can both be myself and find myself. Far from being druglike or opiumlike, this experience of unburdening and expressing one's woes leads to new life and new determination. The language of "rebirth" and "redemption" now reflects an intensely personal experience. One can go on because one has *named* one's troubles, looked them in the face—and not been defeated.

Joseph Bethea also reminds us to what extent the black experience has been a church experience. Only in those modest clapboard or brick churches could blacks stay in touch with their African past. This requirement not to reject experiences was one of the reasons for the sometimes "unruly" character of black worship: hand-clapping, shouting, dancing. More to the point, black worship has been *the* way in which blacks have celebrated and affirmed life, themselves, God. The "formalities" taken for granted in white churches may not be present here; black worship has its own forms or structures, directly related to this goal of life-affirmation. The key to these structures is black preaching, which is at the very core of black worship. The "story" of the Lord is told, and in this story blacks begin to recognize themselves. Bethea is not trying to idealize black religion. What he wishes us to see is how blacks can find and have found a life-giving word, even while living in grinding hardship. They have done so precisely by *not* running away from the realities of the here and now. We can all learn from this combination of realism and hope.

This section concludes with a piece that briefly exhibits Hispanic-American, or more exactly Mexican-American, theology. Virgilio Elizondo's reflections arise from a sense of *mestizaje*—the realization of descent from two disparate peoples. One of the things this leads to *religiously* is an intense devotion to the cross and to a reverence for Good Friday, best represented by the living Way of the Cross. To the Nordic mind, this Hispanic interest in the death of Jesus often appears morbid, but that is because this same mind fails to see the connection with the Mexican-American love of *fiesta*. As Elizondo sees it, the Mexican faith in resurrection and triumphant life becomes focused in the remembrance and honoring of *la Morenita*, Our Lady of Guadalupe.

These few pages are included here to remind us that black theology, while probably the most advanced of indigenous American theologies, is hardly the only possible one. Others include Amerindian, Hispanic-American, and Asian-American (each with numerous subdivisions). But does not this emphasis on particularity fragment the unity of the Christian community? Only if we see the embodiment of Christianity within a particular culture as scandalous. And if we do, we probably have not recognized to what extent Christianity long ago became adapted to European and, later, North American modes of thought.

NOTES

1. Cornel West, *Prophesy Deliverance!* (Philadelphia, Westminster, 1982) 103.

2. West prefers "dialectics" to "perspectives."

3. Vincent Harding, "Out of the Cauldron of Struggle: Black Religion and the Search for a New America," *Soundings*, 61 (1978) 339–54.

Chapter 19

James H. Cone

The Gospel of Jesus, Black People, and Black Power

One thing is clear. The damnation of the rich
is as lucid as the promise to the hungry.
Albert van den Heuvel

Contemporary theology from Karl Barth to Jürgen Moltmann conceives of the theological task as one which speaks from within the covenant community with the sole purpose of making the gospel meaningful to the times in which men live. While the gospel itself does not change, every generation is confronted with new problems, and the gospel must be brought to bear on them. Thus, the task of theology is to show what the changeless gospel means in each new situation.

On the American scene today, as yesterday, one problem stands out: the enslavement of black Americans. But as we examine what contemporary theologians are saying, we find that they are silent about the enslaved condition of black people. Evidently they see no relationship between black slavery and the Christian gospel.[1] Consequently there has been no sharp confrontation of the gospel with white racism. There is, then, a desperate need for a *black theology*, a theology whose sole purpose is to apply the freeing power of the gospel to black people under white oppression.

In more sophisticated terms this may be called a theology of revolution.[2] Lately there has been much talk about revolutionary theology, stemming primarily from non-Western religious thinkers whose identification lies with the indigenous oppressed people of the land.[3] These new theologians of the "Third World" argue that Christians should not shun violence but should initiate it, if violence is the only means of achieving the much needed rapid radical changes in life under dehumanizing systems. They are not confident, as most theologians from industrialized nations seem to be, that changes in the economic structure (from agrarian to industrial) of a country will lead to changes in its oppressive power-structure. (America seems to be the best indication that they are probably correct.) Therefore their first priority is to change the structures of power.

The present work seeks to be revolutionary in the sense that it attempts to bring to theology a special attitude permeated with black consciousness. It asks the question, What does the Christian gospel have to say to powerless black men whose existence is threatened daily by the insidious tentacles of white power? Is there a message from Christ to the countless number of blacks whose lives are smothered under white society? Unless theology can become "ghetto theology," a theology which speaks to black people, the gospel message has no promise of life for the black man—it is a lifeless message.

Unfortunately, even black theologians have, more often than not, merely accepted the problems defined by white theologians. Their treatment of Christianity has been shaped by the dominant ethos of the culture. There have been very few, if any, radical, revolutionary approaches to the Christian gospel for oppressed blacks. There is, then, a need for a theology whose sole purpose is to emancipate the gospel from its "whiteness" so that blacks may be capable of making an honest self-affirmation through Jesus Christ.[4]

This work further seeks to be revolutionary in that "The fact that I am Black is my ultimate reality."[5] My identity with *blackness*, and what it means for millions living in a white world, controls the investigation. It is impossible for me to surrender this basic reality for a "higher, more universal" reality. Therefore, if a higher, Ultimate Reality is to have meaning, it must relate to the very essence of blackness. Certainly, white Western Christianity with its emphasis on individualism and capitalism as expressed in American Protestantism is unreal for blacks. And if Christianity is not real for blacks who are seeking black consciousness through the elements of Black Power, then they will reject it.

Unfortunately, Christianity came to the black man through white oppressors who demanded that he reject his concern for this world as well as his blackness and affirm the next world and whiteness. The black intellectual community, however, with its emphasis on black identity, is becoming increasingly suspicious of Christianity because the oppressor has used it as a means of stifling the oppressed concern for present inequities. Naturally, as the slave questions his existence as a slave, he also questions the religion of the enslaver. "We must," writes Maulana Ron Karenga, "concern ourselves more with this life which has its own problems. For the next life across Jordan is much further away from the growl of the dogs and policemen and the pains of hunger and disease."[6]

Therefore, it is appropriate to ask: Is it possible for men to be *really* black and still feel any identity with the biblical tradition expressed in the Old and the New Testaments? Is it possible to strip the gospel as it had been interpreted of its "whiteness," so that its real message will become a live option for radical advocates of black consciousness? Is there any relationship at all between the work of God and the activity of the ghetto? Must black people be forced to deny their identity in order to embrace the Christian faith?[7] Finally, is Black Power . . . compatible with the Christian faith, or are we dealing with two utterly divergent perspectives? These are hard questions. To answer these questions, however, we need to discuss, first, the gospel of Jesus as it relates to black people.

WHAT IS THE GOSPEL OF JESUS?

Christianity begins and ends with the man Jesus—his life, death, and resurrection. He is the Revelation, the special disclosure of God to man, revealing who God is and what his purpose for man is. In short, Christ is the essence of Christianity. Schleiermacher was not far wrong when he said that "Christianity is essentially distinguished from other faiths by the fact that everything in it is related to the redemption accomplished by Jesus of Nazareth."[8] In contrast to many other religions, Christianity revolves around a Person, without whom its existence ceases to be.

For this very reason Christology is made the point of departure in Karl Barth's *Church Dogmatics*. According to Barth, all theological talk about God, man, church, etc., must inevitably proceed from Jesus Christ, who is the sole criterion for every Christian utterance. To talk of God or of man without first talking about Jesus Christ is to engage in idle, abstract words which have no relation to the Christian experience of revelation. Therefore Barth is best known for his relentless, devastating attack on natural theology, which seeks knowledge of God through reason alone, independent of Jesus Christ. Whether one agrees with Barth or not regarding natural theology, he is at least right about what makes Christianity Christian. Wolfhart Pannenberg puts it this way:

> All theological statements win their Christian character only through their con-
> nection with Jesus. It is precisely Christology that discusses and establishes the
> justification and the appropriate form of theological reference to Jesus in a
> methodological way. Therefore, theology can clarify its Christian self-
> understanding only by a thematic and comprehensive involvement with the
> christological problems.[9]
> Its teaching about Jesus Christ lies at the heart of every Christian theology.[10]
> As Christians we know God only as he has been revealed in and through Jesus.
> All other talk about God can have, at most, provisional significance.[11]

One has only to read the gospel to be convinced of the central importance of Jesus Christ in the Christian faith. According to the New Testament, Jesus is the man for others who views his existence as inextricably tied to other men to the degree that his own Person is inexplicable apart from others. The others, of course, refer to all men, especially the oppressed, the unwanted of society, the "sinners." He is God himself coming into the very depths of human existence for the sole purpose of striking off the chains of slavery, thereby freeing man from ungodly principalities and powers that hinder his relationship with God. Jesus himself defines the nature of his ministry in these terms:

> The Spirit of the Lord is upon me,
> because he has anointed me to preach good news to the poor.
> He has sent me to proclaim release to the captives
> and recovering of sight to the blind,
> to set at liberty those who are oppressed,
> to proclaim the acceptable year of the Lord.
> Luke 4:18–19, RSV

Jesus' work is essentially one of liberation. Becoming a slave himself, he opens realities of human existence formerly closed to man. Through an encounter with Jesus, man now knows the full meaning of God's action in history and man's place within it.

The Gospel of Mark describes the nature of Jesus' ministry in this manner: "The time is fulfilled, the kingdom of God is at hand; repent and believe in the Gospel" (1:14–15). On the face of it, this message appears not to be too radical to our twentieth-century ears, but this impression stems from our failure existentially to bridge the gap between modern man and biblical man. Indeed, the message of the Kingdom strikes at the very center of man's desire to define his own existence in the light of his own interest at the price of his brother's enslavement. It means the irruption of a new age, an age which has to do with God's action in history on behalf of man's salvation. It is an age of liberation, in which "the blind receive their sight, the lame walk, the lepers are cleansed, the deaf hear, the dead are raised up, the poor have the good news preached to them" (Luke 7:22). This is not pious talk, and one does not need a seminary degree to interpret the message. It is a message about the ghetto, and all other injustices done in the name of democracy and religion to further the social, political, and economic interests of the oppressor.

In Christ, God enters human affairs and takes sides with the oppressed. Their suffering becomes his; their despair, divine despair. Through Christ the poor man is offered freedom now to rebel against that which makes him other than human.

It is ironical that America with its history of injustice to the poor (especially the black man and the Indian) prides itself as being a Christian nation. (Is there really such an animal?) It is even more ironic that officials within the body of the Church have passively and actively participated in these injustices. With Jesus, however, the poor were at the heart of his mission: "The last shall be first and the first last" (Matt. 20:16). That is why he was always kind to traitors, adulterers, and sinners and why the Samaritan in the parable came out on top. Speaking of Pharisees (the religious elite of his day), Jesus said: "Truly I say to you, the tax collectors [traitors] and harlots go into the kingdom—but not you" (Matt. 21:31).[12] Jesus had little toleration for the middle- or upper-class religious snob whose attitude attempted to usurp the sovereignty of God and destroy the dignity of the poor.

The Kingdom is for the poor and not the rich because the former has nothing to expect from the world while the latter's entire existence is grounded in his commitment to worldly things. The poor man may expect everything from God, while the rich man may expect nothing because he refuses to free himself from his own pride. It is not that poverty is a precondition for entrance into the Kingdom. But those who recognize their utter dependence on God and wait on him despite the miserable absurdity of life are typically the poor, according to Jesus.

The Kingdom which the poor may enter is not merely an eschatological longing for escape to a transcendent reality, nor is it an inward serenity which eases unbearable suffering. Rather, it is God encountering man in the very depths of his being-in-the-world and releasing him from all human evils, like racism, which hold him captive. The repentant man knows that though God's ultimate Kingdom be in the future, yet even now it breaks through like a ray of light upon the darkness of the oppressed.

When black people begin to hear Jesus' message as contemporaneous with their life situation, they will quickly recognize what Jürgen Moltmann calls the "political hermeneutics of the gospel." Christianity becomes for them a religion of protest against the suffering and affliction of man.

> One cannot grasp freedom in faith without hearing simultaneously the categorical imperative: One must serve through bodily, social, and political obedience the liberation of the suffering creation out of real affliction. . . .
> . . . Consequently, the missionary proclamation of the cross of the Resurrected One is not an opium of the people which intoxicates and incapacitates, but the ferment of new freedom. It leads to the awakening of that revolt which, in the "power of the resurrection" . . . follows the categorical imperative to overthrow all conditions in which man is a being who labors and is heavily laden.[13]

If the gospel of Christ, as Moltmann suggests, frees a man to be for those who labor and are heavily laden, the humiliated and abused, then it would seem that for twentieth-century America the message of Black Power is the message of Christ himself.

To be sure, that statement is both politically and religiously dangerous; politically, because Black Power threatens the very structure of the American way of life; theologically, because it may appear to overlook Barth's early emphasis on "the infinite qualitative distinction between God and man." In this regard, we must say that Christ never promised political security but the opposite; and Karl Barth was mainly concerned with the easy identification of the work of God with the work of the state. But if Luther's statement, "We are Christ to the neighbor," is to be taken seriously, and, if we can believe the New Testament witness which proclaims Jesus as resurrected and thus active even now, then he must be alive in those very men who are struggling in the midst of misery and humiliation.

If the gospel is a gospel of liberation for the oppressed, then Jesus is where the oppressed are and continues his work of liberation there. Jesus is not safely confined in the first century. He is our contemporary, proclaiming release to the captives and rebelling against all who silently accept the structure of injustice. If he is not in the ghetto, if he is not where men are living at the brink of existence, but is, rather, in the easy life of the suburbs, then the gospel is a lie. The opposite, however, is the case. Christianity is not alien to Black Power; it is Black Power.

There are secular interpretations which attempt to account for the present black rebellion, as there have been secular interpretations of the exodus or of the life and death of Jesus. But for the Christian, there is only one interpretation: Black rebellion is a manifestation of God himself actively involved in the present-day affairs of men for the purpose of liberating a people. Through his work, black people now know that there is something more important than life itself. They can afford to be indifferent toward death, because life devoid of freedom is not worth living. They can now sing with a sense of triumph, "Oh, Freedom! Oh, Freedom! Oh Freedom over me! An' befo' I'd be a slave, I'd be buried in my grave, an' go home to my Lord an' be free."

CHRIST, BLACK POWER, AND FREEDOM

An even more radical understanding of the relationship of the gospel to Black Power is found in the concept of freedom. We have seen that freedom stands at the center of the black man's yearning in America. "Freedom Now" has been and still is the echoing slogan of all civil rights groups. The same concept of freedom is presently expressed among Black Power advocates by such phrases as "self-determination" and "self-identity."

What is this freedom for which blacks have marched, boycotted, picketed, and rebelled in order to achieve? Simply stated, freedom is *not doing what I will but becoming what I should.*[14] *A man is free when he sees clearly the fulfillment of his being and is thus capable of making the envisioned self a reality.* This is "Black Power!" They want the grip of white power removed, that is what black people have in mind when they cry, "Freedom Now!" now and forever.

Is this not why God became man in Jesus Christ so that man might become what he is? Is not this at least a part of what St. Paul had in mind when he said, "For freedom, Christ has set us free" (Gal. 5:1)? As long as man is a slave to another power, he is not free to serve God with mature responsibility. He is not free to become what he is—human.

Freedom is indeed what distinguishes man from animals and plants. "In the case of animals and plants nature not only appoints the destiny but it alone carries it out. . . . In the case of man, however, nature provides only the destiny and leaves it to him to carry it out."[15] Black Power means black people carrying out their own destiny.

It would seem that Black Power and Christianity have this in common: the liberation of man! If the work of Christ is that of liberating men from alien loyalties, and if racism is, as George Kelsey says, an alien faith, then there must be some correlation between Black Power and Christianity. For the gospel proclaims that God is with us now, actively fighting the forces which would make man captive. And it is the task of theology and the Church to know where God is at work so that we can join him in this fight against evil. In America we know where the evil is. We know that men are shot and lynched. We know that men are crammed into ghettos. Black power is the power to say No; it is the power of blacks to refuse to cooperate in their own dehumanization. If blacks can trust the message of Christ, if they can take him at his word, this power to say No to white power and domination is derived from him.

Looking at the New Testament, the message of the gospel is clear: Christ came into the world in order to destroy the works of Satan (I John 3:8). His whole life was a deliberate offensive against those powers which held man captive. At the beginning of his ministry there was a conflict with Satan in the wilderness (Luke 4:1–13; Mark 1:12ff.; Matt. 4:1–11), and this conflict continued throughout his ministry. In fact, every exorcism was a binding and despoiling of the evil one (Mark 3:27). It was not until Christ's death on the cross that the decisive battle was fought and won by the Son of Man. In that event, the tyranny of Satan, in principle, came to an end. The Good News is that God in Christ has freed us; we need no longer be enslaved by alien forces. The battle was fought and won on Good Friday and the triumph was revealed to men at Easter.

Though the decisive battle against evil has been fought and won, the war, however, is not over. Men of the new age know that they are free, but they must never lose sight of the tension between the "now" and the "not yet" which characterizes the present age (II Tim. 1:10; Eph. 1:22; Heb. 2:8, 10:13). The crucial battle has been won already on the cross, but the campaign is not over. There is a constant battle between Christ and Satan, and it is going on now.

If we make this message contemporaneous with our own life situation, what does Christ's defeat of Satan mean for us? There is no need here to get bogged down with quaint personifications of Satan. Men are controlled by evil powers that would make them slaves. The demonic forces of racism are *real* for the black man. Theologically, Malcolm X was not far wrong when he called the white man "the devil." The white structure of this American society, personified in every racist, must be at least part of what the New Testament meant by the demonic forces. According to the New Testament, these powers can get hold of a man's total being and can control his life to such a degree that he is incapable of distinguishing himself from the alien power. This seems to be what has happened to white racism in America. It is a part of the spirit of the age, the ethos of the culture, so embedded in the social, economic, and political structure that white society is incapable of knowing its destructive nature. There is only one response: Fight it!

Moreover, it seems to me that it is quite obvious who is actually engaged in the task of liberating black people from the power of white racism, even at the expense of their lives. They are men who stand unafraid of the structures of white racism. They are men who risk their lives for the inner freedom of others. They are men who embody the spirit of Black Power. And if Christ is present today actively risking all for the freedom of man, he must be acting through the most radical elements of Black Power.

Ironically, and this is what white society also fails to understand, the man who enslaves another enslaves himself. Unrestricted freedom is a form of slavery. To be "free" to do what I will in relation to another is to be in bondage to the law of least resistance. This is the bondage of racism. Racism is that bondage in which whites are free to beat, rape, or kill blacks. About thirty years ago it was quite acceptable to lynch a black man by hanging him from a tree; but today whites destroy him by crowding him into the ghetto and letting filth and despair put the final touches on death. Whites are thus enslaved to their own egos. Therefore, when blacks assert their freedom in self-determination, whites too are liberated.[16] They must now confront the black man as a person.

In our analysis of freedom, we should not forget what many existentialists call the burden of freedom. Authentic freedom has nothing to do with the rugged individualism of *laissez faire*, the right of the businessman to pursue without restraint the profit motive or the pleasure principle which is extolled by Western capitalistic democracies. On the contrary, authentic freedom is grounded in the awareness of the universal finality of man and the agonizing responsibility of choosing between perplexing alternatives regarding his existence.

Therefore, freedom cannot be taken for granted. A life of freedom is not the easy or happy way of life. That is why Sartre says man "is condemned to freedom." Freedom is not a trivial birthday remembrance but, in the words of Dostoevsky's Grand Inquisitor, "a terrible gift." It is not merely an opportunity but a temptation. Whether or not we agree with the existentialists' tendency to make man totally autonomous, they are right in their emphasis on the burden of freedom.

In the New Testament, the burden of freedom is described in terms of being free from the law. To be free in Christ means that man is stripped of the law as a guarantee of salvation and is placed in a free, mature love-relationship with God and man, which is man's destiny and in which Christ is the pioneer. Christian freedom means being a slave for Christ in order to do his will. Again this is no easy life; it is a life of suffering because the world and Christ are in constant conflict. To be free in Christ is to be against the world.

With reference, then, to freedom in Christ, three assertions about Black Power can be made: First, the work of Christ is essentially a liberating work, directed toward and by the oppressed. Black Power embraces that very task. Second, Christ in liberating the wretched of the earth also liberates those responsible for the wretchedness. The oppressor is also freed of his peculiar demons. Black Power in shouting Yes to black humanness and No to white oppression is exorcising demons on both sides of the conflict. Third, mature freedom is burdensome and risky, producing anxiety and conflict for free men and for the brittle structures they challenge. The call for Black Power is precisely the call to shoulder the burden of liberty in Christ, risking everything to live not as slaves but as free men.

GOD'S RIGHTEOUSNESS AND BLACK POWER

To demand freedom is to demand justice. When there is no justice in the land, a man's freedom is threatened. Freedom and justice are interdependent. When a man has no protection under the law, it is difficult for him to make others recognize him, and thus his freedom to be a "Thou" is placed in jeopardy. Therefore it is understandable that freedom and justice are probably the most often repeated words when the black man is asked, "What do you want?" The answer is simple: freedom and justice—no more and no less.

Unfortunately, many whites pretend that they do not understand what the black man is demanding. Theologians and churchmen have been of little help in this matter because much of their intellectualizing has gone into analyzing the idea of God's righteousness in a fashion far removed from the daily experiences of men. They fail to give proper emphasis to another equally if not more important concern, namely, the biblical idea of God's righteousness as the divine decision to vindicate the poor, the needy, and the helpless in society. It seems that much of this abstract theological disputation and speculation—the favorite pastime for many theological societies—serves as a substitute for relevant involvement in a world where men die for lack of political justice. A black theologian wants to know what the gospel has to say to a man who is jobless and cannot get work to support his family because the society is unjust. He wants to know what is God's Word to the countless black boys and girls who are fatherless and motherless because white society decreed that blacks have no rights. Unless there is a word from Christ to the helpless, then why should they respond to him? How do we relate the gospel of Christ to people whose daily existence is one of hunger or even worse, despair? Or do we simply refer them to the next world?

The key to the answer, in the thinking of the black theologian, is in the biblical concept of the righteousness of God. According to the Bible, God and not man is the author of justice; and since justice is a part of the Being of God, he is bound to do justly. Whatever God does must be *just* because he is justice.

It is important to note that God's righteousness refers not so much to an abstract quality related to his Being in the realm of thought—as commonly found in Greek philosophy—but to his activity in human history, in the historical events of the time and effecting his purpose despite those who oppose it. This is the biblical tradition. Israel as a people initially came to know God through the exodus. It was Yahweh who emancipated her from Egyptian bondage and subsequently established a convenant with her at Sinai, promising:

> You have seen what I *did* to the Egyptians, and how I bore you on eagles' wings and brought you to myself. Now therefore, if you will obey my voice and keep my convenant, you shall be my own possession among all peoples; . . . You shall be to me a kingdom of priests and a holy nation [Exod. 19:4–6].

Divine righteousness means that God will be faithful to his promise, that his purpose for Israel will not be thwarted. Israel, therefore, need not worry about her weakness and powerlessness in a world of mighty military powers, "for all the earth is mine" (Exod. 19:5). The righteousness of God means that he will protect her from the ungodly menacing of other nations. Righteousness means God is doing justice, that he is putting right what men have made wrong.

It is significant to note the condition of the people to whom God chose to reveal his righteousness. God elected to be the Helper and Saviour to people oppressed and powerless in contrast to the proud and mighty nations. It is also equally important to notice that within Israel, his righteousness is on behalf of the poor, defenseless, and unwanted. "If God is going to see righteousness established in the land, he himself must be particularly active as 'the helper of the fatherless' (Ps. 10:14) to 'deliver the needy when he crieth; and the poor that hath no helper' (Ps. 72:12)."[17] His vindication is for the poor because they are defenseless before the wicked and powerful. Barth writes:

> For this reason, in the relations and events in the life of his people, God always takes his stand unconditionally and passionately on this side alone: against the lofty and on behalf of the lowly; against those who already enjoy right and privilege and on behalf of those who are denied it and deprived of it.[18]

This is certainly the message of the eighth-century prophets—Amos, Hosea, Isaiah, and Micah. Being ethical prophets concerned with social justice, they proclaimed

Yahweh's intolerance with the rich, who, as Amos says, "trample the head of the poor into the dust of the earth" (2:7) and "sell the righteous for silver, and the needy for a pair of shoes" (2:6). God unquestionably will vindicate the poor.

And if we can trust the New Testament, God became man in Jesus Christ in order that the poor might have the gospel preached to them; that the poor might have the Kingdom of God (Luke 6:20); that those who hunger might be satisfied; that those who weep might laugh.

If God is to be true to himself, his righteousness must be directed to the helpless and the poor, those who can expect no security from this world. The rich, the secure, the suburbanite can have no part of God's righteousness because of their trust and dependence on the things of this world. "God's righteousness triumphs when man has no means of triumphing."[19] His righteousness is reserved for those who come empty-handed, without any economic, political, or social power. That is why the prophets and Jesus were so critical of the economically secure. Their security gets in the way of absolute faith in God. "Earthly possessions dazzle our eyes and delude us into thinking that they can provide security and freedom from anxiety. Yet all the time they are the very source of all anxiety."[20]

What, then, is God's Word of righteousness to the poor and the helpless? "I became poor in Christ in order that man may not be poor. I am in the ghetto where rats and disease threaten the very existence of my people, and they can be assured that I have not forgotten my promise to them. *My righteousness will vindicate your suffering!* Remember, I know the meaning of rejection because in Christ I was rejected; the meaning of physical pain because I was crucified; the meaning of death because I died. But my resurrection in Christ means that alien powers cannot keep you from the full meaning of life's existence as found in Christ. Even now the Kingdom is available to you. Even now I am present with you because your suffering is my suffering, and I will not let the wicked triumph." This is God's Word.

Those who wish to share in this divine righteousness must become poor without any possibility of procuring right for themselves. "The righteousness of the believer consists in the fact that God acts for him—utterly, because he cannot plead his own case and no one else can represent him."[21] The men of faith come to God because they can go to no one else. He, and he alone, is their security.

It is within this context that men should be reminded of the awesome political responsibility which follows from justification by faith. To be made righteous through Christ places a man in the situation where he too, like Christ, must be for the poor, for God, and against the world. As Barth puts it:

> . . . there follows from this character of faith a political attitude, decisively determined by the fact that man is made responsible to all those who are poor and wretched in his eyes, that he is summoned on his part to espouse the cause of those who suffer wrong. Why? Because in them it is manifested to him what he himself is in the sight of God; because the living, gracious, merciful action of God towards him consists in the fact that God himself in his own righteousness procures right for him, the poor and wretched; because he and all men stand in the presence of God as those for whom right can be procured only by God himself. The man who lives by the faith that this is true stands under a political responsibility.[22]

No Christian can evade this responsibility. He cannot say that the poor are in poverty because they will not work, or they suffer because they are lazy. Having come before

God as nothing and being received by him into his Kingdom through grace, the Christian should know that he has been made righteous (justified) so that he can join God in the fight for justice. Therefore, whoever fights for the poor, fights for God; whoever risks his life for the helpless and unwanted, risks his life for God. God is active now in the lives of those men who feel an absolute identification with all who suffer because there is no justice in the land.

NOTES

1. The most notable exception is Joseph R. Barndt, *Why Black Power?* (New York, Friendship Press, 1968); see also Kyle Haselden's perceptive treatment in *The Racial Problem in Christian Perspective* (New York, Haper & Row, 1959), as well as Liston Pope, *The Kingdom Beyond Caste* (New York, Friendship Press, 1957), and Daisuke Kitagawa, *The Pastor and the Race Issue* (New York, Seabury, 1965). Among the best treatments by black theologians, see George Kelsey, *Racism and the Christian Understanding of Man* (New York, Scribner's, 1965) and Joseph R. Washington, *The Politics of God* (Boston, Beacon, 1967); compare the latter with his *Black Religion* (Boston, Beacon, 1964). For an excellent analysis of black power and some of its theological implications, see Nathan Wright, Jr., *Black Power and the Urban Unrest* (New York, Hawthorn, 1967).

2. See Harvey Cox, *God's Revolution and Man's Responsibility* (Valley Forge, Judson, 1965) and several excellent essays by other authors in Cox, ed., *The Church Amid Revolution* (New York, Association Press, 1967), essays prepared for the World Council of Churches' Geneva Conference on Church and Society; see also John C. Bennett, "Christians Look at Revolution," *Christian Century* (Feb. 1, 1967).

3. See Cox, *Church Amid Revolution*, and the report of the Theological Commission of the (Prague) Christian Peace Conference, Oct. 1966, in "The Just Revolution," *Frontier* (Spring 1967).

4. In the future I hope to analyze in more detail the structure of Christian theology from the point of view of oppressed blacks.

5. Maulana Ron Karenga, quoted in Vincent Harding, "The Religion of Black Power," in *The Religious Situation: 1968,* D.R. Cutler, ed., (Boston, Beacon, 1968) 8.

6. Ibid., 28–29.

7. Social scientists, theologians, and others have already shown the destructive nature of racism. Few writers would even attempt to reconcile racism and Christianity. See Kelsey, *Racism*, for an excellent theological analysis of the incompatibility.

8. Friedrich Schleiermacher, *The Christian Faith* (New York, Scribner's, 1922) 9.

9. Pannenberg, *Jesus: God and Man* (Philadelphia, Westminster, 1964) 11.

10. Ibid., 19.

11. Ibid.

12. For support of this translation, see Günther Bornkamm, *Jesus of Nazareth*, (New York, Harper & Row, 1960) 79, 203 n. 29; and Joachim Jeremias, *The Parables of Jesus* (New York, Scribner's, 1955) 100 n. 54.

13. "Toward a Political Hermeneutics of the Gospel," *Union Seminary Quarterly Review*, 23/4 (Summer 1968) 313–14.

14. See Helmut Thielicke, *The Freedom of the Christian Man* (New York, Harper & Row, 1963) 10.

15. Ibid., 15.

16. Washington makes this point, drawing a parallel between black people and Israel, a people "chosen" not merely for self-liberation but also for the liberation of her captors; see *The Politics of God*, p. 157.

17. N.H. Snaith, "Righteous, Righteousness," in Alan Richardson, ed., *A Theological Word Book of the Bible* (New York, Macmillan, 1950) 203.

18. Barth, *Church Dogmatics*, vol. 1, part 1 (Edinburgh, Clark, 1957) 386.

19. Ibid., 387.

20. Dietrich Bonhoeffer, *The Cost of Discipleship* (New York, Macmillan, 1961) 158.

21. Barth, *Church Dogmatics*, 1/1, p. 387.

22. Ibid. Used with permission.

Chapter 20

Albert B. Cleage, Jr.

Brother Malcolm

"Thou art my beloved Son, in whom I am well pleased" (*Mark 1:11*).

Each year we pay tribute to Brother Malcolm, Malcolm X. It is wonderful to have this opportunity each year to look objectively at the struggle in which we are all engaged, and to try to see where we have been and where we are going, in the light of Brother Malcolm and what his life means for us. It is strange how the life of a man takes on new meaning in terms of the changing conceptions of a people. His life means more and more as the years go by. We can say, in a sense, that the shooting down of his physical body a few short years ago brought to pass a kind of miracle. Brother Malcolm, his message, his personality, the things for which he lived and died have not changed, but we have changed.

JESUS AND MALCOLM

I cannot resist the temptation to compare Brother Malcolm to Jesus, the Jesus whom we worship, the Black Messiah. The conditions which both faced in many ways were so similar. The conditions faced by Jesus in trying to bring into being a Black Nation two thousand years ago were in many ways similar to those faced by Brother Malcolm just a few years ago. Both tried to bring black people together, tried to give them a sense of purpose, and to build a Black Nation.

Yet in many ways their situations were very different. At the time Jesus was born, men were expecting a savior. The Nation Israel realized that it was fragmented, that its people were despised, that they looked down on each other and upon themselves. They realized their oppression, and even though they betrayed each other to the oppressor, even though they did what the white man wanted them to, they knew that they needed someone to save them from this kind of degeneration and make them a Nation.

So they longed for a savior. Every prophet talked of the coming of a savior. The people organized and waited for the coming of a savior. The most depraved individual in Israel still hoped and longed that a savior would come who could bring him back into a Nation of which he could be proud. This was the kind of a world into which Jesus came, a world anticipating the coming of a savior.

Remember how, at the time of his baptism, it was recorded that a dove lighted upon

First published in *The Black Messiah* (New York, Sheed and Ward, 1968), pp. 186–200. Used with permission of Sheed & Ward, 115 E. Armour Blvd., Kansas City, MO 64141.

his shoulder, and a voice spoke from heaven saying: "This is my beloved son in whom I am well pleased." This was the reaction of men who were thinking, "Perhaps this is the savior we have been waiting for, the Black Messiah who can make us a Nation again." As he came forward to be baptized, John the Baptist is reported to have hesitated saying, "I don't think I should baptize you," because he, too, had a sense that this might be the Messiah Israel was waiting for. The sense of expectation was everywhere. The disciples had to tell the children to stay away and let the master alone. They were taking up too much of his time. Even the little children were waiting for a Messiah.

Remember the shepherds on the night that Jesus was born? According to the Christmas story, they heard the angelic choir, and said, "The Messiah has come, this must be the night of his birth." Wise men came from the East, seeking the Messiah who was to be born in Israel, the Black Messiah who was to bring back into a Nation the black people of Israel. The people were waiting when Jesus came. They did not receive him, only because they wanted a different kind of Messiah.

How different it was for Brother Malcolm! The same fragmentation of black people, divided, exploited, oppressed; the same white Gentiles with their system of oppression; the same degeneration of a people who had lost pride in themselves—who fought against each other, who had no sense of dignity or of their future as a people. The Nation Israel waited for a Messiah that they might again become a Nation. But Brother Malcolm came to a people who waited that they might disappear as a people, a people who prayed every night that God would make them cease to be a people. You know what I am talking about. You didn't want to be black people. Every night you said your prayers and hoped to God that you would wake up in the morning white. Everything you believed in was white. Everything you tried to imitate was white. Everything you had been taught was white.

No. Brother Malcolm didn't come to a people who were waiting for a Messiah. He came to a people who were tired of being a separate people. Fragmented as they were, disorganized as they were, each man looked upon his brother as his enemy. He hated him because he was black. It reminded him that he, too, was black. He hated his own children because they were born black and wished that there had been some kind of miracle that could have permitted at least his children to be born white.

This is the kind of people that Brother Malcolm came to, a people lost beyond any comprehension that Jesus might have had of how lost a people can be. The people that Jesus preached to wanted to hear the message of the Nation. But the last thing in the world the people Brother Malcolm came to wanted to hear was any word about a Black Nation. They wanted to forget everything black they could forget, as fast as they could. Each individual had a dream of escaping from his blackness. Get enough money, get an education, dress nice enough, talk nice enough, get a white man to like you and you can stop being black. That is what everybody was looking for, "integration." Get out of that old black ghetto and get over there where the white man is, where things are good.

Don't look surprised! Admit you felt like that yourself! When you hoped that your child wouldn't have it as hard as you did, you meant that you hoped he could get over there with the white people. You worked and scraped to send him to college so he wouldn't have to be a Nigger, he could be just like white folks. That's what you were working for, that's what Brother Malcolm had to deal with!

SEPARATION AND SHAME

We can look back now and say, "Oh, it's wonderful to be black! Black is beautiful!" but that is not what Brother Malcolm faced. When Brother Malcolm went anywhere to speak, most black people were ashamed even to go in and listen to him. Some would slip in and try to hide in a corner some place, saying "That's right! That's right!" but not saying it too loud. We were a black people who had been debased as far as a people could be debased, because when you stop loving yourself and your brothers and sisters, you have hit bottom. That's where we were. We hated ourselves, we hated each other, and we were looking for some way to escape from ourselves, some way to get out of this thing we were in and to pretend that we weren't black. All the wigs, and processes, and bleaching creams were to help us fool each other.

I remember Brother Malcolm would be talking and the women would reach up and pat their wigs every once in a while because as he talked, they began to know something was wrong. And the Brother in there with the beautiful processed curls hanging would kind of reach up and touch them. He knew something was wrong because of what Brother Malcolm was saying. Malcolm didn't have to say, "Take off your wig." He didn't have to say, "There is something wrong with your process." He just began to give people a sense of pride in being black, and this was hard to do."

Jesus had it hard; the Uncle Tom preachers were all against him. They betrayed him; they went out and organized the people against him. They were afraid because the exploitation they were carrying on was getting more and more difficult, as Jesus began to awaken people. Brother Malcolm faced all that, too. Remember, we had to go to court in Detroit to permit him to speak at King Solomon Baptist Church. After the contract was signed, they tried to call the whole thing off when they found out Malcolm X was to speak. All over the country, black preachers were warning black people, "Don't follow that man who is so filled with hate and who is preaching separation." Everywhere you went black people were saying, "He's preaching hate. He's talking about separation." For black people to say that a black man was preaching hate because he wanted separation from white people who had done everything to destroy black people, was weird.

They said, "He's preaching hate against the white man; he's telling us to hate the white man." They thought there was something wrong with that. It just shows you how far down we were. We were even ashamed to hate a people who had hated, oppressed, and exploited us for almost four hundred years, who had brought us to America in slave ships, sold us on slave blocks, raped our women and lynched our men! Not to hate people like that was a sign of mental illness. But you wouldn't say that to black people. "He's preaching hate," black people would say. Brother Malcolm did not preach hate, but when he got through telling it like it was, you did your own hating. He didn't have to do anything but preach the truth.

"He's preaching separation," the white folks said, and black folks started echoing, "Oh, he's preaching separation." And they had been separated all their lives by the white man. You were born separate, and you'll be buried separate. Malcolm didn't have to preach separation. All he had to do was say, "Look around you, fool. You run around talking about integration. Everything you've got is separate." And that's what we did—we began to look around.

Remember, that was just a few years ago. We have come a long way in a few years because all those wrong ideas I'm talking about are not just things that other people used to believe, but things that most of you believed. Some of you still have a lot of it in the back of your head right now, today. You know how the thing goes, "We settle the whole thing by integrating, one by one. You get your family straight; I'll get my family straight, and we will all be taken care of one of these days." We were hemmed in by a separate existence which the white man had given us, which we thought was temporary but which he knew was permanent.

Inside this all-black thing which the white man had given us, we kept talking, each one saying, "I don't believe in anything all-black." We were in a black ghetto together, hating ourselves and hating each other, and looking enviously out at him on the outside, because wherever he was, that was the place we wanted to be. We wanted to look like him, and we wanted to live over there with him. We wanted to get away from these people who looked just like us. We were separate, but we were ashamed of our separateness. We were ashamed of everything that made us what we are, we wanted to be like the enemy who was oppressing us.

As long as we felt like that, we were helpless, we couldn't do a thing. That's the way we were in every community. Everything we had was just a temporary, stop-gap operation. We didn't really want it, we wanted to get out of it. Even if we were running a business, we didn't have any idea of making it a first-class business. We operated it from the very beginning on the premise that "I'm just operating a nigger business here, you can't expect too much from me." We didn't wash the windows. We just sat there trying to get by because we didn't want that kind of business anyway, we wanted to be in some kind of integrated business. We knew that a black business, even if it was ours, had to be no good because it was black and black is automatically no good. Our houses, our streets, our neighborhoods were all temporary—we were just staying there with these inferior people until we could get out, so we didn't work too hard at fixing things up. Our whole community life was geared to this feeling that we were living a kind of temporarily separate life.

We thought that it was temporary because we believed in the American dream. The white man told us that America is a huge melting pot. Everybody comes in and wherever they come out, they are American. We just couldn't seem to find the spot where you come out. But we had faith that there must be some way to escape from this blackness. If we had a child who showed any promise at all, what did we dream about, day and night? We were going to get him out of these black schools, we were going to move to some neighborhood where he could go to school with white children and really learn. That was a dream. Parents would sit down and talk about how they were saving, how they were trying to get out—for their children. We were not concerned with improving the schools in our black ghettos, with improving the situation for all black children. Each one of us by his own little lonely self was going to find a crack in the ghetto wall and get out some way. That was the dream.

That was the kind of thinking, or useless dreaming, that Malcolm had to deal with. That is why it's so important to remember him and the things he said.

Jesus was distorted by the institution that was set up in his name. Jesus didn't organize anything except a few people who believed in him, some revolutionaries who followed him in a nationalistic movement. Jesus didn't organize any kind of Church. He brought together people who believed in doing what was necessary to create change. That's what Jesus did. But after Jesus was killed, they organized a Church in his name. The Apostle Paul, who was really a great organizer, set up Churches everywhere and said, "This is Christianity. All of you who follow after Jesus, come right on in here. " And then he changed the whole thing around. No longer was it building a Nation, it was tearing down a Nation. It was leading people right back to the same old individualistic kind of thing that Jesus had fought against all of his life. In the name of Jesus they created a new kind of individualism. "Come into the Church, be washed in the blood of the lamb and you will become white as snow."

We did all that. We came in and were washed in the blood of the lamb. But we stayed black, and the white man kept us in black Churches. That old individual thing had us. You said to yourself, "Well, I'm white on the inside, even if I am black on the outside."

And no kind of washing seemed to make any real difference. That is what they did to Jesus and to his teachings about the Black Nation. The teachings of Jesus were destroyed. The Church which carried his name went back to individualism, telling people, "You can find escape from your problems in heaven, after death."

That is why the text which opens the fourth chapter of Ecclesiastes is so important. It says, "Again I saw all of your oppressions that are practiced under the sun. And behold the tears of the oppressed, and they had no one to comfort them. On the side of their oppressors there was power, and there was no one to comfort them." This was true during the lifetime of Jesus; it was also true during the lifetime of Brother Malcolm.

Two saviors came to a black people. The people were different in each instance, but both saw the oppression that black people suffered and each saw the power of their oppressors—and they saw that there was no one to comfort those who were oppressed. So today as we remember Malcolm, and as we remember our weaknesses and how far we have come, let us remember the basic things that Brother Malcolm taught that are so important for us. Because we too can forget, we too can distort Malcolm's teachings as the Apostle Paul distorted the teachings of Jesus. We can make something else out of them to suit our purposes if we forget what Brother Malcolm actually taught.

THE WHITE MAN: THE BLACK MAN'S ENEMY

Brother Malcolm taught us that the white man is the black man's enemy. He didn't beat around the bush and try to say it in some acceptable way. He just looked at black people and told them simply that the white man is an enemy. This was basic because you can't engage in a battle until you know that you have an enemy and you know who he is. Brother Malcolm explained the whole thing. It is not accidental that black people everywhere are poor, that black people everywhere are uneducated, that black people everywhere live in slums, that black people everywhere are exploited. It didn't just happen, it's a system. It's set up that way. The white man doesn't leave anything to chance, he organizes your oppression. You are systematically oppressed. You are supposed to be oppressed. You think that it just happened because you are unlucky or that there is something wrong with you or you made a wrong turn some place. You tell yourself, "I should have gone on to school, then I would have had it made." I tell you, if you had gone to school for a thousand years, you would still be oppressed in this white man's country. Don't drop out of school, but don't think that school is going to solve anything. We are oppressed by a total system of oppression which includes all of us.

You can't escape from it until we can all escape from it together. When you are overcharged three or four thousand dollars for a house, that means that the banks, the insurance companies, the mortgage lending agencies, the real estate boards, all of them together have arranged for your exploitation. They confine us to an area, open up a new area when they want to, and let us in at the price they want us to pay. It's a system. You go into a ghetto store and you pay ten to twenty-five percent more for everything you buy. You drive five miles out to the white suburbs and you pay less. That's no accident either. You send your children to school and their achievement is two to four grades below grade level. That's not an accident. In most of Detroit schools there is a teacher shortage, so they are transferring the good teachers out of inner city schools, and putting in unqualified emergency substitutes. Do you think that just happens? Do you think they don't know that they are dealing with a black school when they take the good teachers out and put in inexperienced and untrained teachers? Do you think that when they transfer a principal who has been kicked out of five schools to your black child's school, they do it by accident? They know what they are doing. They are doing it on purpose. You ask, "Why would they want to do that?" Because without a good education your child is economically and socially disadvantaged in the 20th century. Your child is less of a competitive threat to white children with a better education.

They want your child ignorant because it's easier to oppress an ignorant people. They want to break his spirit so that he'll accept oppression, so they treat him like a dog in school day after day, ridicule him, rob him of his dignity, don't let him see a black person in a position of authority or power, make him feel inferior. It's not by accident. When your child comes home and everything he says is ridiculous, that didn't just happen. They are programming him for inferiority.

The white man is an enemy. I know that you wish we could say the same thing some other way. But there is no other honest way of saying it! That's why Malcolm said, "The white man is your enemy." That's why Brother Malcolm frightened white people so much. That was the last thing they want the black man to know. As long as you think that he is not your enemy, that he is just as concerned about you as he is about himself, and that he is trying to do right by you, but that you are just a little slow-witted, you cannot possibly change conditions, because you are blaming yourself for a situation over which you have no control. You can hate yourself, but you cannot change the way a black man is treated by white people. As long as you go along that path, he doesn't have to worry about you. But when you stop and recognize the simple fact that the white man is your enemy, then he faces an entirely new situation.

Now you are saying, "I have got to draw some lines; there are some good white people." Then you can start naming them: this one that died down there, and that one who was run over by a tractor lying down on some construction site in Cleveland, those were good white people. Go on, you can name them all on two hands and have some fingers left over. The "good white people" in this world are so insignificant that we don't even have to worry about them. They're not going to solve our problems. They are individuals without either power or a power base. Where do they operate, these good white people? In our neighborhoods, at our meetings, in our organizations. What can they do out in Bloomfield Hills or Grosse Pointe or Dearborn? What can they do against organized white racists? Nothing. But they mess us up because they make us think that there are a lot of different kinds of white people. For all practical purposes, there is just one kind, and that kind is out to destroy you and your children, and your children's children.

That's why it was a turning point when Malcolm would stand up and say, "You've got an enemy, the white man is your enemy." And you would sit there and squirm and twist, but you would know that it was true if you sat there long enough. And some people couldn't stand it. They would squirm and twist and then they would get up and go out. Sometimes they would get a drink of water and smoke a cigarette and tiptoe back in. It was hard because they had never faced it before. I have heard people who come here to visit say, "I couldn't go to work the next day. Those white people I work with—I didn't know how to face them, I didn't know how to look at them."

Well, just look at them as they are, as you would look at any enemy. Perhaps two people who can face each other honestly as enemies will someday face each other honestly as equals. So Brother Malcolm taught us. He said it out loud, he went everywhere and said, "The white man is our enemy." It was important. It is so important, that as far as I can gather from all the evidence, white people had to have him killed. I am not worried about the charges we heard against the Honorable Elijah Muhammed. Malcolm wasn't hurting Mr. Muhammed. He wasn't that important to Mr. Muhammed. But he was that important to the enemy.

Malcolm was willing to accept the implications of his statement. You might say that the white man is your enemy, so be careful. But that's not enough: he is our enemy; therefore, we must confront him, we must fight against his oppression. We must protect ourselves against genocide. When you recognize an enemy and you know that he is trying to destroy you, you must do whatever is necessary to guarantee your own survival. That's why Malcolm said that we must forget all this non-violent foolishness in a violent world. The white man has had one basic attribute ever since he climbed down out of the trees, and that is a love of violence, a genius for violence, a commitment to violence, and a willingness to use violence to take anything he wants.

And so, you have an enemy and your enemy believes in violence. Those two things have to be considered together. If you had an enemy who was off praying against you somewhere, you wouldn't have to worry about him. But this enemy believes in violence. You can see what he is doing in Vietnam. He is treating the Vietnamese people just like he has treated us for four hundred years.

White people have a peculiar sex thing with their violence. I'm sure Freud could have explained it. In Vietnam the torture method used by American soldiers is a sexual thing. They attach batteries and generators to the genitals of Vietnamese prisoners to torture them. The same sexual torture was used against us during slavery and reconstruction. Don't look so horrified. It was your own people they did it to. They would cut off a man's genitals and make him eat them while he was still alive. "Good white people" may be good for white people, but they cannot be good people for us. They are an enemy, and they believe in violence.

THE IMPORTANCE OF POWER

Malcolm said that our struggle against these people who are an enemy, who have a system built up to oppress us, and who believe in violence, must be a power struggle. That's why we ourselves were so afraid of him at first, and why white people were so afraid of him. He was developing a concept of struggle. Our struggle is a power struggle. We didn't have to wait for Stokely to scream "Black Power" down on some country road. Malcolm had defined "Black Power" when he said that our whole struggle against the white man as an enemy is a power struggle. We are not going to solve it if we are powerless. We must get power if we are to participate in a power struggle. You can't get down on your knees and beg the man, "Please give me equality. Please give me freedom." You will never get it. Our basic struggle, then, is to get some kind of power. We must not be ashamed of power. We must mobilize the entire black community to secure political and economic power. Without power we are helpless and psychologically sick.

So Brother Malcolm had a message that hung together. You could listen to him and you wouldn't find a hole in it. You might not like his words, and you might wish that he had said it more gently, but you had to say, "That's right." Gradually people began to understand that not only was it true, but Brother Malcolm's message offered the only basis for salvation for black people. To identify an enemy, to understand him, to realize that he is violent, and to recognize the fact that we are engaged in a power struggle—this was Brother Malcolm's message. You can picket and march and scream and sing. If those things lead to power, then they are good. If they do not lead to power, then they are a waste of time. So he gave us a yardstick by which we can judge our organizations, our Churches, and our institutions. Do they lead to power for black people?

That's why this Church, The Shrine of the Black Madonna, is building a Nation, because we believe in Black Power. We are trying to organize for power. In every area, we are trying to secure power for black people, so that we can deal with white people on a basis of equality. We believe in it, and we believe that this was the message of Jesus as well as Brother Malcolm. That's why there is no inner conflict when we have a memorial for Brother Malcolm in a Christian Church which is dedicated to rebuilding the Nation of the Black Messiah.

We believe that the things which Brother Malcolm taught, Jesus taught two thousand years ago. Our struggle is a struggle for survival. Malcolm knew that. You can think of many little things he said that were terribly important. He talked about the "house nigger" and the "field nigger," to illustrate the problem of identification with the enemy. That has always been one of our basic problems. The more you get, the higher you climb above your black brothers and sisters, the more your identification with the enemy becomes a problem for you. That's why the people who serve the Black Nation best are usually those who don't have anything. You wonder why some brothers don't have any qualms about fighting the enemy any time and any place. Usually it's because they can see the problem clearly because they don't have too much to lose. But give them a job (that's the reason for the poverty program) and let them buy a house, or a car, and their whole attitude changes. So we have to be careful, all of us. We have to be wary of any position where a few little possessions tend to separate us from the struggles of black people. A power struggle demands the total involvement of all black people, identification with black people, accountability to black people, and the severing of any identification with white people.

In his last days Brother Malcolm was trying to do the most difficult of all the tasks which he undertook. He was eloquent, he had a philosophy, he could make people understand it. The basic task that he was not spared to do was that of organization. He didn't leave any organization. He left a revolutionary spirit. There are certain benefits to that. If he had left an organization, probably the organization would have distorted his message because they would have tried to use it. He didn't leave anything but a spirit and a memory, and a love in the hearts and minds of people. But this revolutionary spirit must be channeled into a knowledge of organization.

How do we organize to struggle for survival in this second Civil War which has already begun? If the white is getting ready for genocide, it's not enough for us to just walk around saying "Brother." We have got to organize. That is the point to which Brother Malcolm brought us. If we can't move beyond where he left us, into the kind of organization which is essential for struggle, then we still will not survive. We must organize to secure power, and we must organize to use power.

Organization is one thing that we don't know too much about. We have never done it. Our organizations are all loose, helter-skelter, and harum-scarum, and we tend to tear up any organization on a personality basis. We can get a thousand people together, and two people will tear it all up, for no better reason than the simple fact that they don't like each other. In almost every northern urban center, you will find black people fragmented a thousand different ways. We're closer together right here in Detroit, in the Nation, than black people are anywhere else in America. We are also learning the lessons of organization. We have our differences, but we try to avoid fighting each other up and down the street for entertainment of the white man. When we move into real organization, we are moving a step beyond Malcolm. Malcolm couldn't do it in New York and all across the country. We haven't been able to do it. This is the next step in the Black Revolution.

On this occasion, when we remember Malcolm, and review how far we have come, let us keep clearly in focus the simple fact that unless we can learn to organize and submerge ourselves in a Black Nation without regard for individual self-interest, we will not be able to survive the critical decade ahead as black people. We can no longer afford the luxury of individualism. The question is now one of survival. Even if you don't like somebody, if he is black you must work with him because it's the only way you can survive. Our survival will depend upon our ability to work together, to organize and to trust each other.

So on this occasion, in memory of Brother Malcolm, we say that the Black Nation which we are building here, is carrying on his spirit and teachings which we believe to be compatible with the spirit and teachings of Jesus, the Black Messiah. Within the framework of this philosophy, we are trying to do the things which he would have done if the white man had let him live a little longer. Some of us are going to live long enough to finish the job.

Brother Malcolm was tremendously important to all of us because he articulated what we felt. He spelled out a philosophy and we are building on that philosophy.

Heavenly Father, be with us. Give us a sense of the importance of this moment in history and of our importance as a Nation. Help us to submerge ourselves in the cause of black people. Be with us to guide us and strengthen us in all that we do. Keep bright our remembrance of Brother Malcolm. These things we ask in the name of Jesus Christ, the Black Messiah. Amen.

Chapter 21

James H. Cone

Who Is Jesus Christ for Us Today?

To say that Jesus Christ is the truth of the Christian story calls for further examination. It is one thing to assert that the New Testament describes Jesus as the Oppressed One who came to liberate the poor and the weak; but it is quite another to ask, Who is Jesus Christ for us today? If twentieth-century Christians are to speak the truth for their sociohistorical situation, they cannot merely repeat the story of what Jesus did and said in Palestine, as if it were self-interpreting for us today. Truth is more than the retelling of the biblical story. Truth is the divine happening that invades our contemporary situation, revealing the meaning of the past for the present so that we are made new creatures for the future.

It is therefore our commitment to the divine truth, as witnessed to in the biblical story, that requires us to investigate the connection between Jesus' words and deeds in first-century Palestine and our existence today. This is the crux of the christological issue that no Christian theology can avoid.

SOCIAL CONTEXT, SCRIPTURE, AND TRADITION

The interplay of social context with Scripture and tradition is the starting point for an investigation of Jesus Christ's meaning for us today. The focus on social context means that we cannot separate our questions about Jesus from the concreteness of everyday life. We ask, "Who is Jesus Christ for us today?" because we believe that the story of his life and death is the answer to the human story of oppression and suffering. If our existence were not at stake, if we did not experience the pain and the contradictions of life, then the christological question would be no more than an intellectual exercise for professional theologians. But for Christians who have experienced the extreme absurdities of life, the christological question is not primarily theoretical but practical. It arises from the encounter of Christ in the struggle of freedom.

The question, "Who is Christ?" is not prior to faith, as if the answer to the christological question is the precondition of faith. Rather, our question about Christ is derived from Christ himself as he breaks into our social existence, establishing the truth of freedom in our midst. This divine event of liberation places us in a new sociopolitical context wherein we are given the gift of faith for the creation of a new future for ourselves and for humanity. It is because we have encountered Christ in our historical situation and have been given the faith to struggle for truth that we are forced to inquire about the meaning of this truth for the totality of human existence.

[Black Christians] bore witness with songs of praise and joy to Jesus' power to make the crooked straight and the rough places plain. With Jesus' coming, they contended, Isaiah's prophecy was being fulfilled: "Every valley shall be exalted, and every mountain and hill shall be made low. And the glory of the Lord shall be revealed, and all flesh shall see it together: for the mouth of the Lord hath spoken it" (Isa. 40:4-5 KJV). Because the people believed that Jesus could conquer sorrow and wipe away the tears of pain and suffering, they expressed their faith in song:

> When my way grows drear,
> Precious Lord, linger near.
> When my life is almost gone,
> Hear my cry, hear my call,
> Hold my hand lest I fall.
> Take my hand, Precious Lord,
> Lead me home.

It is therefore the people's experience of the freedom of Christ in the context of injustice and oppression that makes them want to know more about him. Who is this Christ who lightens our burdens and eases our pain? It is our faith in him, born of our deliverance by him here and now, that leads us to the christological question.

On the other hand, the truth of Jesus Christ, whom we meet in our social existence, is not exhausted by the questions we ask. The meaning of Christ is not derived from nor dependent upon our social context. There is an otherness which we experience in the encounter with Christ that forces us to look beyond our immediate experience to other witnesses.

One such witness is Scripture. The Bible, it is important to note, does not consist of units of infallible truth about God or Jesus. Rather, it tells the story of God's will to redeem humankind from sin, death, and Satan. According to the New Testament witnesses, God's decisive act against these powers happened in Jesus' life, death, and resurrection. According to Luke's account in Acts, Peter told the story in this manner:

> You know about Jesus of Nazareth, how God anointed him with the Holy Spirit and with power. He went about doing good and healing all who were oppressed by the devil, for God was with him. And we can bear witness to all that he did in the Jewish countryside and in Jerusalem. He was put to death by hanging on a gibbet; but God raised him to life on the third day, and allowed him to appear, not to the whole people, but to witnesses whom God had chosen in advance—to us, who ate and drank with him after he rose from the dead. He commanded us to proclaim him to the people, and affirm that he is the one who has been designated by God as judge of the living and the dead. It is to him that all prophets testify, declaring that everyone who trusts in him receives forgiveness of sins through his name.
>
> Acts 10:38–43 NEB

This passage is one of several succinct accounts of the early apostles' witness to the revelatory significance of Jesus of Nazareth. The variety of these testimonies enriches our perception of Christ while reminding us that words cannot capture him. The Gospel of Mark speaks of him as the Son of God, while John's Gospel says that he is "the offspring of God himself," "the Word [that] became flesh to dwell among us" (1:13-14 NEB). For the writer of I Timothy, Jesus was:

> He who was manifested in the body,
>   vindicated in the spirit,
>   seen by angels;
> who was proclaimed among the nations,
>   believed in throughout the world,
>   glorified in heaven.
>
> I Timothy 3:16 NEB

In contrast to I Timothy's emphasis on Jesus as a manifestation of the divine glory (with no stress on his pre-existence), the apostle Paul declared that the divine glory is not revealed, but hidden in the form of a slave: "For the divine nature was his from the first; yet he did not think to snatch at equality with God, but made himself nothing, assuming the nature of a slave, . . . and in obedience accepted even death—death on a cross" (Phil. 2:6,8 NEB).

The New Testament is the early Church's response to the history of Jesus Christ. That response is important for our christological reflections, because the Bible is our primary source of information about the Jesus we encounter in our social existence.

Black people in America had great confidence in the holy Book. This confidence has not been shaken by the rise of historical criticism and its impact on the Bible as reflected in theological writings from Rudolf Bultmann's "New Testament and Mythology"[1] to James Barr's *The Bible in the Modern World*.[2] This does not mean that black people are fundamentalists in the strict sense of the the term. They have not been preoccupied with definitions of inspiration and infallibility. Accordingly, their confidence in the Book has not been so brittle or contentious as that of white conservatives. It is as if blacks have intuitively drawn the all-important distinction between infallibility and reliability. They have not contended for a fully explicit infallibility, feeling perhaps that there is mystery in the Book, as there is in the Christ. What they have testified to is the Book's reliability: how it is the true and basic source for discovering the truth of Jesus Christ. For this reason there has been no crisis of biblical authority in the black community. The Jesus of black experience is the Christ of Scripture, the One who was born in Bethlehem, grew up in Nazareth, taught in Galilee, and died and was resurrected in Jerusalem.

The authority of the Bible for christology, therefore, does not lie in its objective status as the literal Word of God. Rather, it is found in its power to point to the One whom the people have met in the historical struggle of freedom. Through the reading of Scripture, the people not only hear other stories about Jesus that enable them to move beyond the privateness of their own story; but through faith, because of divine grace, they are taken from the present to the past and then thrust back into their contemporary history with divine power to transform the sociopolitical context.

This event of transcendence enables the people to break the barriers of time and space as they walk and talk with Jesus in Palestine along with Peter, James, and John. They can hear his cry of pain and experience the suffering as he is nailed on the cross and pierced in the side:

> They nail my Jesus down
> They put him on the crown of thorns,
> O see my Jesus hangin' high!

> He look so pale an' bleed so free:
> O don't you think it was a shame,
> He hung three hours in dreadful pain?

They also can experience the divine victory of Jesus' resurrection:

> Weep no more, Marta
> Weep no more, Mary,
> Jesus rise from the dead,
> Happy Morning.

When the people are thrown back into their present social context, they bring with them this sense of having been a witness to Jesus' life, death, and resurrection. Through the experience of moving back and forth between the first and the twentieth centuries, the Bible is transformed from just a report of what the disciples believed about Jesus to black people's personal story of God's will to liberate the oppressed in their contemporary context. They can now testify with the apostle Paul: "For I am not ashamed of the Gospel. It is the saving power of God for everyone who has faith . . . because here is revealed God's way of righting wrong, a way that starts from faith and ends in faith" (Rom. 1:16–17 NEB).

Who Jesus is for us today is not decided by focusing our attention exclusively on either the social context alone or the Bible alone but by seeing them in dialectical relation. The true interpretation of one is dependent upon viewing it in the light of the other. We must say unequivocally that who Jesus Christ is for black people today is found through an encounter with him in the social context of black existence. But as soon as that point is made, the other side of this paradox must be affirmed; otherwise the truth of the black experience is distorted. The Jesus of the black experience is the Jesus of Scripture. The dialectic relationship of the black experience and Scripture is the point of departure of Black Theology's christology.

Serving as an authority, in addition to Scripture, is the tradition of the Church. Tradition is important because it is the bridge that connects Scripture with our contemporary situation. While tradition does not carry the same weight of authority as Scripture, our understanding of the meaning of Jesus Christ in the latter is mediated through the former. Tradition then represents the Church's affirmation of faith in Jesus Christ at different periods of its history. By looking at the meaning of Jesus Christ in the latter, he is mediated through the former. By looking at the meaning of Jesus Christ in different church traditions, we are given clues to ways of understanding him today. Tradition, like Scripture, opens our story of Christ to other stories in the past and thus forces us to move outside the subjectivity of our present. Tradition requires that we ask, What has my experience of Christ today to do with the Christ of Nestorius of Constantinople and Cyril of Alexandria?

However, we must not forget that what is usually called "tradition" represents the Church's theological justification of its existence on the basis of its support of the state in the oppression of the poor. What are we to make of a tradition that investigated the meaning of Christ's relation to God and the divine and human natures in his person, but failed to relate these christological issues to the liberation of the slave; did the Church lose the very essence of the gospel of Jesus Christ?

Whether we answer the foregoing question negatively or positively, it is no less true that American black people have a tradition of their own that stretches back to Africa and its traditional religions. We are an *African* people, at least to the degree that our grandparents came from Africa and not from Europe. They brought with them their stories and combined them with the Christian story, thereby creating a black religious tradition unique to North America.

African culture informed black people's perspective on Christianity and made it impossible for many slaves to accept an interpretation of the Jesus story that violated their will for freedom. The passive Christ of white Christianity when combined with African culture became the Liberator of the oppressed from sociopolitical oppression. Under the influence of this Christ, Richard Allen and James Varick led black people to separate themselves from the white Methodist Church. At another time, Nat Turner saw Jesus as the spirit of violent revolution against the structures of slavery.

Again this Christ takes the black believer out of history entirely and places him in a new heaven where the streets are gold and the gates are pearl. But in every case, Christ is the *otherness* in the black experience that makes possible the affirmation of black humanity in an inhumane situation. We must turn to this tradition of black christology for a perspective on Jesus Christ that will enable us to address the right questions to the "classical" tradition and also locate the Christ of Scripture in our contemporary situation.

By focusing on the black tradition, we not only recieve a check against the inordinate influence of the "classical" tradition but also gain a fresh perspective for interpreting Scripture in the light of Christ. The black tradition breaks down the false distinctions between the sacred and the secular, and invites us to look for Christ's meaning in the spirituals and the blues, folklore and sermon. Christ's meaning is not only expressed in formal church doctrine but also in the rhythm, the beat, and the swing of life, as the people respond to the vision that stamps dignity upon their personhood. It does not matter whether the vision is received on Saturday night or Sunday morning, or whether the interpreter of the vision is bluesman B. B. King or the Rev. C. L. Franklin. Some people will be able to participate in both expressions without experiencing any contradiction. Others will feel at home with only one, whether blues or spiritual. But the crucial point is that both expressions represent the people's attempt to transcend, to "step over,"[3] the limitations placed on them by white society. This is the context for a black analysis of Christ's meaning for today.

To summarize: the dialectic between the social situation of the believer and Scripture and the traditions of the Church is the place to begin the investigation of the question, Who is Jesus Christ for us today? Social context, Scripture, and tradition operate together to enable the people of God to move actively and reflectively with Christ in the struggle of freedom.

JESUS IS WHO HE WAS

The dialectic of Scripture and tradition in relation to our contemporary social context forces us to affirm that there is no knowledge of Jesus Christ today that contradicts who he was yesterday, i.e., his historical appearance in first-century Palestine. Jesus' past is the clue to his present activity in the sense that his past is the medium through which he is made accessible to us today. The historical Jesus is indispensable for a knowledge of the Risen Christ. If it can be shown that the New Testament contains no reliable historical information about Jesus of Nazareth or that the kerygma (early Christian preaching) bears no relation to the historical Jesus, then Christian theology is an impossible enterprise.

In this sense Wolfhart Pannenberg is correct in his insistence that christology must begin "from below" with the historical Jesus and not "from above" with the divine Logos separated from the Jesus of history. Pannenberg writes:

Jesus possesses significance for us only to the extent that this significance is inherent in himself, in his history, and in his person constituted by this history. Only when this can be shown may we be sure that we are not merely attaching our questions, wishes, and thoughts to his figure.[4]

If we do not take the historical Jesus seriously as the key to locating the meaning of Christ's presence today, there is no way to avoid the charge of subjectivism, the identification of Christ today with a momentary political persuasion. Although it cannot "prove," by historical study alone, that Jesus is the Christ, the historical record provides the essential datum without which faith in Christ is impossible.[5]

The error of separating the historical Jesus from the Christ of faith has a long history. The Church Fathers, including the great theologian Athanasius, tended to make Jesus' divinity the point of departure for an understanding of his humanity. Therefore, whatever else may be said about the limitations of Harnack's perspective on the *History of Dogma,* he was not too far wrong in his contention that "no single outstanding church teacher really accepted the humanity [of Jesus] in a perfectly unqualified way.[6] For example, Athanasius stressed the humanity of Jesus because, without becoming human, Christ could not have divinized us. "For he was made man," writes Athanasius, "that we might be made God".[7] Here, as with other church teachers, soteriology determined christology.

Who Christ is was controlled by the Greek view of what God had to do to save man. Few, if any, of the early Church Fathers grounded their christological arguments in the concrete history of Jesus of Nazareth. Consequently, little is said about the significance of his ministry to the poor as a definition of his person. The Nicene Fathers showed little interest in the christological significance of Jesus' deeds for the humiliated, because most of the discussion took place in the social context of the Church's position as the favored religion of the Roman State. It therefore became easy to define Jesus as the divinizer (the modern counterpart is "spiritualizer") of humanity. When this happens, christology is removed from history, and salvation becomes only peripherally related to this world.

This tendency continued through the Middle Ages and, as Schweitzer demonstrated, into the modern German tradition.[8] The historical Jesus was separated from the Christ of faith, and the result was docetism. The historical component of the New Testament witness was subordinated or discredited, leaving Christ's humanity without support. This was the danger of Kierkegaard's contention that "from history one can learn nothing about Christ"[9] and of Bultmann's program of demythologization. If the historical Jesus is unimportant, then the true humanity of Christ is relegated to the periphery of christological analysis. At best Christ's humanity is merely verbalized for the purpose of focusing on his divinity.

This error was evident in the early developments of "dialectical theology" as represented in Emil Brunner's *The Mediator*[10] and in Karl Barth's emphasis on Christ as the Revealed Word. Barth's stress on Christ as the Word of God who stands in judgment on man's word led him to subordinate the historical Jesus in his analysis of the Christian gospel. For example, he admitted in the "Preface to the Second Edition" of *The Epistle to the Romans* (1921) that his system is "limited to a recognition of what Kierkegaard called the 'infinite qualitative distinction' between time and eternity."[11] And since the historical Jesus lived in time, Barth's avowed concern to hear God's eternal Word caused him to play down the human side of Christ's presence. To be sure, the 1920s and the 1930s needed that emphasis, and later Barth corrected much of this one-sided view in *The Humanity of God* (1956).[12] But he never really recovered from the early theme of God's absolute transcendence and thus did not achieve the proper dialectical relationship between the historical Jesus and the Christ of faith.

Contemporary theologians have attempted to correct the one-sidedness of the early Church and the implied docetism of dialectical theologians. Pannenberg is a case in point: "Where the statement that Jesus is God would contradict his real humanity, one would probably rather surrender the confession of his divinity than to doubt that he was really a man."[13] In my perspective, this means that christology must begin with an affirmation of who Jesus was in his true humanity in history, using that point as the clue to who Jesus is for us today.

The docetic error crossed the Atlantic to North America in the seventeenth century. Particularly during the nineteenth century, it displayed special "made in U.S.A." features, as white theologians and preachers contended that slavery was consistent with the gospel of Jesus. Like their German contemporaries whom Schweitzer criticized for allowing subjective interests to determine their analysis of the historical Jesus, the white American Church's analysis of Christ was defined by white people's political and economic interests, and not by the biblical witness.

Black slaves, on the other hand, contended that slavery contradicts the New Testament Christ. They claimed to know about a Christ who came to give freedom and dignity to the oppressed and humiliated. Through sermon, prayer, and song, black slaves bore witness to the little baby that was born of "Sister Mary" in Bethlehem and "everytime the baby cried, she's a-rocked Him in the weary land." He is the One who lived with the poor and died on the cross so that they might have a new life.

The white minister preached to black people about the joys of heaven from a white viewpoint, saying: "Now you darkies need not worry, for God has some mighty good asphalt streets and cement streets for you to walk on." But Uncle Jim's prayerful response to the white minister put the situation quite differently: "Lawd, I knows dat I's your child and when I gets to heaven I's gonna walk any damn where I please."[14] Now if there is no real basis for Uncle Jim's faith in the historical Jesus, then the distinction between the white minister's and Uncle Jim's claims about God are limited to a difference in their social contexts. The same is true of contemporary white theology and black theology. Unless the latter takes seriously who Jesus was as the key to who he is today, then black theologians have no reason to complain about white people using Jesus Christ for the advancement of the present system of oppression.

My assertion that "Jesus is who he was" affirms not only the importance of Scripture as the basis of christology. It also stresses the biblical emphasis on Jesus' humanity in history as the starting point of christological analysis. For without the historical Jesus, theology is left with a docetic Christ who is said to be human but is actually nothing but an idea-principle in a theological system. We cannot have a human Christ unless we have a historical Christ, that is, unless we *know* his history. That is why the writers of the four Gospels tell the good news in the form of the story of Jesus' life. The events described are not intended as fiction but as God's way of changing the course of history in a human person.

The historical Jesus emphasizes the social context of christology and thereby establishes the importance of Jesus' racial identity. *Jesus was a Jew!* The particularity of Jesus' person as disclosed in his Jewishness is indispensable for christological analysis.

On the one hand, Jesus' Jewishness pinpoints the importance of his humanity for faith, and on the other, connects God's salvation drama in Jesus with the Exodus-Sinai event.

Through the divine election of Jesus the Jew as the means of human salvation, Yahweh makes real the divine promise that through Abraham "all the families of the earth shall bless themselves" (Gen. 12:3 RSV). In order to keep the divine promise to make Israel "a kingdom of priests and a holy nation" (Exod. 19:6 RSV), Yahweh became a Jew in Jesus of Nazareth, thereby making possible the reconciliation of the world to himself (ICor. 5:19). Jesus' Jewishness therefore was essential to his person. He was not a "universal" man but a particular Jew who came to fulfill God's will to liberate the oppressed. His Jewishness establishes the concreteness of his existence in history, without which christology inevitably moves in the direction of docetism.

The humanity of Jesus was the emphasis of black slaves when they sang about his suffering and pain during the crucifixion:

> Were you there when they crucified my Lord?
> were you there when they crucified my Lord?
> Oh! sometimes it causes me to tremble, tremble, tremble;
> were you there when they crucified my Lord?

With deep passion and a transcendent leap back into first-century Jerusalem, black people described the details of Jesus suffering on the cross: "Dey whupped him up de hill," "dey crowned him wid a thorny crown," "dey nailed him to de cross," "dey pierced him in de side," "de blood came twinklin' down, an' he never said a mumbalin' word, he jes hung his head an' he died." Unless the biblical story is historically right in its picture of the humanity of Jesus, then there is no reason to believe that he shared our suffering and pain.

The authenticity of the New Testament Jesus guarantees the integrity of his human presence with the poor and the wretched in the struggle of freedom. In Jesus' presence with the poor in Palestine, he disclosed who they were and what they were created to be (Heb. 2: 17-18). Likewise, we today can lay claim on the same humanity that was liberated through Jesus' cross and resurrection. Because Jesus lived, we now know that servitude is inhuman, and that Christ has set us free to live as liberated sons and daughters of God. Unless Jesus was truly like us, then we have no basis to contend that his coming bestows upon us the courage and the wisdom to struggle against injustice and oppression.

NOTES

1. Included in *Kerygma and Myth,* H.W. Bartsch, ed. (New York, Harper Torchbooks, 1961) 1–44. Bultmann's essay was originally published in 1941.

2. New York, Harper & Row, 1973.

3. See Ernst Bloch's comments in *Atheism in Christianity* (New York, Herder and Herder, 1972): "To think is to step over, to over step" (p.9).

4. *Jesus—God and Man* (Philadelplhia, Westminster, 1968) 48. Of course, Pannenberg intends to say much more in this statement than is suggested in my use of it here. He speaks, I think wrongly, of "revelation as history," and not simply of the latter as the foundation of the former. Consequently he insists upon Jesus' resurrection as a historical event. See also his *Revelation as History* (New York, Macmillan, 1969); see also James M. Robinson and John B. Cobb, Jr., eds., *Theology as History* (New York, Harper & Row, 1967).

5. While insisting on the necessity of the historical Jesus for christological reflections, I am aware of the historical difficulties associated with the four Gospels, the primary source for knowledge of Jesus. See my discussion in *God of the Oppressed,* chap. 4, note 4. See also *A Black*

Theology of Liberation, chap. 6. My point here and elsewhere is clear enough: The truth of Jesus Christ stands or falls on the historical validity of the biblical claim that Jesus identified with the poor and the outcasts. That historical fact alone does not provide the evidence that Jesus is the Christ, for the same could be said of other people in history; but without this historical fact, the claim that God has come to liberate the weak in Jesus is sheer illusion.

Of course I do not intend to make the Christian faith dependent upon scholarly investigations, for scholars are not immune to social and political interests. But the truth of the faith is not threatened by critical scholarship. Furthermore, the risks involved in academic pursuits are related to the risk of faith itself, from which no one is excluded. Indeed the honest acceptance of risk and its implications for faith provides an openness in faith and thus the willingness to listen to other viewpoints. The result of scholarship is merely one viewpoint which must be weighed in the context of human experience. For an excellent analysis of the historical Jesus' relation to the Christian faith, see Leander E. Keck, *A Future for the Historical Jesus* (Nashville, Abingdon, 1971).

6. Harnack, *History of Dogma,* vol. 4 (New York, Dover, 1961) 139.

7. Athanasius, "On the Incarnation," in *The Library of Christian Classics,* vol. 3, Edward R. Hardy in collaboration with Cyril Richardson (Philadelphia, Westminster, 1954) 107. For a more recent interpretation of the function of deification in the development of the early Church doctrines, see Jaroslav Pelikan, *The Christian Tradition,* vol. 1 (University of Chicago Press, 1971).

8. See Albert Schweitzer, *The Quest of the Historical Jesus* [original German title, *Von Reimarus zu Wrede,* 1906] (New York, Macmillan, 1961).

9. *Training in Christianity* (Princeton University Press, 1941) 28. In his *Philosophical Fragments* (Princeton University Press, 1962), he says: "If the contemporary generation had left nothing behind them but these words: 'We have believed that in such and such a year that God appeared among us in the humble figure of a servant, that he lived and taught in our community, and finally died, it would be more than enough" (p. 130). See the comparison of Kierkegaard and Bultmann in Herbert C. Wolf, *Kierkegaard and Bultmann: The Quest of the Historical Jesus* (Minneapolis, Augsburg, 1965).

10. London, Lutterworth, 1934.

11. London, Oxford University Press, 1933.

12. Richmond, John Knox Press, 1960.

13. *Jesus—God and Man,* p.189. For another contemporary perspective on christology that emphasizes the humanity of Christ, see W. Norman Pittenger, *The Word Incarnate* (New York, Harper & Row, 1959); idem, *Christology Reconsidered* (London, SCM, 1970). An excellent treatise on the importance of Jesus' humanity is John Knox, *The Humanity and Divinity of Christ* (Cambridge University Press, 1967). On the issue of humanity and divinity in Jesus Christ, he writes: "If we should find ourselves in the position of having to decide between the pre-existence and a fully authentic human life, there is no doubt what our choice should be. Although it would be a grievous error to suppose that the humanity of Jesus is surer or more important than his divinity—the two are equally sure and more important than the pre-existence" (pp. 73-74). Another example of the importance of Jesus' humanity, and thus history for christology is Peter C. Hodgson, *Jesus—World and Presence* (Philadelphia, Fortress, 1971).

14. J. Mason Brewer, *Worser Days and Better Times* (Chicago, Quadrangle Books, 1965) 103.

Chapter 22

Cornel West

Prophetic Afro-American Christian Thought and Progressive Marxism

. . . The prevailing conception of black theology of liberation remains inadequate. I believe that a new conception of black theology of liberation is needed which preserves the positive content of its earlier historical stages, overcomes its earlier (and inevitable) blindnesses, and makes explicit its present challenges. The positive content of the earlier conceptions of black theology of liberation is as follows:

1. The theological claim (or faith claim) that God sides with the oppressed and acts on their belief.
2. The idea that the religion of the oppressed can be either an opiate or a source of struggle for liberation.
3. The idea that white racism is a cancer at the core of an exploitative capitalist U.S. society.

The limitations and shortcomings of earlier conceptions of black theology are:

1. Its absence of a systematic social analysis, which has prevented black theologians from coming to terms with the relationships between racism, sexism, class exploitation, and imperialist oppression.
2. Its lack of a social vision, political program, and concrete praxis which defines and facilitates socioeconomic and political liberation.
3. Its tendency to downplay existential issues such as death, disease, dread, despair, and disappointment which are related to, yet not identical with, suffering caused by oppressive structures.

The present challenge to black theologians is to put forward an understanding of the Christian gospel in the light of present circumstances that takes into account the complex ways in which racism (especially white racism) and sexism (especially male sexism) are integral to the class exploitative capitalist system of production as well as its repressive imperialist tentacles abroad; and to keep in view the crucial existential issues of death, disease, despair, dread, and disappointment that each and every individual must face within the context of these present circumstances.

This theological perspective requires a move into a fifth stage: "Black Theology of Liberation as Critique of Capitalist Civilization." In short, black theological reflection and action must simultaneously become more familiar with and rooted in the progressive Marxist tradition, with its staunch anticapitalist, anti-imperialist, antiracist, and antisexist stance and its creative socialist outlook; and more anchored in its own proto-Kierkegaardian viewpoint, namely, its proper concern with the existential issues facing individuals.

So black theologians and Marxist thinkers are strangers. They steer clear of each other, content to express concerns to their respective audiences. Needless to say, their concerns overlap. Both focus on the plight of the exploited, oppressed, and degraded peoples of the world, their relative powerlessness and possible empowerment. I believe this common focus warrants a serious dialogue between black theologians and Marxist thinkers. This dialogue should not be a mere academic chat that separates religionists and secularists, theists and atheists. Instead, it ought to be an earnest encounter that specifies clearly the different sources of their praxis of faith, yet accents the possibility of mutually arrived at political action.

The primary aim of this encounter is to change the world, not each other's faith; to put both groups on the offensive for structural social change, not put black Christians on the defensive; and to enhance the quality of life of the dispossessed, not expose the empty Marxist meaning of death. In short, both black theologians and Marxist thinkers must preserve their own existential and intellectual integrity and explore the possibility of promoting fundamental social amelioration together.

Black theology and Marxist thought are not monolithic bodies of thought; each contains different perspectives, distinct viewpoints, and diverse conclusions. Therefore it is necessary to identify the particular claims put forward by black theology and by Marxist thought, those claims which distinguish each as a discernible school of thought. Black theology claims:

1. The historical experience of black people and the readings of the bibilical texts that emerge therefrom are the centers around which reflection about God evolves.
2. This reflection is related, in some way, to the liberation of black people, to the creation of a more abundant life definable in existential, economic, social, and political terms.

Marxist thought contains two specific elements: a theory of history and an understanding of capitalism. These two elements are inextricably interlinked, but it may be helpful to characterize them separately. The Marxist theory of history claims:

1. The history of human societies is the history of their transitional stages.
2. The transitional stages of human societies are discernible owing to their systems of production, or their organizational arrangements in which people produce goods and services for their survival.
3. Conflict within systems of production of human societies ultimately results in fundamental social change, or transitions from one historical stage to another.
4. Conflict within systems of production of human societies consists of cleavages between social classes (in those systems of production).
5. Social classes are historically transient, rooted in a particular set of socioeconomic conditions.
6. Therefore, the history of all hitherto existing society is the history of class struggles.

The Marxist theory of capitalist society claims: Capitalism is a historically transient system of production which requires human beings to produce commodities for the purpose of maximizing surplus value (profits). This production presupposes a fundamental social relationship between the purchasers and the sellers of a particular commodity, namely, the labor power (time, skill, and expertise) of producers. This crucial commodity is bought by capitalists who own the land, instruments, and capital necessary for production. The aim of the former is to maximize profits; that of the latter, to ensure their own survival.

I shall claim that black theology and Marxist thought share three characteristics. First, both adhere to a similar methodology: they have the same way of approaching their respective subject matter and arriving at conclusions. Second, both link some notion of liberation to the future socioeconomic conditions of the downtrodden. Third, and most important, both attempt to put forward trenchant critiques of liberal capitalist America. I will try to show that these three traits provide a springboard for a meaningful dialogue between black theologians and Marxist thinkers, and possibly spearhead a unifying effort for structural social change in liberal capitalist America.

DIALECTICAL METHODOLOGY: UNMASKING FALSEHOODS

Black theologians have either consciously or unconsciously employed a dialectical methodology in approaching their subject matter. This methodology consists of a three-step procedure of negation, preservation, and transformation of their subject matter, of white interpretations of the Christian gospel and their own circumstances. Dialectical methodology is critical in character and hermeneutic in content.[1] For black theologians, it is highly critical of dogmatic viewpoints of the gospel, questioning whether certain unjustifiable prejudgments are operative. It is hermeneutic in that it is concerned with unearthing assumptions of particular interpretations and presenting an understanding of the gospel that extends and expands its ever-unfolding truth.

Black theologians have, for the most part, been compelled to adopt a dialectical methodology. They have refused to accept what has been given to them by white theologians; they have claimed that all reflection about God by whites must be digested, decoded, and deciphered. The first theological formulations by Afro-Americans based on biblical texts tried to come to terms with their white owners' viewpoints and their own servitude. Since its inception, black theology has been forced to reduce white deception and distortion of the gospel and make the Christian story meaningful in the light of their oppressive conditions.

The reflection by black theologians begins by negating white interpretations of the gospel, continues by preserving their own perceived truths of the biblical texts, and ends by transforming past understandings of the gospel into new ones. These three steps embody an awareness of the social context of theologizing, the need to accent the historical experience of black people and the insights of the Bible, and the ever-evolving task of recovering, regaining, and repeating the gospel.

Black theologians underscore the importance of the social context of theological reflection.[2] Their dialectical methodology makes them sensitive to the hidden agendas of the theological formulations they negate, agendas often guided by social interests. Their penchant for revealing distortions leads them to adopt a sociology of knowledge approach that stresses the way in which particular viewpoints endorse and encourage ulterior aims.

An interpretation of the black historical experience and the readings of the biblical texts that emerge out of this experience constitute the raw ingredients for the second step of black theological reflection. By trying to understand the plight of black people in the light of the Bible, black theologians claim to preserve the biblical truth that God sides with the oppressed and acts on their behalf.[3] Subsequently, the black historical experience and the biblical texts form a symbiotic relationship, each illuminating the other.

Since black theologians believe in the living presence of God and the work of the Holy Spirit, they acknowledge the constant unfolding process of the gospel. Paradoxically, the gospel is unchanging, yet it is deepened by embracing and encompassing new human realities and experiences. The gospel must speak to every age. Therefore it must be recovered and repeated, often sounding different, but in substance remaining the same. For black theologians, it sounds different because it addresses various contexts of oppression; it remains the same because it is essentially a gospel of liberation.

Marxist thinkers, like black theologians, employ a dialectical methodology in approaching their subject matter. But they do so consciously and their subject matter is bourgeois theories about capitalist society. The primary theoretical task of Marxist thinkers is to uncover the systematic misunderstanding of capitalist society by bourgeois thinkers; to show how this misunderstanding, whether deliberate or not, supports and sanctions exploitation and oppression in this society; and to put forward the correct understanding of this society in order to change it.

Marxist social theory is first and foremost a critique of inadequate theories of capitalist society and subsequently a critique of capitalist society itself. The subtitle of Marx's magnum opus, *Capital*, is "A Critique of Political Economy," not "A Critique of Capitalism." This work takes bourgeois economists to task for perpetuating falsehoods, which then results in revealing the internal dynamics of capitalism and the inhumane consequences. For Marx, a correct understanding of capitalist society is possible only by overcoming present mystifications of it; and this correct understanding is requisite for a propitious political praxis.

Marxist thought stresses the conflict-laden unfolding of history, the conflict-producing nature of social processes. Therefore it is not surprising that Marxist thinkers employ a dialectical methodology, a methodology deeply suspicious of stasis and stability, and highly skeptical of equilibrium and equipoise. This methodology, like that of black theologians, is critical in character and hermeneutic in content. It is critical of perspectives presented by bourgeois social scientists, questioning whether certain ideological biases are operative. It is hermeneutic in that it is obsessed with discovering the correct understanding underneath wrong interpretations, disclosing latent truths behind manifest distortions. For Marx, to be scientific is to be dialectical and to be dialectical is to unmask, unearth, to bring to light.[4]

This conception of science, derived from Hegel, attempts to discern the hidden kernel of an evolving truth becoming manifest by bursting through a visible husk. The husk, once a hidden kernel, dissolves, leaving its indelible imprint upon the new, emerging kernel. This idea of inquiry highlights the moments of negation, preservation, and transformation. By presenting his theory of history and society from this perspective, Marx provided the most powerful and penetrating social criticism in modern times. Dialectical methodology enabled him to create a whole mode of inquiry distinctively his own, though often appearing hermetic and rigid to the untutored and the fanatic.

Despite the similar procedure that black theologians and Marxist thinkers share, there has been little discussion about it between them. This is so, primarily because a dialectical methodology is implicit, hence undeveloped and often unnoticed, in black theology. This failure to examine the methodological stance embodied in black theological reflection obscures its similarity with that of Marxist thought.

LIBERATION: ITS CONSTITUTIVE ELEMENTS

Black theologians all agree that black liberation has something to do with ameliorating the socioeconomic conditions of black people. But it is not clear what this amelioration amounts to. There is little discussion in their writings about what the liberating society will be like. The notion and the process of liberation are often mentioned, but, surprisingly, one is hard put to find a sketch of what liberation would actually mean in the everyday lives of black people, what power they would possess, and what resources they would have access to.

There are two main reasons for this neglect among black theologians. First, a dialectical methodology discourages discussions about the ideal society and simply what ought to be. Instead, it encourages criticizing and overcoming existing society, negating and opposing what is.

The second reason, the one we shall be concerned with in this section, is the failure of black theologians to talk specifically about the way in which the existing system of production and the social structure relate to black oppression and exploitation. Without a focusing upon this relationship, it becomes extremely difficult to present an idea of liberation with socioeconomic content. In short, the lack of clear-cut social theory prevents the emergence of any substantive political program or social vision.

Aside from James Cone in his latest writings, black theologians remain uncritical of America's imperialist presence in Third World countries, its capitalist system of production, and its grossly unequal distribution of wealth. Therefore we may assume they find this acceptable. If this is so, then the political and socioeconomic components of black liberation amount to racial equality before the law, equal opportunities in employment, education, and business, and economic parity with whites in median income.

Surely, this situation would be better than the current dismal one, but it hardly can be viewed as black liberation. It roughly equates liberation with American middle-class status, leaving the unequal distribution of wealth relatively untouched and the capitalist system of production, along with its imperialist ventures, intact. Liberation would consist of including black people within the mainstream of liberal capitalist America. If this is the social vision of black theologians, they should drop the meretricious and flamboyant term "liberation" and adopt the more accurate and sober word "inclusion."

Marxist thought, like black theology, does not elaborate on the ideal society. As we noted earlier, a dialectical methodology does not permit this elaboration. But the brief sketch that progressive Marxist thinkers provide requires a particular system of production and political arrangement—namely, participatory democracy in each. Human liberation occurs only when people participate substantively in the decision-making processes in the major institutions that regulate their lives. Democratic control over the institutions in the productive and political processes in order for them to satisfy human needs and protect personal liberties of the populace constitutes human liberation.

Progressive Marxist thinkers are able to present this sketch of human liberation primarily because they stress what people must liberate themselves from. They suggest what liberation is for only after understanding the internal dynamics of the society from which people must be liberated. Without this clear-cut social theory about what is, it is difficult to say anything significant about what can be. The possibility of liberation is found only within the depths of the actuality of oppression. Without an adequate social theory, this possibility is precluded.

SOCIAL CRITICISM: CLASS, RACE, AND CULTURE

Black theology puts forward a vehement, often vociferous, critique of liberal capitalist America. One of its most attractive and alluring characteristics is its theological indictment of racist American society. An undisputable claim of black theology is America's unfair treatment of black people. What is less apparent is the way in which black theologians understand the internal dynamics of liberal capitalist America, how it functions, why it operates the way it does, who possesses substantive power, and where it is headed. As noted earlier, black theologians do not utilize a social theory that relates the oppression of black people to the overall makeup of America's system of production, foreign policy, political arrangement, and cultural practices.

Black theologians hardly mention the wealth, power, and influence of multinational corporations that monopolize production in the marketplace and prosper partially because of their dependence on public support in the form of government subsidies, free technological equipment, lucrative contracts, and sometimes even direct transfer payments. Black theologians do not stress the way in which corporate interests and the government intermesh, usually resulting in policies favorable to the former. Black theologians fail to highlight the fact that in liberal capitalist America one half of 1 percent own 22 percent of the wealth, 1 percent own 33 percent of the wealth, the lower 61 percent own only 7 percent of the wealth.[5] Lastly, black theologians do not emphasize sufficiently the way in which the racist interpretations of the gospel they reject encourage and support the capitalist system of production, its grossly unequal distribution of wealth, and its closely connected political arrangements.

Instead of focusing on these matters, black theologians draw attention to the racist practices in American society. Since these practices constitute the most visible and vicious form of oppression in America, black theologians justifiably do so. Like the Black Power proponents of the '60s, they call for the empowerment of black people, the need for black people to gain significant control over their lives. But neither Black Power proponents nor black theologians have made it sufficiently clear as to what constitutes this black control, the real power to direct institutions such that black people can live free of excessive exploitation and oppression. The tendency is to assume that middle-class status is equivalent to such control, that a well-paying job amounts to such power. Surely, this assumption is fallacious.

The important point here is not that racist practices should be stressed less by black theologians, for such practices deeply affect black people and shape the perceptions of American society. What is crucial is that these practices be linked to the role they play in buttressing the current mode of production, concealing the unequal distribution of wealth, and portraying the lethargy of the political system. Black theologians are correct in relating racist practices to degrees of black powerlessness, but they obscure this relation by failing to provide a lucid definition of what power is in American society. Subsequently, they often fall into the trap of assuming power in American society to be synonymous with receiving high wages.

Marxist social criticism can be quite helpful at this point. For Marx, power in modern industrial society consists of a group's participation in the decision-making processes of the major institutions that affect their destinies. Since institutions of production, such as multinational corporations, play an important role in people's lives, these institutions should be significantly accountable to the populace. In short, they should be democratically controlled by the citizenry; people should participate in their decision-making processes. Only collective control over the major institutions of society constitutes genuine power on behalf of the people.

For Marx, power in modern industrial society is closely related to a group's say over what happens to products produced in the work situation, to a group's input into decisions that direct the production flow of goods and services. The most powerful group in society has the most say and input into decisions over this production flow; the least powerful group does not participate at all in such decisions. In liberal capitalist America, the former consist of multiple corporate owners who dictate policies concerning the mass production of a variety of products produced by white- and blue-collar workers who receive wages in return. The latter consist of the so-called underclass, the perennially unemployed who are totally removed from the work situation, precluded from any kind of input affecting the production flow, including negotiation and strikes available to white- and blue-collar workers.

Racist practices intensify the degree of powerlessness among black people. This is illustrated by the high rate of black unemployment, the heavy black concentration in low-paying jobs, and inferior housing, education, police protection, and health care. But it is important to note that this powerlessness differs from that of white- and blue-collar workers in degree, not in kind. In human terms, this difference is immense, incalculable; in structural terms, this difference is negligible, trifling. In other words, most Americans are, to a significant degree, powerless. They have no substantive control over their lives, little participation in the decision-making process of the major institutions that regulate their lives. Among Afro-Americans, this powerlessness is exacerbated, creating an apparent qualitative difference in oppression.

This contrast of the social criticism of black theologians and Marxist thinkers raises the age-old question as to whether class position or racial status is the major determinant of black oppression in America. This question should be formulated in the following way: whether class position or racial status contributes most to the fundamental form of powerlessness in America.

Racial status contributes greatly to black oppression. But middle-class black people are essentially well-paid white- or blue-collar workers who have little control over their lives primarily because of their class position, not their racial status. This is so because the same limited control is held by white middle-class people, despite the fact that a higher percentage of whites are well-paid white- and blue-collar workers than blacks. Significant degrees of powerlessness pertain to most Americans and this could be so only if class position determines such powerlessness. Therefore, class position contributes more than racial status to the basic form of powerlessness in America.

I am suggesting that the more black theologians discard or overlook Marxist social criticism, the farther they distance themselves from the fundamental determinant of black oppression and any effective strategy to alleviate it. This distancing also obscures the direct relationship of black oppression in America to black and brown oppression in Third World countries. The most powerful group in America, those multiple corporate owners who dictate crucial corporate policies over a variety of production flows, are intimately and inextricably linked (through their highly paid American and Third World white-collar workers and grossly underpaid Third World blue-collar workers) to the economies and governments of the Third World countries, including the most repressive ones. Marxist social criticism permits this relationship to come to light in an extremely clear and convincing way.

The social criticism of black theologians reflects the peculiar phenomenon of American liberal and radical criticism. This criticism rarely has viewed class position as a major determinant of oppression primarily because of America's lack of a feudal past, the heterogeneity of its population, the many and disparate regions of its geography, and the ever-increasing levels of productivity and growth. These facts make it difficult to see class divisions, and, along with other forms of oppression, make it almost impossible. But, like protons leaving vapor trails in a cloud chamber, one is forced to posit them in the light of the overwhelming evidence for their existence. Only class divisions can explain the gross disparity between rich and poor, the immense benefits accruing to the former and the depravity of the latter.

Region, sex, age, ethnicity, and race often have been considered the only worthy candidates as determinants of oppression. This has been so primarily because American liberal and radical criticism usually has presupposed the existing system of production, assumed class divisions, and attempted only to include marginal groups in the mainstream of liberal capitalist America. This criticism has fostered a petit bourgeois viewpoint that clamors for a bigger piece of the ever-growing American pie, rarely asking fundamental questions such as why it never gets recut more equally or how it gets baked in the first place. In short, this criticism remains silent about class divisions, the crucial role they play in maintaining the unequal distribution of goods and services, and how they undergird discrimination against regions, impose ceilings on upward social mobility, and foster racism, sexism, and ageism. As has been stated above, with the exception of James Cone in his most recent writings, contemporary black theologians suffer from this general myopia of American liberal and radical criticism.

Despite this shortsightedness, black theologians have performed an important service for Marxist thinkers, namely, emphasizing the ways in which culture and religion resist oppression. They have been admirably sensitive to the black cultural buffers against oppression, especially the black religious sources of struggle and strength, vitality and vigor. They also have stressed the indispensable contribution the black churches have made toward the survival, dignity, and self-worth of black people.

Contrary to Marxist thinkers, black theologians recognize that cultural and religious attitudes, values, and sensibilities have a life and logic of their own, not fully accountable in terms of a class analysis. Subsequently, racist practices are not reducible to a mere clever and successful strategy of divide and conquer promoted by the ruling class to prevent proletarian unity. Rather, racism is an integral element within the very fabric of American culture and society. It is embedded in the country's first collective definition, enunciated in its subsequent laws, and imbued in its dominant way of life.

The orthodox Marxist analysis of culture and religion that simply relates racist practices to misconceived material interests is only partially true, hence deceptive and misleading. These practices are fully comprehensible only if one conceives of culture, not as a mere hoax played by the ruling class on workers, but as the tradition that informs one's conception of tradition, as social practices that shape one's idea of social practice.

The major objection to the orthodox Marxist analysis of culture and religion is not that it is wrong, but that it is too narrow, rigid, and dogmatic. It views popular culture and religion only as instruments of domination, vehicles of pacification. It sees only their negative and repressive elements. On this view, only enlightenment, reason, or clarity imposed from the outside can break through the cultural layers of popular false consciousness.[6] Therefore, the orthodox Marxist analysis refuses to acknowledge the positive, liberating aspects of popular culture and religion, and their potential for fostering structural social change.

This issue is at the heart of the early stages of the debate over the adequacy of a Marxist analysis between black theologians and Latin American liberation theologians.

The latter tended to adopt the orthodox Marxist view, paying little attention to the positive, liberating aspects of popular culture and religion.[7] They displayed a contempt for popular culture and religion, a kind of tacit condescension that reeks of paternalism and elitism. They often spoke of the poor possessing a privileged access to truth and reality, but rarely did they take seriously the prevailing beliefs, values, or outlooks of the poor. Instead, Latin American liberation theologians stressed the discontinuity and radical rupture of progressive consciousness with popular culture and religion, suggesting a desire to wipe the cultural slate clean and begin anew.

To the contrary, black theologians recognize the positive and negative elements, the liberating and repressive possibilities, of popular culture and religion. To no surprise, they devote much attention to the armors of survival, forms of reaction, and products of response created by black people in order to preserve their dignity and self-respect.[8] Black theologians view themselves as working within a tradition of political struggle and cultural and religious resistance to oppression. They emphasize their continuity with this tradition.

It is possible to account for this important early difference between black theologians and Latin American liberation theologians by appealing to the different histories of the particular countries about which they theorize. But there is possibly a deeper reason for this disagreement. It relates directly to the composition of the two groups of theologians.

For the most part, Latin American liberation theologians belong to the dominant cultural group in their respective countries. As intellectuals educated in either European schools or Europeanized Latin American universities and seminaries, they adopt cosmopolitan habits and outlooks.[9] Like their theoretical master Karl Marx, a true cosmopolitan far removed from his indigenous Jewish culture, they tend to see popular culture and religion as provincial and parochial. It is something to be shed and ultimately discarded, replaced by something qualitatively different and better. They do not seem to have encountered frequently situations in which they were forced to rely on their own indigenous cultural and religious resources in an alien and hostile environment. So their own experiences often limit their capacity to see the existential richness and radical potential of popular culture and religion.

In contrast to this, black theologians belong to the degraded cultural group in the United States. As intellectuals trained in American colleges, universities, and seminaries, they have firsthand experience of cultural condescension, arrogance, and haughtiness. They know what it is like to be a part of a culture considered to be provincial and parochial. Hence, they view black culture and religion as something to be preserved and promoted, improved and enhanced, not erased and replaced. In short, black theologians acknowledge their personal debts to black culture and religion, and incorporate its fecundity in their understanding of American society.

Latin American liberation theologians and black theologians can learn from each other on this matter. The former must be more sensitive to the complexities and ambiguities of popular culture and religion; the latter should relate more closely their view of black culture and religion to a sophisticated notion of power in liberal capitalist America. And both can learn from the most penetrating Marxist theorist of culture in this century, Antonio Gramsci.[10]

HEGEMONIC CULTURE

Gramsci provides a valuable framework in which to understand culture, its autonomous activity and status, while preserving its indirect yet crucial link with power in society. Unlike the Latin American liberation theologians, he does not downplay the importance of popular culture; unlike the black theologians, he does not minimize the significance of class. Instead, he views the system of production and culture in a symbiotic relationship, each containing intense tension, struggle, and even warfare. Class struggle is not simply the battle between capitalists and the proletariat, owners and producers in the work situation. It also takes the form of cultural and religious conflict over which attitudes, values, and beliefs will dominate the thought and behavior of people. For Gramsci, this incessant conflict is crucial. It contains the key to structural social change; it is the springboard for a revolutionary political praxis.

According to Gramsci, no state or society can be sustained by force alone. It must put forward convincing and persuasive reasons, arguments, ideologies, or propaganda for its continued existence. A state or society requires not only military protection but also principled legitimation. This legitimation takes place in the cultural and religious spheres, in those arenas where the immediacy of everyday life is felt, outlooks formed, and self-images adopted.

Gramsci deepens Marx's understanding of the legitimation process by replacing the notion of ideology with his central concept of hegemony. For Marx, ideology is the set of formal ideas and beliefs promoted by the ruling class for the purpose of preserving its privileged position in society; for Gramsci, hegemony is the set of formal ideas and beliefs and informal modes of behavior, habits, manners, sensibilities, and outlooks that support and sanction the existing order.

In Gramsci's view, culture is both tradition and current practices. Tradition is understood, not as the mere remnants of the past or the lingering, inert elements in the present, but rather as active, formative, and transformative modalities of a society. Current practices are viewed as actualizations of particular modalities, creating new habits, sensibilities, and worldviews against the pressures and limits of the dominant ones.

A hegemonic culture subtly and effectively encourages people to identify themselves with the habits, sensibilities, and worldviews supportive of the status quo and the class interests that dominate it. It is a culture successful in persuading people to "consent" to their oppression and exploitation. A hegemonic culture survives and thrives as long as it convinces people to adopt its preferred formative modality, its favored socialization process. It begins to crumble when people start to opt for a transformative modality, a socialization process that opposes the dominant one. The latter constitutes a counter-hegemonic culture, the deeply embedded oppositional elements within a society. It is these elements the hegemonic culture seeks to contain and control.

Basing my study on the insights of Gramsci, along with those of the distinguished English cultural critic Raymond Williams, I shall present a theoretical framework that may be quite serviceable to black theologians, Latin American liberation theologians, and Marxist thinkers.[11] Cultural processes can be understood in the light of four categories: hegemonic, pre-hegemonic, neo-hegemonic, and counter-hegemonic.

Hegemonic culture is to be viewed as the effectively operative dominant world views, sensibilities, and habits that sanction the established order. Pre-hegemonic culture consists of those residual elements of the past which continue to shape and mold thought and behavior in the present; it often criticizes hegemonic culture, harking back to a golden age in the pristine past. Neo-hegemonic culture constitutes a new phase of hegemonic culture; it postures as an oppositional force, but, in substance, is a new manifestation of people's allegiance and loyalty to the status quo. Counter-hegemonic culture represents genuine opposition to hegemonic culture; it fosters an alternative set of habits, sensibilities, and world views that cannot possibly be realized within the perimeters of the established order.

This framework presupposes three major points. First, it accents the equivocal character of culture and religion, their capacity to be instruments of freedom or domination, vehicles of liberation or pacification. Second, it focuses on the ideological function of culture and religion the necessity of their being either forces for freedom or domination, liberation or pacification. Third, it views the struggle between these two forces as open-ended. The only guarantee of freedom rests upon the contingencies of human practice; the only assurance of liberation relies on the transformative modalities of society. No matter how wide the scope of hegemonic culture may be, it never encompasses or exhausts all human practice or every transformative modality in a society. Human struggle is always a possibility in any society and culture.

In order to clarify further my four categories, I shall identify them crudely with particular elements in contemporary American society. Hegemonic culture can be seen as the prevailing Horatio Alger mystique, the widespread hopes and dreams for social upward mobility among Americans. This mystique nourishes the values, outlooks and lifestyles of achievement, careerism, leisurism, and consumerism that pervade American culture. Pre-hegemonic culture is negligible, owing to the country's peculiar inception, namely, that it was "born liberal." Subsequently, American conservatives and reactionaries find themselves in the ironic position of quarreling with liberals by defending early versions of liberalism. Neo-hegemonic culture is best illustrated by the counter-cultural movement of the 1960s, specifically the protests of white middle-class youth (principally spin-offs of the black political struggles) which with few exceptions was effectively absorbed by the mainstream of liberal capitalist America. The continuous creation of a counter-hegemonic culture is manifest in the multifarious, though disparate, radical grass-roots organizations; elements of the socialist feminists groups; and aspects of Afro-American culture and religion.

A present challenge confronting black theologians is to discover and discern what aspects of Afro-American culture and religion can contribute to a counter-hegemonic culture in American society. They may find Gramsci's conception of organic intellectuals helpful on this matter.[12] Gramsci views organic intellectuals as leaders and thinkers directly tied into a particular cultural group primarily by means of institutional affiliations. Organic intellectuals combine theory and action, and relate popular culture and religion to structural social change.

Black religious leadership can make an enormous contribution to a counter-hegemonic culture and structural social change in American society. Black preachers and pastors are in charge of the most numerous and continuous gatherings of black people, those who are the worst vicitms of liberal capitalist America and whose churches are financially, culturally, and politically free of corporate influence.[13] This freedom of black preachers and pastors, unlike that of most black professionals, is immense. They are the leaders of the only major institutions in the black community that are not accountable to the status quo. Needless to say, many abuse this freedom. But what is important to note is that the contribution of black religious leaders can be prodigious, as exemplified by the great luminaries of the past, including Nat Turner, Martin Delaney, Martin Luther King, Jr., and Malcolm X.

BLACK THEOLOGY AS CRITIQUE OF CAPITALIST CIVILIZATION

I will try to explain what I mean by the vague word "critique." First, I understand this term in a Marxian way; that is; critique is not simply moral criticism of a state of affairs. Rather, critique is a theoretical praxis which:

1. Presupposes a sophisticated understanding of the internal dynamics or power
relations of a society or civilization. This understanding requires a social theory
whose aim is to demystify present ideological distortions or misreadings of society,
to bring to light those who possess power and wealth, why they do, how they
acquired it, how they sustain and enlarge it, and why the poor have little or
nothing.
2. Is integrally linked with a praxis of faith or political movement which is capable in
the near future of fundamentally transforming the present order.
3. Is capable of ushering forth a new order, of organizing, administering, and
governing a more humane social order.

Therefore the crucial characteristics of an acceptable and appropriate critique are
moral sensitivity to the plight of the exploited and oppressed; high-level social analysis
of the sources of exploitation and oppression; objective possibility of weakening the
present order; and praxis of faith or political movement with organization, power, and
social vision, with leaders of impeccable integrity.

NOTES

1. Dialectical methodology is a complex procedure useful for grasping, comprehending,
interpreting, explaining, or predicting phenomena. Aside from the foundation laid by Plato, this
procedure was first fully developed by Hegel and deepened by Marx. Hegel's most succinct
discussions of this approach can be found in his lesser *Logic*, trans. William Wallace, #81, pp. 115–
119, and *The Phenomenology of Mind*, trans. A. V. Miller (New York, 1977), pp. 9–45. For Marx's
brief formal presentation of this approach as it relates to his social theory, see *Grundrisse*, pp. 83–
111.
2. The most explicit and extensive treatment of the social context of theological reflection by a
black theologian is found in James Cone's *God of the Oppressed* (Seabury Press, 1975), Ch. III, pp.
39–61.
3. The most sophisticated dialogue among black theologians has focused on the status of this
biblical truth. William Jones has claimed that black theologians do not provide sufficient empirical
evidence to warrant this truth. He suggests that black theologians have not taken seriously the
possibility of a malevolent deity. For Jones, an acceptable black theology must deal adequately with
the problem of theodicy. James Cone has responded to Jones's argument by claiming that Jesus'
victory over suffering and death constitutes the necessary and sufficient evidence for the belief that
God sides with the oppressed and acts on their behalf. In short, Cone holds that empirical evidence
is never a reliable basis of a biblical truth; the problem of theodicy is never solved in a theoretical
manner, only defeated by one's faith in Jesus Christ. For Jones's incisive and insightful discussion,
see his *Is God a White Racist?* For Cone's reply, see his *God of the Oppressed*, pp. 187–194.
4. This conception of science pervades Marx's mature writings. For example, he states, "But all
science would be superfluous if the outward appearance and the essence of things directly
coincided." (Karl Marx, *Capital*, Vol. 3, ed. Frederick Engels, p. 817; International Publishers Co.,
1967.) Notice also the demystifying aim of theory in the first few paragraphs of the famous section
4 entitled "The Fetishism of Commodities and the Secret Thereof" of Chapter 1 in *Capital*, Vol. 1,
pp. 71ff.
5. These figures come from the nearest thing to an official survey on the maldistribution of
wealth in America conducted by the Federal Reserve Board in 1962. As one of its authors, Herman
Miller, noted, "the figures were so striking as to obviate the need to search for trends." For a further
exposition and elaboration on this study, see Gus Tyler, "The Other Economy: America's Working
Poor," *The New Leader* (Special Issue), May 8, 1978, pp. 20–24.
6. This point illustrates the undeniable link of the orthodox Marxist view to the Enlightenment.
More specifically, it portrays the inherent elitism and paternalism of such a view. We need only
recall Vladimir Lenin's well-known claim (in *What Is to Be Done?* 1902; China Books, 1973) that
the working class can achieve only trade-union consciousness on its own, thereby requiring a
vanguard party to elevate it to revolutionary consciousness. For Lenin, this party brings enlightenment to the benighted proletariat.
7. This view is illustrated clearly in an essay by José Míguez-Bonino, a leading Latin-American

liberation theologian, entitled "Popular Piety in Latin America" in which he states: "From a theological as well as a political perspective the popular piety that used to exist and that still predominates in Latin America can only be considered as a profoundly alienated and alienating piety, a manifestation of an enslaved consciousness and, at the same time, a ready instrument for the continuation and consolidation of oppression. The intent to transform the mobilizing power of that piety to goals of transformation without radically altering the very content to the religious consciousness seems psychologically impossible and theologically unacceptable." This essay appeared in *Cristianismo y Sociedad* (Buenos Aires), No. 47 (first issue, 1976), pp. 31–38, trans. James and Margaret Goff. Gustavo Gutiérrez, another prominent Latin-American liberation theologian, understands popular culture and religion in a more subtle and sophisticated way. I base this judgment on my cordial and provocative discussions with him during his visiting professorship at Union Theological Seminary in the fall of 1977. It seems to me his own cultural roots and his serious study of cultural Marxist thinkers, especially Antonio Gramsci and José Carlos Mariátegui (the father of Latin-American Marxism), principally account for his sensitivity to popular culture and religion. I must add that Gutiérrez's viewpoint is now more widely accepted among Latin-American liberation theologians.

8. This serious concern of black theologians and religious scholars is exemplified best by Charles H. Long's highly suggestive essay, "Perspectives for a Study of Afro-American Religion in the United States," *History of Religions*, Vol. 11, No. 1 (Aug. 1977), pp. 54–66; Gayraud S. Wilmore's solid study, *Black Religion and Black Radicalism*, esp. pp. 298–306; and James H. Cone's speculative work, *The Spirituals and the Blues* (Seabury Press, 1972). The "armors, forms, and products" of Afro-American culture I have in mind here are the spirituals, blues, gospels, jazz, folktales, and sermons. What is not sufficiently emphasized by black theologians, religious scholars, or cultural critics is the radical potential embedded within the style of these art forms. The most important aspect of them is not what is conveyed, but how this "what" is conveyed. It is this "how" which bears the imprint of struggle and constitutes the distinctive imposition of order on chaos by black people. It is this "how" or style that contains the real message or genuine content of these works of art. To my knowledge, only the essays of Ralph Ellison and Albert Murray explore this frontier of Afro-American art forms. See Ralph Ellison, *Shadow and Act*, and Albert Murray, *The Omni-Americans: New Perspectives on Black Experience and American Culture* (E. P. Dutton & Co., 1971).

9. This point is best illustrated by the words of Hugo Assmann, one of the most radical Latin-American theologians. "In my opening address I was sometimes aggressive because, as a Western-ized Latin American, I don't feel at ease with my colour, my 'gringo' face, my German origin. I don't feel happy with the fact that my theological dissertation was written in German. I have a psychological necessity to say to you in Western language that I am not Western. We Latin Americans are still in the early stages of our search for a Latin American identity. If you look in my library you will find books by German authors, French authors, Italian authors, Marx, Moltmann, etc. There is something false in this . . . Something which is not Latin American." This quote is from the publication *RISK* (p. 62), which is based on the Symposium on Black Theology and Latin American Theology of Liberation, May 1973, at the Ecumenical Center in Geneva, Switzerland.

10. It is not surprising that Gramsci comes from a degraded cultural region in Italy, namely Sardinia, and had intense experiences of ostracism owing to his hunchback, poor health, and short height (he was barely five feet tall). A sample of his writings can be found in *Selections from the Prison Notebooks*, trans. and ed. Quintin Hoare and Geoffrey Nowell Smith.

11. The book by Raymond Williams I have in mind is his *Marxism and Literature* (Oxford University Press, 1977), esp. Ch. 2, pp. 75–141.

12. Gramsci discusses this conception in his seminal essay, "The Intellectual Selections from the Prison Notebooks," pp. 5–23. Although he completely misunderstands the nature of the radical potential of Afro-American culture and Afro-American intellectuals, this does not harm his theoretical formulation of the notion of organic intellectuals.

13. I should add that this also holds to an important degree for white poor and Hispanic Pentecostal churches.

Chapter 23

Robert T. Osborn

White Need for Black Theology

Ever since its advent, black theology has puzzled and troubled whites. We have not known what to do with it. It has been so black as apparently to exclude whites, yet on the other hand it appears to some extent to be addressed to us. We can neither copy it and do it as our own, nor contain it as a chapter within our own theology. The waters have been troubled and muddied further by analogous efforts of other minorities and women to do their theologies. In terms of liberation, following in the path of black theologies of liberation have come women's liberation, gay liberation, Latin American liberation theology, etc.

Ironically, one effect of this proliferation has been an apparent ratification of the authority and dominance of white male theology, insofar as it has put upon the dominant theology the responsibility for clarifying, comprehending, and ordering the situation which otherwise remains chaotic and confused. The thesis of this paper is, however, that the prevailing white (male) theology is not so easily off the hook. I contend that black theology is *sui generis* and singularly significant for white American theology (male and female), that while it cannot be appropriated by whites, neither can it be ignored or co-opted by them.[1] The reason for this judgment, to anticipate the argument that follows, is that blacks are uniquely objects of oppression and that among all oppressed groups in North America they present a uniquely Christian self-understanding. Only they speak so radically with both the vision of the oppressed and the responsibility of Christian faith.

I propose that in the biblical story of Joseph and his brothers we have a key to understand our situation as white theologians who find ourselves addressed by this unique black experience and the theology which comes out of it.[2]

Let us recall the story of Joseph. He was sold into slavery by his brothers. Many years later when he had risen to power in Egypt, and his father and brothers were suffering famine in the land of Canaan, he found himself in the position of being able to deliver his brothers from the oppression of their poverty and hunger. When they came to Egypt to find relief from their impending starvation and discovered to their dismay that their anticipated benefactor was Joseph, they were distressed and justly fearful. Joseph, realizing that their guilt and anxiety were curable, spoke to them the memorable word of liberation: "As for you, you meant evil against me, but God meant it for good" (Ex. 50:20).

First published in *The Journal of the Interdenominational Theological Center, 4* (Fall 1976), pp. 45–50. Used by permission.

Whereas they had meant it for evil when they sold Joseph into slavery, God, in spite of their evil, meant it for good—for their good, for their salvation and survival ("to bring it about that many people should be kept alive, as they are today" [Gen. 50:20]).

In the United States, a similar story was told when the white man sold his black brother into slavery, and is still being told insofar as he continues to oppress the black brother and sister through racist institutions and conventions. However, the difference in the stories to date is more striking than the similarity—namely, that the American white person has yet to hear how radically he did and continues to do this for evil, and that whatever good comes from it has been and will be the gracious consequence of the divine intention alone. To the contrary, the white oppressor has remained confident of the goodness and righteousness of his intentions, and of their immediate identity with those of God. He argued that he sold blacks into slavery and oppressed them in a subsequent racist society for the good of both black and white. Both he and God meant it for good.

In his account of the alleged goodness and godliness of the white man's intentions, Shelton Smith cites the testimony of one Iverson L. Brookes (1850): "Next to the gift of his Son to redeem the human race, God never displayed in more lofty sublimity his attributes, than in the institution of slavery." Nowhere, he continues, "had God's benevolence ever been more marvelously displayed" than when he permitted the Africans to be brought to America. For, as Smith observes, "as a result of their enlightenment under slavery, 'thousands [of blacks] will rejoice in redeeming mercy, in every generation, down to the judgment trumpet' " (Brookes).[3] Professor Smith also cites the Virginian Thomas Roderick Dew who recognized that not only was slavery liberating of the blacks but also of all mankind: "We have no hesitation in affirming, that slavery has been perhaps the principal means for impelling forward the civilization of mankind."[4] As far as his contemporary oppressors are concerned, the black has to contend with two expressions of white righteousness—that of the "red-neck" who admits openly but scarcely penitently to his racism, and that of the liberal who admits to his but alleges to cover and overcome it with good and righteous "liberal" intentions and deeds, and who therefore cannot understand his failure to persuade and conciliate his black brother and sister. As I stated, unlike Joseph's brothers, not only were and are the intentions of whites righteous and divine, but this truth is immediately self-evident to them.

In the story of Joseph the most significant element is that Joseph, the former slave and victim of his brother's oppression, was the voice of the clarifying and liberating word of God. Were it not for that word, his brothers would have feared Joseph and not deigned to ask for or accept relief and liberation from him. And Joseph did indeed speak and incarnate in his deed the word of liberation to his brothers and oppressors. However, we must note that while Joseph spoke the liberating word, he was not its author. It was God, not Joseph, who "meant it for good." It was God who liberated Joseph and overcame his oppression and who by that deed spoke and incarnated the liberating word he was then to speak in forgiveness and love through Joseph to Joseph's brothers. So *God* spoke the liberating word to the oppressors, but he spoke it through *Joseph,* the oppressed.

GOD AND JOSEPH, GOD AND THE BLACK

And as he spoke then through Joseph, so today God is speaking his liberating word to the white person through the black Christian in his black theology. So far, whites hear and receive this word only reluctantly, with little trust or faith, as if it were not truly a necessary word from God for them. (Similarly, Joseph's brothers found Joseph's gracious word unbelievable and so sought ground other than God's grace to secure their position with Joseph.) Instead of hearing and accepting the liberating word of the oppressed, we who are white would rather speak it ourselves, in declaration and witness of the alleged fact that we are for our part already liberated and thus free to speak a promising word of liberation to the black.

And so when Martin Luther King spoke to whites and gave his word flesh in his own life, whites did not, nor do they now, perceive that at stake in that word is their own liberation from bondage to a deadly past. Rather, in confirmation and witness of the alleged goodness of white intentions, what ensued was a gracious white word of black liberation embodied in civil rights legislation. We remained unaware, essentially, that the good in that legislation was from God, working through the oppressed to overcome our sin; we did not know that it was *not* continuing, convincing evidence of the essential white goodness.

That this is the case, that even while legislating civil rights for the blacks, as if we were the liberator, we nevertheless remained and remain victims of our oppressive racism, is manifest in our continuing blindness to expressions of racism in our society and in our white impatience with and incomprehension of continuing black discontent and protest. Having spoken to blacks the liberating word, we are puzzled that they continue to speak out and demand a hearing of us. We have spoken the word of liberation! What more is there to be said? What need is there within the Methodist church, for instance, of a black caucus, when the Methodists (white) have spoken and said that there shall be no more Central (black) Jurisdiction? Our intentions are indeed honorable and of God and therefore liberating of us all. Just as whites once said to blacks that in their slavery to whites they were liberated from the darkness of their pagan past, so today we would again presume to speak to them the word of their liberation from white racism and oppression.

From such presumption one can conclude only that white intentions are indeed good, that unlike Joseph we did not and do not mean it for evil, but for good, and therefore are in no need of a divine and gracious word that would overcome our evil word. As were we God or very godlike and as were our evil not radical, we can speak ourselves beyond and out of our own bondage to sin and thus the black out of our oppressive racism. On the other hand, if our intentions were and are evil, if indeed we are the oppressed victims of our own sin, where but through the oppressed sufferer of our sinful word and deed can our liberation come?

Clearly, here is the place and function in the white world of black theology. Remember, Joseph, the oppressed, spoke a word of God to his brothers, the oppressors. Today, the oppressed (blacks) are speaking a word of God (theology) to the oppressor. It is the thesis of this paper that God is also speaking that word; it is God who means it for our white good, just as it was God who spoke through Joseph and who through Joseph meant good for his brothers.

Black theology is not a "minority" theology which white theology may patronizingly and gratuitously take into account; it is not just another chapter to be appended to an otherwise white theology.[5] To the contrary, it is the very possibility of white theology. Joseph's word to his brothers, like the black's word to his white brothers, is a primal, originating word. As such it was an incomprehensible word, a word that the brothers could neither speak themselves nor believe. It was a word of judgment that revealed and condemned their sin and brought them to their knees. It was not a word they were to comprehend in the power of their reason or heart; rather, it was a powerful, creative word that delivered them from their cunning minds and darkened hearts, and liberated them for a new and promising future. In short, it was the word of God. The word of the black as the word of God is such a word. For the white person it is not an optional word; it is the very *sine qua non,* the very liberating word of authentic white theological existence.

However, we must be clear on two points. First, neither Joseph nor blacks are the liberators, nor are they authors of the liberating word. It is God who liberates and who speaks this word. It is not the *black* word as such, but the black *theological* word that liberates. Concretely, it is Jesus Christ who sets free. It is God in Christ who, through and as the oppressed Jew, spoke the liberating word to his oppressor. I am not talking, therefore, about a black Messiah, but about a Jewish Messiah who through the black would liberate the white.

Second, it is evident that this view of our (white) salvation neither requires nor even permits efforts on our part to adopt black theology. White theology is not and cannot be black theology; rather it is white theology made possible by black theology. And, as with black theology, it is *Christian* theology. It asks about the truth and meaning of Christ for the white person, albeit with the understanding this Christ comes to him as one who is one with the oppressed who, for our American world in the twentieth century, is most concretely and inescapably the black. It asks about Christ in light of the black experience rather than in terms of the white history of sin and racism, which is inimicable and alien to him. White theology must seek Christ today with regard to the black experience of oppression, wherein Christ has always been at home. For us who are white, he comes into our past not to justify us, but brings us into our future to liberate us.

Many will object, white women for instance, to this focus on the black experience in contrast to the experience of other victims of oppression. The reason for this focus is two-fold: first, the black is the most unequivocal and most explicit focus of white male (and female) oppression. Secondly, and this is most important, blacks more than any other oppressed group perceive and witness that it is God who means it for good. He more than any other has been claimed by Christ's promise of his liberation and thus has and is a liberating word to the white man (and woman).

What all this may mean is yet before us, hopefully. As of the moment it is not clear that we as whites have identified the liberating word of God. We do not understand that the word must be spoken to us before we speak, that we must hear before we have anything to say. We continue to do theology of sorts, and, though there is much evidence to suggest it, we have failed to be persuaded that without God first speaking to us our theology so-called is a great to-do about very little.

In conclusion, I would point out what I trust is obvious, namely, that this paper intends to be heuristic only and hardly a program for a responsible white theology. I do understand it as faithful to the intentions of the kind of response black theology registered by my colleague Frederick Herzog in his *Theology of Liberation.* When he translates Jesus' words to Nicodemus to mean for us (whites) that we cannot see the kingdom "unless (we) become black," he is saying only that the white experience is *not* that in which Christ comes to us but rather that from which Christ must save and liberate us.[6] Our white experience is not the context for a faithful hearing of God's word; it is not hermeneutically sound. If we are to hear faithfully the word of God addressed us in Christ, Christ himself must translate us into that context in which he was and is heard— namely, in the midst of the oppressed who, for us who are white, is the black. (At least, for while there are other oppressed peoples in our white American world, these are the most obvious and inescapable. One should be very suspect of avoiding oppression and oppressed people if he avoids the blacks in the name of other oppressed groups.) There, in his newborn blackness, by virtue neither of blackness nor of whiteness, but of the grace of God, the white Christian seeks not to be black or to do black theology but rather to hear Christ and Christian theology. To be "born black" is not to do black theology but to be able to do faithfully white Christian theology.

NOTES

1. Quite commonly in the eighteenth and nineteenth centuries, blacks interpreted their experience in light of the Joseph story. Indeed, it is the cornerstone of black faith during this period that God was using the evil of slavery to build up the black church and black faith. See Bishop J.W. Hood, *One Hundred Years of the African Methodist Episcopal Zion Church* (New York, AME Zion Book Concerns, 1895). It was not so common, however, to realize that God was using the black experience for the liberation and salvation of the white oppressor.

2. H. Shelton Smith, *In His Image But . . .* (Duke University Press, 1972) 145.

3. Ibid., p. 147.

4. "The black religious experience is something more than a black patina on a white happening" (James H. Cone, *A Black Theology of Liberation* [Philadelphia, Lippincott, 1970] 28).

5. Frederick Herzog, *Liberation Theology* (New York, Seabury, 1972) 61.

6. Ibid.

Chapter 24

Cheryl Townsend

The Black Church as a Therapeutic Community

"EARTH HAS NO SORROW THAT HEAVEN CANNOT HEAL"

Redefining Black Religious Experience as Therapeutic

. . . There are several practices unique to the black religious experience either in form or in content. These practices can be organized into four possibly therapeutic functions: (1) articulation of suffering; (2) location of persecutors; (3) provision of asylum for "acting-out"; and (4) validation of experiences. Also, the social organization of black religion provides for an alternative set of positions which provide self-esteem and role continuity (especially for women and the aged). The rest of this paper will highlight some practices which should be systematically researched in terms of their effects on the participants in the black religious experience.

"BEEN IN THE STORM SO LONG"

Speaking and Singing about Suffering

The songs of the slaves (spirituals) and the songs of the children of the slaves (gospels)[1] have been criticized for their "pie in the sky" emphasis. They have been characterized by some black activists briefly quoting Marx as "opiates of the people."[2] However, besides speaking of the better life in heaven, there are a few other themes contained in the spirituals which provide black people with a shared perspective on the world and its troubles. If social life is constructed from a collective conversation of gestures and symbols from which shared meanings are derived creating a situational culture, then the spirituals and the gospel songs represent a base for communication upon which black folks have built a collective perspective on their situation as oppressed people in America. Linguistic and moral duality ("stealing" vs. "taking"),[3] deception ("the drinking gourd"), and resistance ("let my people go") were part of the culture which emerged from the slave songs.

Another function of these songs, a function which has survived into modern

---

First Published in *The Journal of the Interdenominational Theological Center,* 8 (Fall 1980), pp. 32–42. Used by permission.

times and remained in the gospel songs, is the legitimate collective expression of the suffering experienced by black people in America. It is this articulation of suffering through music and speech which seems to have a major therapeutic function within the black community.

In attempting to reconcile the labeling theory of mental illness with the reliability of mental stress and personal and social change, Thomas Scheff, in *Labeling Madness,* links the repression of emotion to the creation of an adult who is well adjusted to the social situation in which hierarchy, order, and predictability are emphasized.[4] For black culture to produce an adult who is well suited to this type of human situation would be to produce a people unwilling to struggle for change and therefore willing to accept their downtrodden and oppressed lot in American society. In support of his corollary to the labeling theory of mental illness, Scheff describes a "speak bitterness" session in the People's Republic of China:

> People confessed, not their sins, but their sorrows. This had the effect of creating emotional solidarity. For when people poured out their sorrows to each other, they realized they were all together on the same sad voyage through life, and from recognition of this they drew closer to one another, achieved common sentiments, took sustenance and hope.[5]

Scheff also mentions that this type of social form can also be found in fundamentalist churches and in black churches in the United States.[6] Such meetings:

> Stimulate collective catharsis in such a way that the needs of individuals to release tension or distressful emotion are met. At the same time, this collective catharsis gives rise to heightened solidarity and a sense of cultural community within the group. As long as this form leads to genuine and spontaneous emotional release, it serves a vital need for the members and develops an extremely cohesive group.[7]

In many black churches, this type of session occurs in the Tuesday or Thursday evening prayer meetings.[8] Members of the church recount sources of suffering in their life and ask for prayers by the membership to alleviate their sufferings. They ask for help in bearing their burdens in the same manner that Jesus did in order not to be crushed by them. Prayers by deacons recount collective situations of suffering, many times referring to the south and the tiredness of body that overtakes blacks because of the types of occupations in which they work. The songs sung are also accounts of suffering which symbolically represent the suffering of blacks. James Cone describes how Jesus and God are not distinct entities within the black church. It is not that He is just "the deliverer of humanity from unjust suffering"[9] or a "comforter in time of trouble," but also someone to whom blacks can tell all about their troubles because he suffered. "Jesus is pictured as the Oppressed One who could 'do most anything.' "[10]

When various members in prayer meetings or revivals testify or pray, the congregation usually shares the account of their suffering with numerous "amens" and "tell Jesus."[11] It is at once a communicating to fellow members that they understand their troubles and a way of communication to the Lord that this brother or sister's trouble is like their own.

Besides the Sunday morning church service and its collective representations of suffering through prayer, song, and sermon, there is the gospel choir concert which parallels another type of group device witnessed in the People's Republic of China and used by Scheff to support his theory of emotional catharsis: "Dramatic scenes depicting the oppression of the old society caused mass weeping."[12] William Hinton describes such a scene in *Fanshen:*

> The women around me wept openly and unashamedly. . . . tears were coursing down their faces. No one sobbed, no one cried out, but all wept together in silence. The agony on the stage seemed to have unlocked a thousand painful memories, a bottomless reservoir of suffering that no one could control. . . . Men were weeping, and I along with them.[13]

Choirs and gospel singers also depict the past and present suffering of blacks in the rural and the urban setting. Not only do men and women weep at these concerts, but a good number of them also faint, shout, and cry out "thank you" to Jesus for helping them endure. The singing is a representation of accounts of suffering endured personally and collectively; insults—"everybody talking 'bout me"—and scorn are sung about. Besides the endurance of suffering, there is an expression of the aloneness that blacks have endured, overcome, and will overcome.

It is this ability to collectively talk about their troubles within the context of the church that may account for the low rates of depression found among black psychiatric diagnoses. According to James Blackwell, rates of manic-depressive behavior and involutional psychoses are lower among blacks.[14] Combined with a lower suicide rate, these positive differences may be accounted for by this function of the church. No matter what the political or ideological stance of the church, these structures—the prayer meeting, the gospel chorus-choir, and the area-wide and professional gospel festivals—exist at all levels of religious life within a black community. These aspects of black social organization have not been the subject of much research. Considering their similarities to the healing ceremonies of many other cultures, an exploration of them with an eye to their therapeutic value may prove fruitful.

"AND THE WICKED WILL CEASE FROM TROUBLING"

Locating the Persecutors

When lecturing several years ago on the politics of psychiatric diagnosis, Dr. R. D. Laing commented that it was interesting that psychiatrists had a word for people who believed that they were being persecuted—paranoia. He went on to say that it was also interesting to note that they did not have a word[15] for people who were being persecuted and did not know that they were. Even more interesting, he continued, was the lack of a word for the person who persecutes and does not know that he is persecuting, and more importantly the person who persecutes and knows that he is persecuting. Along with delivering accounts of suffering, black religious practice provides a setting for accounting for the causes of both personal and collective suffering.

Black women, particularly, are able to avail themselves of the forum of the prayer meeting to talk about their troubles with their husbands and sons.[16] They ask not only for the collective support of the membership in helping them to endure their personal trouble—an arrest, a lost job, a drinking problem, a drug problem, and even adulterous affairs—but they also ask the prayers of membership in changing the behavior of the person or persons responsible for the trouble. It is a very pragmatic form of prayer and testimony. The prayers toward the end of the meeting rendered by the deacon or preacher in charge can range from pleas for effecting a change in the erring son or husband's behavior to a prayer that a family be able to endure and struggle against "that racist policeman" or "that racist store owner."

Not only are prayers offered up against the offender, plans of action may be formulated to attempt to change the offending behavior. Ministers and deacons may pay visits to the offending spouse. Peer pressure, therefore, can be an extra benefit. Bail money may be raised. If the problem is no food on the table because of a welfare worker, food may be provided, as well as clothing. There is the notion and belief that suffering accounted for is caused by the acts of real persons in the real world and the right to "tell God all about our troubles" means just that—*all* of our troubles.

Students in my sociology of mental health courses who work as aides in state hospitals have told numerous stories of women on their wards whose feelings of persecution stem from troubles with their husbands. Their suffering in silence emerges in the form of symptoms which become the province of the psychiatrist, while the offending husband is left with more freedom than ever to continue his behavior. The hospital is left trying to rid the wife of her symptoms, but it is impossible for the hospital personnel to attempt to control the husband. He is usually the chief complainant against the wife. Within the context of the church, people are able to give accounts of some of the saddest and most troubling aspects of their personal lives without fear of punishment. In my experience within the church, I have personally witnessed these types of accounts and the intervention of ministers and deacons in order to attempt to alleviate the situations.

When problems such as unwed motherhood and divorce arise, the prayer meeting is both a forum for announcing the impending trouble and for gathering the social supports necessary to endure and actively cope with the situation. Church members may render various forms of social support besides prayer. Church members may organize "showers" for the offending daughter, thus removing some of the punitive social pressure from the stricken parents. Also, ministers in the black church regularly christen or bless the illegitimate child, including the grandparents in the ritual so that the child is made a member of the community and the grandparents are socially supported in their new responsibility. Although these practices may not depress the rates of social disorganization, they do have the effect of alleviating the personal disorganization which can attend these occurrences. Black divorce, separation, and illegitimacy rates may be public issues, but they are not personal troubles to be suffered through and endured alone.

Many black churches are used as forums for dealing with community problems and civil rights issues. Prayer meetings and gospel singing were an important ritual before many of the civil rights demonstrations. Sermons and testimony both speak directly to the structures of oppression which cause black suffering. Prayers delivered by black ministers during the Civil Rights movement and at various church services occurring during local community crises usually include the naming of the people responsible for the specific or general problem faced at the moment. Generally depending upon the specific political context of the moment, certain aspects of religious practice within the black church help to keep an accurate account of just who the enemies of black people really are. At some times and under some conditions, churches provide an organizing base for action against these named enemies.[17]

"THERE IS A BALM IN GILEAD, TO MAKE THE WOUNDED WHOLE"

The Church as an Asylum

There are very few appropriate settings in American society where one can go specifically to discuss one's personal troubles. The affluent have access to various kinds of therapy groups. Again it is the affluent and the medically insured who can avail themselves voluntarily of the services of a social worker or an out-patient psychiatric clinic. Studies have shown that Alcoholics Anonymous works best with middle-class populations.[18] Private social agencies tend to screen out those personal troubles with which they may have the least success. Given the overall economic status of the black population in the United States, therapy is an expensive solution to private troubles with a limited availability. Where economic factors do not intervene, cultural factors such as language barriers, divergent life experiences, and family background are also counter-vailing forces limiting access to therapeutic facilities.

Within the context of the labeling paradigm, a major factor in the labeling process is the society's overall view that having a psychiatric personal trouble is shameful.[19] Besides mental illness, other aspects of personal disorganization such as alcoholism, illegitimacy, criminal involvement, and marital troubles are also considered shameful and the "fault" of the person involved.[20] In middle-class America, seeking help for personal troubles, therefore, holds socially punitive overtones. Suburban ministers, when counseling their parishioners, sometimes exchange offices with ministers in another town so that the neighbors of the church member will not know that he or she is seeking help. William Ryan has shown how the inability of blacks to hide or disguise their personal pathologies in the same manner as whites had led to the distorted view of the black population as pathology ridden and therefore somehow inferior.[21]

It is the punitive aspects of treatment for the mentally ill that has given rise to many of the radical critiques of psychiatric diagnostic categories and the structure and function of institutions for the mentally ill.

One of the most outspoken critics of the punitive and possibly damaging aspects of the mental health treatment setting is R. D. Laing. His theory of mental illness and particularly schizophrenia maintains that what is now called a disease should possibily be redefined. His research,[22] combined with studies "conducted at Palo Alto, California [Bateson] . . . [and] the Pennsylvania Psychiatric Institute [Speck][23] . . . have shown that the person who gets diagnosed [as schizophrenic] is part of a wide network of extremely disturbed and disturbing patterns of communication."[24] Laing later suggests[25] that schizophrenia may be the natural analogue to a 6-12 hour LSD experience. He suggests that this natural analogue be called, instead of schizophrenia, "a *metanoiac* voyage (from metanoia: change of mind). The nature of the metanoiac voyage may be 'good' or 'bad,' largely depending on the *set* and the *setting.*"[26] He goes on to say:

> Mental hospitals define this voyage as *ipso facto* madness *per se,* and treat it accordingly. The *setting* of the psychiatric clinic and mental hospital promotes in staff and patients the *set* best designed to turn the metanoiac voyage from a voyage of discovery into self of a potentially revolutionary nature and with a potentially liberating outcome, into a catastrophe: into a pathological process from which the person requires to be cured.[27]

Such treatment, given the nature of the organization of the treatment of the mentally ill, becomes punishment for personal failure.

Laing goes on to ask the question "what would happen if we began by changing our set and setting, to regard what was happening as a potential healing process through which the person ideally may be guided and during which he is guarded?" This was Laing's idea of the asylum and has been expressed by the famous Kingsley Hall experiment and seven presently functioning community households in London. Laing also describes the similar function of the "rebirthing experience" made famous by the Elizabeth Fehr Natal Therapy Institute in New York City.[28]

I maintain that some black churches, those characterized by extreme emotionalism, prove a similar asylum (read "refuge" or "shelter") which is a non-punitive setting within which blacks are able to act-out and work-through whatever happens to be troubling them on Sunday morning or prayer meeting evening. This "change of mind" which occurs in the church setting has several names within the black community. In the community in which I was raised it is called "getting happy." Churches characterized by this type of behavior were known to us as "a shouting church" and those not characterized by this behavior were called "a dead church."[29]

For the white or the black person socialized in the Episcopal or Catholic faiths, entering one of these churches can be a frightening experience.[30] Men and women scream and cry and leap about. Bodies seem to be wracked by uncontrollable spasms of both grief and joy. People, both young and old, leap about in the aisles, dance at the altar, and fall out on the floor. Those not engaged in such behavior usually attend to those who are, to guarantee that they do not hurt themselves or others while expressing their feelings. A pair of elderly women can lead a young woman through her first experience of "getting happy" by forming a little circle around her with their arms while lending both physical and emotional support, verbally encouraging her on with phrases like: "Tell Jesus"—"Let it all out, child!"—"Tell your troubles to God"—"Shout" and other encouragements. Members of the congregation develop predictable patterns of acting-out, such that other members move to assist them before they actually begin to shout. When certain church members begin to cry, people can be seen changing their seats so that friends can provide comfort and remove infants from possible harm. Choir members who "fall out" during the performance are supported by other choir members and I have personally witnessed choirs singing six or seven choruses of a song until the lead singer regains consciousness in order that she may finish the song with the choir properly.

No matter how severe the pandemonium within the church service, I have never witnessed a church service in which every single person's episode of "getting happy" or "shouting" was not resolved, worked through, or finished before the singing of the final hymn and the recessional. When the participants leave, they usually appear as unruffled as they did when they came into the church.

In the process of the service, church members become therapists for their fellow church members in that they attend to their shouting, encourage them in their feelings, and guard and protect them from possible harm.[31] Every person takes responsibility for the person nearest him or her. Ministers, taking their cues from the congregation, act and speak in ways which encourage the behavior. Choir directors [32] also gauge the length of a song or the number of songs according to the amount of shouting and clapping that is taking place. Sometimes a choir will finish a song and the congregation will keep up a steady rhythm until the choir starts up again. It is a collective therapeutic experience. Those not actively engaged in shouting speak about "I feel full" or "the spirit gets over me" or " 'it' gets over me." The congregation is actively encouraged to lay its burdens on the altar, and it does.

Such songs as "Come Ye Disconsolate," "There is a Balm in Gilead," "Precious Lord (Take my Hand)," "It is Well with my Soul," "Amazing Grace," "How I Got Over," and "I've Decided to Make Jesus my Choice" are particularly effective in rousing the congregation. During the 1960's, a song called "Peace Be Still" was particularly popular for ending a concert or a prayer meeting.

The entire experience is defined as "good." With this, church members speak of the process of becoming members of the church as being "reborn," "saved," or "redeemed." There is the feeling that a person is "new." There is also the notion that a person may re-enter or be "reborn" an infinite number of times. Testimony concerning members' not always being a "child" of God is often heard as they "rededicate" themselves to being "reborn." In effect, certain black churches have become institutions in which a person possesses an infinite amount of social resources so that it is almost impossible to become defined as an "outsider." The wayward child or the persecuting husband who shows up on Easter Sunday can be greeted with overwhelming enthusiasm, even though it may be well known that he won't be seen again until Christmas or next Easter.

Participants are guarded, welcomed, and sheltered. A person's shouting is rarely discussed outside the church, although impersonal gossip or particularly legendary episodes may travel about the community and across generations. Legends abound concerning particular incidents associated with famous gospel singers.[33] However, the folklore (including memories of older relatives concerning particularly colorful shouters) supports the social institution of shouting and defines it as good. The cultural supports of shouting within the black church functions in much the same way that Scheff maintains that the imagery and stereotypes of insanity in American society function to define the mentally ill as outsiders. However, the imagery and folklore surrounding the social institution of shouting within the black church function to define the participants as "insiders" and good people.

Laing, in discussing his idea of the non-punitive therapeutic setting, comments that "No age in the history of humanity has perhaps lost touch with this natural *healing* process that implicates *some* of the people whom we label schizophrenic."[34] He suggests:

> Instead of the mental hospital, a sort of reservicing factory for human breakdowns, we need a place where people . . . can find their way further into inner space and time, and back again. Instead of the *degradation* ceremonial of psychiatric examination, diagnosis, and prognostication, we need, for those who are ready for it . . . an *initiation* ceremonial, through which the person will be guided with full social encouragement and sanction into inner space and time, by people who have been there and back again.[35]

In this place of healing, Laing suggests "Among physicians and priests there should be some who are guides, who can educt the person from this world and induct him to the other. To guide him in it and to lead him back again."[36] The ministers, choir directors, singers, nurses, ushers, and fellow church members who aid the "shouters" in their "getting happy" seem quite similar to the personnel in Laing's true asylum. Some of the newer therapies such as primal scream and Rash Neesh Meditation therapy bear similarities to church activity.

"ASK THE WATCHMAN HOW LONG"

Validating Black Experiences[37]

The feelings of suffering and persecution experienced by black people in America are not successfully experienced or shared by the wider society. What blacks in American society experience as normal everyday racism is hardly noticed by whites or if noticed is denied. According to James Comer:

> Much of white America does not see, feel, or think that a wrong has been done and is still being done. It does not understand compensation, justice, and change

are necessary. . . . In Homestead, Florida, after a black student protest, the South Dade High School voted 1,010 to 47 to keep the symbols of injustice that angered blacks: the nickname "Rebels," "Dixie" as the school song, the Confederate flag as the school emblem, Confederate uniforms for the band, blue and gray as the school colors, and the name "Rebel Review" for the student newspaper. . . . Few things could be more insulting to black students.

A white girl asked the leader of the black student group why he was so angry. The black student told of his feeling as a band member. There I was, wearing the uniform of the man who fought to the death to keep my ancestors in slavery. That I looked ridiculous was not important. It actually hurt. It really does mean a lot to me.[38]

This and the protestations of white Bostonians that there was no racism in Boston prior to busing are only some of the examples of the different definitions of the situation by a white majority with which black people are forced to contend in their everyday lives. According to Laing, "If we deny official definitions of public events, we are regarded as mad."[39] In order to maintain their sense of reality in American society, blacks must continuously disregard the offical definitions of public events which affect their lives. Sometimes feelings of self-blame can only be blocked by some sort of public, yet in-group, accounting of troubles.

The black church represents the most stable and resourceful institution for providing this function. Ministers are usually notified concerning community crises, and they have the stature and the authority to get to the truth of a situation when others in the community cannot or when the media have seriously misrepresented the matter. When a black neighbor of mine was charged with murder while defending his home against the attack of a white teenage gang, black ministers in the community all took time to announce the facts of the matter to their congregations because the media had seriously misrepresented the matter. The family's ability to bear the death threats and the cost of legal defense was greatly aided by the material and emotional support that came to them after that Sunday morning. Members of the various churches in which ministers had given a true account of the incident called, visited, and raised money for the family. At that time the family held no church membership.

IN MY FATHER'S HOUSE

Conclusions

According to Charles V. Hamilton:

One of the most crucial facts about black people in the United States is that they have been subjected to . . . traumatic experiences involving abrupt cultural transformations. . . . These occurrences [have] had serious implications for the disruption of social institutions of the race and for the ways in which black people have attempted to meet and adapt to these abrupt changes in their lives. . . . The one institution the blacks had to rely on in bridging these transitional periods were the church and the preacher. The preacher became, then, a linkage figure, having to link up the old with the new, the familiar with the unfamiliar, tradition with modernity. . . . The black church was an adaptive institution. It was not wholly African, and it was by no means entirely Anglican or Western. Improvisation was required, and the black preacher was the master improviser. . . . He knew his people, and he came to know the many new obstacles and forces with which they had to cope in order to survive—not to mention thrive. . . . The black preacher linked up things. And for a people who had had their lives and their cultures shattered, fragmented, and torn asunder so often and so abruptly, this linkage figure was important. . . . By their mere presence and continued leadership, the black preachers offer a steady figure with which their people can identify. They represent continuity and, in an important sense, stability—the only stable strand in the lives of many people who have been wracked by instability and abrupt changes.[40]

To be able to know that their troubles are not the result of personal defects; that their inferiority is not a certified fact; and that people in certain positions in white society are actively persecuting them prevents for black people the disjuncture between personal experience and feelings, and the realities with which they are coping—which for many other people renders them vulnerable to incarceration within institutions for the insane.

The black church validates the experiences and feelings that the media of the wider society attempt to invalidate. The black church because of its differential social organization provides a sphere of activities in which black people can perform, function, feel, and express themselves without the invidious distinctions which white judgments bring to bear.[41] If positive mental health is defined, as Jahoda found, as mastery of the environment, self-actualization, self-esteem, integration of self, autonomy, and adequacy of perception of reality, then the black church represents a social institution which acts as a support to black sanity. Given the crisis in the delivery of mental health care in America, and the miracle of black survival in America, sensitive and systematic exploration of the possibly therapeutic functions of the black religious experience is indicated.

NOTES

1. According to James Cone (*The Spirituals and the Blues* [New York, Seabury, 1972]), gospel music and the blues are post-emancipation phenomena that speak to the problem of emancipation dislocation and later urban dislocation. The blues and the gospels represent two parallel cultural developments dealing with the dialectic of despair and hope: blues fall within the secular experience and gospels fall within the religious experience. A good discussion of the division between the religious and secular audiences within the black community can be found in Tony Heilbut, *The Gospel Sound: Good News and Bad Times* (New York, Simon and Schuster, 1971).
2. Marx's statement is often taken out of context. A study of the experience of black men in America gives vivid confirmation to the words that Karl Marx wrote, "Man makes religion. . . . Religion is the general theory of this world, its encyclopedic compendium, its logic in popular form, its spiritual point d'honneur, its enthusiasm, its moral sanction, its solemn complement, its general basis of consolation and justification. . . . Religious suffering is at the same time an expression of real suffering and a protest against real suffering. Religion is the sigh of the oppressed creature, the sentiment of a heartless world, and the soul of soulless conditions. It is the opium of the people" (St. Clair Drake, *The Redemption of Africa and Black Religion* [Chicago, Third World Press, 1970] 23).
3. Grace Sims Holt, "'Inversion' in Black Communication," in Thomas Kochman, *Rappin' and Stylin' Out: Communication in Urban Black America* (University of Illinois Press, 1972) 154.
4. Thomas J. Scheff, *Labeling Madness* (Englewood Cliffs, N.J., Prentice-Hall, 1975) 83.
5. Ibid., 86.
6. Ibid., 85.
7. Ibid., 86.
8. Hortense Powdermaker's discussion of the black church and "getting religion" (*After Freedom: A Cultural Study in the Deep South* [New York, Atheneum, 1967] 223-85) is valuable because of the ethnographic description of religious experience in the rural south of the 1930s. St. Clair Drake and Horace Cayton, in their *Black Metropolis: A Study of Negro Life in a Northern City* (New York, Harcourt, Brace, and World, 1962) 412-29, 611-57, provide analysis of the social

functions of religious experience in the urban north of the 1930s and 1940s.

9. Cone, *Spirituals,* 47.

10. Ibid., 50.

11. Many times the person giving the account will pause and interject the phrase "Can I get a witness?" or "Can I get a witness here tonight?" and will continue after hearing an "amen" or "yes" from a fellow member of the congregation. Preachers will also do this during sermons and prayers. See Grace Sims Holt, "'Stylin' outta the Black Pulpit," in Kochman, *Rappin' and Stylin' Out,* 189-204.

12. Scheff, *Madness,* 86.

13. William Hinton, *Fanshen: A Documentary of Revolution in a Chinese Village* (New York, Random House, 1966) 314-15.

14. James Blackwell, *The Black Community: Diversity and Unity* (New York, Dodd, Mead, 1975).

15. Meaning, an official psychiatric diagnosis.

16. See Holt, "'Stylin'," 191-95; Powdermaker, 253-73.

17. Charles V. Hamilton (*The Black Preacher in America* [New York, William Morrow, 1972]) gives a good survey of the variety of roles played by the black church and its clergy in racial uplift as well as in keeping the status quo.

18. See Harrison Trice and Paul Michael Roman, "Delabeling, Relabeling, and Alcoholics Anonymous," in Frank R. Scarpetti and Paul T. McFarlane, eds., *Deviance: Action, Reaction, Interaction* (Reading, Mass., Addison-Wesley, 1975).

19. See Thomas J. Scheff, *Being Mentally Ill: A Sociological Theory* (Chicago, Aldine, 1966) 55-101.

20. The "blaming the victim" ideologies enumerated by William Ryan (*Blaming the Victim* [New York, Random House, 1971]) reflect a Protestant American value system that sees humans as "ruggedly individual" masters of their fate. This problem of "shame" and "guilt" over personal troubles is just one consequence of growing up in a society built upon the ideologies of social Darwinism. To some extent, it affects everyone, not just minorities.

21. Ibid.

22. R. D. Laing and A. Esterson, *Sanity, Madness, and the Family* (Baltimore, Penguin, 1964).

23. Ross V. Speck and Carolyn Attneave, *Family Networks* (New York, Random House, 1973).

24. R. D. Laing, *The Politics of Experience* (New York, Ballantine, 1967) 114.

25. See Hendrik M. Ruitenbeck, *Going Crazy: The Radical Therapy of R. D. Laing and Others* (New York, Bantam, 1972).

26. Ibid., 12.

27. Ibid.

28. R. D. Laing, *The Facts of Life: An Essay in Feelings, Facts, and Fantasy* (New York, Random House, 1976) 72.

29. These perspectives on audience styles of churches arise from the variety of interchurch organizations which exist at local, regional, and national levels within the black community. In my own community, gospel singers would comment upon just how hard they might be required to work at any particular concert or service.

30. Members of my Baptist Youth Fellowship and I took a black Catholic friend with us on one of our many Friday night visits to a local "shoutin'" Baptist church. A short while later she ran out of the church with a look of extreme terror on her face. She later told one of the members that she had never been so frightened in her life.

31. In large churches black nurses and nurses aides form voluntary associations for this specific purpose. Church ushers are expected to perform this role as well.

32. The National Association of Gospel Choirs and Choruses maintains a director's bureau as well as holding seminars and competition in order to train directors at these conventions. Choir directors often build up their very own following. They occupy an extremely important but unresearched role within the black church. Some of them are divinity students or assistant ministers.

33. Heilbut, *Gospel Sound.*

34. R. D. Laing, *The Politics of the Family and Other Essays* (New York, Random House, 1969) 127.

35. *Politics of Experience,* 128.

36. Ibid., p. 139.

37. Laing, in "The Family and Invalidation," notes that public family events and internal experience do not always match:

["Jack and Jill were married in 1960. There were over 100 wedding guests. . . . But Jill was not satisfied. She does not want a pretence of a marriage. . . . One night she started to say in front of the children that he wasn't a real husband. That she was married to him, but he wasn't married to her. He became upset and phoned the doctor in the morning. *People are sent to psychiatrists and into hospitals if they persist in such statements" (Politics of Family,* 68-69)].

Laing in distinguishing between the experiential structure (A) and the public event (B) asserts "To preserve convention, there is general collusion to disavow A when A and B do not match. Anyone breaking this rule is liable to invalidation." The invalidation of the individual's experience by others is the beginning of one's career as mentally ill. At the societal level, the ideologues of equality spoken by American society (public event or B) do not match the experience (A) of oppression suffered by blacks. It is my feeling that the church provides a counter-collusionary force validating the mismatch of American ideology and the black experience.

38. James P. Comer, *Beyond Black and White* (New York, Quandrangle Books, 1972) 113.

39. *Politics of Family,* 68.

40. Hamilton, *Black Preacher,* 32-36.

41. See Comer, *Beyond,* 17.

Chapter 25

Joseph B. Bethea

Worship in the Black Church

In an article entitled "Religious Education and the Black Experience" which was published in *The Black Church,* a journal of the Black Ecumenical Commission of Massachusetts, President Grant Shockley of the Interdenominational Theological Center in Atlanta wrote: "Being Black in the United States of America is a peculiar experience."[1] It is an experience and a condition whose roots are in Africa and whose history is a long and bitter night of slavery, segregation, discrimination, oppression, deprivation, exclusion, alienation, and rejection in this country. This is the experience in which the black church had its beginning and has its continuing history and development. This is the experience out of which emerges a peculiar black theology and a distinct black worship tradition.

For the most part, black churches in America were established in three basic ways.

First, black churches were established on slave plantations where owners were, for one reason or another, sympathetic toward the Christianizing of slaves. In some cases, slave owners were genuinely concerned about the religious development of their slaves and felt some moral or religious obligation to share the Gospel with these "heathens." In many cases, however, slavemasters used Christianity to further exploit their slaves. It was thought and it was taught that making slaves Christians would make them better slaves. Such evangelizing was usually conducted by white preachers; sometimes black preachers thought to be sympathetic toward the slave system were the evangelists; in both instances, such evangelizing was always under the strict control of the master.[2] It was designed to serve his goals and purposes. Other considerations were at least secondary and, more often than not, taboo. This was the beginning of a long history of biblical misinterpretation and manipulation in American Christianity to support black slavery, segregation, discrimination, and oppression. And as recent as today, instances can be cited where the biblical faith is still misinterpreted and manipulated to victimize ethnic minorities in this country.

Secondly, black churches were established on plantations where slaveowners were opposed to the Christianizing of black Africans. Religious exercise among them was prohibited.[3] But, being religious as they were, slaves devised their own ways and forms of relating to deity. They stole away to Jesus and held secret meetings in their huts, or in the woods, or in other places of safety; they devised means to muffle their sounds so that unfriendly masters would not hear them as they worshipped their God, told him about

First published in *Duke Divinity Review,* 43 (Winter 1978), pp.44–53. Used by permission.

their troubles, found assurance that it will be all right after a while, and prayed for strength to sustain them until the day breaks and their long and bitter night of sub-human condition and existence would be over.

And thirdly, black churches were established in direct protest of the subordinate and inferior status that was forced upon black people in white churches. Dr. D. E. King, writing in *The Black Christian Experience,* describes how black people have always been denied the right and privilege of participation in white churches:

> From slavery until now blacks have been humiliated, embarrassed, harassed, brutally attacked, arrested, and imprisoned for even attempting to worship in white churches of all denominations. Even when they were admitted to worship and membership in a few white churches, they were relegated to the rear or to the balconies. They were also forced to wait until whites were served the Lord's Supper before they were served.
>
> From the treatment suffered by blacks in the white church it is indeed a miracle that they did not renounce Christianity altogether. Perhaps they would have if they had not, psychologically, separated Christ from the white church.[4]

Blacks did separate Christ from the white church. If God and his Son could condone the oppression and the inhumane treatment they experienced in the white church, the God of black folks had to be separated from that institution. Thus the failure of "American Christianity" to accord humanity to black people necessitated the establishment and development of black churches.

Obviously, this same failure of "American Christianity" inevitably precipitated a black interpretation of the faith and a black worship tradition. When the churches compromised the civil and spiritual rights of black people and yielded to the assumption that black persons were less than persons—less than human—the formation of a different church, a particular theology, and a unique style of worship ensued. If the God of "American Christianity" could deny blacks freedom and acquiesce in their slavery and brutal oppression, there must be some other interpretation of God, persons, and the world. Black people developed this particular interpretation through a combination of their African heritage and their daily experience of depersonalization with the Bible and the religion of their masters. They formed a church and forged a theology and fashioned a worship tradition to respond to their peculiar needs.

"Being Black in the United States of America is a peculiar experience." The black church, through its interpretation of the faith and its worship, has been the most relevant and adequate response to that experience and that condition. In the "sermons, spirituals, prayers, and Sunday School teachings of the black church," Grant S. Shockley asserts that "Black people came to terms with their blackness, their expressional gifts, and their social situation of slavery and brutalizing oppression in a white racist church and society."[5]

In their churches and in every other aspect of their existence, black people worshipped and proclaimed an almighty sovereign God in whose image they are made. They worshipped a God who was against slavery and oppression, and those who perpetrated this evil. They worshipped a God who wills liberation and sent his Son to be the Liberator of oppressed peoples. They worshipped a God whose Spirit works for the liberation and freedom of all peoples. It is said that a black preacher was heard to remark that it all began when a group of black people, in protest of the inferior and subordinate status forced upon them in a white church, left that church singing:

"Ev'rybody talkin 'about Heab'n ain't goin dere, Heab'n. . . ." Do you know that spiritual?

> I got a robe, you got a robe,
> All God's chillun got a robe.
> When I get to Heab'n gonna put on my robe,
> Gonna shout all over God's Heab'n.
>
> I got shoes, you got shoes,
> All God's chillun got shoes.
> When I get to Heab'n gonna put on my shoes,
> Gonna shout all over God's Heab'n.
>
> Heab'n, Heab'n.
> Ev'rybody talkin bout heab'n ain't going dere,
> Heab'n, Heab'n,
> Gonna shout all over God's Heab'n.

The black experience and the black condition: we have to have some appreciation of that experience and that condition before we can begin to understand the worship tradition of the black church.

Nor can we begin to understand the worship tradition of the black church except we recognize and accept the reality that black people did not come to America bereft of any religious experience. This is important because Western historians and sociologists alike have accepted the myth that the black American has no meaningful past. E. Franklin Frazier, the celebrated Negro sociologist wrote *The Negro Church in America*. In it he said:

> From the available evidence, including what we know of the manner in which the slaves were Christianized and the character of their churches, it is impossible to establish any continuity between African religious practices and the Negro church in the United States.[6]

Frazier goes on to describe how, in the process of enslavement, the Negro was completely stripped of his social, cultural, and religious past. American Christianity became the "new basis of social cohesion" for black Americans; and Frazier concludes, "There was one element in their African heritage that was able to survive capture in Africa and the 'middle passage'—dancing, the most primitive form of religious expression."[7]

The tremendous contribution of Black Power has been its emphasis on black awareness and black identity. It has led black Americans to seriously question Frazier's position; it has led to a new appreciation of the work of Melville J. Herskovits and others who assert that the prevailing attitude upon which this nation bases its racial policies is a "myth." To believe that black Americans have no meaningful past, to believe that African religion has not had some influence on the black church in the United States, is to embrace a myth, a fictitious imagination that cannot be supported by the facts of history.[8]

Alex Haley spent twelve years studying the seven American generations of his family. He researched the history of the slave trade, the slave ship crossings, and the history of the Kinte family in Africa. In *Roots,* Haley told the story of his family; but more than that, he told the story of black people in America. It is a story that declares for all time that African life and culture has influenced black life in America, and African religion has impacted the black church in the United States.[9]

It is not to be doubted that very early in our existence in this country, black people were exposed to Christianity. The missionary efforts, and the warmth of the style and message of the Methodists and Baptists at that time won for those churches large followings from among the slaves. Nor can it be denied that those early religious communities provided the slaves some otherwise prohibited social cohesion. But to think that the black church in America has ever been without some continuing African influence is to be mistaken.

At the turn of the century, W. E. B. DuBois published his findings on the Negro Church which was his report to the Atlanta University Conference for the Study of Negro Problems in 1903. DuBois wrote of the black church:

It was not at first by any means a Christian Church, but a mere adaptation of those heathen rites which we roughly designated by the term "Obe Worship" or "Voodooism." Association and missionary effort soon gave these rites a veneer of Christianity, and gradually, after two centuries, the Church became Christian, with a simple Calvinist creed, but with many of the old customs still clinging to the services.[10]

And more recently, within the decade, Professor Henry Mitchell has insisted that "Black Preaching and Black Religion generally are inescapably the product of the confluence of two streams of culture, one West African and the other Euro-American."[11] Acknowledging the influence of Euro-American Christianity on the Black Church, Professor Mitchell goes on to say:

Black scholars now have proven beyond doubt that the religion of the black masses of the United States is so clearly distinguishable from the white Protestant tradition not only because of the unique experience of oppression but, even more so, because the basic culture/religion continuum from Africa was never broken. . . . It is true that slavery was hard, but not quite that hard; and African religion is still alive and doing well in the Black Church and even the black street culture of today.[12]

That is the backdrop against which we must cast any consideration or discussion of worship in the black church. It is the black experience, a tradition which cannot be known nor fully appreciated except by those who have lived it. It is the black experience in America, with its roots in Africa and a history of dehumanizing oppression in this country.

In his book, *The Souls of Black Folk,* DuBois described preaching, music, and frenzy as some of the distinctive "characteristics of Negro religious life as developed up to the time of Emancipation."[13] Can you give a definition for "frenzy"? When black people have church today, when *black people* have church today, when black people have *church* today, the experience is still characterized by preaching, music, and frenzy. One need only recall the meeting in Memphis on April 3, 1968, where Martin Luther King, Jr., spoke and reported that he had been to the mountaintop and had seen the Promised Land. He said "I may not get there with you, but my eyes have seen the glory of the coming of the Lord." And the resounding refrain was heard: "Glory, Hallelujah." If you saw that meeting, or if you witnessed the choir at Hubert Humphrey's funeral singing,

"Goin Up Yonder," or if you visit a black church where black masses gather today—the distinctive features are preaching, music, and frenzy.

Attention must be given to the acculturation of black "middle-class" worship before this article is concluded with some additional features of authentic worship in the black tradition. The writer served a "middle-class" Negro church in a town where Sunday worship was broadcast from several of the "leading churches in the city." It was at the height of the civil rights movement and we were appalled that none of the black churches had ever participated. We approached the management of the radio station to protest this discrimination. They simply could not identify a "colored" church in the city that could fit the guidelines. They wanted the call to worship at 11:01 A.M. and the benediction at 11:58 A.M. They did not want long breaks or loud preaching, and they could not broadcast shouting. Our church was insulted. We certainly fitted the guidelines; in fact, we could do it better than any of the churches that had had their worship broadcast. We became the only black church in that town that could participate. And we were proud of it. We were better than the other "colored" churches because we did things as well as, or better than, white folks.

I cite this incident to document how well black people have been taught that the right way to worship and do anything else in this country is the way white people do them. There used to be a saying in the black community: "If you're white, you're right; if you're brown, stick around, if you're black, get back." "Black" was the term used to denote error, rejection, and evil. "White" was used to denote truth, acceptance, and goodness.

In an article, "The Black Church in White Structures," Gil Caldwell described the dilemma of many black churchpersons in predominantly white churches:

> The Black Christian in a predominantly white institution has to make a decision early in his or her church life as to whether or not all that represents the white Christian experience will be internalized. Today around the nation there are black people in white Churches who assume that there is a rightness, a correctness, a historical validity to white Church life that is not present in a Black local church or denomination. They have been deluded into thinking that because their Black physical presence represents some form of racial desegregation . . . all might be right.[14]

Caldwell offered a possible solution to the dilemma:

> There are other Black Church people (their number is increasing daily) who have not bought the false concept of the inherent rightness of white Christianity. They are devoted to instilling the best of Blackness into non-Black Church life and preserving the Black experience in other settings.[15]

We would be remiss if we ignored those who insist that there can be no authentic black church life in a predominantly white church structure. Some define the black church as that Christian community whose organization, administration, and programs are originated, controlled, and staffed by black people. Others insist that if black people are going to remain in predominantly white churches, we should forget our blackness. This latter position led me to raise some questions about the black presence in my own United Methodist Church. Are we United Methodist black people? Or are we black United Methodist people? What claims our first priority, our blackness or our United Methodism? Black people must answer for themselves; and it makes all the difference in the world about how we see ourselves and how we fulfill our ministry and mission in and through the church.

I happen to believe that I must be both black and United Methodist. That means that I must try to bring to bear upon this church the black heritage and the black experience. It means that my church can and must be relevant and responsive to the needs and aspirations of black people and the black community at the same time as it is faithful to the doctrines, beliefs, and practices of the United Methodist Church.

What, then, are some additional distinctive features of authentic worship in the black church? I have already mentioned DuBois' distinctive characteristics—preaching, music, and frenzy. I also alluded to the fact that authentic black worship may or may not be limited to a specific time schedule. When people have faced the experience of dehumanizing oppression all the week and in every other setting, they are not so anxious to get away from the one setting that gives them personhood and assures them that they are somebody.

If worship is designed to bring people into a conscious relationship with God and into a spiritual relationship with their brothers and sisters in Christ, then authentic black worship must be designed to bring black people into a conscious relationship with God and into a spiritual relationship with their brothers and sisters in Christ. And when you do that with black people, you cannot determine beforehand what is going to happen. Rigid rules of order give way to freedom—freedom of expression and freedom of movement.

Authentic black worship is celebration. Black worshipers celebrate the sovereignty of an almighty God. Life is hard. In all of our trials and troubles, God has been with us. God has brought us safe thus far. God is with us now. "If it wasn't for the Lord, what would I do?" God will give us the victory through Jesus Christ. We celebrate the sovereignty of our almighty God who "can do anything but fail."

Black people also celebrate our survival in a hostile environment. Before emancipation, the life of a black slave had worth as this nation built its economy on the blood and sweat and toil of black people. When emancipation struck down legal slavery, blacks lost their worth, as this country has never really found a need for free black people. It is all right to kill us, or for us to kill each other. Even our predominantly white churches have mixed feelings about a strong and viable black presence. But here we are! We have survived slavery, segregation, discrimination, injustice, and bitter hatred. But here we are! We have survived! And we celebrate it:

> How I got over,
> How I got over;
> My soul looks back and wonders,
> How I got over.

Authentic black worship is celebration.

And now there abide, uniquely in authentic black worship, preaching, music, frenzy, freedom, celebration, prayer, ritual, emotion, etc. But the greatest of these, in black worship, is preaching. Preaching and the preacher are always at the center and core of the black church. Describing the black preacher's ability to tell a story, D. E. King recalls an incident in the ministry of John Jasper at Sixth Mt. Zion Baptist Church in Richmond, Virginia:

It is said that on one Easter Sunday morning, he was preaching and demonstrating how Jesus raised Lazarus from the grave. In the balcony was a white student from the Richmond Union Seminary with his son. John Jasper created an almost visible grave as he had Jesus bring Lazarus forth. Several times he said: "Jesus said to Lazarus, 'Come forth.' " The student's little boy said: "Dad, come on let's go." The student and the congregation were transfixed as Jasper had Jesus bring Lazarus forth. Finally, the son got up and said, "Daddy, let's go before he makes the man get up." That is spiritual creativity when a preacher is able to raise the dead on Sunday morning.[16]

Preaching the Gospel, telling the story, and raising the dead is at the heart of authentic worship in the black tradition.

This is but an introduction to any serious study of worship in the black church. It may well be concluded and summarized with a quotation from an address which Bobby McClain delivered at the National United Methodist Convocation on the Black Church in 1973:

Black worship . . . is based on the cultural and religious experience of the oppressed. Its liturgy and its theology are derived from the cultural and religious experience of black people struggling to appropriate the meaning of God and human life in the midst of human suffering. Worship in the black tradition is celebration of the power to survive and to affirm life, with all of its complex and contradictory realities. The sacred and the secular, Saturday night and Sunday morning, come together to affirm God's wholeness, the unity of life, and his lordship over all of life. Such a tradition encourages responses of spontaneity and improvisation, and urges worshipers to turn themselves loose into the hands of the existential here and now where joy and travail mingle together as part of the reality of God's creation. It is in this context that black people experience the life of faith and participate in the community of faith.[17]

In 1978, being black in America is yet a peculiar experience. Recent "progress" in race relations and the increased visibility of a black "middle class" may delude many into believing that we have found the answer and that all will soon be well in this country. It just isn't so! Black people still live at the bottom of the employment and economic ladder. Justice is still not just as it relates to black Americans. In every relationship with white people, blacks are expected to assume an inferior and subordinate status. It is still a peculiar experience. It promises to be for some time to come. Thus it is still incumbent upon black churches to help black people come to terms with what it means to live and move and have our being in this oppressive society.

The renewal and enhancement of our worship, in terms of its music, its freedom, and its preaching, is but one aspect of the total renewal of the church for its mission and ministry with black people and the black community:

> Didn't my Lord deliver Daniel,
> Deliver Daniel, Deliver Daniel,
> Didn't my Lord deliver Daniel,
> And why not every man?

NOTES

1. Grant S. Shockley, "Religious Education and the Black Experience," *The Black Church Quarterly* (Boston, The Black Ecumenical Commission of Massachusetts), 11/1 (1972) 94.

2. Leon L. Troy and Emmanuel L. McCall, "Black Church History," in *The Black Christian Experience,* compiled by Emmanuel L. McCall (Nashville, Broadman Press, 1972) 22.

3. Ibid., p. 21.

4. Dearing E. King, "Worship in the Black Church," in McCall, *Black Christian Experience,* 33–34.

5. Shockley, "Religious Education," 96.

6. E. Franklin Frazier, *The Negro Church in America* (New York, Schocken, 1974) 13.

7. Ibid., p. 86.

8. See Melville J. Herskovits, *The Myth of the Negro Past* (Boston, Beacon, 1941) 1–2. Herskovits outlines the myth that "validates the concept of Negro inferiority" in this country. He moves to the conclusion that "the Negro is thus a man without a past."

9. See Alex Haley, *Roots* (Garden City, N.Y., Doubleday, 1976). This "saga of the Afro-American family" was long overdue and its impact on American race relations cannot now be measured.

10. W.E.B. DuBois, *The Negro Church* (Atlanta University Press, 1903) 5.

11. Henry Mitchell, "Two Streams of Tradition," in C. Eric Lincoln, ed., *The Black Experience in Religion* (Garden City, N.Y., Anchor Books, 1974) 70.

12. Ibid.

13. W.E.B. DuBois, *The Souls of Black Folks* (Greenwich, Ct., Fawcett Publ., 1961) 141–42.

14. Gilbert H. Caldwell, "The Black Church in White Structures," *The Black Church Quarterly,* 1/2 (1972) 14.

15. Ibid.

16. King, "Worship," 38–39.

17. William B. McClain, "What is Authentic Black Worship?" in James S. Gadsden, ed., *Experiences, Struggles, and Hopes of the Black Church* (Nashville, Tidings, 1975) 70–71.

Chapter 26

Virgilio Elizondo

Mexican-American Religious Symbolism

THE CROSS

It should not be surprising that devotion to the crucified Lord—scourged, bleeding, agonizing—is one of the deepest traits of the Mexican-American faith. *Cruz* ("cross") is a not uncommon name given to their children.

El Viernes Santo (Good Friday) is the Mexican-American celebration *par excellence.* The commemoration of the Lord's crucifixion is the celebration of their life—a life of suffering. Their daily life is assumed in his death and therein defies the anomalies of life.

Why is the "scandal" of the cross as necessary for salvation today as it was for Jesus? Because the cross continues to reveal the impurity of the pure and the purity of the impure, the innocence of criminals and the crimes of the innocent, the righteousness of sinners and the sin of the righteous, the wisdom of the foolish and the foolishness of the wise.

Some persons working with Mexican-Americans have thought it would be better to shift the emphasis from the cross to the resurrection. I would agree *if* the situation were changing in such a way that we could say that resurrection was indeed becoming a meaningful symbol. But this is not yet the case. I agree with Jesuit theologian Jon Sobrino that the point is not to do away with the people's celebration of the cross, but to help them appreciate better Jesus' active march toward the cross, and not just the passive aspect of suffering on the cross. In the long run, of course, this march would be meaningless without the resurrection; human suffering, as imaged in the crucifixion, would be devoid of sense. Jesus did not *start* with the cross, nor was it the only element in his salvific ministry.

The drama of Good Friday is not just celebrated ritually in the churches but lived out by the Mexican-American people. Beginning on Holy Thursday with the agony in the garden, on Good Friday the way of the cross is reenacted by the people, then the crucifixion, and the seven last words of Jesus from the cross. Finally, in the evening, there is the *pésame a la Virgen* ("visit to the Virgin"). Never was the distance between the

---

First published in *Galilean Journey: The Mexican-American Promise* (Maryknoll, N.Y., Orbis Books, 1983), pp. 41–45. Used by permission.

"official" church and the church of the people more evident to me than on Good Friday in Mexico City where there might be as few as 100 persons in a *barrio* church for the official services, and as many as 60,000 outside the church, taking part in a living way of the cross.

To "academic" theologians and liturgists this may seem a folkloric, nostalgic, emotional, childish expression of religion; they would not call it *real* liturgy. But for a people for whom a sudden arrest, speedy trial, trumped-up charges, circumstantial evidence, quick verdict, and immediate sentencing are a way of life—as is true for the millions of poor and oppressed throughout Latin America and in the U.S.A.—this ritual reenactment of the way of Jesus is the *supreme* liturgy. It is the celebration of their creed. It is not academic theorization; it is life.

Mary's role in the crucifixion of her Son is relived by millions of women in Latin America—grandmothers, mothers, wives, girlfriends. They stand by silently as injustice, violence, is done to their loved ones. They are silent not because they are afraid or because they agree with the civil authorities, but because they do not even understand the language. They are silent because they know, through their collective experience with other women who have gone through similar experiences, that they are powerless against the authorities: "*Pues no sé, Padrecito, se lo llevaron las autoridades . . . no hay nada que se pueda hacer*" ("I don't know, the authorities took him away, Padre . . . there's nothing to be done"). They are silent because if they said something, reprisals might be taken against other members of the family.

Thousands of persons watch their loved ones be taken away, accused of some crime, condemned, and sentenced by the "justice of the powerful"—and all they can do is stand silently by them to the very end. I have myself met many such men and women in the jails of San Antonio. They do not even know why they are there. Some just happened to be standing by when a crime was committed. Their family has no money for bail. They do not know their way around. All they could do was pray and patiently wait and hope that something would be worked out.

The final Good Friday reenactment is the burial service. Some ridicule this popular rite of the burial of Jesus and attribute its popularity to the "morbid" inclinations of Mexican-Americans—"always preoccupied with death." But when it is realized that even in death this people is rejected, the quiet, almost clandestine, burial of Jesus takes on a deeper significance for them. Segregated cemeteries are still a commonplace, even if not segregated as in the past—along skin-color lines.

The Mexican-American people has a very special devotion to *nuestro Diosito en la cruz*. Good Friday is *nuestra fiesta*, the cultic celebration of *nuestra existencia*. It is not an "other-worldy" make believe; it is a celebration of *nuestra vida*.

OUR LADY OF GUADALUPE

The happiness and joy of the Mexican and Mexican-American peoples is immediately obvious to outsiders. The tragedies of their history have not obliterated laughter and joy, warm friendship and the capacity to love.

The Mexican-American propensity for celebration is something that others find extremely difficult to understand. Outsiders may enjoy but they cannot enter fully into the spirit of a fiesta or imitate one on their own. But anyone who has attended a Mexican-American fiesta knows that celebration has taken place. There is spontaneity and ritual, joy and sorrow, music and silence.

Fiesta is the mystical celebration of a complex identity, the mystical affirmation that life is a gift and is worth living. In the fiesta the fatalistic/pessimistic realism and the adventuresome/optimistic idealism of the Mexican heritage are blended into the one celebration of the mystery of life—a series of apparent contradictions never fully comprehended but assumed, transcended, celebrated. In the fiesta the Mexican-American rises above the quest for the logical meaning of life and celebrates the very contradictions that are of the essence of the mystery of human life.

Two Mexican-American celebrations stand out as the most universal: the collective celebration of the fiesta of Our Lady of Guadalupe and the family celebration of the baptism of an infant. The two celebrations are interrelated in the identification of the people as *la raza* as a cultural and religious entity.

Because of the historical process that has been taking place over the past four hundred years and continues today, the cultural elements in the Mexican-American identity cannot be fully separated from the religious elements. The gospel and the culture are not fully identified with each other, but they cannot be fully separated. The gospel has been transforming the culture and the culture has been reactualizing the gospel through its own vital expressions.

If Ash Wednesday stresses the earthly belonging and present suffering of the people, and Good Friday marks their collective struggles and death, the feast of Our Lady of Guadalupe shouts out with joy the proclamation that a new dawn is breaking: the collective resurrection of a new people. Out of their own earth—Tepeyac—and in continuity with the life of their ancestors, a new mother emerges, pregnant with new life. She is not a goddess but the new woman from whom the new humanity will be born, *la raza cósmica de las Américas*. She is herself the prototype of the new creation. She is *la Mestiza*. She combines opposing forces so that in a creative way new life, not destruction, will emerge. On December 12 is celebrated the beginning of the new human-divine adventure.

It is important to remember that *flowers* were the sign that *la Morenita* gave to prove that she was God's messenger. In ancient and contemporary Mexican culture, flowers are a sign of new existence. From the seeds that fall to earth, watered by the heavenly dew, and fertilized by the ashes and remains of previous life, new life comes forth.

The resurrection of Christ was the beginning of the new Christian people, uniting and transcending natural peoples without destroying them. Something similar happened to Guadalupe. Mexicans discovered that they were a new people, reborn.

On the feast of Our Lady of Guadalupe, the people come together early in the morning to celebrate the irruption of new life—the dawn of a new humanity. This is the Easter sunrise service of the people. Before the first rays of the sun, they come together to sing *Las Mañanitas*, which is our proclamation of new life. It is the roses of Tepeyac that take the place of the Easter lilies of Western Christianity.

Guadalupe was also a *pentecost* event: it opened the way to true dialogue between Europeans and Mexican Indians. It was a symbol of unity over and above their many and serious diversities. It marked the beginning of the fusion of two mother cultures—the Spanish and the Mexican Indian—which in turn gave birth to a *mestizo* culture. *La Morenita* became the "mother of all the inhabitants of this land." Individuals who found themselves divided and segregated on the basis of human barriers—external differences—discovered that they were united in something far more important than what divided them: a common mother. Mexico is a very divided nation, and there is no doubt to anyone working with Mexican-Americans in the U.S.A. that they constitute a very divided people. But there is likewise a very strong unity and spirit of *familia* among this divided people.

It has been held that the symbolism of Guadalupe works to canonize and maintain *divisions* among the Mexican-American people. I have to admit that in some ways this does happen. But there is another function to the symbol: it gives a basis for a much deeper unity than does any class-struggle model. The power of Guadalupe is that it signals a common motherhood for all the inhabitants of the land. As new models of society are proposed and begin to be worked out, as long as they lead to or allow some individuals to think of themselves as inferior and others as superior, the conviction of a fellowship of equals under a common mother cannot find realization. Conversely, when individuals have become aware of their basic equality and see that it is not embodied in their society, they will work and struggle to bring about new lifestyles more reflective of the fundamental reality that all are children of the same mother.

La Morenita is found not only in the basilica in Mexico City but in numberless shrines throughout the Americas, in the homes of millions of persons, on medals around the necks of men, women, and children, tattooed on the arms and chests of men, sung about in pop songs, painted on the walls of *barrios* from California to Texas. Our Lady did not appear once and for all in 1531: she continues to appear wherever Mexican-Americans find themselves in the world today.

Our Lady did not simply tell the Indians to build her a temple. She sent them to the bishops—the representative of the institutional church. It was to be the *people*—the whole church—that would build the new temple of compassion. The message was twofold: the Indians, in the person of Juan Diego, were to go to the bishop (the church), and the church (in the person of the bishop) was to build a temple among the people.

In her telling the people through Juan Diego "Go to the bishop . . . ," we can glimpse a reflection of her telling the waiters at Cana "Do whatever he tells you . . ." (John 2:5). And what she tells the church is to "build a temple . . . of compassion"—a way of life in which compassion, mercy, love will reign. In other words, her command, understood in this broader sense, was: "Incarnate the gospel among this people, so that Christ will not come as a stranger but as one of them."

Mary's command to the Mexican church in 1531 was echoed by the Synod of Bishops in 1977, when it recognized and stressed the obligation on the part of the church to inculturate the gospel among peoples of diverse cultures, in order for it to be understood and lived by them. Without this inculturation—*mestizaje*—of the gospel into the natural substratum of a people's life, the gospel will never truly be implanted and a truly local church will never emerge.

PART FOUR

RELIGION AND THE NEW RIGHT

The appearance of the New Right in this volume may present the reader with problems, even aside from ideological differences. Does it fit? Is there a clearly distinguishable social movement to which the new Christian right corresponds? And are there new religious notions emerging from this movement, in the same way that we saw a number of ideas and suggestions coming out of other movements?

To what extent is the New Right a movement? It is sometimes disputed how wide and how important the New Right is as a social and political force in this country. Politically, the leaders of this movement do not seem quite so potent as they did, say, in early 1982. In the election of that year, very few candidates for Congress were defeated solely through the work of the New Right. If it had a hit list, its aim was wide of the target. Also, Jerry Falwell and the Moral Majority were forced to retreat from their plan to act as self-appointed censors of the television networks. Their agenda for social reform, at least to the extent that it would include school prayer and a constitutional amendment against abortion, appears stalled in Congress. No one has suggested that President Reagan's reelection landslide was due in any substantial way to this group.

Nevertheless, it is my belief that there is undeniably a social movement on the far right of American life, and that it is probably quite strong. Its political power was perhaps first felt in the election of Jesse Helms to the Senate in 1972. Members of the New Right have had an important effect on the political resolution of social issues. For example, although it is impossible to measure their influence scientifically, they have undoubtedly played an important role in torpedoing the ERA, once almost certain to be enacted into law.

Have significant *religious* changes resulted from this movement? There certainly are religious emphases that one can pick out in the rhetoric of New Right leaders. Are these new or are we simply more aware of them? After all, Evangelical movements have figured prominently in American history. The question becomes more complicated when we note that New Right writers present themselves as merely returning to a more traditional Christianity from which more liberal Americans have wandered. David Harrel, in his instructive article, argues that the Moral Majority is nothing more than a reappearance of the fundamentalist phenomenon that has surfaced in American life many times previously.

Still, *his own* listing of doctrinal concerns suggests that there is after all something new in the New Right, even from a religious perspective. Besides such traditional theological concerns as creationism and the inerrancy of the Bible, these rightwing Christians have stressed two other themes. The first is a sharp-edged view of what the family should be, and of the role of women in particular. The second is a fusion of religiousness with certain political values, notably a strong nationalistic sentiment. If one takes passion as a barometer, social and political concerns are at least as important to them as are theological concerns.

We also need to note that changes in religious perceptions have occurred not only among New Right advocates, but also among their critics. This volume concentrates more on the latter, but with an eye to those whose comments have included more than a purely negative project, with the expectation that important insights might emerge from which both left and right might learn. Even from a liberal point of view, it is unlikely that a movement so strongly felt and so widespread would have nothing of value in it. There is something troubling about a sentiment that would claim to be liberal or egalitarian, but would dismiss its opposition as "redneck," "backwoods," or "small town."

"Mainline" Protestant churches have begun to recognize the dangers of condescension, as Jeffrey Hadden points out. Although individuals from these churches have been quick to join groups opposed to the Moral Majority, the churches themselves have unanimously avoided anything resembling condemnation. In addition to political problems and right wings in their own churches, they recognize that they can hardly claim consistency in deploring the activism of conservative churches. They have themselves fought more or less successfully for the right to speak out on political issues in the name of Christianity.

Everybody's favorite representative of the new Christian right is Jerry Falwell, even if a number of other names appear over and over in literature on the movement: Ed McAteer (Religious Roundtable), Pat Robertson (700 Club), Paul Weyrich, et al. But Falwell heads the Moral Majority, which for many unfamiliar with the movement *is* the Christian New Right. He also obviously relishes the task and opportunity of being the spokesman. There is certainly something of the slick promoter ("snake-oil salesman," to Theresa Carpenter of *The Village Voice*[1]) in the smooth, genial, yet opinionated Virginian. Or to put it in another way, he is the classic small-town booster (and boaster).[2] Typical of such boosters, he frequently gets carried away by his own rhetoric, so that liberal listeners are horrified. But then he may cheerfully moderate an extreme statement, so that it is not nearly so offensive.

The result is that when we read one of Falwell's more thoughtful pieces, such as one of his numerous interviews or the afterword of his *The Fundamentalist Phenomenon,* we find that we are at least partially disarmed. He does *not* believe that fundamentalism requires no slacks for women, that homosexuals should be persecuted, or that segregation is biblically warranted. He even admonishes his fellow fundamentalists not to make religious doctrines out of conservative shibboleths.

The *thrust* of Falwell's message is to preserve the integrity of the church, or more exactly, of the gospel. With this in mind, it is easy to see why he would inveigh against secular humanism. For him, secular humanism represents the inattention and self-absorption that results from replacing the Christian word with a purely human word. One might be willing to grant that Falwell and his fellow preachers have a point here, but it is disquieting to see how quickly and how surely they determine where their secular "enemies" are. They locate them so easily to the outside of the white middle class of America: among hippies and homosexuals, within the Soviet Union, even in organized labor.

In this section, I am at least as interested in the religious reaction to the New Right as in the New Right itself. This perhaps reflects some of my own liberal bias; if so, I plead guilty. It does seem to me that some of the most interesting reflections on this movement have come, if not from the shock caused by it, then from responses and defenses by those who are outside it.

There are two principal groups, very different in themselves, that have responded strongly to the New Right. The first is the liberal wing of American Christianity. This group, generally liberal in politics as well as theology, has been closely identified with well-established Protestant churches and with the National Council of Churches in particular. The other group consists of Evangelical writers. By "Evangelical" I am referring to that branch of Protestant Christianity that has stressed the centrality of the Bible and personal conversion to Christ, and has deemphasized church organization and doctrine. Politically, these Christians have not always been conservative at all. In fact, Evangelical Christians were prominent in the movement to abolish slavery and to secure suffrage for women, as well as frequently siding with labor in the early part of this century.

In both of these groups, we can find two important kinds of reaction. On the one hand, they reject those elements of New Right religion that they see as betraying Christianity. On the other, there are some writers in each group who recognize that the New Right perhaps offers an opportunity to other Christians—that of testing their own assumptions. For example, although the New Right may not be correct in the *way* it rejects secularism, it may be sounding an alarm we need to hear in raising the issue. They may assist us in avoiding too easy and too uncritical an acceptance of fashionable values.

Robert McAfee Brown makes no pretense of being sympathetic with the aims of the New Right. He gives a scathing account of the contradictions implicit in this movement. The basic problem is that it is socially conservative first and last, and then seeks to disguise its political commitment with religious rhetoric. Its religious individualism is far less significant than the political individualism of raw capitalism that it strives to support. It takes the Bible out of context, to attack what it sees as the real evils of our society: pornography, homosexuality, abortion, trends toward socialism. It is utterly myopic concerning social or structural sin, which may have far more devastating effects on the family and on personal morality in the long run. It has no interest in plumbing the Bible for its real social message, which is acutely aware of the danger of corporate evil. In short, New Right Christianity is not biblical at all, but rests on "political ideology."

More chilling, because it includes the personal experiences of the author, is the brief account of Virginia Doland. The Evangelicalism of the New Right has an innate tendency to totalitarianism and the suppression of the individual, according to Doland. It emphasizes rules and conformity, directly attacks all signs of individuality and creativity, and puts a premium on passivity. It has the same characteristic found in all totalitarian societies: paranoia vis-à-vis the outside world. "Fitting in" becomes all-important, and what is most disturbing about this is that in places like her Bible college there is a highly detailed, predetermined view of what it takes to be a Christian, to "fit in." All this is of course a perversion of Christianity, if God's word is indeed liberating, if we are meant to be on pilgrimage to "hard" (i.e., unexpected and undefined) places where we might meet God on God's terms.

Martin Marty finds the weakness of the New Right precisely where it has always mistakenly thought its strength to be: in its Manichean compulsion to divide the entire world into good and evil. It is thus instinctively hostile to humanism without recognizing how the believer necessarily lives *in* the world, even if in some ways *against* it. Marty has a number of other telling observations to make concerning American Evangelicalism, including its penchant for moralizing. Where else is a movement to go that has never been able to agree on doctrinal issues, whether infant baptism or the nature of the millennium?

Still, the left ought not to dismiss this movement. Marty has the classic liberal strength (or weakness) of finding some good even in what repels many. The New Right may appear cartoonish to the rest of us but, like a Hirshberg drawing, it helps us see something we would otherwise miss. The right may be necessary *especially* to liberals in showing where they have gone wrong, or at least may go wrong.[3] Liberals may also learn from the sense of urgency with which the right seizes on the Bible, although they need not imitate their sense of assurance about what the biblical message is.

To my mind, the most telling criticisms of the New Right have come from fellow Evangelicals. They share a certain religious tradition; there is less likely to be a fundamental misunderstanding concerning premises. Like all traditions, it has problems intrinsic to it, but there are certainly dangers in other Christian traditions as well.[4] In the face of the New Right, fellow Evangelicals are attempting to recover the genuine tradition.

And there *is* another side of Evangelicalism, well represented in *Sojourners* and *The Other Side*. As Jim Wallis, editor of *Sojourners,* points out, these journals and their supporters share with black Evangelicals the vision of the Bible as a liberating document. After all, Wallis says, the gospel is "good news." The New Testament shows Jesus taking as his own the text "The Spirit of the Lord is upon me . . . to set at liberty those who are oppressed, to preach the acceptable year of the Lord." To identify the gospel exclusively with the lives of white middle-class persons is to be part of what Wallis calls "the Great Reversal."

The problem is not that the New Right mixes religion with politics, for the Bible is radically political. The problem is that the right never lets biblical faith truly affect its politics. The "acceptable year" that Jesus preached was no doubt a reference to the year of jubilee in the Old Testament, a time when debts were to be forgiven, a time for equalizing material assets. What Wallis terms "the theology of Empire" is directly opposed to this kind of self-examination. It is instead a legitimation of a national and international status quo in which social and economic life is fundamentally unequal and unjust.

Paris Donehoo and Mortimer Arias also stress the need to stand more directly in the light of the word of God. In Donehoo's brief article, the challenge is to regain the sense of sin that has always been part of Evangelicalism. This sense of sin forces us always to be at some distance with regard to human creations, to avoid absolutizing them. Whether they are scientific, artistic, or political, these works always contain something limited and ambiguous, and are therefore never to be worshiped or raised to the level of the supernatural. The New Right, though, has always been willing to forget this, and to identify divine providence with the good of the United States.

Arias develops another Evangelical theme, discipleship. He notes, correctly, that this perception is also present in the Catholic tradition, in the *comunidades de base.* Jesus did not found a church; he called disciples. As the etymology of the word suggests, the disciple is one open to "learning." The disciple thus enters a process, a journey. Jesus' legacy was a community of disciples, men and women who had experienced the kingdom of God and who were to take the news of that experience to the world. The gospel has little to do, then, with blessing or privilege for those called. It is a summoning to mission, a lifelong vocation.

Kingdom, discipleship, and evangelization all go together for Arias, and none of them has anything to do with "belonging" or being "certified." The picture he offers of Christian faith is radically dynamic. Conversion is necessary, but it is not an entry into a special "state." Nor can it be confined to a particular moment. It is for all the other moments in our life, and for the persons we encounter in those moments.

What we have in looking at the New Right is no integrated set of religious reflections at all. Rather, we are presented with the views of men and women in fundamental disagreement. What *is* noteworthy is how this disagreement too is leading, if painfully, to new dimensions of religious understanding.

NOTES

1. Theresa Carpenter, "Jerry Falwell," *Village Voice,* 47 (Nov. 18, 1980).

2. Jeffrey Hadden and Charles Swann make this point effectively in their chapter "The Mobilization of the Moral Majority," in *Prime Time Preachers* (Reading, Mass., Addison-Wesley, 1981).

3. Peggy Shriver, *The Bible Vote* (New York, Pilgrim Press, 1982) 48.

4. One exceptionally well-balanced account of the three principal Christian traditions found in the United States—mainline Protestant, Catholic, and Evangelical—is found in Martin Marty's *The Public Church* (New York, Crossroads, 1981).

Chapter 27

David Harrel

The Roots of the Moral Majority: Fundamentalism Revisited

DOMESTICATED EVANGELICALS

Billy Graham

In the fifty years from 1925 to 1975 only Billy Graham drew American attention seriously back to the Bible-believing base of American society. Riding the wave of anti-Communist conservatism in the 1950s, Billy rose from the simplicity of his North Carolina Baptist upbringing to international Christian stardom. By 1981 he had been beheld personally by more people than any other human who ever lived (50 million) and had gathered one and a half million "inquirers." He has known, and possibly in some cases influenced, every president since Harry Truman. When he finally found in Richard Milhous Nixon an Israelite in whom was no guile, he gave himself wholeheartedly to politics. Chastened by Watergate, Billy survived, a wiser but no less respected man, a prophet with immense honor in his own country.

Billy did all of this by preaching the Bible, fundamentalist style. It was all there: hell, sin, the soon-coming of the Lord, repent or perish, let every head be bowed and every eye be closed, just slip your hand up right where you are sitting, send your offerings to Billy Graham, Minneapolis, Minnesota—all delivered with piercing eyes fixed on awed listeners and bony finger that seemed to search out backsliders. It is still there, more mixed now with occasional pleas for social justice and less certain about such subjects as the exact dimensions of heaven, but Billy still believes in sin and salvation, and he is not ashamed to preach it.

Through it all, however, Billy Graham was different. In his earliest campaigns he received the backing of fundamentalist leaders, but they soon dropped him. Carl McIntire concluded that Billy was "the greatest disappointment in the Christian world."[1] In spite of his sometimes threatening glare, Billy always ended up with a smile; his spirit was basically ironic. Often attacked by liberals in his early years, he rarely fought back.

As time passed, points out sociologist Bill Martin, Billy seemed to waffle: he hinted that there might be Christians among Communists, and made inquiries about holding a

First published in *Currents in Theology and Mission* 9, April 1982. Copyright © 1982 by The Order of St. Benedict, Inc. Published by the Liturgical Press, Collegeville, Minnesota. Used with permission.

campaign in the Soviet Union; and he spoke well of Catholics and implied that he might preach in Rome "if the Coliseum could be made safer for Christians than the last time it was extensively used."

Jimmy Carter

Billy Graham certainly represents a broad segment of American religion. Bernard Weisberger's characterization of Charles G. Finney is equally true of Graham: "He did not study the popular mind; he had it."[2] It was a mind brought to political eminence by Jimmy Carter, full of assurance, religious openness, earnestness, and zeal. This warm and friendly religious affirmation astonished and disturbed many sophisticated Americans; Graham remained a curiosity and Carter a paradox.

In spite of Carter's fairly orthodox liberal politics, many liberals were embarrassed by a president who taught a Baptist Sunday School class and "witnessed" to visiting heads of state. It seemed fitting in the 1970s that there should be a professing Christian in the White House, but not one who actually believed it. Surely, thought concerned liberals in 1976, fundamentalism had returned from the dead. Not yet.

Billy Graham and Jimmy Carter represented a variety of domesticated evangelicalism that increasingly angered fundamentalists. In fact, the immediate beginnings of the new religious right date from 1978 when a deep disillusionment settled over fundamentalists whose hopes had risen with the election of Jimmy Carter. "It was a tremendous letdown, if not a betrayal," they thought, "to have Carter stumping for the ERA, for not stopping federally-paid abortions, and for advocating homosexual rights."[3] "I've had about all the born-again diplomacy I can stand," said Cornelius W. Pennell, pastor of the huge Forrest Hills Baptist Church in Decatur, Georgia, in July 1980.[4] About all Jimmy Carter had proven, said Jerry Falwell, in a 1979 sermon, was "that America can live without a president."[5]

It was clear by 1978 that there were fundamentalists still around and that they were growing more and more restive about being identified with the likes of Graham and Carter. The election of 1976, with its apparent religious tone, was no adequate preview for what was to come. Jimmy Carter's religion seemed amusing; the Moral Majority was not funny. On his return from Dayton, H. L. Mencken wrote to a friend, "I set out laughing and returned shivering."[6] Religion provided color stories in 1976; in 1980 the new right was labelled by the *Christian Century* "the most significant religious news story of 1980."[7]

THE ELECTRONIC CHURCH

By the 1970s conservative American religion had bred a new generation of leaders, leaders with unparalleled financial power and communications resources. Some of them were evangelists of the old school who admired Billy Graham and Billy Sunday, but others rarely preached; they were religious television personalities, the products of the modern media revolution.

Threatened by science, conservative religion has always been fascinated by technology, from neon signs to satellite television. Revivalism has been religion's Wild West; it beckoned bold entrepreneurs and speculators. Since the time of the early 100,000 watt radio stations in Chicago and Del Rio, Texas, independent evangelists have played a game of survival of the fittest. They skillfully built clienteles and experimented with every new communications advance. When cable and satellite television made relatively cheap programming possible, the fundamentalists and charismatics were miles ahead in knowing how to market their product.

By 1980, the power and breadth of the electronic church, composed mostly of independent ministries, was staggering. An estimated 130 million Americans tuned in a religious television program each week, approximately 47 percent of the population, while only 41 percent attended church services. Of the 8,000 radio stations in the United States, 1,400 are religious; 30 of the nation's 800 television stations and 66 of the 800 cable systems are religious. Including small local ministries, radio and television evangelists probably take in over one billion dollars each year, the largest being Oral Roberts at $60 million, Pat Robertson at $58 million, Jim Bakker at $51 million, Jerry Falwell at about $50 million, Rex Humbard at $25 million, and Jimmy Swaggert at $20 million. With a touch of braggadocia, Ben Armstrong, executive secretary of the National Religious Broadcasters, reported in 1980 that "broadcast religion touches more people than all the churches combined."[8]

Curious as it seems, the growth of the electronic church took place outside the attention of most Americans, certainly most American intellectuals. It is true that the preachers were there when one spun the television dial (Garry Trudeau lingered long enough to do a couple of Doonesbury strips on Jimmy Swaggert), but they seemed relatively irrelevant. Then, early in 1979, Jerry Falwell formed the Moral Majority. He caught the attention of the news media, increasing numbers of politicians, and some suggest as many as four million voters. When the post-mortem began in November 1980, the Moral Majority claimed to have been crucial not only in the election of Ronald Reagan, but to have cleansed the Senate of the likes of Gravel of Alaska, McGovern of South Dakota, Bayh of Indiana, Church of Idaho, Culver of Iowa, and Nelson of Wisconsin. They clearly swayed state elections, especially in the South. Alabama elected its first Republican senator in 100 years and first Catholic ever, former POW Jeremiah Denton; Birmingham voters unseated Congressman James Buchanan, a Republican and the only Southern Baptist minister in Congress, because he had voted "immorally" on several women's rights and civil rights issues. The Moral Majority intended for 1980 to be a trial run, a preparation for an all-out assault in 1984. Even they were astonished by their success.

POLITICAL TIES

The general outline of the formation of the new right political coalition has now been thoroughly explored by the press. Generally regarded as the organizational genius behind the movement is Paul Weyrich, an Eastern Rite Catholic and veteran Washington lobbyist. Weyrich operates a school in Washington for conservative political candidates and heads an organization called the Committee for the Survival of a Free Congress.

One of a bewildering variety of conservative lobbying organizations in Washington, Weyrich's group has been characterized as a "little to the left of the John Birch Society and a little to the right of the American Conservative Union."[9] Joining Weyrich in building the coalition in 1978 and 1979 were Richard Viguerie, professional fund-raiser and publisher of the *Conservative Digest,* and Terry Dolan of the National Conservative Political Action Committee.

The influence of this political triumvirate literally exploded in 1979 when they established contact with several of the important electronic evangelists. As early as 1976 Viguerie predicted that the "next major growth area for the conservative ideology" would be among evangelical Christians.[10] Perhaps the key figure in making the linkage was Ed McAteer, a former Colgate-Palmolive marketing executive and later field director for the Conservative Caucus. McAteer was a Baptist and, apparently, an electronic church groupie; he knew many of the evangelists and he introduced them to the conservative political lobbyists, opening the door to what Weyrich now likes to call "the sleeping giant."

In January 1979, Falwell was persuaded to establish the Moral Majority, appointing Robert Billings, a former Weyrich aide, as its director. Billings later became Ronald Reagan's religious affairs advisor, before establishing his own organization in 1980 called the National Christian Action Coalition. In February 1979, McAteer became head of the Religious Roundtable, an elite organization founded after a high-level meeting in Washington attended by Weyrich, Viguerie, and representatives of a score of religious and industrial organizations. The Roundtable initially included just 56 members, but it listed many of the most prominent television preachers and a number of important new right politicians. Perhaps the most important of the other religious organizations which blossomed in this hothouse environment was the California-based Christian Voice.

Each of these Christian organizations chiseled out a special area of responsibility. Christian Voice publicized a congressional "hit list" naming 36 congressmen with poor moral voting records. The Moral Majority, aided by Falwell's fund-raising, began registering conservative voters, sometimes in church buildings. The groups funneled information to several hundred thousand evangelicals in their newsletters and in grassroots conferences featuring Weyrich and his cohorts.

Perhaps the most important single event marking the emergence of the religious right was a mass meeting in Dallas, Texas, sponsored by the Religious Roundtable on August 21 and 22, 1980. Organized by conservative Southern Baptist television evangelist James Robison, the meeting was attended by perhaps 10,000 fundamentalist ministers. An impressed Ronald Reagan was the only political candidate attending and he pleased the audience by announcing that he also believed that evolution was only a theory. Then, recognizing the strictly religious nature of the gathering, Reagan reportedly announced: "I know you can't endorse me. But . . . I want you to know that I endorse you."[11]

The mushrooming of the religious right in 1979 resulted from two skillfully-orchestrated but quite unstable coalitions. The first was the alliance of the professional political lobbyists in Washington with the conservative religious leaders. Some liberals saw the union as completely manipulative, the deceptive use of "a religious issue as a front for what is in reality a right-wing political campaign."[12] But, in fact, each of the evangelists had his own reasons for becoming politicized; it seems totally unrealistic to picture them as weak-willed dupes being suckered by Washington con men.

In some ways more remarkable than the political-religious alliance of 1979 was the religious diversity within the new right. For half a century conservative American religion had been divided into countless warring sects, generally most angry at one another. "One thing fundamentalists do better than anything is fight," remarked Falwell. "It's all we know how to do and if there isn't an issue we'll start one."[13] But, for reasons which should later become apparent, and always asserting they would not "compromise our theological principles," an astonishing group of individualistic ministers began treating one another civilly.

THE CAST

Jerry Falwell

Most visible in the religious right are evangelists from the fundamentalist tradition. Their acknowledged leader is Jerry Falwell, pastor of Thomas Road Baptist Church in

Lynchburg, Virginia, an independent Baptist church with 17,000 members, an elementary and high school, a college, a seminary, an alcoholic treatment center, a summer camp, and a foreign mission. In addition, Falwell broadcasts "The Old Time Gospel Hour" over 324 television outlets to an estimated audience of fifty million viewers. His ministry employs 950 people and has an operating budget of just over one million dollars a week. Cherubic and rosy-cheeked in the pulpit, Falwell is tough and articulate.

Born into a family of "brawlers," Falwell was a good student and excelled on his high school football team. Jerry found the Lord in 1952. After four years in Bible school he returned to Lynchburg to establish a new congregation in an abandoned pop factory. Since that time, Falwell has had every reason to believe that God liked what he was doing and it was clear that many Americans did. By 1981 he was receiving support from three and one-half million families.[14]

James Robison

Probably the second most visible of the fundamentalist evangelists is Southern Baptist revivalist James Robison, whose crusade ministry has been second only to Billy Graham's for two decades. Robison is Texas born and based and his style is tough and abrasive. "That's how I witnessed," says Robison, "tear 'em up. I'd have truck drivers push back their beer and start crying and say 'tell me more.'"[15] In 1980 Robison's ministry reportedly employed 125 people and was growing; he budgeted $15 million for prime-time television specials during 1981.

Robison is a key figure in the conservative push to control the Southern Baptist Convention. Since the mid-1970s he has turned increasingly political and is a leader in the Religious Roundtable and the Moral Majority.

Jim Bakker

The charismatic wing of the electronic church, which is by far the largest segment, has been far less committed to the political right. Conspicuously absent from almost all of the coalition meetings have been Oral Roberts, Rex Humbard, and Jimmy Swaggert. The main links of the charismatics to the religious right have been Jim Bakker and Pat Robertson, the powerful hosts of PTL and The 700 Club.

Bakker's support for the right has been strong and consistent. An Assemblies of God minister, Bakker first gained fame as Robertson's employee, but in the mid-1970s he broke to establish his own Christian network. Bakker has received constant criticism both because of his unsophisticated theology and because of chronic financial difficulties and high pressure money-raising techniques.

All through 1979 and 1980 Bakker fought a running battle with the FCC over alleged misuse of funds. Critics suggested that PTL (originally signifying Praise the Lord or People that Love) should be christened Please Throw a Lifesaver or Pay the Lawyer. But in spite of this "shaky public image,"[16] in 1980, Bakker's two-hour talk show was aired daily on over 200 television stations, his headquarters was contacted daily by 20,000 people, and he received monthly support from 700,000 contributors. Deeply angered by his legal bouts with government agencies, Bakker apparently gave his full support to the new political right.

Pat Robertson

Pat Robertson, host of the theologically more serious 700 Club and founder of the Christian Broadcasting Network, gave important but more limited support to the new right. Robertson, a charismatic Baptist minister whose father was a senator from Virginia, has consistently denied any direct political interest and publicly avowed that "God isn't a right-winger or a left-winger."[17]

Robertson was one of the major sponsors of the Washington for Jesus rally which drew about 200,000 Christian demonstrators to Washington in April 1980. The charismatic-dominated organizers of the event were "careful to avoid identification with New Right politics or specific controversial causes," a stand which probably accounted for Falwell's inability to fit the rally into his schedule.[18] One prominent charismatic leader privately expressed the belief that Robertson later regretted the limited support he had given to the political right.[19] And yet Robertson's influence was important to the conservatives.

The Washington for Jesus rally featured such militant conservatives as James Robison and Southern Baptist Convention president Adrian Rogers; Robertson's 700 Club was a litany of support for conservative causes, if not candidates (particulary a millennialistic backing for military spending and support of Israel). He also reportedly supported several of the new religious right organizations, particularly the Christian Voice.[20]

Even more unlikely than this loose coalition of evangelists was the shocking fundamentalist flirtation with the formerly polygamous and heterodox Mormons and that fetching lady who sits on the seven hills. Conservative Roman Catholics had long looked upon fundamentalists as eccentric but potential partners against worse evil. In 1955, when Billy Graham was under bitter attack by the liberal religious press in America, the editor of *America* wrote, "We wish Billy Graham well in his mission of recalling God to the minds of the secularized world. We would also wish that there were more like him where he came from."[21] As it turned out, there were many more like him where he came from and they received substantial Catholic support. The audience of Pat Robertson's 700 Club is about 15 percent Catholic and "it is estimated that Catholics contributed about twice as much money last year to 'The 700 Club' as they did to the bishops' communications collection."[22]

TRADITIONAL VALUES

The focus of this unstable coalition has been necessarily quite narrow. Pro-life has been the most important unifying issue, though it seems inaccurate to see the religious right as a single-issue movement. Three areas of concerns are generally shared by the religious right and political candidates are graded in each area.

One set of religious right issues has to do with the preservation of traditional moral values. Specific concerns include curbing abortion; opposing ERA, gay rights, and other alternative lifestyles as destructive of the family unit; and banning pornography. The pro-life issue comes closer than any other to being, especially for Catholics, what the *Christian Century* has called "one of the most intense 'single issues' yet to plague the American political system."[23]

At the huge Convocation '81 rally held by religious conservatives in Washington in February 1981, pro-life groups seemed particularly confident that they were the "vital element of the whole New Right package deal."[24] Several pro-life constitutional amendments have been proposed, all aimed generally at defining life as beginning at conception.

If pro-life is the most important single issue in the coalition, the most hysterical moral issue for most fundamentalists is the open flaunting of alternative lifestyles. Fundamentalism is a masculine movement, its language filled with militant, aggressive imagery.

"Men have led women and children a long way; now it is time for an 'army' of spiritually concerned men to lead America the right way."[25] The Equal Rights Amendment is seen as a threat to traditional sex roles; Falwell has warned that it would allow honosexual marriages. But it is gay rights which receives their most severe abuse; fundamentalist sermons are filled with attacks on "homosexual perverts." James Robison's politicization can be dated from a legal confrontation with a Dallas television station in the summer of 1979 when his program was cancelled because of his withering attacks on homosexuals.

Homosexuality quite obviously disgusts fundamentalists, and a recent critic of the religious right charges that "while Falwell piously informs us that it is our duty to love homosexuals, he makes it clear that God wants them killed."[26]

In general, this set of issues symbolizes what conservatives believe is a pervasive decay in the moral fiber of American society.

ANTI-EVOLUTION

The second set of issues which unites the religious right concerns schools, and, at least partly, reflects old doctrinal concerns. At the center is the still unresolved issue of teaching evolution. Nell Seagraves and her son Kelly, of recent television fame, have led an attack in California for the past 18 years through their San Diego-based Creation Science Research Center to require that textbooks specifically acknowledge that evolution is a theory and not a fact. Most anti-evolutionist plans are more ambitious.

While it is clear that laws prohibiting the teaching of evolution are unconstitutional (the Supreme Court finally ruling in 1968 that the 1927 Arkansas law violated the First Amendment), most recent efforts have tried to force the teaching of creationism. A 1973 Tennessee law requiring teachers to explain the Genesis account was declared unconstitutional because it gave preferential treatment to a particular faith. Creationists have since pressed for the teaching of "scientific creationism" in schools where evolution is taught. In more than 30 states legislation is now pending on that subject. A bill which almost surely will be introduced in Congress this year would require equal federal funding for creationist research, equal federal allocations for creationists' museum exhibits, and restrict evolutionary teaching in schools. Despite a string of judicial setbacks, the creationist assault has had its impact.

Many widely used textbooks now approach evolution with great caution, and many school boards, in order to avoid confrontation with the fundamentalists, have either deemphasized evolution or omitted it entirely. "Quite likely," writes one critic, "many students graduating from today's schools have no knowledge of evolution."[27]

SCHOOL PRAYER

More emotional is the effort to nullify the 1963 Supreme Court decision banning prayer in the public schools. Angered by this symbol of the secularization of the school system, the issue has become a test case for fundamentalists. In recent testimony before the House Judiciary Committee, James Robison charged that banning prayer in the schools was followed by "plagues" which include "acceleration of the Vietnam War, escalation of crime, disintegration of families, racial conflict, teenage pregnancies, and venereal disease."[28] Senator Jesse Helms introduced a bill in 1980 which would have banned federal court review of any case involving prayer in the schools; other conservatives favored a constitutional amendment guaranteeing that right.

PRIVATE SCHOOLS

By far the most important of the school issues, however, relate to the mushrooming private school movement, which Jerry Falwell has called the most significant phenomenon of this era. The dimensions of the private school explosion are startling indeed, from 1,400 Protestant schools in 1960 to 16,000 in 1980; an increase of 150 percent in the number of students between 1965 and 1975. Robert Baldwin, executive director of Citizens for Educational Freedom, recently reported that "independent schools are currently being founded at a rate of about three a day . . . [and that] if this pace continues, by 1990 there will be more independent schools in the United States than government schools."[29] Falwell claims that there are 108,000 fundamentalist churches in the country, each anxious to establish its own parochial school.

These new schools clash with the federal government on a number of points and have provided the religious right with a whole set of legislative needs. Senator Daniel P. Moynihan has introduced one of a variety of bills designed to provide tax credits for the parents of students in such schools. More pressing has been an impending war between the schools and the IRS. In 1978 the IRS threatened to revoke the tax-exempt status of any school that could not prove it did not discriminate by enrolling a quota of minority students. Inundated by letters, Congress passed a law which forbade the IRS to spend money investigating such cases, but the resentment between the schools and government regulatory agencies remains sharp and a major motive for the politicization of the religious right. [Ed.: The Treasury Department recently announced a policy shift ending the practice of denying tax-exempt status to private schools that discriminate against minorities.]

MILITARISM

The third set of issues uniting the religious right includes support for military spending, an aggressive foreign policy, and, especially, vigorous support for Israel. It is at this point that the conservative alliance is probably weakest, since many conservative businessmen favor an accommodation with the Arabs. It is also at this point that the religious right seems to its critics to be least Christian. And yet, the militant pro-Israel foreign policy of the religious right is probably the issue most directly related to its doctrinal beliefs. More ominously, as several critics have observed, this is the point at which the religious right might well make its largest contribution toward the dramatic world-ending cataclysm they are confident is rapidly approaching.

THE 80s AND THE 20s

Such, then, are the general outlines of the rise of the religious right. Considerably more intriguing is the question, why? To discover why, one must look at the religious, intellectual, social, political assumptions that undergird the movement. Viewed from these perspectives, the fundamentalist uprising in 1925 offers striking insights into the dynamics of the religious right in 1980.[30]

In the first place, both movements are distinctively religious. Whatever their political ramifications, they began as religious fusses. In 1925 the Northern Baptist and Presbyterian churches were in the throes of a life-and-death struggle to determine who would control the denominations. At stake were consciences, jobs, and money. The besieged conservatives looked for allies wherever they could find them, mostly in the uniformly conservative but only mildly involved Southern churches. They exerted immense pressure on the moderates within their own denominations and in 1925 appeared to be on the verge of winning.

In the 1970s a clear siege mentality was typical of conservative Catholics and Southern Baptists. Fundamentalists seemed to gain control of the Southern Baptist Convention in 1978 and have dared the liberals to come out fighting. Many observers of that church believe it will suffer a major division in the 1980s. Fundamentalist Baptists and conservative Catholics, looking for support, found conservative allies in the increasingly respectable Pentecostals and Mormons. Out of these denominational pressure-cookers have come the warriors ready to press the battle throughout American society.

INERRANCY

Theologically, two main planks from the 1920s' fundamentalist crusade still undergird the religious right platform. The first is a belief in the inerrancy of the Bible. Falwell believes in Jonah and the whale just as firmly as did William Jennings Bryan. Falwell has said:

> The basic tenet of . . . fundamentalist Christianity is that we have one basic document on which we predicate everything we believe . . . the inerrancy of scripture not only in matters of theology, but science, geography, history, et cetera—totally and entirely, the very word of God.

Falwell, claiming as allies Billy Graham, Pope John Paul, and "over half the preachers in America," warned, "People want what they have always wanted: they want a message from God."[31] He may be right. A poll sponsored by the *St. Cloud Daily Times* (Minnesota), in March 1981, revealed that 54 percent of the people in its reading area favored teaching creationism in the public schools.[32]

PREMILLENNIALISM

The second major theological tenet shared by most of the religious right leaders is dispensational premillennialism, a theory that became widely accepted by American evangelicals in the late nineteenth century. The idea has been popularized most recently in Hal Lindsey's *Late Great Planet Earth,* which at last count sold over nine million copies.

The main points of premillennial belief include dividing world history into seven dispensations, the interruption of this scheme by the church age, and the imminent beginning of a period of tribulation to be followed by the return of Christ and the beginning of a period of the millennial reign of Christ on earth. A whole new vocabulary has been introduced into evangelical thought. Many Americans had assumed, along with Martin Marty, that "rapture" was something achieved in the back seat of the car at a drive-in movie, but to the initiated it meant the instantaneous pretribulation "catching up" of the righteous, a remarkable event which any day now will empty assorted fundamentalist churches and leave cars with appropriate bumper stickers driverless, while at the same time leaving untouched the entire faculty and student body of Yale Divinity School.

The impact of premillennial theology on the religious right is strangely ambivalent. It clearly places history outside human manipulation and anticipates that change can come only by cataclysmic supernatural intervention. Dispensational premillennialists have historically been pessimistic and little given to political and social reform. Yet in both the 1920s and the 1970s premillennialists have launched political crusades. This is a source of considerable tension in the movement. The feature story in a recent Arkansas Southern Baptist Church Newsletter, appropriately named *Good News,* was "Global Gloom." The "good news" was that the "world won't be fit to live in by 2000 A.D.," but "Those who have trusted in Jesus Christ" will be survivors.[33]

The more direct influence of premillennialism has been the identification of the establishment of Israel with the coming end of the church age, confidence that most Jews would soon become Christians, the marking of Russia as the evil power of the North which would lead the final persecution ending in Armageddon, and the belief that the United States was destined to be Israel's protector in the struggle that would precede the end-time.

ANTI-INTELLECTUALISM

While one could hardly understand the rise of the religious right apart from this religious content, it is clear that the movement also reflects some other widely-held intellectual assumptions. Most obvious is the virile anti-intellectualism that is never far beneath the surface in American society. In its extreme form it was voiced by Brother Joe Leffew in an outdoors Pentecostal revival during the Scopes trial:

> I ain't got no learnin' an' never had none. . . . Glory be to the Lamb! Some folks work their hands off'n up'n to the elbows to give their young-uns education, and all they do is send their young-uns to hell. . . . I've got eight young-uns in the cabin and three in glory, and I know they're in glory, because I never learned 'em nothin'.[34]

While many fundamentalists would have expressed shock at such statements, Bryan was as sure as Joe Leffew that "it is better to trust in the Rock of Ages, than to know the age of the rocks."[35] Every fundamentalist knows how to list academic credentials: M.A., Ph.D., A.S.S.

But fundamentalist anti-intellectualism was not simply obscurantism. It was a protest against the chopping up of life in the twentieth century. The explosion of knowledge, the communications revolution, and the endless specialization of modern society seemed to rob people of control over their own lives, giving it over to experts. The intellectual protest of conservative religion in the 1920s and in the 1970s has been aimed at what many common people believe to be scientific elitism which encroaches on their right to make religious choices and to nurture their children in their beliefs. They were being arrogantly manhandled by "conceited professors," "conceited skeptics," "the high-brows," and "biological baboon boosters."[36] Bryan said in 1925:

> There are only 11,000 members of the American Association for the Advance-ment of Science. I don't believe one in ten thousand should dictate to the rest of us. Can a handful of scientists rob your children of religion and turn them out atheists? We'll find 109,000,000 Americans on our side. For the first time in my life, I'm on the side of the majority.[37]

Falwell viewed the modern struggle in the same democratic terms: "The problem is that we don't agree with those buzzards—and that we outnumber them!"[38]

Anti-elitism is powerful medicine in 1980. Millions of people feel they have little control over the politicians who rule them, the intellectuals who instruct them, and the churches and other institutions which allegedly represent them. Editor James M. Wall of the *Christian Century* wrote of this resentment:

> Secular elites who control much of our national media consistently show a disdain for and rejection of the overt expression of religious conviction. Small wonder, then, that the New Right can appeal to so many conservative Christians. Persons threatened by change will retaliate if they do not feel understood. . . . If we are troubled by the prospect of the New Right's determining what is "acceptable" in order to be saved, we must not forget that the current religious and secular liberal establishment has also been guilty of defining for the nation what was pure and right.[39]

Considerably more subtle, and more important, the intellectual base of fundamentalism rests on its continuing loyalty to a nineteenth-century Baconian definition of science.[40] Fundamentalists have never been by definition anti-intellectual, although it sometimes provided a route of final retreat or might be used as a tool for rallying popular support. But creationists have always been inordinately interested in scholarship. A recent survey found many "highly technically trained people" in the religious right movement.[41]

For over half a century creationists have maintained a frantic search for "scientific verification" of the Biblical record. One fundamentalist evangelist summed up their feelings in 1920:

> I am a Christian because I am . . . a scientist. . . . I do not mean that I devote all my time to scientific investigations, but I believe in the scientific method of "gaining and verifying knowledge by exact observation and correct thinking."[42]

AN ERRANT SCIENCE?

The problem, believed conservative Christians, was that science had lost its way. And, in fact, in the late nineteenth century science did begin adopting a new interpretative model, a model, notes a modern historian, "more willing to see perception as an interpretative process. Hence they were more open to speculative theories." Historian George Marsden continues:

> In America between 1860 and 1925 something like the general acceptance of a new perceptual model took place in both the scientific and theological circles. Similarly, the modern theological community adopted a model of truth that in effect stigmatized theologians who rejected evolutionary views as neither scientific nor theologically legitimate.[43]

It seemed outlandish to many conservative theologians to label as scientific that which could not be subjected to observation and verification (such as the theory of evolution); it seemed to return to the superstition of the Middle Ages. The presence of many conservative Christians at the technological level of the modern scientific community is surely partly related to their commitment to the old science of observation and their resistance to the speculative content of contemporary science.

CLASS RELIGION

The presence of large numbers of fundamentalists in middle-level technological jobs also points to the social roots of the religious right. It is clear that from the time of Dwight L. Moody, through the fundamentalist revolt of the 1920s, to the contemporary religious right, conservative religion has appealed primarily to the "predominantly white, aspiring middle-class."[44] Fed by first-generation urban dwellers, the major fundamentalist explosions have come at times when large, new, upwardly mobile groups were pressing into the middle class and this change in status has typically caught liberal Americans by surprise.

A recent critic of the Moral Majority wrote:

> Don't think that these are wicked people; they bear no resemblance to the sort of ex-rednecks recruited by central casting to depict bigots in late-night movies. They're clean, kindly, upstanding folk, the best people in their towns, the pillars of their churches, kings and queens of the covered dish supper.[45]

"The image of American evangelicalism that goes out from the pulpits and over the air waves," bemoans Jim Wallis of *Sojourners,* "is a religion for those at the top, not those at the bottom of the world system."[46]

Nor is the religious right unaware of its new class status. Falwell acknowledged that the success of his movement was directly linked to the presence of doctors and businessmen who could finance fundamentalism in a way hardly possible since the 1920s. Their new middle-class status creates two tensions in fundamentalists, which partly explain their sense of crisis. First, they are appalled by the wicked society in which they find themselves, and which for the first time they sense to be within their power to influence. In short, the fundamentalist vanguard is not so much a frustrated middle-class which is losing control as it is an emerging middle-class flaunting its newly acquired respectability and power. Second, this upwardly mobile class is deeply insecure about its own virtue. How can you keep the wholesome innocence of the farm when there is no more farm, and the church seats 10,000 people, and the pastor wears a pastel double-knit suit?

An advertisement touting James Robison's recent television campaign summed up these tensions:

> If you sense that our country and our world are headed for disaster, that the Church and even you may have become too comfortable, too complacent, please watch these programs. We're running out of time.[47]

Of course, this new militant middle class has made contact with an older middle class which for at least the past 100 years has been engaged in a classic battle of elites in American society. This is the linkage which was hastened by Paul Weyrich and the conservative lobbyists in the 1980 elections. In a sense, the new religious right has simply run headlong into what sociologist Peter Berger calls the "current class struggle . . . between the new knowledge class and the old business class." Berger writes:

> As in all class struggles, this one is over power and privilege. The new class [knowledge class] is a rising class, with its own very specific (and identifiable) vested interests. But, in the public rhetoric of democracy, vested interests are

typically couched in terms of the general welfare. In this, the new class is no different from its current adversary. Just as the business class sincerely believed (presumably still believes) that what is good for business is good for America, the new class believes that its own interests are identical with the "public interest." It so happens that many of the vested interests of the new class depend on miscellaneous state interventions; indeed a large portion of the new class is economically dependent on public-sector employment or subsidization.[48]

Each of these classes has its own symbols which allow people to identify friends and enemies. Berger continues:

Thus a young instructor applying for a job in an elite university is well advised to hide "unsound" views such as political allegiance to the right wing of the Republican party (perhaps even to the left wing), opposition to abortion or to other causes of the feminist movement, or a strong commitment to the virtues of the corporation. Conversely, a young business school graduate seeking a career with one of *Fortune* magazine's "500" had better not advertise his or her career in the new politics, or views associated with the environmentalists, antinuclear or consumer movements.

From this perspective, the new middle-class fundamentalists were simply fresh reinforcements slamming vigorously and patriotically into the old conflict. They were attracted to the side of the old elite both because of the presence of their religious enemies in the opposing camp and because they were defending their newly-born status.

NEW MILITANCY ON THE RIGHT

The spontaneous politicization of the religious right beginning in 1978 calls for one more immediate explanation. Why did this generally apolitical, theologically separatist movement suddenly turn militant? Political action does not come naturally to conservative Protestantism. Every fundamentalist and pentecostal has been fed a diet at least partly seasoned with world separation and expectation of the imminent second coming.

A part of the answer may lie in the general sense of well-being in American society. In spite of complaints about the economy and other discomforts, both in the 1920s and in the 1970s, most Americans were enjoying remarkable prosperity. In his famous book on the paranoid style in American politics, historian Richard Hofstadter pointed out that voters were most likely to be preoccupied with their identity in society rather than with specific personal needs. In short, the kinds of problems that concern the radical right, that in fact possess it, have to do with the collapse of society rather than personal privilege.[49]

THE TABLES TURNED

But there is a more immediate reason why millions of religious Americans, inspired by their evangelist leaders, swarmed to the polls in 1980. It was because they had been attacked. Liberal religion and liberal politics put tremendous pressure on conservative Christians in the years immediately before 1920 and 1975, and then recoiled in shock and indignation when the fundamentalists fought back. If you don't want to fight, don't hit a fundamentalist. Though the parallel is not exact, it brings to mind Commodore Vanderbilt's remark after being outfoxed by Daniel Drew in their war over the Erie Railroad. Moralized the subdued Commodore: "Never kick a skunk."

In 1917 the *Christian Century* and the Chicago Divinity School declared war on the still fairly moderate fundamentalist movement. During the next three years the *Christian Century* published 21 articles denouncing the "premillennial menace." In one of the ironies of history, the liberal attack centered on the lack of American patriotism among the fundamentalists who had refused to support World War I.[50] Stunned by the attack, the fundamentalists by 1919 had shifted their position on the war and were ready to engage the liberals in full warfare. Protestantism was suddenly caught in a battle between extremes.

H. L. Mencken wrote with considerable perception in the *American Mercury:*

> One half of [Protestantism] is moving, with slowly accelerating speed, in the direction of the Harlot of the Seven Hills; the other is sliding down into voodooism. The former carries the greater part of Protestant libido. . . . There is no lack of life on the higher levels, where the more solvent Methodist and the like are gradually transmogrified into Episcopalians, and the Episcopalians shin up the ancient bastions of Holy Church, and there is no lack of life on the lower levels, where the rural Baptists, by the route of Fundamentalism, rapidly descend to the dogmas and practices of the Congo jungle. But in the middle there is desiccation and decay.[51]

The same kind of pressure from the extremes was clearly present in American society by 1975. The 1960s and 1970s brought rapid, even reckless, social change to America and finally stretched the tolerance of moderate American society to a breaking point. In an editorial pondering the massive conservative religious entry into politics, *Newsweek* columnist George F. Will wrote in September 1980: "More important . . . is the question of why so many people are so aroused. The answer is they have been provoked."[52]

The virulent pro-Americanism of the religious right must be understood partly as a reaction to the virulent anti-Americanism that flourished in so many Christian agencies and seminaries in the 1960s and 1970s. As Peter Berger has noted, many American Christians felt they were faced with a choice between flag-burning and flag-waving.

In sum, in the twentieth century, American conservative evangelicals have entered politics only when it seemed to them that the very structure of society was seriously threatened by modernism and liberalism. Generally, fundamentalists' deepest interests have been religious, with forays into politics on questions of personal morality. But on two occasions in the twentieth century religious conservatives have felt compelled to launch crusades to save society. And, although the Scopes trial made it appear that the controversy was over evolution, most fundamentalists believed the issue was the survival of Christian civilization. And, in truth, the stakes were high, the issues profound.

Reacting to J. Gresham Machen's *Christianity and Liberalism,* a sophisticated and well-received defense of theological conservatism, editor Charles Clayton Morrison of the *Christian Century* wrote: "Two worlds have clashed, the world of tradition and the world of modernism. One is scholastic, static, authoritarian, individualistic; the other is vital, dynamic, free, and social."[53]

SECULAR HUMANISM

The evil that called for all-out war in 1980 was "secular humanism," the name given by fundamentalists to the general philosophy behind the specific changes occurring in

American society. They believed the philosophy was unalterably connected with the theory of evolution. "The ultimate end of secular humanism," according to Falwell, will be "amorality, atheism, and developing a permissive society where there is no authority for right or wrong." The results will include "the wipeout of the family, the wipeout of all traditional values that have made the United States, in my opinion, the greatest free society in the world for many years."[54]

It is hard to gainsay much of what Falwell says. Wrote William F. Fore of the National Council of Churches:

> Jerry Falwell is partly right, and this makes him far more dangerous than if he were totally wrong. It is true that the nation needs spiritual reform, that the family is endangered, that ordinary people need to assert themselves politically. It is true that our society has fallen into a moral cynicism that feeds corruption."[55]

Fundamentalists became more and more convinced in the 1960s and 1970s that America was not witnessing a minor rearranging of social customs. Society was in the throes of a revolution which was being supported by American intellectuals and liberal Christians. It was only when the stakes reached that lofty level that the fundamentalists laid aside their preparations for the rapture and turned to the job of saving America.

PROGNOSIS

Finally, what of the future of the religious right? The first fundamentalist alliance collapsed in 1925 with incredible speed. Liberal opposition is mobilizing after the success of the Moral Majority in 1980. A distinguished group of Jewish and Christian leaders has formed Moral Alternatives in Politics to encourage pastors to speak from their pulpits against the New Right. The American Way, an organization which includes Theodore Hesburgh on its board, has raised a million dollars to produce television commercials supporting religious pluralism. And yet, the opposition at this point seems quite unequal to a major battle with the conservative evangelists. In the foreseeable future their budgets are likely to remain infinitesimal compared to the bankrolls of the electronic evangelists.

More important are the internal tensions within the religious right. First is the highly visible split between the fundamentalists and the more moderate evangelicals, most notably Billy Graham. In a showdown, it is not clear whether Graham would side with the fundamentalists or mainstream American religion. Second, not far beneath the surface fester all of the old doctrinal questions which have historically divided conservative religion. Only under severe stress can fundamentalists, Pentecostals, Catholics, and Mormons pray before a common altar. Cracks in the alliance are visible and threatening.

In January 1981, Dr. Curtis Hutson, editor of the *Sword of the Lord,* the largest traditional fundamentalist paper in the country, withdrew from a James Robison Bible Conference, reportedly "to avoid appearing with antifeminist leader Phyllis Schlafly because she is a Roman Catholic." Hutson explained, or rather reminded his fellow fundamentalists, that Catholicism was "a growing accumulation of error through the years, with new doctrines being added continually."[56]

Perhaps even more ominous was the fierce competition for leadership. Given fundamentalists' feelings about popes, and the increasingly keen competition for the religious dollar, there is little likelihood that any individual can establish himself as the dominant figure in a broad alliance. In the 1920s Bryan was a unique figure, the only man who could pass easily through the maze of fundamentalist organizations and communicate with the competing evangelists. There is no such figure in 1980. Weyrich and his colleagues have more savvy than Bryan, but they have no control over their religious partners if the coalition begins to unravel.

Finally, the religious right is threatened by success. At their recent Convocation '81 in Washington, Billy Graham warned the new evangelists, "that the most difficult thing in life to handle is 'success.'"[57] The revivalists are, indeed, faced with a dilemma. You preach on sin, you warn of the troubles ahead, you pray for the Lord to come, and, my Lord, how the money rolls in. The religious right is big business. One disgusted visitor to Convocation '81 called it a "sorry circus of crass commercialism."[58] In the midst of such luxury, one could forget the urgency of his message. And the people are pretty cagey. Gerald W. Johnson watched the revivalists of the 1920s come and go in Raleigh, North Carolina, and concluded that by and large they bought their own medicine, else they could not "put it over." He wrote, "You can fool all of the people some of the time, and educated people, perhaps, all the time, but you cannot fool the riff-raff all the time."[59]

When Jerry Falwell finally confessed that he had been less than honest about Jimmy Carter's remarks on homosexuality, he candidly confided that a preacher could get by with anything except digging into the till and hanky-panky with the sisters. Actually, several American evangelists have gotten by with at least one of those indiscretions and probably both. What one cannot get by with is loss of conviction and public confidence. Exuberant Tammy Bakker, surrounded on the PTL set by the most luxurious and technically-advanced television production studio in the world, recently burst forth, "This life is so great—I just love it whether or not it's true."[60] The luxury is all right, but it better be true. If it is not, the crackers will flip that dial right back to secular humanism.

NOTES

1. Quoted from William C. Martin, "Billy Graham" This essay has been published in David Edwin Harrel, Jr., ed., *Varieties of Southern Evangelicalism* (Mercer University Press, 1979). I have leaned heavily on Martin's interpretation of Graham, and in this paragraph, particularly, the text is sprinkled with his wording.

2. Ibid.

3. Allan J. Mayer et al., "A Tide of Born-Again Politics," *Newsweek* (Sept. 15, 1980) 31. See Jerry Falwell, *How You Can Help Clean Up America* (Lynchburg, Va., Liberty Publ., 1978) 40.

4. Roland Evans and Robert Novak, "Southern Preachers vs. Jimmy," Danville, Ky. *Register* (July 4, 1980).

5. Birmingham, Alabama, July 30, 1979.

6. Bode, ed., *New Mencken Letters* 189.

7. "New Right Tops 1980 Religion News," *Christian Century* (Dec. 31, 1980) 1283.

8. Edward Plowman, "Carter's Presence Confirms Clout of Evangelical Broadcasters," *Christianity Today* (Feb. 22, 1980) 49.

9. L. J. Davis, "Onward Christian Soldiers," *Penthouse* (Feb. 1981) 59.

10. Robert Zweir and Richard Smith, "Christian Politics and the New Right," *Christian Century* (Oct. 8, 1980) 938.

11. Mayer, "Born-Again Politics," 36.

12. James M. Wall, "The New Right Exploits Abortion," *Christian Century* (July 30, 1980) 747.

13. Sermon, Birmingham, Alabama, July 30, 1979.

14. For sketches of Falwell, see Davis, "Christian Soldiers"; "Penthouse Interview"; Kenneth L. Woodward and Howard Fineman, "A $1 Million Habit," *Newsweek* (Sept. 15, 1980) 35.

15. John Maust, "Evangelist James Robison: Making Waves—and a Name," *Christianity Today* (March 21, 1980) 52.

16. "PTL and the FCC: They're Still Sparring," *Christianity Today* (March 21, 1980) 52.

17. Mayer, "Born-Again Politics," 29.

18. Edward E. Plowman, "Washington for Jesus: Revival Fervor and Political Disclaimers," *Christianity Today* (May 23, 1980) 45–46.

19. Interview with Thomas Zimmerman, Springfield, Mo., Oct. 1980.

20. See James M. Wall, "God's Piece of Cheese," *Christian Century* (Feb. 27, 1980) 219–20; Ted Moser, "If Jesus Were a Congressman," *Christian Century* (April 16, 1980) 444–46.

21. "Billy Graham in England," *America* (June 4, 1955) 254–55.

22. Clancy, "Fundamental Facts," *America,* May 31, 1980, 455.

23. Wall, "New Right Exploits Abortion," 747.

24. Richard V. Pierard, "An Innocent in Babylon," *Christian Century* (Feb. 25, 1981) 190.

25. Falwell, *Clean Up America,* 19.

26. Davis, "Christian Soldiers," 138.

27. Gerald Skoog, "The Textbook Battle of Creationism," *Christian Century* (Oct. 15, 1980) 976. A good survey of the legal clashes is that by John M. Swomley, Jr., "The Decade Ahead in Church-State Issues," *Christian Century* (Feb. 25, 1981) 199–203. See also Niles Eldredge, "Creationism Isn't Science, " *The New Republic* (April 14, 1981) 15–20.

28. See Martin E. Marty, "Things Fall Apart," *Christian Century* (Sept. 10, 1980) 863.

29. M. Stanton Evans, "The Private School Room," *National Review* (May 16, 1980) 602.

30. In the interpretation of fundamentalism that follows I am particularly indebted to the brilliant work by George M. Marsden, *Fundamentalism and American Culture: The Shaping of Twentieth-Century Evangelism, 1870-1925* (Oxford University Press, 1980).

31. "Reverend Jerry Falwell," Penthouse, 1981, 151–52.

32. "54% Back Teaching Creation Theory," March 23, 1981, pp. 1A, 6A.

33. Boulevard Baptist Church, Fayetteville, Arkansas, n.d.

34. Allene M. Sumner, "The Holy Rollers on Shin Bone Ridge," *The Nation* (July 29, 1925) 138.

35. Quoted in Marsden, *Fundamentalism,* 212.

36. See William E. Ellis, "The Fundamentalist-Modernist Schism over Evolution in the 1920's," Kentucky Historical Society *Register* (April 1976) 120.

37. "Tennessee's Coming Battle on Evolution," *The Literary Digest* (June 6, 1925) 36.

38. Mayer, "Born-Again Politics," 31.

39. "A Changing Political Climate," *Christian Century* (Sept. 24, 1980) 868.

40. I am particularly indebted in my discussion of this point to the chapter "Fundamentalism as an Intellectual Phenomenon," in Marsden, *Fundamentalism,* 212–21. An earlier book that emphasized the accommodation of 19th-century religion to Baconian science is Theodore Dwight Bozeman's *Protestants in an Age of Science: The Baconian Ideal and Antebellum American Religious Thought* (University of North Carolina Press, 1977).

41. Pat Horn, "The New Middle-Class Fundamentalism," *Psychology Today* (Sept. 18, 1976) 24–25.

42. Quoted in Marsden, *Fundamentalism,* 217.

43. Ibid., 215.

44. Ibid., 91.

45. Davis, "Christian Soldiers," 54.

46. "Recovering the Evangel," *Sojourners* (Feb. 1981) 3 (see chap. 34, below).

47. *Christianity Today* (June 8, 1979) 37.

48. "The Class Struggle in American Religion," *Christian Century* (Feb. 25, 1981) 197–98.

49. See James M. Wall's comment on this point in "A Changing Political Climate," *Christian Century* (Sept. 24, 1980) 867–68.

50. See Marsden, *Fundamentalism,* 141–53.

51. H. L. Mencken, *A Mencken Chrestomathy,* (New York: Alfred A. Knopf, 1974) 76.

52. "Who Put Morality in Politics?" *Newsweek* (Sept. 15, 1980) 108.

53. Quoted in Marsden, *Fundamentalism,* 175.

54. "Reverend Jerry Falwell," 59.

55. "Forms of Self-Deception and Hypocrisy," *Christian Century* (Oct. 22, 1980) 1004.

56. "Baptist Shuns Catholic Schlafly," Tampa, Fla. *Tribune* (Jan. 29, 1981) 3A.

57. Pierard, "Innocent in Babylon," 191.

58. Ibid.

59. "Saving Souls," *American Mercury* (July 1924) 366.

60. Philip Yancey, "The Ironies and Impact of PTL," *Christianity Today* (Sept. 21, 1979) 32.

Chapter 28

Jerry Falwell

A Biblical Plan of Action

Listen, America! Our nation is on a perilous path in regard to her political, economic, and military positions. If America continues down the path she is traveling, she will one day find that she is no longer a free nation. Our nation's internal problems are direct results of her spiritual condition. America is desperately in need of a divine healing, which can only come if God's people will humble themselves, pray, seek His face, and turn from their wicked ways. It is now time that moral Americans awake to the fact that our future depends upon how we stand on moral issues. God has no reason to spare us if we continue to reject Him.

America has been great because her people have been good. We are certainly far from being a perfect society, but our heritage is one of genuine concern for all mankind. It is God Almighty who has made and preserved us as a nation, and the day that we forget that is the day that the United States will become a byword among the nations of the world. We will become nothing more than a memory in a history book, like the many great civilizations that have preceded us. America's only hope for survival is a spiritual awakening that begins in the lives of her individual citizens. It is only in the spiritual rebirth of our nation's citizens that we can have a positive hope in the future. The destiny of America awaits that decision.

We are facing many serious issues at this time. Action must be taken quickly in the areas of politics, economics, and defense. But the most brilliant plans and programs of men will never accomplish enough to save America. The answer to America's continued existence rests with the spiritual condition of her people. When a person allows biblical morality to be the guiding principle of his life, he can have the confidence that "righteousness exalts a nation."

I do not believe that God is finished with America yet. America has more God-fearing citizens per capita than any other nation on earth. There are millions of Americans who love God, decency, and biblical morality. North America is the last logical base for world evangelization. While it is true that God could use any nation or means possible to spread the Gospel to the world, it is also true that we have the churches, the schools, the young people, the media, the money, and the means of spreading the Gospel worldwide in our lifetime. God loves all the world, not just America. However, I am convinced that our freedoms are essential to world evangelism in this latter part of the twentieth century.

First published in *Listen, America!* (Garden City, N. Y., Doubleday, 1980), pp. 243–54. Used by permission.

I am seeking to rally together the people of this country who still believe in decency, the home, the family, morality, the free enterprise system, and all the great ideals that are the cornerstone of this nation. Against the growing tide of permissiveness and moral decay that is crushing our society, we must make a sacred commitment to God Almighty to turn this nation around immediately. I know that there are millions of decent, law-abiding, God-fearing Americans who want to do something about the moral decline of our country, but when you ask the average person what can be done about revival in America, he will often reply, "I'm just one person. What can I do, anyhow?" As long as the average moral American believes that, the political and social liberals in this society will be able to pass their socialistic legislation at will. We are late, but I do not believe that we are too late. It is time to put our lives on the line for this great nation of ours.

THE POWER OF BELIEVING PRAYER

In his last epistle, the Apostle Paul gave this plan of action to Christians who were living in the pagan Roman Empire of their day:

> I exhort, therefore, that, first of all, supplications, prayers, intercessions, and giving of thanks be made for all men; for kings, and for all that are in authority; that we may lead a quiet and peaceable life in all godliness and honesty. For this is good and acceptable in the sight of God our Savior; who will have all men to be saved and to come to the knowledge of the truth. For there is one God, and one mediator between God and men, the man Christ Jesus; who gave himself a ransom for all, to be testified in due time (1 Tm. 2:1-6).

In this passage the Apostle Paul emphasized the importance of prayer for those in positions of authority and leadership. He urged that prayers and intercessions be made for all men, including kings and those in authority. Why would a Christian preacher urge other fellow believers to pray for those in authority? The answer to that question is found in Paul's statement in verse 2: "That we may lead a quiet and peaceable life in all godliness and honesty." It is essential that peace prevail in order to mobilize Christians to spread the Gospel of Christ effectively so that all men might have the opportunity to be saved and come to the knowledge of the truth. I am convinced that many Christians have failed to pray genuinely for our President, his Cabinet, the legislature, and those in judicial positions. These people, representing the highest offices of our country, have a great deal of personal and corporate responsibility placed upon them by the citizens of this free nation. They desperately need our prayerful support. It is easy to become a critic of their failures and shortcomings, while forgetting to hold them up before God in prayer.

Every great revival in the history of the Christian church has been bathed in prayer. God gave Israel a wonderful promise: "If my people, which are called by my name shall humble themselves and pray and seek my face, and turn from their wicked ways, then will I hear from heaven, and will forgive their sin, and will heal their land" (2 Ch. 7:14). Throughout Israel's history, there were times when her kings, like Jehoshaphat and Hezekiah, went to the Lord in prayer and experienced miraculous intervention of God on their behalf.

The great prayer-warrior, E. M. Bounds, wrote that God's greatest movements in this world have been conditioned upon, continued, and fashioned by prayer. He pointed out that God has always responded just as men have prayed. E. M. Bounds saw prayer as a means of moving God to do what He would not otherwise do if prayer were not offered. He knew prayer to be a wonderful power placed by Almighty God in the hands of His saints, to accomplish great purposes and to achieve unusual results. He knew that the only limits to prayer are the promises of God and His ability to fulfill those promises. Like E. M. Bounds, we too have at our disposal an unbelievable resource in the power of prayer. Recognizing this power, we must return to the priority of believing prayer!

In the middle of the nineteenth century, when our nation was divided over the issue of slavery and people were living in a selfish, materialistic approach to life, God raised up Jeremiah Lamphier to lead a revival of prayer. In 1857 he began a prayer meeting in the upper room of the old Fulton Street Dutch Reform Church in Manhattan. Beginning with only six people, the prayer meeting grew until the church was filled. In time virtually every church in New York City was filled with praying people. By February of 1858, nearly ten thousand people a week were being converted. The impact of these prayer meetings spread from city to city across the United States—Cleveland, Detroit, Chicago, Cincinnati. City after city was conquered by the power of believing prayer.

In 1904 a great revival movement began in Wales; the movement was led by Evan Roberts, a young man who was moved by God to pray for revival while studying for the ministry. In a short time, revival swept over Wales like a tidal wave. The impact on the moral condition of the nation was overwhelming. Judges had almost no cases to try. There were virtually no rapes, robberies, or murders. Drunkenness was cut in half, and many taverns were forced to close for lack of business. The illegitimate birth rate dropped 44 percent within a year of the beginning of the revival. All of this happened because one man began to pray.

As Christians living at the close of the twentieth century, we must again learn how to pray in faith, believing that God will hear from heaven, that He will forgive our sin, and that He will heal our land! The key to prayer is faith. God is not impressed with the length or the volume of prayer, but with the sincerity of the faith in which it is uttered. Scripture says, "He that cometh to God must believe that he is, and that he is a rewarder of them that diligently seek him" (Heb. 11:6). Even when the condition of our nation seems most desperate, we must believe that God is still on the throne and that He has the power and authority to answer. Our priorities must merge with His priorities. God will give revival when we meet His conditions. If we expect Him to move miraculously on our behalf, we must be moved in faith to believe Him.

THE NEED FOR NATIONAL REPENTANCE

In light of our present moral condition, we as a nation are quickly approaching the point of no return. There can be no doubt that the sin of America is severe. We are literally approaching the brink of national disaster. Many have exclaimed, "If God does not judge America soon, He will have to apologize to Sodom and Gomorrah." In almost every aspect of our society, we have flaunted our sinful behavior in the very face of God Himself. Our movies, television programs, magazines, and entertainment in general are morally bankrupt and spiritually corrupt. We have become one of the most blatantly sinful nations of all time. We dare not continue to excuse ourselves on the basis of God's past blessing in our national heritage. The time for a national repentance of God's people has now come to America.

The great English statesman, Winston Churchill, once said, "The moral climate of a nation will be in direct proportion to the amount of hellfire and damnation that is preached from its pulpits." As a preacher of the Gospel, I could not more heartily agree! Pastors and religious leaders do not enjoy pointing out the sins of people. I entered the ministry nearly thirty years ago because of a genuine love and concern for people. I wanted to see their lives changed, their problems solved, and their families put back together to the glory of God. As much as I labored to help people and to encourage them and to understand their hurts and problems I soon realized that one of my vital responsibilities was to expose sin even in my own life as well as in theirs. The Bible clearly teaches that it is the preacher's responsibility to "warn every man" against the consequences of sinful living.

Abraham Lincoln once observed:

> We have been the recipients of the choicest bounties of heaven. We have been preserved, these many years, in peace and prosperity. We have grown in numbers, wealth, and power, as no other nation has ever grown, but we have forgotten God. We have forgotten the gracious hand which preserved us in peace, and multiplied and enriched and strengthened us; and we have vainly imagined, in the deceitfulness of our hearts, that all these blessings were produced by some superior wisdom and virtue of our own. Intoxicated with unbroken success, we have become too self-sufficient to feel the necessity of redeeming and preserving grace, too proud to pray to the God that made us.

Wallowing in our materialism, self-centeredness, and pride, we decided that we really didn't need God after all. We began to tamper with His absolute standards, making them subject to our own opinions and decisions. We did not immediately discard all of God's laws; rather, we began to tolerate variations in them. That which God says is never right, we determined could sometimes be right, depending on the situation. Our courts, which had once legislated against immorality, began to grant freedom to every man to do that which was right in his own eyes. As people who no longer felt accountable to a holy God, we began to accept and even admire immoral behavior. Where once we were openly shocked at the outwardness of sin, we have now become gradually conditioned to accepting it.

Today we tolerate, laugh at, and even enjoy what twenty years ago would have deeply shocked us.

Having pushed God out of our conscience, we soon discovered that as a nation we could get away with almost anything. All we had to do was change the terminology. What God called a sin, we called a sickness. Man as always tended to find a euphemism to cover the reality of sin. What God called drunkenness, we call alcoholism. What God called perversion, we called an alternate life style. What God called immorality, we called the new morality. What God called pornography, we called adult entertainment. What God called murder, we called abortion.

Is God blind to the sin of our nation? Will He continue to allow us to live in rebellion to His moral standards while He looks upon our idols of silver and gold, on our pride of personal achievement, our monuments to ourselves? Can God bless that which He ought to curse?

The Bible clearly states: "Righteousness exalteth a nation; but sin is a reproach to any people" (Pr. 14:34). God will not be mocked, for whatever an individual or a nation sows, that shall he also reap. America is not big enough to shake her fist in the face of a holy God and get away with it. Sodom and Gomorrah fell under the judgment of God, so did Israel, Babylon, Greece, Rome, and countless other civilizations as well. Like

Israel of old, we are "oppressed, trampled in judgment, intent on pursuing idols." Our crumbling economy, our fractured family structures, and unrestrained immorality, as well as our international reproach are all signs of the fact that we are already headed on a collision course.

Is there no hope? Is our doom inevitable? Can the hand of God's judgment not be stayed? Many of us are convinced that it can. We believe that there is yet an opportunity for a reprieve in God's judgment of this great nation. But that hope rests in the sincerity of national repentance led by the people of God.

First, God's people must be humble. Humility, however, is the very opposite of pride, which so often besets us. Scripture says, "God resists the proud, but gives grace to the humble" (James 4:6). We must acknowledge that we are not deserving of God's favor. We must realize that we are totally inadequate to deal with the sins of our own lives, let alone those of our entire nation. We must acknowledge that we are utterly dependent upon God and His grace to deliver us. Our financial resources will not turn this nation back to God, and our elaborate church structures will not cause Him to change His mind and restrain His judgment. We must allow Him to strip us of all that we put our confidence in, so that we may trust in Him alone.

Second, we must pray. We must not just talk about praying, we must pray! We must lay aside our pious and structured prayers in order to beseech the God of heaven to have mercy on us. Let us echo the prayer of confession offered by Ezra the priest as he fell on his face before God and acknowledged, "O my God, I am ashamed and blush to lift up my face to thee, my God; for our iniquities are increased over our head, and our trespasses are grown up into the heavens."

Third, we must learn to seek the face of God. When King Jehoshaphat called the people of Judah together to seek the face of God, they acknowledged, "We have no might against this great company that cometh against us, neither know we what to do; but our eyes are upon thee." We must turn our eyes from ourselves and seek the face of Almighty God. We must be willing to give up ourselves as the measure of all things, and acknowledge that He alone is the measure of truth.

Fourth, God's people must turn from their wicked ways. It is one thing for us to be concerned about the sins of our nation, but before we are prepared to confess the sins of an unbelieving society, we must repent of our own sins. We have not fulfilled our function as the "salt of the earth." We have failed to speak out for God on serious moral issues. We have often endorsed what we should have opposed. We must repent for judging the wickedness of our nation while ignoring the sin in our own homes. More than ever before America needs fathers who are willing to be godly leaders and moral examples in their own homes. We need mothers who are determined to be models of virtuous living, and we need children who are committed to live in obedience to the moral leadership of their parents. May God forgive us who claim His name for tolerating things in our own lives that are not holy, pure, and undefiled. We need to turn from our sinful ways in our churches as well, for we have all too often substituted playing for praying; feasting for fasting; religion for righteousness; organizing for agonizing; and compatibility for confrontation. We need a return to the kind of churches that lead the vanguard of decency while upholding the moral conscience of our nation.

The Bible is filled with examples of national confession. Both Nehemiah and Ezra poured out their hearts before God in confessing the sins of Israel. The Prophet Daniel, looking back over the seventy-year period of the Babylonian captivity before Christ and, realizing the imminent release of his spiritually unprepared countrymen, announced:

We have sinned, and have committed iniquity, and have done wickedly, and have rebelled, even by departing from thy precepts and from thy judgments . . . yea, all Israel has transgressed thy law, even by departing that they might not obey thy voice (Dn. 9:5–15).

The time has come for America's Christians to confess the sins of our nation as well. While it is true that we are not a theocracy, as was ancient Israel, we nevertheless are a nation that was founded upon Christian principles, and we have enjoyed a unique relationship toward God because of that foundation. In order to confess sin, we must have a genuine conviction of sin based on an awareness of sin. We need to define and articulate the issues of sin and sinful living, which are destroying our nation today. The secularist will argue: What right do you have to define sin? If our definition rested only upon our personal opinion, he would have every right to reject our message. That is why it is essential that our concept of sin be based clearly upon Scripture itself. One reporter recently asked me if this would not lead to a kind of censorship or a kind of Christian Nazism. My reply was that we cannot allow an immoral minority of our population to intimidate us on moral issues. People who take a weak stand on morality inevitably have weak morals.

We need moral leadership today more than ever before. We need that kind of leadership in the media as well as in our schools and in our churches. Leadership must always be responsible to society. Our freedoms certainly guarantee the right to free speech, but they do not give us the right to use our speech irresponsibly to the harm of others. Just beause we have free speech doesn't mean that a person has a right to make obscene phone calls or to yell "Fire!" in a crowded building when there is no fire. I believe that the family is the cornerstone of America, and whatever undermines the family is wrong. If our leaders are to care about this country at all we must care about its people and its families. It is time that we no longer be driven by economic considerations and political favors but instead be determined to stand for right whether it is convenient or not, popular or not.

FACING OUR NATIONAL SINS

While sins of America are certainly many, let us summarize the five major problems that have political consequences, political implications, that moral Americans need to be ready to face.

Abortion

Nine men, by majority vote, said it was okay to kill unborn children. In 1973, two hundred million Americans and four hundred thousand pastors stood by and did little to stop it. Every year millions of babies are murdered in America, and most of us want to forget that it is happening. The Nazis murdered six million Jews, and certainly the Nazis fell under the hand of the judgment of God for these atrocities. So-called Christian America has murdered more unborn innocents than that. How do we think that we shall escape the judgment of God?

Homosexuality

In spite of the fact that the Bible clearly designates this sin as an act of a "reprobate mind" for which God "gave them up" (Rm. 1:26–28), our government seems determined to legalize homosexuals as a legitimate "minority." The National Civil Rights Act of 1979 (popularly referred to as the Gay Rights Bill) would give homosexuals the same benefits as the 1964 Civil Rights Act, meaning they could not be discriminated against by any employing body because of "sexual preference." Even the ancient Greeks, among whom homosexuality was fairly prevalent, never legally condoned its practice. Plato himself called it "abnormal." If our nation legally recognizes homosexuality, we will put ourselves under the same hand of judgment as that of Sodom and Gomorrah.

Pornography

The four-billion-dollar-per-year pornographic industry is probably the most devastating moral influence of all upon our young people. Sex magazines deliberately increase the problem of immoral lust and thus provoke increased adultery, prostitution, and sexual child abuse. Jesus said that if a man looks upon a woman and lusts after her in his heart, he has committed adultery with her already! Pornography is certainly the No. 1 enemy against marital fidelity and therefore against the family itself. Recent psychological studies are showing without a doubt that divorce caused by adultery is having a devastating effect upon children. Pornography is not a victimless crime—the real victims are wives and children!

Humanism

The contemporary philosophy that glorifies man as man, apart from God, is the ultimate outgrowth of evolutionary science and secular education. In his new book *The Battle for the Mind,* Dr. Tim LaHaye argues that the full admission of humanism as the religion of secular education came after prayer and Bible reading were excluded from our public schools. Ultimately, humanism rests upon the philosophy of existentialism, which emphasizes that one's present existence is the true meaning and purpose of life. Existentialism has become the religion of the public schools. Applied to psychology, it postulates a kind of moral neutrality that is detrimental to Christian ethics. In popular terminology it explains, "Do your own thing," and "If it feels good, do it!" It is an approach to life that has no room for God and makes man the measure of all things.

The Fractured Family

With a skyrocketing divorce rate, the American family may well be on the verge of extinction in the next twenty years. Even the recent White House Conference on Families has called for an emphasis on diverse family forums (common-law, communal, homosexual, and transsexual "marriages"). The Bible pattern of the family has been virtually discarded by modern American society. Our movies and magazines have glorified the physical and emotional experience of sex without love to the point that most Americans do not even consider love to be important at all anymore. Bent on self-gratification, we have reinterpreted our moral values in light of our immoral life styles. Since the family is the basic unit of society, and since the family is desperately in trouble today, we can conclude that our society itself is in danger of total collapse. We are not moving toward an alternate family life style; we are moving closer to the brink of destruction.

Chapter 29

Jeffrey K. Hadden and Charles E. Swann

Responding to the Christian Right

In 1977 Albert Menendez published a book about voting behavior in which he concluded that evangelical Christians in this country constitute a "sleeping giant."[1] Even before the 1980 political campaign began to gear up, evangelical leaders were making bold assertions about the potential of an evangelical vote. Prophesying that the giant was about the awaken, Robert Grant, co-founder of Christian Voice, told his followers, "If Christians unite, we can do anything. We can pass any law or amendment. And that is exactly what we intend to do." Pat Robertson often expressed the same confidence to viewers of The 700 Club, saying, "We have enough votes to run the country. . . . And when the people say 'we've had enough,' we are going to take over the country."

The shock of the election results, plus the high visibility of the Rev. Jerry Falwell and his political arm, the Moral Majority, in the weeks leading up to the election gave credibility to the boastful threats made by the New Christian Right leaders. After the election, Falwell wasted no time in claiming credit for the many upsets in the name of the Moral Majority and their allies. Pollster Louis Harris agreed with Falwell's assessment. So did several of the defeated senators and congress members. It seemed—and the media played up the idea—that the televangelists had created a force to be reckoned with.

The mobilization of any group is certain to trigger the countermobilization of those who stand to lose something if the new organization gains political power. Months before the press even recognized the potential for the emergence of a New Christian Right, or the existence of the televangelists who would lead this movement, the mainline religious establishment was putting together a countermobilization.

During the decade of the 1970s several television programs produced by mainline churches either disappeared or lost most of their audience. The reason for this can be traced directly to the entrepreneurial success of evangelicals on television. Sunday morning broadcast time, once thought to be commercially useless, and thus good time to give away in order to meet public service requirements, became very profitable as the growing crop of televangelists outbid one another for the best time slots. The result was the disappearance of the sustaining or freetime that mainliners had used to air their programs.

Persons engaged in departments or divisions of religious communication were, thus,

First published in *Theology Today*, 39 (January 1983), pp. 377–84. Used by permission.

highly conscious and critical of the televangelists. Their concerns were broader than a potential political agenda, but they were also sensitive to this possibility.

In early 1980 the National Council of Churches and the U.S. Catholic Conference sponsored a Consultation on the Electronic Church. Robert Liebert, one of the keynote speakers, described the ensuing political battles between the electronic preachers and the mainline churches as a "holy war." Colin Williams, former dean of Yale Divinity School, was called upon to respond to a presentation by Pat Robertson. His remarks focused on the political message the electronic church is sending to American society. Because its message is essentially personalistic, Williams argued, its attitude toward politics is conservative. Moreover, it is a nostalgic conservatism which plays upon innocent emotions without providing constructive responses to real problems:

> It calls us to go back to good old-fashioned American attitudes toward the capitalist system, or to good old-fashioned support for America, say in our struggles against communist enemies, etc. And what this does is to draw deeply on the disappointments and fears of the people in a deeply personalistic way. It doesn't help people to think about politics. It doesn't help people to analyze and struggle with the depth of theological issues. It draws upon the feelings of disappointment and fosters estrangement toward the political process.

The Consultation was widely covered by the media. More importantly, it served to alert religious leaders to the significance of television religion and the political agendas of some of its leaders.

"WASHINGTON FOR JESUS"

The first concrete evidence of political thunder from evangelical Christians occurred late in April 1980, when about 200,000 went to Washington, D.C., for two days of prayer and repentance. The involvement of the televangelists in "Washington for Jesus" was abundantly apparent. Pat Robertson and Bill Bright of Campus Crusade were co-chairmen of the program. A total of ten syndicated television preachers were listed on WFJ literature as "national sponsors." Eight of them spoke during the twelve-hour meeting on the Mall.

Robertson and Bright spent a good bit of their time trying to convince a skeptical press corps that the event was not political. Several factors made it difficult for these otherwise effective communicators to do so. A highly partisan document called "A Christian Declaration" was widely circulated, though it was withdrawn before it became an official statement of purpose of Washington for Jesus. Someone who identified himself as a congressional liaison for the rally sent a letter to all members of Congress, inviting them to contact Washington for Jesus to learn how they should vote on a variety of issues. Furthermore, the rally's leaders had organized the gathering by congressional districts so that participants could call on their elected representatives while they were in Washington.

Aside from a credibility gap between what WFJ people were saying and what they were doing, one important reason they received a good bit of negative publicity for mixing prayer and politics can be attributed to mainline church leaders. In the weeks leading up to WFJ, mainline leaders strategically planned news releases critical of the rally. Several assisted in organizing a group called April Alliance, a loose coalition of over 65 secular and religious groups, which held a rally and press conference on the day of the WFJ gathering. On the eve of the rally, 20 nationally prominent Protestant,

Catholic, and Jewish leaders stationed in Washington released a statement challenging the political agenda of WFJ. And on the day of the rally, the Lutheran Council in the USA, on behalf of its constituent bodies, released a statement on religion and politics which denounced "Christians or coalitions of Christians who plan political action under any guise of religious evangelism, worship, or revivalism." Further challenging the assumptions and rhetoric of WFJ leaders, the statement asserted:

> It is a misuse of terms to describe government and politics as godless or profane, because God rules both the civil and the spiritual dimensions of life. Thus it is unnecessary and unbiblical for any church group or individual to seek to "Christianize" the government or to label political views of members of Congress as "Christian" or "religious." It is arrogant to assert that one's position on a political issue is "Christian" and that all others are "un-Christian," "immoral," or "sinful."

For a gathering of its size, the Washington for Jesus rally received only moderate press coverage. But when the 200,000 faithful had picked up and returned home, and the leaders paused to assess their accomplishments, it was clear that the critics had received more than a fair proportion of the press coverage—especially if one measured their investment in contrast to the time and cost required to stage the rally. They succeeded not only in challenging the WFJ claim to be non-political; they also sounded the alert to constituencies all over the nation that the evangelicals were about to enter politics with a vengeance.

MORE NEW CHRISTIAN RIGHT GROUPS AND OPPOSITION

It would be yet another three months before the American public got another good look at the televangelists' movement into the political arena. This occurred when Jerry Falwell showed up in Detroit at the National Republican Convention with his Moral Majority and his Liberty Baptist College students. Falwell's presence in Detroit caught the attention of editors much more forcefully than did the presence of 200,000 Christians who assembled to pray on the Mall in Washington. A few weeks later, they sent more than 250 reporters to cover "The National Affairs Briefing," in Dallas, a gathering of conservative Christians who came to hear Ronald Reagan, Senator Jesse Helms, Congressmen Philip Crane and Guy Vander Jagt, and several of the big television preachers—Jerry Falwell, Pat Robertson, and James Robison.

After that session, there could be no doubt as to the intentions of the televangelists to lead their followings to the ballot box. But much of the mainline church leadership already understood that back in April or before. Democratically governed bodies are not quickly mobilized to action, but this did not prevent individuals and ad hoc groups from responding to the evangelical challenge. As the 1980 campaign built up steam, so also did the attacks on the New Christian Right from the mainline religious establishment. And criticism of the born-again politicians by mainline Protestant, Catholic, and Jewish leaders was extensively reported by the press.

New groups mushroomed into existence. For example, Daniel Maguire, a nationally known theologian and ethicist from Marquette University, organized a group called Moral Alternatives in Politics. He hastily assembled a board of directors that included such prominent figures as Martin Marty of the University of Chicago, Charles Curran of Catholic University, and Rabbi Balfour Brickner of the Stephen Wise Free Synagogue in New York.

Most mainline leaders did not limit themselves in their fight against the New Christian Right to working exclusively through religious organizations. Indeed, they saw every reason to cooperate with and encourage other groups to become involved. The most visible group organized to combat the New Religious Right was People for the American Way. Spearheaded by Norman Lear, creator of "All in the Family," "Maude," "Mary Hartman, Mary Hartman," and several other television sitcom successes of the 1970s, PAW assembled a board of advisors that included some of the most prominent religious leaders in America. Fifteen of the 39 members of the board were religious leaders.

The perception that the Moral Majority had decisive effects in the outcomes of the 1980 elections served to enhance the visibility of the organization and its leader. Through a combination of luck and skillful manipulation of media, Jerry Falwell has scarcely disappeared from the mass media for more than a few days at a time. This high visibility, plus the absence of a challenge to Falwell's claims of organizational strength and accomplishments, has given credence to the belief that the Moral Majority constitutes the nexus of a burgeoning social movement.

Predictably, we have witnessed the emergence of a veritable counter social movement to check the perceived power of the New Christian Right. Almost immediately after the elections, defeated Senator George McGovern announced the formation of Americans for Common Sense. He defined one of his principal goals to "serve as an effective counter to the single issues put forward by the radical right." Within the month, the American Civil Liberties Union launched an attack on the New Christian Right with a full-page advertisement in the Sunday edition of the *New York Times* whose banner headline read: "If the Moral Majority has its way, you'd better start praying." As 1980 unfolded, other left-of-center groups joined ranks with those warning against the ominous threat to civil liberties posed by the Moral Majority and the radical right. Common Cause is the most recent to tell us that "it's time to take a stand" in opposition to the Moral Majority and their friends in Congress, such as Jesse Helms.

MAINLINE COUNTERMOBILIZATION

Religious leaders have continued to be outspoken in their denunciation of the New Christian Right. Religious periodicals have been filled with critical articles, and few gatherings of religious leaders have concluded without addressing the perceived threat of the Moral Majority. Indeed, scores of conferences have been organized for the explicit purpose of assessing the impact of the New Christian Right on American culture.

What is particularly noteworthy, however, is the dearth of organized religious opposition to the New Christian Right in general, or the Moral Majority in particular. This stands in sharp contrast to the response of the mainline churches following the 1954 desegregation decision of the Supreme Court. Campbell and Pettigrew documented no less that 31 official statements of policy, from 23 religious bodies, condemning racial separation and affirming the Supreme Court decision.[2] There were doubtless hundreds of state and local resolutions.

To date, we have failed to locate a single denominational policy statement or resolution dealing with the New Christian Right. Some may have been introduced at national gatherings, but since the Moral Majority has been the biggest religious news story of the year, it is hard to imagine that such resolutions, if passed, would have failed to make the wire services.

Whether such resolutions exist or not, it is obvious that there has not been a rush to pass policy resolutions condemning the activities of the New Christian Right. It is also clear that the absence of such policy action stands in sharp contrast to the flurry of individual and ad hoc group actions. One can argue that the case of desegregation is non-commensurable with the issues raised by the emergence of the New Christian Right. That may be true. But the fact remains that many mainline leaders believe with Norman Lear, George McGovern, Archibald Cox, and others that the New Christian Right poses an egregious threat to our system of government. Why are they apparently unwilling or unable to carry this message to their own church bodies?

The answer rests in the brittle truce that exists between liberals and conservatives within almost every major religious body in America. Ever since the late 1960s when the political activities of liberals in mainline church bodies were discovered, they have been either on the defensive or in retreat.

Virtually every mainline church body has experienced the emergence of conservative caucuses. In the late 1960s, the conservatives cut off funds for liberal social programs. In the 70s, they fought back liberal resolutions. As we enter the 80s, there is an uneasy feeling that conservatives are either going to have things their own way or create unprecedented schisms. Already some 70 congregations have pulled out of the United Presbyterian Church denomination.

In many instances the battle lines are drawn on issues of biblical inerrancy. But just beneath the surface of biblical disputes rest profound disagreements regarding the implications of these disputed truths—the ordination of women, the churches' stance toward homosexuals, abortion, etc. The Southern Baptists went to battle over biblical inerrancy, but the social agenda of the triumphant conservatives closely parallels that of the Moral Majority.

It seems unlikely that the Episcopal, Presbyterian, Lutheran, or Methodist church bodies are going to experience conservative takeovers as sweeping as that experienced by the Southern Baptists. But it also seems apparent that liberal church leaders view the risks of schism to be too great to take on the conservatives in their ranks—even though many liberals believe the Moral Majority is really "fascism masquerading as Christianity."

If we correctly assess the reluctance of mainline church leadership to challenge conservatives within their respective organizational structures, the consequences for the countermobilization of opposition to the New Christian Right are rather significant. Individuals as well as agencies of the major religious bodies will certainly find ways to join in the struggle against the New Christian Right. But this does not carry the same weight as if their views represented the official policy of their respective church bodies.

The unique role of religious institutions in social conflict is to confer legitimacy on a particular definition of reality. The inability to put the full weight of their respective church bodies behind public pronouncements certainly constrains potential effectiveness. How can you speak for God when you lack the authority to speak for your own religious group?

This portends a different strategy in the countermobilization of mainline church resources to oppose the New Christian Right than they pursued during the 50s and 60s in support of civil rights. It would appear that mainline church leaders must substantially limit their engagements to those that do not directly involve their respective institutions.

What this really boils down to is that most of them will be free, individually, to support groups that do stand in active opposition to the New Christian Right. We noted earlier that 15 of the 39 advisory board members of People for the American Way are prominent religious leaders. From the onset, PAW has worked closely with leadership from the three major faiths in America. A close working relationship can be expected to be strengthened over time.

ALTERNATIVE STRATEGIES

We believe there is a potentially more effective strategy mainline church leaders could pursue. This would be to create a religiously grounded alternative organization to the Moral Majority. The scenario for success involves two critical ingredients. The first is a very attractive charismatic leader. The second is a platform which acknowledges the legitimacy of the issues raised by the Moral Majority, but deals with them in carefully reasoned ways that more nearly express the moral sentiments of the real majority of Americans.

One can take a highly skeptical view and conclude that charismatic leaders like Martin Luther King, Jr., are not manufactured by those who seek to launch a social movement in opposition to the Moral Majority. But what about Jerry Falwell? There is good reason to believe that Falwell's influence would still be largely limited to the 1.5 million viewers of the Old-Time Gospel Hour had it not been for the vision and determination of a few New Right leaders who saw the possibilities of a man of God leading their conservative cause.

The task is one of identifying persons with the potential to lead a moderate religiously-based social movement and then providing them with the resources to grow into the role.

As for a platform to challenge the Moral Majority agenda, a group calling themselves the Chicagoland Committee on Fair Play drafted a statement last year which is a creative effort in the right direction. Following the Moral Majority platform, which professes to be pro-traditional family, pro-life, pro-morality, and pro-America, the Committee affirmed eight social convictions: (1) pro-human, (2) pro-family, (3) pro-justice, (4) pro-creationism, (5) pro-morality, (6) pro-nation, (7) pro-peace, and (8) pro-human rights.

A very substantial proportion of what is affirmed by the Moral Majority is also affirmed in "The Chicago Statement." But on each point, the statement goes beyond the rather limited concerns of the Moral Majority. For example, Falwell is pro-life, but he seldom elaborates on this beyond his denunciation of abortion. "The Chicago Statement" begins with "We affirm the sanctity of all human life." It then continues:

> We deplore the devaluation of personhood whether by irresponsible abortion, genetic manipulation, infanticide, euthanasia, capital punishment, economic manipulation, or nuclear proliferation. Therefore, we call upon the church to affirm and honor such actions as respect all human life: the fetus, the mother, the poor, the disadvantaged, the hungry, the aged, the disabled, the guilty on death row, the innocent victimized by guns and brutality, and all caught in fear.

Whether this kind of statement will prove effective as an alternative to the Moral Majority remains to be seen, but we wish simply to illustrate the point that mainline churches do have alternative strategies to deal with the perceived threat of the New Christian Right.

To recapitulate the argument, mainline churches realized early the potential for the televangelists to use the airwaves and their mastery of modern communications technology to organize a conservative political movement. They were instrumental in sounding the alarm which resulted in a rapid countermobilization. However, mainline churches are limited in their efforts to resist the New Christian Right because of the precarious balance of power between liberals and conservatives within their own groups. To maximize their own influence in the ensuing struggle, mainline groups should endeavor to develop leadership and religious organizations which can function outside existing church structures. Finally, the appropriate strategy for such organizations would be to acknowledge the goals of the New Christian Right, but raise the issues to a higher level, thus appealing to a broader constituency than the Moral Majority currently enjoys.

NOTES

1. Albert J. Menendez, *Religion at the Polls* (Philadelphia, Westminster, 1977).
2. Ernest Q. Campbell and Thomas F. Pettigrew, *Christians in Racial Crisis* (Washington, D.C., Public Affairs Press, 1959) 137–70.

Chapter 30

Robert McAfee Brown

The Religious Right and Political/Economic Conservatism

There are numerous analyses that can be made of the new religious right. . . . The concern of the present article is to demonstrate how proponents of the religious right provide a theological cover and sanction for extremely conservative politics and economics. To keep the analysis within reasonable boundaries, we will use the television evangelist Jerry Falwell as a kind of case-study. Mr. Falwell and others like him perpetuate and strengthen the image of the Christian faith as a sanctifier of the *status quo* by providing a bulwark of theological support for right wing political commitments and economic structures.

Mr. Falwell wears many hats, but at least two of them he claims never to be wearing at the same time. One hat is his role as evangelist, a television preacher for twenty years on "The Old-Time Gospel Hour," which originates out of his Thomas Road Baptist Church in Lynchburg, Virginia. In this role, Mr. Falwell claims not to be "political," but to deal exclusively with the subject matter of Christian (which means "individual") salvation. Wearing another hat he claims that, purely as a private citizen, he heads Moral Majority, a political pressure group with a clear political agenda that he pushes unstintingly when not in the pulpit. Unfortunately, it is a little difficult for people who are not named Jerry Falwell to be as clear as he that the two hats are not worn simultaneously, particularly when he tells readers of his direct mail campaigns that he created Moral Majority because God showed him, as he puts it, that "I have a divine mandate to go right into the halls of Congress and fight for laws that will save America . . . laws that will protect the grand old flag." Divine mandates are pretty strong stuff, tending to engulf the whole of life, and we find that when Falwell writes, as he does copiously in *Listen, America!* (Doubleday, 1980), the evangelist and the politician are hard to disentangle.

It seems clear that the recent incursion of members of the religious right into politics has belied their traditional claim, usually offered polemically against "liberals," that "religion and politics don't mix." Today, not only for Mr. Falwell but for almost all like him, that claim has been discarded. With a zeal bent on making up for lost time, they now enact a belief that religion and politics most emphatically do mix. Our concern, in

First published in *Radical Religion*, 5/4 (1981), pp. 14–17. Used by permission.

response, must be with the nature of the mix: what *kind* of religion, what *kind* of politics? The mix that emerges makes them seem almost indistinguishable from one another. Both the religion and the politics can be described by the same words: conservative, right-wing, individualistically oriented, deathly opposed to "liberalism."

THE BIBLE INTERPRETED

The Bible is ostensibly normative and it is the Bible interpreted in a certain way. Mr. Falwell's Biblical stance, for example, is unambiguous: "The Bible is absolutely infallible, without error in all matters pertaining to faith and practice, as well as in areas such as geography, science, history, etc." (*Listen, America!*, p. 63). Even without the "etc.," that is a pretty wide laundry list of infallible subjects, and we can be sure that Mr. Falwell includes politics and economics in his all-inclusive rubric.

So the Bible will provide us with a political and economic stance. A cooperative economy, for example, is ruled out by the Bible and a competitive one is sanctioned: "Competition in business is Biblical. Ambitious and successful business management is clearly outlined as a part of God's plan for His people" (p. 13). So what is the conclusion of the infallible Word of God about economics? Easy: "The free enterprise system is clearly outlined in the Book of Proverbs in the Bible" (p. 13).

If that is the economic philosophy the infallible Word of God espouses, what will be the political consequences for Bible-believing Christians? Clearly to support in political life those who affirm such a position, and that makes it easy for Mr. Falwell to claim that "Mr. Reagan is the greatest thing that has happened to our country in my lifetime" (*Christianity Today*, September, 1981, p. 1099). Q.E.D.

With such a political-economic Biblical base firmly nailed down, Mr. Falwell can go on to draw very clear-cut Biblical consequences. Capital punishment, for example: "The death penalty is a deterrent to crime. In the Book of Romans in the Bible we find in Chapter I that God has given government the responsibility and authority to punish by death" (p. 166). (One of the Moral Majority's regional leaders in the San Jose area of California carried the argument to its logical conclusion by proposing that the government invoke the death penalty against homosexuals, homosexuality being one of the chief "crimes" of our era, according to the Moral Majority viewpoint. To his credit, Mr. Falwell disassociated himself from his overzealous underling.)

If capital punishment is a Biblically appropriate penalty against our own citizens, how much more appropriate is death against those outside our national boundaries who threaten us. "Nowhere in the Bible," Mr. Falwell informs us, "is there a rebuke for the bearing of armaments" (p. 98), a bit of exegesis that reverses the swords into ploughshares bit and overlooks such admonitions as the warning that they who take the sword will perish by the sword. Consequently, one of the most consistent attitudes in Mr. Falwell's writings, and in the handouts of the Moral Majority, is the need to spend more money on defense, because of the threat of the godless Russians. Moral Majority, he explains, is "pro-American, which means strong national defense" (*Christianity Today*, p. 1099). He cites with approval the comment of General Lew Walt of the U.S. Marine Corps, that "No great nation has ever existed any longer than the supremacy of its military power" (*Listen, America!*, p. 103) and comes to the conclusion that "It is only common sense that disarmament is suicide" (p. 10) and that "It is now time that emergency action be taken to increase American military preparedness" (p. 100). Robert McNamara is scored, not for his role in prolonging the Vietnam War, but because he is "the man who started our gradual unilateral disarmament" (p. 100), a characterization that will undoubtedly come as a surprise not only to Mr. McNamara but to high-ranking Pentagon officials as well.

THE FIVE EVILS

Although most of the evils that are in danger of bringing about the demise of America are individual evils (a matter to which we will return), there is a clear reason for the need to keep armed to the teeth: if we fail to do so, our way of life will be overcome by another way of life, and it is not hard to discover what the other way of life is. It is number 4 among "the evils threatening America in 1980," on Mr. Falwell's "Declaration of War" broadsheet. Evils 1, 2, 3, and 5 are predictable: legalized abortion, defined as "murder," pornography, homosexuality, and the deterioration of the home and family. Evil number 4 is "socialism." And since we have already learned that capitalism is God's plan for our economy, socialism is clearly anti-God, and Mr. Falwell signs (and seals) a promise that "The Old-Time Gospel Hour hereby dedicates itself to spearhead the battle and lead an army of Christian soldiers into this war against evil."

The same broadsheet that identifies "socialism" as one of the five evils of our time, is a further example of how closely intertwined is Mr. Falwell's political posture as a "private citizen," and his role as the Biblical preacher on "The Old-Time Gospel Hour." The five evils are to be fought against "in God's name," and the broadsheet is not issued in the name of the politically-oriented Moral Majority, but precisely in the name of the presumably non-political Old-Time Gospel Hour. Just above his signature Mr. Falwell writes, "With a firm mandate from God I fully commit The Old-Time Gospel Hour ministry in support of this Declaration of War."

Quantitatively Mr. Falwell's fulminations *against* socialism are dwarfed by his eager support *for* the Pentagon, though when one puts these two items together, they turn out to be simply two sides of the same coin. At all events, they just about exhaust Mr. Falwell's concern for *social* issues. The issues to which he devotes most of his public energies are chiefly matters of *individual* conduct which he sees as the ills most demanding social correction. Chief among these, as we have already seen, are the evils of pornography, homosexuality, and abortion. These three items undoubtedly have social consequences, but in each case they represent matters of private sexual conduct and attitude that exercise a widespread fascination for most of those on the religious right.

Mr. Falwell has said some very harsh things about homosexuals, proposing with scary language that they have "*invaded* the classrooms, and the pulpits of our churches" (italics added), and that "the sin of homosexuality is so grievous, so abominable in the sight of God, that He destroyed the cities of Sodom and Gomorrah because of this terrible sin" (*Listen, America!*, p. 181). Such people, he has frequently said, should not hold public office or instruct our youth. When pressed in public debate, however, he sometimes modifies his position, insisting that he is only talking about practicing homosexuals who try to force their attentions on others, particularly the young. Such a constriction of sexual aggressiveness would presumably be appropriate for heterosexuals as well, but the emotional appeal of the position is much stronger when used against homosexuals.

The problems of our society, so runs the analysis of the religious right, are located in the widespread permissiveness in relation to these sexual "sins," and eliminating them will take us well on the way toward a creative future. Thus we are called upon to be *against* sexual "deviants" and socialism and the Equal Rights Amendment, and *for* prayer in school and building more bombs.

STRUCTURES UNVISITED

It is interesting that while "sins" that have to do with evil hearts and imaginations come up for strong indictment, sins related to evil social structures never do. One searches in vain for concern about racism or poverty or hunger or collective economic exploitation in Mr. Falwell's writings. To his credit, he is not unaware of such criticism, but with a marvelous kind of candor he indicates why Moral Majority simply can't be concerned with issues as complex as human poverty:

> Someone will say, What about the poor? We could never bring the issue of the poor into Moral Majority because the argument would be, Who is going to decide what we teach those people? Mormons? Catholics? No, we won't get into that. As private persons and ministers, we make a commitment if we feel convicted. But for Moral Majority, no! If we go in there, create jobs, raise funds, and get involved with the local pastors, the problem is, which pastors? . . . We just have to stay away from helping the poor [*Christianity Today*, p. 1100].

The real task of Moral Majority, he tells us in the same interview, is "to zero in on the vital things" (ibid.).

Nor is the competitive nature of the capitalist system ever challenged; as we against the right of people to decide how to handle matters of sexual orientation or the possible termination of a pregnancy.

What we have in the religious right, in other words, is not a position that has started with a Biblical base and proceeded to draw conclusions from that base, nor even a position that has started with a social analysis of what is wrong with the world when seen through the eyes of the victimized, and then proceeded to "search the Scriptures" for further insight. What we have in the religious right is a position that has started with a basically individualistic analysis of the world, seen through affluent, upwardly mobile, middle-class eyes, and has subsequently "searched the Scriptures" to find ways to vindicate such a posture as the only true Biblical one.

Example: "Individuals should be free to build their own lives without interference from government" (*Listen, America!*, p. 69). This is a good example of "the view from above." It works very well for those who Have It Made, or are well on the way to Getting There. For them, governmental "interference" means regulations that might cut down on profits or impose safety regulations in work places. But for those at the bottom of the heap, "interference" might mean the first chance ever to escape from grinding poverty, or to be assured that work places will be safe and that environments will not be excessively polluted. The notion that businesses are going to put self-imposed limits on profits or voluntarily cease exploiting workers is surely conceivable only from a position of privilege.

"Free enterprise in a capitalist society," Mr. Falwell tells us, "where free men trade with other free men without the interference of other people, works" (p. 73). It clearly "works" for those with wealth and capital and influence and power, but it is highly questionable whether it "works" for those who are victims of manipulation by the wealth and capital and influences and power of those on top.

While he concedes that a few people may need welfare assistance even in a God-endorsed capitalistic free enterprise economy, Mr. Falwell goes on to say:

I believe that, generally, there are now enough jobs to go around. Too many people who could work, do not. Have they forgotten what the word "work" means? Will they live off giveaway programs, supported by those people who work hard for a living, forever? [p. 78].

Such a statement is conceivable only from someone who does not face unemployment, who is not subject to the demeaning experience of trying to find work and being rebuffed, or of going through the depersonalizing experiences of seeking welfare aid since no job is to be found.

The examples could be multiplied. In each case it is assumed that a particular part of the social strata is normative, and that problems need to be examined only from that viewpoint. It is a perspective calculated to bring joy to those already in positions of authority and power, who can continue to reap the benefits of a system that grinds down the rest. It is not surprising, therefore, that when Mr. Falwell wants economic expertise to support his view of the Biblical notion of free enterprise economy, he quotes Milton Friedman, nor that when he wants to deal with the role of government he quotes Jesse Helms. It is all of a piece.

A BIBLICAL VENEER

What we have, then, is not so much a Biblical theology as a capitalist free enterprise ideology, overlaid with a thin (often very thin) veneer of Biblical justification. Any claim that the position has been drawn from Scripture is difficult to maintain. No one going to the scriptures would emerge from an exhaustive study of their contents with the conclusion that the major ills threatening the world today are abortion, pornography, homosexuality, and socialism. A few scattered (and highly ambiguous) verses could be collected, but they would hardly represent the hard thrust of the Biblical witness.

A highly selective screening process has obviously been employed, and those on the religious right who claim Biblical orientation for their position have taken a tiny stratum of the Bible and created their own "canon within the canon." (Let us concede that we all do this, and further concede that the sin is easier to detect in the case of another than in our own. But surely some emphases are more dominant in scripture than others, and the ringing cry of the prophets and Jesus for social justice, a message of "good news to the poor," certainly outranks in importance a total of seven verses dealing, more or less ambiguously, with homosexuality.)

We find a clear example of this textual selectivity in Mr. Falwell's use of Sodom and Gomorrah as a warning of how cultures are destroyed because of the presence of homosexuality within their walls. That, however, is hardly the whole story on Sodom and Gomorrah. It may even be asked whether it is a truly significant part of the whole story. Apparently outside of Mr. Falwell's "canon within the canon" are certain portions of the Book of Ezekiel, which on other occasions he quotes to assure us that we will finally defeat the Russians. Ezekiel engages in a searing analysis of what went wrong in Sodom, and his indictment is somewhat different from that of Mr. Falwell: "Behold, this was the guilt of your sister Sodom: she and her daughters had pride, surfeit of food, and prosperous ease, but did not aid the poor and needy" (Ezekiel 16:49).

Is it too presumptuous to suggest that the latter provides a more basically Biblical account of what was wrong in Sodom, and what is going wrong in the modern Sodoms, than Mr. Falwell's? It sounds like a potential epitaph for our culture, in which destruction may clearly come to those who have "a surfeit of food and prosperous ease," and who do not "aid the poor and needy." One could build a significant Biblical theology for the 1980's out of such a starting place.

Another area where an ideology is imposed both on a worldview and on a Biblical perspective is in the religious right's understanding of sin. For Mr. Falwell, the basic sins tearing our society apart are individual sins of a sexual sort. The implicit remedy is to get individual lives put back together, by external compulsion if necessary, and then the social fabric will take care of itself.

The notion that sin is also in social structures is never considered. And yet surely such social analysis is not only descriptively helpful today (when we look at how corporations assume a life of their own and bring about degradation of vast numbers of human beings in the name of higher profits for a few) but is also supported by the very Biblical witness itself. Without denying that there are individual sins, the prophets attack social structures—the monarchy, the judicial system, the religious establishment, the nation. Yes, there must be individual repentance, but there must also be new social structures, dedicated to justice rather than avariciousness, dedicated to the needs of the poor and not just the aggrandizing power of the rich. Not only must individual priests repent, but the whole concept of priesthood must be rethought. Not only must individual kings be brought to account, but the whole concept of monarchy must be rethought. Not only must corrupt judges be chastized, but the whole judicial system must be rethought.

We must be careful here. The Bible does not furnish us with the blueprints for such new structures, but it does remind us of how easy it is for us to take refuge behind old structures, or remain the beneficiaries of structures that treat us handsomely only at the cost of destroying others.

The old adage is true: where we stand determines what we see. In the case of developing a counterposition to the religious right, we are faced not only with the task of rescuing the Bible from the exegesis of predetermined stances, but of analyzing very critically where our own standing point is located. Dietrich Bonhoeffer, rescued by the events of World War II from the stance of affluent comfort that Mr. Falwell represents, spoke about the need for "the view from below," which he describes as "the perspective of the outcast, the suspects, the maltreated, the powerless, the oppressed, the reviled— in short from the perspective of those who suffer" (*Letters and Papers from Prison*, Macmillan, p. 17).

It is from that perspective that we must affirm the para-theological starting point of which Juan Luis Segundo has reminded us, namely that "the world should not be the way it is." To take seriously the necessity of such a starting point will also put us back in touch with the Scriptures, which for the most part are written from the perspective of the poor, the oppressed, the victimized. If we can begin to see how that world and ours come together, we may be able not only to avoid some of the pitfalls into which the new religious right has fallen, but even begin to offer some significant alternatives.

Chapter 31

Virginia M. Doland

Totalitarian Evangelicalism

Once upon a time a man who taught freshman composition in an evangelical Christian college asked his class to write about what they imagined a truly Christian society would be like (this, by the way, is a true story). When he read the essays he was rather shaken to discover that the worlds his students had described were closer to Nazi Germany or Stalinist Russia than to the Garden of Eden or the millennium. Uncomfortably often, the students proposed thought control, loyalty checks, brainwashing and, most of all, rigid rules of conduct stringently enforced. The commonly perceived need was for control of thought as well as of deeds, with dissent minimized because it was regarded as inherently evil.

Although the teacher was shocked at his class's response, unfortunately the desire to impose one's preconceived pattern on the thoughts and actions of others, even though not biblical, is a dangerous temptation for many evangelicals. Since a society's desire to produce a standard, approved human product through a rigid control of thought and action is basically totalitarian, its existence within a closed evangelical context can properly be called totalitarian evangelicalism.

Because a phrase like "totalitarian evangelicalism" has a frightening ring to it, I will distinguish it from those "goods" and "partial goods"—which have some justification in the facts of life and human nature—by explaining what I do *not* mean by it.

First of all, "totalitarian evangelicalism" is not a simple hierarchical arrangement instituted solely for the purpose of doing things "decently and in order"; obviously, any society needs laws, rules, and modes of accepted conduct. Unlike a simple authoritarian society, in which the purpose of rules and regulations is to maintain order and structure, a totalitarian society institutes order for the purpose of control—control of mind and body, thought and action.

Make no mistake, the difference is one of *kind,* not degree. A simple ordered society will settle for outward conformity: a totalitarian one demands complete inward allegiance. Simply obeying the rules is not sufficient; one must feel at one with such a society in every corner of one's being. Whether such allegiance is achievable, let alone desirable, does not seem to be at issue, for unquestioning allegiance is postulated as the norm even though the bed is, more often than not, a Procrustean one.

A second clarification to be made is that "totalitarian evangelicalism" is neither healthy nor efficient. As Hannah Arendt points out in *The Origins of Totalitarianism,* efficiency is so subordinated to control that the totalitarian society can afford to spend 50 to 75 percent of its energies enforcing control of one sort or another on its citizens.

Such a system of priorities strikes at the essence of evangelicalism, for within a totalitarian evangelical system, thought—or, more insidiously, spirit—control takes precedence over spiritual growth. The process of spiritual growth involves individual struggle, doubt, and one's confrontation with God—tensions that are effectively short-circuited by thought control. Far from being healthy, then, the set of attitudes that I am discussing is inimical to spiritual maturity.

The Bible's life-giving, liberalizing force should encourage the Christian to search for the truth which does indeed make him or her free. But, difficult though it may be, we must enter into the deep places of faith and the soul, and ask the hard questions of Christianity with some kind of faith that answers are really there. They are, of course, but we must descend into them and into ourselves if they are ever to be known. To avoid that journey will change the destination. We need to set aside our fear of getting outside of God, for if we journey in honesty and truthfulness the path cannot end anywhere else but within God. As T. S. Eliot, himself a great journeyer, observes:

> We shall not cease from exploration
> And the end of all our exploring
> Will be to arrive where we started
> And know the place for the first time.

Without such exploration we in all probability will never know the place at all. Far from being biblical, the kind of control that stops spiritual growth seems to verge upon the sinful; it is to self-forge a manacle for one's soul.

DEPERSONALIZATION

Totalitarianism is, almost by definition, religious in its intensity and in the nature of the demands it makes upon the total being of its adherents. In its evangelical form it insidiously rigidifies and codifies the attitudes of the spirit. God frees; humans enslave. To achieve this slavery, four methods have been the most obvious in my own experience.

The first was to break down the person's concept of his or her own individuality; one must think of oneself primarily as a member of a group. Uniform behavior, when it becomes a reflex, admirably depresses one's sense of individuality. Such a reflex was brought about by means of an intricate system of rules which existed for their own sake—for the sake of the psychological conditioning they instilled—and not for any actual necessity. From my own experience I learned how the system worked.

In the totalitarian evangelical society in which I as an undergraduate student spent three years of my life (and the situation there reportedly has not significantly changed over the years), all students were subject to numerous unwarranted demands. Women were required to be in bed at 11 P.M. (not 10:59 or 11:01) and up at 7 A.M. (not 7:01). Disobedience was unheard of, deterred by the prompt and efficient punishment meted out by hall monitors and discipline committees.

Breakfast was served exactly at 7:25, and everyone was required to be there—even those who had no morning classes or who did not want to eat. Dress was strictly regulated (for women, skirts and blouses or dresses, stockings and flats, and no hair curlers), and attendance was checked (by the table monitor). Table manners were closely observed; and as one chewed one's grits in the dull Carolina darkness, "Our Etiquette Rule for Today" was announced. Conversation was evaluated for spirituality and attitude. At 7:45 exactly we would be dismissed to get our room ready for inspection, which was daily and thorough and precisely at 8:05. And the rest of the day was filled with similar restrictive rules.

I want to stress again that such precision and multiplicity of rules were designed primarily to take away the volitional impulse. The way the morning was set up made it impossible for students to decide anything for themselves. And this kind of automatic, volitionless going through the motions distorted one's spirit as it bent one's mind. The rules, we were taught to think, were not important; it was our attitude toward them that was significant. And something *did* happen to my attitude toward myself and my world as I automatically followed the prescribed regimen.

It is interesting that very few students rebelled; that seemed simply not a possiblity. In my three years there, I received a total of nine demerits (a demerit was given for being a minute or two late for class, for example, or for not making one's bed to the satisfaction of the monitor), but that was not an unusually good record since most students received *no* demerits at all. Whether I would or no, I was a member of a group; every day in every way, if I would but accept the patterns of my society, I could be defined from without and therefore was not in need of definition from within.

When regulations existed primarily for the purpose of their effect on the individual's self-concept, simply to observe them was not enough; one had to do so with complete dedication and unquestioning enthusiasm—qualities which often seem to have an inverse relationship to sensitivity, intelligence, and sincerity. This demand that the group's members possess unquestioning loyalty constitutes a second method of totalitarian control.

Not only must one conform, but one's apparent attitude in the midst of external compliance had to be constantly evaluated: Does the student smile as she jumps out of bed promptly at 7 A.M.? Does the student pray often enough and long enough in prayer meeting? Indeed, does the student go regularly and joyfully to the "optional" Sunday school and prayer meetings? Does his or her facial expression sometimes reveal a questioning of decisions made by superiors? Under the totalitarian system these were valid questions, and simply to have done nothing wrong (or noncompliant) was no salvation.

At the college I attended, such evaluation was accomplished by a "spiritual police" system whilch effectively enforced attitudinal and spiritual conformity. Each dorm room had an assistant prayer captain responsible for assessing and reporting on the spirituality of the other students in the room. Every four rooms had a prayer captain to whom the assistants reported; she, in turn, reported to the assistant monitor, who reported to the monitor, who reported to the dorm supervisor, who reported to the assistant dean of women, who reported to the dean of women. At each step the reports were evaluated—and the assistant prayer captain or monitor who observed no spiritual problems among any of her charges would soon become a spiritual problem herself!

A terrifying thing about such a system was the arrogance implicit in the evaluation of unique spiritual beings on the basis of some predetermined, often shallowly conceived quality control. The "product" who fell short of the system's "standards" was hauled out of classes or bed and questioned by the administration! If some perceived defect in spirituality or attitude was indeed found, the hapless student might be expelled with a bad recommendation even the week before graduation. After all, "If you're not an asset, you are a liability"—or so proclaimed the sign in two locations on every dormitory floor.

Yet a third quality inherent in this totalitariam system was a suspension of normal values of common sense and individual judgment. Another sign in our dormitory admonished: "Griping is not tolerated—constructive suggestions are appreciated." To my young ears that sounded minimally acceptable, although even then it seemed to me that sometimes griping can be a valid human need. But in reality, *no* suggestions, constructive or otherwise, were tolerated; to "suggest" implied individual thought and evaluation, the perception of a possible improvement—obviously dangerous qualities in that world.

In my own case, I was branded forever as a "malcontent" whose treason merited permanent admission into her record—for making the innocent suggestion that paper towels be installed in the women's restroom. What I did not realize then, and what I still have a little trouble understanding even now, was the *nature* of my offense. Evidently what was so treasonable was not the suggestion itself but the fact that I had individually exercised my common sense and made an evaluation. The premium, I found, was on passivity, on detachment from one's environment in any thinking fashion. Passive people "belong"; they are easier to lead.

The final quality of the totalitarian evangelical mentality that I experienced was its paranoia about the outside world. The implication seemed to be that in conformity and loyalty lay safety; since the world conspires against us, let us not look at its ideas, participate in its institutions, or understand its needs lest we be led away from the faith. We must "stand," build a wall, patrol the campus with machine guns, and quarter our faculty in on-campus dorm rooms, for if they lived elsewhere they would bring the corruption of the outside world in to the students. While it is true that there was a hostile world which surrounded our community, common sense, and Christ's practice, would indicate that we evangelicals should have tried to change it (or, failing that, to influence it), rather than to exorcise it.

EVANGELICAL TOTALITARIANISM

The totalitarian mind-set becomes even more pernicious when it is combined with evangelicalism. To take the freedom and joy of the Christian life and pervert it into rigid patterns, self-congratulatory judgments on others, mind control, and loyalty checks must pain our Lord deeply.

The inescapable truth about the totalitarian evangelicalism I experienced was that, although the totalitarianism was real, the evangelicalism can scarcely have been. In imposing a rigid pattern of thought control, evangelical totalitarianism had given itself over to the "world system," substituting human power for God's freedom.

Although my experience was with an extreme system, the point is valid in less extreme situations. We evangelicals seem to have a built-in weakness for some aspects of totalitarianism. We worry about those who do not fit in, we are uneasy about questioners and doubters, we feel that there needs to be more "order" and regularity. We seem sometimes to have a prefabricated (and entirely unbiblical) concept of what a Christian should act like, look like, even think like. Rigidity and totalitarianism are bedfellows; they are like a spiritual abomination, making a mockery of the freedom of our Lord.

To cast our lot with such a mind-set is to avoid facing the variety and complexity of

God's world. Those who devise and run such systems do irreparable harm to young people, and as a result they have a negative impact on the future of evangelicalism. Dedication and zealousness will not excuse such "leaders" for, in Christ's words:

> Many will say to me in that day, Lord, Lord, have we not prophesied in thy name? and in thy name have cast out devils? and in thy name done many wonderful works? And then will I profess unto them, I never knew you: depart from me, ye that work iniquity.

Chapter 32

Martin E. Marty

Morality, Ethics, and
the New Christian Right

An encyclopedia of religion may soon have an entry like this:

> The New Christian Right is the generic term for a number of conservative and largely Protestant American political forces that surfaced in the elections of 1980. Best known of these was the Moral Majority, but Religious Roundtable and Christian Voice were among other sometimes overlapping, sometimes competing groups. Members were recruited by radio and television evangelists or through direct-mail techniques. Their clienteles were joined by congregants in fundamentalist local churches. Unlike their evangelistic predecessors, the new leaders advocated explicit political involvement. Theirs was a politics of nostalgia for an earlier "Christian America," and an opposition against "secular humanism" as the agent of moral decline in America. Among the chosen causes were opposition to abortion, disarmament, feminist and homosexual movements, and support of prayer and biblical teachings in Christian schools.

It is difficult to assess the strength of a movement whose leadership makes extravagant claims of size and support, and whose influence the media tend to exaggerate in order to emphasize the dimensions of conflict. Despite the dearth of statistics, one can assemble a profile from studies of the cohort on which the Right draws—the audience of Christian television. This audience is over 60 percent female; 64 percent of the audience is over fifty years of age, and only 15 percent is under thirty-five. Only 15 percent of the very committed television viewers have attended college and 41 percent of them report less than $10,000 a year income. Over 80 percent of those who tell polltakers they favor religious television are from the south or midwest, and town and country people are eight times more likely to watch than are city folk. While a large number of blacks watch religious television, they seem to be under-represented in Moral Majority-type groups.

It is apparent that the New Christian Right has attracted middle-aged and older people (predominantly women), and others of aspirant classes, who are on the move

First published in *The Hastings Center Report,* 11 (August 1981), pp. 14–17. Used by permission.

from the upper-lower or lower-middle class. They seek legitimation of their new status and explanation of what limits their rise. In this sense the New Christian Right is a descendant of what social observers from Ernst Troeltsch through H. Richard Niebuhr called "the religions of the dispossessed."

A December 1980 Gallup Poll found that only 40 percent of the respondents had heard or read about the Moral Majority, only 26 percent were familiar with its goals, and among those "informed," disapproval outweighed approval 13 to 8, with 5 undecided. Thus the New Christian Right gets its power not from huge masses but from strategic locations, computerized mailing lists, and effective organization, which depend heavily on television and publishing to spread the word and fill the purse.

The New Right groups are notoriously close-lipped about their fundraising capabilities. They send out expensive appeals for money describing their financial crises. But these direct-mail and similar electronic appeals on Christian television are proliferating. Audiences are supporting at least thirty religiously oriented television stations, over a thousand radio stations, and four religious networks. In fact, the top ten television ministries now bring in $50 to $90 million each per year, more money than the headquarters of all but the three largest denominations in America can command.

Many of the charismatic leaders have a heavy investment in these television and related publishing networks. To survive, they have to stay in the limelight and justify their investments and intentions. This self-interest leads them to exaggerate the evils of their opposition, to deal less than truthfully with both "secular humanism" and the character of the Christian past, and to overadvertise their own virtues.

When a new force hits American politics, it awakens counterforces. While most critics have opposed the substance—not the rights—of the New Christian Right, many observers argue that "no one complained" when moderate or leftish religious leaders were involved in politics in the 1960s. Was it fair (they argued) to switch the rules on fundamentalists (who had switched their own rules by intruding into politics)?

This, of course, was not true. Americans have never welcomed clerics of any kind in politics of any sort; in the 1960s radical religious leaders were scorned at least as much as the New Christian Right is today. Of course, the New Christian Right is not the first movement to blend religion and politics. Of course, it has rights to speak up; just as its opponents have the right to criticize it, to counter it, and to try to prevent it from transgressing legal boundaries separating civil and religious life in, for example, matters of tax exemption.

ROOTS OF EVANGELICAL CONSERVATISM

In what ways is the New Christian Right "new"? Evangelicalism, which encompassed almost all of Protestantism until the Civil War and which is the "softer" antecedent of the harder-line fundamentalism of the past half-century, has always had a moral and at times moralistic interest. While the heart of the evangelical experience has been conversion from a sinful way of life to God in Christ through the Holy Spirit—the formulas vary, but today the code name is "born again"—this experience has moved followers in two closely related directions.

On the one hand evangelicals have favored doctrinal orthodoxies. Some religions that appeal more to the heart than to the head, to "the affections" or emotions than to reason, could tolerate spontaneity and free-flowing "enthusiasm." But in the modern world, where one continually walks the tight-rope or high-wire, many people feel the need for a net. It is no coincidence that Protestant doctrines of the "inerrancy" of the Scripture arose at about the same period Catholics defined the Pope as "infallible."

Both religions had always held their respective authorities in high esteem, but by the late nineteenth century they were impelled toward more clearly defined and more rigid statements. The New Christian Right derives from a fundamentalist movement that stressed biblical inerrancy and then supported doctrines that it felt modernists were compromising: the virgin birth of Jesus, his substitutionary atonement, his physical resurrection, and the like.

The drive to orthodoxy was paralleled by a hunger for drawing boundaries. Fearing the erosions of modernity, the evangelical conservatives huddled together. They tended to form defensive tribes of the like-minded, so that they would not blend into the secular landscape.

This demarcation has created a Manichaean passion for dividing the world into dual camps: God versus Satan, elect people versus sinners, Christians versus secularists. In this triad of dualism, the latter in each case was seen as forming a conspiracy to oppose the good.

An example of this mode of reasoning is the best-selling paperback by one of the movement's theoreticians, Tim LaHaye—*The Battle for the Mind* (Revell, 1980), a blast against the humanist "conspiracy." "As far back as we can go in recorded history," writes LaHaye, "we find that man has always been aware that life was a battle between good and evil." One way was called "the way of man," and "the good way has always been called 'God's way'." LaHaye goes so far as to trace "man's way" back to Saint Thomas Aquinas, because Aquinas felt free to mingle Bible teachings with those of non-Christian philosophers! LaHaye's conclusion: "We are in a battle—and it takes armies to win wars."

The New Christian Right does not deal in subtleties: it favors conspiracy theories to explain why good America has become corrupt America. For some arcane reasons, most of its leaders claim that a magic number of 275,000 secular humanists have taken 225,000,000 good Americans into bondage.

As evangelism turned hardline it grew more moralistic. Many of the world's religions have been devoted chiefly to worldviews, to myth and symbol, rite and practice. But the biblical and prophetic "religions of the book"—Judaism, Christianity, and Islam—have also stressed the moral implications of conversion and devotion. Within Christianity there have been countless local variations, some of them quite relaxed about morality. But in northwest Europe and Anglo-America the severe sons and daughters of the Reformation, though their faith was to be one of response to "grace," sounded as "work-righteous" as the Catholics they set out to repudiate.

Moralism, labeled "Puritanism" in North America and dismissed by H. L. Mencken and his followers as the haunting fear that someone somewhere might be having a good time, was enhanced when Americans separated church and state. No longer "established," the churches nevertheless remained tax-exempt; and they needed to defend the largesse they received by demonstrating their value to the republic. They had to proclaim their moral contribution to the good society because they could not appeal to the rightness of their doctrine.

The New Christian Right still cannot make such a general appeal, since its participants disagree with each other on everything from baptism to the second coming of Christ. The movement includes some Seventh-Day Adventists who insist on a Saturday Sabbath and everyone else whose Bible allows them Sunday worhsip. There are Baptists who reject infant baptism and members of reformed traditions that connect infant baptism with salvation itself. Most believe in a literal coming of Christ for a thousand-year reign on earth, but they disagree about the basic events associated with it, and they allow "a-millennialists" in their company as well.

Although moralism has often received a bad name, honest historical accounting requires that the ledger be balanced. While the evangelicals in general contented themselves with redressing the grossest evils to victims of industrial change and capitalism, and rarely addressed more basic questions of injustice inherent in the system, they often performed their limited part of the division of labor very well. Moderates and liberals may have talked in high-minded terms, but the Salvation Army, a fervent evangelical organization, actually came to the aid of urban victims. While social gospel theorists with academic tenure advocated structural change, preachers of holiness and perfection effected what a recent historian, Norris Magnuson, has called "salvation in the slums," addressing needs of body and soul *(Salvation in the Slums: Evangelical Social Work 1865-1920,* Scarecrow, 1977).

Evangelicals in England—the people who split off from evangelicalism but kept its moral impulses—became prominent abolitionists in America. When urbanization turned alcoholism from a personal to a social problem—saloons at the entrances to mines and factories lured workers and "enslaved" them—the evangelical temperance movement was a positive social force. The often praised system of voluntarism in American humanitarian life largely derives from evangelicalism's "errand of mercy." In England and America alike there developed a network of busy and efficient charitable and reform agencies.

Between the middle of the nineteenth and twentieth centuries, evangelical moralism took on a character that now colors the more self-assured and belligerent New Christian Right. As moderates and liberals came to advocate the social gospel or other systemic approaches, the conservatives retreated, advocating "virtues" against "vices." No matter what society did, an individual citizen or believer had control over his or her own good actions. The individual could "take the pledge," stop using profane language, refrain from gambling, stay away from prostitutes.

The church, however, dared not work for peace. Seeing history as a series of cosmic battles with the militant church at their center, the New Christian Right has disdained pacifists and looked suspiciously at peacemakers. Descended from a long line of hawks, in any tendency toward national crisis it chooses the military way.

Nor did the church dare seek a new social fabric. For a variety of complex reasons, among them an acceptance of Social Darwinism by these anti-Darwinists, many conservative Protestants tied evangelicalism to laissez-faire free enterprise capitalism. Efforts to effect a measure of social justice, as seen in the civil rights movement from 1954 to 1968, were regarded as signs of the church "meddling" in politics. The political conservatives favored "private" styles of religious life, while the moderates and liberals took on more "public" responsibility. Today that demarcation seems to be blurring. Political liberals now often retreat into experimental religion or faddish therapies, or if they wish to be of help in human welfare causes, they work at keeping the local churches healthy. It is the New Christian Right that now engages in the bolder forays into politics.

WHEN THE MILLENNIUM COMES

The older Protestantism in America, including its revivalist tradition, had advocated what is often stereotyped as "postmillennialism." That is, it believed in an end of history in the event of the second coming of Jesus. The Bible had prophesied signs of evil near the end-time, but these, said postmillennialists, had already occurred in the sixteenth-century Reformation era. Now, upright Christians of good will could cooperate with God to improve the world and make it attractive to Christ so that he would return sooner.

Then in the nineteenth century in Scotland and England new theories about the second coming, this time called premillennialism, began to appear. In this view, the signs of evil lie ahead: Armageddon will come in the Middle East, a superchurch of the Antichrist will form (ecumenism), immorality will grow, Israel will be invaded from the north (Russia). Those who repent and are born again will be swept up in the thousand-year reign and will rule with Christ while others will face destruction.

Curiously, this outlook did not breed pessimism about earthly affairs. So long as believers were saved and went about saving others, and so long as they were personally moral, they could enjoy the "more abundant life" that Jesus promised. They could also survive along with the other fittest, as capitalist competition filtered out the weaker members of society.

This millennial view accounts for some of the puzzling aspects of the New Christian Right. For a time the Right was organizing Christian Embassies, publishing Christian Yellow Pages, and advocating an exclusively Christian America, but as it gained power it also began to make compromises. By the end of the 1980 campaign many of its leaders found it advantageous to work with some religious groups that shared little of the Rightist program. They could form a pragmatic alliance with liberal Catholics on the issue of abortion even if they did not agree on programs of social reform.

This was the case as well with Orthodox Jews, who also oppose abortion. For millennial reasons, the fundamentalists had always favored Israel in international politics, and many Jews applauded them for this support. Yet Jews remain understandably suspicious, remembering how in domestic affairs the forebears of Moral Majoritarians had perpetuated racist stereotypes of Jews as money-lenders and monopolizers of media influence, stereotypes that have persisted down to the present. Among its uneasy alliances, however, one viewpoint is conspicuously absent. There is no theological room for "secular humanists," who are of Satan.

Why would an evangelist of this school care for America in a doomed world, especially since he has no theology to legitimate the political life of those who are not born again? America, the evangelists believe, is the current elect nation, a redeemed "last, best hope of earth," precisely because God has chosen it as the training ground for evangelists who will rescue people in other nations. Meanwhile it must stand up against Russia and other national agents of Satan. So an apparently otherworldly faith has become worldly.

This worldliness shows up in many ways. The new forces, for example, cherish celebrities whose ways they once shunned. Beauty queens, athletic heroes, highly successful money-makers, Beautiful People, and the like are the exemplars. One hears little support for causes that are losing, or people who are unhealed, ugly, and unsuccessful. Every new technological breakthrough in communications lures the Right and costs its backers more funds. There is little standing back from late-stage industrialism and there are few calls at all for the simpler life, a life within limits.

FUTURE PROSPECTS

What shall we expect in the years ahead? The New Christian Right did not win all that it hoped to or claimed in the elections of 1980. The fundamentalist movement was only part of the Republican presidential landslide. Some Congressmen and Senators are now in or out of office as a result of the Protestants Rightists, but not so many as the Rightists had envisioned. Moreover, since the social issues that the New Right champions have taken a back seat to fiscal and defense issues, elected officials will undoubtedly have to make compromises on the social front to garner support for more urgent causes.

By definition the New Christian Right does not favor compromise; it feels snubbed. As the Rev. James Robison, a well-known New Right preacher, has said, being a prophet is not a way to gain popularity; prophets do not negotiate or compromise. Nevertheless, the movement has some power on the federal level.

In linkage with more moderate Catholic, evangelical, and Jewish groups, and in cooperation with many moderate Protestants who find them otherwise too distasteful for alliance, the New Christian Right will be a force for federal legislation or constitutional amendments limiting or prohibiting abortions. It may succeed in making "school prayer" more widely licit, thanks to national legislation. But for the most part the interests of the New Christian Right, which the Administration and the media condense into "social programs," are secondary public policy concerns.

New Right groups are likely to take out their frustration on the local level; and state leaders of the Moral Majority have already made their early moves. In hundreds if not thousands of school boards, library boards, or on main streets where they can protest X-rated films and adult bookstores—anywhere where a few score dedicated people can conquer the apathetic—they will fight their chosen battles and win some.

The movement is likely to fragment. The election served temporarily to unite leaders like Jerry Falwell, James Robison, and lesser lights, as it did when 15,000 chiefly clerical fundamentalists gathered in Texas in the summer of 1980. But the heads of various empires like Falwell and Robison also have to compete, and as rivals in the coalition who are working the same mailing lists for funds, they have competitive interests, clienteles, and egos. Some are total hardliners and others combine self-interest with vision to broaden their appeals, at the cost of some compromise.

Even before the election, major evangelical moderates like Billy Graham and theologian Carl Henry, politicians like Senator Mark Hatfield and Minnesota Governor Albert Quie, and charismatic television talk show hosts like Pat Robertson and Jim Bakker dissociated themselves from the New Christian Right.

As the New Christian Right, in Weberian terms, "routinizes its charisma," bureaucratizes itself, and becomes established—and the appearance of Reverend Jerry Falwell at the 1981 Congressional Prayer Breakfast symbolized his tilt toward establishmentarianism—its leaders seem more moderate, more willing to compromise.

The danegeld in pluralist America is simply too abundant for most would-be national leaders to shun. "Aw, shucks, you think Falwell is bad? He is really rather moderate. You ought to see Reverend. . . ." And the Falwells are finding that Jews and Catholics are not as bad as the movement once thought or as bad as they were portrayed when the movement was young. The leaders cannot go so far as to say good things about liberals or humanists without abandoning their ideology or losing their clientele, but they will seek other alliances.

The New Christian Right is the latest in the string of ethnic and interest group complexes in recent America. Many of these began as "single-issue" and "chosen minority people" causes. But then some blacks, Native Americans, women, ethnics, lower-class WASPS, left-over radicals, and others found that they needed allies, that they had misrepresented the opposition, and that some of the original fires of fury had died down. So they began to coalesce. The New Christian Right may do something like that by participating in some moral-action causes with people who do not share their whole outlook.

Will the New Christian Right have a bearing on ethical and moral issues, and on the way in which they are discussed? After only a year of visibility, it is clear that the Right has already established its profile in public affairs. In a republic that was founded on a belief in reasoned discourse and in which citizens seek some common grounding in shared assumptions or consensus, the Right has announced that it is not in pursuit of either. It has assumed a purely prophetic stance.

The New Christian Right has made it clear that it is not interested in discerning the wisdom in the Enlightenment tradition or philosophical principles like natural law, though from time to time fundamentalists will appeal to these general bases if they seem to square with their interpretation of the Bible. For the rest, human learning is dismissed as just that—human learning—of no significance in the Kingdom of Righteousness.

Spokesmen make strong appeals to absolutes, as revealed in the authoritative word of God. References to philosophy are usually negative, for God chose the foolish of the world to confound the wise. There are no moral dilemmas, since there is only one moral stance. Ethics as a study of good and evil is irrelevant, since there is nothing to study—only the good to emulate and the evil to cast out.

Many outsiders, offended by the New Christian Right's exclusivism and its arrogant-sounding identification of its claims with the Word of God, hope that in the course of time its members will find more elements of that Word of God in their cherished Bible. The Bible *does* have something to say against pornography and obscenity and *may* have something, however ambiguous, to say about the rights of homosexuals and fetuses. The scriptures clearly do have much to say about the misuse of wealth, the alliance between the powerful against the poor, the distribution of resources, stewardship of the earth, and the cause of peace.

Should the vast majority of evangelicals, pentecostalists, and even fundamentalists who are not members of the New Christian Right continue to discover the biblical accents that impel justice and freedom, and should they be joined by more open-minded members of the Right's second generation, it would be folly, would it not, for others to write them off? To lump together all Protestant conservatives and to consign them forever to the place their leaders first chose, outside the circle of civil discourse and public argument, would be as unfair as it would be unwise.

Chapter 33

John L. Kater, Jr.

Sexual Morality, the Family, and the Christian Right

It should come as no surprise that the Christian Right's image of the family rests not on a historical perspective or a critical reading of the scriptures but represents rather the personal side of its ideology of power. The Moral Majority and the women's movement agree on one point: the issue at stake is indeed power—power and weakness experienced within the context of marriage and the American family. The New Right claims that the relationship between the sexes in which the husband holds power on behalf of his weaker and more vulnerable wife is supported by an appeal to American tradition and also to the Bible.

FAMILY STRUCTURES

Historians tell us that the family structure as the New Right envisions it is in fact a relatively recent development, which came into its own only with the advent of the Industrial Revolution and the urbanization of America. In the early days of this country, work was carried on primarily in the home, on the family farm, or in small business or craft enterprises which were located in or near the family living quarters. This was the context for work which Thomas Jefferson considered to be the dominant, and appropriate, means of livelihood for Americans, and it is the form on which the theory of *laissez-faire* economics was built. In such a setting, women were an integral, and necessary, part of the work force. The family depended for its survival upon the wife's constant and productive labor, whether in the home or in the fields:

> She was an artisan as she spun and wove cloth from wool, flax, or cotton, and then made clothing for her family. She knew how to preserve vegetables, meat, and fruits as well as make candles or soap. She may have been an herbalist or a midwife. Depending upon where she lived, she may also have taken care of livestock, worked in the fields, or hunted and trapped. Though she was likely to bear a child every two years for twenty years, the upbringing of the chidren was not solely her responsibility. Mothers trained daughters and fathers trained sons

into the interlocking household where all essential goods were produced. No household member worked for a wage.[1]

Alice Kessler-Harris's work reminds us that the model of the family as preached by the Christian Right stems from the division of labor which took place when men began leaving the home in large numbers to earn their livelihood. This radical social change of a century ago redefined work to mean "work for which wages are paid," while the labor of women shifted from "coproduction" to that of maintaining and sustaining the household.

Among middle-class Americans of the nineteenth century, the image of women as homemakers and guardians of family morality became an ideal, both for themselves and for those families striving for upward mobility and "respectability." Survival on a husband's income became a sign of affluence, and the ability to maintain his family on his earnings alone was a test of masculine responsibility. "Since women 'belonged' in the home, those who worked were relegated to unskilled and low paying jobs on the theory that they were preparing for married life or supplementing a husband's income."[2]

One side effect of this model of the family was to overlook or undervalue the work of women in the home. As Kessler-Harris comments:

> To describe women's household work as merely auxiliary to paid work in the labor force, or to talk about some women as "not working," ignores both the value of housework in sustaining the labor force and its relationship to the wage-working lives of women. Wage work and household work are two sides of the same coin.[3]

The family as the New Right describes it is *not* the "traditional" model of the American family. It is a model related to a particular time in history and one social class, and accepts that middle-class ideal as the absolute standard of respectability and propriety. It is in fact only one among many possible models of family life, and the New Right's insistence on its validity is related to the pervasive ambiguity about power which colors its ideology.

The middle-class image of the family in the form in which the New Right describes it provides a setting where both men and women can be certain about power. For men who experience powerlessness in most of the areas of their life, such a model of the family creates an island where they are in control. Yet even its most ardent defenders sometimes seem uncertain whether their image is actually based on the reality of the nature of men and women or on concerns about status and power. Consider these words of Richard Viguerie: "Our family was thrifty. No money was ever wasted. My mother worked in a paper mill during World War II, doing a man's work. I suspect she actually did the work of several men."[4]

Describing the beginning of his career, he writes:

> It was particularly hard for my wife, Elaine, in our early years. She not only took care of our two small children, but she handled most of all the duties normally handled by the husband, such as repairs to the house and car, yard work, paying bills, etc. This allowed me to spend as many as four hours a day studying direct mail in addition to holding down a full time job.[5]

Both Viguerie and other New Right leaders such as Jerry Falwell applaud the work of Phyllis Schlafly, who chairs the national Stop the ERA movement. In Viguerie's words:

She is also president of Eagle Forum, a national organization of conservative women, author of nine books, syndicated columnist, former CBS radio commentator, wife and mother of six children, an attorney, a debater without equal—the heart and soul of a woman's movement which believes in family, God, and country.[6]

It is difficult indeed to reconcile these testimonies to the energies and stamina of women with the New Right's ideology that they are weak and must be sheltered in the home. We can find a hint of impropriety about a woman "doing a man's work" in Viguerie's comments, but certainly no evidence for his ideology. The values the New Right affirms are the product of convention and status anxieties rather than any ultimate truth about women and men.

DISASTROUS CONSEQUENCES

Some scholars argue that in fact the model of the family which emerged in the nineteenth century and which the Moral Majority defends with such vigor has had disastrous consequences for both men and women. Carolyn Heilbrun suggests that asserting that men are stronger than women forces men to deny their vulnerability and allows women to exercise their will only through secret manipulation. Such dependence denies women an authentic identity of their own. One female opponent of the Equal Rights Amendment remarked, "I don't care to be a person,"[7] prompting Heilbrun to observe that in traditionally structured families, "to be a person and a wife are oddly incompatible."[8] The truth about humankind is that "we are all of us, men and women, complex, superior one moment, frail and helpless the next."[9] By denying this fact, the male-dominated family produces "men incapable of loving, and women incapable of selfhood."[10]

Indeed, Heilbrun argues that the image of the family espoused by the New Right is in fact *responsible* for the widespread breakdown of the family because it is built upon a false understanding of the nature of men and women. She is convinced that an authentic relationship between the sexes depends upon the very intimacy and vulnerability to one another which male dominance denies:

> Marriage is now failing before our eyes, but its preservation depends upon the restructuring of the family, where "strength" and "weakness," "fragility" and "endurance" are not assigned by gender. The irony here, as in all essentially reactionary positions, is that those most interested in preserving the family in its nineteenth-century form are, in that very act, destroying its cornerstone, marriage. . . . Our present family structure produces children incapable of the very heterosexual love it has tried to inculcate. In insisting upon "mothering" as the function only of one female figure, we have made impossible the companionship of men and women.[11]

It should by now be clear that the old family structure is not only crumbling, but where it persists, it is, in fact, making *more* likely the very conditions that the defenders of conventional family life must deplore: homosexuality, divorce, and casual sex.[12]

BIBLICAL NORMS

The Christian Right replies to critiques like Heilbrun's by arguing that its model of the family is based on scriptural norms. Paul's letter to the Ephesians directs:

Wives, be subject to your husbands, as to the Lord. For the husband is the head of the wife as Christ is the head of the church, his body, and is himself its savior. As the church is subject to Christ, so let wives also be subject in everything to their husbands. Husbands, love your wives, as Christ loved the church and gave himself up for her. . . . Even so husbands should love their wives as their own bodies. He who loves his wife loves himself. . . . Children, obey your parents in the Lord, for this is right. "Honor your father and mother" (this is the first commandment with a promise), "that it may be well with you and that you may live long on the earth." Fathers, do not provoke your children to anger, but bring them up in the discipline and instruction of the Lord.[13]

1 Peter is equally firm:

You wives, be submissive to your husbands, so that some, though they do not obey the word, may be won without a word by the behavior of their wives, when they see your reverent and chaste behavior. Let not yours be the outward adorning with braiding of hair, decoration of gold, and wearing of robes, but let it be the hidden person of the heart with the imperishable jewel of a gentle and quiet spirit, which in God's sight is very precious. So once the holy women who hoped in God used to adorn themselves and were submissive to their husbands, as Sarah obeyed Abraham, calling him lord. And you are now her children if you do right and let nothing terrify you. Likewise, you husbands, live considerately with your wives, bestowing honor on the woman as the weaker sex, since you are joint heirs of the grace of life, in order that your prayers may not be hindered.[14]

Certainly the burden of proof is upon those of us who would argue that such advice should not be taken as the last Christian word in the relationship between the sexes.

However, if we are to take a genuinely critical approach to the ideology of the Christian Right, we must measure not only historical traditions but even specific biblical texts against the overall teaching of the scriptures *as a whole*. If we undertake to do so, we will, I believe, discover that in fact there is no single biblical ideal or teaching about marriage. Rather, we will find that there is a whole spectrum of prohibited and prescribed behavior between the sexes which changes radically over the centuries and which owes its institutional forms not to a specifically biblical point of view but to the culture in which biblical religion was being practiced.

Marriage in the early stages of Hebrew religion was not so much a private matter between husband and wife as a legal covenant between families. The Bible is nearly silent on the subject of sexual relationships between unmarried people; the Song of Solomon, which contains some of the most sublime poetry in the Old Testament, is an erotic love song between two unmarried lovers. The commandment against adultery is concerned not with the sanctity of marriage but with protecting a man's property. Wives were bought and sold like all other property, and a man's prosperity could be measured by the number of wives. Their function was primarily to ensure the survival of the family by producing sons, and marriage by no means prevented a man from keeping one or more concubines for personal pleasure, companionship, or family survival.

We find such a marriage in the story of Abraham and Sarah, ancestors of Israel: when Sarah is unable to produce a son for Abraham, she offers him her Egyptian maid in the hope that their liaison might be more fruitful. Their grandson Jacob worked for seven years to purchase Rachel from his uncle Laban, but Laban tricked Jacob into marrying her sister instead. Rachel's purchase price was another seven years of labor, at the end of which Jacob found himself in possession of both sisters, one of whom he loved, the other disdained. He also received a maid from Rachel when she became alarmed that she was barren. The Book of Numbers quotes Moses' command, presumably spoken in God's name, that after the conquest of Midian the Israelite men are to kill all the adults but to save the young girls for themselves.

Such marriage practices persisted throughout much of Israel's history. It is true that the small army of wives and concubines possessed by the kings occasionally troubled the prophets, but what they feared was the intrusion of foreign princesses into Israelite society. They were disturbed not by the *number* of royal spouses but by the possible contamination of Israel's religion by alien cults.

It can be safely assumed that when the Moral Majority speaks of defending the biblical ideal of marriage, the Old Testament model is not what they have in mind.

By Jesus' time, the custom of multiple wives had died out, but marriages remained the basic institution of society and the accepted norm of human behavior. As in earlier periods, producing "sons of the covenant" remained both a duty and a sacred privilege. Women received their status and identity through their family, first through their relationship to their father and then to their husband. Only marriage and the family provided women with a secure place in society. The plight of the widow with no family to support her was pitiable indeed (see, e.g., the Book of Ruth). It was for this reason that the custom of *levirate marriage* survived for many centuries: When a woman was widowed, it was the duty of her husband's brother to take her into his household lest she starve to death. For the same reason, divorce was a terrible fate for a woman, who was then left without any means of support except her own family. We might well interpret Jesus' hostility to divorce primarily in terms of his concern for the plight of its vicitim. Jesus' insistence that a man who has divorced his wife and married another is committing adultery is a notably profeminist position: the Jewish Law was originally concerned not with affront to a wife but with protection of a man's property.

Another hint of the tenuous position of widows in the society of the first century survives in the reminder in 1 Timothy that widows who have no families are the responsibility of the congregation.[15]

In spite of these indications that marriage is part of the accepted world we live in, it must also be said that, for the New Testament, marriage is by no means an absolute. Neither Jesus nor Paul considered the family to be as important as the Reign of God for which they were preparing. Jesus himself, to the best of our knowledge, was never married, and his relationship to his own family seems to have been less than ultimate. On one occasion, when his friends reported that his mother and brothers were looking for him, Jesus replied, "Here are my mother and my brothers! Whoever does the will of God is my brother, and sister, and mother."[16] Nor did Jesus have any hesitation in calling his disciples to abandon their families and follow him. It should be remembered that part of the challenge of his call to them was the necessity of leaving behind their wives and children: "Whosoever loves father or mother more than me is not worthy of me."[17] To a potential follower who asked for time to bury his father, Jesus spoke even more harshly: "Leave the dead to bury their own dead; but as for you, go and proclaim the kingdom of God."[18]

This somewhat casual attitude towards the family makes sense only against the apocalyptic background of the New Testament. Its authors believed that in Jesus, God's Reign had begun and would soon arrive in all its fullness, bringing the justice and *shalom* for which they had been waiting. At that time, every human institution would pass away; all would be made new. That belief seems to have colored Jesus' actions and expectations. His challenges to the social order were concrete and specific; he attacked neither the empire, nor slavery, nor the prevailing customs and mores of his time, except when they clearly violated God's demand for justice. There was neither the means nor the need to make a revolution; everything was about to be transformed.

In his behavior towards women, however, Jesus did contradict the social norms of his own day and culture by assuring them of their dignity and worth and their place in the City of God. Many of his encounters make the point. We have already noted, for example, the attention to the well-being of women in his teaching about divorce. His conversation with a Samaritan woman shocked her as much as his friends; drinking from her vessel as he did violated the ritual law in favor of a gesture of respect and compassion. Jesus' friendship with Mary and Martha and his willingness to talk religion with them demonstrates an attitude of sexual equality unknown in his generation. Perhaps most importantly, he appeared to a group of women on Easter morning even before the Twelve saw him, although women were considered too unreliable to serve as witnesses in Jewish courts. Surely the point is that the Risen Christ trusted himself to their testimony even if his contemporaries did not.

The widely held assumption that they were living in the last days lies behind the social conservatism of the New Testament writers. Neither Paul nor the authors who followed him were interested in radically restructuring society to meet the demands of faith. Books like 1 Peter seemed concerned that Christians draw as little attention as possible to themselves, living quietly in confidence that very soon this world would be transformed into the eternal City of God. In the meantime, they were to behave, as far as possible, as if they were *already* citizens of God's City. The church provides them with a foretaste of what is to come.

Paul himself shared in the judgment that marriage was unimportant in view of the imminent arrival of the Reign of God. He himself never married, and seems to have considered marriage as a distraction from the work of proclaiming the Gospel. He suggested to the Christians in Corinth that it would be better to abstain from sexual relations altogether, but realized that others had more trouble than he in controlling their passions. Marriage is preferable to promiscuity (or in Paul's pithy words, "It is better to marry than to burn").[19] Dealing with a situation which may never have faced Jesus, he even suggested that a non-Christian spouse could be divorced, although he thought it preferable that the marriage continue.

When Paul troubles to spell out his theology, he insists that living as if we were already in the City of God radically changes the demands placed upon us. This is spelled out most clearly in the letter to the Galatians: "There is neither Jew nor Greek, there is neither slave nor free, there is neither male nor female; for you are all one in Christ Jesus."[20] The letter to the Christians in Galatia is a hymn in praise of the freedom into which Christ has called us. Among Christians, power has no place in any human relationship. It has been transformed by the demand for justice and mutual love.

What are we to make of this remarkable spectrum of ideas and visions of marriage and human sexuality? Perhaps the New Testament scholar Walter Wink is correct when he writes that in fact "*there is no Biblical sex ethic*. The Bible knows only a love ethic, which is constantly being brought to bear on whatever sexual mores are dominant in any given country, or culture, or period."[21] The same Book of Leviticus which prescribes death for homosexual behavior also decrees exile for a married couple who have intercourse during menstruation. The mores of the Old Testament are the product of ancient taboos connected with sexuality which far antedate Israelite religion; reactions to the customs of the people they feared; and the forms of marriage and social relationships which prevailed in the Middle East during the time of its writing. New Testament attitudes towards marriage reflect the custom of its time and the apocalyptic expectations of its writers, for whom human relationships of any kind might be a distraction.

MARRIAGE AS SACRAMENT

What this means for twentieth-century Christians is that we cannot hope to fulfill the biblical demand for justice and love by imitating the social institutions of twenty centuries ago, but are called instead to examine our own institutions and mores in the light of the City of God. Marriage is Christian not when it conforms to law, from which we have been set free, but when it becomes *sacrament*.

We believe that in the freely chosen union of man and woman, they find mutual joy, comfort in sorrow and pain, and a setting for the raising of children. More than that, however, the sacramental nature of marriage means that this union is holy: We can see something of God in it. As we come to understand more fully God's self-giving love, a love which abandons power in favor of vulnerability, Christian marriages will conform themselves to the image of God. Dominance has no place in a Christian marriage. It is replaced by service to one another.

Some scholars call the product of such a marriage based on mutual care and openness to sharing one another's pain the "symmetrical family." In such a marriage, husband and wife undertake to support one another and to share in the joy and pain of nurturing not only one another but their children.

The mutuality and sacrificial service which embody the love of God in a Christian marriage define the setting in which human dignity and justice come to their fulfillment and contradict the ideology of the Christian Right which would find God only in domination and power.

Desirable as that goal might be, however, some do not succeed in making it real for themselves. Ideological Christians on the Right have no place for them, since they are viewed as deviants from the norms imposed by God. William Barnwell, a divorced priest, observes that both homosexuals and divorced people find themselves beyond the norms not only of society but of the New Testament. He suggests, however, that the scripture indicates that like Adam and Eve when they were banished from the Garden, they will find that God will meet them where they are and assure them of dignity and protection: "God promises to help us make the best of our situation."[22]

Such theological affirmations can help the church as it finds itself on the threshold of exploring the implications of justice and dignity for those who, perhaps through no fault of their own, find that they do not conform to the ideal of permanent marriage— more than half the population of the United States by 1980. What principles can help us move beyond the ideology of the New Right to a genuinely biblical ethic based on love and justice?

Christians are right to affirm the permanence of freely chosen marriages built on mutual commitment and love which respects both wife and husband. Only such a marriage can be said to embody and reflect fully the justice of God. Such households are indeed "havens of blessing and peace," a prelude to the City of God. But is the cause of justice served by insisting that all marriages are "forever," if to do so perpetuates the violence and abuse which afflict so many households? Was not Jesus' own attitude towards divorce shaped by his concern to defend the rights of women when society had no place for single people, and might there be circumstances in our time when a similar concern might argue *for*, not *against*, divorce? Are there occasions when God's demand for justice might be better served by divorce? Is marriage excluded from the promise of forgiveness and the chance to begin over again? What exactly does it mean for a husband and wife to be "one in Christ Jesus"?

HOMOSEXUALITY

Just as the Christian Right's image of marriage fails to do justice to a critical reading of history and scripture, its attitude towards homosexuality is neither biblical nor based on a uniform reading of Christian tradition.

Almost all Old Testament scholars now agree that the so-called sin of Sodom so important to fundamentalists was not homosexuality at all, but inhospitality. Leviticus's prohibition rests on the fact that homosexual acts were popularly identified with pagan worship. Jesus never once mentions the subject. Although there are three references in Paul's epistles which might refer to homosexual behavior, the meaning of the Greek words in two of them is uncertain; the Revised Standard Version chooses words like *impurity* which seem not to have any reference to homosexuality at all. The one case where Paul does specifically condemn homosexual activity (Romans 1:26–27) has to do with *heterosexuals* who seek out relations with members of their own sex. The Bible seems never to address or consider homosexuality as a condition or orientation, focusing entirely on the acts themselves.

A critical look at Christian history indicates an ambiguous and complex attitude towards homosexuality through the centuries. John Boswell's recent study, *Christianity, Social Tolerance, and Homosexuality*, finds no evidence that the early Christians opposed homosexual behavior. Contrary to the generally accepted belief that homosexuality prevailed during the decline of the Roman Empire and contributed to its collapse, the evidence indicates that it flourished during the classical period and that as the Empire waned, both church and state moved towards an antihomosexual position, rigorously legislating matters of personal morality as Europe's urban culture declined and the church preached an increasingly ascetic form of Christianity.

When city life revived in the eleventh century, homosexuality again appeared in Europe; homosexuals "were prominent, influential, and respected at many levels of society in most of Europe, and left a permanent mark on the cultural monuments of the age, both religious and secular."[23] Between 1150 and 1350, however, attitudes again changed. In 1100, Boswell observes, even figures close to the pope could not prevent the election of a homosexual bishop; by 1300, "a single homosexual act was enough to prevent absolutely ordination to any clerical rank, to render one liable to persecution by ecclesiastical courts, or—in many places—to merit the death penalty."[24]

Boswell is uncertain why the antihomosexual passion unleashed in Europe during the Middle Ages took such a form, but notes that it occurred at a period when all minorities—Jews, other non-Christians, heretics, and those suspected of witchcraft—came under steady and virulent persecution. The sentiment in medieval Europe was less a matter of theology or reason than of prejudice and passion.

The same might be said of the Moral Majority's position. Saint Paul seems to consider homosexual behavior to be on an ethical par with anger, envy, and carousing (see Galatians 5:19ff.); Falwell places it in a category and a level of abomination all its own, and claims that it is a freely chosen state which begins with seduction and ends with addiction. "Homosexuals," he asserts, "cannot reproduce themselves, so they must recruit."[25]

Such statements contradict almost every serious study of homosexuality, which indicate that sexual orientation is not a matter of conscious choice, that it is established extremely early in life, that it can be changed only rarely, that its causes are unknown and probably multiple, that the overwhelming majority of child molestors are heterosexual, and that as many as half of all homosexuals are married, many of them also parents. The Moral Majority's image of homosexuality and its ideological stance help prevent Christians from grappling with the real issue, which is how the biblical promises of justice and love apply to people whose sexuality is oriented towards the same sex.

The Christian Right would have us believe that the marriage bond is summed up in power. Christians who search out the Bible's prophetic message find values far more important in the call for justice and the demand for love and dignity for all God's people. A God who surrendered power for love calls us to do the same. Christians are called to hold up those enduring values within every human relationship, confident that in fulfilling God's demands, we will move beyond ideology to faith.

NOTES

1. "*Women Have Always Worked: A Historical Overview* by Alice Kessler-Harris," reviewed by Olive P. Hackett, *Radical Religion*, 5 (n.d.) 28.

2. Ibid., 31.

3. Quoted ibid., 29–30.

4. Richard A. Viguerie, *The New Right: We're Ready to Lead* (Falls Church, Va., The Viguerie Co., 1984) 28.

5. Ibid., 33.

6. Ibid., 103.

7. Quoted in Carolyn G. Heilbrun, *Reinventing Womanhood* (New York, Norton, 1979), 175.

8. Ibid.

9. Ibid., 189.

10. Ibid., 196.

11. Ibid., 189.

12. Ibid., 196.

13. Ephesians 5:22–25, 6:1–4.

14. 1 Peter 3:1–7.

15. 1 Timothy 5:9–16.

16. Mark 3:34.

17. Matthew 10:34.

18. Luke 9:59–60.

19. 1 Corinthians 7:9.

20. Galatians 3:28.

21. Walter Wink, "Biblical Perspectives on Homosexuality," *Christian Century*, 96 (1979) 1085.

22. William Barnwell, "The Gays and the Divorced: Similar Scars," *Christian Century*, 95 (1978) 17.

23. John Boswell, *Christianity, Social Tolerance, and Homosexuality: Gay People in Western Europe from the Beginning of the Christian Era to the Fourteenth Century* (Chicago and London, University of Chicago Press, 1980) 334.

24. Ibid., 295.

25. Jerry Falwell, *Listen, America!* (Garden City, N.Y., Doubleday, 1980) 285.

Chapter 34

Jim Wallis

Recovering the Evangel

I am an evangelical Christian. The word "evangelical" is a good one. At least, it used to be. It has its origin in the root word "evangel" which means "good news." In fact, the word translated in the New Testament as "evangelist" is the noun from a verb which means "to announce the good news."

To be an evangelical Christian, then, means to identify oneself with the good news that Jesus preached, namely, the gospel of the kingdom of God. Christ's inaugural sermon in the little town of Nazareth made clear how, why, and to whom his message was such good news:

The Spirit of the Lord is upon me, because he has anointed me to preach good news to the poor.

He has sent me to proclaim release to the captives and recovery of sight to the blind.

To set at liberty those who are oppressed, to proclaim the acceptable year of the Lord [Luke 4:18–19].

To the Jewish masses under the yoke of Roman domination, the message was good news indeed. The ruling religious and political authorities, however, found this evangel very bad news and set themselves against Jesus right from the beginning.

Today, the greatest number of the world's people are also poor and oppressed. They too would find the evangel of Jesus to be the best news they had heard in a long time.

But is that the message heard today from our evangelical preachers? Do the affluent millions who comprise the burgeoning American evangelical movement find their identity in the promise of salvation, freedom, healing, and liberation proclaimed by Jesus at the outset of his ministry? Does the word "evangelical" conjure up the vision of a gospel that turns the social order upside down? Listening to modern evangelical proclamations leaves one with the distinct impression that the content of the message has been changed.

The image of American evangelicalism that goes out from the pulpits and over the air

First published in *Sojourners,* 10 (February 4, 1981), pp. 3–5. Used by permission.

waves is a religion for those at the top, not those at the bottom of the world system, and bears almost no resemblance to the original evangel.

It has not always been so. Evangelical movements have in England and the United States led struggles for the abolition of slavery, for economic justice, and for women's rights. Eighteenth-century English preachers and nineteenth-century American evangelists deliberately linked revivalism to social change and proclaimed a gospel that was indeed good news to the poor, the captives, and the oppressed.

However, in what sociologist David Moburg has called "the great reversal," twentieth-century evangelicalism in the United States came to thoroughly identify with the mainstream values of wealth and power. As the country became rich and fat, so did its evangelicals, who soon replaced the good news of Christ's kingdom with a personal piety that comfortably supported the status quo.

For many years now, U.S. evangelicals have implicitly endorsed a vision of America that is white, prosperous, and number one in the world. In the last few years, however, that vision has been made much more explicit and highly politicized.

Conservative political forces have successfully penetrated and recruited a large segment of evangelical Christianity by forging an ideological alliance with a new breed of evangelists: the television preachers of America's electronic church. These forces have for some time seen in the nation's growing evangelical population fertile ground for a new right-wing movement.

EVANGELICAL NATIONALISTS

The preachers and their political friends say they have just begun to harvest the crop. Their program is to "restore American morality," interpreted as strengthening the power of the American capitalist system, military establishment, and the affluent majority. These political religionists can be called *evangelical nationalists.*

Their problem is not in mixing faith and politics (biblical faith does have political meaning), but in the fact that this patriotic religion does not stand for the same things as the original evangel. If we are to evaluate every claim to Christian politics by the standard of the gospel, this evangelical nationalism is not genuinely evangelical. The long accommodation of evangelicalism to the values of American power and its recent hardening into a religious vision of zealous nationalism have all but destroyed the integrity of the term "evangelical."

Evangelicals in our day are not known as friends of the poor. Rather, evangelicals are known to have a decided preference for the successful and prosperous who see their wealth as a sign of God's favor.

Ironically, a movement which once fought to free slaves, support industrial workers, and liberate women now has a reputation for accommodating to racism, favoring business over labor, and resisting equal rights for women. In our nation's ghettoes, barrios, and unions, evangelicals are generally not regarded as allies.

Of particular danger is the way the evangelical message has served to further rather than lift the blindness of the nation. Evangelicals have helped to buttress the myths and illusions which have led the American people to believe their nation is the best, greatest, and most blessed nation on earth. With God thought to be on our side, or, rather, with our being the last line of defense against God's enemies, our cause becomes righteous and our foreign policy noble.

Specifically, the evangelical nationalists are perpetuating a theology of empire. Ours is not the old kind of imperial system with occupied colonies named after conquering heroes. Rather, our American empire is based on a complex, global system of economic and political domination which guarantees for us the largest share of benefits and goods by insuring that we have our way in the world. Our control over world events is declining, but America still leads an international economic system where 20 percent of the world's people control 80 percent of the wealth. Most modern-day evangelicals have never challenged that system but, on the contrary, have been on the side of every commercial conquest, political intervention, and military action undertaken by the United States in this century.

The "acceptable year of the Lord" Jesus came to proclaim was, many New Testament scholars suggest, a reference to the Jubilee year of the Old Testament which provided for a periodic redistribution of land and wealth along with the freeing of slaves. The Jubilee was a corrective measure aimed at our sinful human tendency toward the accumulation of wealth at the expense of the poor.

However, evangelicals today have not been the ones calling for economic redistribution. Instead, they have tended to favor tax breaks for the middle class and for big corporations, as well as increased military spending and budget balancing by cutting the amount of public resources allocated for the poor. Simplicity, stewardship, and redistribution are all biblical values no longer associated with the evangelical message.

As an evangelical, I am deeply grieved by the evangelical image presented to the public by the television preachers and their New Right allies. The super-patriotism of their movement flies in the face of the biblical vision of the people of God who know no national boundaries but live among the nations as ministers of reconciliation.

The evangelical nationalists exalt the nation at a time when America needs to be humbled. They extol the virtue of wealth and power when most of the world is poor and powerless. They call for unrestrained economic growth in a world where resources are running out and much of God's creation is ravaged by industrial exploitation. They join in the national frenzy of fear and hostility toward our adversaries and call for more military buildup in a world already on the brink of total destruction; acceptance of nuclear weapons and strategy has made evangelicals morally complicitous in a potential holocaust.

RADICAL EVANGELICALS

We must recover the evangel. The public image of evangelicalism in this country is a distortion of the best of that tradition. The evangelical nationalists offer a political vision that is a corruption of the original gospel message and the radical impulses of evangelical movements in more recent times.

Meanwhile, those in the evangelical center have become alarmed by the excesses of the evangelical nationalists. However, after serving so long as apologists for the established order and lacking any alternative social vision of their own, evangelical centrists now have nothing much to say. Their leadership has been eclipsed by the evangelical nationalists, and they will not regain it without decisively breaking away from their past conformity and embracing the social vision of the evangel.

The civil rights movement in the South was one place where the evangel was upheld in recent decades. That movement was initially led not by northern white liberals but by Bible-believing, black Christians who appealed to the Old Testament prophets and the teaching of Jesus for their inspiration and authority.

There are other evangelicals in the land today. For more than a decade, a radical evangelical movement has been quietly growing that seeks to return to the original meaning of the evangel. It is an evangelical movement with strong affinity to the revivals of the eighteenth and nineteenth centuries which spawned great movements of social compassion. It is a movement in which biblical faith is transforming former class biases and where Christians are learning to view their society and their world from the bottom up instead of the top down.

Radical evangelicals are remembering the simple biblical truth that the gospel is to be good news to the poor and that the children of God are to live in the world as peacemakers.

In Christian congregations and communities around the country, a new style of evangelical faith is emerging that is a clear alternative to the evangelical nationalists and centrists. Its numbers are still small, but its circle is already substantial and is growing. The radical evangelicals have captured few headlines. Their concerns are more long-term and deeper than the pursuit of political power that always attracts the attention of secular reporters and much of the religious media.

Radical evangelicals didn't have any candidates running for election. They have been busy changing their personal lives, cutting their consumption, building community, raising families with new values, creating marriage patterns based on mutuality, learning to cope with the daily stress and tension of living and working among the poor, organizing for economic justice, working against racism, standing up for women, and speaking out for peace.

They often can be found working for subsistence salaries in housing shelters, medical clinics, daycare centers, half-way houses, food cooperatives; or struggling within larger institutions to challenge vested economic interests and unresponsive political policies. Together they are seeking to forge a new shape for the church's life.

It would be a great tragedy to allow a militant religious nationalism to change the meaning of the evangelical tradition. Rather, we must stand in that tradition and build a confessional movement in this country that testifies to the presence of the kingdom of God, and in so doing, opposes the American power structure.

We long for evangelicals to once again be friends of the poor, adversaries of evil in high places, and makers of peace. We can still redeem the evangelical tradition and recover it from the corruption of right-wing ideology.

Radical evangelicals are deeply ecumenical, drawing from both Protestant and Catholic evangelical traditions and welcoming all who would proclaim and live by the evangel of Jesus.

We want to restore the true meaning of the word evangelical. Our defense of the unborn must be connected to defending the lives of enemy populations targeted for nuclear genocide. Our concern for the family must be extended to children of families who are starving because of the present way the global economic system is arranged. Our support for sexual morality must include support for women in a culture that still exploits them and refuses to grant them equality. Our criticism of welfare bureaucracies which control the poor must be linked to a radical call for economic justice. Neither "conservative" nor "liberal," we call for an evangelicalism that espouses a radical social vision rooted in the Bible's concern for the poor and for peace.

Evangelical preachers and strategists claim credit for the victory of Ronald Reagan and the conservative Congress. Whether or not their influence was decisive is less important than is their public identification with that new regime and its nationalistic vision for America's future. Their enormous support and energy expended on behalf of the political Right has now saddled them with responsibility for the results of the 1980 elections.

The evangelical nationalists will not go unchallenged. The resistance will not simply be from "godless secular humanists," as they frequently describe their opponents, but from their fellow evangelical Christians whose public dissent to their agenda is rooted firmly in the gospel that once was good news to all the afflicted.

The compelling evangelistic power of the early church, many historians agree, was due in large part to the reputation of the Christian community as a radically open, inclusive, caring and sharing fellowship where the poor and oppressed were especially welcomed.

Aristides, a non-Christian, described the Christians to the Roman emperor Hadrian in this way:

> They love one another. They never fail to help widows: they save orphans from those who would hurt them. If they have something, they give freely to the man who has nothing; if they see a stranger, they take him home, and are happy, as though he were a real brother. They don't consider themselves brothers in the usual sense, but brothers instead through the Spirit, in God.

To live in such a way is to be evangelical indeed.

Chapter 35

Paris Donehoo

The New Right and the Sin Problem

A statement made May 21, 1981, by Under Secretary of State James L. Buckley should have caused quite a stir among religionists of all stripes. But for the most part, it was either ignored by the media or lost in the shuffle of the day's news.

Speaking before the Aerospace Industries Association in Williamsburg, Virginia, Buckley outlined the Reagan administration's decision to institute a policy of unlimited arms sales to U.S. allies. This was necessary, he said, because the Carter administration had "substituted theology" for sound military thinking.

Given recent events, such a statement seems rather strange. The Moral Majority, Religious Roundtable, and other proponents of the new religious fundamentalism have had a field day denouncing Washington for its *lack* of theology in the past. The trouble with the Carter White House and several others before it, we are told, was its blatant disregard for public policy based on biblical principles. Now that Ronald Reagan is in the saddle, the United States has a chance for a little more theology in government.

So how is one to interpret the implication by Buckley that this administration will substitute something other than theology into its policies? The answer says a great deal about this country's capacity for legitimizing its moods and desires under the cloak of religion. Jerry Falwell can enjoy phone calls from Menachem Begin and give advice to the president. But his coalition with Washington's new direction is founded upon shaky ground.

One major doctrinal pillar of fundamentalism (and of evangelicalism and Christianity in general) is belief in the sinfulness of humanity. "There is none righteous, no, not one." "All our righteousness are as filthy rags." "For all have sinned and come short of the glory of God." It is our sinfulness that prompted Jesus' death on the cross. Without him, humanity is a goner.

The doctrine is stated in a variety of styles. The old-time gospel preacher rebukes his parishioners about the darkness of their hearts, the sinfulness of their souls, the one-way ticket to hell they are about to cash in. Take away the doctrine of sin and you have shaved a good twenty minutes off most sermons.

The more sophisticated young people explain Law Two of the "Four Spiritual Laws." Adults in three-piece suits point out Romans 3:23 to strangers on an airplane. But whatever the packaging, there is universal agreement on this truth. Indeed, almost all theological fronts accept some formulation of it. We all know something is inherently wrong with humanity.

First published in *The Other Side,* 137 (February 1983), pp. 30–31. Reprinted with permission from *The Other Side,* 300 W. Apsley St., Philadelphia, Pa. 19144.

It is fascinating, therefore, to find fundamentalism embracing so many of the political theories of the era. Upon close examination, it becomes clear that Washington's new wave takes much for granted in the arena of human nature. A confident, almost naive trust in our capacity for choosing right over wrong, the best over the worst, and the sublime over the ridiculous is basic to their policies.

If people are sinful at heart, that is a pretty big assumption.

In the area of economics, for example, the fundamental tenet of the Reagan administration is that a market with little or no government interference will be fair and equitable for all. "I don't believe government should stand in the way of the free market," says Secretary of the Interior James Watt, "and I'm here to do what I can to make sure it doesn't." Only the limits of supply and demand are needed to build an economy which is healthy and productive.

The Reagan administration wasted no time in applying its beliefs. In only a few months, it scrapped virtually all remaining vestiges of gasoline and crude oil controls and rolled back conservation and solar research programs. The budget of the Consumer Product Safety Commission has been cut by nearly 30 percent and thirteen regional offices have been closed. Administration lobbyists are working to have it killed outright or buried in the mostly probusiness Commerce Department.

Efforts are also under way to undermine or drastically curtail the effectiveness of the Occupational Safety and Health Administration and the Federal Trade Commission. Regulations which impede the speedy testing of new drugs are under study, and the Department of the Interior is rethinking strictures on strip mining.

All of this sounds fine if you believe that people left to their own scruples will make choices for the good of others. But it is hard to swallow if you believe "there is none righteous, no, not one."

Apparently, neofundamentalists would have us presume that persons gathered in a church are selfish to the core. Gathered in the marketplace, however, they will somehow take an interest in the welfare of others. It simply doesn't add up. What's true about human nature in one place is true in another.

Of course, there is naiveté on both sides of the political and theological spectrum. If current policy denies our sinfulness, past practices have denied our common sense. Government regulations designed to save us from each other have often been taken to silly extremes.

A motel operator in the west, for example, was recently embroiled in a controversy over whether employees could take their uniforms home to launder. The workers did not mind, but the government said the motel would have to pay them extra. Such strictures do not serve the cause of justice, only manipulation.

But we need not exchange one set of misconceptions for another. Gary Trudeau, author of the "Doonesbury" comic strip, struck at the heart of the matter. One of his cartoons depicted a man praising James Watt for his probulldozer conservation policies. The man's wife asks, "Then what will keep big business from destroying the countryside and taking advantage of people?" "The goodness of our hearts," comes the reply. The wife responds, "Is that sort of like states' rights?"

If the fundamentalists won't point out such inconsistencies, maybe they would do better to start quoting Adam Smith. His classic, *The Wealth of Nations,* has become something of a badge worn proudly by those claiming camaraderie with the new administration. Smith did, of course, advocate laissez faire economics and an unfettered market, but he was not simple-minded as to the nature of humanity.

In regard to government, Smith declared:

As far as it is instituted for the security of property, it is in reality instituted for the defense of the rich against the poor or of those who have some property against those who have none at all. . . . People of the same trade seldom meet together, even for merriment and diversion, but the conversation ends in a conspiracy against the public or in some contrivance to raise prices.

Obviously, Smith knew something the Reaganites do not.

In defense spending, there is an even wider gulf. The idea seems to be that if the world community becomes an armed camp, war will then be unlikely. After all, if you know ahead of time that your enemy is likely to return your fire, you will be less eager to pull the trigger first. Thus Charles Flowerree, U.S. representative at the Geneva Disarmament Conference last year, defended the neutron bomb by reasoning, "Enhanced radiation weapons are designed not to make nuclear war more thinkable, but to make aggression less so."

The president, therefore, has embarked on a path not only to rearm our allies but also to make our military defense stronger than it's been since World War II. "The argument, if there is any," he says, "will be over which weapons to build, not whether we should forsake weaponry for treaties and agreements." Once we can match the Soviets bomb for bomb, once NATO can match the Warsaw Pact tank for tank, once El Salvador can match Libya bullet for bullet, all will be safe. At that point, everybody will have the good sense not to shoot at each other.

Again, that's pretty hard to believe if one is convinced that something is inherently wrong with us. If everybody east and west and north and south on the globe is sinful, it would be foolish to make such weapons of destruction easily accessible.

Most die-hard Moral Majority types would cringe at the thought of putting a bottle of whiskey in the hands of an alcoholic. But they have yet to bat an eye at the thought of putting automatic rifles in the hands of peasants reared on violence. Neither are they bothered with the notion of nuclear destruction at the fingertips of an American public tired of being "pushed around" by third-rate nations. It's like locking a group of ten-year-old boys in a room full of fine china and telling them, "Don't break anything."

This kind of incongruity is difficult to reconcile. No one denies the problems of translating biblical ethics into public policy. But a little uniformity is called for in those religious leaders currently shouting the loudest about how to do it. How one can be pessimistic about human nature in one set of circumstances and optimistic in another is a bit hard to figure. If that is bringing biblical standards back into government, some of us are not reading the same book.

So maybe Buckley was right. Maybe Carter did "substitute theology" for more practical thinking in his policies. But if the religious conservatives wish to be consistent with the doctrines they preach, they might start substituting a little theology into the current scene before things have gone too far.

They might learn how to apply their beliefs like former diplomat George Kennan has. In a speech in West Germany in October 1981, he pleaded with the nations of the world to prophesy to the superpowers:

For the love of God, for the love of your children and of the civilization to which you belong, cease this madness. You are mortals. You are capable of error. You have no right to hold in your hands—none of us are wise enough and strong enough to hold in our hands—destructive powers sufficient to put an end to civilized life on a great portion of our planet.

That may not get an amen at a revival meeting, but that's some pretty good theology.

Chapter 36

Mortimer Arias

Announcing the Kingdom

Discipleship as Evangelism

Jesus announced the inbreaking kingdom as a call to radical discipleship. Today we are watching a recovery of discipleship in the life of the church and in evangelistic strategy. Some years ago, Robert Coleman wrote a book entitled *The Master Plan of Evangelism*, which has become a classic manual for evangelism courses and workshops. It stresses the fact that the "master plan" of Jesus was the training of his disciples.

The "church growth school" based in Pasadena, California, has also insisted that the so-called great commission is essentially a mandate to "make disciples." It is true that the church growth understanding of discipleship evangelization may be seen as limited to a primer introduction to Christian faith, enabling the candidate to make a quick decision, but the movement has stimulated the personal work of "discipling" in place of an excessive dependence on mass evangelization.

Among evangelicals in the United States, probably the most creative and challenging movement has been the radical discipleship stream, represented by the publications *Sojourners* and *The Other Side*. This radical discipleship stream is less naive about some traditional stereotypes of evangelical piety and style of life and has been strongly critical of "cultural Christianity"—the illegitimate marriage between evangelical faith and the American way of life or American politics. Through publications and community experiments its participants have been trying to respond to the call to discipleship in the kingdom and to engage in costly discipleship evangelization both inside and outside the church.

The same is true of the extraordinary renewal of the Roman Catholic church in Latin America during the last fifteen years. At a phenomenal rate, the basic Christian communities (*comunidades de base*) have emerged, which show a wholistic type of discipleship, including common celebration, Bible study, interpersonal growth, and social engagement. It is estimated that there are 150,000 of these communities all over Latin America, 80,000 of them in Brazil alone.

DISCIPLESHIP

It is a fact of the biblical record that "disciples" is the oldest name for Christians: "It was in Antioch that the disciples were for the first time called Christians" (Acts 11:26).

First published in *Sojourners*, 12 (September 1983), pp. 17–19. Copyright © 1984 by Fortress Press. Used by permission.

In the book of Acts, the name Christians appears only twice, while disciples is used thirty times. The point is that even if we call ourselves Christians or evangelicals, we are Christians-in-the-making; we are still learning, still following. We are disciples in the kingdom, followers of Jesus on the way. In fact, "followers of the way" is the other name for Christians in the book of Acts.

To be disciples of the kingdom and to make disciples in the kingdom is what evangelization is all about. At least this was Jesus' way of evangelization in the kingdom perspective.

Jesus invented discipleship. Of course, there were teachers and disciples in the Greek schools of philosophy, and the rabbis in Israel had their own disciples of God who were taught in the Torah. But a rabbi would never call a disciple to himself; he would be sought out by the would-be-disciple, while Jesus called his disciples and challenged them to forget everything else and follow him. A disciple of the rabbi might dream of some day becoming even better, if possible, than his master; but a disciple of Jesus could never expect that some day he would be the Son of God.

Jesus discipleship is one of a kind. Juan Stam, from the Seminario Evangélico Latinoamericano of Costa Rica, has made a list of seven distinctive features of an invitation from Jesus. One of them is its life-long character: "Jesus discipleship was permanent. The invitation was for life. Consequently, nobody could expect to be graduated!"

Jesus discipleship was discipleship in the kingdom. Jesus started his proclamation of the reign of God by calling his first disciples. He called them to be with him, and he sent them "to announce the Kingdom of God" (Matthew 10:7).

Jesus discipleship was the model for kingdom-evangelization. His disciples would have a taste of the kingdom that had come in Jesus' ministry: they were going to be a sign and anticipation of the new order of God; and they were going to be witnesses of the kingdom to the end of time.

Jesus left behind two things: the message of the kingdom and a community of disciples. As George Ladd has said, Jesus left no other structure:

No separate synagogue, no special place of meeting, no fixed teachings, no new legislation . . . no organization. The one thing which bound them together was their personal relationship to Jesus and his message about the Kingdom of God.

Discipleship is in itself anticipation of the kingdom. Jesus' community of disciples was indeed an eschatological sign. As Ladd also says:

Those who accepted Jesus' message are also an eschatological fellowship in the sense that they have already experienced the kingdom: forgiveness, fellowship, commitment to God's reign.

Eduard Schweizer, New Testament professor at the University of Zurich, after almost 400 pages of careful exegesis of the Gospel of Mark in which the theme of discipleship runs as a golden thread, concludes that "discipleship is the only form in which faith can exist." Christian faith is nothing other than to follow Christ on the way of the kingdom.

This may seem an overstatement. But for those acquainted with the unforgettable little book by Dietrich Bonhoeffer, *The Cost of Discipleship*, the affirmation will be familiar. Bonhoeffer says, "Christianity without the living Christ is inevitably Christianity without discipleship, and Christianity without discipleship is always Christianity without Christ."

Werner Kelber, in his recent and most provocative study of the *The Kingdom in Mark* insists also on the intimate relationship between the kingdom and discipleship: "The enlistment of Simon, Andrew, John, and James into the service of discipleship, from the very outset accords a communal dimension to the Kingdom. In consists of people and it bids for people."

Is not this also the description of the church? The church is not the kingdom, but it is a sign of the kingdom. As such, it "consists of people and it bids for people." And what is evangelization but to bid for people? Kingdom evangelization is people's business—it has to do with the totality of life for people.

COMMUNITY AND SOCIETY

The church, being entrusted with good news for the world, "bids for people" in its evangelization. Indifference to people, unconcern for those who do not know the good news of the reign of God, is not faithful discipleship. The church, however, doesn't bid only for souls, but for people, real people who are called to enter into the reign of God. This multidimensional reign has to do with the totality of life for people.

And the church doesn't bid for people for its own sake, just for church growth. Church growth is never the aim of the church, but the fruit of its witness to the kingdom, the outcome of its ministry to the world, the free blessing of the Lord. The book of Acts, *after* describing the quality of life and ministry of the early church, spells out God's gift of growth: "And the Lord added to their number day by day" (Acts 2:47).

Discipleship evangelization, then, means recruitment—invitation to participate in the blessings of the kingdom, to celebrate the hopes of the kingdom, and to engage in the tasks of the kingdom: discipleship in the kingdom and for the kingdom.

Here is where we need to correct our almost invincible tendency to present the gospel in terms of blessings or benefits to be received, answers to all our questions, remedy to all our evils, new life to be enjoyed, a future state to be secured, without also presenting the challenges, demands, and tasks of the kingdom. We need to remember Bonhoeffer's warning about reducing "costly discipleship" to "cheap grace."

The emergence of the basic Christian communities in the most deprived areas of Latin America during the years of major oppression and repression throws a new light on and poses a challenge to the meaning of discipleship in and for the kingdom. A *comunidad de base* is actually a discipleship community of 25 to 35 people, or sometimes up to 100 people in a neighborhood or town. Some of these grassroots Christian communities exist among urban middle classes, students, or professionals, but the great majority of them are among city workers, slum dwellers, peasants, people from small towns, river ports, or the rubber plantations in the jungle.

These people are in discipleship of the kingdom and for the kingdom. They may be destitute, but they know of God's love for them, they know of Christ's passion and resurrection, they know of the hope of the kingdom, and they are beginning to move, to walk toward the kingdom. They describe their experience of coming together—mobilizing for the life of their communities, constituting the church that is "born from the people"—as a *caminhada* (meaning a journey, in Portuguese). Great variety exists among them, but basically one can find a common element with other Christian cells throughout history: Bible study, hymn singing, catechetical instruction, fellowship, sharing of experiences and concerns.

What is remarkable, however, and not so common in other grassroots Christian groups, is the prominence of issues of community and society in general. The Bible reading is related to the surrounding reality, to the people's life and problems. The community sets the agenda of concerns: water or transport, schools or sanitary posts, eviction of peasants from the lands, police brutality, manipulation by politicians, unemployment, government indifference, corrupt authorities, and personal and family problems.

The Bible and life are not separate—they are the two books from God. The people read them both. They read their lives with the eyes of the Bible, and they read the Bible with the eyes of their lives. They can see themselves pictured in the Bible, in the persons and events of the people of God; they can discover the liberating power of God through history, both in the past and present. They can hold the promise and vision of the kingdom, and the challenge to search for justice, love, freedom, and dignity, according to God's purpose.

They do not separate "evangelization" from "social action," and perhaps most of them don't know the difference, not being used to our neat definitions and dichotomies. But they can understand that what God promises and God demands is to be done.

Evangelization in this kingdom perspective is natural and effective. It is not only verbal proclamation, but also the incarnation of the gospel in the lives of the people and the community. The Catholic bishops, who did not invent or promote these basic Christian communities, when they met in Medellín in 1968, had to recognize the evangelistic potential of this movement, saying in one of their pastoral documents:

> The basic Christian community is the first and fundamental ecclesial nucleus . . . the initial cell of the ecclesial structures, and the focus of evangelization, and it currently serves as the most important source of human advancement and development.

Evangelization and human development go together. Most of the people participating in the basic communities were already nominal, baptized Christians, but now they have become disciples. This is not numerical church growth (all of them were considered members of the church), but it is evangelization, making the gospel real and effective in their lives and their community. This is evangelization inside the church.

Even more, it is becoming the evangelization *of* the church, challenging the traditional church and its hierarchy to new understandings of the gospel. The great discovery of this century for the Latin American church has been that not only is the church evangelizing the poor but the poor are evangelizing the church. Consequently, the church can reach a new authenticity, a new credibility, to proclaim the good news of the kingdom to those outside. Only God knows the impact of a church that is able to present a new face and new life to unbelievers, agnostics, indifferents, and people of anti-Christian ideologies.

SELF AND NEIGHBOR

Bonhoeffer spoke of "costly discipleship" in his classic exposition on the Sermon on the Mount. In time, as a prisoner of Hitler—and finally executed by a firing squad—he would know by personal experience how costly it might become to be a consistent disciple in this world. Many Christians in Latin America today (as in other parts of the world) are discovering the meaning of discipleship in the kingdom and paying the price for it.

As Jesus said, the kingdom "makes violence" and "suffers violence." He told his disciples in advance that he was sending them "as sheep among wolves" (Matthew 10:16). They should have no illusions. Jesus had been hated and rejected, and the disciples should not expect different treatment. Jesus warned, "A disciple is not above his teacher" (Matthew 10:24); and "If they persecuted me, they will persecute you too; if they obeyed my message, they will obey yours too" (John 15:18–20).

Discipleship in the kingdom takes place in the world where the forces of the anti-kingdom are operating. Before the kingdom, we have to make a choice: for or against it; with the kingdom or with the anti-kingdom; with life or with the anti-life; for Christ or against him. In Jesus' words, "Anyone who is not for me is really against me; anyone who doesn't help me gather is really scattering" (Matthew 12:30).

One of the most difficult challenges for Christians today is to test the spirits, to read the signs of the times, to see clearly where the line of division between the kingdom and the anti-kingdom is passing. In Bonhoeffer's times the Confessing Church in Germany came to this point of division and confronted Nazism, while many others were silent or cooperating with it. In today's Latin America, many Christians have found the line of division and confession in the defense of human rights.

As we have seen in Jesus' evangelization of the inbreaking kingdom, the challenge of the kingdom issues a call to conversion, to give one's allegiance to the kingdom. This call to the kingdom is something that we need to discover in our present evangelization, in which conversion is focused on a purely personal and individualistic transaction between God and the soul. Certainly conversion is a most personalizing experience, when we are face to face with God and called to make the most eventful decision of our lives. Jesus' call to discipleship always began by looking at the individual—Levi at the tax-collector's counter, Zaccheus in the tree, the Samaritan woman at the well—and loving that person.

This was also the case with the rich, young ruler. Jesus called him to turn to God and God's kingdom present in him. It was an invitation to enter into a community and a movement. But while Jesus' call is personal, it is not individualistic. To turn to Christ is to turn to the kingdom, to turn to others. Jesus asked the rich, young ruler to give to the poor and then come and "follow me" (Matthew 19:21).

Salvation was declared for Zaccheus because he was ready to put his economic and social relationships in line with the kingdom.

No means for relationship with God in the New Testament exists that is not connected through the neighbor. To love God and your neighbor are the first and second commandments. You cannot love God if you do not love your sisters and brothers, because to love them is to pass from death to life (1 John 3:17–18 and 4:20). The reverse is also true: "We love because we are loved first" (1 John 4:19), and "The new commandment is to love as he loved us" (John 13:34).

No vertical reconciliation with God is possible without horizontal reconciliation with your sister or brother who has something against you. Nor is forgiveness of sins possible if you do not forgive those who sin against you. To serve "one of the least of these" is the only way to serve the King before inheriting the eternal kingdom.

CONVERSION

Conversion to Christ means conversion to our neighbor, conversion to Christ in our neighbor. We need to incorporate this idea into our call to conversion if we want to be faithful to the gospel of the kingdom and to the total witness of the Scriptures in our evangelization.

Gustavo Gutiérrez, the well-known Latin American theologian of liberation, tells us that this conversion has been a long process in the present generation of Christians in Latin America. They began unaware and unconcerned about people's living conditions, making a radical separation between the religious and the secular, this life and the next. Then they became aware of the suffering and the problems of the Latin American people and tried to respond with aid programs, applying social principles from the church. Then they moved into politics in an attempt to change the situation through legislation.

Gradually they evolved a rigorous analysis of poverty and exploitation, its sources in international and national structures, and entered a process of "radicalization." With this process came the major discovery of our generation: the "other"—the neighbor. This discovery amounted to a real conversion experience.

The fascinating thing about conversion in the kingdom is that even though it has a first moment of turning, of radical decision, of new beginning, it is also an ongoing process: the conversion of the evangelizer in the process of evangelization. We grow in understanding of the gospel the more we share it, and we learn from those with whom we want to share it.

That was precisely Peter's experience. When we speak of conversion, we think of Paul's unique experience or somebody like the jailor from Philippi. We seldom go to Peter for a conversion sermon. The reason may be that we don't know exactly when he was converted—he had so many conversion experiences.

The first event was Peter's entrance into discipleship through his brother Andrew (John 1:40–42). The second conversion was his awareness of being a sinful person in the presence of Jesus' authority and power (Luke 5:1–11). He then came to his third conversion: he was illuminated to confess Jesus as Christ, the son of the living God, and to make a profession of faith before the others (Mark 8:27–30). After Peter's shameful negation of Jesus, he was rehabilitated and reinstated by the resurrected Lord as a shepherd of the sheep through his triple affirmation of love for Jesus Christ (John 21:15–19). Then he had what might be considered a fifth conversion: his experience of the Holy Spirit at Pentecost (Acts 2:4, 36–38).

Even the Pentecost experience was not enough. Peter received the visions and call to go to Cornelius's house, another spiritual crisis of conversion and growth. However, this time Peter was theologically blocked by his attitude toward the Gentile world, illustrated by the separation of clean and unclean food. He needed three visions and a visit to be persuaded to go to Cornelius's house. There he saw how the Spirit of God was already working among the non-Jews. "Now I understand," he said. "I now see how true it is that God has no favorites" (Acts 10:34).

This is the exciting thing about conversion in the kingdom and discipleship evangelization: like Peter, we are always on the way, following Jesus, witnessing to the kingdom in every imaginable situation. We are in a process of constant conversion, until the day when the kingdom will come in its fullness and "God will be all in all."

PART FIVE

RELIGION AND THE THIRD WORLD

To speak of input from the Third World is to speak not of one but of many movements, and perhaps of impulses, spasms, and even simple touches as well. That is almost self-evident when we reflect even briefly on the burden of geography and history (cultural and political) that the term "Third World" carries with it, and of the consequent variety it implies.[1] Still, we *can* recognize a fairly definite shape or pattern in the very shiftings of religious consciousness, which allows us to speak of a single contribution or impact from the Third World.

One can quite clearly discern the Third World's influence on religion in two distinct areas. The first is in the religious consciousness of Third World countries themselves. The actual alterations of course take on different textures depending on what area of the world we are discussing. And yet different themes such as contextualization, indigenization, and liberation tend to reappear in quite different regions. Peoples throughout the Third World are insisting on their autonomy, on affirming themselves and their heritages. Their determination is having important influences on religious attitudes and religious consciousness.

On a symbolic level (not to be underestimated), this may take the form of the emergence of native religious leaders and theologians. Also, new rituals and liturgies are being forged that reflect local traditions and sensibilities. On the more abstract level of religious concepts, their understanding of Christianity, and indeed of other religions, is going through equally thorough reformulations.

In Western nations such as the United States, the emergence of Third World cultures has also had an important influence. Insofar as their reflections have been significantly political, the international standing of the United States has inevitably become an issue. This in turn has motivated many Americans to rethink what political responsibilities are implied by their faith. Other Westerners have found Third World religious life and statements instructive in another way: as a model of what Christian practice can and should be, as a return to a more authentic and integrated form of Christianity. Thus, in the pages following, Fred Morris, Henri Nouwen, and Philip Berryman offer reflections on Latin American Christianity, as well as on its sometimes very painful social realities. Significantly, each of these writers has spent a fairly sizable length of time in Latin America. In contrast, we have another North American, Monika Hellwig, giving a much needed academic summary of liberation theology and its intellectual credentials.

In the chapters that follow, representatives appear from Latin America, Africa, and Asia, but they do not appear in equal numbers. The greater emphasis placed on Latin America in no way implies a theological priority; what it probably does reflect is the somewhat greater *awareness* in the United States of currents emerging from that continent. And this can be explained at least partly on geographical grounds. Latin America is closer, and American missionaries have been very active there. There is also the factor that Latin America is the initial source of liberation theology, the first great attempt by the Third World to develop a truly indigenous political theology. Religious men and women in South Africa, the Philippines, South Korea, and Indonesia, among other areas, have pondered over Latin American liberation theology. They have accepted and modified it, and indeed, in some cases, rejected parts of it.

What, then, are the dominant religious strains currently emerging from these three areas of the world? It has been suggested that each of these regions—Latin America, Africa, and Asia—is assisting the West to understand a different dimension of Christianity. In this interpretation, Latin America has concentrated on faith as liberating, Africa upon incarnation, and Asia on revelation. Without suggesting that these concerns are exclusive, I think it can be argued that the selections herein tend to confirm these relationships. These Latin Americans force us to ponder liberation and development; the Africans are concerned with the relationship of Christianity to culture and to political structures; the Asians lead us to meditate on the relationship between a compassionate God and a world of pain.

LATIN AMERICA

Fred Morris's account is that of a nightmare become real. Against all his expectations, he finds himself in a torture cell, in a repressive Third World regime. He is so American: innocent (or so he sees himself), friendly, naively confident that his good intentions will be reciprocated. Through his horrific experience, he deepens as a person and as a believer. So do we in reading him. His story reminds us of Jacobo Timmerman's book *Prisoner Without a Name, Cell Without a Number.* But we perhaps identify even more with Morris because he is an American.

It is the same phenomenon that made the film *Missing* so effective in bringing home the reality of struggle and pain in Latin America. We become outraged when an American is blatantly mistreated. Never mind that many thousands of Latin Americans may be undergoing much worse. The plight of the American speaks to us, and that of the Latin seems much more distant. Perhaps we should not spend too much time regretting this, but instead allow the natural movement of emotions to occur, from our understandable identification with American victims to pity for the far more numerous Latin American victims.

Ultimately, though, we must listen more attentively to the voices from Latin America, including those speaking from Christian faith. Since the mid-1960s, a story has been unfolding from that continent that may well reach epic proportions. It is an account of unimaginable suffering, but also of struggle and of hope. Without doubt, religion has played a substantial part in that story. Not only have religious men and women been thoroughly involved, but the very understanding of religion itself has been profoundly altered.

What are the concerns or emphases that characterize the new Latin American religious consciousness? I shall list four here, although there are undoubtedly more. The first is the contention that Christianity is essentially political. Hellwig is helpful here. What these Latin Americans have come to understand is that their experience is radically conflictual. Objective forces are working to thwart human aspirations. This is not to dismiss joy and harmony as experiential possibilities, but to stress only them is to ignore, more or less deliberately, the relationship between the frustration of human needs and the *causes* of that frustration. As has often been remarked, it is nothing new for the church to be political. What *is* new and indeed challenging is for it to see its political vocation, not in terms of cooperating with secular power, but in oppositional terms.

So the church must be political, but political for whom and for what? This brings us to a phrase, "preferential option for the poor," which appears over and over in liberation theology and even in such official church documents as those of Medellín and Puebla. Theology is necessarily partisan. A "neutral" stance inherently favors entrenched interests. To counteract the inevitable gravitational pull toward power, the Christian needs to consciously opt for the poor. This choice or bias does not simply involve a practical agenda. It alters one's entire perception of the gospel: of the meaning of faith, of God, of history, church, revelation, sacraments, sin.

For example, Gutiérrez, in the selection below, points out that the Bible sees sin at the root of poverty, injustice, and oppression. Sin creates serious dislocations in the world we inhabit. Nouwen shows how focusing on the sufferings of the poor alters our view of God. We see suffering as present in the very inner life of God when we identify the sufferings of the poor with those of Christ. And Berryman wisely observes that basic Christian communities seem to flourish only among the poor. The rich already have the official churches. They have no need for this new kind of Christian community, and probably do not even understand it.

This brings us to perhaps the most familiar of Latin American theological insights: the need for human liberation. It is not enough for Christians to be sympathetic to the poor. They must be fully committed to their liberation. Perhaps the best known exponent of Christian liberation is Gustavo Gutiérrez, whose path-breaking work is entitled simply *A Theology of Liberation*. In the piece included here, Gutiérrez reflects on the relationship between development and liberation. Many Latin Americans have dismissed "development" as the (uncritical) suggestion that Third World countries should simply imitate the economic and social development of industrial nations (in the face of industrial and trade policies that make such development very difficult or impossible).

Characteristically, Gutiérrez goes further. The notion of development has a positive humanistic meaning that Third World Christians ought to recover. Quoting Joseph Schumpeter, he points out that genuine development "*breaks* the circle of capitalism." It includes (negatively) a social analysis of the factors that have retarded development, and (positively) an understanding of the autonomy of the individual. Gutiérrez is able to clarify how both secular and religious traditions have contributed to the latter. On the secular side, this tradition is best exemplified by the Enlightenment, but Descartes, Hegel, Marx, and Freud ought also to be mentioned. In the Catholic tradition, papal documents such as *Populorum Progressio, Mater et Magistra,* and *Pacem in Terris* have moved with some hesitation in the same direction.

· Gutiérrez connects the ultimate meaning of development to "the need to be free from dependence," taking one's own destiny into one's own hands. The religious tradition in particular has shrunk from the conflictual implications of this, however, and so "liberation" is probably a more useful concept for Latin America today. Thus the 1968 meeting of Latin American bishops at Medellín made liberation virtually the linchpin for its set of theological statements. Gutiérrez approvingly cites Bonhoeffer for having seen that freedom is not a possession but a relationship. In Latin America, it might perhaps be described as a network of relationships. As such, it has three levels or perhaps dimensions, ranging from the aspirations of oppressed peoples to extrication from sin.

The fourth and final theme is that of the priority of praxis. This term, which can be something of a catchword, particularly in North American imitations of liberation theology, is simply the hermeneutical principle that "truth is in action," according to Hellwig. That is to say, not only should right thinking result in right living; concrete living is the necessary filter through which reality can be glimpsed and ultimately understood. Or as Jon Sobrino puts it, the principle is not a justification of action, but is itself the product of action. It is because of their identification with the victims of political and economic oppression that some Christians now have new perceptions of God and of Christ. Henri Nouwen offers a poignant example of how truth can come out of praxis in his story of the women of Jalapa, Nicaragua. Their willingness to give forgiveness to the touring Americans is not an exceptional case, but in fact reveals the genuine *meaning* of forgiveness. Just for this reason, the Americans find it difficult to grasp—and perhaps to accept.

AFRICA

The final form of an African theology is not yet clear, but we can be sure that it will bear very decisively the marks of indigenization. In the two selections reprinted here, the trend is already present. On the one hand, John Mbiti speaks for black Africa and its right to represent Christianity to itself and to the world in distinctively African forms. African Christians have a right and a duty to find their own cultural way. Some of the shapes that these forms will take are already visible. Africans are very comfortable with the language and style of the Bible; with its respect for the aged and for parents, its special place for children, its clear concern for justice, its mystical ties to the land. Africans need a worship that reflects their cultural forms and tastes, including their physicality.

In short, Africans will be living out an age-old principle of the gospel in forging a uniquely African Christianity: that the gospel enters into and traverses culture. It does not consecrate the impurities to be found in any given culture, but neither does it keep itself aloof from culture. Because the gospel is meant for human ears and hearts, it enters into culture, yet precisely for that reason does not absolutize it or remove it from criticism.

Alan Boesak's letter to the South African minister of justice is reminiscent of Martin Luther King's letter from a Birmingham jail. Yet this document is unmistakably African. It is also thoroughly Reformed. The spirit of Reformed Christianity, says Boesak, is not to "stay out of the politics," but to obey God and to obey the state when truly representative of God. Boesak has many of the sensibilities one finds in the Latin American liberation theologians, including the perception of the disadvantaged as being at the center of God's loving plan. They, not civil authority, are the criterion by which Christians are to be guided in determining what are their social responsibilities. What *is* peculiarly South African is the institution of apartheid. Christians must make clear the nature of this institution: as opposed to the law of God and sinful.

ASIA

Asian religious writers, too, are increasingly concerned with themes of justice. The Greek Orthodox Metropolitan Ostathios sees the kingdom of God as a new kind of social order that transcends human divisions. The kingdom itself is the gift of the Trinity. The point of view here is quite different from that of the liberation theologians who consistently see theology as rising up from below. This Orthodox churchman moves from the vision of the Trinity as egalitarian (as only love can make equal) and overflowingly rich, to a world that ought to reflect its divine calling, thus overcoming a one-sided distribution of goods. In this scenario, every sect and every political division need repent: capitalist for being individualistic; communist for being atheistic and materialistic; developed nations for being guided only by self-interest; developing nations for yielding to idleness and jealousy.[2]

What perhaps emerges most powerfully from the two final theologians is the awareness of human pain, more than offset by a compassionate God. In this passage from *Waterbuffalo Theology,* Kosuke Koyama sees much of Asian history as bearing pain. The Portuguese commander Albuquerque came to Malacca bringing guns, and turned them against Asians. Along with the guns, however, Koyama sees "ointment." Westerners brought with them the sense that history could change and even change for the better. There is an amazing forbearance in Koyama; a willingness to give more than his due to the Western usurper and colonizer. Perhaps part of the reason for this is his wise perception that Asia too has had its history of guns and ointment. The key is to mingle these two ointments together to avoid the "impatient" history of the West.

Choan-Seng Song continues this line of thought in his meditation on the relationship of Christian and Asian spirituality. Both spiritualities have struggled to penetrate the darkness surrounding "the Heart of Being," but each has done so in its own distinctive fashion. A specific example of how each has gone about it can perhaps be seen in Kazo Kitamori's "theology of pain." Song sees Kitamori as ultimately isolating his pain to an excessive degree by locating it within God. It seems to me that there is an alternative explanation. Seeing pain as the very "essence of God" may be not to absolutize it, but to allow room for it to be expressed, to give it a name—and thereby to affirm the human potential for transcending it. In Asia, where there has been far too much pain, it may well be that a theology is being developed that will make somewhat more comprehensible this universal phenomenon.

NOTES

1. I have no desire to become ensnared in debates concerning the exact ambit of the term "Third Word." For my purposes, it will designate those countries that belong neither to the developed industrial world of the North Atlantic, nor to the sphere of the socialist countries allied with the Soviet Union. Thus I understand it as applying especially to Asia (excluding Japan), Africa, and Latin America, and to be roughly equivalent to "less developed" or "developing."

2. I have difficulty with the term "idleness," but if one substitutes "despair," one can recognize similar paralyzing effects.

Chapter 37

Fred B. Morris

In the Presence of Mine Enemies

Faith and Torture in Brazil

It was by the merest chance that I happened to run into my friend Luis Soares de Lima, as I then thought his name was, that Monday morning last year [1974]. I had gone to the factory at seven o'clock, as usual. Then about nine o'clock, I got into my car and started toward Recife, about twenty minutes away, where I planned to make some calls from my apartment, as the company telephone was out of order. Luis was walking along the side of the road toward the factory. I honked and stopped, and he came over and got into the car.

Luis was a very close friend who, at the end of 1973, had moved to João Pessoa, about 120 miles away. Now I saw him only occasionally, when he returned to Recife to visit his girl friend. We talked about her as we drove to my house, and he inquired about Tereza, my fiancée. At the apartment I made four calls; then, at exactly 10 A.M., I looked at my watch and told Luis I had to be at the Bank of Brazil in ten minutes and must leave. He said he would get off on the way and do some errands and then come back for lunch about 12:30.

We went down the stairs, still talking about our girls. As we left the building, I noticed a well-dressed bearded man entering. I nodded to him and proceeded on out to my car. I had just opened the door when the bearded man rushed up behind Luis and pointed a revolver at his back, yelling something I couldn't understand. At the same instant, I became aware of being surrounded by three men armed with machine guns. I looked at Luis. It was now our turn.

Sometimes, late at night over a beer, Luis and I had talked about the friends and many others who had been imprisoned and tortured by the Brazilian army and its secret police apparatus. Luis once told me of a man he knew of who had died under torture rather than betray his friends. How can that be? I asked. How can anyone resist pain like that? And why?

These conversations began in the hurt we felt over imprisoned friends, in our anger and frustration over a military dictatorship that had terrorized and exploited the people

---

Published in *Harper's*, 251 (October 1975), pp. 57–60. Copyright © 1975 by Harper's Magazine.

of Brazil for ten years. We also wondered about ourselves, as I suppose every man wonders on thinking of such things. How would *I* bear up if they came for me? How would *I* do under torture? Yet such questions were for me quite academic. I was an American, and if the army should become unhappy with me for any reason—and in Brazil since 1964 it could be *any* reason—the worst possibility was that I would be deported.

The army had been interested in me for several months, ever since the June 24 issue of *Time* appeared with a story about Dom Helder Camara, the archbishop of Olinda and Recife. I was *Time*'s stringer in Recife, and so they assumed (erroneously, as it happened) that the story was mine. I had been called in for questioning in July, by Colonel Meziat, head of Fourth Army Intelligence in Recife. Three times I sat in his office, answering questions about my relations with Dom Helder, *Time,* the Associated Press (for which I was also a stringer). Though cold enough at first, Colonel Meziat became quite *simpático,* and at the end said that if I avoided communicating with the archbishop and ceased to meddle in journalism, I would have no problems with them. Well aware that this was no idle comment, I sent word to Dom Helder through a monk friend and simply stopped filing material with *Time* and the AP: I was not happy with this kind of censorship and control, but I wanted to stay in Brazil and would pay the price.

Apart from a two-year interval, I had been in Brazil since 1964, primarily as a missionary of the United Methodist Church. In 1970 I was assigned to Recife, in the northeast, to organize a community center there. In doing so I became a close friend of Dom Helder, an outspoken critic of the military regime in Brazil.

In January of 1974, nine months before my arrest, I'd taken a leave of absence from the Methodist Board of Global Ministries and gone to work in a small industrial firm in Recife, while continuing to serve the community center as a lay volunteer. Apparently, however, neither my new "civilian" status nor my promise to sever contact with Dom Helder satisfied the authorities. So it was that on September 30, 1974, they came to get me.

THE HUMMING INQUISITOR

The cell was small and not quite rectangular. It was about seven feet long and four feet wide. There was no window, and the only ventilation was an opening at the bottom of the door for the passing of food trays. The door was made of iron bars, but a half-inch plywood panel had been placed on the outside so as to cut off any view. There was a sliding panel, at eye level, maybe four by twelve inches, that served as a kind of peephole. The roof was of clay tile, with one glass tile in the middle, giving some illumination. About seven feet off the floor, a grate of iron bars was embedded in the walls, giving a cage effect to the cell and preventing any athletic prisoner from removing the tiles and thus escaping. The walls had recently been painted a blood red for about four feet up from the floor, and then a flat white on up. The floor was of concrete tile slabs, in alternating yellow and black squares. I was naked except for my shorts.

For some reason, I wasn't afraid. I realized that I could be tortured; I could already hear Luis's voice screaming from somewhere not too far away. But the kind of fear I would have expected to feel was absent. I found myself repeating, for the first of dozens of times, the Twenty-Third Psalm. "The Lord is my shepherd; I shall not want. . . ." I felt a calm that the situation didn't warrant, but for which I was grateful. After about fifteen or twenty minutes, they came for me.

Before opening the door, they ordered me to replace the cloth hood they had put over my head immediately after my arrest. Because of the hood, I was to see my torturers only once in the days to come. Then they came in and handcuffed my hands behind my back, and with much pushing and shoving and dragging they took me down the corridor, through a door, up another short passageway, and into a room that was to be, for me, a torture chamber.

I was pushed to one end of the room and the questions began. I said immediately, "I am an American citizen. I want to see my consul." That was the first time they hit me. "Here is your consul," cried one of them, as he hit me in the abdomen.

"Where were you taking Alanir?" someone shouted. "Who," I asked, never having heard that name before. More blows. "Luis. Where were you taking Luis?" "Nowhere. I was going to the Bank of Brazil and he was going to get off on the way somewhere. He hadn't said where." Now the blow came to the groin, the first kick a bit off target, the second too accurate. I fell to the floor in agony.

"Get up, you son of a bitch," someone cried, and I was kicked in the back while on the floor. There were more questions and more blows in rapid succession, with people constantly coming in and out of the room. I could hear Luis's screams from the next door. Then a voice I was to recognize later as that of Luis Miranda Filho, a notoriously sadistic Recife policeman, said, "We've already sent a car for your fiancée. Tereza will be here soon. We'll strip her and work on her till you decide to talk." I knew they were perfectly capable of doing this, but I simply had to ignore the idea and think of something else.

There were more questions and blows. "Who are your commie friends? Why does an s.o.b. American like you come down here to subvert our country? Your own country's gone to hell. Can't even keep your President. We'll teach you!"

Then it all stopped, and I heard the man who was to be my principal interrogator in the days ahead humming to himself. Water ran into a bucket, then splashed at my feet. Still humming cheerily to himself, the man walked to the other end of the room and returned with a wire, which he proceeded to fasten to the second toe of my right foot. Knowing what this was leading up to, I tried to retreat, but was harshly ordered to get back where I was. Then my interrogator returned with another electrode which he fastened to the nipple of my right breast with a spring clip that cut into the flesh. Once again, and now not at all academically, I wondered: oh God, can I stand it?

Still humming softly, my inquisitor returned to the other side of the room where I heard him pull up a chair and sit down. Then, in a very calm voice, he started the questions again. "Where were you taking Alanir?" "Nowhere," I replied. "I was going to the Bank of Brazil, and he was going to get off on the way." The first jolt was a light one, a sort of tickling and pulling at my breast. But then he increased the current and I began to jump around on the wet floor as though that might relieve the pain. I clamped my mouth shut as hard as I could, not wanting to scream and give him any satisfaction, but as the current increased, my mouth flew open with a great bellow of rage and pain. The current kept on increasing until I was thrown to the floor, doubled over in a vain attempt to diminish the pain. Then it stopped. "Get up," he yelled at me. My hands were handcuffed behind my back, and, as I slipped around trying to get up, he gave me light jolts, just to prod me on, like a steer being loaded into a truck.

As soon as I was on my feet again, the same questions were repeated, accompanied by more shocks. Again I fell to the floor, wondering how long this could go on, how long I could endure. Up again. More questions, more shocks, falling once more.

Finally the shocks stopped, and my inquisitor came near. He took the electrode from my breast, but, before I could feel any sense of relief, he began pushing down my shorts, the only clothing I had left. Oh no! I groaned to myself. This I can't bear. I know I can't.

"Nervous, huh?" he inquired. "Now we can have some real fun. And if you don't talk, we'll shock it right off you." With this he fastened the spring clip to the base of my penis and returned again to his chair.

Then the same questions and some light jolts that made me dance from side to side. I was screaming, now almost in anticipation of the shocks, when he turned up the voltage hard, provoking spasms in both legs that caused them to fly out in front of me. I fell with all my weight on my back and my hands, which were still manacled behind me. The current continued as I squirmed and wriggled on the wet floor. This must have seemed a pratfall, for the room filled with laughter from three or four men now gathered to watch the proceedings.

Then, once again, came the command to get up. This time it was harder even than before, as I had sprained my left wrist in the fall. I was now aware only of a world of agony and torment from which I could not escape, but the pain was so great and so constant that it had almost ceased to register. Perhaps, after their years of experience, they realized this. At any rate, after a few more rounds, they stopped. The electrode was removed from my penis and from my foot; then, with the usual pushing and shoving and threats, I was led back to my cell. There the handcuffs were removed from one wrist, brought around in front of my face, passed through a bar of the cell door at eye level, and refastened. Still hooded and trembling all over, I was left alone, hanging from the door of my cell. I could still hear Luis screaming as I had been.

It couldn't have been more than fifteen minutes before they came for me again. The hood was pulled down over my face and I started the short walk to the torture chamber. Once more I repeated the Shepherd's Psalm. "The Lord is my shepherd; I shall not want. . . ." And again I found myself calmed by those ancient words. I wondered for a moment how many people through the centuries have used that psalm at similar moments. I was also curiously surprised at how it helped. I knew that no one, not even God, was going to save me from the hands of these men, even if they decided to kill me. They had killed many others. But the psalm confirmed in me their limited capacity to touch me where it really mattered. It strengthened me even in the face of my weakness before them.

I was questioned with electric shock and more beatings for about another hour, then hung up again in my cell. Two or three times that afternoon, they repeated the procedure. Then I was taken into a different room. I was to sit, the handcuffs were removed, and my arms and legs were firmly strapped to the chair. One electrode was placed on my breast and the other on my right ear. These were the worst shocks of all. I felt like the top of my head was actually going to burst. I screamed, jumped in the chair, tried to break the straps, and finally, on at least two occasions, was rendered unconscious.

At one point my chief inquisitor launched off on a long and emotional tirade against Dom Helder, saying he was a shameless traitor to his country because he traveled all over the world denouncing torture in Brazil. This surreal harangue was punctuated by my screams as he turned the current on and off at random. At another point, one of my torturers got down on the floor in front of me and lifted up the hood so I could see his face and yelled, "If you don't cooperate, I'll kill you!" The face, I learned later, was that of Luis Miranda Filho, a man clearly proud of his role as a defender of Christian culture in Brazil, willing to kill for the cause. He left then, only to return shortly afterward with a Major Maia, the chief, as I later learned, of the Fourth Army torture operation. Miranda announced that they were now going to bring in Luis: they wanted me to ask him for his address. They said that he was a rotten, no-good, communist son of a bitch, and they wanted his address to round up the rest of his group. If I cooperated with them, they would let me go: if not, they would keep on torturing me until he gave in.

I recalled my late-night talks with Luis about the futility of cooperating with the enemy. Even if one talked, we reasoned then, his torturers would only demand more, and more, and more again. Better to remain silent from the outset. At the same time, I was confusedly aware that, if I adopted a determined resistance, they would conclude that I had something to hide and was really guilty. I had no desire to help them, but I didn't want to be tortured anymore. Neither did I want to hurt Luis. I didn't know if he was really involved in anything subversive. I *hoped* that he was, and if so I didn't want to cause him to betray himself. In the midst of my confusion the door opened, and I heard them dragging Luis in. He was breathing with obvious difficulty as they shoved him over to stand near me.

"Tell Fred your name," someone ordered.

There was a pause and I heard Luis take a deep breath.

"My name is Alanir Cardoso." He spoke with a defiance that startled me, but also made me proud of him. I still don't know why he had become Luis Soares de Lima, as I knew him; but I imagine that, like hundreds of others of his age, he had probably been in some sort of student troubles in 1968–69 and had had to change his identity to avoid imprisonment. He had never spoken to me of his past, and in Brazil I had learned not to ask questions. People told you what you needed to know. At that moment I was truly glad: knowing nothing, I had no secrets to tell.

"Fred," Luis (or Alanir) continued, "I'm sorry that our friendship has led to this. I really didn't think it would happen." He was interrupted by a violent body blow that I could feel sitting strapped to the chair next to him. As he fell against me, his hair brushed against my arm, and I realized that he was not hooded, though he might have been blindfolded. I wanted to reach out to him and help him.

"Fred," he started again, "I'm sorry." "I know, Luis," I said. "I understand." At this point they gave me a heavy jolt that forced another bellow from me.

"Alanir," someone said, "Fred wants you to give us your address. We know he is innocent, but we will torture him to death, if necessary, if you don't give us your address."

"Fred, do you want me to give them my address?"

"If you can," I said, rather weakly, hoping he would understand that I didn't want him to. "You know what you have to do." With that I received another violent shock and, as soon as it was over, I was struck violently on the side of the head two or three times.

"This son of a bitch isn't going to tell us," one of our tormentors said. "Give it to Fred." With that they turned on the current again, and I began my screaming. As they dragged Luis out I heard him say "I'm sorry, Fred" once more.

I was unstrapped, handcuffed again, and dragged back to be hung on my cell door. But the routine was established, and went on. Hood on head, handcuffs behind back, half-shoved, half-dragged down the corridor, repeating the Twenty-Third Psalm to myself, once more feeling an inner poise that the circumstances didn't in any way warrant, strapped to the chair again, wires in place.

Then Luis was there again. "Alanir," one of them said, "Fred wants to ask you something. He wants to know your address."

"Beg him," a voice whispered in my ear. "Beg him." With that I received a blow on the side of the head.

"Luis," I started. "How are you doing?"

"Not too badly," he replied, noticeably weaker than in our earlier encounter. "How are *you*?"

They jolted a scream from me at that point with a sudden shock of current. "I don't know, Luis. They want me to ask you to give them your address. Can you?"

"Do you want me to, Fred?" he asked.

Oh, I wished he hadn't asked that. Yes, yes, I wanted him to give it to them. "Beg him!" insisted the tempter's voice at my side. "Beg him, or we'll kill you right now!"

"If you can," I mumbled, hoping Luis would understand.

Then came another shock and another bellow from me.

"Okay," Luis said. "I'll give the address." No, don't, I cried inwardly, afraid to voice my plea.

Then began a marvelous game of delay and tease. They stopped all the rough stuff with anxious expectation, waiting for Luis to speak. But he merely repeated, "Okay, I'll give the address."

"All right, what is it?" someone yelled.

"My address is . . ." but he didn't say anything more.

"My address is . . ."

Then came another shock and a scream from me.

"Wait!" cried Luis. "I'm giving the address." Another pause. "My address is . . ."

Incredibly, I found myself laughing inside. They were so anxious to get the address that they hung on every word, but it just didn't come. "I live in a *pensão*" [boarding-house], he offered. "I live in a *pensão* downtown." Another pause. I could feel that he was trying to buy a bit more time before giving up the information. "I live in a *pensão.*"

"Where, goddamn it? Tell us now, or we're going to kill Fred." Another violent shock went through me, accompanied by my cries.

"I'm giving it. I'm in a *pensão* downtown in Recife." It must have been nearly an hour later when Luis finally gave them an address of a cheap hotel in downtown Recife. There was a scuffle as some of them rushed out, obviously to raid the hotel. Then, as Luis was being led out, he said, finally, "I gave it to them, Fred."

FANTASIES OF FREEDOM

I was unstrapped, handcuffed, and then dragged off, again to be hung on the cell door. I was to pass the rest of the night standing up, my hands shackled to the door directly in front of my eyes. My left wrist was quite swollen by now, and the handcuff was cutting into the flesh, cutting off the circulation. My body was aching all over, my head was throbbing, I was thirsty and very tired, but I had a strange feeling of exhilaration. I had made it through the day. They had done everything at least once, and I had survived. I didn't have any idea what Tuesday would bring, except probably more of the same, but I had made it through this day; I could make it through the next. For some reason, I remembered the AA dictum that one should stay sober one day at a time. Can one survive torture the same way, one day at a time?

Now I began fantasizing that they would release me. I knew that prisoners were often dumped on the street at night when the army was through with them, and, though I didn't really believe their promise to let me go after getting Luis's address, they might do it. I desperately *wanted* to believe they might. I began to think about what I would do. I conjured up the image of myself arriving at my fiancée's house, the embrace we would have, the joy I would have in reassuring her that I had survived. It was an image I was to nourish often during the days ahead.

I knelt to relieve my aching legs. Often, at intervals, I took advantage of the symbolic position and prayed. I didn't pray for deliverance; my idea of God does not include the Lone Ranger. But I gave thanks for having survived so far and prayed for strength.

A couple of hours after daylight, they came again. I was ordered to replace my hood, the door was opened, the handcuffs were removed and refastened behind my back, and I was led off for more questioning. Again I found myself affirming the psalm: "The Lord is my shepherd. . . ."

After about an hour of torture, I was returned to my cell and left hanging on the door again. I could still hear Luis. His screams were more varied now, mostly weaker, and occasionally he burst forth with a series of barkings. I couldn't imagine what horror they were practicing on him; nothing they had done to me had produced that kind of noise.

Sometime Tuesday morning I was taken to another room and seated in the armchair again, my arms and legs strapped as before. But this time no wires were attached to me. Now a new voice began, saying quietly, "Fred, how are you feeling?"

I immediately thought to myself, this must be the "good guy" of the team. I felt like laughing at the transparency of their technique, yet it was bliss to hear a pleasant voice. I had nothing to hide from them; they could get no more out of me by kindness than by force. I decided to enjoy the respite. It lasted an hour or so. The next session was with the "bad guy," as were all subsequent ones that Tuesday.

Sometime in the evening, while hung on the cell door, I was surprised by the turnkey opening the peephole and wordlessly offering me a piece of bread and a glass of water. As I had had no food or water at all since my breakfast Monday morning, I was nearly overwhelmed by the unexpected humanity of the gesture, especially as his clandestine manner suggested he was acting on his own. The jailer asked me if it was true that I was a pastor and I said it was. He shook his head in obvious confusion and closed the peephole again.

I was taken back for another hour or so of questioning and then returned to the cell, with a bathroom stop on the way. Now, however, for the first time, I was not hung on the door, but simply shoved into the cell, the handcuffs removed. There was no bedding at all, not even a blanket. I was still wearing only my shorts, but I was so tired that I'm not sure I even missed the amenities as I took off the hood and folded it for a pillow and lay down on the bare concrete and fell asleep. Once or twice during the night I awoke as someone opened the peephole to look in at me, but I was otherwise allowed to sleep through till morning.

At about 6:30 the jailer woke me by opening the peephole to ask if I wanted some bread and coffee. I did, and afterward I started off to the first of the day's encounters, affirming once again the Shepherd's Psalm. I felt much rested from the night's sleep and was hopeful that maybe we were reaching an end.

In the chamber, my hopes were dashed. Instead of being strapped to the chair, I was hung by the handcuffs from a hook high over my head and close to the wall.

My chief tormentor began by saying that they were tired of my lying and that today I was going to confess my sins one way or another. He started by asking when I had introduced Luis to Dom Helder, and, when I said never, he struck me in the middle of the back with his fist, then slapped me on the back of the head. Even though I was hooded, as always, the blow smarted and stunned me. These blows were followed by a rapid-fire series of questions and more beatings. I could hear them questioning Luis in the next room, since they apparently had left the door open. He sounded only semiconscious; his answers to their questions were only moans and grunts.

My inquisitor now produced a new (to me) gadget. He began rolling what must have been a spiked wheel over my back, scratching the skin. As I flinched, he laughed and pushed down harder, closing some sort of electric circuit and giving me a shock. This was to be the procedure: the wheel was passed back and forth, and each time I refused to answer he pressed the device down into my naked back, closing the circuit.

After what seemed like forever, he stopped and walked away, leaving me semiconscious and dangling by the handcuffs on the wall. Suddenly I felt someone coming up to me again and I braced myself for the pain. A piece of cold metal was placed on my chest and I flinched. A voice said, very quietly, "It's all right. I'm not going to hurt you." The cold metal moved to another spot and I perceived that it was a doctor's stethoscope. Apparently they wanted to check my heart to see how I was bearing up. Nothing more was said, but as soon as he finished I was taken down and returned to my cell. The day passed, periods of questioning and torture alternating with fitful rest.

A CHANGE OF CHARGES

That evening I dozed off, only to be awakened when Major Maia, chief inquisitor of the Fourth Army, opened the peephole about an inch and said, "Fred, we're beginning to have second thoughts about you. We're beginning to think maybe you're connected to official organs." "Uh," was my only response. "Yes, we know you're guilty, or we wouldn't have brought you here," he said, "but we think now you might be working for the CIA. How about it?"

"No, thank you," I said. "I've got enough trouble already." With that he shut the peephole and I lay there for a moment. Then I began to laugh to myself. They must really be confused by now, I thought. They bring me in for being a communist and want to send me out as a CIA agent. I flirted with the idea of leading them along a bit on the CIA line, to see if I didn't fare better, but I soon decided it was too risky. Moreover, if I ever got out, I didn't want to have to answer questions from the American government about having pretended to be a CIA agent. With that I drifted off to sleep.

It must have been around midnight when they came for me again. I obediently put on my hood, still warm from having served as my pillow, the handcuffs were fastened behind my back, and once more I made the thirty-yard trip to the torture chamber, to the accompaniment of the Twenty-Third Psalm. There I was made to sit down and was greeted by the major and one of his colleagues. "Fred," began the major, "to be or not to be, zat is the question." Obviously he had been practicing that little bit of English for a while. He continued in English, "Are you a communist, or are you a CIA agent?"

"Did it occur to you that I might not be either," I replied, in Portuguese. "Can you imagine that I might be just what I am, a former missionary who is trying to make an honest living in business here in Recife and who happens to have some friends that you don't like?"

"Fred, we wouldn't have brought you here if we weren't sure you are guilty. Your case was discussed and discussed before we had you brought in. I can say that we suffered much more trying to decide if we should bring you in or not than you have suffered here."

"I doubt that very much," I answered. "But if you were so sure of my guilt, then why all the questions? If you have any real evidence, which you haven't mentioned yet, why not just take me to court, rather than torturing me?"

"Look, you are here to *answer* questions, not *ask* them." He then proceeded to rehearse the string of coincidences and circumstantial evidence that they had against me, most of it based on depositions made by people I had never met who had implicated me while being tortured. My friendship with Dom Helder and with Luis, which I had never denied, were the only concrete things on the whole list. We went round and round a few more times before I was taken back to my cell and hung on the door to spend the rest of the night standing up.

That night was the worst. I began thinking once again about what I would do when and if I finally got out. Would I be allowed to stay in Brazil? What would I do if I went back to the States? It was then that I resolved to tell my story to as many people as would hear me. Afraid that I might forget the details of these days before I could set them down, I rehearsed everything verbally, from Monday morning to that moment. I went over every session of torture, remembering every word said and every barbarity practiced. I recalled my own feelings, moment by moment up to that hour. I decided to do that at least once a day until I got to a typewriter or tape recorder, even if it took months, or years. I knew that that was the only way to keep the story straight.

After a couple of hours, I had told myself the whole thing. Then I started composing, in Portuguese, a poem of protest, dedicated to my fiancée. I had never before written a poem, but I found it diverting, and even exciting, trying to tell something of myself and my beliefs to my future wife. I would compose a strophe, repeat it a dozen times so as not to forget it, and go to work on another. I was to spend many hours in the next few days on this project, composing, rearranging, polishing.

Dawn finally came, and a new jailer arrived with coffee and a piece of bread. After breakfast I was allowed to take a bath in the wretched bathroom next to my cell. This was a great relief since I was beginning to find my own smell one of the worst parts of the torture. Back in my cell I was permitted to lie down.

It must have been about 8:30 when they came again. One of my interrogators now explained that the reason I was always hooded was that I would then be unable to recognize them on the streets and so could not try to kill them. The questions continued much as they had the day before, with particular efforts being made to persuade me to confess to being a CIA agent. I was not beaten or shocked during the sessions on Thursday, and most of the time I was allowed to sit down. In the afternoon the major returned. "Fred, how do you feel? Everything okay?" he asked cheerfully. "Just great," I responded. "Never better." I don't know why I had the courage to be sarcastic, but his cheery friendliness provoked me.

"Well," he continued, "as you know, Brazil belongs to the community of nations. We have treaties with many countries, including the United States. One of those treaties gives you the right to see your consul, so of course we are going to let you do that. We are going to have you take a bath, shave, put on your clothes, and we will take you to see your consul. I just want you to remember that you are to speak only in Portuguese since we want to know what you are saying. Afterward you will be coming back here, so be careful not to exaggerate anything that has happened to you up to now."

I was standing in front of him, my head hooded, naked except for my shorts, my hands menacled behind my back. My wrists were cut and bruised, the left one sprained, I had no feeling in either hand, and my back was scratched and bruised, as were my buttocks. I had spent two of the past three nights standing up, had had only one meal of any sort in four days, had been threatened, beaten, cajoled, kicked, and shocked into unconsciousness. But at the end of his little speech I burst out laughing.

"What in hell are you laughing about? There's nothing funny about your situation."

"I'm sorry, but I just thought of a joke."

"Jesus Christ! How can you think of jokes? What is it?"

I told him I had remembered, while he was talking, the old story about President Eisenhower's visit to Moscow. The Russians, wanting to show that theirs is an open and free society in which everyone is happy, brought in a peasant from the interior, put him on TV and told him he could say anything he wanted, as the American president was there and people all over the world were watching him on TV. The peasant, thoroughly intimidated, remained silent. They insisted repeatedly that he should say anything he wanted, until finally he took courage, looked straight at the TV camera and said, "Help!"

The major was so taken aback that he had to laugh too, but immediately went on to warn me again not to say too much to the consul, as I would be coming back to my cell.

As it happened, I told the consul everything, and he, for his part, offered me the strongest assurances that the highest authorities would see to it that I be tortured no longer. He could do nothing, however, about any charges that might be brought against me, and I would of course have to return to my cell. His very presence was a welcome reminder of a world of reason and predictability, and he also brought news that my fiancée's parents had hired a lawyer for me. This was very risky for them, and I was moved to tears by the gesture.

Once again in my cell, after the interview, I was required to give up my clothes and all other symbols of so-called civilized man. Once more I found myself sitting on the floor of my cell in my shorts, wondering if that interlude of quasi reality had been only a hallucination.

It must have been about 7:30 when they sent for me again. Hooded and handcuffed, I was led off to the chamber where my principal torturer was waiting for me. In a most businesslike fashion, he told me that I was to make a formal statement about my ten and a half years in Brazil, all that I had done, my relations with Dom Helder, *Time,* and Luis. He was going to take it all down, it would then be typed, and I would be asked to sign it the next day.

It must have taken three or four hours, but at last we were done. He called the jailer to escort me back to my cell, and then he decided to go along. As we came near my cell, he said, "So you turned us all in, huh?" With that he gave me a violent kick and walked away. I confess that it didn't hurt at all; I saw how frustrated he was and realized that I was, in fact, safe from real harm at his hands.

I woke on Friday with the certainty that the worst was over, and with the hope that I would soon be released. My jailer said that all the little signals were that they were getting ready to let me go. I assumed, and he confirmed, that people were almost always released at night, so I waited impatiently for nightfall.

This was to become a pattern. Each day began with the promise that it would be my last one in prison. After my morning coffee, I would do some exercises in my cell—push-ups, sit-ups, running in place; then a bath, dressing (my clothes getting riper each day), off for a ride, head covered, through the streets of Recife for about fifteen minutes, only to return to Fourth Army Headquarters for a fifteen-minute encounter with the consul, Richard Brown, in Colonel Meziat's office. Mr. Brown would bring me news of Tereza and my friends and family, and tell me how things were going in general. He would inquire about my treatment in great detail, and, through much insistence, gradually secured the return of some of the amenities of life. (After five days I was given a mattress; in a few more I began to get edible food.) He had no word ever about my possible release.

The questioning continued, but only sporadically. Sometimes I wasn't questioned for an entire day; then I would be grilled for five or six hours at a stretch, once even all night. But each day began with the hope that it would bring an end to the nightmare, and each night saw that hope fade into the darkness.

Twice I heard someone taking a shower in the bathroom next to my cell. Thinking it might be Luis, I began singing hymns in a loud voice so he would know I was all right. The jailer confirmed my suspicion by motioning for me to be quiet. Then I heard Luis begin to sing softly a famous Brazilian protest song, *"Disparada,"* and my heart truly leapt with joy.

On Tuesday afternoon, October 15, I was officially informed that I was to be expelled from the country and was delivered over to the federal police. I was taken to my home to pack a suitcase and to sign a power of attorney over to my fiancée's father to handle my affairs in Brazil. Then I was taken to the Federal Police Headquarters, where I spent the night on the floor of an office.

Arrangements had been made for me to meet with my future father-in-law again on Wednesday morning to go over my affairs. I was also to go to the bank and get some money, and was promised an hour with my fiancée for making our plans.

However, on Wednesday morning, at 8:10, I was informed that I should get ready, as I was taking the 9 A.M. plane to Rio. In ten minutes I found myself in a station wagon racing, with siren screaming, toward the airport.

When I arrived, I saw Mr. Brown and four friends at the other end of the terminal, waiting for me. The police agents clearly didn't want me to speak to anyone, but I delayed, fussing about my suitcase until they caught up with me. Then, ignoring the mutterings and fussing of the police agents, I embraced my friends, one by one, thanking them for coming and tearfully receiving their good wishes. Then I was taken by the arm and, accompanied by Mr. Brown, was led to the waiting plane. Mr. Brown said my fiancée was on her way, but he didn't know if she would make it, as there had been an accident, and traffic was jammed up.

On the plane I was seated in the front row with an armed guard by my side. Major Maia came on board to bid me farewell, and after hesitations that I meant to be obvious, I shook his extended hand. I thanked Richard Brown profusely for all he had done for me, and he was escorted off the plane by the major.

At 8:55 I saw some commotion at the foot of the stairs leading up to the plane and saw Tereza, with Mr. Brown in tow, coming up the stairs. Without even thinking, I climbed over my startled guard and met her at the head of the stairs for what can only be described as a Hollywood embrace. With tears streaming down both our faces we hugged and kissed for about ninety seconds while being pulled into the plane where the press wouldn't see us until Tereza, having promised to follow me as soon as she could, was forcefully taken from me and off the plane. At nine o'clock, we took off for Rio where I was to pass the day in a jail cell before being placed on a Varig flight to New York, by armed guard, at 11 P.M., that evening.

(I was to discover later that Tereza, arriving late, had actually jumped over the wall separating visitors from the apron and had run out to the plane, with no authorization from anyone. When Mr. Brown saw her he ran to meet her and insisted that she be allowed to say goodbye to me.)[1]

As the plane arrived at Kennedy Airport in New York at about 8 A.M., on Thursday, October 17, the man seated next to me looked up from the Rio English-language paper he was reading, pointed to a headline saying that I was about to be expelled from the country, and said: "I wonder where that poor son of a bitch is now?" I replied: "That poor son of a bitch is me." He was shocked into total silence and only recovered in time to say "good luck" as we got off the plane.

As my passport had been given to the crew, I was escorted by a crew member straight to immigration. The immigration officer looked at my passport with the brand new rubber stamp saying "EXPULSO" covering one whole page and said, "What did you do?" "I was too friendly with the archbishop," I replied. "Well," he said, "sometimes they do strange things down there. Welcome home."

NOTE

1. Tereza was eventually allowed to leave Brazil. She and the author were married on Dec. 18, 1974, and are now living in Virginia. Since this article was written, conditions have improved noticeably in Brazil, but have remained the same or even worsened in other Latin American countries.

Chapter 38

Monika K. H. Hellwig

Liberation Theology: An Emerging School

Liberation Theology represents a movement in theology that began to shape itself clearly in Latin America in the year 1970. Five international, but predominantly Latin American, conferences of theologians and biblical scholars in that year established the basic vocabulary, the key questions, the general direction of inquiry, and some agreed assumptions concerning method.[1] These conferences, like the authors who subsequently emerged as leading spokesmen, were ecumenical but with a strong concentration of Roman Catholic scholars and churchmen.

There was, of course, an earlier history behind the conferences of 1970. Events in the secular world had been provoking a pastoral and then a theological response from the churches. The 'take-off' point in the series of secular events was the Bandung Conference of 1955 which promoted the notion of the 'Third World'. The Third World was defined to include those peoples and areas which belonged neither to the developed capitalist economy of the West nor to the communist politico-economic bloc of nations. The Third World was further defined as the 'underdeveloped' area of the world, still in need of development, beside the developed, wealthier areas. The Bandung Conference implied a kind of moral obligation on the part of the wealthier and more powerful nations to aid and stimulate this process of 'development'.

National and international secular structures were not the only ones to respond. Due in part to pressure from missionaries—and from technical experts who were consultants to missionary societies—many churches and many church-supported organisations became heavily committed to technical and development aid with personnel and with resources. In the Protestant realm the World Council of Churches and various national church bodies became involved, as did some of the Free Churches. In the Catholic realm, national hierarchies called for volunteers and funds to help in the task of development of underdeveloped nations. The term and idea of development had been mentioned rather casually once by Pius XII. It was explicitly developed early in the sixties by John XXIII's encyclical letters *Mater et magistra* and *Pacem in terris*. It was also considered in some detail in the Vatican II Constitution *Gaudium et spes,* and developed further by Paul VI's encyclical letter *Populorum progressio,* thus acquiring

---

First published in *Scottish Journal of Theology,* 30 (1979), pp. 137–51. Used by permission.

by 1967 the full weight and authority of official Catholic social teaching, closely linked to Catholic doctrinal theology.[2]

In the same decade after the Bandung Conference, however, deep disillusionment characterised the secular sequence of events, and that disillusionment was confirmed by competent economic and socio-political studies. The poor nations, or at least the poorer of the poor nations, were becoming progressively still poorer. The crumbling of traditional social, cultural, and ecological patterns was giving rise to widespread disorganisation, rootlessness, alienation, lawlessness, and disease. A general brutalisation of the conditions of human life was evident in most parts of the Third World.

Out of this disillusionment with the consequences of development efforts and development aid, arose the cry that what was needed was the *liberation of persons and peoples to be the subject of their own history* rather than the objects of someone else's history, whether benignly or selfishly conceived. Liberation was proposed as the antithesis to dependence. Development was seen as a way of shaping more coherent patterns of dependence. Dependence in this context does not mean the interdependence that is the necessary and universal condition of human life. It has a narrower meaning, probably most aptly described as 'being the object of someone else's history and therefore valued only as instrumental to someone else's destiny'.

The above statements, of course, describe conditions in Latin America at least as accurately as conditions elsewhere in the Third World. Although nominally almost entirely Roman Catholic, the Latin American continent has in fact been considered mission territory by the Catholic as well as by the Protestant Churches. Clergy and supporting personnel have been supplied largely from outside the continent, and funds raised for the missions have been pouring in. Latin America was a favorite target for development efforts by church organizations, particularly those based in the United States of America and in Germany.

With the growing cry for liberation, church leaders in Latin America were hard pressed. The local churches were being accused of complicity with oppressive regimes— certainly with a great deal of truth—and the development efforts from foreign churches were being characterised as imperialist attempts to consolidate dependence on the wealthy nations and subservience to their interests. The full brunt of the accusations fell on the lower clergy in pastoral positions among the poor, but it was quickly referred to seminary professors and university chaplains, confronted with the radical and urgent questions of the younger thinking segment of the population.

As is now well known, there was in these years in Latin America, as in France in the years that led up to the French Revolution, considerable sympathy among the lower clergy for the lot of the poor and for the protests that were being made on their behalf. Many Latin American and foreign clergy openly aligned themselves with revolutionary platforms, exposing themselves to ecclesiastical and civil penalties, in some cases even where the revolutionary cause was being carried forward by explicitly Marxist groups. The pressures mounted, therefore, for a pastoral response from the Latin American hierarchy.

This response came with unexpected intensity and coherence, within the Roman Catholic Church, at the Second General Conference of CELAM (Latin American Bishops' Conference) at Medellín, Columbia, in 1968. While concerned with the promotion of a radical and total renewal of the Church in Latin America, at all levels and in all aspects, the Medellín Conference focused on large-scale and searching questions of social justice. It called for action that would certainly demand technically competent critiques of socio-economic and political structures, and it sketched plans for very comprehensive pastoral action, as well as indicating some doctrinal bases for the stand taken by the Conference.[3]

It was in the experimental process of implementation of the Medellín conclusions that the more theoretical reflections on the pastoral dilemmas acquired sharp focus and overwhelming urgency, and became the central topic of theological conventions. Questions were being raised constantly, particularly by church-related and often theologically trained social scientists, concerning the theological correlates of the dichotomy between faith and social responsibility that was so apparent. The meetings of 1970 brought together many theologians and biblical scholars who shared this concern.

Out of the first of these meetings, held in March in Bogotá, Columbia, came two hastily produced volumes of essays,[4] all still very tentative, and a mimeographed bulletin, *Teología de la Liberación,* circulated privately in several countries to those known to be interested. (It must be remembered that in much of Latin America the publication of anything deemed critical of the government or social establishment is extremely dangerous for author, editor, publisher, printer, and distributor down to the lowliest errand boy.)

Key Catholic authors who emerged at that first meeting were Gustavo Gutiérrez, J. A. Hernández, and Gustavo Perés Ramírez, to be joined in later publications by Juan Luis Segundo, Juan Carlos Scannone, Hugo Assmann, Ronaldo Muñoz, Alex Morelli, Leonardo Boff, Segundo Galilea, Joseph Comblin, Porfirio Miranda, and others. Two general characteristics are noteworthy in these authors. Almost all studied in Europe and all are well versed in the mainstream of contemporary European Catholic and Protestant theology. All have been (and are at the time that this is being written) in good standing with the hierarchy of the Catholic Church. Most have some official duties with CELAM.

The third of the 1970 meetings, an explicitly ecumenical one held in Buenos Aires in August, brought to the fore three significant Protestant authors, Rubem Alves, Julio de Santa Ana, and Noel Olaya, whose papers were circulated in mimeograph and were reproduced in part in local church periodicals. These were joined later by José Míguez Bonino, Richard Shaull, and others whose names occur much less frequently in the literature that has grown up since then.

This cluster of theologians, Catholic and Protestant, has adopted the term 'liberation theology' to describe the common endeavours of its members, which have developed such a strong common framework for theological discussion that they may well be considered an emerging 'school' of theology. An interesting feature of their work is that they do not proceed from inspirational or provocative writings of one original figure, whose thought is subsequently developed, challenged, refined, and further elaborated. On the contrary, there is a growing convergence from multiple origins. While there are, of course, important differences in individual authors, there are certain general characteristics that may be predicated of Latin American liberation theology.

POLITICAL INTERPRETATION

In the first place, liberation theology is based on a political interpretation of the gospel, often expressed in the slogan 'history is one'.[5] This is a protest against a common assumption in Christian theology: that the history of the world, with its political structures and economic and social dispositions, is irrelevant to the Redemption, because the saving intervention of God affects only a narrow strand of history, namely the history of the Jews up to the time of Jesus and of the internal affairs of the Christian churches since the time of Jesus. For the liberation theologians the only valid use of the common term 'salvation history' is that which equates it not with the history of salvation seen as a particular strand of history, but rather with the salvation of history seen as the subverting by the power of the gospel of all those structures which are obstacles to the full human and spiritual development of the human community.

When the liberation theologians write or speak of a political interpretation of the gospel, they are using the word 'political' in the comprehensive sense in which it includes all that pertains to the building up of the city of man. They are concerned to emphasise that the Christian gospel is not, and cannot be, merely a message about the saving of individuals out of the world but a message about the saving of the world—of that tangled and sinful complex of human relations which largely determines the possibilities of becoming of the individual. In this they are more closely allied to the traditional theology (though not necessarily the spirituality) of Roman Catholicism than they are to major Protestant trends. Yet they differentiate themselves also from traditional Catholic lines by opposing all church-state alliance, all establishment of churches, all concentration of power in church officials and church structures. The role of the churches is seen, as in the 'political theology' of the German Catholic theologian J. B. Metz, as an oppositional one. The task of the churches is at all times to protest against injustice, to challenge what is inhuman (in the light of Jesus in whom the truly human is revealed), to side with the poor and the oppressed.

Liberation theology has been taken by some as a new attempt at a political ethics, and therefore as a branch of applied theology. The liberation theologians do not accept this, but claim to be working with a perspective or focus or framework for the asking of all theological questions. It is a way of approaching and formulating and answering the questions in relation to God, revelation, creation, sin, christology, soteriology, grace, sacraments, ecclesiology, and eschatology. It engages the central core of Christian credal affirmations and radically questions some commonly unquestioned assumptions in the interpretation of those credal affirmations.

When the liberation theologians claim to be engaged in a Latin American political theology, based on a political interpretation of the gospel, they do not mean that their central concern is with the government of the country, much less that their concern is to provide a theological validation for the violent overthrow of governments—a charge that has frequently been levelled against them from Europe. Their focus is on the promise and the task of redemption of the community of all human persons, called to respond to God. Seeing the close and intricate interdependence of the whole range of decisions, actions, and experiences of human persons and human societies, these theologians are asking what is the meaning of salvation in terms of the contemporary experience of the human. All their other questions follow from this.

IDENTIFICATION WITH THE OPPRESSED

A second characteristic of liberation theology is that is arises directly out of the experience of the oppressed. This is treasured as an essential component by its participants, so that no one should claim the title of liberation theologian who is not personally and concretely identified with the oppressed in their struggles for liberation, and therefore able to reflect on the experience and action in which he participates. It is a practical implementing of the theology of the cross of Christ as propounded by J.B. Metz, namely that 'the future is in the memory of suffering'.[6] It is only in the experience of the marginated, the bitterly oppressed, the vanquished and disregarded wretched of the earth, that the need of redemption and the content of redemption is sharply evident, or the urgency of redemption is revealed. The cross symbolises the need to write history 'upside down' from the perspective of the loser, in order to discern the unfinished business.

The Latin American liberation theologians claim to be reflecting on the basic theological questions from the perspective of their own participation in the awakening consciousness of oppression of their people, the nascent struggles for liberation from those facets of oppression that are recognised as such, the terrible frustration of all efforts, and the need to go back and ask the most radical questions about the content of the hope that human beings have an authentic right to cherish.

In continuity with the Medellín documents, the liberation theologians regard the task of the recollection or memory of suffering, not as something that the church does over and above its sacramental ministry and its life of prayer and faith, but rather as the center of that ministry and life. The life of prayer and faith are not seen as side by side with social concerns but as coincident with them. Theology is not found alongside concern with the causes of suffering but arises out of that concern.

CRITIQUE OF PRAXIS

The third characteristic of liberation theology arises directly from this. It is an assertion concerning the method proper to theology, namely that theology is properly the critique of the praxis of the life of the believing community.[7] Its continuity with the authentic gospel and the authentic tradition of the church (in the Catholic sense) is not primarily logical but spiritual. It is not primarily a theology that is to be handed on intact so that the Christian life of the community may result from its application. It is primarily the Christian life of faith and hope (and action appropriate to that hope) that is to be extended from person to person and from community to community. Reflection upon that praxis follows and constitutes theology, by bringing the praxis into juxtaposition with the revelatory person of Jesus the Christ, testified from the beginning and interpreted through the ages. In itself this is not such a new perspective. What makes it new is that for the liberation theologians the critique of Christian praxis requires a much closer relationship between theology and the human and social sciences than is usually acknowledged on the theological side.

The clearest and most comprehensive example of this is in the understanding of charity and justice. These are seen as having an objective as well as subjective dimension, both subject to scrutiny. The objective dimension is to be scrutinised in terms of statistical and scientific analysis of outcomes. The subjective dimension is to be judged in terms of the relationships of dependency or freedom that are created by the interaction.

This leads to some rather stringent and radical critiques of what has been understood as Christian charity—leading to the diagnosis, in particular, that the unwillingness of conventional Christian theology and preaching to acknowledge conflict as a universal condition of human history invalidates much of the explicit and implicit theology of charity, and therefore further invalidates much of the conventional theology of grace and salvation. These questions, it is claimed, must be brought into confrontation with the findings of the social sciences, because such findings are simply refined observations of human experience. If theology is the critique of the praxis of Christian life, that praxis is properly observed and critically analysed by the human and social sciences before it becomes matter for theological reflection.

Taken one step further in specificity, this involves (and explains) the close relationship of liberation theology to Marxist economic and social analysis—which usually presents either an enigma or a serious scandal to theologians from the wealthier countries of the Western world. The liberation theologians make a distinction between the acceptance of a closed Marxist ideology or 'theology' on the one hand, and a rational, critical acceptance of the Marxist analysis of the politico-economic functioning of society on the other.[8] The former is embraced with the fervour and totality of religious faith, and includes a comprehensive anthropology and ontology. The latter is a qualified acceptance based upon, and further subject to, rational scrutiny, offering an analysis of socio-economic structures but not thereby committed to a comprehensive anthropology.

The contention of the liberation theologians is that, if the Marxist economic analysis offers the most coherent and rational account of the Latin American situation at the present (a matter to be judged rationally), then a Christian is committed to use it as a tool, because charity must be efficacious, and therefore must be based on the best possible analysis of the causes of suffering and oppression.

HISTORICAL TRUTH

A fourth characteristic of liberation theology is the epistemological and hermeneutic principle that undergirds the foregoing, namely that truth is in action. This principle, as a fundamental postulate of liberation theology, is not drawn from philosophical speculation but rather from the biblical interpretation on which liberation theology rests. It is the direct correlate of an understanding of revelation and its relationship to creation. As explained by a Protestant spokesman, José Míguez Bonino,[9] it is not an assertion that pre-existent truth is to be humanly ascertained or recognised in action, but rather that the truth is constituted in actions, in fidelity, in the realisation of promises.

In other words, truth is not suprahistorical, casting its shadows in history, but is essentially historical. This is not a denial of the transcendent God. It is the assertion that the transcendent God does not communicate to us 'truths' or even 'truth' about himself or about us, that have been constituted outside history and independently of it. The transcendent God communicates himself in the constitutive experiences in which we are called into relationship with the one who calls. In those constitutive experiences it is not possible factually or chronologically to distinguish between the call and the response, between the act of the redeeming God and the act of the redeemed human person or community.

The claim that truth is in action clearly involves a certain understanding of revelation and of redemption. This is seldom spelt out explicitly by the liberation theologians, but it does seem to be an implicit understanding held in common by them. Revelation is understood as the receiving of knowledge of God and knowledge of the human person, in personal engagement of greater or lesser intensity. It is rooted in creation, in the receiving of being, and therefore is a dimension of the personal experience of every member of the human race, no matter how deprived or undeveloped.

What brings God's self-revelation to a focus or high point in such moments as Exodus, Sinai and the Paschal mystery of Christ, is the intensity of the engagement of human response in an historically constituted situation of crisis. In such moments the ever-present summons of the creating and redeeming God becomes urgent, exigent, and decisive. Such an understanding clearly requires an explicit statement on christology— what it is that makes Jesus the Christ and how the Christian claim of divinity for Jesus is to be understood. Up to this time such a statement is still lacking—a lack which several of the liberation theologians have acknowledged and lamented

Within their contention that the truth is in action, the liberation theologians do not seem to be maintaining any novel position as to the 'content' or scope of revelation. What is revealed is God himself, welcoming and exigent towards the human person, summoning and empowering the actualisation of a free human community of free human persons. The self-revelation of God in every instance has as its other aspect the revelation of the human—the self-revelation of what is human and inhuman in us.

PARTISAN THEOLOGY

The fifth general characteristic of liberation theology is its acknowledgement that all theology is necessarily partisan. Every theology arises out of the perspective of a particular experience and a particular pattern of response within the experience. There is no such thing as a general, objective, or universal perspective for theology. Taking this for granted, liberation theology asserts as a Christian axiom derived from the prophets of Israel the thesis that among the many possible perspectives, one is privileged: the perspective arising out of the experience of the most oppressed, the sufferings of the excluded and the marginated.[10]

This is in the first place a rejoinder to European and North American theologians who have been willing to write off liberation theology as 'partisan', frequently without having read much of it. Beyond this, however, it is also an understanding intimately related to other points of liberation theology: the theology of the cross as question rather than answer; the understanding of the Eucharist as focus for the Christian task in the world but not as identical with that task; the doctrine of salvation interpreted in terms of its roots in the Hebrew Scriptures; and the teaching of the imitation of Jesus the Christ reexamined in the light of Christian spirituality traditions.

Clearly, the central theological issues raised by the efforts of the liberation theologians to approach the interpretation of the Christian gospel in this way are the following. What is salvation; what is the content of Christian hope? Further, what is the relation of eschatology to history? What is the relation between creation and history, that is, between God's creation and man's creation? What has Christian hope to contribute to politics and public affairs? How does the Christian stand in relation to class struggle, conflictual situations, and violence? What is meant by Messiah-Christ? How is Jesus properly proposed for imitation? Finally, what are the implications for ecclesiology?

To date there are no systematic theologies that claim to answer, or even to discuss, all these questions. The fullest presentations available are *Theology for Artisans of a New Humanity* (5 vols.), by Juan Luis Segundo (Maryknoll, N.Y., Orbis Books, 1973–74), translated from the Spanish original published in 1968, and *A Theology of Liberation,* by Gustavo Gutiérrez (Orbis Books, 1973; London, SCM Press, 1974) translated from the Spanish original published in 1971. . . .

SALVATION

From these it is possible to attempt a synthesis of the way liberation theology interprets the salvation offered in the Christian gospel. Salvation is seen as liberation of the whole person, present and future, individual and social, not opposed to humanisation, but rather finding its proper expression in personhood and peoplehood. Moreover, this liberation is necessarily the gift of God.[11] To speak of it as gift of God, however, is not to set God's freedom and action over against, or alongside of, human freedom and action. The gift of God is given within the freedom of human persons, and can only be received by human liberating action. Salvation is understood as accessible to experience, not by feelings of emotional exhilaration or serenity, but by a transformed life experience and expression characterised by the ability for self-forgetfulness. More specifically, what is envisaged is the authentic possibility for community with others, for altruistic action on behalf of others, for the focusing of attention outside oneself because the self-consciousness rests unshakably in the love and welcome of the creating and redeeming God.

It is understood in liberation theology that persons do not make a mysterious once-for-all transition into a state of salvation, but grow progessively more confirmed in it, and that this happens through the mediation of a community of persons in whom the love and welcome of the creating and redeeming God is expressed. That mediation is seen as including the totality of life experience, the provision of sustenance, of identity, of community, of education, and goals in life—all commensurate to the demands of human freedom and to the particular situation.

This understanding of salvation clearly sees the destiny of each person as being at risk not only through that person's own decisions and actions, but also through the decisions and actions of others. It also reasserts the traditional emphasis on the continuity between grace and salvation, which means that present action appropriate to Christian hope can be searched for and found by human understanding.

Grace also is seen as accessible to human experience. Principally it is the gift which we have in the event of Jesus. That event gives understanding (based on personal experience) of what man is and what God is. It also gives power which arises out of the experience of the presence of true man and the presence of true God. Grace is mediated whenever the presence and effect of Jesus in human society is mediated, even though it be without Christian name or claim. In this, liberation theology pursues a line of thought introduced anew in our times by Karl Rahner and presently very strong in Roman Catholic theology. In the general understanding of salvation, grace, and Christian hope, the liberation theologians also follow fairly closely the positions taken by Jürgen Moltmann in the later elaborations of his 'theology of hope'.

Liberation theology has its own response to a question that has haunted the writings of Moltmann, of Wolfhart Pannenberg, and of J. B. Metz, namely the question: What is the action appropriate to Christian hope? That action is discovered continuously by reflection on praxis, specifically by attempting to discern what is true freedom and personal fulfillment. The reference point for the Christian (in this process of reflection and discernment) is the person of Jesus as known to the faith community, especially in the Paschal mystery of the death and resurrection.

Crucial criteria drawn from this reference point are: first, that true liberation (salvation) is possible for all, not only a few; secondly, that true liberation encompasses the totality of the person; thirdly, that true liberation has an external and an internal dimension (sometimes called the political and mystical dimension among the liberation theologians); and finally, that true liberation is such as to transcend death and all other possible disasters.

From the engagement in contemporary socio-political praxis, some conclusions have been drawn which are of universal pastoral and theological interest. The first conclusion is this: to work for liberation from oppressive economic and socio-political structures is to find those oppressive structures very closely linked to some conventional categories in Christian redemption theology, namely, fear of death, greed, mistrust, lack of personal integration or self-control, and fear of freedom and responsibilty. Further, the praxis of the contemporary liberation movements and the analysis of outcomes of revolutions, suggests a close continuity between means and end. In other words, actions of hatred and vengeance may lead to a take-over of power, but not to a fundamental improvement in the quality of life and of human relationships.

On the other hand the conclusion has been drawn with equal conviction that the historical situation of mankind is conflictual and therefore calls for confrontations and challenges. The historical situation of mankind is also distorted by sin, that is, by the consequences of evil deeds (those destructive actions that spring from greed, mistrust, and so forth). Though not always immediately apparent, all such sinful distortion of the human situation is violent, inasmuch as it crushes and destroys persons. In liberation theology this is often called chronic or systemic violence. The unmasking of such violence for what it is, is part of the task of redemption.

The presence of Jesus himself in history was acutely provocative because it unmasked such violence in his own time and even in other times and societies. Sinful structures, values, and actions must be challenged, but to challenge will inevitably mean to heighten the manifestation of violence, often to make chronic violence erupt in acute forms. When challenged, people will demonstrate how far they will go to protect and maintain their advantage within the existing system, perhaps shooting picketers and trade unionists, perhaps clubbing demonstrators to death and wreaking havoc on innocent populations not even involved in the issue.

If conflictual relations are the stuff of history and society is shot through with great networks of hidden violence on the one hand, while it is clear on the other hand that there is continuity between the means and the end, then a further conclusion follows. The praxis of the gospel demands a constant assessment of both action and inaction, to discern what is basically a de-escalation of violence and what is simply a further accumulation of it. In this as in most human issues there is no way to guard against all errors of judgment. To remain inactive in the public sphere is not safer or more Christian. It is simply collusion with the hidden violence in the situation. There is no political situation in history in which the Christian is not called upon to take an oppositional stance in some aspect, in some way.

The gospel is understood, therefore, as a challenge to, and source of, 'creative non-violent action', that is, action to de-escalate the violence of a given situation. This means: to discern the truth of the situation by identifying with the oppressed; to challenge injustices on the basis of human dignity and solidarity; to cope creatively with the reaction to the challenge which is never two times the same. This conviction is leading, in the literature, to its own kind of casuistry, for any act of creative non-violence, if it provides an effective challenge at all, will be seen by those challenged as violence. Moreover, the maintaining of smooth and equable relationships within a gravely unjust situation may, in the results it effects, be the most violent action of all. Hence there is an acute need for criteria for discernment as to how possible actions are to be ranked.

Because of its tough and immediate engagement with difficult questions to be asked today in the public realm, liberation theology appears to be at the 'cutting edge' of theological endeavour. It does not yet have a fully developed systematic, but it appears to have a promising framework for shaping a systematic that is resilient enough to deal with new and unpredictable questions. It also has the merit of relating speculative theology very closely to church life and to the solving of contemporary dilemmas.

NOTES

1. They were the predominantly Catholic, supranational, theological conferences in Bogotá in March and July; a biblical scholars' conference in Buenos Aires in July; an ecumenical pastoral and

theological congress in Buenos Aires in August; and an intercontinental, ecumenical conference in Mexico City in October. What was particularly significant about these conferences was the wide dissemination of the papers that were read, and the immediate widespread interest these papers aroused.

2. The evolution of thought in these official statements is traced and documented with great care in *Liberation, Development, and Salvation,* by René Laurentin (Maryknoll, N.Y., Orbis, 1972), chap. 7. The English edition is a revised version of the original French work, *Développement et Salut,* first published in 1969.

3. All available in *Medellín: Conclusiones,* published by CELAM (Bogotá, 1971), in paperback; now also available in English and French.

4. Gustavo Gutiérrez et al., *Liberación, Opción de la Iglesia en la decada del 70* (Bogotá, Presencia, 1970), and J. A. Hernández et al., *Aportes para la Liberación* (Presencia, 1970). They are no longer easily available, but the papers are quoted *in extenso* in Hugo Assmann, *Opresión-Liberación* (Montevideo, Biblioteca Mayor, 1971).

5. A clear explanation is given in Gustavo Gutiérrez, *A Theology of Liberation* (Maryknoll, N.Y., Orbis, 1973; London SCM, 1974).

6. 'The Future in the Memory of Suffering', in *Church and World: The God Question (Concilium, 8/6)* (New York, Herder, 1972).

7. Perhaps most clearly explained by Gutiérrez in his 'Liberation, Theology, and Proclamation,' in Claude Geffré and G. Gutiérrez, eds., *The Mystical and Political Dimensions of the Christian Faith (Concilium, 6/10)* (New York, Herder, 1973).

8. Explicitly, the distinction is most clearly made by José Míguez Bonino, *Doing Theology in a Revolutionary Situation* (Philadelphia, Fortress, 1975) *(Revolutionary Theology Comes of Age* [London, SPCK, 1975]), chap. 5.

9. Ibid.

10. See Gutiérrez, *A Theology,* p. 59, for a brief, clear exposition and footnote listing Spanish texts relevant to the question.

11. For the formulation of a definition of salvation as here given, I am indebted to an unpublished paper by Dr. Leroy Friezen, working in the occupied West Bank territory of the Holy Land for the Mennonite Central Committee.

Chapter 39

Gustavo Gutiérrez

Liberation and Development

THE CONCEPT OF DEVELOPMENT

The term *development* seems tentatively to have synthesized the aspirations of people today for more human living conditions. The term itself is not new, but its current usage in the social sciences is new, for it responds to a different set of issues which has emerged only recently. Indeed, the old wealth-poverty antinomy no longer expresses all the problems and contemporary aspirations of mankind.

Origin

For some, the origin of the term *development* is, in a sense, negative. They consider it to have appeared in opposition to the term *underdevelopment*, which expressed the situation—and anguish—of the poor countries compared with the rich countries.[1]

It would perhaps be helpful to recall some of the more important trends which helped clarify the concept of development.

First of all, there is the work of Joseph A. Schumpeter,[2] the first economist after the English classics and Marx to concern himself with long-term processes. Schumpeter studied a capitalism characterized by a "circular flow," that is, a system which repeats itself from one period to the next and does not suffer appreciable structural change. The element which breaks this equilibrium and introduces a new dynamism is an *innovation*. Innovations are on the one hand technico-economic, since they are supposed to have originated in these areas; but they are simultaneously politico-social, because they imply contradicting and overcoming the prevailing system. Schumpeter calls this process *Entwicklung*, which today is translated as "development," although earlier renderings were "evolution"[3] or "unfolding."[4]

The work of the Australian economist Colin Clark represents another important contribution.[5] Clark affirms that the objective of economic activity is not wealth, but well-being, a term understood to mean the satisfaction derived from the resources at one's disposal. He proposes to measure well-being by making comparisons in time and space. The differences among countries are shown by various indicators. His calculations show that the highest levels of well-being are found in the industrialized countries.

Excerpts from Chapter 2 of *A Theology of Liberation: History, Politics, and Salvation* (Maryknoll, N.Y., Orbis, 1973; London, SCM, 1974). Used by permission.

Clark designated the road toward industrialization which poor countries are to follow as "progress" (not development).

The Bandung Conference of 1955 also played an important role in the evolution of the term, although on a different level. A large number of countries met there, especially Asian and African countries. They recognized their common membership in a Third World—underdeveloped and facing two developed worlds, the capitalist and the socialist. This conference marked the beginning of a policy which was supposed to lead out of this state of affairs. Although the deeds that followed did not always correspond to the expectations aroused, Bandung nevertheless signalled a deepened awareness of the fact of underdevelopment and a proclamation of its unacceptability.[6]

Approaches

The concept of development has no clear definition;[7] there are a variety of ways to regard it. Rather than reviewing them all at length, we will recall briefly the general areas involved.

Development can be regarded as purely economic, and in that sense it would be synonymous with *economic growth.*

The degree of development of a country could be measured, for example, by comparing its gross national product or its per capita income with those of a country regarded as highly developed. It is also possible to refine this gauge and make it more complex, but the presuppositions would still be the same: development consists above all in increased wealth or, at most, a higher level of well-being.

Historically, this is the meaning which appears first. What led to this point of view was perhaps the consideration of the process in England, the first country to develop and, understandably enough, the first to be studied by economists. This viewpoint was later reinforced by the mirage which the well-being of the rich nations produced.

Those who champion this view today, at least explicitly, are few in number.[8] Currently its value lies in serving as a yardstick to measure more integral notions. However, this focus continues to exist in a more or less subtle form in the capitalistic view of development.

The deficiencies of the above-mentioned view have led to another more important and more frequently held one. According to it, development is a *total social process,* which includes economic, social, political, and cultural aspects. This notion stresses the interdependence of the different factors. Advances in one area imply advances in all of them and, conversely, the stagnation of one retards the growth of the rest.[9]

A consideration of development as a total process leads one to consider also all the external and internal factors which affect the economic evolution of a nation as well as to evaluate the distribution of goods and services and the system of relationships among the agents of its economic life. This has been carefully worked out by social scientists concerned with so-called Third World countries. They have reached the conclusion that the dynamics of world economics leads simultaneously to the creation of greater wealth for the few and greater poverty for the many.[10]

From all this flows a strategy of development which, taking into account the different factors, will allow a country to advance both totally and harmoniously and to avoid dangerous setbacks.

To view development as a total social process necessarily implies for some an ethical dimension, which presupposes a concern for human values. The step toward an elaboration of a *humanistic perspective* of development is thus taken unconsciously, and it prolongs the former point of view without contradicting it.

François Perroux worked consistently along these lines. Development for him means "the combination of mental and social changes of a people which enable them to increase, cumulatively and permanently, their total real production." Going even further, he says, "Development is achieved fully in the measure that, by reciprocity of services, it prepares the way for reciprocity of consciousness."[11]

It would be a mistake to think that this point of view, which is concerned with human values, is the exclusive preserve of scholars of a Christian inspiration. Converging viewpoints are found in Marxist-inspired positions.[12]

This humanistic approach attempts to place the notion of development in a wider context: a historical vision in which mankind assumes control of its own destiny.[13] But this leads precisely to a change of perspective which—after certain additions and corrections—we would prefer to call liberation. We shall attempt to clarify this below. . . .

THE CONCEPT OF LIBERATION

Although we will consider liberation from a theological perspective more extensively later,[14] it is important at this time to attempt an initial treatment in the light of what we have just discussed.

The term *development* is relatively new in the texts of the ecclesiastical magisterium.[15] Except for a brief reference by Pius XII,[16] the subject is broached for the first time by John XXIII in the encyclical letter *Mater et Magistra.*[17] *Pacem in terris* gives the term special attention. *Gaudium et spes* dedicates a whole section to it, though the treatment is not original. All these documents stress the urgency of eliminating the existing injustices and the need for an economic development geared to the service of man. Finally, *Populorum progressio* discusses development as its central theme. Here the language and ideas are clearer; the adjective *integral* is added to development, putting things in a different context and opening new perspectives.

These new viewpoints were already hinted at in the sketchy discussion of Vatican Council II on dependence and liberation. *Gaudium et spes* points out that "nations on the road to progress . . . continually fall behind while very often their *dependence* on wealthier nations deepens more rapidly, even in the economic sphere" (no. 9). Later it acknowledges that "although nearly all peoples have gained their independence, it is still far from true that they are free from excessive inequalities and from every form of *undue dependence*" (no. 85).

These assertions should lead to a discernment of the need to be free from dependence, to be liberated from it. The same *Gaudium et spes* on two occasions touches on liberation and laments the fact that it is seen exclusively as the fruit of human effort: "Many look forward to a genuine and total *emancipation* of humanity wrought solely by human effort. They are convinced that the future rule of man over the earth will satisfy every desire of his heart" (no. 10). Or it is concerned that liberation be reduced to a purely economic and social level: "Among the forms of modern atheism is that which anticipates the *liberation* of man especially through his economic and social emancipation" (no. 20).[18] These assertions presuppose, negatively speaking, that liberation must be placed in a wider context; they criticize a narrow vision. They allow, therefore, for the possibility of a "genuine and total" liberation.

Unfortunately, this wider perspective is not elaborated. We find some indications, however, in the texts in which *Gaudium et spes* speaks of the birth of a "new humanism, one in which man is defined first of all by his responsibility toward his brothers and toward history" (no. 55). There is a need for men who are makers of history, "men who are truly new and artisans of a new humanity" (no. 30), men moved by the desire to build a really new society. Indeed, the conciliar document asserts that beneath economic and political demands "lies a deeper and more widespread longing. Persons and societies thirst for a full and free life worthy of man—one in which they can subject to their own welfare all that the modern world can offer them so abundantly" (no. 9).

All this is but a beginning. It is an oft-noted fact that *Guadium et spes* in general offers a rather ironic description of the human situation; it touches up the uneven spots, smoothes the rough edges, avoids the more conflictual aspects, and stays away from the sharper confrontations among social classes and countries.

The encyclical *Populorum progressio* goes a step further. In a somewhat isolated text it speaks clearly of "building a world where every man, no matter what his race, religion, or nationality, can live a fully human life, freed from servitude imposed on him by other men or by natural forces over which he has not sufficient control" (no. 47).[19] It is unfortunate, however, that this idea was not expanded in the encyclical. From this point of view, *Populorum progressio* is a transitional document. Although it energetically denounces the "international imperialism of money," "situations whose injustice cries to heaven," and the growing gap between rich and poor countries, ultimately it addresses itself to the great ones of this world urging them to carry out the necessary changes.[20] The outright use of the language of liberation, instead of its mere suggestion, would have given a more decided and direct thrust in favor of the oppressed, encouraging them to break with their present situation and take control of their own destiny.[21]

The theme of liberation appears more completely discussed in the message from eighteen bishops of the Third World, published as a specific response to the call made by *Populorum progressio*.[22] It is also treated frequently—almost to the point of being a synthesis of its message—in the conclusions of the Second General Conference of Latin American Bishops held in Medellín, Colombia, in 1968,[23] which have more doctrinal authority than the eighteen bishops' message. In both these documents the focus has changed. The situation is not judged from the point of view of the countries at the center, but rather of those on the periphery, providing insiders' experience of their anguish and aspirations.

The product of a profound historical movement, this aspiration to liberation is beginning to be accepted by the Christian community as a sign of the times, as a call to commitment and interpretation. The Biblical message, which presents the work of Christ as a liberation, provides the framework for this interpretation. Theology seems to have avoided for a long time reflecting on the conflictual character of human history, the confrontations among men, social classes, and countries. St. Paul continuously reminds us, however, of the paschal core of Christian existence and of all of human life: the passage from the old man to the new, from sin to grace, from slavery to freedom.

"For freedom Christ has set us free" (Gal 5:1), St. Paul tells us. He refers here to liberation from sin insofar as it represents a selfish turning in upon oneself. To sin is to refuse to love one's neighbors and, therefore, the Lord himself. Sin—a breach of friendship with God and others—is according to the Bible the ultimate cause of poverty, injustice, and the oppression in which men live. In describing sin as the ultimate cause we do not in any way negate the structural reasons and the objective determinants leading to these situations. It does, however, emphasize the fact that things do not happen by chance and that behind an unjust structure there is a personal or collective will responsible—a willingness to reject God and neighbor. It suggests, likewise, that a social transformation, no matter how radical it may be, does not automatically achieve the suppression of all evils.

But St. Paul asserts not only that Christ liberated us; he also tells us that he did it in order that we might be free. Free for what? Free to love. "In the language of the Bible," writes Bonhoeffer, "freedom is not something man has for himself but something he has for others. . . . It is not a possession, a presence, an object, . . . but a relationship and nothing else. In truth, freedom is a relationship between two persons. Being free means 'being free for the other,' because the other has bound me to him. Only in relationship with the other am I free."[24] The freedom to which we are called presupposes the going out of oneself, the breaking down of our selfishness and of all the structures that support our selfishness; the foundation of this freedom is openness to others. The fullness of liberation—a free gift from Christ—is communion with God and with other men.

CONCLUSION

Summarizing what has been said above, we can distinguish three reciprocally interpenetrating levels of meaning of the term *liberation*, or in other words, three approaches to the process of liberation.

In the first place, *liberation* expresses the aspirations of oppressed peoples and social classes, emphasizing the conflictual aspect of the economic, social, and political process which puts them at odds with wealthy nations and oppressive classes. In contrast, the word *development*, and above all the policies characterized as developmentalist [*desarrollista*], appear somewhat aseptic, giving a false picture of a tragic and conflictual reality. The issue of development does in fact find its true place in the more universal, profound, and radical perspective of liberation. It is only within this framework that *development* finds its true meaning and the possibilities of accomplishing something worthwhile.

At a deeper level, *liberation* can be applied to an understanding of history. Man is seen as assuming conscious responsibility for his own destiny. This understanding provides a dynamic context and broadens the horizons of the desired social changes. In this perspective the unfolding of all of man's dimensions is demanded—a man who makes himself throughout his life and throughout history. The gradual conquest of true freedom leads to the creation of a new man and a qualitatively different society. This vision provides, therefore, a better understanding of what in fact is at stake in our times.

Finally, the world *development* to a certain extent limits and obscures the theological problems implied in the process designated by this term.[25] On the contrary the word *liberation* allows for another approach leading to the Biblical sources which inspire the presence and action of man in history. In the Bible, Christ is presented as the one who brings us liberation. Christ the Savior liberates man from sin, which is the ultimate root of all disruption of friendship and of all injustice and oppression. Christ makes man truly free, that is to say, he enables man to live in communion with him; and this is the basis for all human brotherhood.

This is not a matter of three parallel or chronologically successive processes, however. There are three levels of meaning of a single, complex process, which finds its deepest sense and its full realization in the saving work of Christ. These levels of meaning, therefore, are interdependent. A comprehensive view of the matter presupposes that all three aspects can be considered together. In this way two pitfalls will be avoided: first, *idealist* or *spiritualist* approaches, which are nothing but ways of evading a harsh and demanding reality, and second, shallow analyses and programs of short-term effect initiated under the pretext of meeting immediate needs.[26]

NOTES

1. See Thomas Suavet, "Développement," in *Dictionnaire économique et social*, 2nd ed. (Paris: Économie et Humanisme, Les Éditions Ouvrières, 1962). For L.J. Lebret, "the idea of development originates in 1945" (*Dynamique concrète du développement* [Paris: Les Éditions Ouvrières, 1967], p. 38), but he does not indicate the source of this information. See also the systematic study of Jacques Freyssinet, *Le concept du sousdéveloppement* (Paris: Mouton, 1966).

2. See *Theorie der Wirtschaftlichen Entwicklung* (Leipzig: Dunker & Humblot, 1912); English edition: *The Theory of Economic Development: An Inquiry into Profits, Capital, Credit, Interest, and the Business Cycle*, trans. Redvers Opie (Cambridge: Harvard Univerity Press, 1934).

3. *Théorie de l'évolution économique* [French translation] (Paris: Dalloz, 1935).

4. *Teoría del desenvolvimiento económico* [Spanish translation] (Mexico, D.F.: Fondo de Cultura Económica, 1944).

5. *The Conditions of Economic Progress* (London: Macmillan and Co., 1940).

6. See in this regard Odette Guitard, *Bandoeng et le réveil des anciens peuples colonisés* (Paris: Presses Universitaires de France, 1961).

7. "The word *development* has not been in use long enough for its meaning to have become absolutely determined" (Suavet, "Développement").

8. Among them is a work which due to special circumstances and carefully planned methods of distribution became widely known in the underdeveloped countries: Walt W. Rostow's *The Stages of Economic Growth: A Non-Communist Manifesto* (New York: Cambridge University Press, 1960).

9. "Development is a total social process, and only for methodological convenience or in a partial sense can one speak of economic, political, cultural, and social development" (Helio Jaguaribe, *Economic & Political Development: A Theoretical Approach & a Brazilian Case Study* [Cambridge: Harvard University Press, 1968], p. 4). See also Giorgio Ceriani Sebregondi, *Sullo sviluppo della società italiana* (Turin: Boringhierio, 1965); Raymond Barre, *Le développement économique: Analyse et politique* (Paris: Cahiers de l'Institute de Science Économique Apliquée, 1958).

10. For a fuller discussion of developmentalism, see chapter 6 of *A Theology of Liberation* (Ed).

11. "La notion de développement," in *L'économie de XXe siècle*, 2nd ed., enl. (Paris: Presses Universitaires de France, 1964), pp. 155 and 171. Perroux had already addressed himself to this perspective in "From the Avarice of Nations to an Economy for Mankind," *Cross Currents* 3, no. 3 (Spring 1953): 193-207. "Development for us," writes Lebret, "is *the object itself of human economics*. . . . This is the discipline of the transition . . . from a less human to a more human condition as fast and as cheaply as possible, bearing in mind the solidarity among subpopulations and populations . . ." (*Dynamique concrète*, p. 28). The same idea is expressed in another definition of development by the same author: "To have more in order to be more." As is well known, both of these expressions were used in the encyclical *Populorum progressio*. See also Luis Velaochaga, *Concepción integral del desarrollo*, pamphlet (Lima: Universidad Católica, 1967).

12. See the themes of the "new man" and the "whole man" of communist society. In it, according to an early text of Karl Marx, man will be defined not by what he has but by what he is: ". . . The positive transcendence of private property . . . should not be conceived merely in the sense of *immediate, one-sided gratification*—merely in the sense of *possession*, of *having*. Man appropriates his total *essence* in a total manner, that is to say, as a whole man" (*Economic and Philosophic Manuscripts of 1844*, ed. Dirk J. Struik, trans. Martin Milligan [New York: International Publishers, 1964], p. 138; the final italics are ours). See also Garaudy, *Perspectives*, pp. 347-51; Henri Lefebvre, *Dialectical Materialism*, trans. John Sturrock (London: Jonathan Cape, 1968), pp. 148-66; Karel Kosik, *Dialéctica de lo concreto* (Mexico, D.F.: Grijalbo, 1963), translated from the Czech, especially pp. 235-69.

13. An example of this inevitable progression to a wider context is the following paragraph of Vincent Cosmao: "We are therefore led beyond the integration of social development with economic development, or in other words of the noneconomic factors with economic development, to a vision of history in which mankind collectively takes hold of its collective destiny, humanizing it for the benefit of the whole man and of all men" ("Les exigences du développement au service de l'homme," *Parole et Mission* 10, no. 39 [October 15, 1967]: 581).

14. Gutiérrez explores the theological dimensions of liberation in chapter 9 of *A Theology of Liberation* (Ed).

15. The work of Jean-Yves Calvez, S.J., and Jacque Perrin, S.J., *The Church and Social Justice:*

The Social Teaching of the Popes from Leo XIII to Pius XII (1878–1958) (Chicago: Regnery Company, 1961), contains no reference to this idea.

16. See René Laurentin, *Liberation, Development, and Salvation*, pp. 102–03.

17. There is an entire chapter devoted to it in the sequel to the work cited in note 15—first published four years later and dedicated to John XXIII: Jean-Yves Calvez, S.J., *The Social Thought of John XXIII: Mater et Magistra*, trans. George J.M. McKenzie, S.M. (Chicago: Henry Regnery Company, 1964).

18. In the texts quoted here the italics are ours.

19. In a less important statement of two years before, there is an interesting text of Paul VI regarding the consequences of technological progress on work styles: "No one foresaw that new work styles would awaken in the worker the awareness of his *alienation*, that is to say, the will no longer to work for others, with instruments belonging to others, not alone but with others. Did no one think that the desire for an economic and *social* liberation would arise, hindering his appreciation of the moral and spiritual redemption offered through faith in Christ?" (Allocution of May 1, 1965, in *L'Osservatore Romano*, May 3, 1965; the italics are ours).

20. See the analyses of René Dumont in "Populorum Progressio: Un pas en avant, trop timide," *Esprit* 35, no. 361 (June 1967): 1092–96; Raymundo Ozanam de Andrade, " 'Populorum Progressio': Neocapitalismo ou revolução," *Paz e Terra* (Rio de Janeiro), no. 4 (August 1967), pp. 209–21; François Perroux, "'Populorum Progressio': L'encyclique de la Résurrection," *L'Église dans le monde de ce temps*, 3: 201–12; Herné Chaigne, "Force et faiblesse de l'encyclique," *Frères du Monde*, nos. 46–47 (1967), pp. 58–74, which proposes "to radicalize the encyclical."

21. It is not our intention to negate the values of *Populorum progressio*, highlighted for example by Ricardo Cetrulo, S.J., " 'Populorum progressio': De la 'animación' de la sociedad al análisis de situación," *Víspera* (Montevideo), no. 3 (October 1967), pp. 5–10. The author comments perceptively on the change of style and perspective in relation to preceding encyclicals. Regarding the encyclical's step forward in the doctrine of the ownership of means of production, see *Comentarios de cuadernos para el diálogo a la Populorum progressio* (Madrid: Ed. Cuadernos para el Diálogo, 1967), especially the observations of Joaquín Ruiz-Giménez (pp. 16–20) and Eduardo Cierco (pp. 31–49). See also the thought-provoking and warm commentary of the Italian Marxist Lucio Lombardo Radice, *Socialismo e libertà* (Rome: Editori Riuniti, 1968), pp. 136–48. Pope Paul VI has taken up these subjects in his recent and in many ways innovative letter to Cardinal Roy, *Octogesima adveniens*. There he says that "today men yearn to *free* themselves from need and dependence" (no. 45; our italics).

22. Reprinted, among others, in *Between Honesty and Hope: Documents from and about the Church in Latin America*. Issued at Lima by the Peruvian Bishops' Commission for Social Action, trans. John Drury (Maryknoll, New York: Maryknoll Publications, 1970), pp. 3–12.

23. We will study these texts in greater detail in chapter 7.

24. *Creation and Fall, Temptation* (New York: The Macmillan Company, 1966), p. 37. Paul VI suggestively points out that freedom "will develop in its deepest human reality: to involve itself and to spend itself in building up active and lived solidarity." And he adds, "It is by losing himself in God who sets him free that man finds true freedom, renewed in the death and resurrection of the Lord" (*Octogesima adveniens*, no. 47).

25. See Laurentin, *Liberation, Development, and Salvation*, p. 63 and also p. 39.

26. An old comparison unexpectedly presented by St. Augustine of Hippo in his own inimitable style is related to the intimate relationship of the different levels of meaning of the term *liberation:* the soul under the control of sin, he says, resembles a country subdued by the enemy. See his commentary on Psalm 9, no. 8, quoted by Congar in "Christianisme et liberation de l'homme," *Masses Ouvrières* (Paris), no. 258 (December, 1969), p. 3.

Chapter 40

Jon Sobrino

Christology and Discipleship

LATIN AMERICAN CHRISTOLOGY

. . . For the most part Latin Americans have not worked out systematic Christologies and full presentations of Christ. The only outstanding exception in this regard is Leonardo Boff's work on Jesus Christ as liberator.[1] But we still can say something about the basic orientation of christological writing in Latin America in terms of the five criteria discussed earlier in this chapter.

The theology of liberation serves as the general frame of reference for Latin American Christology. Unlike European brands of theology, liberation theology does not see itself situated in a broader history of Latin American theology since the latter is of a very recent vintage. So rather than engaging in dialogue with other theologies, philosophies, or cultural movements, liberation theology has faced up to the basic Latin American reality of underdevelopment and oppression: "Liberation is then seen as a setting in motion of a process which will lead to freedom."[2]

This facing up to reality itself rather than to mediating factors engaged in pondering reality has taken place in the midst of real-life commitment to the cause of liberation. Thus liberation theology has not arisen primarily as an effort to *justify* real-life involvement. Instead it has arisen as a by-product of a concrete faith that is pondered and lived out in terms of the questions raised by involvement in the praxis of liberation. Its aim is to make that involvement "more critical-minded and creative."[3]

Pondering the real-life situation only after it has been experienced in concrete terms, Latin Americans have been prompted to see Christ in very new and different terms. As Boff puts it: "Each generation brings a new *parousia* of Christ because in each age he is given a new image, the result of the difficult synthesis between life and faith. . . . Today, in the experience of faith of many Christians in Latin America, he is seen and loved as the liberator."[4] So the basic locus of Christology is the place where faith and life meet.

It is not the first stage of the Enlightenment that seems to pose the real challenge today. It is not such movements as liberalism, freemasonry, and theosophy that raise questions for Latin American theology today. It is the whole problem of *reality* and concrete life itself, of the second stage of the Enlightenment, that now holds center

First published in *Christology at the Crossroads: A Latin American Approach* (Maryknoll, N.Y., Orbis, 1976), pp. 33–37, 118–22. Used by permission.

stage. The problem of the believing *subject*, who may now find it hard to see the import or truth of faith, has taken a back seat. And the sinfulness of the situation is not something just to be explained; it must be concretely transformed. That is why Latin America is not much interested in clarifying people's understanding of such traditional theological problems as transubstantiation, the hypostatic union in Christ, and the relationship between divine and human knowledge in Christ.

Such problems are ignored, I believe, for two basic reasons that have nothing to do with disdain. First of all, theological clarification of that sort does not seem to have any direct repercussions on the social sphere. Second, and more important, to dally over such questions is to play the game of traditional theology, which is seen to be alienating and totally uninvolved with real issues. We are hiding from real problems and serving the interests of ideology if we focus on the traditional theological problems of transubstantiation and the hypostatic union while such issues as underdevelopment and its implications go unexplored.[5]

So Latin American theology aims to be critical and operative, taking life as a whole rather than the individual Christian as its point of departure. From the horizon of liberation, good theologizing means real service.[6]

The impact of the second stage of the Enlightenment is readily seen in the use which is made of Marx's social, religious, and political analyses, though Latin Americans claim to use them with a critical eye. It is even more evident in the fact that Marx's epistemological revolution plays a great role. We come to know reality really only insofar as we come to realize the necessity of transforming it. The second stage of the Enlightenment also exerts an influence on Christology, however sketchy that Christology still may be. Emphasis is placed on those christological elements that serve to constitute a paradigm of liberation (e.g., the resurrection as utopia and the kingdom of God) or to highlight practical ways of understanding and realizing it (e.g., the socio-political activity of Jesus and the obligation to follow in his footsteps).

So hermeneutics becomes a hermeneutics of praxis, and the implications for Christology are clear:

> It is not enough simply to read about the figure of Jesus purely in the light of his *ipsissima vox et facta* and within the apocalyptic framework and the sociological background of his time. Exegetes, using more and more sophisticated methods, have done this and their work is very valuable, but it is not a science in itself. . . . The elements that give permanent validity to this message, above the pressures of history, can only be adequately grasped in a hermeneutic approach. From this, the *ipsissima intentio* of Jesus emerges.[7]

And the aim of studying Jesus' intention is to pave the way for "effective collaboration" with him.[8]

The course that Jesus took is to be investigated scientifically, not just to aid in the quest for truth but also in the fight for truth that will make people free.[9]

The basic quandary that inspires Latin American theology is summed up in the term "liberation." It is embodied concretely in the coexistence of two fundamental and contradictory experiences: the felt need for liberation as an absolute necessity on the one hand, and the impossibility of achieving it in history on the other. The resulting situation is experienced as one of bondage or captivity, where hope for liberation goes hand in hand with concrete experience of unjust oppression.[10]

In theological terms, then, we are dealing with a question of theodicy rather than a question of natural theology. We must try to reconcile the kingdom of God with a situation of bondage. Yet Latin American theodicy has peculiar features of its own insofar as liberation theology arose out of active praxis rather than static contemplation. Faced with a pervasive situation of misery, it does not take the classic tack to be found in the Book of Job, in the work of Dostoyevsky, and more recently in Rabbi Rubinstein's query as to how Jews can believe in God after Auschwitz. It is not concerned with finding some way to contemplate God and captivity in a meaningful relationship. Instead it is concerned with the practical problem of building up and realizing the kingdom of God in the face of captivity.

The quandary is very much lived as such because there is no evident way out of the dilemma. But it is inspired and sustained by the conviction that the real problem is not to justify God but rather to turn the justification of human beings into a reality. The question of justifying God seems to be all too theoretical in the face of the real-life need to make people just. It is reality that must be reconciled with the kingdom of God, and the quandary of theodicy must be resolved in praxis rather than in theory.

What, then, are we to say about the christological concentration of Latin American theology? It is my firm belief that this is one of the most delicate issues in liberation theology. The basic question is, of course, whether the main interest of liberation theology is Christ or liberation. Needless to say, this alternative is not posed as such, either in theory or in praxis, but it will help us to bring the whole matter of christological concentration out into the open. Only the future course of liberation theology will provide an answer to the problem, but even now some observations can be made.

First, it is worth realizing that certain things which seem to be real alternatives for the mind can be united in lived experience. An example from Paul's theology might help us here. In theory we might well ask whether his theology is concentrated on Christology or on justification; in practice we feel sure that the two were joined together in his own experience. We might begin with his christological experience on the road to Damascus in order to comprehend his experience of being justified. Or, on the other hand, we might begin with his personal experience of the need to be justified and the impossibility of ever attaining it, and then see how the problem was resolved in his experience of Christ. Something similar seems to be the case with liberation theology. I think that liberation theology as "theology" is profoundly christological; and insofar as it is concerned with "liberation," its most all-embracing theological concept is "the kingdom of God." . . .

DISCIPLESHIP AND MORALITY

I have already remarked that Jesus is his history, and that the moral values embodied by him must therefore be understood in terms of his concrete realization of them. But we must also consciously realize what those fundamental values are, how they are fleshed out, and how radical they are.

When Jesus calls his disciples to go out and proclaim the "kingdom of God," they understand him. The phrase "kingdom of God" is a utopian symbol for a wholly new and definitive way of living and being. It presupposes renewal in many areas: in the heart of the human person, in societal relationships, and in the cosmos at large. Today we ignore the last dimension because it clearly is bound up with cultural conceptions of Jesus' own age. It simply indicates how total the renewal is to be. The utopian import of the kingdom is a summary way of saying that things should be different than they are— better, of course.

Viewed in terms of its end result, the final goal is one of universal *reconciliation*. People must work for that end, and the morality of specific actions depends on whether they do or do not point in that desired direction. By its very nature, however, the reconciliation stands in opposition to existing reality. To effect reconciliation is to do *justice*, and we can say that the basic general value of Jesus is that of doing justice. But here we should not understand it as retributive or vindictive justice designed to give all persons and situations what is due to them by virtue of what they are. Justice here is meant in the Old Testament sense. It is the liberation of Israel. Yahweh is just, not because he gives all their due, but because he tries to re-create human beings and situations, to "save" them. Thus the justice of God is "the essentially salvific activity of God whereby the people of Israel [in the New Testament, the whole human race] obtain the restoration of the good things promised by God."[11]

Here the question arises as to whether this justice is directed to the individual or to society, and whether people become just as individuals or in structural terms. These modern ways of framing the question are obviously quite alien to Jesus' explicit way of viewing the recipient and subject of justice. Hence we cannot come down apodictically in favor of one side or the other. My belief is that in Jesus we find a dialectical conception embracing both sides, particularly if we consider what Jesus himself does as well as what he says.

Insofar as the first question noted in the last paragraph is concerned, it is quite apparent that Jesus repeatedly addresses himself to the individual in terms of re-creation. When he approaches the poor, the oppressed, and the sinner, he does not simply offer consolation; he offers justice. In other words, he does not propose to leave people as they are and simply console them in their plight; he proposes to re-create their present situation and thus do "justice" to them. This is the quintessence of Jesus' understanding of the kingdom.

But when Jesus addresses himself to oppressed persons the fact is that he is not simply addressing wretched individuals who stand in need of justice. Historically speaking these individuals are in a state of misery because they have been ostracized by society and deprived of status. In approaching these individuals, Jesus is not only doing them justice but also clearing away the barriers of class that have made them not only individuals in misery but also persons ostracized by society. The justice of Jesus, then, points toward some new form of social coexistence where class differences have been abolished, at least in principle.

This shows up even more clearly when Jesus condemns sin, the basic anti-value. Strikingly enough, his harshest condemnations are not directed against the individual sinner who does not fulfill the law out of frailty; they are directed against the collective sins that create a situation contrary to the kingdom. From the de facto evil use of collective power there arises a situation that is the negation of brotherhood and of reconciliation. The resultant sin covers the religious sphere, the economic sphere, the cultural sphere, and the political sphere. There is poverty because the rich do not share their wealth. There is religious oppression because the priests impose intolerable burdens on people. There is ignorance because the Levites have carried off the keys to knowledge. There is political oppression because the rulers rule despotically. In short, the sinfulness of these people is not something that affects only the subjective life of the individual; it is visibly crystalized in the social realm. Jesus' condemnations against these various groups of sinners clearly suggest a desire to re-create the social situation, not just the concrete individual sinner.

The second question is something else again. How did Jesus view the practical realization of the kingdom and its ideals? Was it to come about through personal conversion of the individual or through structural changes? What relationship, if any, did he see between the two? Now it is quite apparent that Jesus wanted to see both come about, that he did not believe in structural change without a personal change in the individual. In that sense I think it is anachronistic to force the data dealing with the historical Jesus in such a way that he is presented as someone who thought that structural change would solve the problem of personal change in the individual. Jesus sees the de facto evil use of power rooted in the will to power—specifically in the power that tries to manipulate God. Insofar as human beings do not let God be God, they themselves cease to be human. And when these nonhumans hold power, they use it against the kingdom. This facet obviously applies to groups with power, not directly to those groups of people who are ostracized by society.

Now we cannot simplify the whole issue by concluding that Jesus was interested in the individual rather than in structures. Even if we were to reduce the problem of conversion to that of individual conversion, we are still left with the problem of relating personal conversion to structural justice. If we take due note of Jesus' demand to bring about the kingdom, and even more of his own personal example, then we are forced to conclude that personal conversion must always be associated with social praxis. Speaking in terms of justice, we are forced to conclude that Jesus sees people becoming just only insofar as they do the work of justice. In systematic terms people become "children" of God by doing the work of "brotherhood." So even the aspect of personal justice is inseparably bound up with some form of social justice.

In analyzing the moral subject as subject, Jesus stresses the danger of a particular temptation. One must make sure that one's yearning for justice does not turn into an affirmation of one's own ego rather than that of others. The human heart must be pure. Jesus poses the limit-case of relations to one's enemy. The good of one's enemy must be sought rather than a vengeful affirmation of the moral subject. That is why Jesus talks about love for one's enemies.

As the history of Jesus makes clear, that has nothing to do with pacifism. Jesus was the first to utter harsh condemnations of the unjust enemy. But this concentration on the moral subject cannot be used as an expression of disinterest in the work of bringing about the kingdom, in the social and structural aspect. His analysis of the moral subject is designed to make sure that in doing justice people really do precisely that, that they do not let themselves be guided by a retributive or vindictive notion of justice rather than a truly re-creative notion. Moral subjects must renounce the will to power, not because that alone will make them just, but because it is through such renunciation that their justice will really be the justice of God and his kingdom.

To sum up, then, we can say that the basic moral value proclaimed and exemplified by Jesus was re-creative justice. That is the value that his followers must realize in the concrete. He does not summon them directly to become just as individuals; he summons them to do justice. Precisely because his interest is in the justice of God as understood by the Old Testament rather than in some substitute form of justice of a retributive or vindictive nature, Jesus analyzes the moral subject in terms of will to power. So long as the moral subject does not renounce that will to power, then in theological terms that person has not yet converted to God. And Jesus doubts that such a person is capable of doing the work of justice proper to God's kingdom.

NOTES

1. Leonardo Boff, *Jesus Christ Liberator* (Maryknoll, N.Y., Orbis, 1978).
2. Leonardo Boff, "Salvation in Jesus Christ and the Process of Liberation," *Concilium*, 96 (New York, Herder and Herder/Seabury, 1974) 78.

3. Gustavo Gutiérrez, "Movimientos de liberación y teología," *Concilium*, 93 (1974) 451.

4. Boff, "Salvation," 78.

5. The point is made forcefully in, e.g., Hugo Assmann, *Theology for a Nomad Church* (Maryknoll, N.Y., Orbis, 1976).

6. "The *verum* of the Bible is not a *factum* already given but a *faciendum* ('something to be done'). That is why any theological reflection based upon a historical *logos* is not content to define reality and the import of what has already been done. On the basis of that determination it also seeks to move in the direction of what remains to be done; to verify, to make real and true in actuality what is already true in principle" (Ignacio Ellacuría, "Tesis sobre posibilidad, necesidad y sentido de una teología latinoamericana," in *Teología y mundo contemporáneo* [Madrid, 1975] 346; also in *Christus*, Mexico City, February–March, 1975).

7. Boff, "Salvation," 79.

8. Raul Vidales, "¿Cómo hablar de Cristo hoy?" *Spes*, 22–23 (1974) 10.

9. Ibid.

10. See L. Boff, "Libertaçao de Jesus Christo," in *Teología y mundo contemporáneo,* p. 267f.

11. S. Lyonnet, *La historia de la salvación en la carta a los romanos*, Spanish trans. (Salamanca, 1967) 50; see his Latin works, *Quaestiones in Epistulam ad Romanos*, 2 vols., and *Exegesis Epistulae ad Romanos*, 2 vols. (Rome, Pontifical Biblical Institute).

Chapter 41

Phillip Berryman

Basic Christian Communities in Latin America

By now the *comunidades eclesiales de base* (CEB's, often translated "grassroots Christian communities") of the Catholic Church in Latin America are well known. There is some tendency to view them as one rivulet within a larger stream, the search for a more face-to-face, more participatory Christian community, as exemplified in the "house church" or even the "underground church." However, the contrasts are noteworthy. The two latter phenomena, found in Europe and the US, are often initiated by lay people, usually middle class, while the CEB's are initiated by priests and sisters; peasants, as an oppressed group, don't initiate much in society. Even more obvious is the political experience of these communities, leading to repression, persecution, and even martyrdom. The history of the CEB phenomenon—though it covers scarcely 15 years—may serve as an approach to understanding it.

There were antecedents to CEB's, most obviously, Protestant or evangelical congregations, which have always been small, Bible-based, lay-led, and close to the people. However, their otherworldly theology and their sense of identity precisely as enclaves set apart from the larger (Catholic) community, have not prepared them to see political commitment as an exigency of their faith.

Catholic antecedents included the *Cursillo* movement, a kind of conversion technique imported from Spain, and the "cell" approach to Catholic Action which formed small groups of "apostles" in milieux of workers, students, and families.

But the real impetus for CEB's was the Second Vatican Council and the ferment it stirred everywhere. The Council's agenda was little influenced by Latin America, but it did encourage questioning and stimulated the Latin American church to examine itself. Many began to critique existing models of pastoral activity: e.g., very often a rural parish with a large territory and perhaps 30,000 baptized Catholics, served by one priest living in the main town, circuit riding, and limiting himself largely to administering sacraments. Some also questioned the existing "popular religion," contrasting it sharply with biblical faith.

One pioneering attempt at an alternative came from a pastoral team of priests from Chicago, headed by Fr. Leo Mahon, who arrived in early 1963 at a Panama City suburb called San Miguelito. Mahon raised some hackles by publishing what amounted to a

First published in *Christianity and Crisis*, 41 (September 21, 1981). Reprinted with permission. Copyright © 1981, Christianity & Crisis, 537 West 121st Street, New York, NY 10027.

manifesto of a new approach to pastoral work: Stop wearing cassocks; live among the people; start working with men rather than only with the traditional female clientele; meet in people's homes rather than the church; stress evangelization and conversion over sacramentalization; present a challenging vision of life rather than abstract or moralistic rules. Mahon and his team combined mystique and pragmatic methodology. In a few years they built up a flourishing network of local communities with lay leaders and continually showed creativity in liturgy and evangelization. Many priests and sisters visited San Miguelito and applied its model elsewhere.

RELATING SCRIPTURE TO LIFE

Others were already doing similar things with less fanfare, especially in Brazil. Typically a team of priests, sisters, and lay people would divide an existing parish into zones, where they would organize evening courses in people's homes. The starting point might be a scripture reading but more typically it would be some basic life experience (work, suffering, friendship, injustice, death, sex/marriage). Through a Socratic method people would be encouraged to tell stories or examine their own ideas and folk wisdom. This experience would then be compared with a biblical passage which might confirm, challenge, or deepen people's awareness. An example: confronting the prevailing machismo with the Genesis 1 vision of the equality of the sexes.

Such a course, besides being a vehicle of evangelization, served to bring together an initial Christian community in the barrio or village. Natural leaders would emerge and after some training they could lead the discussions and eventually lead a worship service every Sunday, following the biblical texts of the season, along with a discussion guide prepared by the pastoral team. Thus from a pastoral point of view such lay leaders (often called "delegates of the Word") were "multipliers."

In my observation in the early days (mid 1960's), this kind of pastoral initiative was more characteristic of foreign than of national priests and sisters, possibly because they were more immediately critical of the existing pastoral model, and even more obviously because they usually had outside sources of support so that they could afford to break with existing practices, such as asking for mass stipends.

The early pioneers of CEB's saw themselves as striving to build a new church. They could call on certain theological themes: the rediscovery of the "house church," a hankering for a pre-Constantinian simplicity, the church as community and event, the minister as prophet rather than priest, biblical faith as opposed to religion. At this phase they operated with the view characteristic of Vatican II: The church as such is not involved in politics but prepares lay people who engage in politics following their own lights.

In 1968 the Latin American Bishops' Conference met at Medellín, Colombia, and produced a series of truly dynamic documents. At that time the bishops gave recognition to the *comunidades eclesiales de base*—the phrase had just been coined—and described them as:

> The first and basic ecclesial nucleus . . . the initial cell of ecclesial structuring, the focal point of evangelization, and at present a primordial factor in the advancement and development of people.

Medellín thus gave official recognition to CEB's, and in the next few years the idea was spread through training courses throughout the continent.

At that same Medellín conference the ideas that were to be the germ of liberation theology also received some ecclesiastical sanction, particularly the notion of "liberation," which represented a challenge to the prevailing evolutionary concept of "development" and implied revolutionary change. Initially, however, liberation theology and CEB's traveled on somewhat separate tracks. Liberation theology arose from the experience of small groups of Christians, for whom Camilo Torres, the Colombian priest who felt conscience-bound to join the guerrillas and was killed in combat in 1966, was an inspiration if not a prototype. Their preoccupation was not "building up the church" but changing a society which they saw as radically incompatible with the Gospel.

As I have mentioned, the original impulse for CEB's came mainly from priests who were searching for a more relevant kind of pastoral ministry. Thus it is not surprising that the movement's concerns were originally church-centered, especially since most of the issues of the period immediately after Vatican II were church-centered: e.g., freedom and authority in the church, ministry, papal authority, the birth control controversy. In Latin America, however, it was the clash with social reality that gave CEB's their own particular shape and style.

In principle CEB's could be set up in any area, rich or poor; in practice they have flourished only among the rural poor and the marginal people of the cities. The upper and middle classes have always had "their" priests and their church movements, but it was a novelty for priests and sisters to come among the poor and share their condition to some extent. It is on one level simply a fact that the poor are more open to accept the Gospel. Moreover, in the CEB they find what the overall society denies them: a community where they are valued, where they have a sense of dignity, where their word is heard with respect. The CEB thus has undeniable political spinoffs, as we shall note.

DIFFERING CONTEXTS

The CEB's process of maturation-through-conflict has taken place in different kinds of contexts which it would be well to distinguish. Schematically we may note four such general contexts: 1) relatively less conflictive countries; 2) repressive countries where there is no foreseeable prospect for "liberation"; 3) countries where serious revolutionary movements are struggling to take power; 4) countries in revolutionary transformation. Obviously a country may pass from one kind of context to another (e.g., Chile during the Popular Unity government seemed to be in a revolutionary process).

By "relatively less conflictive" countries I mean those in which the power structure does not need to employ widespread and extreme repression, even though most of the people are poor and the economic structure works against them (Mexico, Venezuela, Costa Rica, Panama, Ecuador). Elections may give the appearance of democracy although they offer no channel for significant change. No one imagines that revolutionary upheaval is on the horizon.

In such a context the focus of the CEB may well be church-centered, focusing on biblical formation, regularizing commonlaw marriages and improving family life. Often enough a man's decision to be faithful to his wife is a conversion analogous to an evangelical Protestant conversion, one of whose focal points is foreswearing liquor.

In such a context the CEB's may be accompanied by development projects, clinics, agriculture courses, or cooperatives. In a rhetorical way there may be talk of liberation but what is missing is what Latin Americans call a viable *proyecto de liberación*.

The most usual context for CEB's in Latin America today is one of repression with no real liberation foreseeable (Brazil, Chile, Argentina, Uruguay, Paraguay, Bolivia and, until recently, Central America). Some of these countries have experienced moments when they seemed on the march toward a new land, but today they are in the exile of military domination. Economic policies have been deliberately skewed to favor the rich; unions and real opposition parties are forbidden or extremely circumscribed; there is no free press, at least for the poor.

In such a context the CEB becomes a space where truth can be spoken and heard, where the poor can hear that they are the image of God, and that indeed God chooses them over the rich. The symbols of the Exodus, the faithfulness of God, Jesus' challenging the powerful of his time, being crucified and triumphing through the Resurrection, become motives for hope and for resistance.

A participative sermon ultimately becomes subversive. Some readers may have seen transcriptions of Ernesto Cardenal's dialogue sermons in *The Gospel in Solentiname*. Although he is one of Nicaragua's leading poets he seems admirably to have resisted any temptation to edit or dress up these group commentaries on the gospels and simply lets the peasants and other members of the island community speak. They are quite similar to the kinds of commentaries I have heard in many places for fifteen years. In this case apparently innocuous details of the gospel narrative became anti-Somoza weapons.

I would imagine that few of the participants in those dialogues in the early 1970's seriously thought that before the end of the decade a revolutionary movement would be in power in Nicaragua. By the same token no one in Brazil or Chile today can give a likely scenario for revolution. But when I put this to a Brazilian sociologist several years ago, he replied, "We have to be prepared for surprises. Who predicted the OPEC oil boycott?"

Nevertheless, you cannot plan such surprises. In many places CEB's are communities of resistance and hope. Such was the situation in El Salvador in the early 1970's when a number of pastoral teams began to come closer to the poor especially in rural areas. In the space of a few years the country has moved to a period of insurrection, and CEB's have played a vital role.

One of the most notable examples was the work of Jesuits led by Fr. Rutilio Grande, in the area of Aguilares, a town about a half hour from San Salvador. Their method was to go to a village and spend two weeks using a revitalized version of the traditional "mission." During the day they would be with the people, participating in their work and activities and at night held meetings. By the time they moved on there would be the beginnings of a local Christian community.

A DANGEROUS AWARENESS

In March 1977 Grande, then 50 years old, was machine gunned to death in the cane fields along with two other people, the first of El Salvador's martyrs. The story of the persecution of the Salvadoran church is well known and need not be repeated here, but it may be worthwhile to examine the "crime" which led to this attack, the crime of raising people's awarenss. It is well known that church people have documented human rights abuses and denounced them, offered legal aid to the victims' families, and cared for refugees from the violence. To a great extent, these activities stem from a prior fact: the close connection between CEB's and what are called the "popular organizations."

These large mass organizations with a peasant base—which also include labor unions, shantytown dwellers, and students, and which are the core of the opposition to the junta—began in the mid 1970's. Peasants with Christian formation have participated in them, and particularly in the Revolutionary People's Bloc, which is the largest of these organizations. For some time they have been directly linked to the guerrilla organizations.

What is new about the situation in El Salvador is that large groups of Christians have gone into these organizations which themselves have become radicalized. Initially their tactics were strikes, occupations of lands and public buildings, and demonstrations, but as they were met with increasing violence they moved closer to the guerrilla organizations. Many of the leaders and members of these organizations came from CEB's, and, indeed, at the village level it might sometimes be hard to distinguish between the CEB and the peasant organization.

In 1978 Archbishop Oscar Romero wrote a pastoral letter called "The Church and Popular Political Organizations" (signed also by Bishop Arturo Rivera y Damas, who subsequently replaced Romero). [see Oscar Romero, *Voice of the Voiceless* (Maryknoll, N.Y., Orbis, 1985) 85–113]. It was remarkable enough that Romero should devote a pastoral letter to the topic—and at the same time an indication of how much symbiosis there was between CEB's and these organizations.

The letter insists that political commitment and faith are united without being the same thing, that no one should be told that it is a Christian obligation to join any particular movement and, most importantly, that if a person's being a leader in both the CEB and the popular organization is a source of confusion, one of the two leaderships should be dropped, after suitable discernment.

Differing sharply with this essentially positive view of the popular organizations, the other four bishops of El Salvador issued a statement in effect denying any relation between the church and the organizations and warning of the dangers of Marxism. Simultaneous and opposed pastoral letters are unheard of in the Catholic Church, but they serve to illustrate the degree of polarization in El Salvador. Romero evidently sympathized with the popular organizations and knew some of their leaders well, though he would not shrink from criticizing them.

A fourth context for CEB's is that of revolutionary transformation, after political power has been taken. Since the Cuban Revolution took place before Vatican II and in particular circumstances, Christians have not been very present in the revolution, especially not in the form of CEB's. During 1970–1973 Chile lived the appearance of being in a period of transition to socialism, and this affected the life of CEB's at the time (e.g., how do you handle diverse ideological positions in the CEB?).

Nicaragua's Sandinista revolution has had input from Christians in numerous ways. Today in CEB's they are rereading the Bible in the light of the new situation; some, for example, have looked to the book of Nehemiah for images of a "theology of reconstruction."

In short, in diverse contexts, the common experience of CEB's throughout these years has been one of having to confront the political realities, and this experience is an integral part of their evangelization.

I have limited myself to Catholic CEB's for several reasons: Catholics are the overwhelming numerical majority and the Catholic Church as an institution is inevitably an important social force, while Protestant churches in general have the status of private associations. Individuals and small groups of Protestants have played important roles, but it is rare that a whole congregation, much less a denomination, becomes politicized in the manner here described. The more usual case is that the individual is estranged from his or her congregation and gravitates to some ecumenical network. Today a significant exception is Nicaragua, where Protestants and evangelicals are entering wholeheartedly into the Sandinista "process" and seeking to retool theologically and pastorally.

Earlier I mentioned that initially CEB's and liberation theology traveled on somewhat separate tracks. Hence, for example, the documents produced at the 1972 Christians for Socialism meeting in Chile do not mention CEB's. By the same token, I think some proponents of CEB's at one time thought that they were simply the way the church should be: The future of the church would be CEB writ large.

NO SINGLE FORM

Now it is simply an observable fact that many people live a Christian commitment without belonging to a CEB. Much of the Sandinista leadership learned Christian ideals at the Catholic high schools they attended, along with other members of the middle class. Some workers may see Jesus as a "revolutionary" without ever attending a neighborhood CEB meeting.

In the late 1970's there appeared the term *iglesia popular* (people's church) which seeks to express this notion (although, in fact, it resists a clear definition, at least to my Anglo-Saxon mind). A more dynamic phrasing is *iglesia que nace del pueblo*, the "church being born among the people." (The Spanish *el pueblo* has more emotional resonance than the English "the people.")

One group of theologians met in Venezuela in 1978 to reflect on the *iglesia popular*, which they called a "new manner of living the church in Latin America." They see it as embodied in groups "forming among the poor and those who have allowed themselves to be evangelized by the poor":

> The church will be the people of God when it is really the church of the poor, when it understands itself from the viewpoint of, and as existing for, the oppressed, and when they are the ones who speak up and tell us where the Spirit is blowing today in Latin America.

Doctrinal, sacramental, and administrative structures are a secondary aspect of the church, meant to serve the primary aspect of being a church of the poor. From this angle, CEB's are one way of being the church, but not the exclusive way.

The group reflection of those theologians was meant as a contribution to the discussion preparatory to the Latin American Bishops' Conference meeting at Puebla, Mexico, which took place in early 1979. Since the Puebla conference, machinery was in the hands of conservatives who largely set the agenda, the process we have been describing here made relatively little impact on the final documents. Thus, CEB's are treated largely in their church-centered aspects, with considerable stress on their relation to their "legitimate pastors," the bishops. The only reference to the relation between politics and CEB's seems to be a regret that some political interests try to "manipulate" them. Other Puebla themes, such as the "option for the poor," which is a kind of leitmotif, are, of course, a reflection of the process we have been sketching. The Puebla documents consider the term *iglesia popular* unfortunate because it seems to deny that the church is born "from above."

But reflection on the *iglesia popular* has continued and was advanced considerably at a São Paulo conference of Third World theologians in 1980 titled "The Ecclesiology of Popular Christian Communities." Parallel to the theologians' meeting was a meeting of representatives from such communities themselves. The theologians begin their reflection by noting that there is a new phenomenon. The poor are massively breaking through into each society, with new organizational forms. Similarly they are breaking through in the church, which is a form of God's judgment:

> The Christian current within the popular movement and the renewal of the church, starting from an option for the poor, are an ecclesial movement which is one and the same.

They mention CEB's and "popular Christian communities," which seems to have a broader connotation. In any case, both of them have a liberating service within the overall population, exercised through the formation of consciousness, popular education and developing ethical and cultural values. These communities are the "first fruits of the whole people," at whose service they exist. Since the basic division in society is between rich and poor, and since the popular Christian communities, Catholic and Protestant, share the same historical and eschatological *proyecto*, the poor open the way toward ecumenical unity.

Evidently the term "popular church" is meant to relativize a certain notion of "Christian base communities." The intuition is that in some way the church is being born wherever people are struggling for liberation in a Christian way, whatever be their relation to the official church.

Thus CEB's themselves, as exciting a development as they might be when compared to the traditional form of the church's presence, are best seen as but one step toward a still to be discovered future. It occurs to me, for example, that CEB's, for all their merits, still show the marks of an oppressive society by the very fact that the initiative normally does not come from the poor themselves, but from the church's pastoral agents. Certainly they are intended to be a means whereby "masses become a people" as the São Paulo meeting put it, but even in their functioning they inevitably retain many features of a class society.

Implicit in the intuition of the "popular church," then, is the conviction that today's struggles are leading to victory and that these societies will be transformed and people will relate in new ways. It is impossible for us to imagine what forms the church will take in that context, to what extent it will look like today's CEB's and to what extent there might be other forms. Is it possible that in such a society an important form of liturgy might be analogous to large political rallies (where there is no intimate face-to-face dimension)? The existing CEB's are only one pointer toward a future whose full dimensions cannot be measured.

Chapter 42

Henri J. M. Nouwen

Christ of the Americas

When I came to the United States in 1971, not for a visit, a course or a sabbatical, but to make my home here, I had an intuition that would grow stronger as the years went by. It was the intuition that the spiritual destiny of North America is intimately linked to the spiritual destiny of South America. Somehow I sensed that in order to come to know the living Christ among the people in the northern part of the Americas, I had to be willing to expose myself to the way the living Christ reveals Himself in the southern part of the Americas.

This intuition at first was very vague and even seemed somewhat farfetched, but it was strong enough to make me spend summers in Bolivia and Paraguay and familiarize myself increasingly with the language and the life of the Latin American people. During the 1970's I started to explore more and more the ways in which North and South were interconnected, not just in socioeconomic and political ways but also and even more so in spiritual ways.

Could it be possible that the pain and struggles of the North American people are an intimate part of the pains and struggles of the people of South America? Could it be said that the experience of loneliness, guilt, shame, and disconnectedness that I had shared so fully with the students I taught at universities in the United States cannot be fully understood without the experience of poverty, oppression, and exploitation that I came to know in Latin American cities? Could it even be true that underneath all the political and socioeconomic dependencies that have been so powerfully described by contemporary historians, there is a deeper spiritual dependency the nature of which we have hardly explored?

These questions have been with me during the last ten years, though I hardly had words for them. When, however, I went to Central America and witnessed the immense agony of people there, these questions suddenly became burning questions asking for an immediate response. In Central America, that inflamed cord binding the two continents together, my hesitant intuition became an undeniable vision, the vision of the living Christ stretched out on the cross of the American continents from five centuries of human unfaithfulness.

I came to realize that the word of Jesus had come to Central America during the end of the 15th and the beginning of the 16th century and had spread north and south over

First published in *America,* 102 (April 21, 1984). Reprinted with permission of America Press, Inc., 106 West 56th Street, New York, NY 10019. © 1984. All rights reserved.

the continents. I came to see that that Word was a Word of reconciliation, unity, and peace, a Word that wanted to become flesh in human history. I came to understand that this living Word of Jesus wanted to form one body of people bound together by a love stronger and deeper than the fear that divides races, cultures, and nations. And I came to the painful insight that the Word has not been received but is being tortured and broken by the same people who are called to witness to its reconciling power. Christians are imprisoning Christians, Christians are torturing Christians, Christians are murdering Christians, and an immense darkness covers the world in which the incarnate Word is dying again.

When I saw that divine event taking place, I knew that indeed the suffering Christ of North America and the Suffering Christ of South America were one. They cannot be separated or divided without reenacting the crucifixion over and over again. Jesus Christ is not just a historical person who died long ago outside the walls of Jerusalem and whose life we remember as a source of inspiration for us. Jesus Christ is the Lord of history whose death, Resurrection, and coming in judgment is the deepest and most revealing event of our own daily history.

As Christians, we are challenged to recognize that the tragic political, economic, and military events that we are living today are the symptoms of a spiritual event of which we are part. We are challenged to manifest to the world that Christ is dying among us, that Christ is being raised up among us, that Christ is coming again and again in judgment among us. It is this divine knowledge that allows us to see what is really happening, to continue to have hope even when we see death and destruction, and to recognize the concrete task that this vision reveals to us. Thus we may slowly grow in the understanding of the mysterious spiritual connection among the continents and find new ways to live as people of light in the midst of an ever deepening darkness.

Let me therefore try, though with much trepidation, to speak about Central America with the words that summarize the mystery of our human pilgrimage: Christ has died, Christ is risen, Christ will come again.

CHRIST HAS DIED

The Word of the living God, in and through whom all have been created, became flesh in Jesus Christ who died for us humans so that we may have life everlasting. This central affirmation of the Christian faith has profound implications for the way we understand and relate to the agonies of the Americas.

When we say "Christ has died," we express the truth that all human suffering in time and place has been suffered by the Son of God who also is the Son of all humanity and thus has been lifted up into the inner life of God Himself. There is no suffering—no guilt, shame, loneliness, hunger, oppression or exploitation, no torture, imprisonment or murder, no violence or nuclear threat—that has not been suffered by God. There can be no human beings who are completely alone in their sufferings since God, in and through Jesus, has become Emmanuel, God with us.

It belongs to the center of our faith that God is a faithful God, a God who did not want us to ever be alone but who wanted to understand—to stand under—all that is human. The Good News of the Gospel, therefore, is not that God came to take our suffering away, but that God wanted to become part of it.

All of this has been said often before, but maybe not in a way that makes a direct connection with the agony of the world that we witness today. We have to come to the inner knowledge that the agony of the world is God's agony. The agony of women, men, and children during the ages reveals to us the inexhaustible depth of God's agony that we glimpsed in the garden of Gethsemane. The deepest meaning of human history is the gradual unfolding of the suffering of Christ.

As long as there is human history, the story of Christ's suffering has not yet been fully told. Every time we hear more about the way human beings are in pain, we come to know more about the immensity of God's love, who did not want to exclude anything human from his experience of being God. God indeed is Yahweh Rachamin—the God who carries His suffering people in His womb with the intimacy and care of a mother. This is what Blaise Pascal alluded to when he wrote that Christ is in agony until the end of times.

The more we try to enter into this mystery the more we will come to see the suffering world as a world hidden in God. Outside of God human suffering is not only unbearable but cannot even be faced. Understandably, many people say, "I have enough problems of my own, do not bother me with the problems of the world. Just making it from day to day in my family, my town, my work is enough of a burden. Please do not plague me with the burdens of people in Central America or other places. They only make me feel more angry, more guilty, and more powerless." Outside of God even small burdens can pull us down and destroy our physical, emotional, and spiritual health. Outside of God burdens are to be avoided at all cost. Seeing people's misery and pain outside of God becomes a burden too heavy to carry and makes us feel darkness inside.

But when we come to know the inner connectedness between the world's pain and God's pain, everything becomes radically different. Then we see that in and through Jesus Christ God has lifted up all human burdens into his own interiority and made them the way to recognize His immense love. Jesus says, "My yoke is easy and my burden light," but Jesus' burden is the burden of all humankind. When we are invited to carry this burden of Jesus, we are invited to carry the burden of the world. The great mystery is that this very burden is a light burden since it is the burden that makes known to us the unlimited love of God.

Here we touch the spiritual dimensions of all social concern. The hunger of the poor, the torture of prisoners, the threat of war in many countries, and the immense human suffering we hear about from all directions can only call us to a deeply human response if we are willing to see in the brokenness of our fellow human beings the brokenness of God, because God's brokenness does not repulse. It attracts by revealing the loving face of the One who came to carry our burdens and to set us free. Seeing the agony of the people then becomes the way of coming to know the love of God, a love that reconciles, heals and unites.

One of the most remarkable—and disturbing—aspects of our relationship with the people of South and Central America is that we know so little about them. It seems that we feel closer to the people of Europe than to those who live below our southern border. Few North Americans know where Honduras, El Salvador, Guatamala, Nicaragua, and Costa Rica are located. It might even be easier for us to draw a map of Europe than a map of Central or South America. And who knows much about the long and often torturous history of its peoples? It seems that we are afraid to pay attention to their struggles, vaguely realizing that when we start connecting our lives with their lives, our lives cannot remain the same.

And still the peoples of South and Central America are our brothers and sisters who belong to the same body of Christ as we do. That bond can help us overcome our fears and face each other as members of the same family who need each other. It is the bond of Word and Baptism by which we are united in the same Lord that allows us to let down our defenses and reach out to each other. We have to come to know each other, not just in general terms but in the concrete context of our daily lives. We have to come to know each other's names, each other's families, each other's work, and most of all each other's hopes.

So much violence comes from fear, and so much fear is the tragic result of the artificial distance we have kept between us. "Do not fear; it is I," Jesus said. That means for us that we will meet the Lord of love when we let go of our fears and look each other in the eyes, take each other's hands, and carry each other's burdens.

Once we know that we can come together without fear, we can enter into each other's pain and grow together—even where many problems remain unsolved and many questions unanswered. The complexity of the situation in Central America is often a reason for us not to become involved and to withdraw behind the misleading slogans of communism, Marxism, imperialism, democracy, and free enterprise. These words mostly hide the concrete reality of the human struggle and offer us an easy way out. But as a people of God we are called to stay close to one another and to travel together, even though we might be unable fully to grasp or comprehend the situation in which we find ourselves.

For me personally, one of the most difficult challenges in Central America was to face the divisions within the church. When I went to Nicaragua, I had hoped to find a Christian community that could speak clearly and unambiguously the Word of God and thus be a true sign of hope in the midst of the struggle of the Nicaraguan people to find a new national identity. To come to the awareness that the words "Christ has died" not only refer to the physical and emotional pains of the people, but also to the divisions among the Christian communities, was extremely painful for me. The Word of God was clearly torn and the body of Christ tortured by dissent and conflict among its members. But I knew that I had to dare to face this even though it might shake the foundations of my own faith and hope.

One Sunday I attended three different Catholic services. The same Gospel was being proclaimed and the same Eucharist was being celebrated, but there was no unity among them. It seemed that the Word of God meant totally different things at each place.

At 8 A.M. I went to a church where I found some poor people, mostly elderly, gathered around the altar. After reading the Gospel the priest said:

> Dear brothers and sisters in Christ, four years ago you had no voice. Four years ago nobody paid any attention to you. Four years ago you couldn't write or read. Four years ago you were afraid that the national guard of Somoza would suddenly appear to kill and destroy. Four years ago you felt like slaves without any freedom of word or action. But now you have a voice. Since the triumph of the revolution you have become people whose experience and opinion count in the making of a new future. Now you can read and write, now you can walk without fear on the streets of Managua, now you have a new-found freedom. You no longer are like the Israelites in Egypt. You have been led out of Egypt and are on the way to the promised land. And I'd like you to realize that as Christians we have a new opportunity to come to know more fully what it means to live a Christian life. There is no contradiction between the revolution and Christianity. The revolution makes it possible to become better Christians who can claim their human dignity and fully express the gifts God has given them. Let us therefore work together with all those who want to make our land a free land, a land that can determine its own destiny and its own course. We do not have to hesitate, because God is with us in this new and exciting journey.

At 10 A.M. I went to another church very close to the one I had just attended. The church was a beautifully decorated place. There were many people, young and old, mostly families who looked as if they belonged to the middle and upper classes of Nicaraguan society. After the priest had read the Gospel he said:

If you think that you can truly love God without obeying your bishop, you fool yourselves. These people of the so-called popular church or the so-called base communities who think they can be Christians of the revolution do not understand that the Sandinista regime is not at all interested in their religion, but only uses them for its own political interests. Anyone who has read Karl Marx knows that during the first phase of a leftist revolution there is always a certain tolerance toward Christianity. But when the second phase starts it aims at the establishment of an atheistic society. As a priest who has fought Communism all my life, I am willing to protest loudly and clearly together with our bishop against the atheistic and totalitarian regime that wants to destroy our church and persecute its leaders and its members. I am willing to give my life in the struggle against the Communist regime that increasingly robs us of our freedom. Because I know that when those Christians of the revolution will appear before the throne of God on the day of judgment, the Lord will say to them, "I do not know you," and He will send them to the eternal fire.

After the Mass I asked the priest if I could talk with him. He welcomed me into his house and spoke to me openly and freely. There was little doubt in my mind that he was as sincere in his convictions as the priest I had heard at the earlier Mass.

Finally at 5 P.M. I attended a Eucharistic celebration by a group of small Christian base communities. During the dialogue homily one of the women rose and said:

Do you remember how four years ago we all thought that now the good time had come? Do you remember that we expected enough food for all, a good job, a decent house, and our own plot of land? Do you remember how we all had fantasies about an ideal country with an ideal government? But today, four years later, there are long lines of people waiting for bread, there are many unemployed people, there are only a few of us who have a good house to live in or a good piece of land to work on. Things did not work out as smoothly as we had hoped. Our government made more mistakes and our people became more divided than we had expected. But, brothers and sisters, let us not fall into the temptation of wanting to return to the time of slavery and oppression. Let us not be seduced by the flesh pots of Egypt, saying, "Under Somoza we at least had enough to eat!" Although we have not yet reached the promised land, we are no longer in Egypt. We have left the land of oppression and exploitation, and are now together in the desert, tempted to become morose and even resentful. But let us realize that we are moving toward something new and that we need patience and perseverance to let it become true. Let us not look back, but forward, trusting that what we have begun will come to its fulfillment one day.

When I came home that night after having heard these three sermons, I felt confused and very sad. Three times I had heard the Word of God, but it sounded like words from three different gods. Whom to believe, whom to trust, whom to learn from? In the following days I listened to many more people—not only priests but also Protestant ministers, leaders in the government, leaders in the church, people in the marketplace and working on the tobacco farms. And when I returned to the United States, I spoke there to three senators, to representatives, lobbyists, and many American citizens belonging to different churches, living in different states, and coming from different backgrounds. But the same questions kept returning: Whom to believe, whom to trust, whom to learn from?

Some say, "What is happening in Nicaragua is nationalism: a country trying to determine its own future." Others say, "No, it's internationalism: a country becoming the victim of Cuban-Soviet domination." Some say, "What you see in Nicaragua is the best example of a revolution in which Christian values are truly integrated." Others say, "No, it is a revolution based on atheistic principles and bent on the eradication of all religious beliefs." Some say, "What Nicaragua is trying to accomplish is a socialistic society in which all the people can equally enjoy the fruits of the land and the products of human labor." Others say, "No, Nicaragua is gradually becoming the subject of a totalitarian regime in which the state will control every part of life and in which even the little bit of freedom that existed under Somoza will be taken away."

And so we see words being used in all directions whether they are used in the government, the church, or the marketplace. My first inclination was to make up my mind quickly and choose sides. But who am I to take sides, a stranger in a land whose history I have not lived and whose people I hardly know? There is a great attraction to solving ambiguities by quickly taking one side or the other. But this type of solution, while giving a sense of security, might become the fertile ground for more conflict and violence. In order to prevent myself from moving in that direction, I had to remind myself constantly that underneath those conflicting political and socioeconomic evaluations it was being made manifest to me that Christ was dying among His people. I had to hold on to the truth that the tearing apart of the Word outside as well as inside the church was the bitter fruit of five centuries of unfaithfulness. The poverty and oppression that gave rise to the revolution in Nicaragua, as well as the way the powerful nation of the North responded to that revolution, show in a dramatic way that "He came to His own domain and His own people did not accept Him" (Jn. 1:11).

The increasing tensions and the rapid escalation of war and violence in Central America have to be understood far beyond the range of the discussion that takes place in the circles of psychologists, sociologists, historians, economists, and politicians. Their arguments are valuable and important, but for those who have eyes to see and ears to hear, something is taking place the dimensions of which can only be perceived by people of faith. And for them there is a call, not first of all to solve all ambiguities but to stand in the midst of them and become part of the suffering of the living Christ, a suffering that leads to salvation. Maybe after all is said the real question for us is not what to do about it all, but how to repent for the sins that led to the crucifixion of the Lord who came to bring life.

CHRIST IS RISEN

Can we face the death of Christ without knowing about His Resurrection? The Good News of the Gospel is that the death of Christ was the gateway to new life. I think that the story of Christ's death can only be told as a story of hope by those whose faith is deeply anchored in His Resurrection. Just as sin can only be truly known to us in the light of forgiving grace, so death can only be faced squarely in the light of the new life to which it leads. This is important to realize when we want to see not only the death but also the Resurrection of Christ as part of the historical reality in which we live. Maybe we have to say that only in the context of the new life that we see being born out of human agonies are we able to face these very agonies. I say this to suggest that all that I wrote in the previous section somehow presupposes what I will write in this section. Just as the story of Christ's death was written after the knowledge of His Resurrection, so too were the previous thoughts only possible in the light of the following.

"Christ Is Risen" means that guilt, loneliness, hunger, poverty, war, and devastation no longer have the last word. Death and all its symptoms in our individual and communal lives are not the final reality any more.

This has been stated many times in many ways, but it remains one of the greatest challenges to affirm this in our concrete life situation. The constant temptation is to experience a concrete appearance of the power of death as too much to resist and look beyond. Depression, resentment, revenge, and hatred are all forms of surrender to the power of death and signs of our inability to see that, in and through Christ, death has lost its final power.

When it comes to the nitty-gritty of daily life, it is very, very hard to believe that the "sting" has been taken out of death. When your child dies from a sudden illness, when you lose a dear friend in an accident, when your job and your source of income are taken away from you, when you feel without support from anyone, when your son is kidnapped or your husband tortured or your friends killed, when an earthquake destroys all you had carefully built, when you are surrounded by constant threats on your life, when every one around you wonders if this world will still be here when the year 2000 comes—when any of these or other death situations arise, it is very hard not to be seduced by their darkness and not to surrender to the despair they bring.

From a certain distance it sometimes seems easy to speak about hope when we hear or read about death and destruction, but when we ourselves experience the power of death right where we are, it seems close to impossible to call death powerless and to perceive it as a gateway to new life. The feeling of doom that haunts so many people today reminds us how hard it is to say: "Death no longer has the final word."

And still, that is precisely what the Christ event is all about. Our Lord who died on the cross has overcome death, has conquered the evil one, and has triumphed over the powers of this world. There is no power of death, not even a nuclear holocaust, that has not been conquered in the Resurrection of Christ. Just as there is no human suffering in time and place that has not been lifted up into the intimate life of God through the death of Christ, so there is no human suffering that has not been overcome in His Resurrection. This is not just a statement about a past event, saying "Jesus Christ overcame death when He rose from the grave." It is also a statement about the life of the Christian community as the living body of Christ saying: "Jesus is being raised up among us."

When we recognize that Christ is dying among us on the cross of the continents, we have seen at least a glimpse of the new life His death brings among us. The great mystery of the presence of Christ among the people is that it is a life-giving presence that continues to become visible in the most horrendous death situations. Something totally new is being born among the suffering and dying people in South and Central America, and it is that new life that is being given to us for our conversion.

I would never have been able to say this with such confidence if I had not witnessed the presence of the risen Lord among the suffering people of Nicaragua. It was, in fact, a very concrete event on the border between Nicaragua and Honduras that made it possible for me to say: "Christ is risen, He is risen indeed." I even dare to say that what I saw and heard there was the most revealing experience of my visit to Central America, an experience so deep and powerful that it gave me the strength and courage to return to the United States and call the Christians here to a new task of peacemaking.

With 150 North Americans I went to Jalapa, a small Nicaraguan town very close to the Honduran border. Jalapa had been the victim of many attacks by the counterrevolutionaries who have their camps in the southern part of Honduras and regularly enter Nicaragua with the purpose of establishing a bridgehead there and gradually undermining the Sandinista regime. During the month prior to our visit, many people in the Jalapa area had suffered severely from these hostilities. This was the reason we wanted to go there. We wanted to have some firsthand experience of the war going on at the border between Honduras and Nicaragua and pray for peace with the people who suffered from that war.

I vividly remember how during the prayer vigil five Nicaraguan women joined us. They stood very close to one another and quietly spoke to a group of about twenty North Americans. It was an intimate gathering of the people huddling together and trying to understand one another. One of the women raised her voice and said, "A few months ago the counterrevolutionaries kidnapped my 17-year-old son and took him to Honduras. I have never heard from him anymore, and I lie awake during the night wondering if I will ever see him again."

Then another woman spoke: "I had two boys and they both have been killed during the last year. When I grieve and mourn, I grieve and mourn not only because they have been killed but also because those who killed them dismembered their bodies and threw the parts over the fields so that I could not even give them a decent burial."

Then the third woman spoke: "I had just been married and my husband was working in the fields. Suddenly the contras appeared—they burned the harvest, killed my husband, and took his body away. I have never found his body."

There was a long and painful silence. Out of that silence a voice was heard. One of the Nicaraguan women said, "Do you know that we found U.S.-made weapons in our fields? Do you realize that your government paid for the violence that is taking place here? Are you aware that our children and husbands are being killed because your people make it possible by their support? Directly or indirectly, willingly or unwillingly, you are causing our agony. Why? Why? What have we done to deserve this? What did we do to you, your people, or your country to be subjected to so much hostility, anger, and revenge?"

For a long time no one said a word. What could be said? But then a question came from us that sounded like a prayer. Someone quietly asked, "Do you think you can forgive us? Do you think it is possible for you to speak a word of forgiveness?" I saw how one of the women turned to the others and softly said, "We should forgive them." She then turned to us, looking us in the eye, and said clearly: "Yes, we forgive you." But it seemed that we could not yet fully hear it.

Someone else said, "Do you really forgive us for all the sorrow and pain we have brought to your village and your people?" And the woman said, "Yes, we forgive you." Another voice spoke: "Do you truly forgive us for killing your husbands and children?" And the women said, "Yes, we forgive you." And there was another voice, "Do you also forgive us for all the fear and agony we have brought to your homes?" And the women said, "Yes, we forgive you." And as if we still were not hearing it fully, another begging question was heard, "But do you forgive us too for the many times we have invaded your country in the past and for the fact that we have made you subject to our decisions and rules for most of this century?" And again the women said, "Yes, we forgive you."

Suddenly I realized that I was being lifted up in this litany of forgiveness: "Do you forgive us?" "Yes, we forgive you." "Do you forgive us?" "Yes, we forgive you." As this prayer was going on, it was as if I could see for a moment that the broken heart of the dying Christ, stretched out on the cross of the Americas, was being healed. The five women appeared as representatives of all men, women, and children of South and Central America. Their voices were like the voices of millions of people who had suffered during the last five centuries, bringing all the agonies of poverty and oppression together and lifting them up to us. They opened our eyes to the immense suffering that is being suffered by the poor of our countries and said, "Do not be afraid to look at it. We show it to you not to make you feel guilty or ashamed, but to let you see the immensity of God's forgiveness." The five women of Jalapa are the women standing under the cross. They speak for us that divine prayer: "Father, forgive them, they do not know what they are doing" (Lk. 23:34). They are the voices of the dying Christ speaking of new life being born in suffering.

No hatred, no revenge, no lashing out in anger, but repeated words of forgiveness that create unity and community. As these words were spoken, the women of Nicaragua and the men and women of North America became one people. They embraced one another, cried together, and said over and over again, "Peace, peace, peace be with you." As that was taking place, I and many of us had a glimpse of the Resurrection. The risen Christ, the Christ who came to take our sins away by His death, rose to make us into a new body, a new community, a new fellowship, a church. When the North Americans and Nicaraguans became one, they revealed that the power of divine love is stronger than death and reaches far beyond ethnic, national, or cultural boundaries. The forgiveness of the women of Jalapa, offered to us as the fruit of their suffering, gave us a vision of the unity that God's Word came to bring us.

At that moment we saw again that the sting has been taken out of death and that Christ indeed is victorious over the power of evil. It is the vision of the risen Christ emerging in the midst of human suffering. Because precisely at the moment that we saw human agony as we had never seen it before, the light of God's forgiveness was revealed to us. Precisely when we touched the deepest human sorrow, a moment of gladness became visible. Precisely when we were most tempted to despair, words of hope were being spoken. That is the mystery of the Resurrection:

> I tell you most solemnly, you will be weeping and wailing while the world will rejoice; you will be sorrowful but your sorrow will turn to joy . . . . I have told you this so that you may find peace in me. In the world you will have trouble, but be brave: I have conquered the world [Jn. 16:20, 33].

Here all the ambiguities vanish. While I felt called to live in the midst of the diverse opinions, convictions, and evaluations concerning the political events in Central America and suffer the ambiguities as part of the dying of Christ, I realized in Jalapa that there is an undeniable clarity arising out of the ambiguities. It is the clarity of the risen Christ who is the Lord of life and who reaffirms in His Resurrection that God is a God not of the dead but of the living. I might not be able to have a final word about the meaning and direction of the revolution in Nicaragua. But I do have a final word about the U. S. intervention in that country, because the forgiveness of the Nicaraguan women who had been victims of U. S.-supported violence and murder made our sins undeniably manifest.

What the American government, and indirectly the American people, is doing is unjust, illegal, and immoral. It is unjust because we intervene in a country that in no way threatens us; it is illegal because we break every existing international law against intervention in an autonomous country; and it is immoral because we inflict destruction, torture, and death on innocent people. As Christians we should have no doubts or hesitation in protesting clearly and loudly against any form, covert or overt, of U. S. intervention in Nicaragua. Christ is risen means that Christians are a people of reconciliation, not of division; people who heal, not hurt; people of forgiveness, not of revenge; people of love, not of hate; in short, people of life, not of death.

When I heard the words of forgiveness spoken by the five Nicaraguan women in Jalapa, my paralysis about how to speak about Central America was gone. I knew that these women had empowered me to return to my people and to call them in the name of the Risen Christ to their task of peacemaking. I could do this now, not because I feel guilt-ridden and want to clear my conscience, but because I had heard the words of God's reconciling forgiveness that are words for all the people of North America.

Now I can announce: "Have hope! We have been forgiven, we no longer have to be afraid! We no longer have to hide behind walls stacked with bombs. We no longer have to speak words of suspicion and hatred. We no longer have to prepare ourselves for war. Now the time has come to accept the forgiveness offered to us and realize that we belong to one body. Now the time has come to reach out to our suffering sisters and brothers and to offer food, shelter, and health care. Now the time has come to heal the wounds of centuries and make visible to the whole world that Christ is risen indeed. Let us be peacemakers as we are called to be and thus come to realize that we and all the people of South and Central America belong to the household of God and can indeed be called His children."

It seems essential that we start realizing that our first task toward the South and Central American people is not to do something for them, not to help them with their problems or to assist them in their needs. All of that is very important, but all forms of help become forms of violence when giving does not presuppose receiving. Our first task is to receive from the suffering people the fruits of their suffering. Only then can we truly give.

We need the people of South and Central America as much as they need us. We need one another as much as members of the same body need one other. In the midst of the present international crisis, we are becoming aware in a new way that not just our physical and emotional well being but also our spiritual destiny—our salvation—cannot be realized without the people of South and Central America. We need them for our salvation. They offer us forgiveness, gratitude, joy, and a profound understanding of life as mature fruits of their struggle for freedom and human dignity. They offer us these fruits for our conversion, so that we too may be saved. By their suffering they have indeed been ordained to be our evangelizers. It may be hard for us to recognize this divine irony by which the oppressed become the healers of the oppressor, but it is this recognition that might be the beginning of our conversion.

While it is true that the Resurrection of Christ has become manifest in a totally unexpected and new way among our suffering and dying fellow Christians in South and Central America, we will only be able to become real witnesses of the Resurrection when we allow these Christians to become our spiritual guides. Then and only then are we free to help them, not out of obligation, guilt, or fear, but out of gratitude for the gifts we already have received. Thus we can become together again one people, the people that manifest the risen Christ to our despairing world.

CHRIST WILL COME AGAIN

The Christ event embraces more than His death and Resurrection. It will only be complete when it will also include His coming again to judge the living and the dead. Just as Christ's dying and rising not only refer back to past events, so His coming again not only refers to a future event. As Christians, we are called to recognize in the concrete events of our daily lives not only the dying and rising of Christ, but also His coming again.

The coming again of Christ is His coming in judgment. The question that will sound through the heavens and the earth will be the question that we always tend to remain deaf to. Our lives as we live them seem lives that anticipate questions that never will be asked. It seems as if we are getting ourselves ready for the question, "How much did you earn during your lifetime?" or, "How many friends did you make?" or "How much progress did you make in your career?" or, "How much influence did you have on people?" or, "How many books did you write?" or, "How many conversions did you make?" Were any of these to be the question Christ will ask when He comes again in glory, many of us in North America could approach the judgment day with great confidence.

But nobody is going to hear any of these questions. The question we all are going to face is the question we are least prepared for. It is the question: "What have you done for the least of mine?"

It is the question of the just judge who in that question reveals to us that making peace and working for justice can never be separated. As long as there are people who are less than we, in whatever way or form, the question of the last judgment will be with us. As long as there are strangers; hungry, naked, and sick people; prisoners, refugees, and slaves; people who are handicapped physically, mentally, or emotionally; people without work, a home, or a piece of land—there will be that haunting question from the throne of judgment: "What have you done for the least of mine?"

This question makes the coming of Christ an ever present event. It challenges us to look at our world agonized by wars and rumors of war, and to wonder if we have not fallen into the temptation to think that peace can be separated from justice. But why would there be wars if all people have enough food, enough work, enough land? Why would there be so many guns, tanks, nuclear warheads, submarines, and other instruments of destruction if the world were not divided according to those who have the most, those who have more than enough, those who have just enough, those who have less than enough, and those who have the least?

When we look at the painful struggles of the people in South and Central America, it is not hard to realize who the least are. In most of the countries below our southern border, a very few have the most, and most have the least, and there is little in between. This state of flagrant injustice that causes the oppression and exploitation of many by a few is artificially maintained by the nations in which most people have the most, and a few have the least.

"Protecting our vital interests" has become the standard euphemism for maintaining inequality among peoples and nations. It also is the main rationale for an internationally interlocking military network built on the illusion that an ever-increasing power is the only thing that keeps this world from disintegrating into chaos. Thus the world becomes an absurd world in which every year thousands of people die from hunger and violence, and in which those who cause these deaths are convinced that they do this to defend the great spiritual values of the free world.

As Jesus predicted, many will commit crimes thinking that they are doing something virtuous in the name of God. And as death and destruction increase, there are fewer people who can explain what is happening for what reason. Thus the world plunges itself deeper and deeper into absurdity—which literally means "Deep deafness"—becoming less and less able to hear the question of the coming Christ, "What have you done for the least of mine?"

It is my impression that most people understand the question of the coming Christ as a question directed to individual persons. All through Christian history there have been men and women who have listened with great attentiveness to this question and radically changed their lives in response to it. Many have dedicated their entire lives to work with the poor, the sick, and the dying. Thus we can say that the question of the day of judgment has already borne fruit.

But when we read the 25th chapter of Matthew's Gospel carefully, it becomes clear that the question of the coming of Christ is not directed to individuals alone but to nations as well. The story of the last judgment opens with the words, "When the Son of Man comes in His glory, escorted by all the angels, then He will take His seat on His throne of glory. All nations will be assembled before Him" (Mt. 25:31–32). These words open a new perspective on the final question: "What have you done for the least of mine?" They make us wonder what it means that we not only will be judged as individuals but as nations as well.

Often it seems that we have heard the invitation of Jesus to be humble, compassionate, and forgiving, to take the last place, to carry our cross, and lose our life as an invitation for our individual lives, our family lives or our lives within the communities of prayer and service. We even "encourage each other to follow this gentle way of the Lord and praise those who follow the advice always to consider the other person as better than ourselves" (see Phil. 2:3, 4). But when it comes to the relationship among nations, when we are dealing with decisions that have implications for our nation's role in the world, when we are thinking about our national security and its political ramifications, then we suddenly reverse our attitude completely and consider the Gospel demands as utterly naive.

When it comes to politics, power is the issue, and those who suggest that the powerless way of Christ is also the way to which the nations are called find themselves quickly accused as betrayers of their country. As nations—so we hear—we cannot seriously listen to the question, "What have you done for the least of mine?" Looking at small nations, struggling to overcome their hunger, thirst, estrangement, nakedness, and imprisonment as the least of our brothers and sisters would require a radical change in the use of power; a change from using power to dominate to using power to serve. Many would consider such a change political suicide.

When Nicaragua, a country of 2.8 million people, threw off the yoke of decades of oppression and tried to determine its own destiny, the powerful nation of the North did not respond by encouraging her sister nation with food, clothes, words of welcome, and friendly visits, but by arrogant rejection, isolation, and hostile threats. The United States did not reach out to help one of the least of the nations but soon considered it a potential Soviet missile base that needed to be brought back under absolute control as soon as possible.

The response of the United States towards Nicaragua is the response of a fearful power. Words such as "Marxist-Leninist regime," "Cuban-Soviet domination," and "atheist-totalitarian development" are used to insinuate that a direct danger exists for the safety, security, and well-being of the people of the North. A boycott is organized to prevent Nicaragua from receiving necessary aid and loans, thus paralyzing its economic life. Honduras is made into a huge military base. The counterrevolutionary forces in Honduras and Costa Rica receive increasing support for their attacks on Nicaragua. Meanwhile naval forces are sent to the Pacific and Caribbean waters off the Nicaraguan coasts.

Thus a small country of mostly hungry, poor, and oppressed people is being regarded by the most powerful nation of the world as a serious menace to its "vital interests," treated with suspicion, isolation, and hatred, and pushed in a direction that its Northern "masters" feared it would go. Thus the cry of a people asking for the recognition of their human and national dignity is misinterpreted as part of the seduction of a Communist totalitarian state far away trying to subvert the free democratic state close by. Thus the East-West dimension of the Nicaraguan problem is so stressed and manipulated that the obvious North-South dimension is pushed into the background. Thus the less powerful Southern countries, desiring only to live their own lives, make their own mistakes, and celebrate their own successes, are being cut off by their sister country from the sources that could provide help. Thus the wounds of five centuries of unfaithfulness are torn open and deepened.

The Apostle Paul writes, "In your minds you must be as Christ Jesus. His state was divine, yet He did not cling to His equality with God but emptied Himself to assume the condition of a slave and become as we are" (Phil. 2:5, 7). Are these words also words for the nations? Is it possible that a nation can become one among the nations as Christ became one among us? If it is true that the question of the returning Christ is also a question for the nations, then that question requires not only an individual but also a national conversion.

As long as the overarching goal of the United States is to be at all costs the most powerful nation of the earth, we may become the reluctant participants in the hastening of the Judgment Day, since in this nuclear age the cost for remaining the most powerful nation on the earth quite likely is the end of all human life on this planet.

Thus we are faced with the greatest spiritual challenge ever presented: to be converted as a nation and follow the humble way of Christ. Is that a possibility? It has become a necessity for our survival. It has become our most urgent task to find our true identity among the nations and to let go of the illusory identities that continue to breed one war after another.

The tragedy is that the political discussion among our people and their representatives has been narrowed down so much that no truly political concern can be brought to the foreground without threatening political survival. When the main question has become, "Should the Sandinista regime be overthrown overtly or covertly?" politics has already become the victim of the totalitarianism it is trying to stop from coming close to its borders.

The real issue that faces us today is, "What does it mean to be a nation in a world that is able to destroy itself at any moment?" That is the issue that has to be brought to the center of the attention of our people. If ever, it is today that politicians are called to be wise people, that is, women and men who can raise the issue of national identity and offer a vision of how to be a nation living in harmony among nations freely using its power to serve rather than dominate.

I sense that many personal sacrifices in the political arena will be necessary to reach the point of national discussion aiming at national conversion. Many who possess political power today will need to risk their own political futures and will have to be willing to let go of oppressive power in order to empower other nations and thus further justice and peace in the world. Without such sacrifices there will no longer be a true dialogue in the world of politics, but only a tyrannical monologue leading to the absurd silence not only of politicians but of all human beings. Then we will have created our own day of judgment and will have become our own judges.

This is precisely what the last judgment is all about. The Lord who becomes one of us in humility does not really judge us. He reveals to us what we have become to one another. The day of judgment is in fact the day of recognition, the day on which we see for ourselves what we have done to our brothers and sisters, and how we have treated the divine body of which we are part.

Thus the question, "What have you done to the least of mine?" is not only the question of injustice and the question of peace, it also is the question by which we judge ourselves. The answer to that question will determine the existence or nonexistence of our human family.

"Christ has died, Christ is risen, Christ will come again." That is the divine event taking place in the continents of the Americas, which we as Christians are called to recognize. Without this recognition we cannot truly be peacemakers. Jesus Himself makes this clear when He says, "May you find peace in Me. In the world you will have trouble, but be brave: I have conquered the world" (Jn. 16:33). Peacemaking means to find peace in Christ, the dying, rising, and coming Christ who reveals Himself among the peoples of the Americas.

Recognizing the dying Christ among His people allows us to live in the midst of confusion, ambiguity, and agony; recognizing the risen Christ among His people allows us to receive the fruits of suffering as gifts offered to us for our conversion; recognizing the coming of Christ among His people allows us to search for a new identity not only as individuals but also as a nation. Thus we can find peace in Christ, a peace that does not make us stay aloof from the bitter reality of our history, but a peace that makes us stand in the midst of our world without being destroyed by its seductive powers.

There is one question left. It might prove to be the most important one. "Can we see Christ in the world?" The answer is, "No, we cannot see Christ in the world, but only the Christ in us can see Christ in the world." This answer reveals that the Christ within us opens our eyes for the Christ among us. That is what is meant by the expression "Spirit speaks to Spirit." It is the Spirit of the living Christ dwelling in our innermost being who gives us eyes to contemplate the living Christ as he becomes visible in the concrete events of our history. Christians who become interested in Central America, therefore, do not move from prayer to politics, they move from prayer to prayer.

All that I have been trying to say about the Christ of the Americas was meant to broaden the spectrum of our life of prayer. The Christ whom we encounter in the center of our heart is the same Christ we see stretched out on the cross of the American continents. Without interior prayer we will remain blind to the spiritual nature of what is happening in Central America. But without the prayerful recognition of the living Christ among our sisters and brothers below our southern borders, we can easily slip into a world denying piety that does not lead to the transformation Christ calls for. This explains why prayer continues to be our first—and in a sense—our only task.

Describing the end times, Jesus says, "When you hear of wars and revolutions, do not be frightened, for this is something that must happen. . . . Nation will fight against nation and kingdom against kingdom . . . people dying of fear as they await what menaces the world . . . watch yourselves . . . stay awake, praying at all times for the strength to survive all that is going to happen, and to stand with confidence before the Son of Man" (Lk. 21:9, 36). Praying at all times means keeping our eyes always fixed on Jesus the Christ. As Peter began to sink as soon as he moved his eyes from Jesus to the restless waters on which He walked, so will we lose heart as soon as we stop praying. But as long as we keep the eyes of our hearts and minds focused on Him, we can walk confidently in this world, bringing peace wherever we go.

Chapter 43

Geevarghese Mar Osthathios

The Holy Trinity and the Kingdom of God

Theology is holistic only when it is Trinitarian. In the Patristic period the title "theologian" meant one who dealt with the theology of the Holy Trinity. There is no doctrine of God, specifically based on the Christian Revelation, which is not related to the teaching about God as triune. The Incarnation is that of the Second Person of the Blessed Trinity. The Holy Spirit, according to St. Basil, is not sub-numerated, but connumerated with the Father and the Son. The Church is not only the extension of the Incarnation in the power and under the guidance of the Holy Spirit, but also the sharing fellowship (*koinonia*) in the model of the Holy Trinity.

The Church baptises the catechumen in the name of the Father, the Son, and the Holy Spirit. The worship of the Church is the adoration of the Holy Trinity. The mission of the Church is the expression of the love of the Blessed Trinity manifested in the Incarnation that the world may believe and be brought to baptism in the name of the Trinity and for the deification of the world. The eschaton to which humanity is called through the Church is to the fulness of life in the fellowship of the Trinity.

According to Karl Barth, the Kingdom of God is the Community, but the Community is not the Kingdom of God. This is a subtle difference which differentiates the divine community from the human community:

> The Kingdom of God is the lordship of God established in the world in Jesus Christ. It is the rule of God as it takes place in Him. He Himself is the Kingdom of God. Thus we cannot avoid a statement which Protestantism has far too hastily and heedlessly contested—that the Kingdom of God is the Community. We do not refer to that Kingdom or dominion of God in its completed form in which it obtains for the whole world in the person of the one Son of Man, the one Holy Spirit, and in which it will be directly and universally and definitely revealed and known at the end and goal of all history. . . . The Community is not the Kingdom of God. But the Kingdom of God is the Community.[1]

First published in *The Indian Journal of Theology*, 31 (January–March 1982), pp. 1–14. Used by permission.

In fact, the call to repentance is the call from selfish individualism to the joy of the Trinitarian fellowship of the Church. In another context, speaking of the Kingdom, Barth says, "If it is the case that man is given a promise for his own future in this as yet unrevealed depth of fellowship with God, it cannot be otherwise than that the content of the promise should correspond to the being of God."[2] Life in the Kingdom is life in the fellowship of the Triune God, revealed in history by Christ and the Event of the Pentecost, and manifested in the practice of the Pentecostal sharing and caring community.

There is no doubt, the lack of brotherly fellowship by the Church obscures the face of the Kingdom of which we preach in our mission. Bishop Stephen Neill identifies four areas of vulnerability of the Church in the present day and the third is our lack of brotherhood:

> More serious still is the allegation that we have wholly failed to produce brotherhood in Christ. The Muslim claims—and not without reason—that the brotherhood of Islam is far better than anything that Christianity has to offer. With two suicidal civil wars to our discredit in this country, there is not much that we can say in our defence. It is perhaps possible to claim that we have improved a little.[3]

LOVE IS DECISIVE

The Kingdom of God is the Kingdom of love and so Trinitarian. Love, like God, is all-embracing and self-emptying, and so is the grace of the Kingdom. To quote Hans Urs von Balthasar:

> The obedient love of the Son for the Father is certainly the model for human love before the majesty of God, but, more than that, it is the supreme image of divine love itself appearing. For it is precisely in the Kenosis of Christ (and nowhere else) that the *inner* majesty of God's love appears, of God who "is love" (1 Jn. 4:8) and therefore Trinity.[4]

This love is a gift and a promise, a blessing and an obligation, a joyful responsibility to be evidenced in the life of the Christian in the fellowship of the Church, which is a foretaste and manifestation of the Kingdom of God. Trinitarian love (*agape*), the distinguishing mark of life in the Kingdom, in the model of the Incarnation and the Cross, accepts self-emptying voluntarily and the Cross joyfully for the salvation of the world. Justice, which the whole world craves today more than ever before, should be hastened by the Church's self-denial, cross-bearing, and identification with the poor to strengthen them. "For the Kingdom of God does not mean food and drink but righteousness and peace of joy in the Holy Spirit; he who thus serves Christ is acceptable to God and approved by men" (Rom. 14:17f.).

Life in the Kingdom is marked by the three theological virtues of faith, hope, and love; faith in what God has already done, hope in what He will be perfecting in the future, and love in our present-day thoughts, words, and deeds. Faith in the Holy Trinity will express itself in love, which is the fruit of the Spirit and will instil in us a strong anchor of hope in the consummation of the Kingdom of God at the Parousia. As Jürgen Moltmann points out, "The Kingdom of God becomes present in history through the rule of God. The rule of God is manifested through world and faith, obedience and fellowship, in potentialities grasped, and in co-operation for the life of the world."[5] Love, which is the supreme virtue, actualised fully only in the Holy Trinity and in the Incarnation and the Atoning death of Christ, has to be emulated in the new life in the Kingdom by the power of the Holy Spirit.

There is no sexual distinction in the Godhead, but the virtues of Fatherhood, Motherhood, and Sonship are in God. "Spirit" in Hebrew is in the feminine gender as in Syriac. In a family there is the provision of the father, the love of the mother, and the fellowship of the son. We can speak of God as "Our Father" as He provides everything for us. Similarly, we can speak of God as "Our Mother" as God is the source of love. In Christ the Logos we have our Brother in the Godhead. These distinctions are not water-tight compartments as *perichoresis* unites the three in one and shares the one in three. In the touching utterance of Jesus about Jerusalem, he compares his love for Jerusalem to that of a hen: "O Jerusalem, Jerusalem, killing the prophets and stoning those who are sent to you! How often would I have gathered your children together as a hen gathers her brood under her wings, and you would not" (Matt. 23:37f.).

During the morning walk today through the high range, I was touched by the haste of a cow to climb up the hill to give some milk to her calf crying in the cowshed for some milk. God cares for His children with such a motherly affection and so there is no harm in comparing the Holy Spirit to a mother to show the warmth of God's love for us. After all, all language is symbol. If we can address God as "Our Father who art in Heaven," we can also address Him as "Our Mother who art in Heaven," or "Our Brother who art in Heaven." God is not just one of these, but all these and much more. When Christ taught us to pray "Our Father . . . ," he wanted us to understand God as Father, Mother, Brother, and everything else that we need for our fulness. God is all-sufficient, almighty, all-loving, all-judging, all-giving, all-sovereign, *el shaddai*. His all-inclusive virtue is love. Gal. 5:22 says "the fruit of the Spirit is love," though St. Paul goes on to enumerate eight more virtues which are all included in love.

COMMON GOOD AND PERSONAL PROPERTY

The solution for the tug-of-war between capitalism and communism is in the Trinitarian economic life in the model of the Kingdom of God. Capitalism justifies private property and communism attacks it. Thomas Aquinas justified private property on the basis of the natural law, but the Fathers of the Church attacked it and saw it as the result of the Fall. To quote Emil Brunner:

> Brentano, in the work which has already been mentioned on the economic theories of Christian antiquity, has shown incontestably that "the Fathers of the Church in no wise regarded property as something which has been ordered by the Law of Nature; to them the natural thing is communism, to them property seems only an evil which has become necessary owing to the Fall," and indeed that is true, not only as Troeltsch thought, of the later Church Fathers, but of Tertullian, Irenaeus, and Cyprian. The one who goes furthest in the assertion of communistic ideas in Chrysostom; in his exposition of the story of Ananias and Sapphira he outlines an absolutely communistic theory, which even extols communal consumption as the most natural method. St. Thomas, on the other hand, not only asserts that private property is the best order for the world as it is at the present time, but he tries to modify the patristic communistic doctrine of the Primitive State; modern Catholicism alone, however, has "proved" that private property is an original order of creation, and from the time of Leo XIII this thesis has been sacrosanct, in spite of the reiterated opposition from some isolated individuals.[6]

As I have shown elsewhere,[7] the whole wealth of the whole world belongs to God the Father and all His children have a right to it and no one can claim absolute right to private property. It is selfishness to accumulate wealth when one's own brothers and sisters are without work and food. Emil Brunner, who attacks both capitalism and communism, says, "Although we are convinced that the theory of equality is contrary to the Biblical idea of Creation, we are also convinced that *this* kind of inequality is still more contrary to it."[8] He goes on to say that the "postulate of a Christian economic ethics is not equality, but balance." Again, "The divinely willed meaning of the economic order is not the profit of the individual, but 'the common good,' maintenance of the human life of the community and this knowledge ought to determine his desires and actions."[9]

"Be ye therefore perfect as your heavenly father is perfect" is the ultimate commandment. There is distinction (inequality?) and equality in the Holy Trinity. This paradox is to be applied in the economic order also. In an ideal family, even in the fallen world, every member works for the common good. The brother who is paid higher contributes more to the family than the one who does not get so much salary.

There are so many brothers of the same [Indian] family in the Persian Gulf areas. The one who went there first worked hard and took other brothers and sisters also to their lucrative jobs. As the Indian Government is not socialistic, only a few families are thus better off. The Chinese Government, on the other hand, takes the salary of their citizens abroad for the common good of the Chinese family. The Chinese experiment has bridged the gulf between the rich and the poor more than the Indian. But it is pointed out that there is a monotonous equality in China without the beauty of variety. In order to strike a balance between equality and variety, we can allow a limited quantity of personal property, but no private ownership of instruments of production. The need of all has to be met by the work of all and yet incentive must be given for greater dedicated work. He who comes at the eleventh hour and works only for one hour must also get sufficient to meet the need of the members of his family (Matt. 20) as he was waiting for a job from the morning. But the one who makes five talents ten by hard work must get an incentive (Matt. 25:14–30).

FREE AND RESPONSIBLE KINGDOM

"Freedom means," says Karl Barth, "being in spontaneous and therefore willing agreement with the sovereign freedom of God."[10] Freedom to do *anything* is not freedom, but licence. True freedom is divine responsibility. Freedom is the birth-right of the good, but not of robbers, murderers, exploiters, and thieves. The Kingdom of God is the realm of the free and the kingdom of the devil is the realm of the slaves to passions. God alone is absolutely free. Those who are attuned to the Holy Trinity are truly free. When Jesus told the Jews ". . . you will know the truth and the truth will make you free," they said that they were the descendants of Abraham and were never in bondage. (In fact they were in bondage in Egypt, Assyria, Babylon.) Jesus answered them, "Truly, truly, I say to you, everyone who commits sin is a slave to sin. . . . So if the Son makes you free, you will be free indeed" (Jn. 8:31–36).

Freedom is not individualistic, but social. As Barth points out:

> The kingdom of freedom is not one in which he can act as lord. It is not for him to try to act in it according to his own judgment. If he did, he would certainly not be free, he would secretly have left that place. It is the house of the father, and he needs the father's guidance to act in it and therefore to be free.[11]

The story of the prodigal son shows the truth of Mk. 8:35 that whoever would save his life will lose it and whoever loses his life for God's sake will find it. The younger prodigal ended up in slavery when he wanted to be his lord, but regained freedom and life when he returned to his father's good pleasure. The elder prodigal was a slave all along and ended up in slavery when the brother returned and he was not ready to accept him as his brother. We do not read in Luke 15 that the elder son came into the house. He could not with his proud individualism and irresponsibility.

There is no real freedom in the dehumanising *laissez faire* capitalism which does not treat employees as persons and brothers, but as tools and machines, nor in the atheistic communism, which does not show the ultimate meaning and purpose of life in God and eternal life. The thesis of capitalism which produces the antithesis of communism should find its synthesis in a responsible theistic human brotherhood, an approximation to the Kingdom of God to be fully manifested in the second coming of Christ. The dominating interest of the USA and Soviet Union today is in manufacturing the most destructive bombs conceivable, and not in eradicating poverty from the face of the earth. Emil Brunner is right in saying, "The expression, 'Monster,' which Sombart frequently uses of capitalism, is no exaggeration."[12] In another sense communism is also a monster. Both the monsters are preparing to kill each other without self-destruction, which is an impossibility. It is now agreed on all sides that a Third World War will not be a war to end all wars, but a war to end the world. If the super powers will ever be able to overcome their madness and have good sense, they will stop praying "My kingdom come!" and start to pray "Your Kingdom come" and stop the armament race and build up a responsible brotherhood.

Brunner is wrong in contrasting Stoic egalitarianism and the Christian doctrine of creation. God did not create the class-structure but a human family. It is the Fall that made the brother kill his own brother. The Trinitarian model was in the image of God given to Adam and Eve personally and collectively. Christ died and rose up again and the Holy Spirit descended to give us back that model in a higher and better manner in the Kingdom of God. Life with God in Paradise was a happy fellowship of freedom. Pentecost gave it back to the redeemed. We have no right to ask "Am I my brother's keeper?" I *am* my brother's brother.

TRINITARIAN DISTINCTION AND EQUALITY TO BE AIMED AT

The kingdom of darkness we live in is getting darker and darker. The disparity between the rich and the poor in the same country and between the developed and developing countries is becoming intolerable. The following statistics are taken from the excellent book, *Towards the Church of the Poor*, edited by Julio de Santa Ana and published by the World Council of Churches. World Military expenditure in 1974 was $2,608,000,000,000, whereas the world economic aid in the same year was a tiny $125,000,000,000. Per capita income of the developed nations in that year was $3974 over against $315 for the developing nations. The growth of consumer prices, which was 100 in 1960, grew to 617 in 1974 for the developing nations and only to 189 for the developed. Further discrepancies are charted in Table 1.

These staggering differences have been the result of the power of the powerful to exploit the powerless who could not prevent the rich exploiting them through transnational corporations, military power, unjust trade and tariff rates, and the monopoly of scientific knowhow.

A just international economic order will never be brought about voluntarily by the developed rich nations. Even Emil Brunner agrees that "it will need the assistance of the

Table 1

Discrepancies between Developed/Developing Countries (1977)

	Developed Countries	Developing Countries
Per capita public education expense (dollars)	229	13
Teachers per 1000 school children	37	16
Adult literacy percentage	98	49
Public health expenditure per capita (dollars)	144	4
Physicians per 10,000 population	19	3
Life expectancy (years)	72	56
Percentage of world population (1976)	28	72
Percentage of world GNP (1976)	80	20
Percentage of world export earnings (1976)	73	27
Percentage of international reserves (1977)	57	43
Percentage of world military expenditure (1974)	77	23
Percentage of world public education expenditure (1974)	87	13
Percentage of world public health expenditure (1974)	93	7
Growth of per capita income, from 1960 to 1976	from $1396 to $5036	from $128 to $494
Deaths per 1000 population between 1960 and 1975	9	17

law, with its powers of compulsion; on the other hand, it is also evident that the individual Christian can never be satisfied with the measure of compulsory adjustment effected legally by the community."[13]

The first thing to be done is a new understanding of the sin of the present disparity, selfish accumulation of wealth, consumerism, love of luxury, callous disregard of the need of the neighbour, social injustice, economic exploitation, cultural alienation, and religious individualism.

In order to do this, the Christian ethic must be taught with the basis of Trinitarian theology and kenotic Christology which would reinstate the double commandment in its central biblical position. We must teach that even if capitalism had a role to play to exploit the resources of the world on a competitive system of the "survival of the fittest," the time has now come when the survival of the fittest is intertwined with the survival of the unfit and that stewardship of depleting resources is indispensable.

THE KINGDOM AS THE GIFT OF THE HOLY TRINITY

The preaching of John the Baptist and of Christ was, "Repent for the Kingdom of God is at hand." "Now after John was arrested, Jesus came into Galilee, preaching the Gospel of God and saying, 'The time is fulfilled, and the Kingdom of God is at hand, repent and believe in the Gospel' " (Mk. 1:14f.; Matt. 4:12–17; Lk. 4:14, 15). God the Father is the source of Kingship; Christ the Son inaugurated it in history, and the Holy Spirit is here to consummate it, although the full manifestation will be only when the new heaven and the new earth will take the place of our aeon. "Then comes the end, when he delivers the Kingdom to God the Father after destroying every rule and every authority and power. For he must reign until he has put all his enemies under his feet. The last enemy to be destroyed is death" (1 Cor. 15:24–26).

Each Christian and the divided Church must repent to receive the joy and the glory of the Kingdom. Capitalistic order must repent of its selfish profit-motive and exploitation. Communistic order must repent of its materialism and atheism. The developed nations must repent of their self-interest which keeps the poor in their dire poverty and need. The developing nations must repent of their idleness, indifference, and jealousy. "For there is no distinction; since all have sinned and fall short of the glory of God" (Rom. 3:22f.). Orthodox Churches must repent for the lack of missionary zeal to save the world, Roman Catholicism of its pyramidical hierarchy and class-structure, and Protestantism of its ultra-individualism.

If we do not repent and change our ways of life, the kingdom of darkness will overtake us. Sin is very real and pays its wages. The wrath of God may allow Satan to be the instrument of God's punishment for the sinful world. Brunner says that "even to the Reformers Satan is never an independent power, but always merely the being which executes the wrath of God."[14] And St. Paul speaks emphatically, "For the wrath of God is revealed from heaven against all ungodliness and wickedness of men who by their wickedness suppress the truth" (Rom. 1:18). History shows that many rich nations have fallen by inner corruption and power-mongering. Arnold J. Toynbee's *Study of History* has proved this fact. The question is whether the rich will repent and learn to live simply that the poor may simply live. Will the present greed-based economy of the rich change to a need-based economy?

The Church has rightly emphasized the unknowability and the inscrutability of the mystery of the Trinity, which will ever be a mystery as long as we are in the finitude of our existence. She has also taught that the mystery of the Trinity is not to be scrutinised but to be adored and worshipped. But she has not taught with definite clarity that the

Trinity is to be emulated as far as we can by the power of the Holy Spirit. The various analogies of the theologians about the Trinity have been from nature (like spring, pond, and river) or psychology (like memory, understanding, and will) and from philosophy (like one substance [*ousia*] and three persons [*hypostasis*]), but seldom from the human family of the Father, the Mother, and the Son. This may be due to the fear of being branded as tritheists. But as St. Basil asks, "What is number in the Godhead?" God is beyond number. He is the fulness of all number and includes within Him singularity and plurality. It is to this unity in plurality that the Church must move as the Kingdom of the triune God. God wants to give it to us, but are we ready to receive it?

BEAR THE CROSS AND WEAR THE CROWN

The Cross was not an anti-climax of the life of Christ, but the natural coronation of the one born in a manger, brought up in infancy as a refugee, who worked as a carpenter for his livelihood, moved about as an itinerant preacher without a place to lay his head, rode into the temple on a borrowed ass, had the last supper with his disciples in a borrowed room, and was crucified on somebody else's cross to be buried in another's tomb. But all the seven words from the Cross were sermons of forgiveness from the gallows. Hence, naturally the thief from the right prayed to Him, "Remember me when you come into your kingdom!" "For you know the grace of our Lord Jesus Christ, that though he was rich, yet for your sake he became poor, so that by his poverty you might become rich" (2 Cor. 8:9). Writing about the dignity of the Cross, Karl Barth says:

> He endured it in the act of reconciling the world with God, as the man in whom God humbled Himself in order that man should be exalted. . . . And in so doing He tore down the wall of partition which separated man from God. Offering and losing His life, He was the living and true and royal man, as was revealed in His resurrection. This is the law of His crucifixion. It is in accordance with this law that a term is set for Christians and they have to bear their cross.[15]

This last sentence is very important. Christ bore the Cross to save the world and we have to bear our crosses to follow Him in fulfilling today what he has fulfilled for all times. It is here that Christianity has failed ever since Constantine, except in the example of the desert fathers and others who have accepted voluntary and vicarious suffering in mission fields for the extension of the Kingdom of God.

God, being love, could not remain in Heaven when His own children, created by Him in His own image, were labouring, suffering, and dying. The question we have to ask ourselves, if we are Christians, is whether we are worthy to be called Christians as long as we do not take up the Cross and follow the Master to Calvary. The path to Easter is always through Good Friday. But we want to have the golden crown without the Cross of thorns. Christ is our Redeemer as well as our Model. As Moltmann says:

> On the Cross, there takes place what Luther so vividly calls 'the merry exchange,' as he draws on the bridal imagery of medieval mysticism, in which Christ and the soul become one body. Christ makes the soul's sin and suffering his own, conferring on her in her poverty his own righteousness, his freedom, and his divinity. Here man's sufferings become Christ's history and Christ's freedom becomes man's history. As the community of Christ, the Church is in solidarity with the men and women who are living in the shadow of the cross.[16]

Our tendency today is to see the Cross only as that of Christ and accept the Kingdom without paying the cost of discipleship. This is a very dangerous tendency. One of the ways in which we can take up our cross, and follow the Lord in our times is by taking the side of the poor and the oppressed, and strengthening them to stand squarely against exploitation and oppression by the rich. The result will be fresh crucifixion of us by the oppressors, as happened to Archbishop Romero in March 1980 and is happening to many others in El Salvador, Brazil, Argentina, Korea, S. Africa, and many other parts of the world today. Mere identification and solidarity with the poor is not enough. We must do everything to conscientise them and to make them self-reliant. Exploiters will not stop exploitation unless they are forced to do so. There are many ways of doing it non-violently.

WHAT IS TO BE DONE?

Are we to be complacent and allow the kingdom of darkness to extend its passion for power? No, we are to wait upon the Lord for the power of Pentecost again in the Church. The seed that waits for rain sprouts and grows into a tree. The worm that patiently waits in the cocoon comes out as a butterfly. The egg that waits in the incubator changes itself into a chicken and comes out of the shell, breaking its strength. The apostles and their companions who waited in the upper room received a new courage to bear witness to Christ to their enemies and become martyrs for Christ. They could finally break the power of the Roman Empire.

Once we are renewed by the person and power of the Holy Spirit, we can challenge the citadels of the oppressors and bring their fortress down. Jesus Christ was very vehement in his attack on the rich. Zacchaeus became volutarily poor when Christ visited his home. John the Baptist had some strong words for the corrupt officers and Roman soldiers (Lk. 3). St. James was the prophet of social justice who told the rich to "weep and howl for the miseries that are coming upon you" (5:1ff.). We must also join the company of the apostles and take our stand squarely against the rich. If the Father's property is for all His children, those who are rich in a poor world have robbed their brothers to become rich. This truth must be brought home to both the rich and the poor. The fruit of hard work by any must be for the welfare of the human family and not for islands of luxury in an ocean of poverty.

St. Thomas Aquinas would not have defended private property if he were alive today. The teachings of St. John Chrysostom and other Fathers of the Church must be taught in the Sunday Schools and Churches over against what Aquinas taught about the justification of private property. The biblical teaching on stewardship and private property cannot go together. If God is the Owner of everything, we are not the owners, but only stewards. The duty of the steward is to act in accordance with the will of the Owner. The New Testament makes it clear what is the will of the Father. We are to love our neighbours as we love ourselves. This means that the neighbour and I are one.

Though the Church as such cannnot enter party politics, the faithful must be taught to enter politics and to stand with the party that stands for freedom and justice, for human brotherhood under the Fatherhood of God. The life of these faithful who enter politics must be simple, incorruptible, proletarian, and courageous. They must take their stand against liquor, luxury, laziness, and licentious freedom. They must take their stand with the oppressed, the exploited, the jobless, and rally them all around the few exploiters. As the establishment will be against them, they should be ready to be persecuted and killed by the vested interests of existing governments and the rich who control the rulers.

An *agape* army must be recruited by the Church to rush to areas of tension. They must help those who are having collective bargaining for just wages by supporting them during the period of strike. Unless the poor are helped by the Churches of the rich countries also to become self-reliant, the present rate of exploitation of the poor by the rich will only increase in spite of all our sermons. But it is extremely difficult to conscientise the Churches in rich countries, though a few Christians may develop a Christian conscience in spite of the cultural onslaught on them. It is an uphill journey and yet we cannot postpone it.

The question we must ask ourselves and others is whether the present tyrants must reign or Jesus Christ should reign. If we are convinced that Christ must reign, the way is that of the Cross.

NOTES

1. Karl Barth, *Church Dogmatics* (Edinburgh, Clarke, 1961), vol. 4, part 2, pp. 655f.

2. Ibid., part 1, pp. 112f.

3. Stephen Neill, *Salvation Tomorrow* (London, Lutterworth, 1976) 146.

4. Hans Urs von Balthasar, *Love Alone the Way of Salvation* (London, Burns & Oates, 1968) 71 (quoted in Michael Gouldered, *Incarnation and Myth* [London, SCM, 1977] 97).

5. Jürgen Moltmann, *The Church in the Power of the Spirit* (London, SCM, 1977) 192.

6. Emil Brunner, *The Divine Imperative* (Philadelphia, Westminster, 1947) 661.

7. Geevarghese Mar Osthathios, *Theology of a Classless Society* (London, Butterworth, 1979) 51, 102.

8. Brunner, *Imperative*, 408.

9. Ibid., 140.

10. Barth, *Dogmatics*, vol. 4, part 2, p. 101.

11. Ibid., 100.

12. Brunner, *Imperative*, 422.

13. Ibid., 408.

14. Ibid., 482.

15. Barth, *Dogmatics*, vol. 4, part 2, p. 603.

16. Moltmann, *Church*, 86.

Chapter 44

Choan-Seng Song

The Double Darkness

As long ago as the sixth century B.C., Lao-tzu, the master of aphorisms and reputed founder of Taoism in China, made the following statement:

> Impenetrable is the darkness where the heart of Being dwells,
> This Being is Truth itself and Faith itself.
> From eternity to eternity, they will never perish,
> Who saw the beginning of All?
> The beginning of All, one knows only through the perennial Spirit.[1]

The darkness surrounding the heart of Being—this has been the center of human spiritual inquiries both in the East and the West from time immemorial to the present day. Consciously or unconsciously, human beings seem to be aware of the Being from whom they derive the power and meaning of their existence. Therefore, it is only natural that they are intent on discovering who and what that Being may be. In Augustine's famous words, human souls are restless until they find rest in God. And in the process of the search for that Being, human beings become conscious of their spirituality, which relates them to that Being in a very special way. They are bound to the Being who is the source and destiny of their being. They are thus conditioned by this spirituality. They are conditioned, to use a biblical expression, by the image of God within them.

This does not mean that inquiries of the human spirit in all ages have taken the same form and expression. On the contrary! These inquiries often take vastly different forms of expression for people in different cultural situations. Why is this so? One possible answer is that the darkness surrounding the heart of Being defies a complete grasp by human beings of the mystery of that Being. In fact, religions and folklores are full of stories about those who impudently seek to penetrate the darkness of mystery to gain a glimpse of the secret of that Being. In the darkness of Being human beings are confronted with their ultimate puzzlement, anxiety, and fear. All kinds of religious images and symbols are testimonies of such an awesome encounter. Consequently, from highly developed religions like Buddhism, Hinduism, Islam, or Christianity to the primitive religions of nomads and others who live on the fringe of modern civilization, each faith has developed its own ways and systems to account for whatever insight each is enabled to gain into the mystery of Being.

First published in *Third-Eye Theology: Theology in Formation in Asian Settings* (Maryknoll, N.Y., Orbis, 1979), pp. 17–18, 22–25, 59–63. Used by permission.

Speaking of religion in Africa, John Mbiti, an African religious historian, points out that within traditional life in Africa:

> Man lives in a religious universe. . . . Names of people have religious meanings in them; rocks and boulders are not just empty objects, but religious objects; the sound of the drum speaks a religious language; the eclipse of the sun or moon is not simply a silent phenomenon of nature, but one which speaks to the community that observes it, often warning of an impending catastrophe.[2]

It should be added that this is not a phenomenon unique to African society. A similar religious phenomenon can be observed in Asia and in other parts of the world. What we see here is a transformation of the inscrutable and mysterious Being into tangible, visible forms—a substitution that incurred the great wrath of the Old Testament prophets and of modern western missionaries.

MYSTERIUM TREMENDUM ET FASCINOSUM

At a highly sophisticated and theological level, Rudolf Otto in his important book *The Idea of the Holy* terms this sense of reverence and awe before the objects of worship a *mysterium tremendum et fascinosum*. The *mysterium* is something before which we tremble on the one hand and experience fascination on the other. In the presence of the *mysterium* our whole being is exposed to that which defies human intellect and cognition. In Otto's own words:

> The truly "mysterious" object is beyond our apprehension and comprehension, not only because our knowledge has certain irresistible limits, but because in it we come upon something inherently "Wholly Other," whose kind and character are incommensurable with our own, and before which we therefore recoil in a wonder that strikes us chill and numb.[3]

As we know, Karl Barth powerfully exploited the concept of God as the Wholly Other in the early stage of his long, distinguished theological career. With the powerful theological language at his command, Barth initiated the era of neo-orthodox theology, stressing the absolute and qualitative difference between God and human beings. In retrospect, it is only fair to say that Barth must have been impressed as much by the darkness that surrounds the heart of Being as by the finiteness and sinfulness of human beings. . . .

THE PROBLEM OF HEART-TO-HEART COMMUNICATION

. . . It is clear that in our theological efforts we are confronted by what I would call a "double darkness": the darkness surrounding the heart of Being and the darkness separating Christian spirituality from other Asian spiritualities. To overcome this double darkness is the task of third-eye theology, especially the darkness that makes different spiritualities unable to communicate with each other. Only when the darkness that surrounds different spiritualities is lifted can we begin to see the love and compassion of God for the world in a fuller and richer light. The following story is illustrative of what is meant here.

A Japanese Christian engaged in theological teaching in the northern part of Thailand encountered a typical example of alienation between one spirituality and another.

Finding himself at the bedside of a Thai woman who was suffering from cancer, the Japanese missionary tried to talk to her about the Christian faith and Jesus Christ the Savior. A little annoyed, the woman said:

> You missionaries are always trying to teach people while you really do not understand the people. The Buddhist monks are much better than you missionaries. I will call in a monk right now. I will listen to him. He will understand me. He can comfort me with his *dharma*. He can speak my own language. You are wasting your time here. Go home![4]

As the Japanese Christian missionary correctly observed, the Thai woman was not referring to a problem with the spoken language. In saying that a Buddhist monk spoke her own language, she was implying that she and the monk shared a common cultural and religious heritage, that they were on the same wavelength in spiritual matters, and that sympathy and understanding could be taken for granted within that same spiritual and cultural framework.

Language is an essential vehicle for expressing and conveying the totality of what it means to be and to live and die in a certain cultural context. Language is therefore not just a matter of sound but a matter of substance, not just a problem of grammar and syntax but a problem of the mind and the spirit. Thus, when the Japanese missionary concluded self-reproachfully that the woman was objecting to his "imperialistic one-sidedness," he was missing the real issue. Maybe he was too conscious of what his western predecessors had done in the so-called mission field. Still the woman's statement posed an issue that went much deeper than that of imperialistic one-sidedness.

What was at stake here, it seems to me, is this: a heart-to-heart communication did not take place between the Japanese Christian teacher and the Thai Buddhist woman. Both were anxious to penetrate the darkness of Being at a critical time in the woman's life, but the darkness between the spirituality of Theravada Buddhism and that of Christianity stood in their way. This darkness prevented them from seeing each other in the heart of Being. *Dharma* and Christ did not meet in the hearts of those two people. The woman had to call in a Buddhist monk who could speak her own language, and the Christian missionary had to go away, deeply troubled by his apparent failure to communicate to her in his own Christian language.

The central issue here is heart-to-heart communication between one spirituality and another. What is it that prevents communication from taking place freely and fruitfully among people of different religious and spiritual allegiances? The mistrust, hostility, and conflict that have developed over a long period of time—partly because of misunderstandings and distortions, and partly because of a lack of sympathy and empathy—disrupt communication. For some reason tension is particularly heightened between Christianity and other world religions. Numerous examples can be cited to illustrate this: the confrontation of Christianity with Islam in Palestine during the Crusades is a case in point. Perhaps the Crusades were conceived, motivated, and carried out by the Christian church and the kingdoms of Europe as much for political as for religious motives. It was, in any case, one of the ugliest and saddest conflicts in the history of the world. It stained the image of Christianity and strained the relationship between the two world religions.

Despite this remark, I hasten to add that I have no intention of advocating unconditional recognition and acceptance of Asian spirituality and all that it represents. Unfortunately one has to admit that the integrity of Asian spirituality is also threatened by a breakdown in heart-to-heart communication. On the whole we can say that the language of the heart has gone through a great devaluation in Asian countries. Through inner corruption on the one hand and on the other hand through the invasion of a modern technological culture based on western capitalist structures of economy and lifestyle, Asian spirituality faces the danger of disintegration. At the very least it is on the defensive.

It is no longer self-evident that present-day Asia still preserves the spirituality that enables people to aspire to what is good, beautiful, and true. Disillusioned by their own affluent society, some idealistic youths may leave their western homelands in search of an oriental spirituality which, they hope, will bring peace, joy, and tranquility to their troubled bodies and souls. But as many of them soon find out, spirituality is not lying about in the streets of Calcutta, Bangkok, Peking, or Tokyo, just waiting to be picked up. There has been too much romanticism on the part of western seekers of the oriental meaning of life and also on the part of its Asian advocates. In a very strange way this becomes also evident in the West through the growth of some esoteric religious sects that claim to trace their spiritual origin to the great Asian religions.[5] As a matter of fact, the oriental religious sects that thrive on the consumerism of western society are sad caricatures of their distant spiritual ancestors.

Romanticism apart, the people in Asia are facing a crisis of spirituality that poses a baffling question concerning the meaning of human existence. The feeling is that something has departed from the spirit of Asian culture, which has somehow spent itself and is no longer capable of fulfilling its role in the increasingly demanding situation of Asia today. Asian spirituality seems to have lost its say about the complex social and political problems that confront the people in their everyday life.

This is, of course, not a totally accurate assessment of what has been happening in Asia in recent decades. There is the emergence of a new vitality in Asian spirituality that seeks to help people as they wrestle with the problems of life and death, and face with determination social and political changes. It must be admitted, however, that the Asian spirituality that has allowed itself to become captive to the past and lost its strength to sustain people in their daily struggle tends to be discredited by many enlightened Asians today. In this connection China can be cited as a good example.

Hu Shih, one of the most prominent champions of the Chinese Renaissance in 1919, never ceased to deplore the fatal grip of traditional Chinese spirituality on the people of China. True to a humanistic spirit based on science and democracy, he never tired of challenging the Chinese classical scholars who preached the salvation of China in terms of a revival of the traditional cultural and social values. As he poignantly pointed out:

> The civilization under which people are restricted and controlled by a material environment from which they cannot escape, and under which they cannot utilize human thought and intellectual power to change environment and improve conditions, is the civilization of a lazy and non-progressive people. It is truly a materialistic civilization. Such civilization can only obstruct but cannot satisfy the spiritual demands of mankind.[6]

The turbulent history of China in the succeeding years has more than vindicated Hu Shih's indictment of the old Chinese civilization, which became uprooted from its spiritual soil in the people and as a result deteriorated.

What, then, about Communist China, which has carried out a radical sociopolitical transformation after long years of revolutionary struggle? What we see in China today is a single-minded pursuit of an ultimate reality defined in ideological and political terms. In his June 30, 1949, address on the occasion of the twenty-eighth anniversary of the Chinese Communist Party, Mao Tse-tung stated emphatically: "We . . . declare openly that we are striving hard to create the very conditions which bring about their [classes'] extinction." When this goal is finally achieved, he continued, "human society will move to a higher stage."[7]

What is this higher stage? It is a classless society in which the dictatorship of the proletariat will prevail completely. Political struggle is the vehicle for the realization of this political ideology. It promises to be a long struggle, for class enemies both within China and outside are not going to surrender easily to the vision of a classless society. There is thick darkness, as it were, shrouding the communists' sociopolitical goal—a goal that has acquired intense religious implications for the people of China. To remove the veil of darkness, Mao Tse-tung and his party advocated and engineered a continuous struggle that would involve the people of China in perpetual revolution. This is a religious crusade against the mind and the spirit of a people who have inherited the cultural and spiritual traditions of Confucianism, Buddhism, Taoism, and ancestor worship.

Communism presents itself as a new spirituality promising the utopia of a classless society and fighting the traditional spirituality with formidable ideological and political weapons. The struggle has been a costly one. The spirits of Confucius and other sages are summoned up from time to time from their rest to stand trial before the court of the Communist Party, which declares them to be class enemies. This is a determined attempt to wean people away from the spirituality that has played a great role in the cultural and political history of China.

Stuart Schram, a by no means unsympathetic student of Communist China, describes China under Mao Tse-tung in the following way:

> Being utterly convinced that his own thought was correct, he [Mao] supposed that everyone else would be better off thinking exactly as he did. In his effort to conciliate spontaneity and discipline he was therefore inclined to place the emphasis heavily on conformity.[8]

Conformity is essentially a one-way communication. The leader dictates and the masses follow. Personal relations among people also tend to become distorted on account of the need to conform to ideological and political rules. It is therefore possible to assume that in this vast school of continuous revolution that is China today, heart-to-heart communication between political leaders and the people and between individuals and their neighbors must be disrupted. Individuals must subordinate their hearts to the party's political machine and to its ideological orthodoxy. If the vision of a classless society is realized one day, the people of China as a result of their constant struggles and the rigorous need to conform would perhaps have lost their ability to talk from heart to heart. What kind of a utopia would this be if people have ceased to communicate in the language of the heart? . . .

KAZO KITAMORI'S THEOLOGY OF GOD'S PAIN

At this point, I must refer to the theology of the pain of God propounded with a typically Japanese sensitivity and insight by Kazo Kitamori. His theology was as much a product of the agony and pain of his time as a result of theological reflection on the nature of Christian faith. In the 1940s Japanese culture and spirituality were undergoing unprecedented threats from the militarist government. The Japanese invasion of China had been going on for years, bringing indescribable horror and suffering to millions of

Chinese. The power of darkness had completely overpowered every vestige of goodness, beauty, and truth in Japanese spirituality. The war of invasion took its toll too among the Japanese people. Reports of conquest and victory were accompanied by endless lists of Japanese troops killed on battlefields. Still the invasion continued, involving the United States and many Asian nations in the Pacific war.

It was as if the gate of hell had opened and the monsters lying at the depth of the abyss of terror were suddenly released to wage vengeance on all humanity. In the Japanese invaders we saw human beings who had gone insane; we saw them turn on themselves in fierce hatred and destruction. It was the darkest hour in the history of modern Japan and Asia. And when we take into consideration what was happening simultaneously on the European front, it was the darkest hour in the history of the modern world. In such a grim world situation the theology of the pain of God was born.

As Kitamori read the Gospel in the midst of chaos and destruction, he saw the word *pain* leap out of practically every page of the Bible. God in pain—this is the God of Abraham, of Isaac, and of Jacob. This is the God of Moses and the prophets. This is the God of Christ suffering excruciating pain on the cross. "The heart of the Gospel," Kitamori confides, "was revealed to me as the 'pain of God'."[9] God is in pain because of the terrible pain the world is going through in the confusion and horror of war. Accordingly, Kitamori's theological interpretation of what God is and what he does is based on the motif of pain.

We must understand that Kitamori's emphasis on pain brings depth to our understanding of God and his relation to the world. It challenges a cheap interpretation of the Gospel as all joy, happiness, and success in the world as well as the assurance of life and glory in the world to come. Moreover, it strikes sympathetic cords in Asian spirituality, particularly the one fostered by the Buddhist tradition. Kitamori writes:

> . . . the religious thought closest to the gospel—the pain of God which heals our wounds—is found in the Crown Prince Shotoku's *An Interpretation of Yuima-kyo,* where we find religious thought which closely resembles our gospel of the pain of God who heals our pain. There we find the earth-shaking sentence: "Man's real sickness springs from foolish love; Buddha's responding sickness arises from great mercy. His suffering mercy is man's vice—man's sickness. The sickness of the great mercy saves people by absorbing their sickness. Sickness is saved by sickness."[10]

But the resemblance between the pain of God in the Christian Gospel, Kitamori goes on to declare, and the mercy of Buddha is more superficial than real:

> It must not be overlooked that in their [i.e., Buddhists'] religious thought the echo of an alien note is heard. . . . There can be no inflexible wrath of the absolute in Buddhism, as long as it does not have the God of the first commandment. An absolute being without wrath can have no *real* pain. . . . The pain of God is his love—this love is based on the premise of his wrath, which is absolute, inflexible reality. Thus the pain of God is *real* pain, the Lord's wounds are *real* wounds. Buddhism cannot comprehend this real pain, even in the stages of thought of the Jodo and Jodo Shinshu sects about the mercy of Amida Buddha.[11]

While there is no concept of an absolute being in Buddhism, the pain and suffering that Buddha himself and Buddhist saints down the centuries have felt for humanity is nonetheless real. The problem is that Kitamori relates the absolute God to what he calls "absolute and inflexible" wrath. Even God's love, to use Kitamori's own words, "is based on the premise of his wrath." Here the God of Mount Sinai is dominant in his theological thinking. But we must ask: Is it the God of absolute and inflexible wrath that the Bible as a whole tries to convey? To be sure, the prophets of the Old Testament perceive their God Yahweh as a stern judge who judges the world on account of its wickedness and injustice. But what becomes evident and transparent in the end is the God who loves his own children despite their waywardness and sins. The prophets are never tired of calling people to return to the healing and loving embrace of God. They can do this only because for them God's wrath is neither absolute nor inflexible.

To absolutize wrath is to internalize it. This seems to be what happens in Kitamori's theology of the pain of God. In his theology there is a strong tendency to internalize God's work of salvation within God himself, seeing it as a conflict within God himself between his love and his wrath:

> The pain is God in conflict within himself, God going outside of himself in Christ, God letting his son die: all of which means God conquering his wrath by his love in the interests of loving the unloveworthy.[12]

This is how Carl Michalson interprets Kitamori's theology of the pain of God. In other words, external expressions of God's salvation result from an internal conflict between love and wrath within God himself. Is it biblically and theologically commendable to internalize God's salvation in this way?

By interpreting salvation in terms of the conflict between love and wrath within God himself, Kitamori finds himself within the theological traditions of the West. Since he is himself a Lutheran, his views are particularly in the Lutheran tradition. Here his great sensitivity to Japanese spirituality seems to give way to western theological thought in which he is also versed and steeped. Just to illustrate what I mean here, I want to quote Lutheran theologian Jürgen Moltmann. In his work *The Crucified God* we find these words:

> The theology of the cross must take up and think through to a conclusion this . . . dimension of the dying of Jesus in abandonment by God. If, abandoned by his God and Father, he was raised through the "glory of the Father," then eschatological faith in the cross of Jesus Christ must acknowledge the theological trial between God and God. The cross of the Son divides God from God to the utmost degree of enmity and distinction. The resurrection of the Son abandoned by God unites God with God in the most intimate fellowship.[13]

The cross, according to Moltmann, is the division of God from God to the utmost degree, while the resurrection is the union of God with God in the most intimate fellowship. But the cross and the resurrection have taken place within God, or between God and God, to use Moltmann's rather awkward expression. This is a clear example of theology constructed and developed on what I call the internalization of salvation within God himself. According to such theology, salvation takes place inside an introverted God. There is, in fact, too much theology here and too little salvation for poor sinners. Moltmann even speaks of the cross as "the theological trial between God and God."[14] Does this mean that the cross is a drama of God's own trial and we humans are only its spectators?

This *objective* understanding of the cross and the resurrection deprives God, it seems to me, of his intimate and personal involvement in human suffering and pain. But a more fundamental question is this: How are we to understand salvation? Are we to understand it as a dissolution of the tension between love and wrath within God himself? If the answer is yes, then what does this dissolution of the tension within God himself have to do with our own pain and our own suffering? How is it related to the forgiveness of our sins? In other words, how does this drama played within God himself become our own drama? What makes this *theological* trial become *human* salvation? If the salvation of the world consists in God's love overcoming his own wrath, do we not have to come to the absurd conclusion that the world suffers not so much from its sins as from the wrath of God? Neither Kitamori nor Moltmann, I am sure, wants to suggest this as the implication of their theology. But insofar as the wrath of God is absolutized, and the cross and the resurrection are regarded as something which has taken place internally within God or between God and God, the absurdity I mentioned seems unavoidable. Thus in Kitamori and Moltmann we have a theology that goes beyond the boundary of faith to which people in the Bible bear witness.

To return to Kitamori, I want to point out further that he defines pain as "the essence of God."[15] Once wrath in God is absolutized and love is seen in conflict with wrath, pain becomes an *essential* part of God's being. Pain becomes God's essence. Thus pain acquires an ontological overtone in Kitamori's understanding of God. His God is not only the God who has pain but the God who is pain. Pain seen as an ontological element in relation to God's essence is bound to remain with God for all eternity. Pain will neither leave God nor all of creation. Pain reigns supreme! "What is the essence of the gospel?" Kitamori asks himself. His answer: "It is the cross of Christ, the pain of God, or it is God's tribulation."[16] The cross is the reality and symbol of pain. No one can question this. But there must be a difference between the cross that God in Christ is bearing for the pain and suffering of this world, and the cross that embodies the conflict between God's love and his wrath, between God the Father and God the Son. The cross in the former sense is redemptive or salvific, but the cross in the latter sense is an external symbol of God's internal struggle of himself against himself. Is the cross the pain which God has inflicted upon himself in order to resolve his own internal contradiction? Is it an expression of divine masochism?

Kitamori is essentially in the tradition of western theology, which turns salvation into an intense struggle of God against God within God himself. Consequently, his theology of the pain of God, his *theologia crucis,* stops at the cross. It does not go beyond it. The cross is the final station of God's journey. Is it by accident that there is little reference to the resurrection in *The Theology of the Pain of God?* It cannot in fact accommodate resurrection; it does not have room for it. For resurrection is God's declaration of the end of pain and suffering. It is the eschatological victory over the power of pain. As the seer of the Book of Revelation puts it, God "will wipe every tear from their eyes; there shall be an end to death, and to mourning and crying and pain" (Rev. 21:4). If pain and wrath are absolute and constitute the essence of God's being, how can they be overcome? For God to have done away with pain and wrath would amount to God doing away with his own being. I am sure Kitamori has no intention whatsoever of pressing his theology of God's pain to such a logical absurdity, but how could he avoid it if he made pain and wrath into the essence of God? Moreover, I am sure Kitamori will give as much weight to the gospel of resurrection as to the theology of the pain of the cross. But if the pain and suffering of God are not seen in the perspective of resurrection, theology stops at the painful cross and the wrathful God. There will be no anticipation of a life of joy and jubilation; we are not given courage and fortitude to endure pain in joy and in hope.

It is entirely in line with his thought on the pain of God that Kitamori speaks of it as "the tragedy of God."[17] And of course the cross is the embodiment of this divine tragedy.

Consequently he finds in Japanese tragedy, filled with the typical Japanese feeling of *tsurasa*—"the feeling of inevitable fate and sorrow that overhangs human life," or the feeling of an aching void that makes us helpless and weak—a comparable element that echoes the tragedy of the Gospel. Now the God of *tsurasa* is definitely much more expressive of oriental pathos than is the God of wrath.

It may be, as Kitamori points out, that the element of wrath is missing in most Asian concepts of God. The desert God who pours down his wrath on the enemies of his people, the God of justice who vents his wrath on a wicked and wayward people, does not make his appearance as strongly as he does in the God of the Old Testament prophets. But there are strong indications both in the Old Testament and the New Testament that this angry God is also a God of *tsurasa*. Perhaps it is this God of *tsurasa* that eventually comes close to the heart of the biblical faith. . . .

NOTES

1. See Wade Baskin, ed., *Classics in Chinese Philosophy* (New York, Philosophical Library, 1972) 62.

2. John S. Mbiti, *African Religions and Philosophy* (New York, Praeger, 1969) 15.

3. Rudolf Otto, *The Idea of the Holy* (London, Oxford University Press, 1950) 39.

4. Kosuke Koyama, *Waterbuffalo Theology* (Maryknoll, N.Y., Orbis, 1976) 85.

5. According to Ronald L. Johnstone, "There are more people attracted to religious cults in the United States today than were in the past. . . . There are over a million and a half Americans in the cult movement today." Among these religious cults are Transcendental Meditation, Nichiren Shoshu, Hari Krishna (Ronald L. Johnstone, *Religion and Society in Interaction* [Englewood Cliffs, N.J., Prentice-Hall, 1975] 317).

6. Hu Shi, *Wen-ts'un,* collection 3, pp. 1–11, in William Theodore de Bary, Wing-tsit Chan, and Burton Watson, comps., *Sources of Chinese Tradition* (Columbia University Press, 1960) 854.

7. Mao Tse-tung, *Selected Works* (Peking, Foreign Language Press, 1961) 4:411.

8. Stuart Schram, *Mao Tse-tung* (New York, Penguin Books, 1967) 270.

9. Kazo Kitamori, *The Theology of the Pain of God* (Richmond, Va., John Knox Press, 1965) 19.

10. Ibid., 27.

11. Ibid.

12. Carl Michalson, *Japanese Contribution to Christian Theology* (Philadelphia, Westminster, 1960) 79.

13. Jürgen Moltmann, *The Crucified God* (New York, Harper & Row, 1974) 152.

14. "Der theologische Prozess zwischen Gott und Gott," in *Der gekreuzigte Gott* (Munich, Kaiser, 1972) 145.

15. Kitamori, *Pain of God,* 47.

16. Ibid., 140.

17. Ibid., 148.

Chapter 45

Kosuke Koyama

Patient vs. Impatient History

THE 'GUN AND OINTMENT' PERSPECTIVE

It was in 1511. The Portuguese fleet, propelled by greed for the monopoly of the Asiatic trade (spice!) and hatred of the infidel Muslim, approached the fortress of Malacca. The captain of the fleet, Alfonso de Albuquerque, spoke to his men to inspire them on the eve of the successful assault on the city. The speech contains a highly interesting theological interpretation of the event:

> It is, too, well worthy of belief that as the King of Malacca, who has already once been discomfited and had proof of our strength, with no hope of obtaining any succour from any other quarters—sixteen days having already elapsed since this took place—makes no endeavour to negotiate with us for the security of his estate, Our Lord is blinding his judgment and hardening his heart, and desires the completion of this affair of Malacca.[1]

Contrary to Albuquerque's imperialistic theologizing, I am afraid that God had hardened *his* heart and blinded [*his*] judgment. . . . The heart of the Portuguese captain was hardened, first, by his drive after wealth and his antipathy to the Muslims, and perhaps, secondly, by a very direct application of a biblical doctrine—a doctrine which happens to be a controversial and abstruse one which must not be used without soul-searching!—to his historical situation, for his own advantage. The guns he carried on his fleet symbolize the first hardening, the cross he hoisted high on his fleet symbolizes the second. Albuquerque was convinced that God Almighty was on his side. He was hardened to an intensive degree unknown to the Asians who had not the 'theological maturity' to utilize biblical doctrine to their own advantage![2]

Malacca 1511 stands as an incident burdened with a symbolic historical value. In the person of Albuquerque one can discern the structure and character of the relationship between the West and Asia. In her dealing with Asia, the West has often been hardened by commercial avariciousness and by theological self-righteousness. These two 'hardening' elements constitute the main ingredients of the gunpowder of the West against Asia.

First published in *Waterbuffalo Theology* (Maryknoll, N.Y., Orbis, 1976), pp. 47-56. Used by permission.

Professor K. M. Panikkar's *Asia and Western Dominance* is an extensive historical investigation of the acts of the West's 'gun' since 27 May 1498, the day of the arrival of *San Gabriel* at Calicut. Whether we begin in 1498, or in 1511, or in 1564 (the first Spanish settlement in Cebu by Miguel Lopez de Legaspi), or in 1602 (the formation of the Dutch United East India Company—*Vereenigde Oostindische Compagnie*—to which 'was granted the monopoly of trade in the regions between the Cape of Good Hope and the Magellan Straits for an initial period of twenty-one years, together with power to make treaties, build forts, maintain armed forces and install officers of justice'), we can discern the same psychological structure of the West's aggression on South East Asia.[3] The study of the history of the 'new power' (K. M. Panikkar) since the sixteenth century involves complicated historical processes and accidents which differ significantly from one locality to another. Economic, political, anthropological, and cultural assessment of Asia's experience of the West's expansion, conquest, and empire-building from 1498 to 1914 poses a formidable scientific assignment.

The point I wish to make here is that the twenty-one cannons mounted on the deck of *San Gabriel,* the flagship of the Vasco da Gama expedition, meant far more than some twenty mechanical arrangements in which gunpowder could be ignited. They symbolized the coming of a time of radical crisis and upheaval for Asian life, the shaking up of her economic, political, and cultural life. This process is a process of 'wounding', particularly as it came at the hands of countless 'hardened and blinded' Albuquerques!

Concomitant with the process of 'gun' came 'ointment', also from the West, to Asia. 'Gun' was accompanied by 'ointment'! 'From the same mouth come blessing and cursing. My brethren this ought not to be so. Does a spring pour forth from the same opening fresh water and brackish?' (James 3.10f.). In the West's relationship with Asia, however, history has produced both 'fresh water and brackish' in a remarkable fashion. Sixteenth-century Europe has the unique distinction of being the century from which both 'wounding' and 'healing' began to reach the East. It was a stormy century for the European nations in their political, religious, and scientific life, accelerating the process of the momentous transition from the medieval to the modern which took place between the twelfth century and the eighteenth century.

What is that 'healing' which the West brought into Asia, perhaps as an 'unintended gift' of the age of an extended Albuquerque?[4] It is *modernization*. The impact of modernization upon Asia has been a gradual process of historical development which began its acutely ascending phase at the end of the Second World War. Modernization does not simply mean a spread of modern technological information and practices. It is a new orientation in the life of mankind which has been effecting radical transformations in all areas of human life. It affects political systems, international life, community life, education, health service, employment, labour conditions, public works, and business enterprises. Professor C. E. Black attempts a definition of modernization as 'the process by which historically evolved institutions are adapted to the rapidly changing functions that reflect the unprecedented increase in man's knowledge, permitting control over his environment, that accompanied the scientific revolution.'[5]

Asia's traditional way of life in all these areas of man's existence was 'gunned' by the Albuquerquean invasion. But one discerns at once that the 'dynamic and interventionist' valuation of modernization has 'gunned' the 'static' traditional values, too.[6] Modernization has been attacking, then, with historically creative promises. Here lies the great 'ointment' aspect of modernization.

How far, however, has the Albuquerquean 'wounding' prepared the ground for the modernization 'healing'? Has the colonial 'gun' accelerated or hindered the process of the modernization 'ointment' in Asia? These questions require careful historical investigation. It is true that the simultaneous advent of 'gun' and 'ointment' has produced an unusually compact and fertile history for Asia.[7] Experiencing this accelerated historical process, the Asians began to have a new feeling about history. From this feeling came two convictions: first, a growing conviction that Asians can become the main force in the universal history of mankind today and tomorrow, that through their active participation in history they can *change* history; second, an increasing confidence that history has some definite goal. In the 'goal of modernization' they have found a practical goal toward which they can 'purposefully' move. An 'Asian Drama' has begun. The modernization-ointment consists outwardly in the transformation of every-day life, in increasing physical and environmental comfort, and inwardly in the sense of active participation in history. Modernization is, in this sense, an 'ointment' for a stagnant and traditional Asia.

Thus the West's 'gun and ointment' means the 'colonial exploitation-disruption gun,' and 'modernization ointment'. The results of the former are still quite visible today in South Asia, particularly when viewed from the perspective of the development issue. The modernization ointment must work to foster and restore health to the wounded process of development.

Modernization, however, is not all ointment! This becomes clear when one studies one of the main arteries through which the blood of modernization circulates in the world today, technological advancement. Technology, from the printing machine of Johann G. Gutenberg in 1448 to the American NASA men who overcame both terrestrial and lunar gravitational pulls in 1969, has emancipated mankind, to a signifi-cant extent, from toil and suffering. It has succeeded in putting an unheard-of amount of educational material into the hands of millions. It has achieved miracles in hospitals. Technological advancement stands in a positive relationship with the 'life abundant' for which Christ came (John 10.10; Matt. 11.4–6). *But,* isn't it also technology that changed the twenty guns mounted on the deck of *San Gabriel* to the nuclear missiles delivered by underwater submarines or earth-orbiting bombing systems? The *San Gabriel* cannons, through the apocalyptic touch of technology, have become literally 'cosmic guns'!

Technological efficiency, however fantastic, computers, heart-transplants, nuclear energy—none of these can solve the problem of history. Doesn't there seem to be a demonic alliance between technocracy-psychology and the modern age? 'The modern age, more than any other, has been an age of assassinations, of civil, religious, and international wars, of mass slaughter in many forms, and of concentration camps.'[8] Between 1820 and 1949 the world lost 46.8 million lives in wars.[9] Isn't this 'the agony of modernization'?[10] Modernization itself, then, must be realistically understood as simul-taneously 'gun and ointment'. 'Colonial gun and modernization ointment' and 'mod-ernization ointment and modernization gun' are continuous, co-existing, and mingled.

PARTICIPATION IN HISTORY AND CHRISTIAN MISSION

Great nations, empires, and civilizations existed in Asia prior to the invasion of the West's 'gun and ointment'. Perhaps because of the abrupt onslaught of the West's 'gun and ointment', the modern world has not fully understood or acknowledged the vast and profound contribution of the the Asian civilizations to the life of mankind. Asian sons, Gotama Siddhartha, the writers of the *Upanishads,* Confucius, Lao-tse, partici-pated in the 'axial period' of mankind with Elijah, Isaiah, Jeremiah, Deutero-Isaiah, Zarathustra, Homer, Parmenides, and Plato.[11] Asian histories have had their own 'gun and ointment'.

If I may hazard a limited characterization of Asia's experience of history, I would say it has been *patient,* compared to the West's *impatient* history. This characterization is guided by a theological understanding of history. The strongly linear view of history in the biblical tradition, based on the faith that God is the governor of history, is not indigenous to the life and thought of the peoples of Asia. A linear sense of history, when appropriated by the man of *hybris,* can produce dangerous *impatience* with history.

The biblical God is the God who 'experiences' history.[12] He has his purpose for the history of man. He does 'strange things' in history (Isa. 28.21). He may harden the mind of man according to his purpose. But for the mortal Albuquerque to say that God was on his side and blinding the judgment of his enemy was a distorted and egoistic expression of the biblical sense of the linear view of history! The relationship between the mystery of 'hardening of hearts' and the mystery of the 'linear view of history' produces an extremely dangerous zone for man to walk in. Albuquerque became *theologically* impatient with the city of Malacca, since he was convinced that God, in his holy zeal, was on his side. The Albuquerquean impatience and aggressiveness are thus of a special kind, since they have a theological foundation.[13]

The Albuquerquean theistic impatience was given powerful expression in July 1937, in the land of 'axial' Confucius, in the person of the Chinese atheist Mao Tse-tung (what a development!):

In the present epoch of the development of society, the responsibility of correctly knowing and changing the world has been placed by history upon the shoulders of the proletariat and its party. This process, the practice of changing the world, which is determined in accordance with scientific knowledge, has already reached a historic moment in the world and in China, a great moment unprecedented in human history, that is, the moment for completely banishing darkness from the the world and from China and for changing the world into a world of light such as never previously existed.[14]

Mao Tse-tung, 'the helmsman' of the world's most populous nation, here speaks 'theological' language. The *kairos* has come to the world and to China through his 'proletariat ointment'! He speaks of the once-for-all event of 'banishing darkness from the world'. His interpretation of a participation in history is based on the impatient criticism made by Marx and Lenin of the economic substructure of the West's 'gun and ointment'. Mao's passion and conviction betray their 'Christian origin'. His proletariat ointment is a great historical agent bringing change into Asian life today.

Mahatma Gandhi's life (1869–1948) was a continuous story of active participation in history. He organized campaigns of civil disobedience; he was imprisoned because of his conviction of the direction of history; he founded the *ashram;* he advocated *swaraj* (home rule); he improved the status of the untouchables. He experienced, through his own life and the life of his people, the whole range of implications of the West's 'gun and ointment' upon India. He appreciated the effects of the Christian missionary ointment. But for his part, he presented to the millions of his fellow Indians *'ahimsa* ointment' (non-killing, non-violence), the first principle in the *satyagraha* (holding to the truth) movement.[15] The *ahimsa* ointment used by the Hindu Indian has been repeatedly referred to by the Burmese Theravada Buddhist U Thant, when Secretary-General of the United Nations:

It was in an effort to assert the dignity and worth of the human person that Gandhiji started the first passive resistance movement called Satyagraha in South Africa at the beginning of this century. As its connotation so clearly shows,

Gandhiji believed that the weapon of truth, if firmly grasped and purposefully used, could lead to peaceful change without resort to violence. This was indeed one of the great ideas of our century. Gandhiji has rightly been regarded as the apostle of Ahimsa or non-violence, a concept enshrined in the teaching of practically all the great religions. It is really one of the basic tenents of my own religion, Buddhism. Intolerance, violence, and the spirit of persecution are foreign to Buddhism. . . . A familiar phrase one often hears is that 'the end justifies the means.' Gandhiji categorically rejected this idea; he did not believe that a noble end could be achieved by ignoble means.[16]

The former Secretary-General of the United Nations endorsed the *ahimsa* ointment as 'in line with the principles and purposes of the Charter of the United Nations' and enshrined in 'all the great religions'.[17] *Ahimsa* ointment is rooted in man's conscience, which echoes back to the messages of the axial epoch. At the same time, it has cogently relevant application for today's violently torn world. This great ointment activated itself in recent history through the Hindu man, who himself met a violent death. I must mention here, too, the name of Martin Luther King, Jr., the American Christian negro who also stood for the *ahimsa* ointment and came to a violent end.

I have chosen two Asian ointments centered in the two great countries of ancient civilization, China and India, whose spiritual and cultural influence upon the whole of Asia have been immense and profound. In speaking of the present proletariat ointment and the ancient *ahimsa* ointment, I am not intending to be comprehensive. There may be several other important Asian ointments. My aim is to clarify, if at all possible, some of the critical challenges the Christian mission is facing in Asia while speaking of the encounters between representative great 'ointments' in the perspective of Asia's historic encounter with the West's 'gun and ointment'.

Both proletariat ointment and *ahimsa* ointment have histories. They are two outstanding examples of Asian participation in history. They are not just ideas. They have influenced millions of people in more than a superficial way. They intend to heal the wounds of man. Here are concrete ointments working in the concrete history of the Asian man.

As has been pointed out, both ointments have come out of frictions and irritations with the West. They are not ignorant of the history of the acts of the West's colonial-expansionist and modernization guns. Both realize the presence of a strange ointment called the missionary ointment, which is trying to heal the wounds of history by the name of a man crucified two thousand years ago. Whether they realize it or not, it is true that the missionary ointment has influenced, to a great measure, their commitment towards the establishment of social justice in the community of man. The name of Jesus Christ does not, however, occupy centrality in these two Asian ointments.

The very necessity for these two Asian ointments (Mao Tse-tung; Gandhi and U Thant) connotes to Asians a criticism of the 'almighty' West's ointments, both modernization and missionary. They see, rightly or wrongly, that both missionary ointment and modernization ointment have not really healed the wounds of history. Modernization is valuable, says the *ahimsa* ointment, as long as it increases the *ahimsa* value. It is valuable, says the proletariat ointment, as long as it contributes to the creation of the classless society. The same points must be made with the missionary ointment. The proletariat ointment positively accepts the proposition 'the end justifies the means' because it is intensely 'impatient' with history. Its rejection of religious value is also rooted in the same impatience with history. Religious interpretation of and participation in history is too lenient and patient! The Chinese proletariat eschatological movement engages in a radical surgery of history. It cuts history open, puts its hand inside, and extracts the cancer of all evils from the body of history once and for all! The *ahimsa* ointment, reflecting the ancient Indo-Aryan wisdom, does not work or develop according to historical scientific dialecticism. It is not impatient with history. It desires to speak to the history of man through a simple *satyagraha.* It proposes to 'hold all things' (Col. 1.17) by the invisible power of the eternal truth.

Against the background of the proletariat ointment ('impatient' in the tradition of Albuquerque) and the *ahimsa* ointment ('patient' in the tradition of the ancient Indo-Aryan spirituality), a critical event took place in 1964. The 'impatient' China successfully detonated a device containing thermonuclear material in the Sinkiang test ground. Sinkiang 1964 stands out as the point of the Chinese transition from the message of the proletariat ointment to the dread of the naked force of the modernization gun which was, until then, the monopoly of the West. There could be no Sinkiang 1964 without New Mexico 1945. China's apocalyptic gun began to overshadow her message of 'completely banishing darkness from the world'. Her cosmic gun has become a threat to mankind because of her ideologically impatient position that 'the end justifies the means'.

India, the land of the *ahimsa* ointment, bordering on China, watched apprehensively the coming of the modernization gun which can annihilate 46.8 million lives and more perhaps in one strike, into the hands of Mao Tse-tung. She has been threatened by it and has begun to explore the possibility of developing nuclear arms herself, in spite of the obviously devastating cost that the project entails! This move is a tragic Indian departure from the *ahimsa* ointment to the *himsa* gun. The *ahimsa* ointment has been the torch of hope in the world of the *himsa* gun. Sinkiang 1964 thus shook the foundation of both Asian ointments. The demonic fumes of the modernization gun are now beginning to paralyse the nerve-system of the two centers of the great civilizations in Asia— China and India.

The courtship with the modernization gun will immediately exhaust the resources for the projects of the modernization ointment. The modernization ointment has been recognized among Asians for its high value. But the astronomically expensive process has been gravely hindered by the armament drive. In the place of Albuquerquean exploitation and disruption has come slavery to expenditure on armaments. At this point, the West's positive contribution of the modernization ointment is going on, but under the constant threat of the super-gun. How long can the modernization gun and modernization ointment stay together in this crowded history of mankind?

NOTES

1. H. J. Benda and J. A. Larkin, *The World of South East Asia,* Harper and Row, New York 1968, p. 78.
2. Historical and theological investigation into the origin and development of the European background of the 'agressive theology' up to the appearance of Albuquerque in the East would be a worthwhile study. The church's negative attitude towards the Jews and Moslems and the church's powerful position that enabled her to suppress other religious persuasions certainly must have to do with the future appearance of Albuquerque. But we cannot take up this discussion here.
3. D. G. E. Hall, *A History of South East Asia,* Macmillan, 1968, p. 271.
4. Henrik Kraemer, *World Cultures and World Religions,* Lutterworth Press 1960, p. 67.
5. C. E. Black, *The Dynamics of Modernization,* p. 7.
6. Gunnar Myrdal, *Asian Drama,* vol. 1, Penguin Books 1969, p. 73.
7. According to Dr Masao Takonaka, six revolutions in the West which spread over the four hundred years since the Reformation came to Asia all at once, telescoped into five decades. Cf. Hans Ruedi Weber, *Asia and the Ecumenical Movement,* SCM Press, 1966, p. 21.

8. C.E. Black, op.cit., p. 27.

9. Ibid., p. 33.

10. Ibid., p. 20.

11. Karl Jaspers, *The Origin and Goal of History,* Routledge 1953, pp. 1–21.

12. "What concerns the prophet is the human event as a divine experience. History to us is the record of human experience; to the prophet it is a record of God's experience' (Abraham J. Heschel, *The Prophets*, Harper and Row 1963, p. 172).

13. For example, in 1454 Henry the Navigator received Pope Nicholas V's bull: 'We, after careful deliberation, and having considered that we have by our apostolic letters conceded to king Afonso the right, total and absolute, to invade, conquer and subject all the countries which are under rule of the enemies of Christ, Saracen or pagan', quoted in K.M. Panikkar, *Asia and Western Dominance,* Allen and Unwin 1959, p. 27.

14. From Mao's philosophical essay 'On Practice', *Essential Works of Chinese Communism,* ed. W. Chai, Bantam Books 1962, p. 95. What he said in 1937 is reiterated with an equal vigour in 1966: 'Communism is at once a complete system of proletarian ideology and a new social system. It is different from any other ideological and social system, and is the most complete, progressive, revolutionary and rational system in human history. . . . However much the reactionaries try to hold back the wheel of history, sooner or later revolutions will take place and will inevitably triumph' (*Quotations from Chairman Mao Tse-Tung*).

15. 'The Satyagraha movement is an attempt to carry this ancient Indo-Aryan idea into play against what would seem to the eye to be the vastly superior powers of the highly mechanized, industrially supported, military and political equipment of the Anglo-Saxon's victorious machine of universal empire' (Heinrich Zimmer, *Philosophies of India*, Routledge 1951, p. 169).

16. U Thant, 'Non-Violence and World Peace', *Gandhi Centenary Celebrations*, Singapore 1969, p. 15.

17. Ibid.

Chapter 46

John S. Mbiti

Christianity and African Culture

INTRODUCTION

Importance of this Topic

An African proverb says that "the crown of a man is in his hands." Culture is man's crown. Therefore the question of culture and the Christian Faith is very important as exemplified by the fact that, since the time of our Lord and the early Church, it has continued to come upon every generation of Christians in new and demanding ways.

Three recent world gatherings of Christians spoke about culture. I quote some statements from them. The conference on Salvation Today at Bangkok, Thailand, in 1973, said: "Culture shapes the human voice that answers the voice of Christ."

The Lausanne Congress on World Evangelization in 1974 spoke of "the rise of Churches deeply rooted in Christ and closely related to their culture. Culture must always be tested and judged by Scripture. Because man is God's creature, some of his culture is rich in beauty and goodness. Because he has fallen, all of it is tainted with sin and some of it is demonic."

The World Council of Churches Fifth Assembly in Nairobi in 1975 said:

Despite all of our cultural differences, despite the structures in society and in the Church that obscure our confession of Christ, and despite our own sinfulness, we affirm and confess Christ together, for we have found that He is not alien to any culture and that He redeems and judges in all our societies.

Working Definition of Culture

In this address, culture will be used to mean human pattern of life in response to man's environment. This pattern is expressed in physical forms (such as agriculture, the arts, technology, etc.), in inter-human relations (such as institutions, laws, customs, etc.) and in the form of reflection on the total reality of life (such as language, philosophy, religion, spiritual values, world view, the riddle of life-birth-death, etc.).

First published in *Journal of Theology for Southern Africa,* 20 (September 1977). Used by permission.

In this respect, African culture is like any other culture in the world. We can also speak of African cultures in the plural, if we wish to draw attention to regional and local expressions of culture. But for our purposes I will use culture generically in the singular.

GOSPEL AND CULTURE

God Takes the Initiative

"God so loved the world that He gave His only begotten Son" (John 3:16). This is the well known biblical statement about God in His love invading man in his culture. The Incarnation of our Lord was God's act of intercepting human and cosmic history. The Gospel was revealed to the world, in the context and language of culture, and not in an empty vacuum. This revelation took place in a specific cultural place, Palestine, among a specific people, the Jews, at a specific moment, two thousand years ago. Since then the Gospel has been proclaimed, propagated, and accepted within the cultural milieux of the peoples of the world. God gave us the Gospel. Man gives us culture. When the Gospel and culture meet, and if the Christian Faith is generated, then Christianity is the result.

The Gospel Enters and Traverses Culture

Because the Gospel traverses culture, it moved from the Palestine of two thousand years ago, into all parts of the world today. In this global outreach, the Gospel has been carried on the wings of culture. Acts 2 is the classical record of how the Gospel and culture became intimate partners:

"When the day of Pentecost had come, they were all together in one place. . . . And they were all filled with the Holy Spirit and began to speak in other tongues. . . . And at this sound the multitude came together and they were bewildered, because *each one heard them speaking in his own language*. And they were amazed and wondered saying . . . We hear them telling in our own tongues the mighty works of God"[Acts 2:1-11].

Here then is the Gospel being proclaimed, being understood, being believed by people in their different cultures throughout the world. Without cultural transmission, the Gospel might as well have remained and been forgotten in Jerusalem. So the Holy Spirit entrusted the Gospel into the hands of human cultures, and this divine arrangement has remained that way ever since.

African culture is one of these cultures to which God has entrusted the Gospel of His Son Jesus Christ, exactly as He entrusted it to the Jewish, Greek, Roman, German, American, Indian, and other cultures of the world. The Gospel is a stranger in every culture—a stranger who settles down, when it is so accepted by Faith, and yet a stranger who continues to wander on from culture to culture, from generation to generation, calling all people to a newness of life in Christ. The Gospel is greater than any single culture and all cultures put together.

African Response to the Gospel

Conversion to the Gospel takes place within a cultural framework. The Gospel has been and should continue to be proclaimed within the melodies of our African culture—

through words of our one thousand languages, through the vibrant tunes of our three thousand musical instruments, through the joyous rhythm of our bodies and the solemn symbols of our artists. It is within our culture that we have to wrestle with the demands of the Gospel, and it is within our culture that we have to propagate the Gospel of our Lord.

The Gospel does not throw out culture; to the contrary, it comes into our culture, it settles there, it brings its impact on our total life within that culture. It is within our culture that God loves us and calls us to repentance; it is also within our culture that God wants us to love, worship, and obey Him. God does not want us to be aliens to our culture—but only aliens to sin. Our culture is the medium of receiving, diffusing, tuning in, and relaying the Gospel. Without culture we would not hear the Gospel, we would not believe the Gospel, and we would not inherit the promises of the Gospel.

The Gospel: No Cultural Monopoly

And yet, the relation between culture and the Gospel demands that no single culture should imprison the Gospel. The Gospel was first revealed and proclaimed in the Jewish culture, but soon it was proclaimed in the Greek and Roman cultures. So it went on, until eventually it reached our African culture—and it must go on, from culture to culture. We have no right to imagine that we can monopolize the Gospel or keep it only to ourselves.

The Gospel is not the property of European or American culture; neither should we make it the property of our African culture. We must recognize cultural plurality as the Gospel gets to be proclaimed in all societies of the world. One can say: "this is my culture, this our culture"; but nobody can say: "this is my Gospel, this our Gospel". The Gospel belongs to Jesus Christ, and it refuses to be made the exclusive property of any one culture, or nation, or region, or generation.

So then each culture must count it a privilege to have the Gospel as its guest. African culture must extend its hospitality to the Gospel as an honoured guest that, hopefully, may stay for many centuries and millennia as the case may be. Some cultures of the world have rejected the Gospel while others have restricted its effectiveness. It is tragic when a culture—perhaps through no fault of its own—rejects the Gospel, closes its doors to the Gospel, or turns a deaf ear to the Gospel. Each culture is in danger of doing this, sometimes dramatically and forcefully, sometimes slowly and imperceptibly. So let our African culture treat the Gospel with respect, with gentleness, with all due hospitality—for it is a divine message coming into frail cultural vessels.

AFRICAN CULTURE AND CHRISTIANITY

"He who has never travelled thinks that his mother is the only good cook in the world" (an African proverb).

We have established that Christianity is the end result of the Gospel coming into a given culture whose people respond to the Gospel through Faith. As such, there is no divine form of Christianity 100 percent suitable for all peoples and at all times. Every form of Christianity has its impurities—because of man's sinfulness. Therefore every cultural setting has a right to evolve its own form or expression of Christianity. No single form of Christianity should dominate another.

It was very unfortunate, therefore, that Africans were told by word and example, by those who brought them the Gospel, that they first had to become culturally circumcised before they could become Christians (according to the form of Christianity developed in the home countries of those missionaries). There is no theological justification for this kind of burden.

Already at the time of the Apostles the Gentile Christians faced a similar burden from the Jewish brethren who insisted that they should observe Jewish cultural habits. "Unless you are circumcised according to the custom of Moses, you cannot be saved" (Acts 15:2). This sparked off a major controversy in the early Church, which had to be settled in what was probably the first Christian Council to be held. Saint James spoke much sense when he told the assembly that: "My judgment is that we should not trouble those of the Gentiles who turn to God" (Acts 15:19).

I wish that this judgment would have been observed by our brethren from overseas who brought us the Gospel of Christ. Sometimes Africans have been pressured or hypnotised into being converted to a foreign culture, rather than to the Gospel. Consequently, the Church in Africa is paying heavily for this tragic short-sightedness.

Cultural imperialism must terminate first, in order to allow the indigenous culture to relate more effectively to the Gospel, on its own terms and without pressure from outside. With humility and gratitude let us borrow and learn from other cultures, but let us not become their cultural slaves. The only lasting form of Christianity in this continent is that which results from a serious encounter of the Gospel with the indigenous African culture when the people voluntarily accept by faith the Gospel of Jesus Christ. A Christianity which is heavily intertwined with an imported culture may indeed be very impressive, but it cannot be a sufficient substitute for the kind of Christianity that should grow out of the spontaneous, free impregnation of the Gospel in the fertile womb of African culture.

Another African proverb reminds us that: "A bee does not start a new home with honey". Therefore, even imported Christian honey, however sweet, will not be a sufficient basis for a permanent home for Christianity in Africa. Until we can cultivate a genuine Christiantiy which is truly MADE IN AFRICA, we will be building on a shallow foundation and living on borrowed time. Let it be said once and for all, as loudly as technology can make it, that *imported Christianity will never, never quench the spiritual thirst of African peoples.*

The wisdom of our forefathers speaks clearly about this, in a proverb: "That which comes from charity is never sufficient to fill the granary". Thank God for the missionaries from Europe and America who, in recent centuries, have brought us the Gospel. Africa wants and needs the Gospel. But Africa does not require imported Christianity, because too much of it will only castrate us spiritually or turn us into spiritual cripples who can only move on broken and imported crutches.

A Viable African Christianity

The only tools needed to evolve a viable form of Christianity are: the Gospel, Faith, and Culture. Thank God, we have these three fundamental tools now in plenty in our continent. With them we are obliged to fill the spiritual granaries of our peoples. Have we not enough musical instruments, for example, in this continent with which to raise the thunderous sound of the glory of God even unto the heaven of heavens? Have we not enough mouths in this continent to sing the rhythms of the Gospel in our own tunes until it settles in our bloodstream? Have we not enough artistic talents in this continent to expose and express the mysteries of our Faith? Have we not enough hearts in this continent to contemplate the marvels of the Christian Faith? Have we not enough problems and spiritual needs in this continent with which to concern the riches of the Gospel? Have we not enough intellectuals in this continent to reflect and theologize on the meaning of the Gospel? Have we not enough feet on this continent to carry the Gospel to every corner of this globe?

What more, then, do we need? Why, then, have we to continue living on borrowed Christianity when all the necessary tools are present with us? Thanks be to God for His Gospel, thanks to the missionaries who brought it across the seas to our forefathers, thanks to the riches of our cultural heritage by means of which this Gospel can be understood, articulated, and propagated. But shame be to those who think falsely that God speaks only English or French or Latin.

God has a thousand tongues in this continent by which to speak to us about the mystery of His will and plan for the world. If God did not speak through African languages, there would not be today 180 million Christians on this contintent. Let us, therefore, not put to silence any of these tongues by which He speaks; let us not erase these channels of communication through which He makes Himself known; let us not tread under our feet these cultural vessels of African peoples by means of which He is worshipped, adored, proclaimed, believed, and hoped in.

Unless we can adequately become the depositories of the Gospel, unless it can stretch out its roots in our cultural setting, we as the peoples of this continent shall be found unfaithful in the sight of God, and a day would come when He would take away the Gospel. The Gospel is like a submarine: it does not sit on the water, but moves deep down in the depths of the ocean—and if that water is not deep enough for it, then it moves away to other regions. It is my belief that our cultural waters are deep enough to contain the Gospel.

AFRICAN CULTURE AND CHURCH LIFE

I see the specific revelance of African culture in the following areas of Church life.

Worship

Christians are called to worship God in a spirituality which bears witness to their Faith. Worship takes on many forms which are culturally determined. African culture needs to be studied, analysed, and utilised in the evolution of relevant spirituality and worship life of the Church. This has many aspects such as architecture, traditional African music and prayer forms, the home and family in worship life, the community approach to worship, the Sacraments, the use of religious dancing in worship, clapping of hands, confession of sin, exorcism of troublesome spirits, visions and dreams, symbols, etc.

Community

African traditional life is largely built on the community. Since the Church is also a community of those who have Faith in Jesus Christ, this overlapping concept should be exploited much more on the African scene, particularly in terms of the family, relatives, neighbours, the departed, the question of mutual interdependence and the sustaining of one another in times of need. It is not enough to reach only the individual with the Gospel—he or she belongs also to other people, as part of a corporate whole.

In the African traditional worldview, the well-being of man is intimately connected with the well-being of the total creation. If man abuses nature or the environment, nature also will abuse man. Similarly, the Gospel has both community and cosmic implications. We cannot, therefore, afford to speak of the salvation of man in isolation from the rest of creation. We read in Romans 8:19, 21f.:

> For the creation waits with eager longing for the revealing of the sons of God . . . because the creation itself will be set free from its bondage to decay and obtain the glorious liberty of the children of God. We know that the whole creation has been groaning in travail together until now; and not only the creation, but we ourselves, who have the first fruits of the Spirit.

There is corporate sinfulness of man and creation, there is also corporate hope of man and creation to be set free at the culmination of the purposes of God. The final vision of the new creation in Christ is one in which there will be "new heavens and a new earth".

Is African Church life going to rediscover, or lead the way, in the broad understanding of Christ's salvation as being not only personal, but also communal, corporate, and cosmic?

Church Nurture and Education

In the African setting, the home has always been the centre of nurture and education for the children. It must continue to be so for Christian families. Church buildings are not the most suitable places for communicating and experiencing the real essence of the Faith. Often these big and beautiful buildings are frightening: they are impersonal, they create a feeling of phobia, they silence people who often have problems but cannot open them up in a Church building, and worse still the buildings are often empty from Monday to Saturday. God is not on a regular weekly holiday from Monday to Saturday.

I suggest that true Christian life must be cultivated and nurtured first and foremost at home, and only in a secondary and broader way in the Church building and through the Church institutions and bureaucracy (if indeed Church bureaucracy is an instrument of Christian nurture). Those who cannot be Christians at home will never know how to be Christians in Church buildings or offices. The early Church emerged on the basis of the Christian home, since Christians did not have their own church buildings. I believe that there is much to be said about "home churches" in Africa. It is at home where the Bible will be read, discussed, and given time to 'sink' into the spiritual book of the faithful.

One cannot overlook the value of schools, seminaries, theological faculties, and departments of religion in our various universities. But a careful study of the curriculum of the seminaries and colleges which train pastors and priests for our Church shows that this curriculum is very much out of touch with the realities of African culture and problems. It is often more mediaeval than mediaeval Europe ever was. Unless theological colleges and seminaries drastically revise and change their curricula, they will become religious anachronisms fit to be only in museums or sold as tourist souvenirs.

One is encouraged, however, by the genuine attempts being made in different parts of Africa to make greater use of indigenous cultural materials and to relate the Faith to the problems of our time. In particular, the Christian curriculum development scheme that has been jointly sponsored by different Churches in East Africa is a very impressive and fruitful attempt to come to terms with the realities in which the Gospel has come.

Christian Values and Ethics

The Christian Faith mediates certain values which sustain the life of the individual, of the community, and of the Church. We can only mention a few examples of these, such as: love, truth, justice, the right of life, the "right" use of sex, freedom, etc. These values and ethics cannot be applied or taught in a vacuum. They have to be related to the living, existential situations of African peoples in their cultural milieux—whether in terms of individuals, communities, nations, or international affairs. Many of them are in fact very similar to those that have developed through African traditional religiosity and insights. These Christian values and ethics are, therefore, close to the African experience and worldview.

Christian Service and Witness

Corporate life, community life, and Church life are not life in isolation. The Christian Faith is not just a private bank account which the depositor uses secretly or privately. It is public property which has to be shared through service and proclaimed through evangelism. It is at the very heart of what our Lord Himself did: He went about preaching the Gospel, healing the sick, raising the dead, feeding the hungry. . . .

African Church life must reflect and incarnate this work of our Lord, within the context of the peoples of Africa. There are many who are ready to listen to the Gospel— but they must hear it in their own languages and life situations. There are many who are sick, and the Gospel must bring them hope, healing, and newness of life. There are many who are spiritually and morally dead, politically oppressed, economically exploited, socially ostracised. The Gospel and the Church must bring healing to them all.

There are many who are hungry—physically starving, eating only the crumbs that fall from their master's table, babies suffering from malnutrition, thousands crying out for the food of love, the food of justice, the food of care. . . . The Gospel and the Church must feed them first. Unless they have enough to eat and drink, unless they are touched by the grain of love, they will be too concerned about their stomachs to hear the Gospel, unless they are socially and economically given to eat (set free), they will not understand what the Gospel is all about. The centre of the hungry man is his stomach, not his heart. The centre of an oppressed man is the chains that bind his legs and hands, not his head. The centre of the destitute is not his soul but his basic rights and his craving for love. . . .

African Church life should address itself to these centres of human life. Another African proverb says: "The home of one's lover is never too hilly to be reached". Since the Gospel has now come to love the African people, it must teach them, wherever they are, even if they be ugly, oppressed, the peripherals of society. After all, we have a saying that: "You should not abandon a child when she has an itching sore".

Evangelism in Africa is making enormous strides. It was initiated by missionaries, often through great difficulties and obstacles. But no sooner did Africans embrace the Gospel than they began to evangelize one another. There is a vast host of evangelists— men and women, young and old, everywhere, at least in the southern two-thirds of the continent. As a result of this evangelistic work, each year the Church is increasing by 5%—partly through new conversions, and partly through demographic increase among Christians.

Evangelism has two dimensions: human effort and the divine superintendence. On the human level, evangelism must be related to the culture of the people concerned. Here, then, African culture becomes supremely important as a vehicle of evangelism. It proclaims the Gospel, it makes it understood, it makes it accepted or believed, and it gives the setting in which Christian growth is possible. Therefore we must take African culture very seriously in Christian evangelism—and use all its tools for the glory of God—tools of language, art, drama, dance, music, symbols, worldviews, technology, mass media, the Bible in different languages, and tools of customs that have produced special meaning for life (e.g., in connection with birth, adolescence, marriage, death, festivals and rituals that do not contradict the Gospel message, etc.). No cultural element should be left out if it can be used in evangelism and for the nurture of the people of God.

Church life in Africa has often been afraid of African cultural elements—such fears are not justifiable in most cases. We should not be afraid that our cultures will make the Gospel rusty—far from it. Since God protects His Gospel, nothing can alter it, nothing can change it, and nothing can make it unclean. The Gospel is beyond culture—even if it depends on human culture to be proclaimed and embraced. God is the only protector of the Gospel: our business is to proclaim it, to believe it, to celebrate it and to be changed by it.

And yet, it must be pointed out that within our culture there are elements that may obscure the preaching or elucidation of the Gospel. Not every element of our culture has the same value and weight in making the mysteries of God known. We have to look out for such elements, in order to exorcise them, eliminate them, avoid them, and if possible destroy them by the power of the Gospel.

Yet the Church should not pose as a spiritual police force of a people's cultural life, since the Church itself is made up of sinful men, women, and children, and its own history is not without fault.

Christians and their Culture

There are several ways by which the Christian relates to his culture. No single way is universally agreed upon. Some Christians withdraw—or wish to—from their culture, as if they could completely disown it. Others regard their culture negatively—as if culture is totally and irrevocably evil. Other Christians depict an attitude of hostility towards culture, condemning it, despising it, fearing it, always regarding it as a temptation to sinfulness. There are those who embrace culture uncritically, as though culture were perfect and always right. Another view regards Christ as having come to "save" the whole person, including the person's culture and history and environment.

While I do not wish to provide a recipe for Christians in Africa, I would tend to favour the last of these views, even if I would accept that the other views have their degrees of validity as well. The Church has a duty to guide Christians in reaching a working view of relating to their culture.

Culture shapes man, and man creates culture. African Christians are also makers of culture. What, then, is the responsibility of Christians in making their contribution to the culture of their society? Many Christians are making contributions which are being utilised in the life of the Church, e.g., musicians and singers, artists, authors, poets, story tellers, dancers, dramatists, newspaper, radio, and television reporters, architects, technicians, craftsmen, doctors, teachers, weavers, makers of handicrafts, etc. The Church should deliberately encourage more of these cultural activities among Christians, with the understanding that they are ultimately using the gifts and talents of God to whom their cultural expressions should be directed and dedicated.

The Bible and African Culture

It is no mean achievement by missionaries and African converts that today we have the Bible translated in part or in full into nearly 600 African languages. Through the translation of the Scriptures the basic elements of the Christian Faith come into intimate links with African culture. Language itself is a major cultural element. In the process of translation, the Biblical world (using this in a very broad sense) is injected into African thought forms and concepts; and in return, African cultural elements enter the Biblical world. The process of translation is, in fact, reciprocal.

At another level the Bible is close to African peoples because of the many items in common, between their cultural life and the cultural life of the Jewish people as contained in the Bible. African readers of the scripture feel much at home in parts of the Old Testament (like Genesis, Deuteronomy, Judges, Samuel, Kings, Chronicles, Psalms, Proverbs) and the Synoptic Gospels. This makes it possible for many to feel that the Bible is literally their book, and there are many things that they can claim to make "sense" to them.

Examples can be given to illustrate some of the important cultural elements and values in African life which find parallels or references in the Bible as well. Thus: respect (for the aged, for parents, for authority), justice, truth, friendship, hospitality, the value of children (and the more of them the better), marriage customs (such as the necessity to get married, marriage gifts, protection of women, divorce customs, plural wives especially for leaders like chiefs and kings, inheriting the wife of one's dead brother, etc.), family coherence, corporate or communal life, festivals of celebration and commemoration, the centrality of God in religious life, the use of artistic and creative talents, mystical ties to the land, etc.

There are cultural elements which are "hated" very much in African life and in a similar way in the Bible. For example: theft and stealing, sexual abuses (like incest, homosexual relations, rape, and adultery), meanness, murder and homicide, telling lies, divorce, witchcraft and sorcery, the curse, disrespect, laziness, slander, plus many taboos.

There are historical and mythological parallels, ethical parallels, and parallels in worldviews, etc., plus the close contact that people have between themselves and both with nature and land. In more recent years African peoples have identified their political struggles, and received inspiration from, the enslavement, deliverance, and exodus account of the children of Israel in Egypt.

We see, therefore, that for African peoples the Bible is not only the book of their Christian Faith, it also gives them a place in which they project their cultural life, history, and experiences. "Officially" the Church has used the Bible only as an evangelistic tool. But one has the feeling that African readers get more out of it than just the questions connected with salvation and evangelism. Obviously there are some basic differences which have no parallels, and these we cannot overlook. In particular we can mention the message of salvation in the Bible, which has no parallel with anything in African culture and religiosity.

While the Bible recommends itself so readily, in many ways, to African peoples, this gives it an opportunity to be used as the objective judge in matters pertaining to the Faith, just as individual conscience is the subjective judge. It is also the Bible that gives us the basis for judging culture. It is necessary for the Church in Africa to sharpen its use of the Bible as a basis of judging or critically evaluating cultural elements and practices. Unless African culture understands the Biblical message, no other culture in the world will be able to mediate this message to African peoples effectively.

Culture and the Gospel: Allies

Without culture, the Gospel cannot encounter people. Yet, by its very nature, even though expressed and communicated within the limits of culture, the Gospel is itself beyond culture. The beyondness of the Gospel derives from the fact that God is the author of the Gospel while man is the author of culture. Culture makes us very earthly and human, the Gospel makes us very heavenly and divine. It is not culture but the Gospel which has the final say over us as human beings. Yet, the Gospel makes us new people in Christ within the framework of our culture and not apart from it. For that reason, the Gospel and culture are not mutually contradictory or in conflict—since man (and not culture) is the sinner and the Gospel changes man, whatever culture makes him to be.

CONCLUSION

African Culture Must Bring Glory to God

If we take it that the Gospel of our Lord is intended for the whole man in the whole world (oikoumene), the whole cosmos, and the whole creation (Mt. 28:19f., Mk. 16:15, Eph. 1:9f., II Cor. 5:17, Col. 1:15–20, etc.), then the Church must take African culture seriously. It must ask how the Gospel is to work on culture and in culture, so that it can manifest the transforming work of Christ in creating all things anew. In the Book of Revelation, the final picture of the new creation is one in which, among other things, the people of the whole world, bring into the holy city, the New Jerusalem, "the glory and the honour of the nations" (Rev. 21). I believe that Africa is spiritually capable of bringing its contribution of glory to the city of God, through the elements of our religiosity and culture—healed, saved, purified, and sanctified by the Gospel.

The Cross of Jesus Christ was, in fact, a fabrication of culture—a Roman method of punishing criminals. But that which was an actuality of torture, oppression, punishment, and death was lifted out of its debasement, into a symbol and actuality of our Salvation. A human cultural form of degradation and affliction was turned by God into a form of glorification (John 3:14; 7:39; 8:28; 12:23, etc.); and human foolishness became God's power and wisdom (I Cor. 1:23f., etc.). Once yielded to the Gospel, even the weakest of our cultural expressions and elements can be used by God to bring glory to Him. We must not, therefore, hide away our culture from the Gospel: instead, we have to lay it before the Gospel, and use it for the Gospel.

The Gospel Must Judge African Culture

While advocating this positive use of our culture in Church life, we must also, without fear or hesitation, bring the Gospel to bear upon our culture in order to evaluate it, to judge it, to transform it. Because culture is created by man, and because man is sinful, what he creates, however beautiful, however great, however highly cultivated it might be, nevertheless bears the imprint of human sinfulness—through individual sins, corporate sins, structural sins, economic sins, social sins, political sins, national sins, and international sins. Culture does not cleanse itself of its own impurities; it does not rescue itself from decay and deformities. Culture has its demons, which only the Gospel is equipped to exorcise and disarm.

So now, it is the duty of the Church, particularly through its leaders and theologians, to guide our people in getting our culture evaluated, judged, and rescued from its demonic powers and sinfulness. I do not advocate a rejection of culture, but I advocate a merciful judgment of our culture by the Gospel of Jesus Christ.

Ecumenical Openness Towards Other Cultures

One must plead for a deep sense of humility in our use of African culture, because the Gospel is present also in other cultures of the world—it is not our own exclusive property. All cultures have a right and access to the Gospel—and they will express its presence in ways that may not be the same as ours. We need, therefore, to cultivate a genuine openness—an ecumenical openness that is willing to share and receive the meaning of the Gospel in other cultures. Indeed, many of the things I have said about African culture in this lecture are equally applicable to other cultures.

We must realise that we belong to the worldwide Church, and Christian fellowship demands that we mutually share the riches of our experience in Jesus Christ. Just as the cultures of Palestine, the Mediterranean, and Europe carried and conveyed the Gospel to other parts of the world—we too should carry the same Gospel and share it with other parts of the world. "Freely you have received, freely give" (Mt. 10:8, cf. John 1:16), so our Lord reminded us. The Church has become truly global in this century; therefore, Christians should seek the ways and means of sharing the grace of God so as to take into account this globalness, and to appreciate the global outreach of the Gospel.

For a large number of Christians, the ecumenical movement—whether expressed locally or in its worldwide manifestations—seems to offer the possibility for sharing this global expression of the Gospel and Christian fellowship. We have to learn to live together, to be Christians together, to share our riches and our problems in response to the will of God for our world. African Church leaders would do well to study carefully the ecumenical movement, to listen carefully to what the Spirit of God is saying to the Church through this movement.

There is nothing secret about it, and that which is based on faith in Jesus Christ as God and Saviour certainly deserves the attention and affection of all Christians. This ecumenical movement also takes cultures seriously, since the Gospel wanders from culture to culture, and the confession or proclamation of Christ is made within the cultures of all mankind.

An Agenda for Further Consideration

1. A clarification of cultural elements that are common and/or different, in the Bible and in African societies.

2. The use of African cultural elements and creativity in Church life.

3. Serious attention to contemporary areas of African cultural expressions and activities, such as modern literature, art, drama, music, dance, entertainment, press, radio, television, etc. This is to enable the Church to keep up with cultural change.

4. The question of the relationship between culture and leadership in the light of the Gospel—both within and outside the Church—in a variety of such issues as hierarchy, respect, authority, human rights, role and dignity of women and children, etc. The New Testament speaks of leaders who are servants rather than masters of their people.

5. Identity as expressed through culture, and identity as expressed in Christ. How can one be simultaneously and harmoniously an African (by culture) and a Christian (by Faith)?

6. Culture and the ecumenical movement—the contexts in which the Christian Faith is embraced and expressed throughout the world today, the mobility of people and ideas, the meaning of Christian fellowship on a global scale, etc.

7. Culture and communication, in terms of sharing information, evangelism, propagation of ideas, ideology and culture, propaganda and culture, indoctrination and culture, etc. What is the role of the Church in Africa, in all these areas?

8. Inter-cultural encounters, particularly through language, social intercourse, symbols, modern technology, and mass media. Where is the Church in this complex world of cultural encounters? What is its specific role?

9. In the area of culture and change, people are both actors and spectators. Africa is going through such change. What, then, is the particular Christian contribution in Africa today in this process?

10. A careful study or understanding is needed about the impact of the Bible on African culture.

11. There is a strong invasion of western and technological cultures upon African culture, producing a dynamic cultural interaction. African culture has also influenced other parts of the world, at different times in history. In this process, there is borrowing, adapting, copying, and imitating. How far has the Church been instrumental in this process, and to what extent should it continue to play that role?

12. What are the areas of cultural bankruptcy and decay as we look at our African culture today? Culture has its limitations, and these should be clearly recognised. What does the Gospel judge and save in our culture?

13. The question of how we can prompt or facilitate the Gospel to deepen its roots in African culture.

14. What is the message of the Gospel to our culture in the areas of human problems and needs, such as oppression, exploitation, poverty, starvation, injustice, destruction of human life, extravagant spoliation of nature, pollution, and dangers to human survival (such as armaments, war, domination, even science and technology)? How can the Gospel raise an alarm through our culture in these areas of urgent concerns?

15. Africa lacks a theology of culture, as indeed of many other issues. The more we open up the issue, the sooner a theology of culture will evolve, hopefully to aid the Church in coming to terms with African culture at all levels.

Christian First, Then African (American, German, etc.)

Christian leadership in Africa should be well equipped to help Christians in responding simultaneously to the demands of the Gospel and the demands of their culture. Sometimes these demands will overlap and be complementary, sometimes they will be neutral to each other, and sometimes they will be mutually opposed or contradictory. The Christian should be enabled to distinguished between these possibilities; and consequently to act, to decide, and to speak with freedom, when confronted by the situation. Culture can be "all powerful" over an individual—at least temporarily. The Gospel is "all powerful", at least ultimately. We need to assimilate this temporality of culture and this ultimatum of the Gospel—simultaneously, meaningfully, and harmoniously.

Culture says to each one of us: "You are mine, you belong to me, I have made you truly an African, a Mugandan, a Nigerian, or an American. You owe me allegiance." To the Christian there comes also the Gospel voice which says: "But you are mine. I have saved you. I have bought you with a Price. You are deeply valuable. You belong to me, and I am jealous because I wish to own you entirely to be mine. . . . I am making you a new creation".

It is not easy for many Christians in the world to say whether they are first and foremost "African", "European", "Asian" or whatever else their culture has made them; or whether first and foremost they are Christian. For many the first choice is what their culture has made them, and later they are Christian.

But the New Testament order is: first Christian, and then Jew or African, beggar or king, male or female. We have no choice other than to be first Christian and then African, cost what it will; first Christian and then American, cost what it will; first

Christian and then Indian or English, cost what it will. The trouble comes when we reverse this Gospel order—and many there are who fall into that temptation.

Eschatology, Culture, and the Gospel

We must finish with the difficult question of the relationship among the Gospel, culture, and the future. Culture has no eschatology: it is concerned with our past and present, and promises no special goal in time and history. It may boast of a golden age, but it knows of no paradise regained.

In contrast, the Gospel of Jesus Christ is intensely eschatological, and draws everything towards its conclusion and finality *(telos)*. Culture knows how to bury the dead, but it does not know what to do with the soul of man in the final analysis, because it has no resurrection, so to speak. Culture has limitations beyond which it cannot take mankind. Therefore, the Gospel must take over from where culture reaches its limits.

While culture and the Gospel may work as allies, it is the responsibility of the Gospel to knock down the cultural idols and chains which may otherwise detain man from reaching the promised land of his Faith in Christ. The Gospel is deeply protective and jealous, to make sure that culture does not monopolise and keep man forever on the cultural level of life alone. There are other values and heights beyond those of culture. Therefore the Christian is a cultural pilgrim, not a settler, moving even with his cultural luggage towards the eschatological goal of the Gospel.

To this end, the Church must equip its people to be faithful and courageous pilgrims under the guidance of the Holy Spirit. In my judgment, that is the essence of Christianity. And here lies the most difficult, and yet most exciting, piece of homework for Church leaders, not only in Africa but throughout the whole world.

As an African proverb says: "he who guides you by night can be trusted by day". I pray that God may enable you to guide His people by night and by day. Amen.

Chapter 47

Allan Boesak

Divine Obedience: A Letter
to the Minister of Justice

The South African Council of Churches (SACC) convened in St. Peter's Church in Hammanskrall, South Africa, in July 1979. The theme of this meeting was "The Church and the Alternative Society." Allan Boesak gave the keynote address at the meeting. The SACC adopted a resolution in which Christians were encouraged to engage in acts of civil disobedience relative to the apartheid laws. This resolution was not related directly to Dr. Boesak's presentation, although his address does provide a theological rationale for civil disobedience. Minister Schlebusch responded to this resolution with a warning in which he stated that the South African government was becoming impatient with such statements as the SACC resolution because they "posed a threat to the stability of South African society." In response to the warning of Minister Schlebusch, Dr. Boesak wrote the following letter.

August 24, 1979

The Honourable A[lwyn] Schlebusch
Minister of Justice
Union Buildings
Pretoria

Dear Sir,

A short while ago you thought it your duty to address the South African Council of Churches, as well as church leaders, very sharply and seriously over radio and television and in the press in connection with the SACC resolution on civil disobedience. Although the resolution was not taken as a direct result of my address, I did express my point of view openly on that occasion and I am one of those who support the SACC in this respect.

You are the minister of justice and it is in this capacity that you have issued your serious warning. I take your words seriously. Hence my reaction, which I express to you

First published in *Black and Reformed: Apartheid, Liberation, and the Calvinist Tradition* (Maryknoll, N.Y., Orbis, 1984). Used by permission.

respectfully and which I ask you to read as a personal declaration of faith.

Your warning has become almost routine in South Africa: the government continually says to pastors and churches that they must keep themselves "out of politics" and confine themselves to their "proper task": the preaching of the gospel.

However, on this very point an extremely important question emerges: What is the gospel of Jesus Christ that the churches have been called to preach? Surely it is the message of the salvation of God that has come to all peoples in Jesus Christ. It is the proclamation of the kingdom of God and of the lordship of Jesus Christ. But this salvation is the liberation, the making whole, of the *whole person*. It is not something meant for the "inner life," the soul, only. It is meant for the whole of human existence. This Jesus who is proclaimed by the church was certainly not a spiritual being with spiritual qualities estranged from the realities of our human existence. No, he was the Word become flesh, who took on complete human form, and his message of liberation is meant for persons in their *full humanity.*

Besides, the fact that the term "kingdom" is such a political term must already say a great deal to us. For example, this fact brought Reformed Christians to believe (and rightly so) and profess with conviction throughout the centuries that this lordship of Jesus Christ applies to all spheres of life. There is not one inch of life that is not claimed by the lordship of Jesus Christ. This includes the political, social, and economic spheres. The Lord rules over all these spheres, and the church and the Christian proclaim his sovereignty in all these spheres. Surely it is the holy duty and the calling of every Christian to participate in politics so that there also God's law and justice may prevail, and there also obedience to God and God's word can be shown.

The Dutch Reformed Church professes this in its report "Race Relations in the South African Situation in the Light of Scripture." The report states plainly that in its proclamation the church must appeal to its members to apply the principles of the kingdom of God in the social and political sphere. When the word of God demands it, the church is compelled to fulfill its prophetic function vis-à-vis the state *even in spite of popular opinion.* The witness of the church with regard to the government is a part of its essential being in the world, says the report. This is sound Reformed thinking, and the Dutch Reformed Church accepts this because it wants to be Reformed. Why, then, are you refusing to grant other churches and Christians (also other Reformed Christians!) this witness and participation?

But there is still another problem. Through its spokesmen your government has often warned that those of us who serve in the church must "keep out of politics." Yet at the same time it is your own colleagues in the cabinet who want to involve the clergy in political dialogue!

The only conclusion that I can come to is that you do not really object in principle to the participation of the clergy in politics—as long as it happens on *your* terms and within the framework of *your* policy. This seems to me to be neither tenable nor honest. In addition, are you not denying your own history by holding to this viewpoint? Did not the Afrikaner clergy speak as leaders of their people, and did they not inspire their people in what you saw as a just struggle? Did not the churches of the Afrikaner, even in the Anglo-Boer War, stand right in the midst of the struggle? Why, then, do you reject today with a sort of political pietism that which yesterday and the day before you accepted and embraced with thankfulness to God?

But, Mr. Minister, there is even more in your warning, which I cannot ignore. It has to do with the exceptionally difficult and sensitive issue of the Christian's obedience to the government.

It is important that you understand clearly that I have made my call for civil disobedience as a Christian, and that I was addressing the church. The context and basis of my call may thus not be alienated from my convictions as a Christian addressing other Christians upon that same basis.

It surprises me that some have tried to interpret this as a call for wanton violence. It is precisely an *alternative* to violence! And I turn to this alternative because I still find it difficult to accept violence as an unobjectionable solution. Or perhaps there are some who fear that should Christians in South Africa perform their duty in being more obedient to God than to humans, the idolized nature of this state will be exposed. Surely a state that accepts the supreme rule of Christ should not have to be afraid of this?

I believe I have done nothing more than to place myself squarely within the Reformed tradition as that tradition has always understood sacred scripture on these matters.

Essential to this is the following: It is my conviction that, for a Christian, obedience to the state or any earthly authority is always linked to our obedience to God. That is to say, obedience to human institutions (and to human beings) is always relative. The human institution can never have the same authority as God, and human laws must always be subordinate to the word of God. This is how the Christian understands it. Even God does not expect blind servility; Christians cannot even think of giving unconditional obedience to a government.

Our past experience has taught us that this is exactly the kind of obedience, blind and unquestioning, that your government expects. I want, however, to be honest with you: this I cannot give you. The believer in Christ not only has the right, but also the responsibility, should a government deviate from God's law, to be more obedient to God than to the government. The question is not really whether Christians have the courage to disobey the government, but whether we have the courage to set aside God's word and not obey *God*.

Over the years, nearly all the Christian churches in this country have condemned the policies of your government as wrong and sinful. My own church, the Dutch Reformed Mission Church, last year at its synod condemned apartheid as being "in conflict with the gospel of Jesus Christ," a policy that cannot stand up to the demands of the gospel. I heartily endorse this stand my church has taken. Your policy is unjust; it denies persons their basic human rights, and it undermines their God-given human dignity. Too many of the laws you make are blatantly in conflict with the word of God.

I have no doubt that your policies, and their execution, are a tremendous obstacle to reconciliation between the peoples of South Africa. There are laws that are most hurtful, or more draconian than others, and these especially have been condemned by the churches. Now the churches have reached a point where we have to say: If we condemn laws on the grounds of the word of God, how can we obey those laws?

In my view, Christians in South Africa today do not stand alone in this decision. Scripture knows of disobedience to earthly powers when these powers disregarded the Word of the living God. Daniel disobeyed the king's law when he refused to bow down before the graven image of Nebuchadnezzar (Dan. 3:17–18), because he regarded the king's law as being in conflict with the demands of his God. Peter's refusal to obey the commands of the Sanhedrin not to give witness to Jesus has always been the classic example of disobedience to a worldly authority. To this day his answer still resounds like a bell in the church of Christ: "We must obey God rather than men" (Acts 5:29). There are other examples. Paul displayed nothing of a servile obedience when the magistrates of Philippi wanted to release him from prison after having confined him unlawfully (without a trial!): "They gave us a public flogging, though we are Roman citizens and have not been found guilty; they threw us into prison, and are they now to smuggle us out privately? No, indeed!" (Acts 16:37).

In the case of Peter and John, the Sanhedrin was the highest authority, not only in religious matters, but in everything that did not lie directly in the sphere of the Roman procurator. In the case of Paul, the magistrates were the highest officials in the Roman colony of Philippi. For both Peter and Paul it was clear that occasions could arise where disobedience to unjust authority was the only honorable way for the Christian.

Furthermore, Luke 23:6-12, Mark 15:1-5, and John 18:8-11 teach us that Jesus himself did not always demonstrate obedience to state authority. Before Herod, on one occasion, "he answered him not a word." Also before Pilate there were those moments when he chose to give reply neither to the questions of Pilate, nor to the charges of the high priests and scribes. John tells us something else of great significance. He tells us that Jesus reminded Pilate of something that every bearer of authority must remember or be reminded of: "'You would have no authority over me at all,' Jesus replies, 'if it had not been granted you from above'" (John 29:11).

I am not arguing that there is "proof" from these actions of Jesus, Peter, and Paul that violent, revolutionary overthrow of a government is justifiable. That is a completely different issue. I am saying, rather, that blind obedience to civil authorities is alien to the Bible; and that, for the Christian, loyalty and obedience to God are first and foremost. May I also point out, parenthetically, that the issue on which everything hinges, and the lesson that South Africa has to learn, is that what is needed is *not* servile submissiveness of citizens to the state, but *rightful co-responsibility* for the affairs of the state? And this is precisely what your policy denies millions of South Africans.

This is not the place to present a full treatment of Romans 13. However, I would simply point out that the first verse of Romans 13, which is often taken as unconditional legitimization of a government's contention that its authority can never be challenged by Christians, is in fact a very serious criticism of that very authority. A government wields authority because, and as long as, it reflects the authority of God. And the power of God is a liberating, creative, serving power. Thus Paul can refer to civil authority as "a servant of God [*diakonos!*] for your good." Thus, throughout the years, it has been taken for granted in Reformed thinking that a government has authority as long as there is evidence that it accepts responsibility for justice, for what is right.

Put another way, the definition of government in Romans 13 does not simply point out that civil authority exists. It also suggests that there is proper authority only where there is a clear distinction between good and evil, so that it is not only important whether a government is "Christian" or not, but really whether it is still truly *government*—that is, understands the difference between good and evil. Where there is no justice and no understanding, the authority of the government is no longer derived from God, but is in conflict with God. Resistance to such a government is both demanded and justified.

Even Augustine, one of the respected fathers of the church, who was concerned particularly with protecting the state and who defended political authority with extraordinary energy, had this to say: "Justice is the only thing that can give worth to a worldly power. What is worldly government if justice is lacking? It is nothing other than a bunch of plunderers."

Calvin echoed this sentiment when he wrote to King Francis in the letter published as the prologue to his *Institutes:* "For where the glory of God is not made the end of the government, it is not a legitimate sovereignty, but a usurpation." And Calvin added, "Where there is no vision, the people perish." Calvin also stated clearly that "worldly princes" lose all their power when they rise up against God. Christians should resist such a power, not obey it.

When, precisely, do the actions of a government collide with the demands of the word of God? In deciding this, the church should be led by the word itself, knowing the demands for justice and peace, and also by the actual experience of the people. It is in the concrete situations of actual human experience that the word of God shows itself alive, and more powerful and sharper than any two-edged sword.

In making this decision, the church should look for criteria not among those who make the laws and who have political and economic power, nor among those who are favored by unjust laws, but rather among those who are disadvantaged by these laws, who are hurt at the deepest level of their being: those who suffer, those who have no voice—the oppressed, the "least of these my brethren." And in the eyes of the least of the brethren in our country, your government and your policies stand condemned. I need not repeat these accusations; I simply want to draw your attention to them, and to the truth that is in them.

The untold suffering of men, women, and children, the bitterness of too many, the wounds caused by your policy through the years can never be forgotten, nor compensated for by the "concessions" your government is apparently willing to make. The superficial adjustments to apartheid already initiated do not touch the root of the matter. It is as one of your colleagues has said: "The fact that a black man is allowed to wear a *Springbok* emblem (as he participates in multiracial sports) does not give him political rights." Indeed, and we may add: it does not give him his God-given humanity either.

You complain that the churches are "against the government." But it is because of your policies that so many churches and so many Christians find themselves against you. In this, we really have no choice, because the church of Christ in South Africa *must* obey God rather than you. I plead with you: stop your disastrous policies.

May I end with a personal word? I am not writing this letter in order to be brave or arrogant. I must honestly confess that I am afraid of you. You are the minister of justice. As such, you have at your disposal awesome powers such as only a fool would underestimate. The victims of these powers are sown across the path of the past and recent history of South Africa.

I, like any other South African, want to live a normal life with my wife and children. I want to serve the church without fear. I want a country where freedom is seen as the right of every citizen and not as a gift to be given or withheld by the government. I want, along with millions of our people, to have co-responsibility for government in our native land, with everything you want for yourself and your children. I, too, want peace, but authentic peace, which is the fruit of active justice for all. However, my longing for a "normal" life must not undermine the service to which God has called me. That would be intolerable. And my service is also to you. That is why I write this letter. I shall surely stand guilty before God if I do not witness against this government.

I think the time has come for your government to make a choice: you are either the "servant of God" of Romans 13, or you are the "beast from the abyss" of Revelation 13. Unless and until the right choice becomes *evident* (through the wholehearted and fundamental change of your policy), Christians in South Africa shall be called upon, *for the sake of their faith,* to resist you as we would the beast of Revelation 13. For the Christian, obedience to God and God's word must be the first priority.

I am aware that the decision to resist the forces of government cannot be an easy one. That is why the synod of the D[utch] R[eformed] Mission Church made this so clear last year: "If a Christian is bound by his conscience to follow the way of criticism, which brings him into conflict with the state, then he should obey God more than humans. In this case, however, he must be prepared to accept suffering in the spirit of Christ and his apostles."

Once again, this is not a matter of being brave. Rather, I should like to use this occasion to urge you to realize that peace and salvation, indeed, the future of South Africa, do not lie in more "security laws," in more threats, or in an ever growing defense budget. They lie, rather, in the recognition of the human dignity of all South Africans, in the pursuit of justice, and in respect for the God-given rights of all.

You as whites are not in a position to achieve this on your own. That is why the churches have pleaded for a national convention where the people could be represented by authentic, chosen leadership. We demand the right to have the vote, so that our citizenship in South Africa may become meaningful. Give us the right to express ourselves and our political will. We need to have the opportunity to participate fully and meaningfully in the political processes in South Africa. Is this not the fundamental thing you grant yourself?

I plead that you make use of the offer and the opportunity to have discussions. Honest negotiations with the intention genuinely to share together in South Africa is always better than to stand against each other as enemies.

I am using this letter as an open witness, and thus will make it available to the press. I thank you for giving me your time.
May God give you wisdom in everything.

Sincerely,
Allan Boesak

PART SIX

RELIGION AND ECONOMICS

"Economics" is not a social movement, is it? It probably is not, but within the sphere of life that we broadly designate as economics, there are at least two powerful economic systems: capitalism and socialism. Since these systems are in fierce competition with one another, it is no surprise that a great amount of energy is spent in their defense. At least an equal amount of energy has probably been consumed in pointing out their flaws (usually by someone rather strongly committed to the opposite system). There are also basic questions that have arisen concerning the production and distribution of material goods in modern societies: questions of justice, of environmental protection, of preservation of the dignity and rights of labor. All these have given rise to movements.

Finally, economics has become most real and most crucial when embodied in concrete situations and, yes, power struggles: the closing of a factory, lines of men and women at soup kitchens, acid rain and *its* fallout, shortages of water, and higher interest rates, to name just a few. Unquestionably, these situations can and do give rise to passionate feelings for and against a particular policy. In short, economics as *lived* is far from being an abstraction, and is in fact almost too intensely real.

Movements rooted in economics also directly affect religion, although from a certain perspective it may appear that religion and economics have little to do with one another. Or that at most, religious attitudes affect economics, but not vice versa. One factor that contributes substantially to this perception is that for many of us economics and religious consciousness may appear to belong to entirely different worlds, never to intersect, never to influence one another. Vertical metaphors contribute to this sense of mutual distancing: thus religion is "up there," economics is "down here." We may even be vaguely ashamed that we have to immerse ourselves in economics, "make a living" as the saying goes.

This very model of religion, however, has itself been one of the casualties from the impact of economic concerns on religion. Christians today, for example, not only call for more attention to the poor, the unemployed, and the homeless; they see these conditions as being the very starting point of faith and therefore of genuine religion. As Thomas Hanks shows us in the following selection, this awareness of the poor is not really new at all, but is a striking feature of the Bible itself. From this starting point, religious men and women have begun to reconsider work, nature, and material goods, and how all these correspond to the contents of faith.

We have in fact reached the stage where it is no longer necessary to apologize for dwelling on material conditions and the need for improving them. Notice that the 1983 statement of the Canadian bishops begins immediately with current economic conditions. The much longer statement of the American Catholic bishops takes a broader perspective, but it too is acutely aware of immediate and pressing needs. Religious representatives such as these make no claim to special economic expertise, but that does not prevent them from pointing out salient features of our economic landscape, nor from developing key principles directly related to religious faith. David Hollenbach makes just this point. It is always necessary for the Christian community to *embody* its religious understanding of justice in the language of contemporary politics and social proposals. There is no guarantee that one will not be mistaken or even manipulated and used, but the biblical understanding of human nature *requires* that we rely on secular reasoning and the human capacity to understand our world, including the man-made world.

Included in this section are two well-known defenders of capitalism, along with two essays (by Davis and Steinfels) highly critical of these defenses. Still, the defenses differ from one another in important ways.

George Gilder has been called the house intellectual of the Reagan administration. In his interview with Rodney Clapp we can see how congenial many of his ideas are to policies the administration is implementing or attempting to implement. Gilder begins by stressing the independence that should exist between religion and politics. He then procedes, though, to make a number of theological statements that have very immediate political implications.

Gilder's book, *Wealth and Poverty,* concentrates on the relationship between prosperity and religious/moral resources. A prosperous economy is literally built upon moral and spiritual capital. The problem of the poor is fundamentally spiritual and can only be cured in a spiritual way. This does not mean that one is not to give to the poor. On the contrary: one of the strengths of capitalism is that there is always room for giving. More importantly, however, capitalism is conducive to Christianity insofar as it guarantees a future that is not predetermined and, yes, has risks. Capitalism requires faith, and so of course does Christianity. Entrepreneurs too must commit themselves to the future, make a "leap of faith." Although Gilder stops short of saying that Christianity requires capitalism (after all, what about all those centuries when there were only Christian noncapitalists?), he does insist that it rejects socialism. The teaching of Jesus "cannot be fulfilled in a socialist system." The attempt to build an entirely self-sufficient system excludes the radical dependence characteristic of Christian faith.

Michael Novak wishes to avoid the individualism implicit in Gilder's defense. He is well aware that this, along with utilitarianism, has been viewed as contrary to the Christian message. Thus his approach is systemic. Capitalism alone of economic systems carefully adheres to the principle of subsidiarity. As Steinfels notes, Novak takes his cue from one of his intellectual heroes, Jacques Maritain. Maritain had suggested that in important respects democracy is intrinsically Christian. But the primary quality of a democratic social system is decentralization. The division of powers found in the American constitution (executive, legislative, judicial) is intrinsic to American democracy and responsible for its remarkable success. But capitalism implies a similar autonomy for the three principal spheres of contemporary life: the political, the economic, and the cultural-moral. It is precisely because "profit is the name of the game" that capitalism possesses its flexibility and power, and indeed its democratic character. *Homo oeconomicus* can go about making a living, while political decisions are made separately. Cultural values, too, do not regulate the marketplace. They are determined, presumably, in the arena of one's personal conscience. (Steinfels, on the other hand, argues that economic power has important cultural effects—in the media, for example.)

Novak also wishes to argue that, contrary to prevailing opinion, capitalism is not atomistic or individualistic. The true representative of capitalism is not the individual "on the make" or "on the fast track," but rather the corporation, which is characterized by "cooperation, trust, covenants, and compacts." Novak wishes to argue that at its core, capitalism is communitarian. Its goal is not individual wealth, but the increase of social wealth, the "wealth of nations" to borrow from Adam Smith's famous work.[1]

But theological critiques of capitalism abound. Some are implicit; others are explicit. David Bryce-Smith and Douglas Meeks offer two of the former. Bryce-Smith is concerned with ecology. Both socialism and capitalism show far too little concern for our environment. Bryce-Smith sees the roots of this indifference as theological: in the (one-sided) notion that humankind is over against and superior to nature. Yet the Bible does not indicate that human beings are only to dominate nature. They are to be its stewards. Indeed, the only genuine kind of humanism is a biblical humanism involving such stewardship, for any humanism that excludes nature is ultimately self-destructive. Bryce-Smith's remedy is the development of "morally adaptive responses," in which we become far more sensitive to our natural environment than we have been to date.

Meeks's examination of economic issues is more theological and more extensive. His article is in fact an excellent example of what reflection on apparently nonreligious forces can do to and for one's religious thinking. Meeks begins with the uneasy position of Christians relative to their church. Christians need the church because they are committed by their faith to the transformation of the world. (On the other hand, Christians also need to know that the churches, particularly the North American churches, can in no way transform the world by themselves.)

Immediately stemming from this relationship to church is the requirement for an internal critique of the church itself, a critique at least as important as the critique of secular conditions. Crucial to such a critique is the God-concept to which the individual is committed. Commitment to change and God-concept are dialectically related. A God who is dynamic and open-ended implies a world that can be altered, and vice versa. This perception has always rested at the heart of Christianity in the doctrine of the Trinity, even if it has often been forgotten.

It is not coincidental that Christians have had special difficulties with "the Holy Spirit." No wonder; it is precisely the notion of the Spirit that forces us to recognize that the Christian God is working economically in the world and at the same time is threatening worldly interests, "the spirit of the world." Meeks relates this other spirit to Max Weber's famous "spirit of capitalism," the spirit of possessive individualism that cuts persons off from one another and makes an idol of consumption.

The Holy Spirit, however, has also to be supplemented by the other "persons" of the Trinity. Father and Son without Spirit lead to a concept of God that is unilateral, hierarchical—the *esse absolutum,* imperturbable, remote. Spirit without Father and especially without Son (characteristic, for example, of the charismatic movement) coalesces in a curious way with hard-boiled libertarianism and even rampant nationalism. What is lost in each one-sided concept is the cross. The Spirit of the New Testament *is* triumphant, but that triumph is meaningless without suffering.

Meeks also connects the New Testament theme of *pleroma* or "fullness" to economic life. Both capitalistic and Marxist perceptions of production begin with scarcity, with need. It is in order to overcome this condition of need that human beings organize for production and develop economic systems. In contrast, the New Testament repeats over and over that the Christian, the "new person," is breathing an air of abundance and superabundance. Only by adding this radical optimism to our economic efforts can we avoid the brutal impersonality and antihuman effects of systems that otherwise assume that one person's gain is another's loss (capitalism), or that a rigid collectivity is required to offset selfish individualism (various versions of socialism).

Prentiss Pemberton and Daniel Finn begin where Bryce-Smith and Meeks leave off. They are more interested in grasping the fundamental concepts assumed by capitalism than in offering a direct critique. In the excerpt included below, they concentrate on five such linchpin notions, including scarcity and, perhaps most important of all, self-interest. Pemberton and Finn want us to realize that what "mainstream economists" assume for their models may be just what Christians need to reflect upon and evaluate. For example, although self-interest does not automatically imply selfishness, it *does* assume a kind of egoism in which one consistently places one's personal interests ahead of the community's. Capitalist theory relies on the interests of others to balance this self-interest. But as the authors make clear, Christianity has always insisted on adding further checks to unrestrained egoism, notably conversion or a personal change of heart, and institutional restrictions. When he exhorted the Corinthians to avoid selfishness and other excesses, St. Paul appealed to both of these.

Finally, it is useful to look at one attempt to combine religious faith and socialism. Dorothy Sölle's essay is scarcely the first such attempt. Many years earlier, for example, the great theologian Paul Tillich offered what he called "religious socialism" as an alternative to the then relatively new Marxist socialism as well as raw capitalism. In his version of socialism, humans would avoid what he termed the "demonry" of material things, in which an economic system transformed objects into instruments of power. Religious socialism would be based on "theonomy," in which the Unconditioned present in each finite moment and thing was permitted to burst forth and realize itself. Religious socialism became then the retrieval of the divine in the context of the material life of individuals, particularly in production.

Sölle takes a less philosophical and more personal tack. For her, what is most crucial are the consequences of religious socialism for the individual believer. It implies, she says, a new language, a new lifestyle, and a new commitment to build community. (This last can be termed "mission" or "organizing," depending on how religious or secular one wishes to be. There is room here for both Mother Theresa and Saul Alinsky.) The outcome for the Christian is literally a new world. Relationships are changed. One may well be ostracized by family and friends at the same time one is discovering new communities. History is changed; "God" becomes more concrete, takes on texture. What emerges, says Sölle, is a new *nontheistic* theology! What she means by this is that we no longer see God as above us, but in the workplace and in the work itself. Thus the Christian socialist develops a new, far more positive, theology of work. Work is seen not as repressive or as a burden, but as a means of self-expression, self-discovery, and self-realization. Just as important, work is now understood as a means of reconciliation—with other human beings and with nature itself.

An appreciation of work and the worker is a thread running through a number of these essays. Economic objects (commodities, capital, profit, etc.) are meant to be for the human community, not the other way around. It follows, as the Canadian bishops point out, that not just workers but the unemployed too must be allowed to participate in decisions involving the harnessing and development of our economic resources. Here, as elsewhere in this section, religious consciousness returns to the simple truth that both religious and economic life is the life of human beings.

NOTE

1. I cannot resist mentioning here that Engels in "Socialism: Utopian and Scientific" long ago recognized that capitalism combined a social form of production with individualistic appropriation. In other words, although we need each other to make automobiles (not to mention selling them), we enjoy and use them very separately. It was just this contradiction, according to Engels, that produced the exploitation characteristic of capitalism as well as its fundamental instability.

Chapter 48

Thomas D. Hanks

Why People Are Poor

If a poll were to be taken in North American churches concerning the causes of poverty, results might be quite revealing. The major cause of poverty is widely assumed to be "underdevelopment." Other prominent factors are believed to be laziness (we've all read about those exemplary ants in Proverbs 6), vices such as drunkenness, and, however subtly and discreetly expressed, the supposed racial and national inferiority of certain peoples. It's a very comforting worldview and one that our most popular politicians delight to propagate.

But if you look up "underdevelopment" in a concordance, even an exhaustive one, it makes for a very short "quiet time": You find precisely nothing. The Bible contains a few scattered references attributing certain instances of poverty to laziness, drunkenness, and other assorted causes, but hardly enough to substantiate any of them as the basic cause.

Looking up the words "oppress" and "oppression" in the concordance discloses an overwhelming avalanche of texts, however, representing fifteen Hebrew roots and two Greek, occurring more than 300 times. Following through the the concordance study with references to standard Hebrew and Greek lexicons uncovers even more references, many of them obscured by traditional translations.

If the biblical vocabulary for oppression is then correlated with the vocabulary for the poor and poverty, we find that in 122 texts oppression is indicated as the cause of poverty. The Hebrew lexicons even indicate an overlapping of meaning in some cases, so some words for poor should be translated the "oppressed-poor." Other causes for poverty, such as laziness, are mentioned in very few texts, though somehow these are the texts we have heard most about.

OPPRESSION IN THE OLD TESTAMENT

Oppression is a major category in the Bible's understanding and approach to reality. The exodus has come to be recognized as playing a central role in the theology of the Old Testament, comparable to that of the cross in the New Testament. And it was in the exodus that a people God recognized as oppressed won their liberation.

In the period of the Judges, or Liberators, Israel repeatedly fell under the oppression of neighboring powers that impoverished them (Judges 6, for example), until they

First published in *Sojourners,* 10 (January 22, 1981). Used by permission.

finally opted for a king. This temporarily solved the problem of foreign oppression. But beginning with Solomon, Israel began to feel the brunt of internal oppression.

In the period of the divided kingdom, both North and South suffered at the hands of an increasingly powerful local oligarchy, which tended to collaborate with the great imperial powers of Assyria and, later, Babylon. After the fall of Jerusalem in 586 B.C., a series of empires succeeded Babylon in dominating the Holy Land: Persia, beginning in 539 B.C., followed by Greece, and finally Rome (the latter for the entire New Testament period).

Clearly there were relatively few years in the entire sweep of biblical history when oppression by foreign superpowers and/or local oligarchies was not the daily experience of the common Israelite. It is no exaggeration to say that 90 percent of biblical history is written from the perspective of a small, weak, oppressed, poor people. Small wonder, then, that oppression and the resulting poverty form so large a bulk of the literature that recounts the struggle.

Nor should we be surprised that theologians from the affluent superpowers miss the boat in seeking to delineate the basic message of the Scriptures. Most of the Bible makes a lot more sense when read from the perspective of the oppressed-poor in the Third World.

Latin American theologians like to point out that after the conversion of Constantine, the church (Catholic and Protestant alike) stopped reading the Bible from the perspective of the oppressed-poor, aligning itself instead with the wealthy and powerful, or at best with the middle class. That would explain why we search in vain in our multivolumes of systematic theologies and Bible encyclopedias for articles on oppression.

The first explicit reference to oppression is in Genesis 15:13 in which the Lord declares to Abraham, "Know for certain that your descendants will be immigrants in a country not their own, and they will be enslaved and *oppressed* [Hebrew *anah*] 400 years." Exodus repeatedly refers to this oppression, using a variety of terms: *nagash,* "treat like an animal"; *labats,* "press, put the squeeze on," etc. So if we ask why the Israelites were poor during their stay in Egypt, the Bible is quite explicit. The Israelites were not racially inferior (Exodus begins with a genealogy tracing their roots to the great patriarchs). Nor were they lazy, though that is the explanation their oppressors preferred (Exodus 5:17). Nor does Exodus ever describe the people as given over to vices or idolatry. Repeatedly they are described as suffering oppression, and the Lord makes clear that in a class struggle between oppressors and oppressed, he does not remain neutral or impartial: God takes the side of the oppressed-poor and acts decisively for their liberation (Exodus 3:7-10; 6:2-5).

The exodus experience of oppression-liberation made such an indelible impression on Israel that the rest of the Bible continually hearkens back to it. Thus, Deuteronomy 26:5-9, often referred to as the "Apostles' Creed" of the Old Testament, reflects the experience as it tells us what Israel confessed annually when they brought their offerings of first fruits. The themes are few: patriarchal wanderings, oppression, resulting poverty in Egypt, the exodus liberation, and possession of Canaan: "The Egyptians mistreated us and oppressed us [*labats*]. So the Lord brought us out of Egypt." In other words, the Israelites were creedally committed to confess every year a sense of solidarity with their oppressed-poor ancestors and to celebrate the great liberation of the Lord in the exodus.

In Psalm 103 (so loved, perhaps, because so little understood) we see how the tremendous experience of the exodus liberation becomes what Latin theologians like to call a "paradigm"—an experience to be repeated by other nations:

The Lord is working liberations
(tsedeqot)
and justice for all the oppressed
(ashaqim)
He revealed to Moses his characteristic
ways of acting,
his miraculous deeds to the people of Israel.
[Psalm 103:6–7]

Thus, in Isaiah we find such a sweepingly universal invitation:

Turn to me and be liberated, all the ends of the earth;
for I am God, and there is no other.
[Isaiah 45:22]

God continually acts in history on behalf of the poor-oppressed to bring them into an experience of integral liberation-salvation.

The perspective of the exodus paradigm on oppression is also abundantly evident in Psalm 72. Commonly we treat this psalm as if it were exclusively a messianic prediction to be fulfilled at Christ's return, but commentators agree that originally it was a prayer for a reigning king.

The justice that is to characterize the king is not like our notion of cold neutrality, but justice that takes sides with the oppressed-poor and leaps into the struggle to liberate them from their oppressors:

May he govern your people with justice,
and your oppressed-poor *(ani)* with just judgments . . .
May he vindicate the oppressed-poor *(ani)* of the people,
May he save-liberate the sons of the needy,
And crush the oppressor *(ashaq)*.
[Psalm 72:2–4]

This option in favor of the oppressed-poor is motivated by compassionate solidarity with them (verse 13a).

The salvation the king brings to the oppressed-poor is first of all a liberation from the tyrannical oppression and institutionalized violence they continually suffer:

May he liberate the needy who cries for help,
the oppressed-poor whom no one else cares for.
May he manifest compassionate solidarity with the poor and needy,
and save the lives of the needy.
May he redeem their lives from tyrannical oppression and from
institutionalized violence—
May their lifeblood be precious in his eyes.
[Psalm 72:12–14]

The New Testament similarly proclaims that this dimension of salvation is expected to flow into human history at the birth of Christ (not just at the second coming). Zechariah, filled with the Holy Spirit, prophesied about a salvation that was to include "salvation from our enemies and from the hand of all who hate us" (Luke 1:71), beginning at the birth of Jesus' forerunner.

A study of the basic biblical word for violence (Hebrew *hamas)* makes clear that violence in the Scriptures is not what someone does to try to defend the oppressed-poor from the injustices that threaten their lives. Rather, violence in the Bible refers to what the oppressed-poor suffer at the hands of their wealthy oppressors:

> This is what the Sovereign Lord says: You have gone far enough, O princes of Israel! Give up your violence *(hamas)* and oppression and do what is just and right. Stop dispossessing my people, declares the Sovereign Lord.
>
> [Ezekiel 45:9]

Thus violence is always unjust, and the Lord hates it (Psalm 11:5).

When we turn to the prophet Isaiah we find that our favorite messianic prophecies speak clearly of liberation from oppression. Perhaps we are so accustomed to hearing Isaiah 9:6 sung in Handel's "Messiah" that our curiosity is not even aroused to ask what is indicated by the "for" (Hebrew *ki)* in the exultant "For unto us a child is born."

If we trace back in the context (verses 4 and 5 likewise begin with "for" *[ki]),* we discover the reference to oppression in verse 4: "For as in the day of Midian's defeat [Judges 6] you have shattered the yoke that burdens them, the bar across their shoulders, the rod of their oppressors *(nagash)."* The liberation from oppression, we should note, is not relegated to the second coming but to the Messiah's birth, which is to mark the beginning of a kingdom characterized by liberation from oppression, continual growth, and the final triumph of true justice (verse 7).

In the fourth Servant Song (Isaiah 52:13–53:12) we find four Hebrew words for oppression occurring six times. In verse 7: "He was oppressed and afflicted." And in verse 8: "By oppression and judgment he was taken away." Rather than referring euphemistically to the "Suffering Servant," we would do well to be as blunt as the Hebrew: He was the "Oppressed Servant."

This more accurate title clarifies considerably the political dimension of Peter's sermon on the day of Pentecost. In denouncing the injustice of Jesus' crucifixion, Peter was denouncing oppression in the tradition of the Old Testament prophets (Acts 2:22–24). Just as Jesus identified with the poor in his birth and ministry (2 Corinthians 8:9), so supremely in his crucifixion he shows his solidarity with the oppressed. The proclamation of the resurrection is thus a declaration of a liberation from oppression that far exceeds what Israel experienced in Egypt.

Only in the light of this Old Testament background can we begin to appreciate the radical nature of the New Testament message. We have to put ourselves in the place of a people living like the Jews of the first century, under the boot heel of Roman oppression, to understand what Jesus said.

OPPRESSION IN THE NEW TESTAMENT

What does it mean to follow this Jesus as a disciple? Traditional theology has taught us to think in terms of ethics, a Greek philosophical category commonly used to describe absolutes unrelated to history. Latin American Christians are redisovering another word that expresses better the biblical understanding: *praxis* (in the original Greek, the title of the book of Acts is the *praxis* of the Apostles). It involves, among other things, a commitment to work for the liberation of the oppressed-poor. Luke makes it emphatically clear (Acts 2:42–47; 4:32–37) that this remained a top priority for the early church.

So does James, the Lord's brother, in his classic definition of true religion:

Religion that God our Father accepts as pure and faultless is this: to care for orphans and widows in their *oppression* (Greek *thilpsei)* and to keep oneself from being polluted by the world.

[James 1:27]

Our common English translations prefer to speak of *affliction* in this text, but Arndt and Gingrich's Greek lexicon correctly recognizes that oppression is the first meaning and the reference to orphans and widows, repeatedly called oppressed classes in the Old Testament, makes the sense unmistakable.

James' reference to oppression in 1:27 is buttressed by his analysis of class struggle. In the strict Marxian sense, of course, class struggle occurs after the rise of capitalism. The Bible, however, abundantly witnesses its awareness of antagonistic classes and the struggle of the poor against their oppressors, particularly in Exodus, the references to "enemies" in the Psalms, and in the eighth-century prophets. This reality of class struggle is largely ignored and evaded in conservative evangelical theology.

In Latin America's theological and spiritual revolution, biblical Christians often are accused of introducing class struggle into the churches. This is utterly naive and shows we have understood neither biblical social analysis nor the most elementary facts that are a daily part of Third World poverty. Latin American theologian José Míguez Bonino, in his book *Doing Theology in a Revolutionary Situation,* goes so far as to conclude:

The ideological appropriation of the Christian doctrine of reconciliation by the liberal capitalist system in order to conceal the brutal fact of class and imperialist exploitation and conflict is one—if not *the*—major heresy of our times.

It is fascinating, though profoundly disturbing, to see the conservative evangelical mentality at work to make James more palatable. In James 4, in a description of the class struggle ("wars," "fights," "ye fight," "ye war," verses 1–2) motivated by greed ("ye covet," verse 2), and expressing itself in all manner of capitalist initiatives ("we will trade and we will make a profit," verse 13), James says directly "you murder" (verse 2b). "Murder?" say the commentators. "Impossible. Free enterprise, capitalist ingenuity, the American way of life, an honest buck; what's good for General Motors is good for the country."

But James says "you murder." The mechanisms of oppression deprive the poor of their land and other means of livelihood and leave them without the essentials for life (1 Kings 21; Luke 16:19–31). The prophet Micah had gone even further than James, denouncing the mechanisms of oppression and institutionalized violence as "cannibalism" (Micah 3:1–3).

A long line of translators and commentators, beginning with Erasmus, have opted for changing the offending word without a shred of textual support: "you murder" (Greek *phoneuete)* is changed to "you are envious" (Greek *phthoneite)*. Even a conservative commentator like J. Adamson, however, provides abundant evidence for the recognition of class struggle in the churches James addressed. Clear lines of class demarcation are referred to repeatedly. Thus in James 4:6, " 'Haughty' signifies especially the arrogant rich contrasted in 1:9 with the humble poor." In 2:6, James delineates one of the common mechanisms of oppression condemned in the Old Testament: "Is it not the rich who are oppressing you [poor]? Are not they the ones who drag you into court?"

Adamson points out that the word for oppress has "violent" overtones. He also describes the merchants in James 4:13–17 as "the materialist core of the contemporary bourgeois prosperity." He recognizes that most of James' readers were drawn from the poor and that the verses in James 5:1–6 "apostrophize the rich . . . as a *class.*"

In his analysis of the class struggle and denunciation of oppression, James does not stand in a tradition different from Jesus (see Matthew 23). Jesus came to fulfill, not spiritualize, the Torah and the prophets, and stands in continuity with them. But we cannot reduce our Lord to one who merely repeats and echoes his predecessors. Jesus gives us a comprehension and approach to oppression that is broader and more profound.

JESUS' TEACHING AND PRAXIS

Jesus takes his stand squarely in his family's prophetic tradition. In his classic definition of his own understanding of his mission, he declares that God's spirit has anointed him to proclaim "good news to the poor . . . freedom for the prisoners . . . liberation for the oppressed," and to inaugurate a jubilee epoch (Luke 4:18–19). Jesus says nothing about needing to energize the lazy, improve the IQ of the racially inferior, develop the underdeveloped, or control the demographic explosion of the excessively prolific.

In fact, careful linguistic examination of the text reveals that Jesus basically directs himself to one group: the oppressed-poor. Prisoners in that time usually were not criminals. More often they were in prison for debt (crimes were commonly punished by fines and execution). The blind to be healed are almost always also beggars in the Gospels.

However, Jesus comes not just to repeat the devastating socio-economic analysis of the prophets regarding the causes of poverty: rather, he comes to incarnate and herald the solution: "The Law and the Prophets were proclaimed until John. Since that time, the good news of the kingdom of God is being preached, and everyone is forcing their way into it" (Luke 16:16, NIV). The emphatically evangelical character of Jesus' approach to the oppressed-poor is everywhere evident throughout the Gospel.

Jesus' teaching and praxis in regard to the oppression that causes poverty can be observed in a number of areas: his liberating approach to women, particularly widows; his simple lifestyle and teaching against accumulated wealth; his denunciations and protests against the local religious-political oligarchy; and his more subtle critique and stubborn policy of non-cooperation with the Roman empire.

The Gospel of Luke begins by stressing Jesus' identification with the poor in his incarnation. It reaches its climax with his death on the cross as God's "oppressed servant." God then liberated him from all his oppressors in the decisive event of the resurrection, through which he became the first fruits of the liberated children of God and all creation (Romans 8:18–23). The Old Testament paradigm was not "spiritualized" or "depoliticized" but made universal, even as God had promised Abraham (Luke 9:31; Genesis 12:1–3).

Even this cursory examination makes it clear that oppression is a major category of biblical theology. More than 100 texts link oppression to poverty; it must be recognized as the basic cause of poverty in biblical theology. This discovery holds implications for the church.

First, in our approach to the poor, whether in our own slums or in Third World nations, we need to stop justifying our privileges and start trying to discover, unmask, and denounce the mechanisms of oppression that make and keep people poor. The biblical prophets were geniuses at this. We need to enter into the depths of their social analysis and not content ourselves with the discovery of occasional messianic proof texts.

Second, we need to examine radically our understanding of the Christian gospel and Jesus Christ. We must ask whether Christ is presented as liberator of the oppressed or as champion of an unjust status quo, and whether our gospel is "good news to the poor" or a rationalization for the rich. Strange that John the Baptist should be portrayed in Luke's version of the good news as declaring: "He that has two coats, let him give to him that has none." That may sound like very bad news in an American suburb, but in a Nicaraguan slum that kind of teaching sparked a revolution. It all depends on whether you have two coats or none. We must study carefully what the Bible teaches about the kind of salvation-liberation Jesus came to bring.

Finally, we need to re-examine our foreign policy as the cultural context in which our missionaries must work. The test is whether we promote a foreign policy dominated by fear (contrary to 2 Timothy 1:7) and anti-communism or a policy characterized by trust in the God of the Bible, the exodus, the cross, and the resurrection—a policy that is firmly and positively pro-justice.

The prophet Amos compared the Lord's speaking to the roar of a lion (Amos 1:2; 3:8). Capitalist ideology has succeeded in domesticating the lion for most North American Christians. In effect, we keep the lion in a cage and parade him around in our circuses. Then we can can declare to the world that we are the proud possessors of an inerrant lion.

In Latin America the domesticated lion has escaped and is recovering his roar. Churches are rediscovering their authentic mission and praxis. Dictators are being toppled; the "gospel to the poor" is being proclaimed. Martyrs are dying.

It is time now for our North American churches to examine what the Bible says about the causes of oppression and let the lion roar.

Chapter 49

David Hollenbach

The Biblical Justice of Politics

I

Justice in the Bible is pre-eminently a *relational* bond which links persons together in a community of mutual responsibility and mutual rights. It is the prime characteristic of the covenant relationship which binds God to the people of Israel and the people to each other. The righteousness which Paul proclaims in the New Testament is similarly relational. It is founded on God's relation of graciousness toward human beings, on the human relation of faith toward God, and on the active relation of love among neighbors.

Biblical justice, in other words, is a quality of mutual bondedness in community. It stands as a critique of all efforts to build society and create policies on the basis of individualism, both the rugged individualism of the free-enterprise capitalist and the narcissistic individualism of the "me generation." In the biblical vision, justice means seeking to protect and enhance the lives of individuals by continually building connections of mutual support in community and society. Where there is no such vision, both individual people and "the people" as a whole will perish.

II

Biblical justice is *creative*. In both Old and New Testaments, the justice of the covenant-community is brought into existence by the gracious initiative of God. This initiative creates a people where once there was no people. It is a justice which ever seeks new and deeper levels of mutual relatedness, not simply the preservation of those familiar bonds which already exist. Thus it goes beyond a *quid pro quo* fairness in social interaction and economic exchanges.

The fairness symbolized by the balanced scales in the hand of the blindfolded Roman goddess "Justitia" is part of biblical justice, but it is only a part. Biblical justice remakes the context of fairness by its drive toward new and deeper forms of relatedness between people. This creativity is rooted in the biblical conviction that a gracious and continually active God is the source of the covenant which is at the heart of all human community.

First published in *Theology Today*, 38 (1980). Used by permission.

Biblical justice is modeled on the justice of a God who labors creatively for the salvation of every person. Thus a just community is one which draws the stranger and the alien into the circle of neighbors. Following the parable of the Good Samaritan, it defines the neighbor by creative, inclusive response to those in need, not by the already existing boundaries of social and political life. Such a community will approach public policy questions ever on the alert for opportunities to incorporate isolated or marginalized persons into a network of mutual support and responsibility.

III

Biblical justice is *liberating*. The Old Testament describes the creative construction of a community of mutual relationship as an exodus from slavery to freedom. In Paul's writings, the community which is truly reconciled with God and within itself comes into being through God's emancipating justification in Christ. In the biblical vision, freedom and corporate responsibility are not opposed to each other but rather are mutually supporting. In the Exodus, the act of liberation and the creation of a true people are identified. Similarly, Pauline justification is a liberation from the futile project of living solely on one's own resources and an incorporation into a reconciled community.

These interconnections of freedom and community suggest that biblical justice calls for policies that overcome the patterns of unfreedom and lack of community which result whenever one social group asserts itself in domination over another.

IV

This liberating quality of justice is linked with another central emphasis of the biblical vision: God's justice brings *vindication to the poor, the outcasts, and the oppressed*. Throughout its history, Israel was continually challenged by the prophets to recognize that the justice of God will raise up the lowly and stand in judgment on those who oppress them. In the New Testament, Jesus is portrayed as the very embodiment of this vindicating and judging justice of God. The complete fulfillment of this vindication will occur only on the eschatological day of judgment. But the resurrection of Jesus is the down payment on its complete realization, and the Spirit of God has been given to a groaning world as the first fruits of the harvest in which vindication and judgment will be complete.

There is need for such liberation from oppression in the life of every human being. It is also sure that every person and society stands judged by the justice of God. Nonetheless, Christians who seek to remain faithful to the Spirit which has been given them are both called and enabled to act in the task of bringing vindication to all who are poor and oppressed. Such action is central in the biblical understanding of the Christian's participation in the justice of God.

V

These four characteristics of justice as a relational, creative, liberating, and vindicating form of life in community are all interconnected and inseparable. In the biblical vision, they are not pitted against each other as competing values or opposed norms. There can be no vindication of the oppressed apart from a creative restructuring of the conditions of exchange and interaction in economic and political life. There can be no liberation which is not simultaneously a movement into a relationship of truly mutual relatedness. The biblical vision acknowledges the reality of injustice and deep conflict in history. Thus it sees the fullness of justice as an eschatological hope.

Injustice is the conflict-ridden exclusion of persons or groups from participation in the richness of social relationship. It leads to oppression and poverty. The remedy for injustice is the struggle to overcome this exclusion and domination, a struggle that is often filled with conflict. But the conflicts of injustice as biblically portrayed are most definitely not conflicts between freedom and social solidarity or between personal faithfulness and corporate responsibility. These are inseparable both in a fully just community and in the process of moving toward such a community.

VI

This rudimentary effort to sketch an evangelically catholic portrayal of justice suggests further considerations as to the proper relationship between Christian faith and civil responsibility. On the one hand, biblical justice is a public reality. It concerns the civil life of society—its laws, its public actions, and, in contemporary American terms, its "policies." Thus advocates of biblical justice need to learn to speak a language and use the analytic tools which are the keys to effectiveness in the contemporary policy process. To be effective, the full meaning of biblical justice must be brought into dialogue with the movements and issues which are at the focus of civil life today. The shape of current public debate should in part determine the form of Christian engagement in the political process.

The adoption of language and social analytic tools which are taken from current debate and from the policy sciences is not without the danger of cultural co-optation, as some evangelical Christians are quick to point out. Nevertheless, reliance on non-biblical categories and forms of analysis is both practically unavoidable and theologically legitimate in the exercise of Christian civil responsibility. It is unavoidable because one cannot even discuss many major current policy concerns in the language and concepts of the Bible.

In the area of economic policies, for example, evangelicals of the Moral Majority persuasion would do well to notice that "the free enterprise system" is a notion which never did and never could have occurred in the biblical text. More leftist Christians should have similar hesitations before making claims about the gospel imperative to participate in the struggle for a particular brand of socialism. Right-to-Lifers and Bread for the World advocates of the right to food both need to recognize that the notion of rights which is employed in the current debates on these issues is largely a product of the eighteenth century, not the Bible. Similarly, specific policies and laws which are up for Congressional consideration today involve a host of empirical and analytic considerations on which the Bible provides virtually no information or guidance at all.

Acknowledgement of this gap between biblical categories and the categories in which policy debate is conducted, however, is not cause for being silent where the Bible is silent. Part of the biblical revelation calls Christians to recognize that as beings created in the image of God, all persons share some measure of participation in the wisdom and freedom of God. Exercising this wisdom and freedom by emphasizing the knowledge and analytic skills which are the human community's common possession is thus not only necessary but also legitimate. Further, when Christians debate public issues, the civil responsibility of having a "decent respect for the opinions of mankind" is part of the biblical call to an inclusive public community. Entering the civil process with a measure of such respect is a precondition for coming to an understanding of concepts and structures not illuminated by the Bible.

This respect for the image of God in others and the presence of "common grace" in the life of public society calls on Christians to back their policy recommendations with what John Coleman has called "secular warrants." Under the conditions of religious pluralism which prevail in the world, an inclusive, relational, and creative vision of justice cannot be realized by efforts to implement policies inspired by that vision without offering reasons for them which are at least plausible to the people affected. Making explicit the secular reasoning which warrants the policy recommendations will also help keep Christian advocates honest. It will help prevent them from confusing God's revelation in Christ with their own partial understanding of the society they live in.

VII

It must also be noted that the biblical vision of justice will sometimes call Christian citizens to question and challenge the presuppositions which underlie current movements in the political process. Pluralism prevails in both national and international communities today to a degree perhaps greater than ever before. This pluralism is frequently in danger of breaking apart into overt ideological and physical conflict. The diverse visions of individuals, groups, and nations often blind them to forms of oppression, exclusion, violence, hunger, and hopelessness which afflict many in the world today. The greatest temptation of a pluralist world undergoing rapid change accompanied by conflict is to lose sight of the common good shared by people bound together in true communal mutuality. In such a situation, Christians are called to press the case once again for the inclusiveness of biblical justice as they enter the political process.

A justice which is integrally relational, creative, liberating, and vindicating of the poor cuts against some of the bias and self-interests of nearly all political movements and ideologies to be found on the political scene. So though Christians need to employ reason and persuasion fully in their civil pursuit of justice, they also need to recognize its tendency to become infected with what Niebuhr called ideological taint. The defense against this danger is not retreat into an uncritical fundamentalism. The pathway of such a retreat is closed off by the fact that the Bible does not contain the concepts or analyses that can fully illuminate real policy choices.

The strongest secular warrant for the biblical vision of justice is its appositeness for a pluralist and conflicted world. Mutual relatedness, creative restructuring, liberating inclusiveness, and a forthright commitment to the vindication of the poor and oppressed are simultaneously the conditions of religious faithfulness and public civility today. Elements of this integral vision are present in diverse parts of the churches and the body politic in the 1980s. The civil task of the public church is to help nurture them and act on them in both the religious and political domains. Failure to do so would be both unbiblical and uncivil.

Chapter 50

George Gilder
Interviewed by Rodney Clapp

Where Capitalism and Christianity Meet

George Gilder is a conservative. To those who have read his books or heard his lectures or seen him with President Reagan's men, nothing could be more obvious. Yet to Gilder himself this assertion is not a dull and colorless fact. To him, political, social, and religious conservatism are the lifeblood of humanity; they constitute the one grand and unifying theme that makes dazzling sense of reality.

Adam Smith set the world talking about laissez-faire economics when he wrote *The Wealth of Nations* (1776). But Smith's capitalist descendants are often surprised that he took an almost Machiavellian approach to the free market, referring to the "mean rapacity," "monopolizing spirit," and "sneaking arts" of merchants and manufacturers.

Gilder does not believe capitalism feeds on the poisoned blood of greed and envy. Instead, he sees capitalism's heart pumped by Saint Paul's three verities of the Christian life: faith, hope, and love. He happily quotes Walter Lippmann to the effect that capitalism finally made "the Golden Rule . . . economically sound." Yes, "for the first time men could conceive a social order in which the ancient moral aspiration of liberty, fraternity, and equality was consistent with the abolition of poverty and the increase of wealth."

In fact, for Gilder, religious faith is necessary to capitalism: capitalism "thrives" on it and "decays without it." In that vein, Gilder the intellectual can leave the tomes of scholars to note that religious figures of average intelligence—not the professors—have got the story right.

Before long, Gilder writes, nonconservatives of all stripes:

> [Will] have to grant, in essence, that Ernest van den Haag and Billy Graham were right about pornography; that Anita Bryant knows more about homosexuality than does the American Association of Psychiatrists; that Phyllis Schlafly is better at defining national priorities than Daniel Patrick Moynihan; that the Moral Majority is a more valuable and responsible movement in our politics than is the Coalition for a Democratic Majority.

George Gilder is a thinker. He studied government at Harvard but has since dived deeply into anthropology, sociology, and economics. His first book, *Sexual Suicide*

First published in *Christianity Today* (Februrary 4, 1983). Used by permission.

(Quadrangle, 1973), enraged feminists by asserting that man is biologically more aggressive than woman. Masculine sexuality is oriented to the immediate. But the child-bearing female's sexuality is oriented to the future. "Women have long horizons within their very bodies, glimpses of eternity within their wombs," Gilder explains. Monogamous marriage thus makes civilization possible:

> Civilized society is dependent upon the submission of the short-term sexuality of young men to the extended maternal horizons of women.

His next book involved Gilder in ghetto life. *Visible Man* (Basic Books, 1978) explored the plight of the poor. Characteristically, his eloquently stated opinions acted like magnets to draw and throw readers into two angrily disagreeing camps. He said that liberal social policies, far from assuaging poverty, were aggravating it.

That theme is resumed in Gilder's latest—and thus far most influential—book, *Wealth and Poverty* (Basic Books, 1981). Something of an inspirational exposition on capitalism, and more specifically, supply side economics, *Wealth and Poverty* was declared the "bible" of the Reagan administration. The President bought several copies and distributed them to political friends and foes. The chief of Reagan's transition team was clear about it. He said the "brilliant book" would serve "as an inspiration and guide for the new administration." And David Stockman, Reagan's once-and-future budget director, declared "*Wealth and Poverty* is Promethean in its intellectual power and insight." With accolades like these from men in such positions, one might not exaggerate in saying that George Gilder has influenced the Reagan administration as much as anyone else who is not a member of the cabinet.

Not everyone is happy about that influence, and those critics are not without daunting ammunition. Those concerned with women's rights have attacked Gilder's "biological determinism," his contention that male and female innately have different functions in life and work. Some say his elevation of woman as the great tamer of man's base passions only makes her queen to chain her to a powerless throne. If Gilder's view restricts women, it also abases men by implying that the male is basically brutal, but insecure and in constant need of female affirmation.

Gilder defends the altruistic nature of capitalism by asserting that the successful capitalist must understand "the needs of others." It is noble to meet such basic needs as food, clothing, and shelter. But some say it is less heroic when one remembers that some capitalists fulfill those basics with Perrier, designer jeans, and vacation cabins furnished with hot tubs.

Gilder's boundless optimism has also produced accusations that he is uncompassionate, especially when he states that tax cuts for the rich will eventually trickle wealth down to help the poor. Cracks liberal economist Lester Thurow, "George says you've got to have faith, but the problem with the got-to-have-faith argument is that we have only one economy to play tiddly-winks with."

Finally, Gilder recognizes but does not conclusively answer a charge made even by those sympathetic to capitalism: that it inflames appetites and can breed unrealistic as well as ugly expectations. Here Gilder shifts the blame to secular humanism and the failure of moral guardians such as the church. He will not allow that some flaw within the economic system itself might lead to an unjust distribution of wealth or the dissolution of society's moral discipline.

What drew *Christianity Today* to Gilder is his insistence on the importance of religion in society. His books are not aimed at an explicitly religious audience, yet *Wealth and*

Poverty contains a chapter entitled "The Necessity of Faith." He has written luminously (to use one of his favorite words) on his thesis that, "if religion is true, its truth must necessarily apply to the economic sphere."

Thus it was that we met George Gilder at the Hartford, Connecticut, airport last June. He was on his way to join Phyllis Schlafly's party celebrating the death of the Equal Rights Amendment. He is tall and wiry, with a basketball player's build. His casually combed black hair makes it clear Gilder is more interested in what goes on inside his head than outside. In a friendly, unpretentious manner he exposed what is inside that head, volunteering many provocative opinions. Most important to *Christianity Today* readers, he made plain the role that religious faith, especially his Christian faith, plays in his thought.

Clapp: Let's begin with your own words. You recently wrote in the *American Spectator*, "The church should devote itself to its own spiritual and religious cause, upholding the laws of morality and faith, and thus redeem the most crucial conditions of capitalistic giving and entrepreneurship." Is the church, then, subordinated to a supportive role in maintaining the capitalist economy? Is that its place in society?

Gilder: No. Like every other human activity, capitalism can succeed to the extent that it accords with the deeper principles that inspire religion. God comes first, obviously. Capitalism comes second. But when churches abandon God through various secular fads and enthusiasms, they are betraying God. When they maintain there's something inherently antagonistic between Christianity and capitalism, they're being obtuse. In other words, the church is perfectly capable of betraying God, and when it does, it betrays its deepest purpose in the world.

Clapp: How does that purpose work out in a concrete, practical manner? What exactly should the church be doing?

Gilder: The church should be evangelizing and persuading people of the truth of the Christian message. To the extent that it succeeds in performing that function it can save the world, and to the extent that it abandons that role it will both destroy itself—as many established churches are beginning to do—and destroy the world as well. Ultimately, the world can only work to the extent that it responds to God and is ordered by God's truth. So it's essential that the church propagate those truths rather than get involved in political conflicts.

Clapp: Is there any place for the church to be involved in politics?

Gilder: Yes. The church can be involved in politics, but that's not its prime role. The church as the church has the essential role of propagating and evangelizing God's truth. Individual people in the church certainly can enter politics. Politics is a perfectly legitimate human activity.

Clapp: So you would see the primary political involvement of the church to be individual Christians and not the church as an organization or body?

Gilder: I think Jerry Falwell makes that distinction very clearly. He is a preacher of the gospel much of the time, but he also performs a political role. He collaborates with a number of people of all faiths, propagating moral propositions that are upheld by many other religions as well as Christianity. I think that distinction is legitimate.

The World Council of Churches and the National Council of Churches routinely accept a lot of socialist propositions and try to infuse them with a kind of holy light they don't deserve—helping the poor, for example. This is a practical problem, not something that can be done through good intentions alone. But the liberal policies some churches have endorsed have hurt the poor in America. The essential proposition of the church has been that anything that's done in the name of helping the poor is holy—as long as it doesn't focus on their spiritual or moral condition. The fundamental and paramount role of the church is to transmit moral, inspirational teachings to the poor. There's nothing more important that can be done for the poor.

Clapp: You would see the church's movement toward more social involvement and away from an explicit proclamation of the gospel as an error, then?

Gilder: Yes, that's an error. It's also been an error to move away from a strong assertion of moral law toward increasing acceptance of the behavioral view that people are not responsible for their actions. The world is wandering in a wilderness of secular hedonism, where people have no sense of what's right or wrong, or of the ultimate divine purposes of their lives. This leads to mental illness and all sorts of diseases of our times. These are ordinarily ascribed to various frailties of social policy or psychological understanding, but, in fact, they are attributable to estrangement from God. The function of the church is to overcome the estrangement from God that results in the chaos of our times. When the church goes to the poor, it tells them that the source of their difficulties lies in some conspiracy by others and in the conditions of the society rather than in their own relationship to God.

Yet in every material way, the American poor today are better off than most in the history of the human race. Their fundamental problem is spiritual. For the church to continue its preoccupation with material problems while denying the centrality of the spiritual estrangement is to betray the poor.

Clapp: Does the plight of the poor mean that they have more spiritual problems than the wealthy or the middle class?

Gilder: Not always. But some do; a good many of the poor do have very serious spiritual problems. But many in the wealthy and middle class also have serious spiritual problems.

Clapp: Yet the spiritual problems of the middle class and wealthy don't leave them in an economic bind. So how can we say that the spiritual problem is the root of poverty?

Gilder: The greed and faithlessness of the upper classes do, in fact, lead to pain and failure, while penniless immigrants full of commitment often prevail under capitalism. The last are often first, in rather short order, in American society. Some 46 percent of those in the top fifth of incomes drop out within seven years, replaced by others from below.

Many in the wealthy and middle class have been fortunate. But there's a sense in which a complete spiritual collapse leads to economic impotence, and many of the poor, the people who are struggling in this society and can't find a way, do suffer from a real spiritual malaise.

The middle class and wealthy, although they are often not more virtuous, depend on the accumulated moral capital of their culture and society to live productive lives. This moral capital has been destroyed in many poor communities. People are lucky. I was lucky to be brought up by a mother who was intensely religious and taught me the Bible from an early age. I depended on my own inheritance of moral and religious values. If moral, religious values collapse, as they have to a great extent in inner-city society (with crime and illegitimacy rates that are beyond belief), the church has to start there. Many behave in a moral way for not particularly good reasons. But nonetheless, the observance of moral law does greatly increase the possibilities for material achievement.

Clapp: I think you've written that hypocrisy is vice's tribute to virtue.

Gilder: Yes, and it's better to have this tribute paid than to have it withheld. I think it has good effects in that paying respects to the law, to God, and to the moral code is a good thing to do. Not to do that is to propagate evil and cynicism. There are gradations of goodness and badness in the world and we're all to some extent sinners. Our hypocrisies are an effort to transcend that sinfulness. Sometimes it doesn't succeed, but it's an effort in the right direction.

But the crucial principle is that there is a link between material achievement and religious values. Complete repudiation of religious values leads to economic collapse as well as moral failure. That does not mean that every wealthy man is good. It does mean that as moral values collapse in a society, it becomes impossible to have productive capitalism. The value of anything is ultimately derived from the values upheld by society, and those values ultimately derive from the religion a society upholds. If that religion is secular hedonism and humanism, there will be a different kind of material manifestation than if the values are moral and Christian.

Clapp: You've noted, "the poor know their condition is to a great degree their own fault or choice" and that "in order to succeed, the poor need most of all the spur of poverty." One critic wrote that Gilder's theology of capitalism is long on faith and hope and short on charity. How do you respond to that?

Gilder: I reject that proposition. I reject the idea that it's good for the poor to destroy their motivation, to destroy their families, and to destroy their moral integrity. These social programs that are allegedly charitable are in fact profoundly destructive. I reject all the assumptions that underlie that particular criticism. But when I say they need the spur of their poverty, I don't mean that they need the spur of destitution.

A welfare system is indispensable to capitalism, because capitalism is based on freedom, on voluntary participation, on voluntary response to the need of others. A society that's based on forcing people to work under the pain of starvation is just as coercive as one that forces them to work at the point of a gun. Welfare is indispensable to capitalism, and capitalist societies generate welfare systems. We have a much more elaborate welfare state than the Soviet Union, which does force people to work under the pain of starvation. However, when the benefits of the welfare state far exceed the needs of subsistence or the possible earnings of an employee at an entry-level job, then it becomes destructive. It violates the principle of moral hazard, which underlies all insurance schemes, and essentially a welfare system is an insurance scheme.

Take fire insurance, for example. When the payoff becomes more valuable than the house, arson often occurs. This has happened in many cities where the houses have become less and less valuable, until the fire insurance payoff is higher. Fire insurance may foster fires. In the same way, where a social insurance system, or welfare, offers benefits far more valuable than work, the welfare state causes poverty. That's what we're doing now: we're causing poverty by paying for it.

Clapp: Back to the "spur of poverty" not meaning destitution—what exactly do you mean?

Gilder: In contemporary American society it means income and benefits are less valuable than working at an entry-level job. When the combination of welfare benefits the poor receive are about equivalent to the median family income, it's catastrophic for them.

As experienced by the poor, our current welfare state rewards family breakdown, unemployment, and consumption. If you save anything, you're immediately forced to spend that savings in order to retain your welfare benefits. It cultivates exactly the pattern of behavior that assures failure in a capitalist system. The spur of poverty means that the welfare state cannot be a cradle-to-grave cushion.

Clapp: Is the capitalist system open to the poor anyway?

Gilder: A capitalist system has millions and millions of small businesses. There are 16 million small businesses in the U.S. In Japan, which has been a more successful capitalist system in recent years, there are as many small businesses as there are in the U.S. with only a little more than half our population. A small business is the crux of a capitalist society, and it's accessible to anybody who doesn't follow the pattern of existence the welfare state prescribes—which is to break down the family into as many welfare-receiving components as possible, forgo all savings, and avoid any kind of regular employment.

There's also something about this dependence on the state that tends to erode religious belief. People begin to orient themselves toward belief in and dependence on the state. The state can become God.

Clapp: You have said capitalism thrives on religious faith and that it decays without it, and that capitalist progress is based on risk "that cannot be demonstrated to pay off in any one lifetime; thus it relies on faith in the future and in providence." How specific can you get about the kind of faith that's required here? Must capitalism be Jewish or Christian?

Gilder: Not necessarily. Though Eastern religions lack the help of Jesus, they do manage to capture some of the essential truths. If you analyze their moral teaching, they often correspond very closely to Christian teachings. Capitalism can thrive in that environment. Christianity offers a deeper and more inspiring exposition of those values, but through a glass darkly other religions can also espy the essential outlines of God and his truth, so I don't exclude them.

Clapp: Why is capitalism, from a religious standpoint, more acceptable than other economic systems?

Gilder: The central truth in capitalism is that its progress is unpredictable. The attempt to predetermine returns, to arrogate to the human mind the capacity to know the future, to calculate carefully its precise outlines and exploit this knowledge in some prescriptive way, leads to catastrophe. Capitalism, because it is based on the unknowability of the future and the conduct of continual experiments that reveal facets of the truth, can in fact partake of providence. The great sin of *hubris* is to imagine that without the help of God we can create a better future through some sort of human planning. It's this desire to have a master plan based on secular analysis that underlies socialism and makes it an evil system. Capitalism is an open system, where people succeed by serving others.

In order to serve others they have to understand others, and this requires that they have an outgoing temperament—an altruistic orientation, if you wish. And what others want is dependent on their values, which in turn is derived from the religious orientation of the society. If the society is irreligious and oriented chiefly toward hedonistic gratifications and sensuous fulfillment, then the operations of capitalism—in attempting to respond to others—will be depraved by these values.

But at the same time, the capitalists themselves have a crucial role in identifying the market's values and in choosing which values they are going to meet. I don't exonerate capitalists at all from their part in this society and their interplay with its societal values. They create goods and services, and because they do take that initiative, they are very important in the determination of the character of the society.

Clapp: Some Christians believe Jesus taught and embodied an ethic that can't be comprehended by any economic system—capitalism, socialism, or whatever. Thus, through the church, he stands in judgment over these temporal systems. Do you agree with that view?

Gilder: No. Obviously, Jesus' teachings far transcend particular economic processes, but I think that his teachings cannot be fulfilled in a socialist system. A planned, socialist system has to be ruled by experts who prescribe the activities of individuals and thus deny to them the moral freedom that is crucial to both Christian behavior and a successful social order. You can't give if the government controls all the property and essentially plans the modes of charity.

"Give and you'll be given unto" is the fundamental practical principle of the Christian life, and when there's no private property you can't give it because you don't own it. When all the returns of enterprise are captured by the state, you can't continue to expand your enterprise in response to your vision of the needs of the society. So socialism is inherently hostile to Christianity and capitalism is simply the essential mode of human life that corresponds to religious truth.

Clapp: So Christ, or the church, does not have to stand in judgment or be a potential critic of capitalism?

Gilder: There are two ways to view it. Capitalism is the economic system that is consonant with Christianity. But it obviously does not in itself produce a good society. You can have a hopelessly corrupt, evil society that's actually capitalistic. Capitalism is dependent on the church for the moral values that redeem it, so clearly the church has to stand in judgment. But it should not imagine that there is some other social system that partakes of Christianity in a better way than capitalism itself.

Clapp: You do not have a high estimate of opinion polls, yet they have increasingly assumed a more significant place in our society. Politics and social movements are largely influenced by Gallup and other polls. Apparently you feel there is some inaccuracy in these polls. Would you elaborate on that?

Gilder: Public opinion polls are in general the alchemy of the modern era. They're about as valid as the scrutiny of the entrails of pigeons conducted by hierophants in ancient Rome. They are virtually meaningless.

Most people do not think about the questions they answer for public opinion polls. They have no concerted opinion of the sort that they would defend under any real stress or circumstances. Polls aren't gathering opinions; they're gathering vague whims—impulses—which are votes elicited by the specific form of the question. If the question expects one answer, it will probably get it. If the question contains words that seem positive and affirmative, it will evoke assent. The polls are thus almost entirely meaningless because of the ignorance dominant in them.

Clapp: Would we be better off without opinion polls?

Gilder: Polls can be used in various ways that mean something. But certainly we'd be better off if the newspapers didn't have this superstition that polls are true and somehow a democratic expression worthy of the greatest respect. When the *New York Times* puts every poll result on the front page it is engaging in a new secular humanist religion that has no more validity than astrology—less, because it has a pretense of scientific truth while astrologers have trouble gaining this pretense.

Clapp: You have said America's economic problems may be straightened out with the help of a technological revolution. What is that revolution?

Gilder: It is the movement into the computer age. This has been predicted for decades, and it's actually happening today. It has happened in all sorts of unexpected ways. The crucial instrument in bringing computers into the home turns out to have been video games, which nobody even began to contemplate as a major use of home computers. The personal computer industry will probably be more important than the auto industry by 1984 or 1985. The shift will be that massive in the orientation of the economy.

Clapp: Will that help to renew the economy?

Gilder: Yes, because these computers make it possible to deal with red tape in a very efficient way. They tend to overcome the glut of paper that is clogging the offices of most American enterprises. And they also give small businesses the same sort of financial planning and inventory control capability that was formerly accessible only to large corporations that assigned whole divisions to these tasks.

The movement of computers into manufacturing is also significant. A technique called CADCAM (Computer Aided Design and Computer Aided Manufacture) means that the designer of the particular product can inscribe all the specifications into a computer, can change those specifications on the computer (which is modeling the product on the screen), can test the product in various ways on the screen, and then produce a program. That program can then be inserted into a manufacturing robot that in turn can produce the product designed on the computers.

This avoids all the processes of blueprinting and translating the blueprint into machinists' language, and the machine tool into the form required for production of a particular device. It can all be performed by the designer himself. This will revolutionize manufacturing around the world. Essentially, it's going to solve the productivity problem that we often speak of. It will also solve in various ways both the energy problem and the problem of food production.

Clapp: You sound optimistic.

Gilder: I'm very optimistic, because if these new ideas are blocked in the U.S. by the interest groups that have a stake in past arrangements, they will triumph in other countries. There is enough of the capitalist vision in the world that these new technologies will prevail. They will relieve people of routine and spiritually oppressive jobs, freeing those people to do more fulfilling work in the service of others.

Of course, the solution of material problems will not answer the deeper spiritual needs of man. But all wealth is ultimately spiritual—a gift of God—and a persistent and resolute defense of the paramount truths of Christianity will foster an ever-more generous and giving capitalism. In that context, the essential human problems of subsistence and production will be largely solved.

Clapp: Christians believe the Bible addresses "central human problems." How important was the Bible to the formation of your views on sociology and economics?

Gilder: It was important. But I arrived at many of my conclusions during a period of my life when I was less religious than I am now. What startled me was the religious explanation of the world. The Bible's explanation is far more convincing than all the secular analyses I've studied. The Bible knows more about such matters as marriage, sexuality, and economics than do most of the sociologists and economists who address these subjects, and also more about the mind than the dominant psychologies.

My first real perception was that most of the problems that are described as mental illnesses are essentially religious problems, and that they can't be solved through secular administration. Psychology can be a mental illness, because it's something of an analytical approach to the mind that tends to exclude the luminosity of the divine. The mind is not coterminous with the brain—our minds partake of the mind of God.

Clapp: That brings us to the idea of creativity.

Gilder: Right. It is human arrogance to believe that intellectual processes alone, rational pursuit alone, can suffice to orient man to his role in the world. The mind must be open to God, to the divine, to Providence, in order to achieve anything worthwhile. It's interesting that almost anybody who does achieve something really stunning and amazing, whether he is a boxer or a scientist, always claims that in some sense he wasn't the one who did it. In some way there was external help. If he is explicitly religious, he refers to God. If he's not, he refers to some mystical transcendence that made possible his achievement.

This is ordinarily regarded as some sort of hypocritical affirmation that's expected of people who achieve great things, but in fact it's the truth. The human mind, moving step by step through rational processes, isn't capable of shooting a basket or hitting a tennis ball or projecting a new vision or a new idea. There's an essential principle of giving up yourself to a higher power in all great human achievement; that is the faith I speak of that underlies capitalist success.

Intellectual creativity—any breakthrough of human achievement—is a willingness to give up yourself to others and to God. It's that essential principle that infuses Christian teaching and that also pervades all human life. Most psychological and sociological analyses say you should be much more self-conscious and rational and introspective and that through these means you can achieve a kind of autonomous mental health. But mental health comes from giving yourself up to others and to God, having faith in others and in the divine truth.

Chapter 51

Winston Davis

The Gospel According to Gilder

George Gilder's *Wealth and Poverty* has been hailed as the manifesto of supply-side economics and the master-plan behind the orgy of tax and budget-cutting now going on in Washington. The fact that the President has given away dozens of free copies to his highly placed colleagues indicates the importance of the book for Reaganomics. That it is now available in paperback speaks further of its impact.

The real significance of the book, however, is its theology, an aspect neglected by most reviewers who have passed it off as an ex-speechwriter's addiction to rhapsodic prose. But it is more than that. As Gilder testified in his interview with *Playboy* (August 1981): "I believe in a free capitalist system in a larger cosmic order, founded on absolute truth."

Capitalism itself, for him, is a kind of religion, a form of idealism in which spirit triumphs over inert matter. It is an "economic noosphere [mental world] governed by emotions, visions, and ideas." Economics is dominated by the "laws of the mind." The more courageous the entrepreneur, the closer he comes to participating in the life of God. In short, free enterprise, a system based on "altruism" and a deep "sensitivity" to the needs of others, is nothing short of a manifestation of the Golden Rule.

Gilder combines this Evangelical Niceness with an emphasis on the need for male aggressiveness in a way that will strain the imagination of readers who have never had dealings with real estate agents or used-car salesmen. The book is laced with other debatable themes: e.g., that women, by their very nature, really do not want to work, that black unemployment in the U.S. has nothing to do with racial discrimination, that "the poor need most of all the spur of their poverty," and that to cure America's present ills all that we need to do is get rid of government regulations and cut taxes and government spending, *radically*.

Since economics has been so deeply affected by the general secularization of social and scientific thought, to write a "theology of capitalism" today would be a *tour de force* indeed. As early as the 17th century, economists eagerly imitated the New Science, banning questions of quality and ultimate purpose, focusing instead on what could be described in purely mathematical terms. In the economic world that developed at that time, perceptive writers like Thomas Hobbes pointed out that labor had become a commodity and that the *worth* of a man was the same as his *price*—which was set by the buyer and not by the individual himself. Indeed, as long as the market dominated society (and not *vice versa*), questions of value could be posed only in terms of price.

First published in *Christianity and Crisis* (February 1, 1982). Reprinted with permission. Copyright © 1982, Christianity & Crisis, 537 West 121st Street, New York, NY 10027.

Even philosophers were forced to admit their helplessness in the face of questions of value. "Poetry" became "as good as pushpin." The debates about "the Good" of man and society—the very stuff of traditional social and political thought—were ruthlessly expelled from economic investigations of "goods" in the market place.

This radically secularizing and value-emptying trend reached its apogee in the trenchant attack by the conservative economist Friedrich A. Hayek on the concept of social justice. Hayek claimed that the term itself was "wholly devoid of meaning or content." From this it follows that corporations have a moral responsibility only to their stockholders, as Milton Friedman periodically reminds us. Thus, while some conservatives still bemoan the lack of a transcendental justification of capitalism, morality and values—and certainly theology—play virtually no role in economic thought at the present. This, however, makes for some "negative externalities" for the economic system itself, raising, above all, the question whether human beings will find a world based exclusively on the maximization of profits meaningful.

Joseph Schumpeter once pointed out that capitalism "creates a critical frame of mind which, after having destroyed the moral authority of so many other institutions, in the end turns against its own." The "creative gales of destruction," which he attributed to capitalist innovation, ultimately come crashing down on the ethical and ideological foundations of society itself.

Writing theology in, let alone *for,* such a world is an intellectually thankless, tricky business. Like other silver-tongued, radical theologians, Gilder tries to disguise his new god under the symbols of the old one—his god likes families, morality, love, faith, masculinity, and women who stay at home. But, in fact, the supply-side divinity has more in common with the pagan gods Tyche or Fortuna than with the God of "steadfast love." Gilder's deity is none other than Chance, god of the anarchy of capitalist production. "Chance is the foundation of change and the vessel of the divine," he writes. Chance or predestination (he assumes they are the same thing) "taps the underlying and transcendent order of the universe."

One of the most crucial themes in the book is faith. While obviously intended to resonate theologically with the traditional religious use of the word, Gilder's faith is really synonymous with economic risk-taking. (He cites the black enterprises of Father Divine's "God, Inc." of the 1930's as an example of "faith"!) It is faith and not planning that makes the noosphere go 'round. Gilder's entrepreneur seems oblivious to planning, taking his leap of faith with Kierkegaard, and zooming valiantly over the mud-flats of the mundane world with Jonathan Livingston Seagull.

The danger is that like Jonathan, Gilder's swooping supply-siders may smash themselves into smithereens against the intractable cliffs of economic reality, taking not a few of us terrestrial types along with them. This danger has been alleged as the reason why Wall Street itself has not responded to recent tax incentives by putting its money in those investments that supposedly will generate a serendipity of wealth for all of us. Asked to accept *on faith* the Administration's supply-side gospel, the original zeal of the financial community and even the *Wall Street Journal* has now grown lukewarm, if not ice cold. It would, in fact, take a strong dose of "faith" to make the clear-headed investor see how one can cure inflation by virtually the same formula Lyndon Johnson used to start it: high military spending financed by enormous government borrowing.

But does this really explain the doldrums on Wall Street? After all, investors knew that the supply-siders had Reagan's ear before the election and supported him all the same. One suspects that we are seeing, in effect, a classical "strike of capital." (Ironically, while Wall Street is out on its investment strike, it can collect "welfare" by taking advantage of the handsome interest rates created by the government's "tight money" policy.) About 60 percent of the Federal budget is now sacrosanct; social security, military spending, and the servicing of the national debt are obligations from which the Administration cannot escape. This leaves about 40 percent of relatively soft money to be used for social services. In spite of recent pillaging on this side of the budget, the financial establishment will not be satisfied until it forces the government to obliterate *all* traces of "dependency" among those whom Gilder collectively styles "the unemployed, the deviant, and the prodigal."

The goal, obviously, is to convince everyone that no one has a right to education, health care, or a secure retirement. This will leave us with only a handful of entitlements—the right to police protection, the right to military protection (against advancing Communism) and the right to federally protected bank deposits— entitlements which, for some reason, even the Reaganauts regard with holy awe.

As theology, *Wealth and Poverty* is much indebted to the spirit of Norman Vincent Peale, Horatio Alger, Richard Bach, and other pop-theologians. It is a good example of the entrepreneurial piety and psycho-babble that have characterized popular American religion for over a century. But there is also a darker side to the book, the side which addresses the center and the left of the political spectrum. Here Gilder's lush prose turns sour and snide. What he has to say about the "New Class" and "humanistic intellectuals" is not far removed in tone from the attacks on "secular humanism" coming from the pulpits of the Moral Majority.

Because the tone of the book is in harmony with the basic themes of American piety, Gilder's economic gospel is bound to be influential. Its fideism (i.e., faithism) easily translates into a pietism of contemptuous indifference to noneconomic social problems. Undoubtedly, it will provide the Right with an ideology that can bridge the gap between the pecuniary interests of Secular Wealth and the domestic imperialism of the Moral Majority. Gilder has met a need that supply-siders must feel: he supplies them with a conscience-salving doctrine that makes them proof against critiques from more orthodox economists, bleeding-heart liberals, outraged church people, social workers, organizers, and those among the poor and the near-poor who know they are being robbed in the name of righteousness.

Chapter 52

Michael Novak

Capitalism and Christianity

Democracy is linked to Christianity and . . . the democratic impulse has arisen in human history as a temporal manifestation of the inspiration of the Gospel. The question does not deal here with Christianity as a religious creed and road to eternal life, but rather with Christianity as leaven in the social and political life of nations and as bearer of the temporal hope of mankind . . . with Christianity as historical energy at work in the world [Jacques Maritain, *Christianity and Democracy*].[1]

Reflect on these words of Maritain. Cannot an analogous claim be made about capitalism—about *the economic system* based on respect for the rights of the individual, on markets, and on incentives? This is, after all, the economic system which grew up stride by stride alongside democracy in Great Britain, the United States, and then a score and more of other nations after 1776. To be sure, in the annals of social revolution, democracy has long carried a favorable reputation (so favorable that even the least democratic of nations insist upon calling themselves by the name which most condemns them). By contrast, capitalism has almost everywhere been held in disdain.

When Maritain first came to America during World War II, he came with a European intellectual's negative judgments on capitalism. To him, capitalism connoted unchecked greed, atomistic individualism, and a merely mechanical view of human relations in the marketplace. The reality as it was actually lived surprised him. Transformations must have occurred within the American economic system, he thought, during recent generations.[2] He described these as revolutionary in import. They startled him by their depth and scope. He believed that a "new reality" had appeared, for which there was as yet no suitable name or even an adequate theory.

In too many peoples' minds, Maritain noted, capitalism "stands for the primitive economic system of the nineteenth century." But something new had appeared. The new system, too, remained "imperfect, but always improving, and always capable of further improvement." In this new system, "men move forward together, working together,

---

Excerpts from "The Economic System: The Evangelical Basis of a Social Market Economy," first published in *The Review of Politics,* 43 (July 1981). Used by permission.

building together, producing always more and more, and sharing together the rewards of their increased production."[3]

Maritain wrote in 1958:

> This new social and economic regime is still in a state of full becoming, but it has already brought human history beyond both capitalism and socialism. [This] new social and economic regime is . . . a phenomenon which gives the lie to the forecasts of Karl Marx, and which came about not by virtue of some kind of inner necessity in the evolution of capitalism which Marx has overlooked, but by virtue of the freedom and spirit of man, namely by virtue of the American mind and conscience, and of the American collective effort of imagination and creation.[4]

Maritain had always been a great believer in human experience, in obscure ways of knowing, in "creative intuition," and in that wisdom which is barely if at all articulate in its profound workings. So it is not surprising that he was able to discern more at work in humble reality than anyone before him had discerned. He wrote: "Here we have a decisive fact in modern history; and this fact is a considerable success of the experiential approach dear to the American mind." He called the chapter in which his reflections on this theme unfolded: "Too Much Modesty—The Need for an Explicit Philosophy," and was explicit: "But now I return to my point, namely to the need for an adequate ideology, or philosophy. And I ask: who in the world is aware of this decisive fact which we have just discussed?" He saw the necessity of a new name for this misunderstood system, and proposed, among others, "the new capitalism," "democratic capitalism," "economic democracy," "mutualism," "distributism," "productivism." He himself preferred "economic humanism," as a term "more pleasing to the ear, and more accurate."[5]

Let us assume for the moment that Maritain had his facts correct; that there has been, in fact, an inner transformation in the very nature of capitalism, not only in the United States but around the world. He traced the roots of this transformation to "the freedom and spirit of man" in "the American mind and conscience." But this "American" mind and conscience has profound Jewish and Christian roots.

Despite its reputation for secularism, pollsters and scholars have long observed that the United States is perhaps the most religious country—in its practices and explicit attitudes—of any modern nation. Is democratic capitalism in its transformed state, then, like democracy itself, evangelical in its roots? Democratic capitalism cannot be understood apart from an ethos of a specific sort; in some cultures of the world it would make no sense, could hardly be realized. A market economy may be as much an expression of the Jewish-Christian "historical energy" in the economic order as democracy is in the political order. Indeed, democracy itself may not be able to be realized apart from a market economy and personal incentives.

Until now, democratic socialists and social democrats have tried to capture the moral *élan* of democracy in order to steal it away for socialism. Socialism has many attractive moral qualities. But as the governing philosophy of a social system it has three grievous difficulties. First, it runs a very great risk of re-creating the ancient patterns of state tyranny. Second, even in its democratic forms, it runs the risk of endowing collectivities, especially the best organized ones, with excessive power at the expense of individual liberties. (This is a real threat in all welfare democracies.) Third, paying too little attention both to markets and to incentives, it runs the risk of slowing productivity and raising the level of inefficiencies, thus reducing societies to a zero-sum game, within which factionalism and other forms of discontent multiply.

Social democracy has had a relatively long period of trial in Western Europe. Its successes are many. Yet it has fallen short of the dreams of its founders. It can go forward toward socialist ideals only at great peril to its liberties. Are there not, then, other ideals? Is there no alternative to "democratic socialism"?

It seems intellectually useful and even urgent at the present time to look with fresh eyes at the experience of democratic capitalism. Christian thinkers have for many years now emphasized the connections between Christianity and democracy. But they have neglected the connections between Christianity and capitalism. Yet questions of economics are of urgent concern to governments today. What ought governments to expect of economic systems? How ought democracies to govern their economic systems? Above all, what have Christian ideas, values, and inspirations to say about economic systems?

It is important to note that capitalism and socialism are not symmetrical concepts. Under the theoretical framework of democratic capitalism, there are three distinct systems, each with its own autonomy and yet each also in part dependent upon the other two: an economic system, a political system, a moral-cultural system. By contrast, socialism is unitary. It tends to collapse these three systems into one. Socialism fuses the economic system and the political system into one, under the aegis of a single, collective moral-cultural system.

Socialism is more like a religion or a moral vision than capitalism is. Socialism proposes to produce the "new man" who will spring forth (like Venus from the sea) under "socialism with a human face." Capitalism has never been so morally pretentious. Morally, it has spoken of itself with what Maritain describes as excessive modesty. By and large, it has left moral visions to the poets, the philosophers, the archbishops. It thinks of itself as only one of three systems. These three systems are relatively autonomous. Each is *coordinate* with the other two. None is *subordinate* to the others.

In this respect, capitalism is not an alternative to democracy or to a Judaeo-Christian culture. It is not so pretentious. It plays only one of three roles. It is compatible with democracy, on the one hand, and with the Judaeo-Christian tradition, on the other. But it does not exhaust either the democratic or the Judaeo-Christian ideal. The coalescence of all three systems into one unitary system, as in the socialist model, may at first seem to be in keeping with the Jewish-Christian ideal of social harmony and social unity. It certainly attracts a certain type of person. But unitary systems are especially vulnerable to tyranny, whether by a majority or by the seizure of collective powers by a small elite.

Democracy is based upon the *separation of powers* (executive, legislative, judicial). A truly differentiated and fully humane social system is based upon the *separation of systems* (political, economic, moral-cultural). Democratic capitalism is such a system of systems. The warrant for this separation of systems is found in Judaeo-Christian views of the nature of the individual, of social life, of history, and of sin.

EVANGELICAL ROOTS

Aleksandr Solzhenitsyn has argued that Western ideas of progress and revolution took a "wrong turn" at the time of the Enlightenment.[6] He attributes to secularism and to materialism modern beliefs in progress (especially material progress), the legalism of democratic life, the free press, the cult of the individual, narcissism, and other modern vices. He holds an ancient Russian Orthodox view of the sinfulness of human beings. In this view, dreams of progress are doomed never to come true. Solzhenitsyn places his trust in Christian virtue—in the power of such virtue in the lives of rulers and among whole peoples who follow in the ways of justice, charity, and peace. He seems at once too pessimistic and too optimistic.

One sympathizes with the great Solzhenitsyn's intentions. Yet his views on the relation of democracy and Christianity are not historically correct. As Maritain shows, it is not the Enlightenment which is the yeast that made the democratic idea grow. It is not the Enlightenment which, as Robert Nisbet has shown in *The Idea of Progress,* taught the West that the future may be different from the past.[7] It is not the Enlightenment which instructed Adam Smith, James Madison, Thomas Jefferson, Benjamin Franklin, and others about the sinfulness of every human being. It is not the Enlightenment which counseled the invention of checks-and-balances against every form of tyranny, even the tyranny of "good" rulers, "benevolent" dictators, and "philosopher kings." It is not the Enlightenment which taught that one must not trust even the virtue of the common people.

Without by any means intending to do so—exactly when trying not to do so—the great Solzhenitsyn, in wishing for a regime of virtuous Christian leaders, apart from democratic constraints, may be paving the path for a regime all too like that of the fabled Grand Inquisitor. In compassion for men, one may seek to make men virtuous by depriving them of liberty. There are too few protections in Solzhenitsyn's vision of the future to protect humankind against the tyranny of virtue.

Thus Solzhenitsyn, like many others, in seeking the true ground and origin of democracy, attributes too much to the Enlightenment, too little to Christianity. Yet, like democracy, so capitalism grew out of specifically Christian soil. Its preconceptions are also Jewish-Christian. Its ethos is in some substantial measure—but not entirely—Jewish-Christian. Its roots are, in significant particulars, evangelical. Time is brief, but we may at least suggest a few themes for further study.

The Communitarian Individual

The characteristic social invention of democratic capitalism in the economic sphere is the corporation. The corporation is a social construct, which springs, however, from individual initiative. Virtually every economic corporation of the present day is founded upon an invention or, at least, upon an organizing idea. In all cases, the idea originated in the mind of a single human individual or a small team of individuals. Around this idea, such persons gathered colleagues, pooled investments, organized enterprises, and risked such resources as they thus invested.

The risk was in every case a social risk. One individual alone would have been powerless. Founders of corporations necessarily rely upon cooperation, trust, covenants, and compacts. Usually, the corporation is independent of the state. It is a collective of individuals who "incorporate themselves" and place at risk, not public funds, but their own funds.

The history of the communitarian individual thus generated by the institutions of capitalism has not yet been written. Such an individual is a new social type. We are accustomed to think of such persons as "robber barons," thus imagining them to be like an *old* social type—that of the feudal aristocracy. We thus omit from consideration precisely what is new about them. When historians one day turn to examining the communitarian individual, however, they will have to turn to the emphasis which Adam Smith placed upon *benevolence, sympathy, fellow feeling,* and the spirit of *fair play* which he explored in his pregnant book, *The Theory of Moral Sentiments* (1759), which set the stage for his invention of the economics of development. The founder of a corporation does not rely, like a baron, on troops of his own enlisting. He does not seek military adventure or glory. He relies upon persuasion, legal compacts, and the productivity of an idea realized in an economic enterprise.

The fundamental nature of capitalism as Adam Smith expressed it in the beginning, and as has been realized before our eyes in history since his time, is *not* "the wealth of individuals," nor yet "the wealth of Great Britain," but "the wealth of nations"—*all* nations, without exception. The driving force of capitalism is social, indeed, universal. (Smith would have been cheered, one thinks, by the immense successes of Japan—and even of OPEC—since World War II, and the "economic miracles" of Germany and Italy. The world has been transformed by the driving force he liberated.)

Moreover, capitalism proceeds even in particular localities only through the organizing of collaborative efforts. It is true that the ideas and initiatives of the individual are important. But the individual alone is not a corporation. Buying and selling are activities as ancient as the human race; they do not constitute capitalism. What constitutes capitalism is an organizing ethos, a corporate enterprise, a collective effort.

Capitalism is far more social in character than its enemies—or its friends—have yet grasped. The growth of organized labor, of collective management, of profit-sharing and pension plans (the transformations which so struck Maritain) have been implicit in the ethos of capitalism from the beginning. It is true that these advances were won only through struggle, but so were those of democracy and many important victories in the history of Christianity, too. They could be won in relative peacefulness and with internal consistency, however, precisely because they were inherent in its inner logic. If, for example, a wage contract is conceived of as a voluntary exchange, both parties to it are entitled to renegotiate it constantly. The original historical weakness of the position of labor was bound, over time, to become a position of strength. The idea of "contract" remains intact as the contract becomes more favorable to labor, as well it ought. Future transformations in the relation of capital and labor are also likely.

The Social Nature of Humankind

British utilitarianism provided a limited intellectual framework for understanding the true import of capitalism. Social Darwinism, which followed utilitarianism by nearly three-quarters of a century, led understanding still further astray. Nonetheless, the early conception of "economic man" was self-consciously designed to be an abstraction, not so much in order to deny the existence of "political man" or "moral-cultural man," as to allow analysts to concentrate upon one aspect at a time. The economic system was never imagined to be coincident with the whole of human social nature.

Capitalism was designed to be for the economic system what democracy is for the political system, and what the family, churches, universities, presses, and other media are for the moral-cultural system. Since it is part of human nature for human beings to require one another's assistance, capitalism was designed to be a complex system in which there is a division of labor, a division of purposes, and a division of talents. It was conceived as a vision of interdependence—not only at the worksite, but in an entire world of "free trade."

Adam Smith, James Madison, and others argued explicitly that a world made interdependent through commerce, trade, and industry would, of necessity, become more lawlike and pacific.[8] They showed no particular respect for, or trust in, men of commerce and industry—quite the opposite.[9] But they observed that both in their typical temperament and in their typical self-interests (to which they attached more importance), such men were unlike the military rulers, clergymen, and feudal lords of the past, all of whom delighted in and benefited from abstract causes, adventures, and conquest. Sinful, and of the lower classes as men of commerce and industry might be, the entire scaffolding of their activities depends upon systems of law, stability, and predictability. Lenin would one day taunt capitalists for selling the communists rope for their own hanging. It was precisely this ideological indifference of the men of commerce and industry which Smith, Madison, and others found hopeful. The interests of such men lies in interdependence, not in barriers or in strife.

Similarly, an economic system based upon markets and personal incentives seemed to them singulary apt as a companion to a system of democratic pluralism. No test of faith or metaphysics is required for entrance into markets. None is appropriate for a pluralistic democracy. This does not mean that faith and metaphysics are matters of indifference. Rather, it means—as Maritain pointed out—that practical cooperation among men of goodwill does not need to wait upon prior resolution of all philosophical or theological disputes.[10] In order for democracy to function, it is not necessary for all to become converted to the same vision of reality. In order for capitalist economy to function, it is not necessary for all who take part in it to share the same faith or metaphysics. Indeed, the notion that each *person* should be free to make his or her own decisions of economic agency is intended to reinforce the ideal of personal integrity in every sphere. This notion in the economic sphere matches that in the moral-cultural sphere which defends each person's conscience, and that in the political sphere which defends each person's human rights.

To be sure, liberty is dangerous. Any free society will give plenty of evidence of sinfulness. Some persons will use their liberty as saints, others as sinners. A market system protects their economic liberties as democracy protects their political liberties. Alas, their moral liberties will be used as humans will use them.

It follows, furthermore, that political liberties without economic liberties are empty. Totalitarianism may be just as effectively enforced through complete controls over economic transactions as through police surveillance.[11] If presses must depend upon state allocations of newsprint, numbers of copies printed, and systems of distribution, such presses are not free. Political liberties require economic liberties. Moral-cultural liberties depend upon both. Thus religions whose essence lies in the free acts of individual conscience—as do narrative religions like Judaism and Christianity—require as their natural expression in human social life systems of political liberty and economic liberty alike.

Emergent Probability

Some thinkers have held that human progess is illusory, since history is inevitably caught in cycles of eternal recurrence. Others have held that human history is determined by forces beyond the liberty of individual human beings. Judaism and Christianity teach a quite different vision of history. Bernard Lonergan has described it in abstract philosophical terms as a vision of "emergent probability."[12]

In this vision, human history is open to new futures, yet the sequences of any one future depend upon the fulfillment of prior conditions in preceding sequences. Human liberty may affect the fulfillment of such conditions. Thus, choices made by humans today affect future probabililties. Humans may fullfill the necessary and sufficient conditions for a future development Y, or fail to fulfill them. They are partly responsible for the emergence or nonemergence of Y in the future. At times, even a single individual may invent new possibilities or set in motion new sets of occurrences which dramatically alter the probabilities faced by others.

The world which humans face is, therefore, open, uncertain, not perfectly stable, subject both to progress and to decline. Ideas count. Moral energies count. For want of them, whole societies may perish. Especially gifted societies may flourish in unprecedented ways. The Lord of History thus respects the liberty of his creatures in the long disorderly pilgrimage of history.

Both democracy and capitalism were invented as experiments. Their founders were not certain that either experiment would endure. Such founders recognized many hazards. They were obliged to argue against heavy opposition. They succeeded, at times, only through the force of arms. Their own sins and failings at times placed the entire experiment in which they were engaged at jeopardy—as Abraham Lincoln observed during the terrible Civil War in the United States, 1861–1865. Every market democracy has experienced the risk of failure or collapse, in one form or another, since its founding. Nothing in the stars guarantees the survival of either democracy or capitalism. Both are creatures of liberty. Both are subject to laws of emergent probability.

Sin

Perhaps the most important contribution of Judaism and Christianity to democratic capitalism is a theory of sin. According to this view, no human is without sin. In social systems, the most destructive potential of human sin lies in errant will-to-power. Democracy is founded upon a theory of sin which holds that, because of the dangers of tyranny, all forms of political power must be diffused. Political power is more dangerous than economic power, since it has at its disposal the coercive powers of the state. In order to attain other social goods, however, modern democracies have judged it necessary to expand the powers of the twentieth-century state beyond those of the nineteenth-century state. The dangers of tyranny are growing once again.

On the other hand, it is the inevitable tendency of economic agents to expand and to solidify their economic power. As Adam Smith warned from the beginning, society and state alike must be ever-vigilant to prevent economic monopolies, however irrepressible the tendency toward them. Modern technology and mass production have dramatically expanded the scope and economic power of the largest corporations. The contest between the expanded powers of the central state and those of the corporation—often operating in an international framework—bears the closest scrutiny. Those concerned to protect human liberty must worry both about the corporations and about the state. Both are creatures of sin, like all things human.

The theory of sin invites us to be vigilant about our liberties. It suggests that the wrong solution to our perplexities would be to increase further the power of either one of these giants in the effort to contain the other. This is why the socialist solution appeals less and less to thinking persons today. If the eleven major oil companies of the United States, for example, are already too powerful, the creation of a single United States government agency to subordinate all of them hardly seems to diminish that threat.

CONCLUSION

My aim has been to extend the work of Jacques Maritain, who showed that democracy has its roots in the Jewish-Christian leaven active in Western history and now in the entire world. I have wanted to propose a hypothesis for further investigation. This hypothesis is that capitalism—an economic system based upon markets and incentives—has, like democracy, evangelical roots. Both democracy and capitalism breathe vital air from a moral-cultural system based on powerful ideas about the communitarian individual, the social nature of human life, emergent probability, and sin. Much else could be said. Perhaps what has been said may contribute to enlarging the discussion.

In any case, democratic capitalism, such as the world has until now experienced it, is not yet at the end of its pilgrimage nor in the final stages of its testing. We will need all the energies our religious traditions offer us, and all the clear-sightedness and courage of which we are capable, if we are to be as inventive as our predecessors were. We have much to do.

NOTES

1. P. 37.

2. Maritain described transformations in the unions, the corporations, the political system, and the beliefs of individuals in *Reflections on America,* 105–11.

3. Maritain, *Reflections,* 112–13; he is here quoting the words of William I. Nichols in "Wanted: A New Name for Capitalism," *This Week,* March 4, 1951.

4. Maritain, *Reflections,* 114–15.

5. Ibid., 113, 115–16.

6. Aleksandr Solzhenitsyn, *A World Split Apart* (New York, 1978) 47–51. See also Ronald Berman, ed., *Solzhenitsyn at Harvard* (Washington, 1980).

7. Robert Nisbet, *History of the Idea of Progress* (New York, 1980).

8. See Ralph Lerner, "Commerce and Character: The Anglo-American as New-Model Man," *William and Mary Quarterly,* 36 (Jan. 1979) 16.

9. Adam Smith, in his criticism of mercantilist theories of political economy, decries the "mean rapacity" and "monopolizing spirit of merchants and manufacturers"; he goes on to say that they "neither are, nor ought to be, the rulers of mankind" (*Wealth of Nations,* p. 460). Later, in his criticism of certain agriculturalist theories of political economy, he paraphrases the commonly held belief that "proprietors and cultivators . . . [exhibit] liberality, frankness, and good fellowship," whereas "merchants, artificers, and manufacturers . . . [exhibit] narrowness, meanness, and a selfish disposition, averse to all social pleasure and enjoyment" (ibid., 632–33). He neither disputes nor endorses this view, but he does find a "capital error . . . in . . . representing the class of artificers, manufacturers, and merchants, as altogether barren and unproductive" (ibid., 638–39). See Duncan Forbes, "Sceptical Whiggism, Commerce, and Liberty, " *Essays on Adam Smith,* Andrew S. Skinner and Thomas Wilson, eds. (London, 1975) 197.

10. Addressing the Second International Conference of UNESCO in 1947, Maritain remarked: "How is an agreement conceivable among men . . . who come from the four corners of the earth and who belong not only to different cultures and civilizations, but to different spiritual families and antagonistic schools of thought? Agreement . . . can be . . . achieved . . . not on the affirmation of the same conception of the world, man, and knowledge, but on the affirmation of the same set of convictions concerning actions" *(Man and the State* [Chicago, 1951] 77).

11. See my "A Lesson in Polish Economics," *Washington Star,* Dec. 15, 1979.

12. See Bernard Lonergan, *Insight* (New York, rev. ed., 1958), esp. pp. 121–28.

Chapter 53

Peter Steinfels

Michael Novak and His Ultrasuper Democraticapitalism

NOVAK I AND NOVAK II

"Michael Novak has written what I think is perhaps the most important book of the decade." The speaker was Michael J. Horowitz, a senior aide to David A. Stockman at the Office of Management and Budget. Horowitz was lamenting the fact that conservatives and corporate leaders had abandoned all the "moral buzz words" to liberals. He suggested Novak's *The Spirit of Democratic Capitalism* as a corrective.

People like Mr. Horowitz have an advantage in reading Michael Novak. Faced with *The Spirit of Democratic Capitalism*, for instance, Mr. Horowitz is most likely not haunted by the image of the Michael Novak of *A Theology for Radical Politics* posed in white turtleneck and lovebeads, advocating a "revolution of consciousness" which would "reintroduce freedom into an industrial, technological state." According to *that* Michael Novak, a Christian could hardly "live in these United States and not protest with every fiber of his being against the militarization of American life, the appalling mediocrity of American imagination and sensibilities, and the heedlessness and irrationality of merely technological progress." Most important, someone had to help the young generation of New Left activists to articulate their intuitive rebellion and "construct a new system of life in America."

"A Christian theologian," wrote Novak in explanation of his own efforts, "does well to commit his life to such an enterprise."

A life, like a generation, is not as long as it used to be. Today Michael Novak devotes his considerable talents to articulating the inchoate ideals of successful executives rather than fledgling revolutionaries, to making the best case for Reaganism rather than radicalism. Those who have observed the successive phases of Novak's evolution are all too tempted to greet his latest performance as defender and explicator of "democratic capitalism" with more than a little cynicism. What they begrudge him is not so much that he has changed his mind—though, to be fair, his evolution would sit a lot better with many had it been, like Garry Wills', from right to left rather than the opposite—but the way he has done it. Each new cause is taken up with the same lack of restraint, the same

---

Excerpts from two articles first published in *Commonweal*, 102 (January 14 and February 11, 1983). Used by permission.

sense that Michael Novak is the first to touch these shores, the same need to bolster his latest enthusiasm with the severest judgments on those whose outlook he had sympathetically portrayed not long before. "Skepticism," said Santayana, "is the chastity of the mind." In that respect, Novak has been ideologically promiscuous.

I understand, therefore, the impulse not to take Novak seriously; indeed, the more I read him, the more I understand it. Yet take him seriously we must, if only because so many of the world's Mr. Horowitzes do. At a time when debates about religion and public policy have grown intense, Novak, with an astonishing energy as well as a grasp of religious language and history uncommon in the political world, has established himself as a kind of one-man battalion in what he calls a "war of ideas." To dismiss him out of hand or to attribute his changing opinions to fashion or opportunism is not only unfair, it suggests to his newest audience that Novak's critics have only *ad hominem* complaints to sustain them. If familiarity with Novak has bred more than a little incredulity, it is important that the reasons be set forth, even at some length. What is more, *The Spirit of Democratic Capitalism* raises a number of basic issues that are always well worth reviewing. Whatever its other flaws, no one can accuse it of not being provocative. . . .

It should be clear that *The Spirit of Democratic Capitalism* represents two massive shifts, even reversals, in Novak's perspective. One is a shift in values, in the norms by which he evaluates the surrounding social system. Formerly, realism and pragmatism, productivity, efficiency, and economic rationality were terms of scorn. Now they are accolades. Formerly, Novak suggested, sometimes by the use of quotation marks, that the claims made by such words were spurious, that what passed for realism, pragmatism, productivity, and rationality was in truth constricted, ideological, destructive, and irrational. Now such notions are taken at face value and honored. Capitalist productivity, efficiency, and economic rationality are conducive to virtue and self-government.

But Novak has also shifted in his description of what actually transpires in the social system. Where once he saw it as corrosive of inner life, pressing toward shoddiness, imposing isolation, and destructive of communities, now he sees it as enriching and humanizing, demanding of excellence, supportive of association, and giving birth to "a new type of human being, the communitarian individual." Where once he saw society as dangerously militarized, now he sees it as vaccinated against the military ethos. Where once he saw cultural institutions in the thrall of economic and political power, now he sees them as vigorously independent; indeed, if anything, the economic institutions are in thrall to the cultural. Where once he found the forces of the economy in conflict with family life, now he sees family and capitalism linked in an ultimately supportive tension. Where once he saw inequalities of wealth and power as scandalous, now he sees them as "in tune with natural inequalities which everyone experiences every day." It is not too much to say that *The Spirit of Democratic Capitalism* marks the intellectual, if not the social, assimilation of Michael Novak into the world and worldview he had previously identified with the WASP establishment and the corporate, professional, and intellectual managers of both left and right.

There is nothing wrong with a person changing his mind. But why should readers be convinced that Novak's later views are any sounder than his earlier ones? What is involved, after all, is quite a lot more than a few deprecations of mass taste or occasional passing lapses in *A Theology for Radical Politics*. It seems too easy to dispose of the matter with the explanation he had not "looked more closely at my neighbors and companions" but had been taken in by "literary conventions." If he had really held his earlier judgments so fiercely and firmly on such slight evidence, what confidence can readers have in his current opinions? Why should they believe that the scales suddenly fell from his eyes in the mid-seventies? Why should they not suspect he has simply traded in one set of "conventions" for another, exchanged those of the "literary" world that evidently dominated his thinking so easily, for those of the world of businessmen, economists, policy planners, and conservative politicians where he now operates?

Novak's major explanation for his change of mind is that in his forties he finally got around to studying economics. He even claims that during all those years of writing about international affairs, ethnicity, and domestic politics, he deliberately preserved his economic virginity: "I saved economics . . . until last." Of Novak's neophyte status in this subject there can be no doubt—his book shows not even passing familiarity with opposing viewpoints at any sophisticated level—but why, exactly, should this be a recommendation of his newfound truth to others?

The Spirit of Democratic Capitalism does not, it should be made clear, rest on economic analysis. It is in no way a tightly argued, thoroughly documented book that contains within itself all the necessary justification for its author's conclusions. Like Novak's other books, it abounds in vast generalizations—about America, about groups of people, about social structures. Insofar as these can be documented at all, Novak leans heavily on the conference papers and favored authorities of the American Enterprise Institute, where he is a Resident Scholar, even as earlier he had relied uncritically on New Left sources. Novak's use of evidence does less to explain than to illustrate or reflect his changed standpoint. Just as the values attached to key words in his vocabulary like *realism* and *pragmatism* have shifted without explanation, whole bodies of literature have dropped from his range of references, to be neither cited nor refuted, as though they ceased to have any factual value or compelling force now that they no longer coincide with his own position.

Even the reference points that do endure prove to be remarkably malleable. Novak has never failed to invoke the blessing of Jacques Maritain, for instance, in every phase of his career. It was Maritain who "provided for me an intellectual path for moving from the conservatism of my hometown" to the tough-minded "liberalism of John F. Kennedy." Nonetheless—this was now the beginning of the seventies—Novak characterized Maritain as "more 'New Left' than 'liberal.' " But by 1982, with Novak returning to something very much like that old hometown conservatism, Maritain was right along with him—the patron saint of democratic capitalism.

Novak's personal history, too, seems subject to sudden revision. Despite that earlier reference to "moving from the conservatism of my hometown," we are now informed that *The Spirit of Democratic Capitalism* represents a break "with the tradition of Christian socialism in which I was reared." Novak continues, "For many of my adult years I thought of myself as a democratic socialist." Although this revelation obviously renders his recent conversion all the more striking, it comes as something of a surprise to those of us who cannot remember a single occasion when Novak, even in his most radical period, declared in print that he was a socialist. Perhaps such occasions can be recovered by the archivist, but one must admit that Novak was extraordinarily discreet about his socialist beliefs in the years when he allegedly held them, compared to his frank confessions now that he has repented. No one should doubt Novak's ability to explain how this "conservatism of my hometown" and this "tradition of Christian socialism in which I was reared" were really one and the same thing; but it is this sheer facility for selectively emphasizing different facets of a reality in order to make the necessary case of the moment that undermines Novak's credibility. All is flux, nothing is stationary; one is reminded of the Heraclitian roots of Greek sophistry. One is also reminded of Marx's line—how appropriate in this case—describing capitalism's unbridled power of transformation: "All that is solid melts into air."

"Democratic Capitalism"

Nowhere does Novak's rhetoric run roughshod over careful thinking so much as in the central concept of his book: democratic capitalism. Recall the old joke about the worker who exits from his East European plant each evening pushing a wheelbarrow. The Communist guard inspects the wheelbarrow, finds nothing being stolen. Every night the same procedure, and never can the guard find any of the plant's property in the wheelbarrow. But suspicion dies hard, and so does curiosity. Finally the guard begs the worker, under a solemn pledge of secrecy, to reveal what he is stealing and how he is concealing it. The answer, of course, wheelbarrows.

"Democratic capitalism" is Michael Novak's wheelbarrow. While so many of his critics are suspiciously wondering whether he has slipped this or that virtue into the container, without its legitimately belonging there, it is the container itself, the very concept of democratic capitalism, that he is boldly wheeling past them.

The mere fact that two words can be put together does not mean they represent a reality. "Democratic Caesarism" was the label that devotees of a flamboyant Latin American dictator pasted on his regime. "Democratic centralism" is the Leninists' way of saying that the party elite makes all the decisions. "Democratic capitalism," however, is a somewhat more complicated phrase. Clearly there are nations that, at the same time, are more or less democratic and more or less capitalist. But then again there are men (Novak and I are both examples) who are at once tall and balding—without that fact justifying a concept such as "tall baldingism." The question, in the former case as in the latter, is what exactly is the relationship between the two elements named. Is their simultaneous presence merely fortuitous? Are they independent of each other, or mutually supporting, or in conflict? Is one the cause of the other? Is one the *necessary* cause of the other? Does their relationship remain the same throughout all stages of development?

Questions like these are simply bowled over by the force of Novak's rhetoric. Democratic capitalism is introduced in the book's first sentence, and by sheer repetition it takes on a life of its own, eventually to roll like a juggernaut through hundreds of pages. It becomes the subject of active verbs, is even personified: "Democratic capitalism . . . glories in divergence. . . ." "It stimulates invention . . . delights irreverently in change, dissent, and singularity." "It instructs nations . . . awakens individuals. . . ." We even learn "its two favorite words." (These turn out to be "new" and "improved," as in, I suppose, "new, improved, long-lasting Sudso.")

Yet for all its overwhelming presence, democratic capitalism, like most of Novak's notions, remains a mightily shifty phenomenon. What purports to be a discussion of democratic capitalism in general is for the most part a discussion of the United States alone, and even that with no reference to the specific history or conditions, other than "democratic capitalism" of course, that have shaped American society. Whenever something beneficial is attributed to capitalism, e.g., the material progress of Europe since 1800, it is attributed to *democratic* capitalism, quite regardless of whether democracy was involved at all. Whenever capitalism shows a less attractive face, e.g., its alliances with dictatorial regimes, this is attributed to "bastard forms of capitalism" and held to be an unstable and transient reality. This is the intellectual equivalent of three-card monte.

"The natural logic of capitalism leads to democracy." Novak believes that this is a fact of history. Yet if there is one thing almost totally lacking from Novak's argument it is any sense of history, better yet, any knowledge of history. "The watershed year," he writes, "was 1776. Almost simultaneously, Adam Smith published *An Inquiry into the Nature and Causes of the Wealth of Nations* and the first democratic capitalist republic came into existence in the United States." Just like that. Democratic capitalism, it seems, was "invented" by its "founding fathers" around the end of the eighteenth century, or rather it sprang, apparently fully-armed, from their Enlightenment brows. (One of Novak's favorite rhetorical devices is to refer to democratic capitalism as "designed" to do this or that; the word suggests a degree of regularity, rationality, and purposefulness belied by history.)

This is hardly adequate even for the narrowly Anglo-American historical viewpoint that, ironically, now dominates the thinking of this once Unmeltable Ethnic. Indeed, there is an embarrassing parallel between the argument of *The Spirit of Democratic Capitalism* and that of turn-of-the-century Anglo-American nativists.

Novak builds his case on a statistical association between capitalism and democracy and a similar association between socialism and dictatorship. In exactly the same fashion, the Anglo-American nativists pointed to a statistical association between free, tolerant institutions and Protestant and North European races, on the one hand, and between corrupt despotisms and Catholic South and East European peoples, on the other. The nativists concluded that you could not preserve political liberty without preserving the numerical and cultural hegemony of Protestant Anglo-Saxons, and that the Catholic culture of South and East European immigrants was incompatible with democracy. In like manner, Novak concludes that capitalism is essential for democracy and socialism incompatible with it.

Both Novak and the nativists are guilty of confusing historical correlations with logical ones, but both are also bad, because ethnocentric historians, Novak, for instance, show no awareness of the stages or process by which capitalism was established in any nation other than Britain and the U.S. Even worse, he is oblivious to the history of democracy. This results in ludicrous anachronisms, as when he scolds Leo XIII and Max Weber for not celebrating the virtues of *democratic* capitalism, without any notice of just how democratic was the capitalism of their generations.

Consider so basic a criterion of democracy as the right to vote. In 1850, outside of Switzerland, not a single European state granted universal suffrage even to males. The United Kingdom granted the right to vote to approximately one million property-owners out of a population of 27.5 million; Belgium had 60,000 voters out of 4.7 million inhabitants—and those were among the most "democratic" of states. Britain's landmark Second Reform Act of 1867 extended the franchise to no more than eight percent of the population. In the post-1870 Kingdom of Italy (which the popes had before their eyes), no more than one or two percent of the population could vote before 1882, seven percent until 1913. Universal male suffrage was not established until after World War I, female suffrage after World War II. Germany, at the time Max Weber wrote *The Protestant Ethic and the Spirit of Capitalism*, maintained a complicated voting system that effectively blocked universal suffrage. Perhaps it is too much to expect Novak to know things like this. After all, he can define democratic capitalism by referring to "social systems like those of the United States, West Germany, and Japan" without reflecting on the fact that two out of three of his leading illustrations existed as decidedly *undemocratic* capitalist societies for a longer period of time than as democratic ones, and that they settled into democracy only after being militarily conquered and occupied by the third.

The Role of Liberalism

Should Novak's capitalism-democracy link be relegated, therefore, to the category of half-educated pamphleteering? Not quite. There is a real historical link between capitalism and democracy, but it is by way of a third "ism" which, for some reason, Novak has preferred not to name. I mean liberalism. Liberalism was the creed which, on both sides of the Atlantic, generally represented the political interests of new economic forces in the late eighteenth and early nineteenth centuries. Liberalism strove to limit the power of the state (except when it came to enforcing contracts, maintaining a stable currency, subsidizing or protecting new industrial enterprises, outlawing labor unions, and breaking strikes). Liberalism demanded "free institutions"—some kind of deliberative parliament, accountable state officials, freedom of religion, freedom from political censorship, independent courts, an end to hereditary privileges.

Modern democracy has been built on this liberal heritage. But liberalism—and in this it spoke for capitalism—was highly ambivalent about democracy. Liberal leaders of the rising economic classes needed the support of the "people" to break the monopoly on political power of the landed aristocracy. But actual rule by the "people" was something else again, conjuring up dangerous leveling and all the excesses of the French Revolution. Liberal principles had democratic implications; liberal politics sometimes encouraged democratic forces; but liberal—and capitalist—self-interest dictated drawing the line far short of genuinely democratic government.

From about the middle of the nineteenth century, the link liberalism had provided between capitalist forces and democratic ones was increasingly broken. In the later industrial powers like Germany and Japan, capitalism was introduced by bureaucrats and aristocrats as much as by the bourgeoisie. In the older capitalist regimes, liberals often turned sharply against democracy. The difficulty that faces any theoretician of "democratic capitalism" is obvious: Since the latter part of the nineteenth century, there has scarcely been an expression of democratic reform toward which most capitalist leaders were not, at best, indifferent or, more commonly, hostile.

Take that basic matter of suffrage again. Universal manhood suffrage did not come to most European nations until late in the nineteenth or early in the twentieth century. The vote for women came later. In the U.S., Southern blacks, whose enslavement had been terminated at least in part because it represented a pre-capitalist way of life, were nonetheless deprived of their voting rights precisely during the heyday of expanding capitalism. The struggles for ballot-box democracy, including, besides universal suffrage, the secret ballot and paid representatives, were led in almost every case by working-class movements or left-wing reformers highly critical of existing capitalism if not explicitly socialist.

Much the same can be said of other efforts to assure or expand democratic liberties in this century. Freedom of belief and expression, freedom to organize in independent unions, guarantees of equal justice in the courts, minimums of well-being that secure a degree of political as well as economic independence for masses of citizens—has capitalist leadership been in the forefront of recent struggles for any of these things? Did it head the resistance to the wave of ideological terrorism that swept over Western Europe between the world wars? Quite the contrary.

DOES CAPITALISM = PLURALISM = DEMOCRACY?

The idea of democratic capitalism is not new. It is one of the charms of Michael Novak in *The Spirit of Democratic Capitalism* that, having spent so much of the fifties in the seminary, he is determined to reinvent that decade. It is less charming that he should inflict his rediscovery on us with such a vengeance. The fifties' apologists for "democratic capitalism" were likely to see it as an expression of "American exceptionalism." It was a recent achievement attributable, perhaps, to this land's special material advantages or uniquely democratic ethos, and only lately exported to Europe and the other continents by American arms and aid. Novak, however, projects democratic capitalism back two centuries and over two continents, and he gives capitalism rather than democracy the causative edge.

In this regard as in many others, Robert Benne, in *The Ethic of Democratic Capitalism* (Fortress, 1981), is more modest. Eschewing larger historical or social schemes, he sticks with the American present and merely argues that its current combination of capitalism and democracy is "morally defensible."

Novak's project is grander. "For two centuries," he writes, "democratic capitalism has been more a matter of practice than of theory"; and he now offers, at last, to "grasp the ideals latent in its practice." . . . What are the "ideals" that he deduces from this cloudily imagined past?

Democratic capitalism, he tells us, is characterized by "three dynamic and converging systems functioning as one: a democratic policy, an economy based on markets and incentives, and a moral-cultural system which is pluralistic and, in the largest sense, liberal." Each one of these systems must be "structurally separated" from the others. Each has its own institutions and its own ethos. Each sphere creates tensions with the others—and offers support. Each develops virtues that the others need or lack. Where all past "traditional" societies and all alternative "socialist" ones are said to be "unitary," democratic capitalism alone promises a pluralism of three systems that are at once balancing and buttressing, sustaining and self-correcting.

Now, this is an attractive scheme, no matter how questionable Novak's claim that it represents the latent ideals of two centuries of democratic capitalism. Novak is a partisan of pluralism, and even his most critical readers ought to agree with him (and with Benne) that a healthy, humane society should have multiple, competing centers of institutional power and of intellectual and moral energy. But does contemporary capitalism in fact insure that such is the case? Among the most abiding sources of discontent with capitalism is the belief that over time it destroys rather than creates genuine pluralism. Benne acknowledges this criticism and addresses it directly, although I believe incompletely, in a chapter entitled "Is There Such a Thing as Democratic Capitalism?" Novak, on the other hand, repeatedly suggests that opposition to capitalism is based on an explicit or surreptitious commitment to a "unitary order." Where Benne tries to marshal empirical evidence to show that capitalism is not antagonistic to pluralism, Novak simply elaborates as a "latent ideal" his scheme of "three dynamic and converging systems."

Does this scheme really reply to the major questions about capitalism, pluralism, and democracy? I believe it does not, and would point out the following difficulties.

Balanced Systems?

Novak offers no criteria except his own subjective judgment for concluding that these three "systems" are in fact sustaining and self-correcting rather than colluding and suborning, or fatally antagonistic and corroding. Novak allows that the "dynamic balance" between systems can be destroyed; indeed, like Ronald Reagan and businessmen generally, he insists that government, allied with anti-capitalist, moral-cultural forces, has gone too far in limiting the proper independence of the economic sphere. But as Joseph L. Walsh perceptively noted in a 1979 *Commonweal* article, "At the very least Novak ought . . . to articulate the basis on which he judges 'too far' or 'not enough.' "

A decade ago, for example, in *The Rise of the Unmeltable Ethnics*, Novak wrote:

> The radical problem of American democracy is economic. We have succeeded, by and large, in separating church and state. We have not succeeded in separating church and economy, or state and economy. The same is true for those organs of the imagination which have replaced the churches in their impact on the human spirit—the media . . . and the schools. Economic power rules.

As usual, we must ask who is closer to the truth, Novak I or Novak II? In part, deciding is a matter of reading the trends, but it is also a question of what end-state in society one considers "balance." This side of the extreme cases of theocracy or totalitarianism, Novak's scheme offers no guidelines.

It is interesting to note the sea change that Novak has wrought on the source of this tripartite framework of economy, polity, and culture, namely Daniel Bell's analysis in *The Cultural Contradictions of Capitalism*. Bell offered a theory of "three realms" as a *descriptive* framework for analyzing not capitalism but contemporary *society* (and perhaps other societies as well); and his analysis emphasized not the harmonious, balancing, and supportive character of these realms but their "disjunctive" and contradictory character. Novak has transmuted Bell's descriptive framework into a normative one, presenting Bell's disjunctive realms as a happy ideal. He has also had to ignore one of Bell's own conclusions about the relationship of the realms: "Though capitalism and democracy historically have arisen together, and have been commonly justified by philosophical liberalism, there is nothing which makes it either theoretically or practically necessary for the two to be yoked."

Novak's "systems" are not, in reality, the discrete and bounded entities he suggests. In particular, the moral-cultural system does not parallel the other two systems.

This might be of academic interest were it not the moral-cultural system with which Novak is preeminently concerned. Institutionally, the moral-cultural system includes government enterprises (public schools, scientific institutes, the courts and the law in their role as articulators of values). It also includes profit-making business ventures (the television networks, the *New York Times, Playboy,* the *Reader's Digest*, Hollywood, and Madison Avenue). And it includes private non-profit institutions based on voluntary mass support (the churches, the Boy Scouts, the National Organization of Women) or on elite wealth sometimes combined with government grants (Harvard, the Committee on the Present Danger, the American Enterprise Institute).

There is therefore no simple way to speak about the capacity of the moral-cultural system to balance the government and the private economy. Consider the withdrawal of federal funds from higher education. Does that render the university more independent of government? Does it make the university more reliant on corporate aid and large private fortunes? Or does it simply weaken the power of the university vis-à-vis both government and the economy? Does pluralism gain or lose if influence shifts from university- or media-based "adversary intellectuals" to those working for Pentagon-funded think tanks or receiving grants from Exxon and the SmithKline Corporation?

Empty Shrine or Moral Vacuum?

Novak celebrates the idea that democratic capitalism demands adherence only to procedures and refrains from prescribing any ultimate values—at its moral core there is only an "empty shrine" which points to transcendence but does not define it. Novak imports a number of religious images into his political argument; the "empty shrine" is one that I find appropriate and moving. (Compare it with his repeated labeling of democratic capitalism in its three systems as "trinitarian"—as though anything in triplicate somehow carried a divine cachet.)

But effective imagery does not resolve the many difficulties that theorists of pluralism have debated and Novak has stumbled upon. Can a society really cohere with an "empty shrine"—some would call it a moral vacuum—at its core? And will the shrine ever really be empty—if there is nothing within, will not the trappings be worshipped instead? Procedural adherence implies substantive values; by overlooking this fact, don't we simply shelter those substantive values from examination, criticism, and renewal?

These are not only theoretical questions; they lurk behind our fierce disputes over numerous practical matters: government policies toward schooling, families, work, wealth, the future of the environment. The problem is a tough one, and I don't complain that Novak's "empty shrine" is an inadequate solution. I only wish he knew it.

Pluralism and Democracy

Novak never examines what exactly the relationship between pluralism and democracy might be; he never asks about pluralism *within* his three systems, nor about democracy within them.

Is a pluralist society automatically a democratic one? Contrary to Novak's sweeping and uninformed statements about "traditional societies" (a category that apparently lumps ancient Rome with Amazon tribes and medieval Europe), there have been societies that were pluralist, i.e., where power was divided and decentralized, without being democratic. Pluralism, like liberalism, appears to be, at least in the modern world, a necessary but not sufficient condition for democracy. Not only that, there are pluralisms and there are pluralisms. Pluralism *within* the broad sectors may be as important as a "balance" between them. "Government," for example, is not a monolith in the United States. The federal government's power is formally limited by the Constitution's division of powers, on top of which various agencies compete with one another for funds and influence. The federal government, in turn, shares power with the states, and power is finally splintered among a myriad of municipalities, counties, school boards, sanitation districts, and so on.

Novak has pointed out that in 1978 "government" in the U.S. employed as many civilian workers as did all 500 top industrial corporations. He assumes that this shows a vast concentration of power on the government side, when in fact it may show just the opposite, those government employees being distributed not among five hundred but among tens of thousands of official units. Indeed it is the dramatic concentration of private power in the economy that took place in the decades before and after World War I and has continued at a slower but steady pace since then that is at the root of much of the corresponding growth in federal power and of today's government-business tensions. This "rise of large-scale enterprise," according to three historians of the American economy highly sympathetic to capitalism, "was the most significant change in the organization of economic decision-making since the development of market orientation and capitalist institutions." Yet of this transformation, and all its implications for pluralism, Novak has virtually nothing to say. He conveys the impression that big business is only a balance to big government, in no way its cause. . . .

In his tripartite map of "democratic capitalism," what Novak has constructed is, in fact, an analysis of the American "constitution" not in the sense of a written document or even an unwritten set of principles to which government must conform, but in the older sense of the existing pattern of institutions, laws, and practices that, with their animating principles and spirits, actually govern a society.

Novak's analysis is analogous to that of the eighteenth-century thinkers who praised England's "mixed" constitution as "a system of consummate wisdom and policy." They, like him, divided society into three social orders—royalty, nobility, and "commons"— which had miraculously been brought into a splendid equilibrium that assured liberty, prosperity, and tranquillity. To depart in any way from that "dynamic balance," as Novak would call it, was to court disaster. Strengthen the monarchy and you risk tyranny; strengthen the nobles and you risk oligarchy; strengthen the commons and you risk anarchic democracy.

It was, of course, the American political thinkers of the Revolutionary period who challenged this pretty scheme. America had always been bereft of a nobility, a troubling flaw in the tripartite "system." Now it was to be done with a monarch as well. How could liberty survive if there were no other social forces to balance the commons? Through trial and error and political genius, the Americans simply discovered that a new kind of pluralism was possible. The separation of powers, the federal system, and the multiplicity of interests in a broad land could assure freedom at the same time as *all* political authority was derived from the "people."

Ironically, in identifying the preservation of liberty with the limited pluralism and alleged "balance" of three immutable orders, and in disregarding the possibility that liberty and pluralism could be strengthened by the democratizing of all the "systems," Novak hearkens back not to American revolutionaries but to their predecessors and adversaries. The odyssey of Michael Novak has indeed taken a peculiar turn: he has become an eighteenth-century British Tory. . . .

Before critics of democratic capitalism gloat over the weaknesses to be found in a book like Novak's, they should face the fact that the same faults abound in the political literature of the religious left. Questionable statistics are thrown about like proof-texts. Concepts like exploitation and imperialism are brandished without inquiry into their precise meaning and applicability. Crude theories of economics and international relations are accepted as self-evident. The specific arguments of opposing theorists are ignored or dismissed as morally compromised.

I do not want to propose an airy, impossible standard for political debate. Obviously, there is not world enough and time for a dispassionate and learned analysis of every problem, nor would such a response be necessarily appropriate. We cannot, in practice, maintain a "single standard." We give the benefit of the doubt to someone, place the burden of proof on someone else. It makes sense to do so in favor of the powerless, the underdogs, the immediate victims. But there must be checks on such a preference.

Novak, too, has always seen himself as speaking for the inarticulate underdog, first student radicals, then ethnics, and now the Fortune 500. However implausible an "underdog" the latter may seem to those who don't judge worldly power by popularity ratings in Ivy League faculty clubs, I think that Novak's excesses in *all* these causes have their roots in his belief that he is representing neither himself nor the truth but some inarticulate group that deserves its day in court. How many of us have done the same, have quelled our doubts and put the best face on the principles or practices of some group—pacifist demonstrators, third-world liberationists, left-wing lobbyists— because "they deserve to be heard?" After a while, we all become lawyers, a fate worse than death.

If there is anything that would serve the religious left well in this uncertain area—and that is currently wanting—it is precisely that historical sense I find absent in Novak— that refusal to yield to enthusiasm over claims that have not been set against the shadowed tapestry of the past. For too many Christian pacifists, the world seems to have skipped from St. Augustine's devising of the just-war theory to Vietnam; if they are interested in the intervening centuries it is mainly to cull Bad Examples.

Christian advocates of liberation and revolution often write as though the twentieth century were something which they had vaguely heard about but which doesn't very much interest them. They acknowledge that the left has made its mistakes, but they are not going to waste much grief and intelligence in pondering exactly what those mistakes were and how they came to be made. Awareness of the tangled threads of history may induce despair or indifferentism; that is its danger. But it can also substitute steady and knowing passion for the kind of skittish infatuation found as frequently on the religious left as in *The Spirit of Democratic Capitalism*.

Chapter 54

David Bryce-Smith

Ecology, Theology, and Humanism

My purpose is, first, to discuss the character of the increasingly serious state of disequilibrium which now manifestly exists in the relationship between *homo sapiens* as a species and the rest of nature—the so-called environmental crisis. Second, I would like to discuss both the fundamental and more immediate causes of this ecological disequilibrium and their origins in certain human attitudes and actions, which stem from, or are encouraged by, various forms of conventional religious and humanistic belief. Third, I shall try to suggest some constructive conclusions arising from this analysis, with particular reference to the essential (as distinct from optional) ecological role of moral laws in the conduct of human affairs. I believe that these conclusions can provide signposts to a healthier, that is, more harmonious, future relationship between man and God's natural world of which he is a part.

I should like to start with the subject of economics. I am not myself a professional economist. But as the professional practice and theory of the subject are so clearly in almost total disarray, perhaps the outsider may be justified in trying to discover whether he can see more of the players in this case. We are all much concerned with economics these days, for it is the economic pressures on individual pockets that belatedly are stimulating most people to recognize that something is seriously wrong with the management of human affairs. The self-indulgent complacency of the "affluent society" is beginning to wear thin under the influence of rising prices, rising unemployment, and the falling value of money. Whom can we blame? people ask.

Well, of course, we ourselves are basically to blame for listening so long to false prophets. But many of the most influential of these false prophets have been economists whose absurd doctrine of the never-ending growth economy has provided the sandy foundation on which the grandiose edifices of modern industrial society have been built.

I believe it was E.F. Schumacher, among others, who drew attention to the important general principle that there are no "free dinners." This principle has little place in conventional economics but is deeply enshrined in folk wisdom. Thus in Spain it appears in the form of the old proverb, "Take what you want, says God; and pay for it." Or in Yorkshire they would say, "Tha can't get owt for nowt."

Excerpts from a paper presented at a conference, "Man's Responsibility for Nature," sponsored by the Science and Religion Forum, Windsor, England, April 1976. Full text first published in *Zygon*, 12/3 (September 1977), pp. 212–31. Used by permission.

On the other hand, many economists have continued to assert that operation of market forces—the laws of supply and demand—can be relied on to solve all problems of material scarcity. As a commodity becomes scarce, it is claimed that its price will rise and the development and use of substitutes will become "economic." Much of this modern economic thinking seems to rest on the tacit assumption that the world is an Aladdin's cave of infinite dimensions and that the job of economists is merely to organize the extraction, processing, and distribution of its supposedly unlimited store of riches. Another assumption is that science and technology will solve all problems by the provision of an infinite supply of substitutes and "technical fixes." Once the childish fallacy of these underlying assumptions of economics is perceived, the causes of such phenomena as inflation become clear.

Thus the general introduction of paper money started off as convenience and as a stratagem to stimulate the production and consumption of material goods. People were induced to trust it by the promise that it could be exchanged for a fixed amount of gold or silver—the traditional monetary symbols whose virtues of permanence and scarcity were becoming an impediment to the concept of a material growth economy. Although the promise has long been revoked and replaced by the almost meaningless rubric which now appears on bank notes, the paper money system appeared to work fairly well for as long as basic material supply comfortably exceeded human demand. At least, it worked for those countries whose technological strength enabled them to control the supply and distribution of money. But now that human demand is beginning to exceed the supply of natural resources, those countries having the greatest natural resources are acquiring greater real power, and the balance is beginning to tip. In these new conditions paper money and credit have come to be used as a sophisticated confidence trick which enables governments to create notional wealth (i.e., the temporary illusion of greater purchasing power) through the printing press without any corresponding increase in real material assets—a form of legalized forgery which it is hoped will deceive the public into an illusion of greater prosperity, at least until the next elections. The resulting excess of purchasing power over material supply is maintained by printing more and more money without material asset backing, and inflation is a wholly inevitable consequence.

We must realize, however, that inflation is a *symptom* of disease, not the disease itself. The disease is malignant growth—a cancer which could destroy human society—and human greed is its dynamic. Thus it is clear that the phenomenon of inflation is a problem which stems from faulty human morality.

But the principle of matching demand to stable and sustainable supply is in practice still widely disregarded by politicians, their economic advisers, industrialists, and most others concerned with directing the short-term course of human affairs; and it is in fact a principle even more fundamental to the long-neglected subject of ecology, of which economics is merely an overinflated subdivision. Thus the most stable ecological systems are those in which the individual living plant and animal species are highly diverse. The ecological diversity so repugnant to the tidy minds of many bureaucrats is in fact a source of strength and stability in nature. It is also a source of stability in ecosystems that the various life forms should be in reasonable balance in their demands on one another, on their food supplies, and on their general physical environment.

In other words, if man as a species wishes to have a stable future on earth, ecologists inform us that he should be very cautious in seeking to manipulate his ecological environment for short-term objectives by reducing its diversity (e.g., by indiscriminate use of insecticides and herbicides, or overselective breeding of food cereals and farm animals), by taking more out of his environment than he returns to it (e.g., through the failure to recycle nonrenewable mineral resources), or by overbreeding beyond the capacity of the food supply.

This will strike most people nowadays as simple common sense. But prior to the 1973 Arab oil crisis the few enlightened commentators such as Paul Erlich and Schumacher who warned that man as a species was embarked on an ecological Rake's Progress were largely ignored or contemptuously dismissed as "eco-nuts" or "doom-mongers." It seems astonishing that prior to 1973 no Western government had even the most rudimentary energy policy. But the Arab oil crisis of 1973 and its continuing aftermath have brought home to an increasing number of people the extent to which we are dependent on finite natural resources and the danger of depleting these. In the West, at least, many thinking people are at long last beginning to question whether the laws of supply and demand, state control, or the supposedly unfailing ability of scientists to provide a technical fix, or whatever, will really enable economic growth to be sustained indefinitely by consumption of nonrenewable resources.

It is indeed a remarkable phenomenon that over the short space of two or three years we have moved from a situation where most people believed (if they bothered to think about it at all) that Western industrially based material societies could continue to grow indefinitely to one where it is recognized increasingly that nearly all material and energy resources, virtually except sunlight (and in theory atomic fusion power), really are finite, that many resources such as oil, natural gas, and some minerals will become in noticeably short supply within one or two generations at present rates of depletion, and that the present rate of population growth superimposes an ever-increasing pressure on the resources which remain. These problems, if unabated by man, will be abated eventually by the force of natural reactions to intolerable human pressure, probably at the cost of vast human suffering and the destruction of most human institutions—including, one may add, the churches. The growing public recognition of these ecological facts of life provides grounds for hope that we may be able to adjust our lives and attitudes to them in time. But how much time do we have? And how must we adjust?

ECOLOGICAL PROBLEMS

Let us try to take stock. As a species, man in the 1970s is faced with ecological pressure from at least three main directions.

First, there is the much-discussed problem of nonrenewable material resources (coal, oil, minerals, etc.) and the depletion or dispersion of these by human demand. This demand stems from two characteristics of *homo sapiens,* one morally deplorable, the other morally admirable. The deplorable characteristic is greed, that insatiable instinctive demand for more with which most of us seem to be cursed to some degree. The admirable characteristic is compassion which, coupled with the working of conscience, leads many good men to try to bring the material benefits of Western civilization to the poor and to the Third World. But this humane objective of bringing our version of the good life to all men is basically unattainable, however unpalatable the fact may be to one's humanistic, liberal conscience.

Thus the various forms of socialism, communism, and "statism" appear to spring from the idealistic desire to create a utopia by sharing more fairly the material resources of the world. These objectives may be politically and ethically desirable, but I see no way in which they could be ecologically possible on any sustained basis. Thus to abolish hunger for even the present world population (some thirty million of whom are believed to die each year from causes related to malnutrition or downright starvation) and to give everybody in the world the material living standards now regarded as normal in Western industrial nations would require us to increase the present rate of consumption of petroleum, iron, copper, tin, uranium, and most other nonrenewable minerals, by factors of tens or even one hundred. With those rates of depletion, even the most optimistic would be talking of exhaustion of many key minerals in terms not of decades as at present but rather of a few months or years. That is an ecological fact of life in massive conflict with much of our present political, social, and economic thinking. Thus, while it is an ecological impossibility to maintain our present Western consumer society much beyond this generation, the objective of making this way of life eventually available to all our fellow human beings must be seen as totally unreal. We must not lose sight of this morally troubling fact in our compassionate attempts to make the world a truly better place.

The depletion of available material resources therefore constitutes one of our major problems. It is a problem caused wholly by man.

The second problem is population growth. The world population has quadrupled since 1850 and is estimated to have exceeded four billion persons on March 28, 1976. At the present 1.8 percent annual rate of increase, today's world population will double by soon after the turn of the century, sometime in the year 2012. Population growth obviously compounds the resources problem and is likewise caused solely by man. Man is a compulsive breeder, and his rutting season lasts for 365 days a year, come famine or feast. Many animals seem automatically to regulate their breeding rates according to the availability of the food supply, but man appears to lack this important natural control, for the highest rates of human population increase tend to be found in the most densely populated and poorest parts of the world where the risk of famine is greatest, whereas in many more prosperous countries the birth rate is now tending to fall. From an evolutionary viewpoint this is a breeding characteristic of positive feedback type which is disadvantageous to the survival of a species. It remains to be seen to what extent its effects will be counteracted by birth-control measures.

It is also uncomfortable to reflect that penicillin and many other life-saving and life-prolonging developments in modern medicine have contributed to population growth by their use to frustrate—for the most humane reasons—the existing natural processes of population control. Medical science can be a two-edged sword. In my view it should be directed more toward improving the quality of life than the quantity.

Man, of course, does control his numbers to some extent by wars, genocide, and the like. Our species has slaughtered something approaching one hundred millions of its own kind over the past sixty years or so, often under terrible conditions of cruelty and degradation. We properly condemn the Nazis for their concept of a "master race" justified in exploiting or exterminating its supposed racial inferiors. Yet we have accepted unquestioningly the equally arbitrary concept of *homo sapiens* as a "master species." Thus, as a scientist, I feel very troubled by a great many of the experiments on animals now coldly carried out in the name of scientific or medical research. It does not flatter God to say that man is made in his image.

The third major ecological problem is environmental pollution. This is a consequence of the first two problems of resources depletion and population growth, and is greatly exacerbated by human ignorance and immorality. There is indeed no lack of industrialists, politicians, and their friends only too ready to justify or excuse pollution on economic grounds. There are many who know that I hold strong views on the subject of chemical pollution and its harmful effects on our physical and mental health. But this is not a subject which I shall consider in detail here, except to make the point that environmental pollution is, like resources depletion and population growth, almost wholly a problem which man has created by his own activities.

We must face the fact that these problems are coming together to produce a gravely critical situation in man's relationship with his earthly environment—an ecological crunch, as it were. They result from human errors. These errors in turn have arisen from human ignorance and old-fashioned sin, especially greed, folly, and self-admiration. We are not faced with those natural phenomena such as earthquakes, floods, plagues, Ice Ages, and the like, which must in the past have challenged the survival of many other species through no conscious faults of their own.

Our key problems of resources depletion, population growth, and pollution are produced by deliberate human behavior. And they could be controlled by human behavior if we were to exercise the free will in which we take such pride. Yet, while no other known species in the long history of earth has been given such combined natural, physical advantages in brainpower, imagination, language ability, and manual dexterity as man, no other species can have so willfully abused these advantages as to imperil its own continued evolutionary survival. If you think I exaggerate, consider the vast arsenals of nuclear weapons which now provide the explosive equivalent of tens of tons of TNT for each man, woman, and child on earth and the chemical and biological warfare weapons which have been forged by equally grotesque perversions of science. Does the past violent history of man offer much promise that weapons once made will not eventually be used?

Moreover, we must expect reasonably that pressures on society from population growth and the scramble for the shrinking store of natural resources will increase the risk of war.

The debate about nuclear power stations well illustrates the way in which man is stacking the cards against his own prospects for survival. As we all know, nuclear energy is being widely canvassed as a technological fix which supposedly will overcome the present energy shortages from fossil fuels and thereby permit us to resume our economic growth into the indefinite future—a prospect pleasing to most shades of political thought from the far left to the far right. But, as Walter Patterson has described in his excellent recent book, *Nuclear Power,* quite serious accidents have arisen in the past— for example, at Windscale in England and the Chalk River in Canada—and there is still no general agreement among nuclear power engineers on the best and safest design of nuclear fission reactors for the future.[1]

Pending the successful development of possibly safer power reactors based on nuclear fusion rather than fission (a remote prospect at present), it seems likely that we shall continue to use nuclear power reactors which produce plutonium as a by-product. Quite apart from its bomb-making potential (which India has demonstrated), this plutonium is one of the most toxic materials known to man and, with other radioactive by-products, will have to be stored and guarded for tens of thousands of years before its radioactivity falls to safer levels. How can we possibly assume that society will be stable over that sort of time period? A lump of plutonium about the size of a grapefruit could be brought together by terrorists, criminals, or other mentally deranged persons to make a crude but effective atomic bomb. Further, an increasing number of politically immature or unstable countries are now acquiring the nuclear power stations which will enable them to construct atomic bombs. It is reported that Israel has built thirteen atomic bombs from plutonium and actually prepared them for use in the 1973 war. So the consequences of keeping this generation comfortable with nuclear energy will be that we bequeath a problem to imperil the well-being and survival of countless future generations.

To bring the picture into sharper focus, consider the situation which might exist now if Newton had discovered atomic fission and a nuclear power technology with its associated radioactive waste and bomb-making potential had been proliferating, not for two or three decades, but for two or three centuries. Might we now be cursing the willfully blind selfishness of our forefathers for this legacy? Possibly we should not be here to curse at all.

Of course, no less immoral is the burning up by one or two generations of petroleum which took some one billion years to accumulate. What a legacy to our children! What will they think of us for bequeathing them a world exhausted of petroleum and other key minerals but brimming over with plutonium and other dangerous by-products of our consumer society? What respect will they have for those guardians of morality, the churches, if they speak out on this problem as little in the future as they have in the past?

On such matters I have heard it said, "Let future generations look after themselves." Or there is the cynical jest, "What has posterity done for me?" Yet consider the evolutionary aspects. We have, to an extent unapproached by any previously known species, now acquired the power to produce an environment hostile to our own survival. So the degree of responsibility to our unborn descendants with which we exercise that power may measure quite simply our fitness in the evolutionary sense to survive as a species.

MORAL ATTITUDES AS AN EVOLUTIONARY NECESSITY

This line of reasoning leads to the interesting conclusion that morally based attitudes on such matters as the development of nuclear energy, consumption of resources, pollution, etc., may not be just a luxury for cranks and unpractical idealists but an evolutionary necessity for man as a species.

So, to sum up the arguments so far, I believe we have strong evidence that *homo sapiens* now faces an essentially Darwinian evolutionary challenge from nature. But this is of a novel type in that it arises as a natural reaction to the greed, narcissism, and other classically immoral behavior which have led man to attempt to subdue nature and organize the whole world according to his own selfish desires. If this analysis is correct, it follows that the evolutionary challenge which we have provoked requires a moral adaptive response. If we as a species can make the necessary moral adaptation, I believe that we shall demonstrate our fitness for a better life. But if we fail to adapt, it may prove that *homo sapiens* comes to exemplify one of evolution's many blind-alley species—and will deserve to do so.

This conclusion—man's ecological crisis results essentially from man's immoral behavior—has a number of interesting philosophical and theological implications. First, Mother Nature appears to be confirming the teachings of moralists and religious writers throughout the ages that morally based attitudes and behavior are essential for healthy spiritual and physical development. This conclusion contradicts the widely held view that moral behavior is irrelevant to the problems which face practical men of the world. It contradicts the pragmatic approach to politics which has now been elevated in Britain almost to the status of genuine political philosophy—and which has so clearly failed. A man, or a nation, without the guidance of a moral sense is like a ship without a compass. We do not see so much these days of the sad-faced chaps who used to parade in sandwich boards bearing "the wages of sin is death," but they seem to have had the truth of the matter.

Another conclusion of special interest to ecologists is that the old moral imperatives to love our neighbors, cultivate humility, and avoid selfishness appear to have the force of a law of nature which we ignore at our peril. Solzhenitsyn recently has drawn our attention to the historical fact that immorality in nations, as in men, usually brings eventual defeat and decay, whereas morality brings success and strength: but it is our tragedy that we seem unable to learn from experience that this is so. Now in the ecological crisis we face the consequences not so much of individual or national immorality as of species immorality—the immorality of the arrogant belief that nature was constructed to serve man and that man, supposing himself the highest form of creation, was justified in exploiting the rest of the natural world for his own selfish ends. I am surprised that theologians do not appear to have perceived the inconsistency of teaching on the one hand that individual selfishness and pride are wicked and on the other that man is innately superior to the rest of creation. Or to put it another way, I fail to understand how that which is evil in men can be good in man.

I would like now to explore some of the ways in which man has acquired the potentially fatal notion of his own absolute natural supremacy. I fear that the theologian and humanist must stand together in the dock to face the charges on this matter. First, the theologian, although I think he is the less blameworthy. Let us remind ourselves of Genesis, chapter 1, verses 26–28:

> And God said, Let us make man in our image, after our likeness: and let them have dominion over the fish of the sea, and over the fowl of the air, and over the cattle, and over all the earth, and over every creeping thing that creepeth upon the earth. So God created man in his own image, in the image of God created he him: male and female created he them. And God blessed them, and God said unto them, Be fruitful and multiply, and replenish the earth, and subdue it: and have dominion over the fish of the sea, and over the fowl of the air, and over every living thing that moveth upon the earth.

While great honor is due to the writer of Genesis for the enlightened (if largely ignored) injunction to "replenish the earth," the ecological force of these words is deflected by the rather imperialistic references to subduing the earth and having dominion over all other forms of life. The unqualified instruction to be fruitful and multiply still finds religious support, especially among Roman Catholics, and cannot escape its share of blame for the consequences of what we now term "population explosion." (Of course, if God really intended the population explosion and its eventual apocalyptic consequences, there the matter rests.)

However, these beautiful verses of Genesis undoubtedly have encouraged the narcissistic belief that man is set apart from all other animals in a qualitative sense as a sort of steward administering and ruling the estate for an unseen landlord. And with the passage of time and growth of knowledge of the estate, the steward has found it increasingly attractive and "rational" to doubt the existence of the landlord and to appoint himself to the honor, as in the ultimate absurdity of humanism, where man the usurper worships himself as a quasi god. Humanists have sought to transmute "man in the image of God" into "God in the image of man." I shall have some more to say about humanism a little later.

Meanwhile, it is true that elsewhere in the Bible (Luke 12:6–7) Jesus says that not a sparrow is forgotten before God, but he assures his audience that they are of more value than many sparrows. And I have always felt he was a bit too hard on the poor fig tree for its inability to bear fruit out of season (Mark 11:12–21). Jesus may have been the first ecologist in his teaching of the power of love, but I wish that he had placed more emphasis on the need to love and respect all the earthly creations of God, including even fig trees, as well as our fellowmen and God himself.

Saint Francis of course spread his love more widely, and he is perhaps an even stronger candidate for the title of the first ecologist. And we should remember that some religions, such as that of the Jains of India, teach a greater reverence for life than do others, for example, Christianity and Judaism.

So the record of religious teaching on man's relation to, and responsibility toward, the natural world is at best like the curate's egg—good in parts. What then of the humanists? I think you already will have gathered that I regard the anthropocentric doctrines of humanism with special disfavour for their role in the human Rake's Progress that I have been describing. Humanists regard themselves as supremely rational beings and describe all religious belief as wishful thinking and the worship of fairy tales. On the other hand, they worship human reason and intelligence, and try to derive an ethic based on human need and interest as a substitute for superhuman morality. We can see in the environmental crisis where the doctrine of "man first" has led the supremely rational and intelligent human race. Was there ever a god with such feet of clay as man?

Some of the early origins of modern humanism can be found in the verses of Genesis I have just quoted; ancient China, especially in the teachings of Confucius; the beliefs of the early Greek Sophists such as Protagoras ("man is the measure of all things"); and in the philosophy of Aristotle, as distinct from that of Plato, with its emphasis on relating "good" to human good, human happiness, and the exercise of human rationality. Saint Augustine recognized man's state of tension between the superhuman moral values of God and the natural ethical values of a God-created nature, and Saint Thomas Aquinas sought to reconcile the Aristotelian virtues of proper living with the theological virtues of faith and love which come from God by divine grace; but both held a firm grasp on the duality of man as body and spirit, and possessed in some measure of the Godlike attribute of free will.

This astonishingly penetrating concept of man as a duality of interpenetrating body and spirit finds a modern parallel in the scientific duality of matter and energy: I believe it to be close to the truth. But it began to be shaken seriously following the abuses of the medieval Roman church which provoked the Reformation.

The success of Luther's courageous challenge to the previously all-powerful Roman church had the side effect of encouraging humanistic thinkers such as Erasmus to speak out ever more boldly in favour of the preeminence of human rationality and even to challenge Luther himself for his resolute theistic beliefs and for asserting that man possesses free will only in relation to temporal matters. Although many early scientists such as Newton and John Dalton were deeply religious men, the increased knowledge of the laws, order, and structure of the material world which came with the growth of scientific discovery was casting growing doubt on the truth of religious belief since this apparently could not be tested by man in the laboratory, and its acceptance appeared to require the suspension of human rationality. Indeed, every schoolboy is told of the scandalous attitude of the Roman church toward Galileo, by which religious bigotry sought to preserve archaic falsehoods and suppress an honest scientist's demonstrated truth. (In fact, the reverence for truth is that which the good scientist and theologian should have most in common.) Darwin's classic studies on the origin of species have been widely assumed to provide a materialistic basis for an understanding of the living world. Some of the most recent developments in cosmology and molecular biology are believed by many humanists to provide the coup de grace to the whole concept of God or any superhuman power or purpose in the universe. Life, according to them, is to be viewed as an interesting mechanistic phenomenon, fully described by the laws of physics and chemistry, which we must suppose to have emerged with the rest of the universe purely by accident from the debris following a "big bang" of some almost infinitely small and dense object some ten billion years ago at time zero. God and intelligent superhuman purpose being declared unnecessary, as in the doctrine of the "death of God," following Nietzsche and others, humanistic man steps into the vacant place as the best-qualified candidate. Scientists are the new priesthood, laboratories the new temples, and science and the technological fix, coupled with Marxist, social democratic, or capitalistic visions of an earthly utopia, the new theology. But the crown is hollow, the ramshackle kingdom is manifestly falling to bits, and many good people are, like Bertrand Russell, gritting their teeth to build "only on the firm foundation of unyielding despair." Other less sturdy spirits are following Camus, Sartre, and other disappointed rationalists into the terrible intellectual and spiritual desert of existentialism or vainly seeking refuge in the shallow hedonism and self-indulgence of the "permissive society." After all, what barrier to despair is there if man is, following the humanistic beliefs, nothing but a glorified clockwork mouse assembled and wound up purely by chance—chance, the very antithesis of intelligent purpose? If that were true, why indeed should the clockwork mouse not grab whatever pleasure is available before decaying into endless oblivion?

Or, to change the metaphor, are we, as A. J. Ayer suggests, only performers in a play which has no author? No doubt he has in mind one of those famous plays which we are told would be written eventually by a monkey flailing randomly at the keys of a typewriter, both monkey and typewriter likewise being assembled by chance.

We may laugh at such an apparently preposterous notion, but we must also consider it very seriously. For the idea that everything, including ourselves, evolved by chance is one which has penetrated human consciousness strongly and has perplexed many theologians and contemporary philosophers. If it were true, and if man were merely the most complex structure yet produced by the blind workings of chance—a sort of prizewinning three-lemons combination in a molecular slot machine—I agree that life would have no meaning other than that we choose to put into it, the highest values would be the human values imposed by the master species man on other species he chooses to regard as lower than himself (as the strong can impose on the weak), and the human senses would be the highest arbiters of reality. These are the essential assumptions of humanism and existentialism, although existentialists in a rather despairing way do recognize the limitations of human senses.

The supposed primacy of human values underlies the doctrines of both Marxism and the modern materialistic consumer society, and by placing man on a pedestal (even a pedestal floating in the infinite sea of chance) these doctrines undoubtedly encourage the anthropocentric attitudes which have provoked the present ecological crisis. Moreover, by replacing the concept of a purposeful superhuman God with the doctrine of blind chance, they remove the ultimate basis of that morality which I hold to be an ecological necessity if human society is to survive. They leave only a residual humanistic ethic based arbitrarily on human need as perceived by the emotions and intellect. And in so doing they help to create that essentially purposeless zeitgeist of our modern times which we can see to be so damaging to the human spirit. It is true that humanistic philosophers such as Ayer have had the insight to perceive the need for morality, but it is sad to see them tying themselves in knots trying to work out how one can have morality without God—which is really the philosophical equivalent of attempting to square the circle.

So can one logically refute the doctrine of chance and the humanistic definition of reality in terms of human sense perceptions? I believe that both in fact can be decisively refuted by exercise of the human rationality so worshipped by humanists. It is not, in my view, sufficient in this day and age merely to assert the primacy of faith and belief over demonstrable knowledge, any more than it was in Galileo's time.

Consider first the doctrine advanced by Jacques Monod in *Chance and Necessity* that all life, including man, evolved by way of a chance succession of physicochemical events at the molecular level.[2] Let me say right away that superficially at least there is considerable support for such ideas from the discoveries of modern molecular biology. The biochemical structures of mice and men have fundamental similarities and differ only in numerous points of detail. To my best knowledge, the biochemical life processes in mice and men obey the same laws of physics and chemistry as the non-life processes which occur in our test tubes and chemical factories. And these processes certainly involve random molecular encounters subject to the laws of chance. It is perfectly possible to conceive that the phenomenon of life arose from the primordial cosmic soup, just as orderly crystals may appear on cooling a chemical solution. But neither life nor crystals will be expected to appear unless certain necessary preconditions are satisfied, that is, unless the potentiality for them to appear already exists in the system. For example, life as we know it could not have appeared if the element carbon had been as rare as the closely related element germanium or if the magnesium required for chlorophyll in plants and for animal nutrition had been as rare as the toxic but closely related element beryllium.

Chance can produce only events which are inherently possible. To illustrate this truth, consider a box in which I have placed 999,999 black balls and one white ball. The laws of chance tell us that there is only a one in a million chance of selecting the white ball but that if we continue trying for long enough we shall obtain it eventually. But if I had not originally added the white ball, no amount of chance selection would ever produce it. Thus even the rarest of chance events, as the evolution of life may well be, requires certain preconditions before it can occur at all. We cannot logically avoid the need for original causes by invoking chance.

Let us now consider whether the anthropocentric beliefs of humanism are really "rational." According to these, man is the highest order of creation (although, unlike the writer of Genesis, humanists deny the existence of a creator). Human needs are paramount, and reality is defined by the ability of man to perceive it. The logical fallacy in this doctrine is apparent from the following considerations.

All living things perceive their environment: flowers will turn toward the sun. The nature and extent of perceptions vary from case to case and depend on the "senses" of the organism. These in turn depend on the physical structures of the sense organs. Man becomes aware of his physical environment through his brain coupled to his physical senses of sight, touch, etc. Now from any purely materialistic view the human perception of objective reality must depend on and be limited by the physical structure of the brain—the number and arrangement of cells, neurons, etc. Since the structure of the brain is finite, the reality which it perceives must also be finite. Humanism is therefore in effect defining the supposedly absolute limits of reality in the arbitrary terms of a finite physical structure—the brain. And since the physical brain is only part of reality, it is not rational to attempt to define and limit the whole of reality in terms of a limited part of the whole. That would be to make the part greater than the whole.

The belief that reality is to be defined in terms of the ability of man to perceive it is a characteristic example of human arrogance. The doctrine of humanism is of course no less arbitrary than, say, cat-ism or dog-ism would be. It would have a special absolute truth above other "-isms" only if one could show that in man consciousness, intellect, and wisdom have developed to an ultimate peak of perfection. And who, contemplating the ravages wrought in the world by human ignorance and folly, would claim that?

I therefore see humanism as a hollow doctrine devoid of real scientific, rational, or philosophical justification. But its influence on the political, educational, and social attitudes of our time has been catastrophic. It has encouraged selfish anthropocentric attitudes, eroded belief in absolute moral standards of behavior, and undermined the simple religious faith which is a necessary psychological support for many people in this complex and stressful world. The effects are clearly recognizable: for example, the often well-intentioned attempts to build materialistic utopias based on scientific technology or politico-economic theories, or both; the widespread cynicism concerning the motivation and corruption of politicians and other leaders of society; the self-absorbed emphasis on human rights as applied to oneself or one's class, race, or sex rather than on one's duties and moral responsibility to others; and the ugly and decadent "permissive society" in which the concept of personal freedom has degenerated into a shallow and hedonistic self-indulgence.

But the most serious effect of all, with which all these other effects are associated, is the environmental or ecological crisis. We have multiplied human populations, pillaged the world's resources, and polluted our environment at rates which our descendants, if we have any, surely will regard as grossly immoral. This is indeed a moral crisis. It therefore requires an adaptive evolutionary response which is moral in character. That is the central conclusion from this analysis. . . .

NOTES

1. Walter Patterson, *Nuclear Power* (New York, Penguin, 1976).
2. Jacques Monod, *Chance and Necessity: An Essay on the Natural Philosophy of Modern Biology* (New York, Knopf, 1971).

Chapter 55

*Prentiss L. Pemberton and
Daniel Rush Finn*

Economics and Christian Values

It is quite natural that in dealing with economic problems Christians should depend heavily on the discipline of economics for a description of the situation. Thoughtful believers have long ago ceased ignoring the social or natural sciences simply because they are "secular."

At the same time, however, the use in Christian ethics of the insights of economics is not so simple and straightforward as most economists believe. Within the discipline of economics it is usually assumed that while economists as ordinary citizens have their own values and convictions, when they act as scientists they are only supposed to describe what is going on in the economy. They are supposed to leave to others the use of that description in judging whether what is happening ought to go on. Most economists see themselves as providing description, not prescription; as social scientists, they want to leave to others the choice about what to value. If things really were this simple, life would be a lot easier. But the economist's usual understanding of the relation of economic science and human values runs into difficulties on two levels.

At the most obvious level, a problem is posed by the fact that on a large number of important issues economists as scientists debate among themselves as to what is going on in the economic realm. Are the major oil companies exacerbating the energy problem for higher profits or is just OPEC to blame? Does less unemployment cause more inflation or must one of these problems be solved before the other will get better? Are multinational firms the best hope for development in the third world or do they actually cause underdevelopment? As we listen to economists from the right, left, and center we can hear different answers to these questions about what is going on in the economy.

At a deeper level, however, we find that in the very process of trying to describe what is (and trying to avoid the question of what ought to be), the economist starts with some basic assumptions which are value-laden and not value-free. In addition, since these assumptions are starting points, they are unproved and, at least within the science of economics, are unprovable. In fact, many of the disputes among different "schools" of economists—conservative, liberal, radical— can be traced to different starting assumptions. Differing schools of economic thought look at the same world, but see it differently. They consequently come to different recommendations for economic policy.

To be sure each of these many descriptions of economic life has some degree of truth to it, and an empirical investigation is always crucial. But the fact remains that different starting points and conflicting visions of the world need to be weighed against each other. It is our contention that the basic insights of the Christian tradition must be employed in assessing the adequacy of those assumptions which operate below the surface of economic description.

Most economists in the United States share a set of assumptions about the human person and economic activity. Technically speaking, these assumptions are a part of the "neoclassical" school of economics. We will simply refer to this as "mainstream" or "orthodox" economic theory. Employing this approach, economists have made highly valuable contributions to the well-being of people here and abroad. At the same time, however, orthodox economic science has had significant negative effects—effects which economists themselves often overlook. Examine, if you will, five basic economic categories of mainstream economics, and you will see how the Christian tradition requires a critique and expansion of each concept.

1. SCARCITY

Mainstream economists today universally take "scarcity" as the fundamental problem with which economics is concerned. The orthodox definition of economic science is "the study of the allocation of scarce resources to achieve alternative ends." For example, with limits on the amount of iron ore and labor available for making steel, we must choose between more tractors or more autos, between more military tanks or more steel girders for buildings. What people would like to have always exceeds what is available. This is what the economist means technically by scarcity.

However, there is a serious problem in taking this definition of scarcity as a starting point for economic science. Nearly everyone sees that "scarcity" is the fundamental problem of economics, but the ordinary person's notion is different from the economist's use of the term. In everyday terms, scarcity refers to not having enough to live a fully human life. This concern over scarcity is represented in fears about whether the food and housing bills can be paid, whether a Social Security pension will be sufficient, whether the unemployed worker can find a job, whether the malnourished child of the third world will live past the age of twelve. The shortcoming of the economist's definition of scarcity is that all these concerns are grouped together in the same category with a desire for ever-larger stereo speakers and ever-longer boats for recreation.

The economist is right in pointing out that people's wants exceed what is available, but this conceals an even more important insight. For economists, the problem of scarcity applies to commodities: the inability of a family to buy food is treated in economics in the same manner as the inability of a family to purchase a yacht. For nearly everyone else, it is untrue to say that a well-to-do family that wishes it could afford a yacht is experiencing the same kind of scarcity as the poor family that wishes it could afford a balanced diet.

From the point of view of the Judeo-Christian tradition, scarcity as deprivation, as the lack of what it takes to live a full life, is an evil which all in the community have the responsibility to eliminate. Scarcity as the gap between unlimited wants and what is available, however, is a sign of human greed, something that the Bible has always referred to as the sin of covetousness.

M. Douglas Meeks has argued (in the November 10, 1980, issue of *Christianity and*

Crisis) [Chap. 56, below] that the economist's preoccupation with scarcity contradicts a truly Trinitarian conception of economics because it overlooks what the New Testament calls the "pleroma" or fullness of God's gifts in the Spirit. This is not to deny that multitudes live in destitution but rather to point out that there is enough to go around if justice prevails. Justice here would imply not only a redistribution of wealth but a realignment of the production system so that, for example, the best agricultural land in the third world would be used to produce basic food for domestic consumption and not the more profitable cash crops grown for export to the industrialized world.

Thus, an ethical assessment of economic arguments will confirm the view that scarcity is a crucial economic problem, but not primarily in the way economists generally mean it. Scarcity as physical poverty is often underrated by economists. Scarcity as the excess of wants over available goods is important but not important enough to render it the starting point of the study of economic life. We do need to choose among alternative ends in the allocation of scarce resources but the most real sense of scarcity is missed if we treat all wants as equally significant. Of course, economists do ultimately make a distinction between different kinds of "wants": some are backed up by expenditures of money and are fulfilled while others are not. In order to understand this difference, we need to examine the economist's notion of the market.

2. THE MARKET

Mainstream economists appreciate "the market." They mean, of course, not the corner store, but that series of social interactions between people who have something which others want and those others who are willing to pay in order to get it. The original "owners" (say manufacturers with goods or laborers with their labor power) look for the best offer for their product or service, while the buyers (say consumers or employers) look for the lowest priced source of what they seek. Competition (with other sellers) keeps owners from charging too much, while competition (with other buyers) keeps each buyer from being able to force sellers to lower their prices unduly. In addition, the hope of profits entices producers to make new products which consumers would like to have. The "free market"—unencumbered by government restrictions—is viewed as a marvelous mechanism for setting national economic priorities without the need for national debate. Consumers' value systems determine where the nation puts its time and resources.

The assumptions implicit in such confidence in the market have been criticized from both secular and religious points of view. The first problem is that wealthy consumers can fulfill far more of their wants than the poor can. Thus, relying on the market to determine what goods the nation will produce allows the wealthy a far greater voice in setting national economic priorities. Our own society, let alone various third-world ones, is characterized by a great disparity in yearly income between the rich and poor, and an even more alarming difference in wealth (the dollar value of the property a person owns at the end of the year). Economists will admit that if the current distribution of income between the rich and the poor is judged to be a bad one from the moral point of view, then the national economic priorities set in the free market will also be wrong until a redistribution of wealth and income is achieved. It is quite clear that the Christian principle of the just entitlement of the poor does in fact require such a redistribution. The obvious conclusion from this moral assessment is that although the market mechanism may be employed to achieve certain goals, Christians cannot have a naïve confidence in market outcomes.

A good number of economists—particularly "conservative" economists—are caught in a problem here. In spite of the concessions just cited, many advocates of the market oppose programs of income redistribution on the grounds that only poverty (euphemistically called "market forces") will provide enough incentive for the poor to exert themselves. This stance bespeaks some important and questionable assumptions about the human person and self-interest which we will examine later.

A second problem raised by relying heavily on the market is the implicit assumption that the firms in the marketplace actually do compete with each other. We need not deal with the technical economic definition of "perfect competition" here, but let us note that most economists do recognize that in many industries, the few very large firms which dominate the industry often do not fully compete with each other in spite of the ideal of competition of the free market. Explicit collusion and outright price-fixing by firms is, of course, illegal in the United States, but there are more subtle ways to "administer" prices.

A significant example of such behavior is "priced leadership," a procedure described even in introductory economics textbooks as prevalent in the American steel industry. One firm announces a price increase to be effective at some future date, and the other firms then generally announce the same price rise effective on the same date. Now and then the first firm is out of line and it later alters its price change to match what the other firms are doing. This adjustment process occurs about four times a year and effectively eliminates much competition (which the firms euphemistically call "cut-throat" competition) where one firm might lower its prices to attract more customers. There are other ways that competition can be and is reduced, but the point here is that to the extent that competition *is* reduced, economists themselves admit that the operation of the market will produce less than optimal results.

At another level it is important to question the wisdom of relying on the market mechanism to set national economic priorities even if we were first to solve the problems of the deprivation of the poor and the failures of competition among firms. Advocates of the market appreciate, first, its automatic operation (no bureaucracy has to act before market adjustments occur) and, second, its impersonal operation (no person or group gets to decide what adjustments are ultimately made). The first of these claims involves the notion of "efficiency" to which we shall return presently. The second—the impersonality of the market—raises a very important quesion for Christian ethics: Is an occurrence better simply because no person or group decided it should happen?

To answer this question it is important to see why proponents of the market respond by saying "Yes." Many of them, though not all, would argue that any person's values or ethical positions are simply personal subjective preferences. If this were true, then a policy decision by Congress or a government agency or a neighborhood council would be just an expression of preferences of the people in that group (and of any others who might be able to have some influence over them). In case of a shortage of gasoline, for example, rather than allowing a government agency to ration gas "arbitrarily," proponents of the market would advocate allowing the price of gas to rise to whatever price would induce consumers to reduce the amount they demand so there would be enough gas to go round.

The tradition of Christian ethics has consistently rejected the first step of this argument. Christianity has always denied the assumption that values are just personal preferences. While it may not always be easy to decide what is the morally best course of action, the careful decision of a deliberative body ought be dismissed as just the efforts of one more "interest group." Some values *are* better than others, and sincere discussion in a group can improve a decision.

Not only do Christian ethics have greater respect for group decisions about the common good than do proponents of the market, the Christian tradition has analogously put less confidence in the initial preferences of individuals than do those same market advocates. While the latter have no standard by which to judge consumers' wants, Christian ethics has always held that some values—like food and shelter—are more basic and more important than others—like luxury consumption. Therefore, the market choices of consumers with money to spend may not be the best basis on which to determine what the economy should produce. In fact, if a decision had to be made about basic economic questions, the discussion and debate about priorities might well change many people's original personal "preferences" (hopefully for the better).

The Christian tradition has never granted ultimate value to the immediate inclination of individuals. Proponents of the market often call this "paternalistic" or "totalitarian." For Christians and others, it is a matter of public morality. Although the action of the free market might at times achieve the best outcome, it does not necessarily do so. This is by no means to say that Christian ethics endorses the excesses of bureaucracy that occur in totalitarian forms of socialism, but rather to assert that major questions of economic priority should be carefully weighed, debated, and decided upon in the light of fundamental moral values.

3. EFFICIENCY

Economists—and just about all other human beings—value efficiency. No one thinks inefficiency is a good idea. So it is particularly difficult for well-meaning people to respond when in response to proposals for humanizing our economy they hear: "That sounds nice but it is quite inefficient." What is efficiency and how is it related to moral concern?

Economists define efficiency as getting the greatest possible production out of any given amount of resources available. Alternatively, it can be seen as achieving any particular goal at the least possible cost in effort and resources. At a sort of common sense level, this is quite straightforward. Problems appear as we dig deeper. Consider two alternate procedures for, say, making steel: an older process and a more recently developed one which is more "efficient." The term "efficient" here means that the newer process produces steel at a lower cost per ton than does the old one. Now, however, consider two alternatives for a steel plant where the only difference between them is that one has a series of complex devices costing $300 million in its smokestacks to reduce pollution by 90 percent while the other simply releases untreated smoke into the air. Which is more "efficient"? Clearly the second plant will appear to produce a ton of steel at a lower "cost" since from the point of view of the firm the costs paid by citizens who must breathe polluted air are not part of the firm's calculation of the "cost" of a ton of steel.

This particular case is a good example of the economic problem of "externalities" which we will examine further on; but like many other examples, it demonstrates the flaw in the usual use of the word "efficiency." In practice, that word generally includes only those costs of production which are measured in dollars and cents in the market. Although the steel mill with pollution control devices must pay for them, the mill with no such device need not pay for the privilege of imposing costs on people living downwind. Thus it is that many have complained about government pollution regulations because they reduce the "efficiency " of American firms. The advantages of lower pollution levels get lost in this casual use of the term.

To be fair to economists here, we must note that the discipline of economics does clearly recognize that the negative effects of polluted air are indeed costs of producing steel—even if the steel mill doesn't have to pay those costs. This particular misuse of the term "efficiency" is most frequent among people in business and financial circles. Still, most economists do periodically lapse from a careful use of the term—as the next example shows.

Today we can see that the gas guzzlers of the 1950s and 1960s were very inefficient in their use of gasoline, although they were nonetheless "efficient" economically since gas was so cheap at that time. Even now, after our energy prices have risen dramatically, we still pay much less for gasoline, heating oil, and other forms of energy than people in Europe and most other places on the globe. The economist will define efficiency in energy consumption with respect to the market price of energy even though from an ethical point of view other concerns, like the availability of resources to future generations, may loom large in the assessment.

Fundamentally, then, the word "efficiency" is forced to do double duty and is misused in the process. The economist wants to use it in a value-free way—to designate achieving any goal with the least effort and use of resources. But even though the idea could apply to any goal and could include all costs, in practice both the goals sought and the costs considered are usually limited to those items which have a price tag designated in the market. The "efficient solution" to an economic problem is generally equivalent to "the market solution."

When Christians reflect on the possibilities for an economic ethic in the modern world, they must keep "efficiency" in perspective. Any time human values are involved which are not adequately represented in the market place—human dignity, the rights of future generations, the interests of the poor, etc.—then an efficient attainment of those goals may look remarkably inefficient from the point of view of the market. Once such values are incorporated into the list of society's goals, even orthodox economists often concede that only government intervention or activities by other nonmarket forces can improve on the deficiencies of the market.

4. PROPERTY

In an effort to describe the economic situation without making a moral judgment about whether it is good or bad, orthodox economists have generally taken the institutional framework of the U.S. economy as given and have proceeded to analyze its workings. As a result, economists operate with the same assumptions about property as do most people in modern industrial society. They generally work with the understanding of private property deriving from the work of John Locke.

Most of us are already familiar with the conflict between the assertion of nearly absolute authority of the owner over the thing owned and the Judeo-Christian insight into possession as stewardship. This disparity requires a rethinking of some of the usual rights and claims of ownership. This, in turn, will affect behavior on an individual and on an institutional level.

One of the moral problems arising most frequently within current American economic institutions is the clash between moral principles and the charter of the firm to produce a profit. From the point of view of the individual manager facing a difficult decision, this is most often felt as a clash between his or her "own" values and a responsibility to the stockholders who have a right to a significant return on their investment. Once, however, we realize that ownership entails not only rights but also the duty to use possessions responsibly, the manager could be allowed as great a discretion in fulfilling the moral responsibilities of the firm as he or she has in creatively seeking a profit.

When we step back and look at the larger issues in the economy, we find that this notion of a more limited ownership has equally important implications. In the last section we saw the example of air pollution by a steel mill. The usual presumption in our competitive society is that one person's rights will act as a limit on the excesses of others. No one is allowed to dump refuse on a neighbor's property, and if someone tries to do this, the neighbor can sue in court. But the release of toxic gases into the air by the plant is not challenged in the courts on the grounds of violation of ownership rights since no one person "owns" the atmosphere. When the system of competing rights breaks down in cases like this, only direct action by government can alleviate pollution.

We should note that from the point of view of the steel company—operating with Locke's notion of property—the government's action appears to be an external and arbitrary limit on its rights. We can even hear assertions that government has "imposed" hundreds of billions of dollars in costs on U.S. business.

Yet, if we really do believe the Judeo-Christian vision of all things as created for the good of humanity, then the atmosphere (like the rivers, lakes, and oceans) is not presumed to be a cost-free dumping ground. Pollution is seen as piracy of the good. If it costs $300 million to reduce a steel mill's pollution to "acceptable" levels, then this amount ought not be seen as a cost imposed on business. Rather, it is a measure, to put it kindly, of the subsidy the firm had previously been receiving from the public in allowing the pollution to go on. More strikingly, it is a measure of legalized theft as real as if the firm had, through a loophole in the law, been allowed to dump solid waste on a neighbor's land.

To widen the context even further, we can consider our nation's role in the international discussions about mining the floor of the world's oceans. At a number of conferences on a "law of the sea," the vast majority of the nations of the world have been calling for a special status for the oceans so that while they may be mined they cannot be "owned" absolutely. A world fund for developing nations could be established by a tax on all such mining. Many in the United States, however, have objected to this notion and, following John Locke, want to assert an absolute right for the firms who do the mining. (See, for example, the article on "Locke and the Law of the Sea" in *Commonweal,* June 1981.) The Christian vision of property points toward some sort of communal possession of these extra-national resources.

The "law of the sea" raises questions about economic structures of ownership in a situation where they are yet to be designed for the first time. The Christian economic ethic should also have a transforming impact on existing institutions of property ownership. The Christian tradition on its own does not provide ahead-of-time any exact definition of how a particular institution like the firm should be structured; the details can only be worked out in an actual historical situation. Still, it seems clear that the firm ought not be viewed solely or even primarily as an organization of investors or owners who hire employees to perform certain tasks. Rather, the firm is an organization of persons of many sorts who have come together to produce goods or services for the benefit of themselves and the rest of society.

Seeing the firm in this way and understanding the limits to private property, there is no reason why the ultimate decisions about the firm should be made by stockholders only. It would seem reasonable, for example, for the board of directors of a firm to be elected not just by the stockholders but by blue-collar workers and lower-level managers as well as upper management. In addition, some representation of consumers and of society as a whole would be very important since, in spite of the best of intentions, there will always be a tendency for the common self-interest of employees and investors to overshadow the rights and needs of persons outside the firm. Various arrangements would have to be tried and tested; some such attempts (entitled "co-determination") are currently being made in West Germany and elsewhere. Although a more limited sense of private property is not sufficient to spell out new institutional forms precisely, it does indicate the direction in which to move.

5. THE HUMAN PERSON AND SELF-INTEREST

The fifth (and last) element we will investigate may not look like an economic category at all. Economists are not in the business of developing and proving theories about human nature. They would like to leave that to philosophers and theologians. Still, in order to think about how people act and react as consumers and producers, economists work with a model of the human person. Mainstream economists think of the person as a "rational maximizer." That is, every individual has a set of preferences or values, and some amount of wealth and natural ability. Using these financial and personal resources, the individual tries to fulfill those preferences to the greatest extent possible.

"Self-interest" is an important part of this understanding of the human person, but it is not always defined or understood clearly by either economists or their critics. On the one hand, the economists' official conception of "self-interest" does not mean that the individual engages in only "selfish" behavior. Some individuals value charitable actions, the economist explains, and thus those individuals get a kind of psychological "return" for activity which assists others. In the language of economics, individuals gain "utility" from actions they choose to undertake, whether those actions include buying heroin for themselves or working as a volunteer at a community service agency. We will return to this notion later, but let us here note that this position can be well described as "psychological egoism," the belief that while not all behavior is consciously "selfish" in the narrow sense, all behavior is ultimately "self-interested."

On the other hand, most mainstream economists believe that the "self-interest" of individuals is so strong that capitalism (which is based on each individual's looking out for his or her own interests) is not only morally better but is more feasible than socialism (which they feel requires that individuals act counter to their narrow self-interest since the government organizes economic activity). Although in orthodox economic theory the category of "self-interest" ought to cover altruistic or charitable acts as well as narrowly hedonistic or self-seeking ones, in practice those economists who judge capitalism to be more feasible than socialism on the grounds just stated in the text are making some assumption about the content (and not just the form) of the self-interest of most people. The assumption is that among the elements in this "self-interest," the "selfish" ones outweigh the "altruistic"ones. It is this belief that selfish activity predominates that leads many proponents of capitalism to oppose any significant redistribution of income to the poor on the grounds that it would tend to destroy the incentive to work.

The Judeo-Christian vision of the human person is more communal than all this. The person is recognized to be constituted in a social setting. The idea of self-interest is treated more subtly. Mainstream economics can say that all actions have some end or goal, and that this end is an interest of the self who takes that action. But this sense of "self-interest" isn't very interesting. Christianity has, rather carefully, made the commonsense distinction between actions where the intended beneficiary is the self (self-interested in the sense of "selfish") and actions where the intended beneficiary is another person or group.

The Christian tradition has always recognized the excesses of sin. But where capitalism counts on competition from other self-interested persons to hold self-interest in check, Christianity has always held out two additional prescriptions: a personal change of heart, and institutionalized requirements and restrictions. The individual can be exhorted to a less selfish way of living, and the structures of the community can be molded so that the basic needs of all persons are met and the self-interest of individuals corresponds more closely with the common good.

In fact, Christianity has always denounced any attempt to base social organization on self-interest alone. Behind this stance is an appreciation for the power of human sinfulness. In its critique of every social and economic system, Christian ethics points out the way those persons with power (i.e., "wealth" under capitalism) can subvert the usual checks and balances, can gain their own ends, and can legitimate this by showing how "just" it is since they are not breaking any laws. In a careful study entitled *Economic Foundations of Political Power* (Free Press, 1973), Randall Bartlett has demonstrated how an economic system based on individuals asserting their self-interest will, in the modern, uncertain world, subvert any democratic government and will render it a servant of vested economic interests:

> Government actions will preserve the economic *status quo* since they arise from patterns of influence generated by the operation of the economic system. In a system such as we have described, the actions of self-interested, rational agents operating in an uncertain world will—rightly or wrongly—cause the structure of political power to rise from a firm economic foundation. This structure and its foundation are inseparable.

At the same time as it challenges the foundations of capitalism, the Christian tradition also chides that naïveté of those Marxists who would hope to eliminate human sinfulness simply by restructuring the economy. While the human person may, over generations, be shaped into a less competitive, less anxious, and less self-interested being than has been the case under capitalism, the doctrine of original sin recognizes that the human condition shall never be free of a tendency to sinful forms of self-assertion.

Chapter 56

M. Douglas Meeks

The Holy Spirit and Human Needs

Toward a Trinitarian View of Economics

It is of the church that one usually thinks as soon as there is a question of denouncing the irrelevance of Christianity. As the praxis of faith, the church does seem outdated in the social as well as the personal sphere. Yet without the church the Christian faith is nothing but an esoteric doctrine. The calling of the Christian faith is to transform the world by spreading obedience to the Gospel of Jesus Christ. This cannot be done without the church. It may be otherwise in theologies born of other traditions, using sources other than the Bible. Christian theology stands or falls with the coming into being of the church. And the church of Jesus Christ comes into being only when it takes part in God's transformation of the world.

According to the preponderance of biblical traditions, an absolute split between the church and the world is unthinkable. The church is not non-world. Rather the church is that part of the world that has been given over to the lordship of Jesus Christ. Thus the very formation of the church will be a transformation of the world. The formation of the *ecclesia* will mean a cultural, political, and economic transformation precisely because whenever the messianic community of Jesus Christ is called into being, the interests, powers, and claims of at least part of the world come under the interest, the power, and the claim of Jesus Christ. That part of the world then witnesses in word and deed to the "righteousness" of God—which is God's power for life against death.

But according to the biblical traditions, we would think onesidedly if we thought only in this direction. We would soon get the impression that the church comes first, then the salvation of the world. But the biblical traditions will not allow us to think exclusively that way. The world is not bereft of God's passion. "God so loved the *world* [not the church, not Christians] that he gave his only begotten Son." It is God's history of transforming the world that first brings the church into existence. It is not that the church first exists and then gets a mission to the world. Rather the mission of transforming the world creates the church. Thus we must say both things at once: The formation of the church means the transformation of the world, the transformation of the world means the formation of the church.

From the biblical perspective, what holds together the formation of the church and

First published in *Christianity and Crisis*, 40 (November 10, 1980), pp. 307–16. Reprinted with permission. Copyright © 1980, Christianity & Crisis, 537 West 121st Street, New York, NY 10027.

the transformation of the world is the presence and the power of the Holy Spirit. To my mind that is the principal reason why the theology of the Holy Spirit has come to be a principal concern of our theological work today. The church and the Holy Spirit: Why has it always been so difficult to speak of both at once? Why are there so many churches that exist without the Spirit? Why are there so many churches that are merely full of spiritualism and the spirits of the world?

The church is meant to be that place in history where God's interests for the world meet the interests of the world *in the presence and power of the Holy Spirit.* The Holy Spirit transforms the world into the church so that, as transformed world, the church may live for the future of the world. According to Paul, the presence of the Holy Spirit means that we have to die either to the world or to the Spirit of God. But if we live in the Spirit of God, this means solidarity with the world: We are to die to the world so that we might live for the transformation of the world.

This is an insight with consequences. If we strive to put church, world, and Holy Spirit together in our time and place, we discover that theology must begin with an ideological critique of the church. Our initial question should be the ancient question: *Cui bono?* For whose good are we doing theology in the first place? Whose interests is the church serving by its existence? If the church is already captivated by the interests of the world, can it serve the transformation of the world?

TRANSFORMING OURSELVES

This is serious business because, in order to engage in such criticism of interests, theology has to name names. It will soon become clear that the church is not captivated by every imaginable interest in the world but by a few particular interests that are often specifically those of my worldly existence and your worldly existence. The more we press this question, the more we realize that the first thing Christian theology should serve is the liberation of the church from many of our own self-interests. And that leads me to the hard thing I want to say: We liberals are ready to talk about the transformation of the world and the liberation of the oppressed (and anybody else you propose), but we find it next to impossible to turn to our own transformation and our own liberation. If the church is already captivated by our economic, political, and cultural interests, can it serve God's liberation of the poor and the dying in the world?

What kind of liberation theology can we do? Is it not farcical for a North American, white, male theologian to talk about liberation or transformation at all? Are not our churches among the most segregated and sexist and perhaps also among the most classist institutions in our society? Has not much of the rest of the world declared a moratorium on even listening to us? Have we not lost the authority and the right to speak to the world? Whenever the North American churches intervene in economics, politics, and culture, there is the suspicion that they are serving their own interests. By what right or whose right can we claim any authority or do anything in the world? The first confusion we should be delivered from is the notion that the North American churches, in their present form, can really bring about liberation and transformation of the world.

But must we not also be delivered from a second confusion, namely, the delusion that as Christian theologians we should give up on the churches in which we find ourselves? This seems to me to be an ever more present temptation among theologians, pastors, and laypersons: Either to give up hope for the church completely, or to think and work theologically on issues that are totally separated from their own church situation. Often, if not always, we focus on the liberation of the poor and the oppressed without even being aware that their poverty and oppression are immediately connected with our sin and our death-serving systems. Is it that everything looks more possible than our own liberation, than the transformation of the churches of which we are a part, than the transformation of that part of the world which is glued together by our values?

If so, then we should turn neither to the right nor the left, but direct our attention to the churches that are before our eyes. Our lives and work as theologians must be directed to the ecclesial revolution which would mean the utter transformation of the world which is our church. For our churches have become the world—but not the transformed world. That is the basic description of our situation. Thus to be a North American theologian means to have a particular focus: We should do theology directed at the transformation of the church for the humane formation of the world.

If theology is so directed, its first task becomes the criticism of the God concepts prevalent in North American churches and society. "God concepts," it will be understood, may or may not use the name of God or the language of theology. To discover them we must discern what it is that we worship, what we regard as having ultimate value, our source of meaning. In this sense all people, including atheists, hold God concepts. And whatever any of us hold to be divine, as divine is understood here, will determine our life interests, the shape of our lives, and the institutions of our society.

So it is that whenever the Gospel is integrally preached and believed, immediately the God concepts reigning in the untransformed world are challenged. Whatever militates against the rule of the Father of Jesus Christ in the Holy Spirit, whatever directs our lives against the interests of God's righteousness in Jesus Christ through the Spirit, is in conflict with the Gospel. The task of theology is to enter actively into that conflict.

In the doing of this task theology is called to hold together church and world (for the sake of God's passion for the world) under the unalterable assumption that *the church does not exist for itself.* The church is not the first word of God. The first word of God is Jesus Christ. Nor is the church the last word of God. The last word of God is God's transformation of everything that is and the rule of God's glory in everything. Thus, only when the interests of the church are the interests of the Father and the Son present in the Holy Spirit is the church the transformed world and thus capable of transforming the interests of the world.

THEOLOGY vs. THE GOSPEL

If Christian theology is to make this one clear point, its resource must be the God concept presented in the Gospel—that is to say, the Trinity. If we have problems in doing this, some of the problems lie with theology's own traditions, not with the Gospel. Traditional trinitarian thinking, as will be shown, has made it almost impossible to do a theology of the Holy Spirit; it is for this reason that the church has suffered and is now suffering outbursts of spiritualism. A thornier problem, however, is that a biblical theology of the Holy Spirit is deeply threatening to our interests in the world today, and this may explain a widespread failure of nerve in contemporary theology.

Yet when Christian theology engages in conflict over God concepts, as it must, it has no choice but to be trinitarian if it is to be a response to the Gospel, which confesses that we intend to serve the interests of God in Jesus Christ through the Holy Spirit. For the Trinity is meant to be an initial answer to the question, *Cui bono?* It is a formula for understanding God's history of righteousness with the world, and thus it is the principle of the transformation of the world. And the transformation of the world begins with the transformation of the God concepts by which our church and world are organized.

I would like now to offer a small contribution to this task under the heading of "The Holy Spirit and Economics." This may seem a strange juxtaposition. Are not the Holy

Spirit and economics at opposite poles from each other? No. They are surprisingly about the same thing.

"Economics" comes from the Greek word *oikonomia*, which means the law or management of the household. Economics is basically about the question whether everyone in the household will get what it takes to be human and live a full life. The Holy Spirit is the presence of the living God "for us" and for the whole creation. The Holy Spirit is God working economically so that God's creatures and the whole creation may live and live abundantly. This is the reason that the Holy Spirit is identified with God's righteousness, which appears paradigmatically in God's raising of Jesus from the dead (Rom. 1:4) and is called the "spirit that gives life" (I Cor. 15:45). As the Holy Spirit, God makes present the power of God's righteousness, which is God's power for life against death.

But the Holy Spirit, God acting economically, causes a severe conflict with the economics of our society today, a conflict that centers on certain God concepts that are reigning in our churches and in the ethos of North American society. What is at stake is the rethinking of the Holy Spirit in relation to what Max Weber called the "spirit of capitalism." I am not going to debate the technical merits or demerits of capitalism here, or compare capitalism with socialism, since I believe that all existing forms of socialism also share basically the same distorted God concepts as those in our economic sphere.

Rather I am interested in three fundamental assumptions of our economic ethos which I think feed on distorted conceptions of God and the Holy Spirit. They are (1) possessive individualism, which cuts people off from one another by making them unable to sense the need of the other and to suffer with the other; (2) the spiritualized compulsion to growth and consumption, which makes us as a society serve the idol of increase at all costs, even when the resulting contradictions obviously close off a human future for our society; (3) a sense of scarcity, which is the overheated, roaring motor behind the senseless injustices of our economic order.

Our liberation from the God concepts underlying these economic assumptions would mean the beginning of the ecclesial revolution which in our situation would be the simultaneous transformation of church and world. I believe that a trinitarian understanding of the cross is the perspective from which we come to know the person and work of the Holy Spirit and the perspective from which we should call into question the reigning God concepts of our economic life.

God without Spirit. In our mainline churches many people worship and think of God as a radically individual and isolated being. The New Testament, however, speaks of God by speaking of a history of communal relationships among the Father, the Son, and the Holy Spirit. Is God a radical individual or is God a community of relationships? This is a crucial question of the economics of salvation in church and world today because the concept of God as a simple individual being gives rise to the notion of the radically separated, individual human being and to the disastrous concept of "possessive individualism."

Traditional doctrines of God have begun by trying to think of God on the basis of a concept of nature in order to talk about the divine essence, which has been defined as one, unchanging, without needs, and incapable of suffering. In general the only basic problem perceived with this approach has been the difficulty of explaining how this essence could be incarnated in Jesus. Another difficulty, less often perceived, is that in this way of thinking the Holy Spirit always get short shrift. The writers of the New Testament, however, did not have the essence of God in mind as the starting point, but rather the experience of Jesus as our salvation and as God's promise for the coming salvation of the world. And it is precisely this experience of Jesus which the New

Testament writers call *pneuma*, Spirit. All New Testament theology is a thematization of this communal experience of Jesus in the Holy Spirit.

IMMOBILIZING THE TRINITY

The problem with the patristic doctrines of God was that they did not begin with this social experience of the Spirit but with the knowledge of God as creator. Thus the first sentence of the Nicene Creed reads: "We believe in one God, the Father all governing (*pantokratora*), creator (*poieten*) of all things visible and invisible." Attention then shifts immediately to the Son. The creed takes a whole paragraph to make clear that Jesus Christ has a different origin from all created things. It was not deemed necessary to say much about the Holy Spirit. The confession *per se* ends simply: "And [we believe] in the Holy Spirit." That we have access to this God only through the Spirit (the New Testament starting point) is not reflected here.

The issue can be seen even more clearly in Thomas Aquinas's doctrine of God. Thomas begins with a description of that which can be called *esse absolutum*, absolute being—and he ends with that, too. Behind the three divine persons is the divine nature. God's absolute existence in and for God's self. God exists for God's self. God is proper to God's self, and that means God's self is the property of God. And of course Thomas is simply following Augustine's notion that we should think about the divine being on the model of the radically individual human person, who constitutes him or herself, is proper to him or herself, and is the property of him or herself.

It is widely believed that this Greek monotheism and divine absolutism has come to an end with the so-called "death-of-God" phenomenon of the last two centuries. But has this God concept of the individual simple being represented as a self-sufficient person really come to an end, or is it still functioning in our churches and our society as a ground for "possessive individualism"? To think of God without the Spirit is to think of God as the private self; and, since *human* life will always be understood in terms of what it regards as *divine* life, it is to think of the human being as the private self. God without Spirit is the being who exists as property of God. God is the being who has no needs and no external relationships, who cannot go beyond God's self and give that self away. God is the being who is free from others through being "apathetic," that is, incapable of suffering.

THE ATOMIZED PERSON

This description of God without Spirit is exactly the description of the human being without spirit in our economic life today. It is the theological background for the statement C. B. MacPherson deduces from his exhaustive historical study of economic anthropology in the modern world:

> The individual in market society *is* human as proprietor of his own person . . . his humanity . . . depends on his freedom from any but self-interested . . . relations with others [*The Political Theory of Possessive Individualism*, Oxford, 1962].

In *About Possession: The Self as Private Property* (Pennsylvania State University Press, 1977), John R. Wikse comments similarly:

> Where human identity is defined by subjectivity, inwardness, or interiority, the experience of being deprived of intimate and enduring associations and relation-

ships with others is discounted and is transformed into the meaning of freedom. This is the freedom and privilege of the *bourgeois* individual, fearfully suspicious that others will deprive him of his possessions, including himself. . . . To be able to think of oneself as "living property" means the logic of socioeconomic relationships has penetrated the psyche. . . . Subjectivity understood in this way is intelligible in terms of private property, as a hidden, private relationship: the self's ownership of itself.

The *homo americanus* is the private individual. Economic freedom comes to mean having no claims laid upon one by others. It is the freedom to make oneself and remake oneself and thus to be "on the make." It is the freedom to view oneself as one's own property. It is the freedom not to have to suffer when the other suffers. It is the freedom to serve one's own interests.

Increasingly Americans are becoming aware, however, that no one really lives as an atomistic individual in the economic sphere. Our lives are becoming more and more collective because of the technological and institutional decisions we make day by day. As Michael Harrington has put it in *Socialism* (Saturday Review Press, 1975):

One need not any longer ask whether the future is going to be collective—if we do not blow ourselves to smithereens, that issue has already been settled by a technology of such complex interdependence that it demands conscious regulation and control.

Factories, unions, corporations, banks, insurance companies, and government bureaucracies are factually putting the lie to any notion that freedom can be gained by denying all but self-interested relationships.

If there is anything certain about the short- and long-range human future, then, it is that we shall live collectively. The only question is: What kind of collective existence shall we have? Bureaucratic, totalitarian, democratic? And that can be answered only by an economics of a public household. But it is precisely the basic tenet of "possessive individualism" that prevents even the recognition of a public household, much less the development of a humane way of distributing whatever is necessary for life to all members of the public household.

The transformation of church and world will begin with the transformation of the concept of "God without Spirit" and of the resulting notion of the possessive human being without spirit.

Spirit without God. But it is not only a God concept which views God without Spirit that urges the church to exist as the world instead of the transformed world. A God concept which views the Spirit without God is also responsible.

Like all spiritualist movements since Montanus, the charismatic renewal movement is a reaction against a static God concept that views the Holy Spirit as an afterthought, and against the resulting spiritless reality of church and world. These movements refuse to think of God as a static, self-sufficient individual—a conception that can be used as an instrument for external control by hierarchical, imperialistic, or totalitarian conceptions of authority. Thus spiritualist and pietist movements are usually in the beginning liberation movements. They fight against domination by moving from the God concept of the self-centered, all-powerful being to the experience of the Spirit as the starting point for everything. There is much in the present charismatic movements that we in the mainline churches need to learn from.

But these movements characteristically tend to separate the Holy Spirit from the

Father and the Son. They thus sometimes understand the Spirit as a distinct third party, an independent second mediator, or even as a separate dynamistic or animistic force. Morever, they see the experience of the Spirit as concentrated in the isolated feelings of the individual (sometimes articulable only in the noncommunal expression of glossolalia). And, finally, they emphasize the affects and effects of the Spirit, the work rather than the divine person of the Spirit, and the subjective power of the Spirit rather than the presence of the Spirit. If the Spirit is the "divine" cut loose from the Father and the Son, then in the end it will be a spirit that can be co-opted for any conceivable purpose of the human spirit.

Recent analyses of neo-Pentecostalism in North America show that this God concept has the effect of strengthening the fundamental capitalist ethos of North America. Many contemporary charismatics reject the criticism of society in the older Pentecostalism and are becoming accommodated to the spirit and values of the prevailing economic system. In fact, the more the Holy Spirit is separated from God in Jesus Christ, the more the Holy Spirit is viewed as the sheer motivation and blind dynamism on which the prevailing economic ethos lives.

One could point to many leaders on the spiritualist circuit who are flagrantly avowing the worst aspects of our economic life: commodity fetishism, profiteering, and consumerism. Some spiritualist conservatives who keep a strict private morality when it comes to sexuality, family, and personal relationships, nevertheless let themselves be caught up in an utter animism when it comes to economics. Over and over their definitions of gifts of the Spirit turn out to be the idols of action, growth, and progress.

The ecstasy of many new spiritualists is not much more than euphoria at being able to believe in the old-time values of American capitalism. Financial success is a sure sign of having been gifted by the Spirit. And that means that everything from money, to the market, to personal relationships can be spiritualized—made into living idols, transmuted from means to ends. The bank commercials would have us all relate to our money animistically as they exhort us: "Make your money *work* for you." Our economic life is filled with animism, not unlike that of many so-called primitive societies.

The concept of Spirit without God serves the spiraling increase of insatiable wants and the doctrine of growth which has become the secular religion of our society.

The Holy Spirit and the Cross. What both of these God concepts ("God without Spirit" and "Spirit without God") do is separate the Spirit from the Father and the Son by denying the cross. The mainline churches and the so-called charismatic churches are often equally guilty of this. But according to the witness of the New Testament, the Holy Spirit can be understood only through the cross, which is the center of the Christian proclamation and faith.

A SUFFERING GOD

Both the Gospels and Paul speak about the relationship between Father and Son as one in which the Father has delivered over the Son and the Son has delivered over himself to death on the cross. The deepest suffering of the Son is his experience of being godforsaken, of being infinitely separated from the one with whom he had claimed the greatest intimacy: "My God, my God, why has thou forsaken me?" (Mark 15:34). The deepest suffering of the Father, on the other hand, is his suffering the death of his Son. This is a deeper suffering, just as our suffering through the death of a loved one is greater than our suffering our own death. The Father gives away the Son, and the Son gives away himself; both go outside themselves and both suffer.

Thus with the cross before us we must criticize every concept of God which defines

God as radically individual, self-sufficient, and passionless, just as we must criticize every concept of the divine which depicts the Spirit as sheer dynamism, motivation, or empowerment without suffering. The Holy Spirit is God compassionately present in the world and among us.

But the cross is not the end of God's history with us. It continues in the history of the Holy Spirit. From the whole context of the New Testament there can be no doubt that this Spirit, through whose power Jesus has offered himself up to the Father (Heb. 9:14) for us, is in the strictest sense identical with the "Spirit which is from God" (I Cor. 2:12). The Holy Spirit *is* this reality of love between the Father and the Son, their sacrifice for us, their going beyond themselves and the self-giving of each for us. Thus we may never speak of God without the Spirit, who is God's going outside the divine communion to be in community with God's creation. Neither may we ever speak of the Spirit without the unique suffering love between the Father and the Son. The Holy Spirit is the presence and the power of God among us and in the world for life.

Scarcity or plethora? This leads us to a final point of conflict between the economics of the Holy Spirit and the economic ethos of our society. It is a conflict between scarcity and what the New Testament calls the *pleroma* or the fullness of God's blessings and gifts in the Holy Spirit. An accepted definition of economics is "the art of allocating scarce goods among competing demands" (Daniel Bell). The most basic assumption of economics in the West is that there is a scarcity of what it takes to be human. I want to suggest that a trinitarian understanding and experience of the Holy Spirit will cause us to call into question the whole enterprise of economics based on this assumption.

Nothing is deeper in the spirit of capitalism, and of socialism as well, than the belief that there is not enough to go around. The church, however, is called to live and organize itself out of the sure faith that God the Holy Spirit is willing and providing whatever is necessary for all persons and the whole creation to live. This is not to deny the shortfall of what it takes to be human in the world. People are dying for lack of food and live in misery for lack of decent housing and clothing. Economic systems are faltering for lack of fuel and natural resources. Human beings are humiliated by the lack of jobs and of caring human relationships. This lack is not an illusion. Scarcity is real enough; yet it may not be made the starting point for a system of economic justice. As *starting point*, scarcity is an illusion, because in almost all situations of human life scarcity has been caused by human injustice.

Thus the church, though it be an incredible scandal to the world, will say with Paul: "He who did not spare his own Son but gave him up for us all, will he not also give us all things with him?" (Rom. 8:32). The early church always spoke of the presence of the Holy Spirit in superlatives, in the language of abundance and superabundance. So in II Corinthians 9:8:

> God is able to provide you with every blessing and abundance, so that you may always have enough of everything and may provide an abundance for every good work.

If we actually lived this faith in the church, it would already mean the transformation of part of the world, because it would mean the elimination of the inhuman spirit of struggle against an alleged scarcity. Moreover, the church of Jesus Christ could then actually be an agent for the transformation of the world's economics. Nothing less than that is what the church is called to do. But, remember, I am talking about a miracle of the Holy Spirit. I'm not talking about a program for the existing churches. For we are still living hour by hour as if there were a scarcity of what it takes to be human.

BEYOND ARISTOTLE

Aristotle held that the aim of economics is to work for and produce what is necessary for life. For him it was clear that "household management is more concerned with human beings than with the acquisition of inanimate property, and with human excellence than with the excellence of property which we call wealth" (*Politics*, Bk. I Ch. 13). What is produced is meant to be used for human needs. Human needs are defined as sufficient food, clothing, and shelter, care during sickness, human intimacy and companionship, and meaning in life. These needs are for the most part biologically derived, limited, and satiable. The art of economics entails recognizing those natural limits. *If we recognize these limits*, there will be enough to go around.

There are similarities to this economics in the biblical traditions, but with the decisive difference that whether there is enough for everyone depends completely on the presence of God's "righteousness." The word *righteousness* has to be redeemed from its moralistic overtones. It is the key word of the biblical traditions. Righteousness is the power by which God creates, nurtures, judges, and creates anew. Righteousness is the power by which God creates justice, without which the humanness of life is aborted. Is there not an Ariadne's thread running throughout the biblical traditions with a twofold assumption: If God's justice is present and embraced, there will be enough to go around. If God's justice is denied, scarcity leads to the systems of death. Thus the premise of God's economics—the distribution of what is necessary for life in the creation—its righteousness: God's power for life.

In his book *The Land* (Fortress, 1977), Walter Brueggman has traced these most basic assumptions of biblical faith through the various traditions. Over and over again it becomes clear that the crucial issue is not how many goods are present, but whether the righteousness of God is present. This is so because the righteousness of God destroys scarcity. The righteousness of God brings the manna in the wilderness; there is enough. The pretense of scarcity is not tolerated as the starting point for economics. The righteousness of God creates the justice which enables 5,000 people to share five loaves and two fishes; there is enough. Even in poverty, there is enough *if* the righteousness of God is present. Persons can then share their poverty. If the righteousness of God is not present, then poverty is hell and people are subjected to death. In that case, some people are poor because others are rich.

Of course there are shortages and limits to plenty in nature. Oil, coal, pure water, arable land, and food are limited (though their limits have always had everything to do with the unjust use of the creation by human beings). But I think we have to be wary of the arguments about physical limits and material scarcity. Do not these ideological arguments used by the economic powers lead to strange solutions of allocation? Since 1973 this has become a standard ploy of the energy corporations. The shrewdness of our faith should prompt us immediately to ask what kind of economics is being constructed on the assumption of such arguments about scarcity. For in general the biblical faith teaches us that there is always enough, *if* the righteousness of God is present and acknowledged as the source of life.

The biblical traditions are in fact aware that the severest economic problems come not when there is scarcity but when there is plenty. The history of modern economics is a history of increasing determination not by human needs but by human wants. With Adam Smith, "consumption becomes the sole end and purpose of all production." The motives for the acquisition of goods are not needs but wants. Psychology replaces biology as the basis of satisfaction. We move from an economics of production for human needs to an economics of consumption for spiritualized human wants.

As has long been recognized, the main problems of capitalism come when it produces a superabundance. Karl Marx thought the creation of an abundance was the great accomplishment of capitalism on which socialism could be built. When industry and technology produce enough for everybody and thereby remove scarcity, then and only then is it possible to create economic justice for all. Like all great "capitalists," Marx believed deeply in scarcity as the greatest evil of the world but also as the surest presupposition of economics. Once the scarcity of physical goods is eliminated and there is enough to go around, then society can struggle for economic justice. But Marx was naive in not being able to see the infinite potential of the human spirit for sin, that is, the ability of the human spirit to create spiritualized, artificial scarcity in the midst of plenty.

THE CREATION OF SCARCITY

The urgent problem of modern economics has always been how to make people work when there is already enough. To solve this problem the spirit of our society has created artificial scarcity. It has created the insatiable human spirit. It is this spirit which feeds the blind compulsion to growth, increase, and success that has a death grip on our society. Many economists today believe that the economic contradictions—unemployment, inflation, defense economy, and other death-serving systems—that are fast closing off the future of our society, have to do with this compulsion to growth. I believe the transformation of church and world in our time depends on the conflict between modes of artifical scarcity and the Holy Spirit, who destroys all our attempts to build economics on scarcity.

There are at least three ways our society tries to create artificial scarcity in order to make people work and to feed the compulsion to growth and increase. For those who stand to gain an ever greater share of the profit and product, work itself can be spiritualized and thus be used to create artificially a sense of scarcity. Work becomes the criterion of what it means to be human. The definition of sickness in our society is not being able to work. The definition of deviancy in our society is refusing to work. If we really believe that we become free and human through work, then the result will be that we cannot work enough. The full meaning of *being* a human being is held to be scarce, unattainable except by those who *earn* meaning through work. And thus is born our lust after work as an end in itself.

But in reality work is never an end in itself: it always produces advantages. Therefore work can be used as the primary way of deciding who will get the allegedly scarce resources. The just principle of distribution then reads: To each according to his or her work, effort, and achievement. One's work thus becomes a justification for one's unequal share of the goods and a way of assuaging one's guilt for having more than others. But because work in the end always fails at the triple task of giving freedom, life, and self-justification, there will be a compulsion to make at least some people guilty and undeserving by nature. Thus the spiritualized work of our economic ethos intensifies racism and the hatred of the poor, just as feudalism intensified the caste system.

The presence of the Holy Spirit brings an end to this form of artificial scarcity. In the presence of the Holy Spirit all we can do is confess the abundance, the richness, the fullness of God's righteousness. The Holy Spirit makes it clear that no one can become human and be justified through work. To be human and to live abundantly is exclusively the gift of God's grace, of which there is no lack. Whenever we acknowledge the presence of the Holy Spirit, there is a deep crisis for us and for our society: we cannot justify ourselves through work and thus work is thoroughly despiritualized. There is no scarcity of what it takes to be human. The gift of God's life to all God's creatures is full, plenipotent, and abundant. And, what is more, God the Holy Spirit gives us the power to do the unthinkable, namely, to accept this gift and become a human being. Despiritualized work will thus be a response to the abundance of God's grace. It will not be an end in itself, but will be a servant, in every sense, of the abundance of life. There is no way to the kingdom of freedom through the kingdom of work. That is why it is that for us the Sabbath comes on the first day of the week as the precondition of work, not on the last day of the week as recuperation from work.

It is a tougher problem to make those people work who do not stand to gain a proportionately greater share of the profit. For these people our economic ethos has developed the system of debt. Even though you are not inclined to work when your family already has enough to eat, if you are in debt and live under laws that will totally restrict your freedom if you are not working to get out of debt, you can be counted on to come to work tomorrow morning.

We live in a debt society. In order to create such a system of debt, we have to spiritualize both money and commodities. We have to convince people that if they do not possess certain products, they are not fully human. And thus a deep sense of scarcity is instilled in the minds and hearts of people through the media and their daily experiences. To want more is a sign that you are alive and valuable. Is it not, quite frankly, impossible to sell any product today if it is not more than you need? Shaving cream has to be "great balls of comfort" or it will not satisfy the sense of scarcity for which consumption is the messianic message of salvation.

Paul wrote to people in the early church at Corinth who were obsessed with becoming ever more rich in spiritualized things and spiritualized human relationships. Paul's message was, "You are already filled. Already you are rich" (I Cor. 4:8). But this *pleroma*, this fullness, has come from "the Spirit who is from God" (2:12), not from the spirit of the world. This fullness and abundance we have from God is nothing other than the power of his suffering love in the cross. To participate in the Spirit, to be in the Spirit, is to be filled with the power to suffer with others and their needs. I believe a faithful future of the churches of which we are a part depends upon the Holy Spirit making plain to us that the abundance of God's love destroys the scarcity we try to create with our spiritualized love of things.

LOSS AND GAIN

This, of course, does not mean that human suffering and human yearning end. In fact, it is the fullness of God's grace among us in the Holy Spirit that makes us yearn, together with the whole creation, for the completion of God's righteousness in everything. We in the North American churches will yearn for God's righteouness, and that means we will relinquish our superfluous store of life's necessities to those whose life needs are not met, when we realize that God really has filled us with the gifts of God's love for life. It is not a loss to give up a sense of artificial scarcity and thus our lusts after the empty promises of fulfillment. It is not a loss; it is the joyful and free embrace of life.

The spiritualization of work and money as a way of forcing work and growth constantly breaks down as we move from a society of production to a society of consumption. The more affluent a society becomes, the more difficult it is to create notions of scarcity on the basis of work or money. Are there other artificial scarcities? According to Philip Slater in *The Pursuit of Loneliness* (Beacon, 1971), society has discovered that sexuality can be used as an almost universal means of creating in human beings an artificial sense of scarcity. Our society has spiritualized sex so that it becomes ahistorical and unrealizable. If spiritualized images of sex are presented often enough as objects which must be attained in order to be really alive, people will feel a constant emptiness in their lives, a scarcity, a gnawing void that keeps them unsatisfied and constantly involved in competitive work and consumptive pleasure to fill that void.

Fred Hirsch has identified another motivating idol in his important book *Social Limits to Growth* (Harvard, 1977). He argues that the more the basic material needs of most of our population are met, the more intense becomes the competition for what he calls "positional goods," which include top jobs, mobility, recreation, education, services, and leisure. The irony is that as more and more people gain access to these things, the less and less satisfying they are. People react by trying to make them more scarce by making them more expensive and more exclusive. This raises year by year the destructive competition for positional goods and lowers the ability of human beings to live together in community, in genuine presence to each other. Society becomes less and less a public household, more and more an arena of frantic competition filled with painful frustration.

The presence and power of the Holy Spirit remove the insatiable hunger after possession and consumption by removing even the most spiritualized sense of scarcity. In this sense the Holy Spirit is the power of the ecclesial revolution of which I have spoken. The Holy Spirit does not remove every hunger. Rather the Holy Spirit transforms every hunger into the hunger for righteousness (Mt. 5:6) and thus creates persons who can give themselves away and relinquish what others need in order to live.

Nothing is more urgent today than an openness to the Holy Spirit who yearns and suffers for the transformation of the church and the formation of a just world. The Holy Spirit criticizes and yearns to free us from our notions of God which make the self an isolated property or a historical spirit animated by a spiritualized world or a compulsive competitor after scarce goods. The Holy Spirit brings righteousness as the condition of life. The Holy Spirit is the bountiful presence of God's power for transforming us and the church so that we may participate in the just formation of the world. And thus does the Spirit teach us that it is of the church that we must speak as soon as there is a question of the relevance of Christianity.

Chapter 57

Canadian Conference
of Catholic Bishops

Ethical Reflections
on the Economic Crisis

As the New Year begins, we wish to share some ethical reflections on the critical issues facing the Canadian economy.

In recent years the Catholic Church has become increasingly concerned about the scourge of unemployment that plagues our society today and the corresponding struggles of workers in this country. A number of pastoral statements and social projects have been launched by church groups in national, regional, and local communities as a response to various aspects of the emerging economic crisis.[1] On this occasion we wish to make some brief comments on the immediate economic and social problems, followed by some brief observations on the deeper social and ethical issues at stake in developing future economic strategies.

As pastors, our concerns about the economy are not based on any specific political options. Instead, they are inspired by the gospel message of Jesus Christ. In particular we cite two fundamental gospel principles that underlie our concerns.

The first principle has to do with the preferential option for the poor, the afflicted, and the oppressed. In the tradition of the prophets, Jesus dedicated his ministry to bringing "good news to the poor" and "liberty to the oppressed."[2] As Christians, we are called to follow Jesus by identifying with the victims of injustice, by analyzing the dominant attitudes and structures that cause human suffering, and by actively supporting the poor and oppressed in their struggles to transform society. For, as Jesus declared, "when you did it unto these, the least of my brethren, you did it unto me."[3]

The second principle concerns the special value and dignity of human work in God's plan for Creation.[4] It is through the activity of work that people are able to exercise their creative spirit, realize their human dignity, and share in Creation. By interacting with fellow workers in a common task, men and women have an opportunity to further develop their personalities and sense of self-worth. In so doing, people participate in the development of their society and give meaning to their existence as human beings.[5] Indeed, the importance of human labor is illustrated in the life of Jesus, who was himself a worker, "a craftsman like Joseph of Nazareth."[6]

It is from the perspective of these basic gospel principles that we wish to share our reflections on the current economic crisis. Along with most people in Canada today we realize that our economy is in serious trouble. In our own regions we have seen the economic realities of plant shut-downs, massive layoffs of workers, wage-restraint programs, and suspension of collective bargaining rights for public-sector workers. At the same time we have seen the social realities of abandoned one-industry towns, depleting unemployment insurance benefits, cutbacks in health and social services, and line-ups at local soup kitchens. And we have also witnessed firsthand the results of a troubled economy: personal tragedies, emotional strain, loss of human dignity, family breakdown, and even suicide.

Indeed, we recognize that serious economic challenges lie ahead for this country. If our society is going to face up to these challenges, people must meet and work together as a "true community" with vision and courage. In developing strategies for economic recovery, we firmly believe that first priority must be given to the real victims of the current recession, namely—the unemployed, the welfare poor, the working poor—pensioners, native peoples, women, young people—and small farmers, fishermen, some factory workers and some small business men and women. This option calls for economic policies which realize that the needs of the poor have priority over the wants of the rich, that the rights of workers are more important than the maximization of profits, that the participation of marginalized groups has precedence over the preservation of a system which excludes them.

In response to current economic problems we suggest that priority be given to the following short-term strategies by both government and business.

First, unemployment rather than inflation should be recognized as the number one problem to be tackled in overcoming the present crisis. The fact that some 1.5 million people are jobless constitutes a serious moral as well as economic crisis in this country. While efforts should continually be made to curb wasteful spending, it is imperative that primary emphasis be placed on combating unemployment.

Second, an industrial strategy should be developed to create permanent and meaning-ful jobs for people in local communities. To be effective, such a strategy should be designed for both national and regional levels. It should include emphasis on increased production, creation of new labor-intensive industries for basic needs, and measures to ensure job security for workers.

Third, a more balanced and equitable program should be developed for reducing and stemming the rate of inflation. This requires shifting the burden of wage controls to upper income earners, and introducing controls on prices and new forms of taxes on investment income (e.g., dividends, interest).

Fourth, greater emphasis should be given to the goal of social responsibility in the current recession. This means that every effort must be made to curtail cutbacks in social services, maintain adequate health care and social security benefits, and above all, guarantee special assistance for the unemployed, welfare recipients, the working poor, and one-industry towns suffering from plant shutdowns.

Fifth, labor unions should be asked to play a more decisive and responsible role in developing strategies for economic recovery and employment. This requires the restoration of collective bargaining rights where they have been suspended, collaboration between unions and the unemployed and unorganized workers, and assurances that labor unions will have an effective role in developing economic policies.

Furthermore, all people of good will in local and regional communities throughout the country must be encouraged to coordinate their efforts to develop and implement such strategies. As a step in this direction, we again call on local Christian communities to become actively involved in the six-point plan of action outlined in the message of the Canadian bishops on "Unemployment: The Human Costs."[7]

We recognize that these proposals run counter to some current policies or strategies advanced by both governments and corporations. We are also aware of the limited perspectives and excessive demands of some labor unions. To be certain, the issues are complex; there are no simple or magical solutions. Yet from the standpoint of the church's social teachings,[8] we firmly believe that present economic realities reveal a "moral disorder" in our society. As pastors, we have a responsibility to raise some of the fundamental social and ethical issues pertaining to the economic order. In so doing, we expect that there will be considerable discussion and debate within the Christian community itself on these issues. Indeed we hope that the following reflections will help to explain our concerns and contribute to the current public debate about the economy.

ECONOMIC CRISIS

The present recession appears to be symptomatic of a much larger structural crisis in the international system of capitalism. Observers point out that profound changes are taking place in the structure of both capital and technology which are bound to have serious social impacts on labor.[9] We are now in an age, for example, where transnational corporations and banks can move capital from one country to another in order to take advantage of cheaper labor conditions, lower taxes, and reduced environmental restrictions. We are also in an age of automation and computers where human work is rapidly being replaced by machines on the assembly line and in administrative centers. In effect, capital has become transnational and technology has become increasingly capital intensive. The consequences are likely to be permanent or structural unemployment and increasing marginalization for a large segment of the population in Canada and other countries. [10] In this context the increasing concentration of capital and technology in the production of military armaments further intensifies this economic crisis, rather than bringing about recovery.[11]

Indeed these structural changes largely explain the nature of the current economic recession at home and throughout the world.[12] While there does not appear to be a global shortage of capital per se, large-scale banks and corporations continue to wait for a more profitable investment climate. Many companies are also experiencing a temporary shortage of investment funds required for the new technology, due largely to an overextension of production and related factors. In order to restore profit margins needed for new investment, companies are cutting back on production, laying off workers, and selling off their inventories. The result has been economic slowdown and soaring unemployment. To stimulate economic growth, governments are being called upon to provide a more favorable climate for private investments. Since capital tends to flow wherever the returns are greatest, reduced labor costs and lower taxes are required if countries are to remain competitive. As a result, most governments are introducing austerity measures such as wage-restraint programs, cutbacks in social services, and other reductions in social spending in order to attract more private investment. And to enforce such economic policies some countries have introduced repressive measures for restraining civil liberties and controlling social unrest.

MORAL CRISIS

The current structural changes in the global economy, in turn, reveal a deepening moral crisis. Through these structural changes "capital" is re-asserted as the dominant organizing principle of economic life. This orientation directly contradicts the ethical principle that labor, not capital, must be given priority in the development of an economy based on justice.[13] There is, in other words, an ethical order in which human labor, the subject of production, takes precedence over capital and technology. This is the priority of labor principle. By placing greater importance on the accumulation of profits and machines than on the people who work in a given economy, the value, meaning, and dignity of human labor are violated. By creating conditions for permanent unemployment, an increasingly large segment of the population is threatened with the loss of human dignity. In effect, there is a tendency for people to be treated as an impersonal force having little or no significance beyond their economic purpose in the system.[14] As long as technology and capital are not harnessed by society to serve basic human needs, they are likely to become an enemy rather than an ally in the development of peoples.[15]

In addition, the renewed emphasis on the "survival of the fittest" as the supreme law of economics is likely to increase the domination of the weak by the strong, both at home and abroad. The "survival of the fittest" theory has often been used to rationalize the increasing concentration of wealth and power in the hands of a few.[16] The strong survive, the weak are eliminated. Under conditions of "tough competition" in international markets for capital and trade, the poor majority of the world is especially vulnerable. With three-fourths of the world's population, for example, the poor nations of the South are already expected to survive on less than one-fifth of the world's income. Within Canada itself the top 20 percent of the population receive 42.5 percent of total personal income while the bottom 20 percent receive 4.1 percent.[17] These patterns of domination and inequality are likely to further intensify as the "survival of the fittest" doctrine is applied more rigorously to the economic order. While these Darwinian theories aptly explain the rules that govern the animal world, they are in our view morally unacceptable as a "rule of life" for the human community.

PRESENT STRATEGIES

There is a very real danger that these same structural and moral problems are present in Canada's strategies for economic recovery. As recent economic policy statements reveal, the primary objective is to restore profitability and competitiveness in certain Canadian industries and provide more favorable conditions for private investment in the country.[18] The private sector is to be the "engine" for economic recovery. To achieve these goals, inflation is put forth as the number one problem. The causes of inflation are seen as workers' wages, government spending, and low productivity, rather than monopoly control of prices. The means for curbing inflation are such austerity measures as the federal 6 and 5 wage-restraint program and cutbacks in social spending (e.g., hospitals, medicare, public services, education, and foreign aid), rather than controls on profits and prices.[19] These measures, in turn, have been strengthened by a series of corporate tax reductions and direct investment incentives for such sectors as the petroleum industry. In effect, the survival of capital takes priority over labor in present strategies for economic recovery.

At the same time working people, the unemployed, young people, and those on fixed incomes are increasingly called upon to make the most sacrifices for economic recovery. For it is these people who suffer most from layoffs, wage restraints, and cutbacks in social services. The recent tax changes, which have the effect of raising taxes for working people and lowering them for the wealthy, add to this burden. And these conditions, in turn, are reinforced by the existence of large-scale unemployment, which tends to generate a climate of social fear and passive acceptance. Moreover, the federal and provincial wage-control programs are inequitable, imposing the same control rate on lower incomes as on upper incomes.[20]

If successfully implemented, these programs could also have the effect of transferring income from wages to profits.[21] Yet there are no clear reasons to believe that working people will ever really benefit from these and other sacrifices they are called to make. For even if companies recover and increase their profit margins, the additional revenues are likely to be re-invested in some labor-saving technology, exported to other countries, or spent on market speculation or luxury goods.

ALTERNATIVE APPROACHES

An alternative approach calls for a re-ordering of values and priorities in our economic life. What is required first is a basic shift in values. The goal of serving the human needs of all people in our society must take precedence over the maximization of profits and growth, and priority must be given to the dignity of human labor, not machines.[22] From this perspective, economic policies that focus primary attention on inflation and treat soaring unemployment as an inevitable problem clearly violate these basic ethical values and priorities. There is nothing "normal" or "natural" about present unemployment rates. Indeed massive unemployment, which deprives people of the dignity of human work and an adequate family income, constitutes a social evil. It is also a major economic problem since high unemployment rates are accompanied by lower productivity, lower consumption of products, reduced public revenues, and increasing social welfare costs. Thus alternative strategies are required which place primary emphasis on the goals of combating unemployment by stimulating production and permanent job creation in basic industries; developing a more balanced and equitable program for curbing inflation; and maintaining health care, social security, and special assistance programs.

An alternative approach also requires that serious attention be given to the development of new industrial strategies.[23] In recent years people have begun to raise serious questions about the desirability of economic strategies based on megaprojects wherein large amounts of capital are invested in high-technology resource developments (e.g., large-scale nuclear plants, pipelines, hydroelectric projects). Such megaprojects may increase economic growth and profits, but they generally end up producing relatively few permanent jobs while adding to a large national debt.

In our view it is important to increase the self-sufficiency of Canada's industries, to strengthen manufacturing and construction industries, to create new job-producing industries in local communities, to redistribute capital for industrial development in underdeveloped regions, and to provide relevant job training programs.[24] It is imperative that such strategies, wherever possible, be developed on a regional basis and that labor unions and community organizations be effectively involved in their design and implementation.

NEW DIRECTIONS

In order to implement these alternatives there is a need for people to take a closer look at the industrial vision and economic model that govern our society.[25] Indeed it is becoming more evident that an industrial future is already planned by governments and corporations. According to this industrial vision, we are now preparing to move into the high-technology computer age of the 1990s.[26] In order to become more competitive in world markets, the strategy for the '80s is to retool Canadian industries with new technologies, create new forms of high-tech industries (e.g., micro-electronic, petro-chemical, nuclear industries), and phase out many labor-intensive industries (e.g., textile, clothing, and footwear industries). This industrial vision, in turn, is to be realized through an economic model of development that is primarily capital-intensive (using less and less human labor), energy-intensive (requiring more non-renewable energy sources), foreign controlled (orienting development priorities to external interests), and export oriented (providing resources or products for markets elsewhere rather than serving basic needs of people in this country).

There are, of course, alternative ways of looking at our industrial future and organizing our economy. This does not imply a halt to technological progress, but rather a fundamental re-ordering of the basic values and priorities of economic development. An alternative economic vision, for example, could place priorities on serving the basic needs of all people in this country, on the value of human labor, and an equitable distribution of wealth and power among people and regions.

What would it mean to develop an alternative economic model that would place emphasis on socially useful forms of production; labor-intensive industries; the use of appropriate forms of technology; self-reliant models of economic development; community ownership and control of industries; new forms of worker management and ownership; and greater use of renewable energy sources in industrial production? As a country we have the resources, the capital, the technology, and above all else, the aspirations and skills of working men and women required to build an alternative economic future. Yet the people of this country have seldom been challenged to envision and develop alternatives to the dominant economic model that governs our society.

At the outset we agreed that people must indeed meet and work together as a "true community" in the face of the current economic crisis.[27] Yet in order to forge a true community out of the present crisis, people must have a chance to choose their economic future rather than have one forced upon them. What is required, in our judgment, is a real public debate about economic visions and industrial strategies involving choices about values and priorities for the future direction of this country. Across our society there are working and non-working people in communities—factory workers, farmers, forestry workers, miners, people on welfare, fishermen, native peoples, public service workers, and many others—who have a creative and dynamic contribution to make in shaping the economic future of our society. It is essential that serious attention be given to their concerns and proposals if the seeds of trust are to be sown for the development of a true community and a new economic order.

For our part, we will do whatever we can to stimulate public dialogue about alternative visions and strategies. More specifically we urge local parishes or Christian communities, wherever possible, to organize public forums for discussion and debate on major issues of economic justice. Such events could provide a significant opportunity for people to discuss: a) specific struggles of workers, the poor, and the unemployed in local communities; b) analysis of local and regional economic problems and structures; c) major ethical principles of economic life in the church's recent social teachings; d) suggestions for alternative economic visions; e) new proposals for industrial strategies that reflect basic ethical principles. In some communities and regions Christian groups, in collaboration with other concerned groups, have already launched similar events or activities for economic justice. And we encourage them to continue doing so.

Indeed, we hope and pray that more people will join in this search for alternative economic visions and strategies. For the present economic crisis, as we have seen, reveals a deepening moral disorder in the values and priorities of our society. We believe that the cries of the poor and the powerless are the voice of Christ, the Lord of history, in our midst. As Christians, we are called to become involved in struggles for economic justice and participate in the building up of a new society based on gospel principles. In so doing, we fulfill our vocation as a pilgrim people on earth, participating in Creation and preparing for the coming kingdom.

GUIDELINES FOR STUDY AND ACTION[28]

The long-range task of developing alternative industrial strategies requires study and action by people of good will in local and regional communities throughout this country. As a step in this direction we encourage more local Christian communities to become involved in a process of:

1. Becoming aware of the local realities and experiences of unemployment. This includes being present with unemployed workers, listening to their problems, and identifying current and future job needs in your region.

2. Analyzing the basic causes of unemployment in your region. This includes some reflection on the structural causes of unemployment to be found in our present economy, which were noted above.

3. Making some ethical judgments about the realities and causes of unemployment. This includes some reflection and education on the Christian meaning of human labor and the primary goal of an economic order as serving human needs (in parishes, families, schools, and community groups).

4. Supporting the specific struggles of unemployed workers in your region. This includes moral and financial support for activities aimed at creating new jobs, obtaining job security for workers, planning shorter work weeks, and generating public awareness about the realities and causes of unemployment.

5. Participating in efforts to develop alternative industrial strategies in your region. This includes assessing the economic potential of your region, developing alternative plans for economic development, and pressing local governments and corporations to change their priorities and industrial strategies.

6. Increasing community ownership and control of industries where desirable. This includes the promotion of cooperatives, worker-controlled industries, and other initiatives to develop more effective community participation and control of economic life in your region.

NOTES

1. Among more recent pastoral statements, see Episcopal Commission for Social Affairs, "Unemployment: The Human Costs" (Canadian Conference of Catholic Bishops, 1980); Comité des affaires sociales, "Luttes de travailleurs en temps de crise" (Assemblée des évêques du Québec, 1982). For an ethical reflection on the economic crisis in France, see the statement of the bishops of France, "Pour de nouveaux modes de vie: Déclaration du Conseil permanent de l'Episcopat sur la conjoncture économique et sociale" (1982).

2. Lk. 4:16–19; 7:22; Mt. 11:4–6.

3. Mt. 25:40.

4. John Paul II, *Laborem Exercens,* 4,6,9,24,25,26.

5. "Unemployment," 5.

6. *Laborem Exercens,* 26.

7. "Unemployment," 15.

8. See, e.g., John Paul II, *Laborem Exercens,* 1981; *Redemptor Hominis,* 1979; Paul VI, *Octogesima Adveniens,* 1971; *Populorum Progressio,* 1967; World Synod of Bishops, *Justice in the World,* 1971.

9. See, e.g., A. G. Frank, *Crisis in the World Economy* (New York, Holmes and Meier, 1980);

Samik Amin et al., *La crise, quelle crise? Dynamique de la crise mondiale* (Paris, Maspero, 1982); S. Rousseau, *Capitalism and Catastrophe: A Critical Appraisal of the Limits to Capitalism* (Cambridge [Mass.] University Press, 1979); *Social Analysis: Linking Faith and Justice* (Washington, D.C., Center of Concern); *La crise économique et sa gestion: Actes du colloque de l'Association d'économie politique, tenue a l'université du Québec à Montréal* (Montreal, Boreal Express, 1982); Cy Gonick, *Inflation or Depression: An Analysis of the Continuing Crisis in the Canadian Economy* (Toronto, Lorimer, 1975).

10. See, e.g., forecasts of the Conference Board of Canada, Nov. 1982. Their forecasts predict moderate recovery with greater unemployment. (With forecasts of economic recovery for 1983 and 1984, unemployment is forecast at 12.7% for 1983 and 11.4% for 1984.)

11. Observers point out that the highly capital-intensive nature of modern weapons manufacture creates a more rapid rate of technological obsolescence of fixed capital and thus leads to greater inflationary pressures and higher unemployment. See M. Kaldor, "The Role of Military Technology in Industrial Development" (U.N. Group of Government Experts on the Relationship of Disarmament and Development, May 1980). For a more extensive analysis of this question, see A. Eide and M. Thee, eds., *Problems of Contemporary Militarism* (London, 1980).

12. See e.g., *La crise économique et sa gestion,* part 1, "La crise actuelle des sociétées capitalistes."

13. *Laborem Exercens,* 12, on the "priority of labor." For a commentary see G. Baum, *The Priority of Labor* (New York, Paulist Press, 1982).

14. *Laborem Exercens,* 13, particularly comments on the error of "economism" and "materialism."

15. *Laborem Exercens,* 5.

16. See CCCB, "A Society to Be Transformed," 1977; *Populorum Progressio,* 33 and 57.

17. For analysis of global disparities, see Brandt Commission Report, *North-South: A Program for Survival,* 1980. For data on disparities in Canada, see *Statistics Canada,* 1980. For more extended analysis, see J. Harp and J. R. Hofley, eds., *Structured Inequality in Canada* (Scarborough, Prentice-Hall, 1980).

18. See the budget statements of the Hon. Alan MacEachen, Nov. 1981 and June 28, 1982, plus the statement on the economy by the Hon. Marc Lalonde, Oct. 29, 1982.

19. See budget statements of the Hon. Alan MacEachen, June 28, 1982. Finance Department officials have stated that the 6 and 5 program will have the "unintended effect of transferring income from wages to profits" (Toronto, *Globe and Mail,* Aug. 28, 1982).

20. It should be noted that: 1) people earning $18,000 who can least afford reductions in their incomes below the inflation rate are subjected to the same rate of control as people earning $50,000 salaries or more, who could afford an income freeze; 2) it is estimated that approximately 30% of the total net national income generated in Canada (1980) came in the form of dividends, interest, and other investment income rather than wages and salaries which are subject to controls.

21. See concerns expressed by the Canadian Labor Congress in their "Statement on Economic Policy," July 8, 1982. For a further perspective, see "Wage Controls Won't Work," *The Public Employee,* Fall 1982. See also the report of the Confédération des syndicats nationaux (CSN), "Du travail pour tout le monde," Feb. 1982.

22. See "Unemployment," 12.

23. See "Unemployment," 9, 14.

24. For examples of proposed industrial strategies, see Canadian Labor Congress, Economic Policy Statement, May 1982. See also the proposals of the Confédération des syndicats nationaux, *La Presse,* Nov. 18, 1982.

25. As an example of thinking about alternative directions, see W. Wagerman, *Christians and the Great Economic Debate* (London, SCM, 1977).

26. See, e.g., the following Science Council of Canada Reports: "The Weakest Link: A Technological Perspective on Canadian Industrial Underdevelopment"; "Forging the Links: A Technological Policy for Canada"; "Hard Times-Hard Choices: Technology and the Balance of Payments."

27. For references to "true community," See Rt. Hon. Pierre E. Trudeau, *Statements on the Economy,* parts 1 and 3.

28. Excerpted from "Unemployment: The Human Costs."

Chapter 58

Jordan Bishop

Episcopal Economics

A Controversy in Canada

Two years ago the Canadian Bishops' Commission for Social Affairs published a statement entitled "Unemployment: The Social Costs." This statement, in the measured and moderate tones which often characterize official statements from the hierarchy, passed for all practical purposes unnoticed. At the end of 1982 the same Commission released another statement, entitled "Ethical Reflections on the Economic Crisis." Embargoed for January 5, 1983, it provoked a major controversy even before it was officially published. The reaction to unofficial press leaks was immediate and virulent. Jean-Louis Roy, publisher of the Montreal daily *Le Devoir*, was appalled at the "simplism" of the statement, and said so in a lead editorial published January 4th. The Archbishop of Toronto, Cardinal Emmett Carter, expressed doubts as to certain ideas and attitudes reflected in the document. At the same time, Bishop Remi De Roo of Victoria, B.C., made it clear that the executive of the Canadian Council of Bishops had approved the controversial declaration.

In Ontario, provincial leaders of all three political parties (including the Liberals who are in opposition there) voiced approval of the position taken by the bishops. Federal Liberals, who rightly saw the paper as an attack on current governmental policy, either avoided making any statements or questioned the economics in the bishops' statement. The Hon. Marc Lalonde, Minister of Finance, said that he had no desire to get involved in a quarrel among bishops. Mr. Trudeau, the Prime Minister, who was in Asia promoting Canadian exports, dismissed the paper as the work of "five prelates" (there are in fact eight in the Commission) whose economics did not appear to be very serious. "The fox is in the chicken coop and I shall let the bishops pick at each other," he said. "I don't want to get involved in this conflict."

This, on the whole, was the line taken by the business establishment: the economics of the statement leave much to be desired. Having said this, none of them took the trouble to examine the economics that underlie the statement in any detail.

Perhaps more important, none of the critics appeared willing to tackle the main thrust of the statement. The Commission had in fact raised some questions that few people in business and governmental circles are prepared to debate publicly: these concern the

First published in *Commonweal*, 102 (February 25, 1983), pp. 104–5. Used by permission.

distribution of wealth in Canada and basic policy options in the management of the economy. In the opinion of the Bishops' Commission, "the current structural changes in the global economy . . . reveal a deepening moral crisis. Through these structural changes, 'capital' is re-asserted as the dominant organizing principle of economic life." Footnoting John Paul II's Encyclical *Laborem Exercens*, they went on to say that "This orientation directly contradicts the ethical principle that labor, not capital, must be given priority in the development of an economy based on justice."

John Stuart Mill, perhaps the last of the classical economists, had affirmed one hundred thirty years ago that while economics had to do with the production of wealth, distribution was a political question. And it is this political question which was addressed by the bishops. Reflecting the Puebla statement on the "preferential option for the poor," the statement proposed that "this option calls for economic policies which realize that the needs of the poor have priority over the wants of the rich; that the rights of workers are more important than the maximization of profits."

Here again, the business establishment was outraged. A number of business spokesmen appeared to assume that the statement amounted to a condemnation of profits as such. In fact, the paper had proposed controls on profits and said—following the well-established tradition of the papal encyclicals—that "the goal of serving the human needs of all people in our society must take precedence over the maximization of profits and growth." This merited a vigorous response from Marie-Josée Drouin of the Hudson Institute:

They forget that the control of profits is an instrument that takes away all incentive on the part of enterprises to control their costs of production and to reduce waste. Is it moral to encourage the waste of our resources? [Montreal, *Le Devoir*, Jan. 15, 1983].

Despite the universal condemnation of the economics of the statement from business and government spokesmen, the statement has not been attacked by serious independent professional economists. For the most part, they have remained silent. Professor John C. Weldon, of McGill University and a former president of the Canadian Association of Economists, said that the economics of the bishops' statement were "decidedly better than those of the last budget, and a full order of magnitude better than those of the recent reports of the Bank of Canada." Another McGill economist, Professor Sydney Ingerman, says that it is unthinkable that the unemployment of millions of people should be used as a policy tool to bring down inflation.

The aim of the statement was quite frankly to "stimulate public dialogue about alternative visions and strategies." In this the bishops appear to have succeeded. On January 27th the Canadian Center for Policy Alternatives hosted a meeting in Ottawa for the express purpose of discussing their statement. In addition to a number of professional economists involved in the Center for Policy Alternatives, members of the Bishops' Commission, labor leaders, and representatives of the Anglican, Lutheran, and United Churches took part in the meeting. Professor Ingerman described the meeting as a "historic event," marked by a profound sense of the importance of the issues and by a great deal of tolerance. For example, old rivals such as the Canadian Labor Conference and Quebec's CNTU sat down together for perhaps the first time. Participants agreed that there is in fact a crisis, not of the management of the economy as given, but in basic areas of public policy. While it is true that the CCPA, as an institution, is dedicated to a critical examination of current social and economic policy, it is remarkable that there was almost no dissent to the main positions taken by the

Bishops' Commission. One speaker did suggest that they may have understated the seriousness of the problem posed by the distribution of wealth in Canadian society—the bishops had cited figures on the distribution of *income* but had not taken on the larger question of the distribution of wealth. This may account for the fact that establishment spokesmen have studiously avoided comment on their critique of the distribution of income.

The statement has been widely criticized in business and establishment circles as being too forthright, too abrasive, too critical of governmental policy. When this objection was made to Bishop Remi De Roo of Victoria, he replied simply that public debate on these questions was urgent, and that the mild and measured statements made on past occasions had been widely ignored. This time they were not.

Chapter 59

Arthur Jones

The William Simon Committee: A Study in Preemption

[On November 8, 1984, a 29-member "lay commission" released the text of Toward the Future: Catholic Thought and the U.S. Economy, a Lay Letter. *The 120-page text had been drawn up after some sixty witnesses had been listened to at six public hearings. This procedure was designed to parallel the lengthier deliberations of the Ad Hoc Committee on Catholic Social Teaching and the U.S. Economy, of the Catholic bishops' national conference, which was to release the first draft of its study six days later (see chap. 60, below). The lay group was co-chaired by social theorist Michael Novak (see chap. 52, above) and former secretary of the treasury William Simon.]*

Toward the Future: Catholic Thought and the U.S. Economy, a Lay Letter, is the Catholic right's preemptive strike at the bishops' economic pastoral. . . .

This is the best that corporate capitalism's collective talent can do. If so, is it enough?

The letter opens by congratulating the bishops for summoning Americans to reflect on the U.S. economy, delves quickly into the origins of the American system, relies primarily on Pius XI (*Quadragesimo Anno*) and John Paul II (*Laborem Exercens*) for any outside comments/criticisms of the capitalist system, and raises interesting possibilities about American influence on Catholic thought.

However, a principal segment, "The Lay Task of Co-Creation," provides but two economic ideas, capitalist and socialist, and makes its way along the capitalist road. In so doing, *Toward the Future* lays bare the fibers of its own straw man not because the letter should have gone along the socialist road, but because the letter pretends this is an either/or situation.

Look at what is being intertwined:

". . . democratic institutions helped lead the church from opposition to openness to democratic principles." No difficulty exists with that, except the Lay Commission on Catholic Social Thought and the U.S. Economy which produced this "letter," calls its product "democratic capitalism," as if democracy and capitalism were the same. They are not shown to be so; it is doubtful they are.

Next. "Social justice is not a euphemism for collectivism. . . . Not all who cry 'social justice' speak for the genuine Catholic conception." But we are not treated to anyone

---

First published in *National Catholic Reporter*, November 16, 1984. Used by permission.

crying "social justice" in the last half-century—except in a paraphrased statement from John Paul II. Whose cries *ought* we to attend to?

No specific charges against capitalism or capitalist exploits are examined. This letter is a conversation between the writer and himself or herself.

". . . the virtues required for pluralistic, democratic, and capitalistic living, far from contradicting Catholic social thought, bring out from its treasure house new things and old. . . . Capitalist living requires a new emphasis on enterprise, invention, social cooperation, and habits of providence." Which? What? When? Where? Why? How? Who?

There is much about "social cooperation" here, nothing about economic cooperation. The cooperative movement does not live. Nothing modern is apparent. The leveraged buy-out (when senior managers buy out a generally publicly held corporation) or worker-ownership (each prime trends in the U.S. economy) are, like all other examples of real-life stuff, absent.

Instead, Jesuit Father John Courtney Murray is quoted: "In sheer point of fact, the church in America has accepted this thing which is the American economy." This was quite correct when Murray wrote it in 1960. But surely the "sheer point of fact" today is that the church in America does not accept the American economy the way it once did. And surely that is the precise point of the pastoral.

At this juncture, *Toward the Future* begins to get a bit deceptive. "Bad" capitalism has nothing to do with the United States; it's a European, continental aberration.

The letter quotes John Paul II as saying the "reversal" of (God's right) order in which (man) is treated as "an instrument of production . . . should rightly be called 'capitalism.' "

Not us, says the letter. "While Pope John Paul II clearly defines the term 'capitalism' in this way," states *Toward the Future*, "and while abuses of this sort do occur here, this is not the meaning of the term in the United States." The letter writers would have done a greater service to the debate underway by examining precisely those areas in the United States and U.S. Catholicism where capitalism is seen in this way.

Then, say the writers, "Pope John Paul II is clearly in favor of 'reformed' capitalism. Yet Catholic social thought needs to examine more carefully the institutional causes of economic creativity."

Whoa! Correct on both counts, but crafty. And this is but a single example of the way this letter slides past the issues. However, when John Paul II talks of reforming, as he did in Canada, he talks of reforming entire economic structures. The reform of capitalism he might have in mind could mean a final structure that might bear no resemblance to today's market economy.

The second point, which the letter does not wrestle with, is that Catholic social thought is now more concerned with examining the institutional causes, not of economic *creativity* (which is a vital topic), but of economic oppression, exploitation, and inequality.

Snippets, and a closing comment:

—"Capital and labor are both human." Agreed, but not to the same degree.

—"Many have come to see that economic activism is as much a vocation for lay Catholics as is political activism—indeed, much more so." Again, agreed. But that is not a license that favors any particular system. Indeed, the weight of the past century of Catholic teaching would favor cooperativism and distributivism over anything else.

—"The term 'capitalism' has negative connotations on the (European) continent which, except among those who approach these matters as socialists do, it does not have in America." One would have thought, looking at surveys that at least go back to the bicentennial period, that it was *because* American capitalism has accrued so many negative connotations deserving to be addressed that this lay commission would have taken advantage of the opportunity the pastoral has presented.

Despite the name change, this bishops' group started as a committee on capitalism. That is what was moved from the floor of the bishops' conference that initiated this process.

—"The aim of capitalism has been to overcome the tyranny of poverty." The aim of capitalism has not been to overcome the tyranny of poverty any more than the aim of capitalism has been to provide employment for the masses or to underpin democracy. The aim of capitalism has been, still is, and will be, to make money for those engaged in the original exploit or for those with money to invest in the continuation of that original exploit, the modern corporation. Everything else is tangential.

The issue before the bishops, the Catholics, and the other Americans who care about the economy and the corporate structure is whether the capitalist system and/or the capitalist corporate structure is morally inert, morally offensive, or morally redeemable.

Tyranny? When Standard Oil was selling petroleum to the Nazis, Nelson Rockefeller, to his everlasting credit, inserted a patriotic (nothing wrong with that) yet moral judgment into the morass. He provided the detailed information that enabled a blaze of publicity to cause Standard Oil to choose sides between the Allies and the Axis.

Those of us who are not opposed to the corporate structure needed this debate to examine the system and the corporations, choosing their "moral" side—between excess or maximized profits, if you will, and the common good or the option for the poor. That the lay commission has not touched on these central themes is entirely their choice, but nor have the writers given us anything remotely useful instead.

Capitalist activity—similar to all other human activities, as this letter constantly reiterates, in that it needs guidance—is capable of error and sin. Oh, for a letter that would have enabled us to face up to capitalism's error and sin. And then to marshal the strengths. One that could then have been counterbalanced (as we do our own sins and errors) with strengths and strong points—which the corporate structure has.

We all needed an honest and fearless and specific defense of what is good and what is possible within the system and the corporations as now structured and/or potentially structured.

The lay commission, to a large extent some of capitalism's most talented exponents, has thrown away these many opportunities with weasel words and Panglossian sentiment.

By making a preemptive strike—though the letter writers do not regard it as such—the lay commission now has no comeback.

How much better would the lay commission have served by risking waiting until the bishops released their first draft. Then they could have built a case, point by point, into the ensuing first-draft discussion.

The document is a crafty work. Capitalism by Candide?

Chapter 60

Kenneth Aman

From Another Quarter

New Jersey's Poor Respond to the Bishops' Pastoral

On November 14, 1984, the first draft of the pastoral letter "Catholic Social Teaching and the U.S. Economy" was issued by the National Conference of Catholic Bishops, Washington, D.C.

Northern New Jersey is probably as good a place as any to observe how that letter has been received. As a heavily industrial area, northern New Jersey has always had more than its share of blue-collar Catholics. In recent years, though, it has begun quietly to make a move as one of the newer concentrations of "yuppiedom." Several national columnists made this discovery in 1984 during the New Jersey presidential primaries. They devoted a number of paragraphs to the conversion of acres of farmland into gleaming new high-tech plants and corporate headquarters in places like Morris County and the area around Princeton. At the same time, New Jersey is perhaps better known for its leadership in such unpleasantries as the number of hazardous waste sites. Not to mention its cities, which have been at or near the top of poverty lists since the violent demonstrations of the late 1960s. (One should perhaps note that there have been considerable signs of gentrification in such places as Jersey City, Paterson, and even Newark as young middle-class whites seek relief from New York's daunting rents. Mayor Gerald McCann put himself solidly behind the rapid real estate development of Jersey City, and thought himself guaranteed of at least 60 percent of the votes in the 1985 mayoral election. But despite brass-knuckle tactics reminiscent of the old Frank Hague machine, a coalition of minorities and reformers succeeded in electing Anthony Cucci, one of the bigger upsets in recent New Jersey political history.)

There is no question that much of New Jersey is doing well—in fact somewhat better than the nation as a whole. And yet there is another part of New Jersey that is anything but pretty and also refuses to be completely forgotten. The bishops' letter on economics has given its representatives a chance to be heard; has in fact forced others to hear them.

But before the poor made themselves audible, another segment of Catholic New Jersey was very active. The "lay commission" that preempted the bishops' pastoral with

First published in *The Journal of Faith and Thought,* 3/2 Fall 1985. Used by permission.

its own letter (see chap. 59, above) was co-chaired by William Simon, former Secretary of the Treasury. Simon also happens to be chairman of Wesray corporation in Morristown, and is a resident of New Vernon, N.J. Immediately after the first draft of the pastoral was released, Catholic business leaders in New Jersey set up a number of meetings with Archbishop Gerrity (of Newark) and other church leaders. One notable meeting of New Jersey businessmen was attended by Gerrity, Archbishop Law of Boston, and Cardinal Bernardin of Chicago. The air of secrecy that clung to some of these meetings did not completely disguise the very real concern of many business leaders concerning the bishops' initiative.

The Archdiocesan Commission on Justice and Peace was asked in December to assist in getting feedback for the bishops of the Newark archdiocese. The commission decided to hold a series of hearings in strategic cities in the four counties that comprise the archdiocese, and a fifth hearing in Newark for the Spanish-speaking. Within the commission there was some discussion about trying to be sure that a cross section of attitudes was represented at the hearings. Commission members decided that they need not worry about the affluent receiving a hearing: they were already getting into print and appearing on television. Choosing appropriate sites was not much of a problem. Even Bergen County, despite its reputation as a home for the elite and the prosperous, has serious pockets of poverty, as the first hearing at Holy Trinity church in Hackensack showed. The vicar (an auxiliary bishop) for each county was invited to attend. Every vicar, including Bishop Arias, vicar for the Spanish-speaking, was there.

What these hearings demonstrated was the need for an instrument for the poor, or at least those who worked with the poor, to respond. The dates for the hearings ranged from January 7 to January 22; they managed to fall on the most bitterly cold nights of the winter. Instead of the dozen or so expected attendants, up to one hundred were present for a single hearing. Many of the speakers brought with them carefully prepared written statements to supplement their oral presentations. They spoke forcefully, even eloquently. And the secular press gave the hearings good coverage. Monica Maske of the *Newark Star Ledger,* for example, wrote half a dozen pieces on them, some of which were quite lengthy.

What did the urban poor of Hackensack, Jersey City, Elizabeth, and Newark have to say to and for the bishops? And who *are* these persons anyway?

To take the last question first, there was no difficulty getting witnesses to testify. Despite the limited time for setting up the hearings (two to three weeks), despite the fact that the time for organization corresponded roughly to the Christmas holiday, and despite the cold, enough persons wished to speak that each had to be strictly limited to ten minutes. A fair percentage represented agencies active in urban areas: shelters, soup kitchens, centers to place the unemployed, elementary schools, traditional churches. They demonstrate the existence of an underground or infrastructure in our cities that continues to fight for the unfortunate of our society, even when they, the activists, are not much noticed even by the churches. They are ecumenical, and this ecumenism extends beyond the churches and synagogues even to some who do not care much about religion any more, or perhaps never did.

The urban underground (one speaker called it a counterintelligence, working to offset prevailing myths about the poor) includes, among others, battle-scarred Jewish liberals, black Evangelical pastors, idealistic young persons intent on doing something practical, and a handful of rather tough nuns. As a group, they tend to be somewhat different from the activists of the 1960s. The issues they care most about are very local ones: getting more beds for the homeless; turning municipal and state bureaucracies around; tapping into the generous or guilty sentiments of suburbanites; helping someone get a good, inexpensive lawyer. They are by no means unaware of how these issues are related to the more global issues discussed by the bishops. On some themes of national interest, notably the growing militarization of our society, they go beyond the bishops. But the local, the here-and-now, is where they wish to begin and where they wish to end (in the sense of having an impact). They are also in this struggle for the long run. They have no illusions about what can be done dramatically and by a single gesture—even by an eloquent pastoral letter. They do not become discouraged easily. Or perhaps more accurately, one should say that if they become discouraged, they do not let that stop them.

What do they have to say? It is impossible here to give more than some of the flavor of the testimony found in the massive materials compiled by the commission.

If these witnesses are right, to be poor in America is worse today than it has ever been. Sister Norberta flatly and unemotionally describes what a medium-sized shelter runs into in Hoboken:

> Each night we were approximately 60 people for supper. During the month of December, 225 different people ate supper with us. That means 2,480 people had meals provided. 775 people found shelter with us. Over 155 volunteers helped us cook meals and wash dishes. There has not been one night that we have not turned people away from the shelter. I believe we could double the number if we were permitted.

According to David Burgess, director of the metropolitan ecumenical ministry in Newark, the situation is getting worse: "Since 1983, 51,000 families have lost their food stamps, 38,000 have been dropped from the Aid to Dependent Children rolls, and Newark's WIC program for mothers has been cut by over one million dollars." According to Thomas McKenna in Hackensack, the poor are largely invisible. Part of the reason for this is that they are inconvenient; they simply cannot make it in the new price structure accompanying the revival of our economy: "We send our poor to Passaic or Hudson or Essex because they can't afford to live here. Those who somehow manage to stay we don't see and therefore they don't exist. The fact is, however, the poor are among us as an invisible minority."

The frustration of those who work and live with the poor is palpable. "Local welfare for a single man or woman is at 127 dollars. I challenge anyone to find either food or shelter for 127 dollars." "The newest thing we have heard is that a person who is totally bedbound, who has no one else to care for them, we can give them homemaker service for three hours, three days a week. Nice! What are they supposed to do for the rest of the time?"

The poor themselves appear to be too much in pain to have energy left over for exasperation:

> On the first of the month, we give the best demonstration of inhuman dignity when the poor stand in lines that are blocks long to cash checks and to receive food stamps. And I wonder if there couldn't be a better system for distributing those checks to these people. Women have little babies and numerous children by the hand that are crying because they are tired and a lot of them are hungry. Why must we exploit the poor to this degree? . . . I wish somebody would say in answer to the famous question "Are we better off this year than we were last year?," will you please tell Mr. Reagan that Mrs. Lang said no [Mrs. Lang is

described by the documents of the hearings as an elderly black woman from Newark].

To the extent that these persons are aware of the bishops' pastoral, they have generally welcomed it. "The bishops' letter has particular relevance to this city" [Newark]. The pastoral is valuable precisely because it has a chance of being heard. It is described as "an eloquent voice." It is on the right track in calling for the opening up of our institutions to the participation of the poor. But the Reverend Dennis Jacobsen, a Lutheran pastor in Jersey City, probably spoke for many when he saw the primary value of the pastoral as confirming those who actually live among the cities' and country's poor. The real statement is "the sacrificial statement of those who confront injustice in the name of the poor." And for Jacobsen at least, the pastoral letter does not go far enough: "Its strategy quite simply does not call for elimination of poverty, but for its alleviation. The strategy offers no real critique of capitalism. I'm amazed that there have been indictments accusing the pastoral of being socialistic."

Are there any striking theological themes that can be drawn from these testimonies in behalf of the poor? Without any claim to profundity or completeness, I think a few can be discerned. I find them conveniently clustered within the area of ecclesiology.

First, the church of the advocates of the poor is both more tangible and less defined than our customary understanding. For them, *any* church of a particular neighborhood is an invaluable resource as well as a battle ground. These activists are quite uninterested in ethereal notions of the church that might unite them with persons of good will elsewhere, but at the same time have little or nothing to do with local needs. Meanwhile, old denominational differences seem to matter little. Protestants and Jews here take a proprietary interest in the concrete decisions and debates of the Catholic Church. One gets the impression that Catholics would respond similarly to initiatives taken by other church groups.

It is also clear that these activists associate the church with advocacy. They are acutely aware of the church's vocation to speak out. At the same time, they are well aware of the shortcomings of the church: of the coziness of ecclesiastical leaders with the economic establishment, of de facto racism in its decision-making, of its blindness to much of the reality of poverty. There is a tension between the church as they see it and the church as they would have it, but this tension seems to me not sterile but fruitful. It is born not of disillusionment but of a hope that the more positive elements in the church will overcome those that are cowardly or slothful or self-serving. There is also the important factor that the church is the only real hope for compassion in these demoralized cities. What other institution will stoop to listen, or is even capable of listening?

Finally, they wish to localize the church in a new and significant way. They are quite aware, perhaps more than the rest of us, of the interconnection between national and international issues on the one hand, and regional and neighborhood problems on the other. But if religion is to mean anything, it must address the concrete needs of the people, and these are always found on the local level. Contrast this new localism with earlier strong but perhaps narrowly exclusive loyalties to this particular church, or that particular congregation.

The pastoral is, then, an important stimulus for new kinds of religious reflection. This reflection is not coming merely from intellectual or religious leaders, but is welling up from below. As such, it reveals the continuing vitality of the American churches; perhaps more important, it offers evidence of an enduring American populism as tough as it is idealistic.

Chapter 61

Dorothee Sölle

Resurrection and Liberation

Last year I went to a conference of the Christians for Socialism in Italy. One evening I got into an argument with two participants, both priests. I felt offended by some of their remarks which seemed to me uncritical, anti-liberal, and anti-Protestant. Finally I asked them: "What exactly do you have against Protestantism?" They kept silent for a while, and then the older one, who came from a small village in southern Italy, said:

> You feel the same way we do about the trouble of being a Christian in the industrialized world. There is a certain incompatibility of Christianity and the modern world. We may easily agree about this. The problem, however, is with the solution you Protestants are offering. You've changed religion to make it compat-ible.

Instead of changing religion until it fits the modern world, what these priests want is to change the world until it fits the biblical view of human beings. Are they not right? I went back to review the years of my theological studies and readings. What essentially was done in Protestant faculties and churches was to adjust religion to the modern world. This world itself was seen as a given, so the task for the theologian was to modernize and shift the outdated religion.

It never came to us as students of theology to think the other way around; to change society until it fits better to the promise of the gospel and its vision of life. In this sense, we did not talk about alienation as a destructive social structure, as sin, but we talked about human rebellion against God. We shortened and reduced the biblical concreteness and accuracy about socio-economic realities. We did not take seriously the biblical talk about the rich and the poor. We spiritualized these notions or forgot them. Working people became invisible in theological circles; we did not know anything about their life conditions. We related sin to the rebellious personality, and we were not taught to think in collective categories. We cut off the concept of sin from our national history as Germans in the twentieth century, and we separated it neatly from our economy. We experienced alienation, but we ontologized it into an everlasting fate, given with human existence. Thus, we failed to call it "sin" and to face it in our society.

This section is reprinted with permission of Institute For A People's Church (P.O. Box 32214, Detroit, MI 48216). This section is Part III of *Beyond Mere Dialogue,* published originally by Christians for Socialism in the U.S. in 1978 and now available through the Institute For A People's Church.

We related the cross to the endurance of the suffering, lonely person. We cut it off from the struggle. Mother Jones says: "I learned in the early part of my career that labor must bear the cross for others' sins, must be the vicarious sufferer for the wrongs that others do." [Mother Jones was a legendary figure in the labor union movement of the early twentieth century—ED.] But we were caught up in academic theology, and we didn't even see the crosses around us. Finally, we thought about resurrection only as a life after death instead of believing in it here and now.

The emphasis was on seeing one's relatives again in the hereafter, on coming home after a long and troublesome journey, on resting in the evening after a hard workday. The old imagery was of the City of God with its golden gates. To walk freely and to speak of justice publicly was forgotten. The change of imagery reveals something about the reduction of a hope that once spoke inclusively and wholistically about this world in terms of the world to come, and now came to speak merely of an after-hope, which desires nothing but rest and peace.

Bourgeois culture thus changed religion instead of changing the world. We Protestants reduced the symbols of our religion and shrank them down to our selves, to our personalities. We used religious notions and symbols for one purpose: to serve the highest value of bourgeois culture—namely, individualism. The starting point of modern economic activity is the individual entrepreneur, and capitalism has managed to eliminate almost all forms of cooperative working and possession. Mainstream religion had to bless this process. Thus religion became a tool in the hands of the bourgeois class and functioned only to console the saddened, to enrich personal life, to give meaning to the individual. Sin became my personal failure, the cross was my unique suffering, and resurrection my individual immortality.

In order to understand what the forgotten resurrection means, let us listen once more to the teaching of the American working class. I am referring to a famous song about the labor organizer and song writer Joe Hill. In January 1914, Hill was arrested in Salt Lake City for alleged murder. Despite vigorous protests from politicians all over the world and public meetings in this country, he was finally executed in November 1919. The night before he was shot, a speaker at a protest meeting cried, "Joe Hill will never die." Twenty years later this song was written:

> I dreamed I saw Joe Hill last night
>   Alive as you and me.
> Says I, "But Joe, you're ten years dead."
>   "I never died," says he.
>   "I never died," says he.
>
> "In Salt Lake, Joe, by God," says I,
>   Him standing by my bed,
> "They framed you on a murder charge."
>   Says Joe, "But I ain't dead."
>   Says Joe, "But I ain't dead."
>
> "The copper bosses killed you, Joe,
>   They shot you, Joe," says I.
> "Takes more than guns to kill a man,"
>   Says Joe, "I didn't die."
>   Says Joe, "I didn't die."

And standing there as big as life
　　And smiling with his eyes,
Joe says, "What they forgot to kill
　　Went on to organize
　　Went on to organize."

"Joe Hill ain't dead," he says to me,
　　"Joe Hill ain't never died.
Where working men are out on strike
　　Joe Hill is at their side.
　　Joe Hill is at their side."

"From San Diego up to Maine
　　In every mine and mill,
Where workers strike and organize,"
　　Says he, "You'll find Joe Hill."
　　Says he, "You'll find Joe Hill."

I dreamed I saw Joe Hill last night
　　Alive as you and me.
Says I, "But Joe, you're ten years dead."
　　"I never died," says he.
　　"I never died," says he.[1]

I am going to share with you my theological understanding of resurrection, which originates in the biblical testimonies but is nourished and fed by other sources as well. I am trying to read the Bible in the light of Joe Hill who never died, and his brothers and sisters.

The Christian faith expresses itself most genuinely in telling the story of the resurrection. Christ has risen from the dead. This has been and is a message of life-changing power. It is the core of the Christian message. It speaks about the final reconciliation of the alienated life, about victory over death and injustice. It is the last liberation.

However, this power is veiled if we look at the resurrection of Christ in an exclusive way. To render the resurrection into Christ's exclusive privilege means to miss its meaning, which is inclusive. He has risen; therefore, we too will rise from death in which we are now. He has left death behind him, but the essence of this message does not end in itself. Otherwise we would fall into the theological mistake that Mary Daly excellently describes as "christolotry." To venerate Christ's resurrection without sharing it means to make an idol out of him.

Sometimes I feel that Christ today is more homeless in our churches than ever before because he finds worshipers there but no friends; admirers, but not followers. This is what we may learn from the song about Joe Hill: there is no worshiping, no admiration, no heroic idolatry. "I never died," says he. "I didn't die." Joe Hill lived on in his friends.

Resurrection as merely objective, as a brute fact, as something that would be true without us, does not make any sense. It is a theological reification under a positivist worldview. But believers in the Bible are as far from this christolatrist reification as the people who sang about Joe Hill. Joe Hill alone, he in himself, he *a se*—to use a scholastic theological term—is dead. If individualism is the ultimate and deepest category for human beings, then we cannot understand what resurrection is all about. The anthropological point, however, is that there is no such thing as he alone, he in himself, he *a se*. We are a part of Jesus Christ, he belongs to our human existence, which is to be defined not by the borderline of our bodies, or by the uniqueness of our personalities, but by our social relationships. Human beings are defined more by their relationships than by their substance. Our being is a living relationship to others, based on mutual aid and furnished with an elementary need for communication. It is only in the capitalistic view of humanity that we become reduced to monads, whose relationship to the world does not consist in communicating but in having, consuming and dominating. In this context, the old principle of the working class, "one for all and all for one," mirrors a view much closer to the Christian faith than a bourgeois maxim like: everyone for oneself and God for the rest.

We have to liberate the concept of resurrection from the stranglehold of individualism. This also means that resurrection is not to be viewed as a single isolated event that happened two thousand years ago. It is rather a process, and it happens again and again and again that persons who were dead rise from the dead. Some people have already risen from death; to remember them is to feed our own hope for resurrection.

This hope is unproved and unprovable. It is a genuine act of faith. The only possible proof of Christ's and our resurrection would be a transformed world, an approximation of the kingdom of God. In this sense socialists are not richer than Christians: Joe Hill is now sixty years dead and the truth of his "I never died, says he" still depends on us.

Resurrection gives us the beginning of the kingdom but not its completeness. The pain of unfulfilled promises is still with us. Tradition itself testifies to the theological differentiation between kingdom and resurrection: Jesus wears the wounds of crucifixion on his body. Paul speaks about cross and resurrection as a unit. This reminds us of the unaccomplished kingdom. The concept of liberation speaks in a similar way about the struggle for liberation, which is liberating in itself, instead of having liberty as a gift received once and forever. Thus, liberation theology implies cross and resurrection as well.

Resurrection is the most encoded symbol of the faith, and it resists decoding. It is the utmost yes to life of which human language is capable, so far as I can see. To give up this language would mean to lose the human power to transcend. The symbol transforms even death into an instrument of life. Different times will attempt different translations of this mystery. Bourgeois theology emphasized the individual dimension, but the new theology on which we are working will emphasize the social dimension of the mystery. Hence we bring together liberation with resurrection because our deepest need is not personal immortality but a life before death for all human beings.

But is there a life before death? How would we describe it? Where does resurrection/ liberation happen? The most important value of a new socialist ethics is solidarity. Where solidarity happens, there is resurrection. The new life begins when we break the neutrality of silence and leave aside the complicity of injustice. Persons who were previously invisible and forgotten become self-conscious and articulate. They stand up for their rights, and this rising up is a part of the resurrection process. It is a long way from alienation through class struggle to liberation, or—in another but convergent terminology—from sin through the cross to resurrection. But on this way we already create here and now, islands of the new life in the midst of the old. I want to describe three elements of this new life: a new language, new lifestyles, and new communities.

Liberated zones emerge; the liberated begin to talk a new language in which the words *mine* and *thine* lose their relevance. One might make a whole list of words that belong to the language of the oppressor and will be replaced. Let me give you an example, something that happened in South Africa in June 1976 when the school children of Soweto protested their life conditions. The government had ordered the mandatory use of Afrikaan as the medium of instruction in black schools. Mathematics, history, and geography had to be taught in Afrikaan, a language alien to black students and their teachers. In those days fifteen thousand Soweto school children marched through the township in protest. Their slogans were: "Do not force Afrikaan down our throats," "Our teachers can't teach in Afrikaan," "Afrikaan—the language of the oppressor."

All of us have learned the language of the oppressor. I learned Nazi German; others were brought up on Donald Duck cultural imperialism.[2] One of the most influential means of mass education is the language of advertisement, which sullies every human feeling because it thinks only of universal saleability. We all learned the Afrikaan of the oppressor. Can we all now begin to learn the language of the liberator?

In Christian tradition, God is defined as love, "the very same love with which we love," as St. Augustine says. But in the theological language of the oppressor, we learned this love was reduced into one between two persons separated from the world and time. Using the word "love" in our preliberation language means to remain on the level of "I am okay, you are okay," and to pawn off this middle-class game as God. It means to forget that God is "the love that fashions human society in history."[3] The new language, which is a sign of resurrection, will teach us, as Juan Segundo puts it, that "despite all our twisted and distorted images, the God that Jesus revealed to us is a God who is a society."[4] In this new language personal existence will not be meaningful *in spite of* the meaninglessness of history, but *in accordance with* the meaning of history.

In this sense we are the heirs of the best parts of the Christian tradition and its unmitigated, undistorted good wishes for all human beings. The great pedagogue Pestalozzi said at the beginning of the eighteenth century: "There is no God and there is no faith in God, as long as the suffering of injustice does not end." The more we will become a part of the historical movement which is ending the suffering of injustice, the more we become ourselves agents of this process and we will rediscover the meaning of the present time and praise God in celebrating new life in liberation societies.

There is a new lifestyle lived in the islands of resurrection. Increasing numbers of small groups in this country have decided to break with the old culture and its standards of education, career, income, and lifestyle. Traveling through this country I am deeply moved to see so many groups who stay and live with the poor. The simplest form of solidarity is what the French worker priests in the 1950s called "presence"—to share the life of the underprivileged and to struggle not "for" but "with" them. Jesus lived with the poor, he visited tax collectors, he had no home of his own. He tried to develop a new language with the poor and for the poor, a very simple language of prayer and of short parables taken from the life context of the wretched of this earth.

Today there are so-called base communities all over Latin America and in some European countries in which Christians try to live together in a new style—that is, without the privileges of the middle classes; to work together in cooperatives—that is, without the emptiness of alienated labor; and to read the gospel together and develop new forms of liberation spirituality based on radical and militant identification with the oppressed. When Mother Jones traveled for the union, she used to live in the shabby and overcrowded huts of the miners; for a time she lived with a woman whose child was working in a mill and died of exhaustion. Sometimes workers were threatened and fired by the mill bosses because of giving her a glass of tea.

What does resurrection mean for us? It means to unlearn the language of the oppressor; it means a transformation of lifestyle; and it means building up community, gaining protagonists for the common cause. I doubt whether I should use the old Christian word "mission" or the socialist word "organization." At any rate, the new life exists only as a shared life. Joe Hill's resurrection is explained in the simple words, "What they forgot to kill/went on to organize." When Jesus sent his friends out to build up the kingdom, he gave them rules, such as having no extra shoes or cloak, and traveling two by two. Perhaps the main organizational rule was the antidomination one:

> You know that in the world the recognized rulers lord it over their subjects, and their great men make them feel the weight of authority. That is not the way with you: among you, whoever wants to be great must be your servant, and whoever wants to be first must be the willing slave of all, for even the Son of Man did not come to be served but to serve, and to give up his life as a ransom for many [Mk. 10:42–45].

The surrender of privilege and domination is a criterion for a liberated life. Jesus washed his disciples' feet, another example for the new life in solidarity. The value of members of the group is not measured by their natural gifts or rank but by how they serve the needs of others. Resurrection means to join the forces of liberation.

There is a suspicion commonly held against socialist Christians, as if their faith were only a disguise, or as if their spirituality would disappear when they begin to agitate, to organize, and to struggle. But what really happens to them is not a loss but a deepening of spirituality.

During the last years of the Franco regime in Spain, a small group of Spanish Christians for Socialism worked strictly in the underground and developed a self-study questionnaire. The first question was: How has your faith changed since you joined the movement of Christians for Socialism? I do not know anyone else's response, but I should like to answer this question for myself and many of my friends.

First of all, joining the movement changed my relationship to others. The radicalization I went through separated me from some of my former friends and destroyed some bonds to others. Neighbors stopped greeting me, and colleagues ceased their chatting when I entered. On the one hand, I became lonelier; on the other hand, my eyes were opened to persons who had been invisible to me before. I learned a new type of relationship based on the common cause. Radicalization liberated me from old fears and considerations because it built up a network of communication.

A second change is related to my reading of history, and I am referring quite simply to an everyday life experience: opening the morning newspaper. I had felt lost in the face of events, saying for example: "I don't understand anything that is going on here or around the world." To feel this way means to be helpless. But in the light of my subsequent transformation, I think it involved a lack of faith as well. When we do not understand our own historical situation, when we are unable to read the signs of the times, then we also do not see the meaning of struggle. All our activities become a mere coming and going. We really do not know why we are visiting this friend, watching this television program, going to this movie. Even if we want to serve others with our work, we do not know how to do it. Our job becomes a waste of time, useful only in terms of making a living. However, when I came to understand participation in unjust social structures as sin, I awoke to a new assessment of events, and it became easier for me to make choices among the activities in which I was involved.

I would even go a step further and say that my hope became firmer. It took on more substance. I was happy when a strike was won; I could celebrate the liberation of the Vietnamese people and not just wish for peace in Southeast Asia. I learned to read the newspaper in the interests of the voiceless and to listen carefully whenever an undertone spoke in their stead.

To put it very simply: God became more concrete for me. One of the theological questions that had troubled me for a long time concerned the relationship between love and power. As a woman, I could not deal easily with a powerful, almighty, supernatural Lord, called Father. I had no interest in being ruled and protected by an independent sovereign. I felt that this God imagery, which had been handed down to me by the guardians of my Christian tradition, was essentially "macho." This God was more concerned about power than about anything else and he wanted to be called "all mighty." He was construed in the image of the free entrepreneur, independent from his workers. His title of "king" insulted my democratic feelings and the name "lord" hurt my solidarity with those who always had to live under someone else's thumb.

It took me a long time to get rid of this god, and it led me to a nontheistic theology, of which the center was the suffering love of Christ. The Son was closer to me than the Father. He revealed what the Father could not communicate to me: love without privileges; love that empties itself and takes on the form of a slave, a proletarian, love that prefers to go to hell as long as others are condemned to stay there. When Mother Jones talked about the mill children who are crucified between the two thieves of their childhood—capital and ignorance—she quoted the gospel: "Of such is the kingdom of heaven, said the great teacher. Well, if heaven is full of undersized, round-shouldered, hollow-eyed, listless sleepy little angel children, I want to go to the other place with the bad little boys and girls."[5]

The more I grew in the socialist movement, the more I discovered a new God-language. The point for me is not merely to overcome a sexist language by changing pronouns, because a female imagery can include domination and protectionism just as well. I think it is more important to overcome the inherent machismo in God-talk, its bourgeois male ideals. The adoration of power and independence established the eternal alien determination of humankind. When one of the main political goals of democratic socialists is workers' co-determination and self-determination, how can we stand a God-talk based on the refusal of democratization and self-determination? If God is not ready to give up power, if God does not want us to determine our own fate, we cannot trust God. God is then nothing but a somewhat liberal capitalist, and our trust in God would make us more childish than we are. The God we are in need of is not a private owner, or a capitalist with a smiling face. There is only one legitimization of power and that is to share it. Power that is not shared, that is not transformed into love, is domination; to adore it means to accept slavery.

The Nicaraguan priest and writer Ernesto Cardenal narrates a conversation about the prologue of the Gospel of St. John that he had with his friends—fishermen and peasants. They were reading the verse: "Through him God made all things; nothing that exists was made without him" (John 1:3). The Nicaraguans gathered around this word immediately relating divine creation with human creation. They said:

> In creating you make something known, like when you write a poem or a song, or when a carpenter makes a table. Every worker becomes known through his creation. The worker is the image of God and everything he produces is good. It enriches man. The things that we have have been made by God and afterwards by workers. The shoes we wear were made by workers. The clothes by other workers. The cities and everything in them and the highways and the bridges. . . . All those things come from the power of the Father, and the Father gave that power to the Son, and the power of the Son is also our power.[6]

What I learned from this passage is how to overcome the alienating God-talk with its feudal and bourgeois connotations. In the prison of the old language, God is essentially separated from us, as lords from bondsmen, kings from their subjects, so-called independent entrepreneurs from "their"—as the telling phrase goes—workers. If you listen carefully to the simple words of these Latin American *campesinos*, you will find in them traces of the Hegelian-Marxist tradition with its deep respect for human work and for the ones who carry it out. A young Nicaraguan continues to talk about workers' power: "It's the greatness of the workers. The workers continue the power of God on earth by working on creation. That's why the workers should be the owners of the earth."[7]

Resurrection means liberation from death and from the adoration of death. It implies a restoration of distorted creation. One of the participants in the talk on the gospel says:

God made matter by means of his word, but there are certain people who are enemies of matter, and they're destroying it with injustice. Now I understand better a poem that Ernesto read to us last night about the stars that said that all matter is moved by the law of attraction, which is the law of love itself. I say this social system is in conflict with reality and that's why the exploiters don't want us to see social reality.[8]

Indeed, this system is in conflict with reality, if we accept the biblical view of reality and cease to consider it a sum of accidentalness. A class society and a class-divided world are in conflict with the law of attraction. Division needs domination and class struggle from above. The systemic injustice of class division disrupts creation and its continuity in human work. There is no brotherhood and sisterhood possible under conditions of inequality.

HUMAN WORK IN A CHRISTIAN-SOCIALIST SETTING

Theologically we are accustomed to separate God's creation from human work. Bourgeois theology does not see the relationship between God and the worker mediated through work. We have accepted the capitalist worldview, which relates work primarily with money and not with creation. We have renounced our dignity as workers; in this view, what we do is what we get money for.

It is very clear that in capitalist societies the understanding of human rights is mainly individualistic. Human rights are seen as one's freedom to move, to talk, to worship, to publish whatever one wants. But this freedom ends at the gateway to the factory. Dictatorship, which we detest as a form of political governance, is tolerated in the working place. The owners of a plant can make a unilateral decision, maybe to move to a place where labor is cheaper, without even asking those whose life is completely changed by this dictatorial decision.

Labor is seen as an exception to the realm of human freedom. One of the basic characteristics of bourgeois societies is the dichotomy of private and public affairs. Within this framework, labor falls under the private sector. It is your private problem how to sell yourself on the job market. It is the private problem of the owner to buy cheap labor. Salary arrangements are a private contract between two unequal contracting parties, one of whom, owning the means of production, has power over the other who does not own them.

When labor was separated from common goals and popular organization in the early bourgeois epoch, there was a deterioration of its meaning. A common experience of work in our society is a sense of futility and meaninglessness. Work is seen primarily as a *means toward personal acquisition*. Work becomes wage labor. Labor is seen as a commodity that can be bought and sold, and the relationship of men and women to their work can only go so far as the relationship to buyable and sellable things goes. Work as a means toward personal acquisition is a distortion and truncation of the understanding of work as I see it in Christian tradition.

We have to distinguish two main streams. The one, which I would name a repressive tradition, was developed out of the story of the fall of Adam and Eve, and understands labor as punishment: "With labor you shall win your food from the ground all the days of your life" (Genesis 3:17). In other words, before the fall it was easy to find food in nature. But the thorns and thistles that the earth will now produce "for you," as the text says, are symbols of the hostility between nature and humankind that resulted from the fall. Labor is understood as God's punishment for sin; it is necessary for survival, but there is no thought of human fulfillment in working, of creativity or joy.

It is not so easy to discover the other stream in the annals of Christianity, a liberating tradition. Here work is understood not as a means for survival in a hostile environment but as an expression of specifically human existence. Work has to do with life and not simply with survival. It is not easy to locate this positive image in the Bible because the Bible assumes it as obvious. Perhaps the most beautiful and telling image of this liberative understanding of human labor is the image of the vineyard and its gardeners, which runs through the whole Bible. It is not by chance that the image of the vineyard, coming out of collective human labor, is also used as a metaphor for the relationship between persons, between lover and beloved.

There are three dimensions in this humanistic view of work: (1) self-expression; (2) contribution to society; and (3) reconciliation with nature.

1. One must be able to discover oneself in the work one does—this is what we mean by saying that work must be "creative." Hegel describes work as a form of positive alienation from myself, in that I am giving my energy to the work I am doing, but it comes back to me. I am leaving myself for, and I am emptying myself into, work. But in losing myself I am finding myself, and therefore the servant is stronger than the idle master, in Hegel's view.

Personally, when I reflect on class differences, the most important one that I experience is that I am able to love my work; it is a part of my life and it is not reified into a means for survival. In our society my situation is a privilege, and so I have an incentive to struggle to overcome an injustice—namely, that most workers are not able to get much more back from their work than a wage sufficient to "keep on going."

2. Work is an activity that relates workers to their society. Work creates community and gives workers pride in belonging to a group and doing something respected and needed by society. Lack of this societal dimension leads to self-deprecation and socially-based inferiority complexes. It is a goal of the cultural, socialist revolution to reinstate workers' pride in their labor, as well as in their products.

3. The earth is allowed to grow not only thistles and thorns for you, but vegetables and fruits. In the christological tradition of the church fathers, Christ is seen as the new Orpheus who tames wild animals by singing and flute-playing so that they follow him. We may understand Christ's work as the fulfillment of this three-dimensional dream of what work is meant to be. The tradition describes what Christ has done for us very often as his labor, his work.

When we look at the Jesus in the gospel stories, we find these dimensions. Jesus works among carpenters and fishermen; what he does is healing, preaching, or "agitating" as Mother Jones said, and community organizing. He expresses himself in his creative love for the people. He relates to the needs of society in caring for the oppressed and outcasts. He envisages new forms of community in which nobody is to be called rabbi or master, communities free from domination. In Jesus' dying, seen as the consequence of his work, the deepest sense of all our work breaks through: instead of wasting the best time of our life with meaningless running after private acquisition, we may join him in understanding that work is the way in which I am personally involved in God's ongoing creation and Christ's redemption of the world. It is the way I personally further and make effective the redeeming transformation of creation, bringing it within the control of the human community.

Before the resurrection things were brutal and meaningless, insubordinate to human social control. We did not participate in creative work, but were subjugated to the masters and the power structures of "this" world, which is in conflict with gospel reality. But now Christ, through his struggle and cross, has gained mastery over all things: he has given the world back to workers' self-determination. He is indeed reconciling all creation to himself through us, through our work. Resurrection as liberation from the power of sin takes place in new forms of work:

> The Son can do nothing by himself; he does only what he sees the Father doing: What the Father does, the Son does. For the Father loves the Son and shows him all his works, and will show greater yet, to fill you with wonder. As the Father raises the dead and gives them life, so the Son gives life to men, as he determines [John 5:19–21, NEB].

The unity of Father and Son is mediated through work and all of us participate in the resurrection of Christ.

In the biblical view, the human being is "little less than a god, [crowned] with glory and honor" (Psalm 8:5). It is the working man or woman come of age who is so crowned and honored. It is they who may participate in both creation and reconciliation. It is this deep respect for human dignity made master over all creatures that is to be realized in work.

The purpose of these theological reflections on work is not to glorify older, happier times but to look at the present in the light of the Christian understanding of human life. This view is traditional and radical at the same time. It is traditional because it refuses to accept the destructive forms of labor in modern times and to try to balance this destruction by personal acquisition, as if a loss of meaning could be offset by an increase of possessions. It is traditional because it criticizes those forms of exchange that stress having rather than being, as if possessing more could compensate for being less. It is radical because it demonstrates once more that there is no possible harmony between the Christian faith and a capitalistic system.

Faith teaches us forms of human dignity we may at best dream of in times when dignity is denied the majority of humans. The exploitation of the working class is not simply that their wages are low and their standard of living wretched, but much more importantly that the increase of social wealth—the result of the manual and intellectual labor of all workers—takes the form of private property in capitalist regimes. The surplus value is not used for the quality of our corporate life but is taken by the commanding elite that owns more than 80 percent of the national wealth. Small increases of wages and benefits have to be understood as a safety valve and bribery to the working masses who are socially impoverished and whose quality of life is declining even if the quantity of consumer goods increases. Faith teaches us expectations and hopes for our living and working that cannot be fulfilled in a system based on private profit-making.

Needless to say, the capitalist system denies all forms of a Christian understanding of work. It does not allow self-expression and creativity. It does not admit any orientation toward the needs of the people, and we are today further from a reconciliation with nature than ever before because the need for profit-making as the overall goal has followed the assumption that "big is beautiful."

I have attempted to explain the incompatibility between faith and capitalism. On the personal level, capitalism causes alienation; on the interpersonal level, competition; on the social level, class division; on the international level, imperialism and war. Peace is inseparable from justice.

It was not my intention to examine the emerging socialist societies. Although I think we can learn much from these new types of societies in transition to socialism, it would be naive to hope and strive for a simple adoption of any one model. What one may call the American way to socialism will be developed with the help of the best traditions of this country, both religious and democratic. It goes without saying that both these traditions are threatened by advanced capitalism. They are like fish in a polluted lake.

However, true faithfulness to these genuine American traditions may well lead to a democratization of the economy and the use of collectively produced surplus value for our needs as communities. The choice, therefore, is not between freedom and totalitarianism, as the ruling class wants us believe. The choice is the oldest one of all, between death and life.

Former Vice-President Nelson Rockefeller once gave a rare insight into some of the major issues facing Americans and other First World citizens. He noted that there is a fundamental conflict between our Christian heritage and the free enterprise system, to which we owe the life we enjoy.

I personally have some doubts about the use of the words "life" and "enjoy" in this society. But in agreement with Rockefeller, we should ask ourselves whether we will opt for the Christian faith or for capitalistic values. This will also be *the* question for the church in this century. Is the church inseparably allied with the old death-producing world, and will it die together with that world?

There are signs of a rebirth of Christianity. Each day a greater number of Christians commit themselves to a socialist option. Which side are you on? This is the question for the labor movement but it is also the biblical question that God asked the people through Moses:

> Today I offer you the choice of life or death, blessing or curse. Choose life, and then you and your descendants will live; love the Lord your God, obey him and hold fast to him: that is life for you and length of days in the land which the Lord swore to give to your forefathers, Abraham, Isaac, and Jacob [Deut. 30:19f].

NOTES

1. "Songs of Work and Protest," 20.
2. See Ariel Dorfman and Armand Mattelart, *How to Read Donald Duck: Imperialist Ideology in the Disney Comic.* This book, first published in Chile (1971), is a profound critique of the supposedly innocent Disney myth, which helps in the education of children to "a constant round of buying, selling, and consuming."
3. Juan Luis Segundo, *Our Idea of God* (1974) 66.
4. Ibid.
5. *The Autobiography of Mother Jones* (1935; 3rd ed., Chicago, 1976).
6. Ernesto Cardenal, *The Gospel of Solentiname* (1976).
7. Ibid., 6.
8. Ibid., 7.

Epilogue

Christianity and Social Change in a Postmodern Age

In the Introduction to this volume, I spoke of two poles within a dialectic that seems operative for many Christians today. One of the poles in this dialectic might be designated "religion" or "faith"; the other might be termed "society." I pointed out how reverberations at one pole inevitably involve alterations in the other. In examining various movements in the intervening chapters, we have seen some very specific examples of this interaction.

It is now possible to go beyond a particular kind of social change or a given movement to raise a more general set of questions. Can we speak of an entirely new tenor, a new mode of religious reflection that marks contemporary religious consciousness? Has theology itself taken a new turn? Is it even possible that theology itself is hardly recognizable as such—that is, is now far less a product of purely academic scholarship and is instead embedded in the matrix of social and cultural life, and indeed in efforts to change aspects of that life? This would not necessarily mean that there is no longer a place for academic or intraecclesial work. After all, Rosemary Ruether, James Cone, and Gustavo Gutiérrez are very respectable academics, in demand at the Harvards and Unions of our land. It would suggest, though, that theologians cannot adequately pursue their studies without being in much closer contact with the problems of our society than was formerly considered necessary. Certainly it would indicate as a bare minimum that contemporary theology must be aware of social change and social criticism. The impact of such forces for change as the women's movement and liberation theology have done more than affect particular regions of religious consciousness. They have altered the very form of religious reflection.

A new kind of religious imperative has arisen precisely because we are so aware of the limitations of our social structures. In the nineteenth century, our most perceptive theological minds were preoccupied with history and culture, and how to grasp these from a Christian perspective. In the last two decades—with movements, for example, intent on establishing black rights, securing sexual equality, and preventing nuclear war—we have become far more aware of the need for social criticism and social change. This awareness may in turn demand that we view theology itself quite differently, as we recognize that religious understanding itself is undergoing change.

The following are some observations on the possible nature of this theology. I would hope that they are connected to one another, but I make no claim to systematic integration. I would argue that we are in no position to demand or expect such a highly developed system. We are not at the point where a comprehensive account of this theological turn can be given; all we can do is point to it. Still, I believe that we can describe some features of what will ultimately be its fundamental shape.

515

We have moved from a modern to a postmodern era. It is this fact more than any other that will condition a theology of social change. At least since the time of Nietzche, prophetic voices have shrilly proclaimed the event—or perhaps have whispered it in our ear. In just the past few years, though, a number of thoughtful commentators have taken up the clarion call again, in a way that I think demands our attention. I am not speaking here of the "death-of-God" theology, although this rather short-lived phenomenon did underline in a memorable manner the limitations of even liberal theology. I have in mind both religious and nonreligious writers who have come to remarkably similar conclusions. In his *The Politics at God's Funeral,* Michael Harrington struggles with the question: What will serve to legitimate modern political systems now that traditional religious ideologies, in particular Christian ones, are totally incapable of it? The problem is just as acute for the nonbeliever as for the religious person: what is at stake is the very underpinnings of civilization. In his *After Virtue,* a sweeping appraisal of the history of philosophy from the Greeks to the present, Alasdair MacIntyre argues that we live in an ethically incoherent universe, in which we do not simply disagree but in which even the terms of disagreement are incomprehensible to those who hold ethically opposing positions. What is striking, he says, is that the very conditions for moral discourse have broken down. What lies behind this breakdown is the utter failure of what might be described as *the* modern project: the attempt to work out a completely rational and autonomous basis for a system of morality.

On the religious side, the most obvious example of a work in the same vein is Harvey Cox's *Religion in the Secular City.* Here the very author who previously celebrated the autonomy of modern humankind, humankind without religion, is able to discern the presence, indeed the transforming power, of religion in our contemporary situation. And welcome it is, for Cox too marks the demise of the modern world. The celebration of modern humanity has gone flat, for the simple reason that modernism has not worked, even on its own terms. Some of the problems are familiar: theoretical obstacles to the advance of science, political developments that have bared dark areas of our collective soul, most of all perhaps the very real possibility of human self-annihilation. Cox, though, particularly concentrates on areas that have also been my concern in this volume: the persistent tendency in the history of the West to what he calls "domination and debasement." The modern world has not been able to meet even the minimum requirements for decent human life. Significant segments of our own society and much larger segments of other populations have undergone severe physical and emotional hardship, and, more importantly, have suffered it would seem unnecessarily. As Cox puts it, what disturbs us today is not so much that we cannot pray, but that we (or others) cannot eat.[1]

In short, the collapse of the modern consensus has been accompanied if not precipitated by all the movements that have appeared so prominently in this volume. In theory, it promised a color-blind, sexually coequal world in which all individuals and all nations would stand on even ground, or at least have access to it. In practice, powerful social forces as well as enduring prejudices have guaranteed that for many the promise resembled a hollow mockery. In addition, the threat of a nuclear holocaust has shaken even those not suffering economic or social discrimination.

Certain other commentators on contemporary Christianity deserve to be at least mentioned here, inasmuch as they assume the same crisis of modernism. Thomas Oden, in his *Agenda for Theology,* mounts a scathing attack on the modern tendency of religious thinkers to accommodate to current social trends, whatever they happen to be. (One might observe, perhaps a trifle unkindly, that Oden himself was a prime example of such a tendency in his earlier books on religion and experimental forms of psychology.) In his *Agenda,* Oden calls for a courageous turning away from modernism to "classical Christianity." He too calls for a postmodern culture, but in his case it is "postmodern Orthodoxy," a return to an earlier and sounder faith. George Lindbeck in his *The Nature of Doctrine* provides a thoughtful essay on the form of religion in an age afflicted by relativism. As his subtitle—"Religion in a Post-Liberal Age"—suggests, he is seeking a new approach to religion, one capable of utilizing certain breakthroughs in the social sciences. Finally, Langdon Gilkey clearly calls for a religiosity that will go beyond subjectivity and a merely individual consciousness in his *Society and the Sacred.* The collapse of modernism has propelled Christians into a new appreciation of the social dimensions of religion. Thus contemporary Christians are prepared to see valid religion as "primarily if not exclusively *critical* or *revolutionary.*"[2] Although Gilkey has some useful cautions concerning this tendency, he recognizes how appropriate it is today.

To the modern era of Western history corresponds modern or liberal or (Gutiérrez's term) progressive theology. Throughout the nineteenth and into the twentieth century, many of the best theological minds in Christianity focused on the relationship between culture and religious faith. Liberal theology attempted to make Christianity relevant to modern culture. It began with the understanding that it was possible to be both modern and Christian. To make the connection plausible, it was necessary to affirm those Western values that explicitly stood outside its religious traditions. Even if it could be argued that some if not all of these secular affirmations were only possible because of the Judeo-Christian roots of the West, the point was not particularly helpful for the Christian caught in the dilemma of contemporary secularism. What was unsettling was that these values had become virtually autonomous from religion, and needed to become even more autonomous if they were to retain their integrity. For example, a Western ethic would be usable only if it were capable of standing on its own. Kant in this sense stood for the ultimate self-understanding of Western culture when he called for an autonomous, not a heteronomous, ethic. Here, to choose ethically was to choose just because something was the right thing to do, not because it would make one happy or get one to heaven or even because God had commanded it.

The logical consequence of this trend was the secularization of religion itself. Here, the Christian mind came to understand the human enterprise as legitimate in itself; as having great value even as independent of God. The collapse of the distinction between the secular and the sacred was inevitable. The sacred could be located primarily or exclusively in this world, and especially in human undertakings. The religion of the Christian took place in no special sphere, somewhere "other," but here at home, on this earth. In fact, it was, or ought to be, religionless.

It is a serious mistake, though, to think that all liberal theologians merely urged capitulation to trends in contemporary culture. On the contrary, much of their thought was a laborious effort to work out equations or correspondences between Christian faith and appropriate modern developments. For example, the German historian and religious thinker Ernst Troeltsch was one of the first to ponder the possibilities of a Christian pluralism. Beginning with the view that there was an absolute qualitative difference between Christianity and all other religions, he moved to "historicism," arguing that Christianity is distinguishably different for every age. In his words, "an unchangeable Christianity would mean the end of Christianity."[3] Yet even the later Troeltsch is intent to add that historicism is not relativism. The former emphasizes that Christianity cannot be separated from its historical and cultural roots. The latter assumes that there is no way to appraise values. It begins with individualism and ultimately gives way to nihilism.

Other liberal theologians were at least as careful in warning against wholesale or uncritical adaptation. Paul Tillich suggested criteria or "correspondences" as a means of mapping out the relationship between contemporary culture and Christian faith. But these very criteria presuppose areas that do *not* correspond, that indeed are likely to be antithetical to the venture of faith. Tillich is also famous for enunciating "the Protestant Principle," which at least implies some mistrust of prevailing values and mores. But as one famous commentator on Tillich has pointed out, the foundations of his theology include both the need to draw near to current social values *and* the necessity to protest against some of them.[4] Indeed, each of these impulses depends on the other.

As for the Niebuhrs, their position was skeptical enough of the modern world that they perhaps do not merit the term "liberal" at all. Yet, they too recognized the need to live within culture to the extent of being closely engaged with it, even if one should take care not to surrender to it. Reinhold Niebuhr in his *Moral Man and Immoral Society* argued that all social structures tend to corrupt. H. Richard Niebuhr in his *Christ and Culture* suggested that Christians should aim at transforming modern culture, rather than coexisting with it or melting into it.

What is the appropriate religious response to the collapse of modernism and the emergence of a postmodern era? No single theological term readily suggests itself. Gutiérrez suggests liberation theology, but it is perhaps too identified with the Third World, if not Latin America, to do service to all the movements discussed in this book, not to mention the many others that could have been discussed. "Radical theology" might do, with the caveat that it not be overidentified with radical politics. The problem is that the term has already been used for several rather unrelated theological movements. I personally am drawn to "critical theology" with its implications not only of reviewing religious tradition but also of looking with a critical eye at society, as well as at oneself. But if one uses this term, one had better avoid any tendency toward armchair theology—a religious reflection that is primarily cerebral and only secondarily, if ever, involved in action. One of the characteristics of the religious reflections we have seen is that they take place in a highly concrete context, one of issues and events.

A theology of social change, then, would be part of this critical theology, just as a theology of culture was part of liberal theology. It too focuses on the interaction between religion and society, but with certain perceptions that mark the breakdown of what might be called "the liberal faith": a faith that accepted the priority of the individual, the crucial character of tolerance within society, the power of rationality, and, last but hardly least, the inevitability of progress.

The crucial difference between liberal theology and critical theology is that the former takes a fundamentally positive position on the values of contemporary culture whereas the latter begins with a profound sense of the limitations of our society. Included in its premises may be such observations as the following. Contemporary American society is racist. The arms race is not only dangerous but produces disastrous social and economic dislocations. Sex discrimination has crippling psychological effects for both men and women. Capitalism carries with it an unacceptable human cost in areas such as unemployment, pollution, and maldistribution of goods. Even the radical right assumes a critical posture with respet to the status quo; it sees social danger in permissiveness, loose sexual morals, "secular humanism."

Critical theology cannot begin simply with the question: What elements in secular life should the Christian embrace? For it has as a prior intuition the notion that society is not anything like what it should be or can be, and that it is the task of the Christian, indeed of all humans, to work to make it better.

What liberal theology and critical theology have in common is that both take culture seriously. They refuse to separate the area of grace and revelation from this earth, this life. They both differ from traditional theology, which attempted to build Christendom, distinct from "this vale of tears." For the liberal, theology needs to be relevant, not for the sake of relevance but in order to be fully Christian. For the critical theologian, theology needs not so much to be relevant as to make a difference. This in turn means occupying the gap between what our world is and what it ought to be. Religion *belongs* in this uncomfortable place. Hence the spatial metaphors that its proponents reach for to indicate its situation. It exists "on the edges," to use Cox's favorite phrase, or "on the underside of history," to adapt Gutiérrez's expression.

Or to employ the metaphor in the title of this book, it takes place on the borders of faith. Borders are far from the safe central places of life where the territory is quite familiar and is more or less clearly mapped out. Border regions are frequently areas of tension, but they certainly need not be only that. They can also be places where exciting interchanges take place. The Alsatians, for example, possess a culture and cuisine which has borrowed from both the German and the French. The dynamism of Istanbul certainly is partly due to its bridging of Asia and Europe. The city of Hong Kong probably draws some of its incredible vitality from its position between the West and socialist China. Nevertheless, to live in a border region is to live under some strain as one grapples with the inescapable reality that at least two alternatives exist: two cultures, two political systems, two ways of life. One may indeed become schizophrenic, but then again one may begin the somewhat painful but invigorating process of development and growth in one's basic point of view. Finally, border regions and central regions are never entirely separate. What goes on in border regions may well affect safer, interior areas, but this influence will take time. It also may be resented. Furthermore, such influence is scarcely ever predictable, much less mechanical. In the case of religious alternatives, those on the fringe may be looked upon with suspicion. They may be regarded as, quite literally, heretical.

Critical or postmodern theology, then, has already begun to take on at least embryonic form. Some of its features are already clear. It rejects any separation between the world of the Spirit and the secular. The God who saves is identical with the God who creates. Yet in affirming this world, it refuses to accept the status quo as sanctified; in fact, it indicts whatever is debasing and dehumanizing in our current life-structures in the name of this God. Its criticism is two-edged: it looks at the social *and* the religious. Each is examined; each is measured. The dialectic between the social and the religious also suggests new concepts and new perspectives for both religion and culture. The reason: those who are the source of this theology are both rooted in Christianity and socially committed. It is, finally, a theology that, because of its dynamic character, is intrinsically multidimensional and multidisciplinary. Feminist theologians dig deeply into anthropology. Bishops crafting letters on values and economics have exhaustive conferences with economists and business executives. Black theologians turn to Africa and African affairs with a new interest.

Finally, a word or two on possible "dangers" in this form of theology. I use quotation marks here because it seems to me that not all "dangers" are equally so in fact. For example, a frequent charge against Cox's *Religion in the Secular City* is that he would have us be as uncritical about postmodern theology as we were formerly with liberal. "What safeguards does Cox invoke to prevent postmodern theology's capitulation to the postmodern *Geist* as much of modern theology seems to have capitulated to modernity? Is the [Christian] tradition merely accommodating to the presumed values of the new age?"[5] In other words, with what will those who critique *be* critiqued? This comment, although telling on the face of it, misses a major difference between a postmodern perspective and the earlier liberal point of view. Our awareness of the limitations of the previous point of view makes the difference. When traditional (philosophical and theological) concepts gave way to radically new (modern or liberal) ones, our understanding of time and history was altered radically. Indeed, one might say that for the first time Western culture took history seriously. Similarly, postmodern life has made us incapable of accepting social, political, and economic structures with the same uncritical faith that marked modern culture. No doubt some of us, perhaps most of us, will forget this occasionally and jump on this or that bandwagon. But to that extent, we will not be postmodern but will have reverted to modernism. Postmodern Christianity ought to have at its very core a sense of self-criticism, not to say skepticism. This critical spirit, though, does not prevent commitment but rather accompanies commitment.

One can see this postmodern point of view already at work in certain assessments of capitalist and Marxist economic and social systems. The religious critique of the former in no way entails an uncritical embrace of the latter. And yet, this certainly does not mean that the postmodern Christian necessarily avoids all systems as flawed. The wealth of detail of the pastoral letter on economics by the American Catholic bishops shows how this kind of Christianity plunges into concrete problems, even at the very real risk of heavy criticism. The Christian needs to, wants to, deal with the realities at hand, whatever they may be. The expectation of reform (social and political, but also religious) is of the very essence of Christian life, and revolution (not necessarily political) is at least conceivable.

Another warning that we very much need to listen to is offered by Gilkey. He reminds us of the realism of the scriptures, which can also be described as their balance. The Bible insists upon both destiny and freedom; upon possibility as well as fatedness; on the subjective as well as the objective character of sin. To take the last: the Bible insists that sin begins with and from inner freedom; indeed much of the Old Testament can be seen as a gradual unfolding of the notion of personal responsibility. At the same time, the Bible continues to affirm that we all inherit the consequences of sin. They finally become embodied in social structures, even in the very earth. Thus the Bible recognizes a genuine and objective unfreedom for the multitudes, where personal creativity and authentic relationships to other persons and to nature become difficult or impossible. Sin is equally present in the lives of the poor as it is in the lives of the rich. Their sinfulness, though, has little impact outside themselves and their immediate surroundings. The objective consequences of their sin are not so appallingly widespread or lasting.

The theology that I am envisioning will be useful to the extent that it recalls us to the biblical vision, which captures both the social and the personal dimensions of human life. As Gilkey notes, we need to pay attention to both dimensions, not because such attention is biblical, but because the truth demands it. We must not lose sight of the other side of the dialectic: of the personal, of the inner freedom already received in the economy of salvation. Gilkey puts it beautifully. The powerful symbols of the Bible, such as creation, redemption and sanctification, "each weave individual and community together into a new fabric, a new world of the inner spirit expressed objectively in and through a community of justice, of reconciliation, and of love."[6] A fully critical theology will not omit this inward and personal dimension.

These reflections do not fully describe a postmodern theology. They certainly do not even begin to organize or systematize one. What they perhaps do accomplish is to suggest some of its qualities. It may be useful to generalize concerning these qualities, but they become fully luminous only when wedded to life. The reflections contained in this volume amply illustrate the power and suggestiveness such reflections can possess.

NOTES

1. Harvey Cox, *Religion in the Secular City* (New York, Simon and Schuster, 1984) 97.

2. Langdon Gilkey, *Society and the Sacred* (New York, Crossroads, 1981) 47.

3. See Robert J. Rubanowice, *Crisis in Consciousness: The Thought of Ernst Troeltsch* (Florida State University Press, 1983) 42.

4. James Luther Adams, *Paul Tillich's Philosophy of Culture, Science, and Religion* (New York, Harper, 1965) Introduction.

5. Robert Imbelli, "What Will Christian Mean?," *Christianity and Crisis,* 5/44 (Feb. 20, 1984) 45. This entire issue of *Christianity and Crisis* was devoted to a discussion and critique of Cox's book.

6. Gilkey, *Society,* 56.

Suggestions for Further Reading

RELIGION AND FEMINISM

Christ, Carol, and Plaskow, Judith, eds., *Womanspirit Rising: A Feminist Reader in Religion*. New York, Harper, 1979.

Daly, Mary, *Beyond God the Father*. Boston, Beacon, 1974.

Fiorenza, Elisabeth Schüssler, *In Memory of Her*. New York, Crossroad, 1983.

Ruether, Rosemary, *New Woman, New Earth*. New York, Seabury, 1975.

Spretnak, Charlene, ed., *The Politics of God's Spirituality*. Garden City, N.Y., Anchor, 1982.

RELIGION, PEACE, AND WAR

Helgeland, John, Daly, Robert, and Burns, J., *Christians and the Military*. Philadelphia, Fortress, 1985.

Heyer, Robert, ed., *Nuclear Disarmament: Key Statements from the Vatican, Catholic Leaders in North America, and Ecumenical Bodies*. New York, Paulist, 1982.

Novak, Michael, *Nuclear Morality*. Nashville, Thomas Nelson, 1984.

Swain, J. Carter, *War, Peace, and the Bible*. Maryknoll, N.Y., Orbis, 1982.

Wallis, Jim, ed., *Waging Peace*. New York, Harper, 1983.

Yoder, John, *The Politics of Jesus*. Grand Rapids, Eerdmans, 1972.

BLACK AND MEXICAN-AMERICAN THEOLOGIES

Boesak, Allan, *Farewell to Innocence: A Socio-Ethical Study on Black Theology and Black Power*. Maryknoll, N.Y., Orbis, 2nd printing, 1979.

Deloria, Vine, "Native American Perspectives on Liberation," *Occasional Bulletin of Missionary Research* 1 (July 1977) 15–17.

Ellis, Carl F., Jr., *Beyond Liberation: The Gospel in the Black Tradition*. Downers Grove, Ill., Intervarsity, 1983.

Stevens-Arroyo, Antonio, ed., *An Anthology on the Hispanic Church in the United States*. Maryknoll, N.Y., Orbis, 1982.

Wilmore, Gayraud, *Black Religion and Black Radicalism*, 2nd ed. Maryknoll, N.Y., Orbis, 1983.

Young, Josiah, *Black and African Theologies: Siblings or Distant Cousins?* Maryknoll, N.Y., Orbis, 1986.

RELIGION AND THE NEW RIGHT

Abraham, William, *The Coming Great Revival: Recovering the Full Evangelical Tradition*. New York, Harper, 1984.

Fachré, Gabriel, *The Religious Right and Christian Faith*. Grand Rapids, Eerdmans, 1982.

Marsden, George, *Fundamentalism and American Culture: The Shaping of Twentieth Century Fundamentalism*. New York, Oxford University Press, 1981.

Quebedeaux, Richard, *The Worldly Evangelicals.* New York, Harper, 1978.

Shriver, Peggy, *The Bible Vote.* New York, Pilgrim, 1981.

RELIGION AND THE THIRD WORLD

England, John, ed., *Living Theology in Asia.* Maryknoll, N.Y., Orbis, 1984.

Gutiérrez, Gustavo, *We Drink from Our Own Wells: The Spiritual Journey of a People.* Maryknoll, N.Y., Orbis, 1984.

Mbiti, John, *African Religions and Philosophy.* Garden City, N.Y., Doubleday, 1969.

Segundo, Juan, *The Liberation of Theology.* Maryknoll, N.Y., Orbis, 1975.

Tutu, Desmond, *Hope and Suffering: Sermons and Speeches.* Grand Rapids, Eerdmans, 1983.

Witvliet, Theo, *A Place in the Sun: An Introduction to Liberation Theology in the Third World.* Maryknoll, N.Y., Orbis, 1985.

RELIGION AND ECONOMICS

Lamb, Matthew, *Solidarity with Victims.* New York, Crossroad, 1982.

Lapide, Pinchas, *The Sermon on the Mount: Utopia or Blueprint?* Maryknoll, N.Y., Orbis, 1986.

Novak, Michael, and Cooper, John, eds., *The Corporation: A Theological Inquiry.* Washington, D.C., American Enterprise Institute, 1981.

Rasmussen, Larry, *Economic Anxiety and Christian Faith.* Minneapolis, Augsburg, 1981.

Sider, Ronald, ed., *Cry Justice: The Bible on Hunger and Poverty.* New York, Paulist, 1980.

Tillich, Paul, *Political Expectation.* New York, Harper, 1971.

Contributors

Kenneth AMAN is associate professor of philosophy at Montclair State College. He has written on the philosophical background of Latin American liberation theology.

Mortimer ARIAS, a Methodist bishop, is professor of Hispanic studies and evangelization at the School of Theology at Claremont, California. He is the author of *Salvation Is Liberation* (1973) and *Announcing the Reign of God* (1983).

Phillip BERRYMAN has worked closely with church groups in Central America and Panama for many years, and has contributed articles to a number of journals. He is the author of *What's Wrong in Central America* (1983) and *Religious Roots of Rebellion: Christians in Central American Revolutions* (1984).

Joseph B. BETHEA is district superintendent of the Rockingham District, United Methodist Church, Rockingham, North Carolina.

Jordan BISHOP is a member of the faculty of the College of Cape Breton, Nova Scotia.

Allan BOESAK is chaplain at the University of the Western Cape, Peninsula Technical College, and Bellville Training College for Teachers, South Africa. In 1982 he was elected president of the World Alliance of Reformed Churches. He is the author of *Farewell to Innocence: A Socio-Ethical Study on Black Theology and Black Power* (1977), *The Finger of God: Sermons on Faith and Socio-Political Responsibility* (1982), and *Black and Reformed: Apartheid, Liberation, and the Calvinist Tradition* (1984).

Robert McAfee BROWN is professor of theology and ethics at the Pacific School of Religion, Berkeley, California, and a contributing editor to *Radical Religion*. He is the author of *Creative Dislocation—the Movement of Grace* (1980) and *Making Peace in the Global Village* (1981).

Barbara BROWN ZIKMUND is dean of the Pacific School of Religion, Berkeley, California.

David BRYCE-SMITH is professor of organic chemistry, University of Reading, England.

The CANADIAN BISHOPS' Social Affairs Commission was headed by Bishop Remi De Roo (Victoria). Other members: Bishops Adolphe Proulx (Hull), Bernard Pappin (Sault St. Marie), John O'Mara (Thunder Bay), Gerard Drainville (Amos), Raymond Saint-Gelais (Saint-Jerome), Peter Sutton (Labrador), and William Power (Antigonish).

Carol P. CHRIST teaches at the Women's Studies Program, San Jose State University, California. She was co-editor of *Womanspirit Rising: A Feminist Reader in Religion* (1979).

Albert B. CLEAGE, Jr., is the author of *Black Messiah* (1969) and *Black Christian Nationalism: New Directions for the Black Church* (1972).

James H. CONE is Charles A. Briggs Professor of Systematic Theology at Union Theological Seminary, New York City. He is the author of *Black Theology and Black Power* (1969), *A Black Theology of Liberation* (1970), *God of the Oppressed* (1978), *For My People* (1984) and co-editor of *Black Theology: A Documentary History, 1966–1979* (1979).

Mary DALY is an associate professor at Boston College, where she teaches feminist courses. She has written *Beyond God the Father: Toward A Philosophy of Women's Liberation* (1973), *Gyn-Ecology: The Metaethics of Radical Feminism* (1979), and *Pure Lust: Elemental Feminist Philosophy* (1984).

Winston DAVIS is professor of sociology at Kwansei Gakuin University, Uegahara, Japan.

Virginia M. DOLAND chairs the English Department at Biola University, La Mirada, California.

Paris DONEHOO is pastor of Lost Mountain Baptist Church in Powder Springs, Georgia.

Robert F. DRINAN, S.J., former U.S. congressman from Massachusetts, teaches law at the Georgetown University Law Center, Washington, D.C.

Virgilio ELIZONDO is president of the Mexican-American Cultural Center and rector of the Cathedral, San Antonio, Texas. He is the author of *Galilean Journey: The Mexican-American Promise* (1983).

Jerry FALWELL is pastor of the Thomas Road Baptist Church (17,000 members), Lynchburg, Virginia, sponsor of the "Old Time Gospel Hour," and founder of the Moral Majority.

Daniel Rush FINN teaches economics at St. John's University, Collegeville, Minnesota. With Prentiss L. Pemberton, he co-authored *Toward a Christian Ethic* (1985).

Elisabeth Schüssler FIORENZA is associate professor of theology at Notre Dame University, Indiana. She is the author of *In Memory of Her: A Feminist Theological Reconstruction of Women's Liberation* (1983).

George GILDER is the author of *Wealth and Poverty*, a book which was particularly influential in the first years of the Reagan administration.

Mary GORDON is the author of *Final Payments* (1978) and *The Company of Women* (1981).

Gustavo GUTIÉRREZ teaches at the Catholic University, Lima, Peru. He is the author of *A Theology of Liberation* (1973), *The Power of the Poor in History* (1983), and *We Drink from Our Own Wells: The Spiritual Journey of a People* (1984).

Jeffrey K. HADDEN is professor of sociology at the University of Virginia, Charlottes-ville. He is the author of several books on the churches and society, the best known of which is *The Gathering Storm in the Churches* (1983).

Thomas D. HANKS teaches the Old Testament at the Seminaro Biblico Latinoameri-cano, San José, Costa Rica. He is the author of *God So Loved the Third World: The Biblical Vocabulary of Oppression* (1983).

David HARREL is on the faculty of the University of Arkansas. He is the author of *All Things Are Possible: The Healing and Charismatic Revivals in Modern America* (1975).

Monika K. H. HELLWIG teaches theology at Georgetown University, Washington, D.C. She is the author of *Understanding Catholicism* (1981) and *Whose Experience Counts in Theological Reflection?* (1982).

David HOLLENBACH, S.J., is associate professor of theological ethics at Weston School of Theology, Cambridge, Massachusetts. He is the author of *Claims in Conflict: Retrieving and Renewing the Catholic Human Rights Tradition* (1979).

Arthur JONES is the Washington, D.C., correspondent for the *National Catholic Reporter,* Kansas City, Missouri.

George F. KENNAN, former U.S. ambassador to the U.S.S.R., is professor emeritus at the Institute for Advanced Study, Princeton, N.J. He is the author of *The Nuclear Delusion: Soviet-American Relations in the Atomic Age* (1982).

John L. KATER, Jr., is the author of *Christians on the Right: The Moral Majority in Perspective* (1982).

Alan KREIDER is on the staff of the Mennonite Center in London, England, and a peace advocate in the English churches.

Kosuke KOYAMA is the author of *Waterbuffalo Theology* (1974), *No Handle on the Cross: An Asian Meditation on the Crucified Mind* (1977), and *Three Mile an Hour God* (1980).

William P. MAHEDY is Episcopal campus minister at the Universtiy of California-San Diego in La Jolla, and at San Diego State University.

Martin E. MARTY is Fairfax M. Cone Distinguished Service Professor of the History of Modern Christianity at the University of Chicago and associate editor of *The Christian Century.* He is the author of many books and articles, including *The Public Church: Mainline, Evangelical, Catholic* (1981).

John S. MBITI is director of the Ecumenical Institute, Bossey (Geneva), Switzerland. He is the author of *African Religions and Philosophy* (1970), *Introduction to African Religion* (1975), and *The Prayers of African Religion* (1976).

M. Douglas MEEKS is professor of systematic theology and philosophy at Eden Theological Seminary, St. Louis.

Thomas MERTON was the well-known Trappist monk and author at Gethsemane Abbey, Kentucky.

Fred B. MORRIS, a research consultant on Latin America, has written on Brazil's recent experience under military dictatorship.

Ched MYERS is a graduate student at the Graduate Theological Union, Berkeley, California.

Henri J. M. NOUWEN was formerly a member of the faculty of Harvard Divinity School, Cambridge, Massachusetts. He is the author of *Reaching Out: The Three Movements of Spiritual Life* (1975) and *Intimacy* (1981).

Michael NOVAK is a syndicated columnist with the *Washington Post*. He has written *The American Vision* (1978) and *The Spirit of Democratic Capitalism* (1982).

Robert T. OSBORN is professor of Religious Studies at Duke University and has written extensively on black theology and on the theology of liberation.

Geevarghese Mar OSTHATHIOS is vice-principal of the Orthodox Seminary, Kottayam, and the metropolitan of Niranam, Kerala, India.

Elaine H. PAGELS teaches in the Department of Religion, Barnard College, New York City.

Prentiss L. PEMBERTON is professor emeritus of sociology of religion and social ethics at Colgate-Rochester Divinity School, Rochester, New York.

Jon SOBRINO, S.J., is professor of theology and philosophy at the Universidad José Cañas, San Salvador, El Salvador. He is the author of *Christology at the Crossroads* (1978) and co-author of *Theology of Christian Solidarity* (1985).

Dorothee SÖLLE teaches at Union Theological Seminary, New York, and the University of Hamburg, West Germany. She is the author of *Revolutionary Patience* (1977) and *Of War and Love* (1983).

Choan-Seng SONG is coordinator of study of the World Alliance of Reformed Churches and professor of theology in the South East Asia Graduate School of Theology. He is the author of *Third-Eye Theology* (1979), *The Compassionate God* (1982), and *Tell Us Our Names: Story Theology from an Asian Perspective* (1984).

Peter STEINFELS is executive editor of *Commonweal*. He is the author of *The Neoconservatives: The Men Who Are Changing America's Politics* (1979).

Charles E. SWANN is vice-president of Union Theological Seminary, Richmond, Virginia. He and Jeffrey K. Hadden co-authored *Prime Time Preachers: The Rising Power of Televangelism* (1981).

Leonard SWIDLER is an editor of *Journal of Ecumenical Studies* and a member of the religion department at Temple Universtiy, Philadelphia.

Cheryl TOWNSEND is a faculty member within the sociology department of Boston University.

Kay TURNER, who has written on several subjects related to feminism, is currently doing graduate work at the University of Texas.

Jim WALLIS is the editor of the monthly *Sojourner's,* Washington, D.C. He also was the editor of *Waging Peace: A Handbook for the Struggle to Abolish Nuclear Weapons* (1982).

Cornel WEST is the author of *Prophesy Deliverance! An Afro-American Revolutionary Christianity* (1982) and is a member of the faculty at Yale University.

Walter WINK is professor of biblical interpretation at Auburn Theological Seminary, New York City.